THE
EAST INDIA
MILITARY CALENDAR;

CONTAINING THE SERVICES OF

GENERAL AND FIELD OFFICERS

OF THE

INDIAN ARMY

BY THE EDITOR OF THE ROYAL MILITARY CALENDAR

VOL. I

The Naval & Military Press Ltd

Published by
The Naval & Military Press Ltd
Unit 10, Ridgewood Industrial Park,
Uckfield, East Sussex,
TN22 5QE England
Tel: +44 (0) 1825 749494
Fax: +44 (0) 1825 765701
www.naval-military-press.com
www.military-genealogy.com

© The Naval & Military Press Ltd 2007

In reprinting in facsimile from the original, any imperfections are inevitably reproduced and the quality may fall short of modern type and cartographic standards.

Printed and bound by Lightning Source

This Work

IS, WITH PERMISSION, RESPECTFULLY DEDICATED

TO THE

HONOURABLE THE COURT OF DIRECTORS

OF THE AFFAIRS OF THE

EAST INDIA COMPANY,

BY THEIR OBLIGED AND FAITHFUL SERVANT,

THE EDITOR.

In concluding this Volume, the Editor has the honour publicly to acknowledge his obligations to many distinguished officers who have, either from personal friendship to him, or a desire to have the services of their contemporaries accurately recorded, aided and encouraged him in his labours. It would be gratifying to the Editor to introduce their names in this notice, but as their assistance was not given with a view to public thanks, he imagines this general acknowledgment of their kindness will be more acceptable to them than a particular specification of their several favours and his obligations.

To the memory of one highly-honoured individual, by whom the Editor was most particularly encouraged to pursue a task, agreeable, as it records the services of honourable characters, yet both laborious and expensive in its execution, the Editor cannot avoid the public expression of his respect and gratitude. The friendship of that individual, the late Maj.-Gen. Sir Henry White, K. C. B., his advice, and his talents, principally influenced the Editor in this undertaking; and if the work should contribute to rescue from oblivion the services of veteran officers of the Indian Army, the memory of that distinguished character is, at least, entitled to this public acknowledgment.

It was observed to the Editor, by a late Lieutenant-General of the Madras Establishment, that " unfortunately during the period of the services of many of the oldest officers of the Indian army, the military transactions in India had not assumed in their detail that historical dress they have of late worn, or had the gratifying medium for individual and subordinate merit of a gazette, and consequently the only record of their services consists in general orders or letters to the government, and frequently in letters to themselves*, that have never been made known to the public." This misfortune it must be acknowledged will, in a degree, be remedied by the EAST INDIA MILITARY CALENDAR; the services of some of the oldest officers of the company's army are introduced in this volume, and the Editor will endeavour to collect and arrange for publication those of others.

* See p. 246.

Allusion is made in this work (p. 420) to the operations of the Indian army not being sufficiently estimated in this country: this remark equally applies to the services of its officers, than whom there are not in any army individuals who have been more constantly, actively, and honourably employed, or who have evinced greater gallantry and military skill: moreover, the officers of the Indian army, as observed by Lord Morpeth*, " to all the qualifications of soldiers unite all the accomplishments of scholars." To the remoteness, therefore, of the theatre of their exploits can only be ascribed the comparatively small degree of attention their operations have frequently excited in this country: and if by recording those operations fairly, and in the case of living officers, without comment, the Editor can contribute to draw the public attention to their importance, he will have performed a task most grateful to his feelings.

As it may excite surprise, that the services of officers inserted in this volume are not arranged according to seniority of rank, the Editor begs to observe, that the chief object which influenced their publication without such reference was, that as several of the retired Lieutenant-Colonels and Majors entered the service prior to some Lieutenant-Generals and Major-Generals of the Hon. Company's army, it would not have been advisable to class them with officers of their own rank now in the service, and whose military career, in some cases, commenced at the period which terminated that of their seniors; and considering also, that in a collection of the services of gallant men all places must be equally honourable, he has thought it best to disregard seniority all together in the arrangement of the services for publication.

As parts of three or four of the services of deceased officers published in this

* On a motion of thanks, in the House of Commons, to the Marquess of Hastings and to the army in India, on the 4th March 1819, by the then President of the Board of Controul, the Right Hon. George Canning, Lord Morpeth observed, "that he thought the Indian or Native part of that army, whose operations had been so warmly extolled, had vied with British soldiers in coolness and deliberation; but there was one circumstance, in regard to many of our officers in India, which had always struck him with peculiar force,—to all the qualifications of soldiers, they united all the accomplishments of scholars. This was exemplified by their scientific labours; they had performed the measurement of mountains, for the purpose of discovering the difference in altitude between those of the old continent and their competitors in the new; they had traced the courses of the Ganges and the Indus, amid the fatigues of war. Many of these very officers had been the companions of the early victories of Sir Arthur Wellesley, and maintain their former glory."

work have also appeared in that respectable miscellany the 'Asiatic Journal,' the Editor has further to observe, that the memoirs in question were placed in his hands by the friends of the deceased officers.

The Editor, in requesting to be favoured with communications from those who are acquainted with the services of old and distinguished deceased officers of the Indian army, need scarcely observe, that as his object is to do justice to the career of the General and Field Officers of the Company's present army, and to rescue from oblivion the names and achievements of those who, from a simple factory on the coast, struggling for its security and existence, mainly contributed to render the East India Company the Governors of a vast Empire; he flatters himself, that officers, and the individuals connected with India, who have the power to assist him in recording the eminent merits and exploits of the leaders and actors in a career, honourable to their friends, families, and descendants, and the knowledge of which is important to history, will cheerfully afford their aid to this undertaking.

Duke-street, Westminster, 1st Sept. 1823.

THE EAST INDIA MILITARY CALENDAR.

THE LATE LIEUT.-GEN. SIR HENRY COSBY, Knt.

(Madras Establishment.)

THIS much-distinguished officer arrived on the coast of Coromandel in the year 1759, soon after the siege of Madras had been abandoned by the French army, commanded by General Lally, and immediately joined the army in the field under Colonel (afterwards Sir Eyre) Coote, as ensign, being then a youth of between fifteen and sixteen. He proceeded*, in 1760, with the army to retaliate on the enemy by the siege of Pondicherry, and was appointed to the first company of grenadiers in the Company's service, with which he acted at the attack of the Bound's Hedge, where the division he was with, commanded by Major (afterwards General) Joseph Smith, consisting entirely of Company's troops, carried the principal post, de-

---

* Whilst on the march towards Pondicherry, Major More, of his Majesty's 79th regiment, was detached to intercept a body of the enemy, who were collecting provisions for the garrison, when a severe action took place; and the enemy being superior in force, the Major found it necessary to retreat under cover of the pagodas of Trivity: during the business of the day, Ensign Cosby, making one of the detachment, offered his service as an Assistant Aid-de-Camp, and whilst attending the Major in that capacity, the latter had his horse killed under him by a cannon-ball, upon which Ensign Cosby remounted him on his, at the risk of being made prisoner himself. Major More, on the return of the detachment, recommended him strongly to the Commander-in-Chief, and offered him an ensigncy in the 79th regiment, which he declined, preferring to remain in the Company's service.

fended by the regiments of Lovaine and Lally with ten pieces of cannon, the latter being all taken, and many prisoners; the main body making a precipitate retreat into the town. Immediately after the investment of the place, Ensign Cosby was appointed to the charge of the Ariancopong redoubt, the southermost one of the Bound's Hedge, a situation of much importance, as it was that by which the enemy expected to receive supplies, and which, though often attempted, they were prevented from effecting by the assiduity of this officer.

He served after this at the siege and taking of Vellore, under General Calliand, and being promoted to the rank of Lieutenant, was sent on duty to Masulipatam, where he was appointed to command a detachment of two hundred sepoys, two six-pounders, and twelve artillery men, to assist the then temporary Nabob of Rajamundry against some refractory Poligars, who resisted his authority, but were speedily brought to terms.

Lieutenant Cosby returned to Rajamundry, where his situation became particularly delicate, there being at that time different claimants for the possession of the Northern Circars, and of course much jealousy respecting the English influence at Rajamundry.

A near relation of one of the candidates, and nominal killedar or governor, who commanded a fine corps of five hundred Arabs, which he had brought with him from the north of India, and who shewed evident marks of discontent at the measures now adopted, was in the fort, and Lieutenant Cosby felt it necessary to keep a watchful eye over him, which many subsequent events justified, as he was one night awakened by a confidential person, and informed, that most of the Arabs had in the course of the evening been secretly collected into the fort from the Petah, and were then in the very act of having ball cartridges served out to them by their commander in the court of his own residence. Not a moment was to be lost; the barracks of the English Sepoys were fortunately close to Lieutenant Cosby's own quarters, and the two field-pieces always kept in front of them, with the artillery men in a shed adjoining. The men were under arms in an instant, and, with portfires lighted, this small body moved directly to the Killedar's residence, which was surrounded by a high wall, and taking possession of the two approaches, obtained that advantage which the smallness of the force rendered necessary. On Lieutenant Cosby sending in a message, that if they did not immediately lay down their arms, the field pieces would compel them to do so; the Killedar, astonished at this unexpected obstacle to his plan, which was nothing less than to make himself master of the place, lost all his confidence, and immediately surrendered, attempting to make many excuses for his conduct. Lieutenant Cosby, however, having reason to think the plot deeper laid than even now appeared, sent off an express to the then Chief of Masulipatam, Mr. Pybus, under whom he acted, with a full account of the business, in consequence of which a strong reinforcement was immediately sent to him for the security of the place, until matters were finally settled between the English government and the Soubah of the Deccan, who assumed the right of disposing of those provinces as he pleased, and which were soon after completely ceded to the English, when Lieutenant Cosby had the honour of being the first to hoist the English colours on the fort of Rajamundry, on the bank of the Godavery; and those provinces still continue an integral part of the East India Company's valuable possessions north of the Kistna.

Lieutenant Cosby was soon after appointed to succeed Captain Long in the command of the garrison of Masulipatam, in which he continued till 1764, when officers being greatly wanted at the siege of Madura, then obstinately defended by the celebrated Isoof Cawn, who had rebelled against the Nabob of Arcot, such was Lieutenant Cosby's zeal, although then most advantageously situated, that he tendered his services, which being readily accepted, he proceeded to join the army under Colonel Charles Campbell, who was so well pleased with his conduct on this occasion, that he immediately appointed him to the command of eight independent companies of Sepoys stationed on the south face of attack, where he continued till the fall of the place.

He was next appointed to the command of Warriorpollam, a place then recently taken from the Rajah of that name, and during which period he was indefatigable in his endeavours to bring the Sepoys under his command to submit to a more regular system of discipline than they had hitherto been accustomed to; and was the first on the coast of Coromandel who succeeded in getting them to submit to a uniformity of dress, and many other regulations, which being afterwards gradually adopted throughout the service, brought them to be what they now are, very little inferior to the best troops in Europe.

In 1767, Lieutenant Cosby was promoted to the rank of Captain*; and the Sepoys, being then formed into regular battalions under the command of Captains Commandant, he was appointed to the command of the sixth.

The government of Madras having at this period entered into a treaty of Alliance with the Soubah of the Deccan and the Mahrattas, for the reduction of the power of Hyder Ally Cawn, which had then become very alarming, Captain Cosby with his corps, now completed to a thousand men, was selected to make part of the English contingent, which was to consist of five hundred European infantry, five battalions of Sepoys, thirty European dragoons, and sixteen field-pieces, twelve and six-pounders, under the immediate command of Brigadier General Joseph Smith, the Commander-in-Chief of the troops on the Madras establishment. Owing, however, to the treacherous policy so common to the native powers of India, this little army had joined the Soubah in the enemy's country but a short time before it was discovered that the Mahrattas, being the first in the field, had, after plundering every thing they could, made a separate peace with Hyder; that the Soubah was on the point of following their example, and that the English were likely to be made a sacrifice to this selfish and perfidious conduct. Precautions were therefore adopted by the Madras government to guard against the

---

* At this period, from there being but few field officers in the Indian service, the rank of captain gave to an officer of the Company's service a command, which in the present days would be considered suitable for a major or lieutenant-general of the " King's army."

J. P.

worst that might happen; and Brigadier General Smith received orders to retire by slow marches into the Carnatic with the greater part of his force, leaving, however, for the present, three battalions of Sepoys, under the command of Captain Baillie, with the Soubah, then advanced near to Seringapatam. This was no doubt risking these corps; but the government had not yet, as they thought, sufficient grounds to withdraw entirely from the league. In order, however, to indemnify themselves, they had appointed a detachment, under Major Bonjour, to take possession of the Biramaul country, lying between the Carnatic and Mysore.

Whilst in this awkward situation, the three battalions left with the Soubah became greatly in arrear of pay, and apprehensions were entertained that they might mutiny, and advantage be taken of their doing so, either by Hyder or the Soubah, to get them into their service; and as they constituted part of the Company's best troops, their relief became an object of most serious consideration to the general. He therefore detached Captain Cosby with five hundred of his own men and twelve dragoons, with a sum of money in specie made up in bags, it being intended in case of extremity that the money so prepared should be divided amongst the dragoons, in order to make a last push with it for Captain Baillie's camp; and, as the whole of the route lay through the enemy's country, and the high road within sight of several of Hyder's garrisons, particularly Bangalore, he was directed to proceed with as much caution as possible.

This delicate service was performed with admirable success, Captain Cosby having so skilfully evaded the corps detached to intercept him, as to return with the loss of only one man, who deserted, after performing a circuitous march, guided chiefly by the compass, of 350 miles in thirteen days, including two days occupied in delivering his charge and refreshing his troops.

The Soubah and Hyder having soon after settled matters, they determined on the invasion of the Carnatic; but, with more honor than was expected, first permitting these battalions of the Company's army to retire. Brigadier General Smith, by orders from the government of Madras, began his retreat from the Biramaul, in order to cover the Company's frontiers, there to wait for further reinforcements, the whole force of the English being at this time only 800 European infantry, 5000 Sepoys, 30 European dragoons, and sixteen pieces of cannon, twelve and six-pounders, and 1000 irregular cavalry belonging to the Nabob of Arcot.

The enemy, consisting of 42,000 horse, 28,000 infantry, and 109 guns, came up with this small force on the 28th September, 1767, just as they had got through the Changama Pass, which divides the Carnatic from Hyder's dominions, and had early in the morning, with a large body of cavalry and light troops, taken possession of a village and hill commanding a narrow defile, through which the English army had to pass. Brigadier-General Smith, having made the best possible disposition, began to move forward with the line, and the corps commanded by Captain Cosby, being one of those in advance, was ordered to dislodge the enemy from the village, which he effected at the point of the bayonet; and finding himself annoyed from the hill, proceeeded with equal success to drive them from that position likewise, while the advance pursued its route, and cleared the difficulties of the pass. From this hill Captain Cosby perceived the rapid approach of Hyder's regular infantry at some distance, on the right flank of the English line, and reporting his observations to Major Bonjour, who commanded the advance, requested, and obtained his permission, to call up the leading corps of the army, commanded by Captain Cowly, to occupy the hill, before he quitted it to join the van to which he belonged,---a judicious suggestion, which essentially contributed to the success of the day. The confederates were entering this position, but had not completely occupied it, when Brigadier-General Smith, on approaching the hill, and hearing the report of Captain Cosby, perceived the necessity of quickening his march, and by so doing got up in time, and by securing the hill and village, gained an advantage that enabled him completely to repulse every subsequent attack, and ultimately oblige the enemy to draw off, leaving him master of the field, and at liberty, soon after dusk, which now approached, to continue his march, which the necessity and situation of affairs obliged him to do all night, in order to reach a depôt, Trinomally, where Brigadier-General Smith expected to be reinforced by troops from Trichinopoly. The enemy suffered so severely as to prevent their following during the night, and Hyder himself was slightly wounded. The loss of the English was considerable.

The battle of Trinomally, or Errour, followed soon after that of Changama, and proved so decisive that the confederates lost the greater part of their cannon and baggage, blew up their ammunition, and went off in the greatest confusion, abandoning a strongly-fortified camp, and ultimately left the Carnatic. In this action Captain Cosby, at the head of his corps, the 6th Sepoys, was particularly mentioned by the Commander-in-Chief as having borne a conspicuous part.

The retreat of the enemy gave, however, but short respite to the Company's army, which was ordered to retaliate by entering the Mysore country; and, in 1768, Captain Cosby was again actively employed, being detached with his own corps, a corps of grenadier Sepoys, and a troop of dragoons, against one of Hyder's most active partizans, Muctum Saib, whom he defeated and dislodged from under the guns of Bangalore, the poligar, or chief, of which place he obliged to accompany him to the English head-quarters.

Captain Cosby was afterwards placed in advance of the army, in command of a force consisting of his own corps, a company of European grenadiers, a corps of Sepoy grenadiers, some European cavalry, and a field train, with orders to reduce the forts of Anicul and Dencanicota in the Mysore country, which service he completely accomplished, whilst the Commander-in-Chief, Brigadier-General Joseph Smith, was making preparations for the attack of the enemy's principal forts; and being soon after ordered to reinforce a division of the army acting under Colonel John Wood, an action took place near Arlier between that officer and Hyder Ally in person, in which Captain Cosby received a severe contusion from a cannon-ball.

In 1769 a peace was concluded with Hyder, and the army went into quarters, Captain Cosby's battalion making part of the garrison of Vellore. In 1771, the army being ordered to take the field, under Brigadier-General Joseph Smith, against Tanjore, Captain Cosby, with his battalion, made a part thereof, but proceeded no further than Vellum, a strong fort belonging to the Rajah, about nine miles from Tanjore, which it was deemed proper to obtain possession of. A breach being accordingly effected, and Captain Cosby's corps then on duty at the batteries, under the orders of Lieutenant-Colonel Bonjour, the latter about midnight observing the fire of the enemy to slacken near the breach, and thinking it a favourable moment for carrying the place, directed Captain Cosby with a few of his men to try how far it might be practicable, which he accordingly did, and having with some difficulty reached the top, and being followed close by more of his people, the enemy, panic-struck, were soon driven from the ramparts, and abandoned the fort by the Tanjore gate (on the opposite side) of which Captain Cosby had but just got possession, and secured, when it was approached by a reinforcement from the garrison of some of the best troops from Tanjore, with orders to defend it to the last; but they were only in time to receive a discharge of musquetry from the new masters of the place, and of which they did not wait a repetition. The general was pleased immediately to appoint Captain Cosby to the command of the fortress, as expressed in the following extract of his letter to the government of Madras.

"*Camp near Vellum, Sept. 27th,* 1771.

" I have garrisoned the fort of Vellum with four companies of Captain Cosby's battalion, and two companies of Topasses belonging to the Nabob, amongst whom are several gunners: as Captain Cosby mounted the breach with part of his battalion, I thought he had the best title to the command. I hope, from his diligence, many discoveries will be made with respect to hidden grain, as I suppose a place of such consequence to Tanjore has not been left without a considerable store in it.

(Signed) "JOSEPH SMITH, Commander-in-Chief."

The Rajah of Tanjore having at last been brought to terms, but not before Brigadier-General Smith had proceeded some length in the approaches, the army went into cantonments; Vellum was however retained in the hands of the English as a security for the fulfilment of the Rajah's engagements; and the garrison being increased, Captain Cosby was appointed to the permanent command, as appears by the following document.

Extract from Brigadier-General Joseph Smith's letter to the Honourable Josias Du Pre, president of Fort St. George, dated " Camp, fifteen miles S. W. of Tanjore, 13th Nov. 1771 :---

" I have left Captain Cosby in the command of Vellum, with his own battalion complete, two companies of European infantry, a subaltern and thirty artillerymen, Captain Alexander's battalion of Sepoys, and a hundred Lascars. Captain Cosby's great care and assiduity during the siege merit my warmest recommendation of him to you, sir; for, I confess, had he not seasonably sent me a supply of rice, which he took from the Polygars, we should have been under the necessity of raising the siege.

(Signed)   " JOSEPH SMITH, Commander-in-Chief."

The distress of the army under Brigadier-General Smith, for provisions during the siege, is further illustrated by the following letter.

" *At the Siege of Tanjore, Oct. 17, 1771.*

" DEAR COSBY,---I have received your several letters and the convoy safe; we had not a grain of rice left when it made its first appearance; and but for the supply you sent, God knows what the consequence might have been, for our Sepoys began to grow very troublesome, and I wonder not at it, considering the fatigue they undergo.

(Signed)   " JOSEPH SMITH, Commander-in-Chief."

In 1772, Capt. Cosby was appointed Brigade-Major to the army, at that period the highest staff situation on the coast, and as such acted under Brig.-Gen. Smith at the reduction of the forts of Ramnadapram and Callacoil, in the southern provinces of the Carnatic. In 1773, he was raised to the office of Adjut.-Gen. with official rank as Lieut.-Col. being the first officer appointed to that situation in India.

In the latter capacity, and as head of the staff under Brig.-Gen. Smith, he served at the second siege of Tanjore; which being at last carried by assault, after a passage had been effected over the ditch, Col. Cosby was deputed by the general to treat with the Rajah, who, with a chosen body of men, had, on the breach being carried, returned into his palace, and appeared determined to defend himself in that position to the last. Col. Cosby, with only an interpreter, was admitted to his presence, after passing through several intricate passages filled with men, who it seems had devoted themselves to die with their chief, and which their gloomy countenances strongly indicated they would have done. He found him in a small chamber, surrounded by a few of the most confidential of his people. The interview was solemn and impressive, but it took not long to convince the Rajah of the imprudence of further resistance; and when Col. Cosby assured him he was fully authorized to promise, not only that his life should be protected by the English, but that also every delicacy and respect should be observed towards himself, the females, and rest of his family, and reminded him of Gen. Smith's well-known honourable character, he, after a heavy sigh or two, asked Col. Cosby if he would swear to that effect by the sword he then held in his hand, and that he was properly authorised to give him protection. The reply being in the affirmative, he arose, said he was satisfied, and gave orders to his people to lay down their arms, as he relied on the honour of the English, and proper guards were immediately appointed by Col. Cosby for the protection of the palace.

In 1775, Col. Cosby was sent to England with despatches of a confidential nature from the Commander-in-Chief, and on this occasion received the following letter from him.

"*To Lieut.-Col. Cosby, Adjut.-Gen.*

" Sir,---As you are proceeding to England, I think it incumbent on me, as your commanding officer, to give you this voluntary testimony, and to assure the honourable court of directors, that during the last ten years of my service on this coast, you never were absent from the field in the many campaigns their troops have made; that your zeal, abilities, and merit, as an officer, have more than once been publicly noticed; and that on every occasion you gained my entire approbation. These proofs will, I hope, recommend you to the countenance and protection of our honourable employers, who, I make no doubt, will have a due sense of your services.---Wishing you a happy passage, I am, Sir, your most obedient Servant,

" Joseph Smith, Brig.-Gen. and Com.-in-Chief."
" *Madras, 4th July,* 1775."

Colonel Cosby returned to his station at Madras in 1777. A few weeks after his arrival, (although somewhat out of the general usage of the army, being still Adjut.-Gen.) he was appointed, by the government of Madras, to command a force consisting of three battalions of Native infantry, with their field train, a battalion of the Nabob's troops, some cavalry, and the forces of the Calastry, and Vencatigherry Rajahs, to take the field against Bom Rauze, a Rajah of the first consideration, possessing an extensive tract of country, about ninety miles N. W. of Madras, which had never yet been penetrated with the least success by an enemy, and, from its peculiar advantages, its capital being in the midst of hills, roads, and ravines, had deterred any serious hostile attacks even from Hyder or the Mahrattas; nor were batteries mounted with cannon wanting to complete its defence, or a large force well disposed to avail themselves of these advantages; yet such was the superiority of English discipline, and the art of tactics brought into use on this occasion, that by diverting the attention of the enemy by false demonstrations, and turning their flanks, while others were making more serious attacks on their principal barriers, they were driven from one to another, until the English gained such a footing in the country as to alarm and thereby occasion a fluctuation of opinion amongst their chiefs as to the probable success of a further resistance; which ultimately induced the Rajah to capitulate, and agree to the terms settled by the Nabob of Arcot, whose tributary he was, or those on which he would be allowed to retain his situation, and admitted Col. Cosby to take possession of Cavaretty, his capital, till every thing was finally adjusted, and military roads cut through the country. The loss on this occasion was trivial, but Col. Cosby had himself a narrow escape, his orderly-serjeant being killed close to him. The whole business was accomplished in the course of six weeks, with so much enterprize and judgment, that Col. Cosby received the thanks of the Madras government on this occasion, who were pleased to say the service had been performed with a celerity that far surpassed their expectation, and particularly fortunate, as the rainy season was just beginning; and the Nabob addressed a letter to government in Persian, dated Oct. 28th, 1777, of which the following is a translation :—

"Lieut.-Col. Cosby, whom the government of Madras appointed with some of the Company's troops to punish Bomrauze, has behaved with the greatest bravery and activity in that affair, and has settled matters to my entire satisfaction. I am, therefore, to return thanks to the Company and the governor and council, and am convinced that they will recommend the colonel to the Company."

In 1778, intelligence being received at Madras, by an over-land despatch, of the breaking out of the war between Great Britain and France, the army on the coast of Coromandel was ordered to take the field for the purpose of attacking Pondicherry. Lieut.-Col. Cosby, being still adjutant-general, had shortly before, in consequence of an application to the government from the Nabob of Arcot, been appointed Commandant of all his regular cavalry, then consisting of seven regiments, 550 each, with 200 light infantry, forty artillerymen, and four six-pounders attached to each regiment, forming together a most complete legion of 5180 men, with twenty-eight pieces of cannon; and although this appointment was of itself no doubt of sufficient consequence to call forth all his exertions, yet, at the particular request of the Commander-in-Chief, Gen. Sir Hector Munro, Col. Cosby readily agreed to act in both capacities during the siege, and actually executed those important duties till the fall of the place, which, being most skilfully defended by Gen. Bellecombe, at that time one of the best officers in the French service, did not surrender till a practicable breach was made in the face of the queen's bastion, and a passage effected across the ditch. On the completion of this important service, Col. Cosby was permitted to resign the office of adjutant-general, and on that occasion received the following flattering mark of approbation from the select committee of the Madras government, and the commander-in-chief of the army:—

"*Fort St. George, 17th Dec.* 1778.
" GENERAL ORDERS.

" Lieut.-Col. Cosby having been permitted, at his own request, to resign the office of adjutant-general, Lieut.-Col. Thomas Burrows is appointed thereto. In justice to Lieut.-Col. Cosby, the select committee think it proper to publish the Commander-in-Chief's approbation of his conduct, which he has expressed to them in the following terms.

" Gen. Munro regrets much the loss of an officer who filled the office of adjutant-general with such ability that he not only gave entire satisfaction to the general, but to the whole army; and that his being appointed to the command of the Nabob's cavalry is the sole cause of his resigning the office of adjutant-general."

In 1780, the Carnatic was suddenly invaded by Hyder Ally Cawn, with a powerful army, consisting of 14,000 of his best stable horse, 12,000 Sillidar horse, 2000 Savenore horse, 15,000 regular infantry, 12,000 select and veteran peons, 18,000 peons selected from the garrison, 10,000 tributary Polligars, 2000 rocket men, 5000 well-equipped pioneers, and 100 guns, making 90,000 cavalry and infantry, and 100 pieces of cannon, many of the corps commanded by experienced French officers.

Col. Cosby, then at Madras, was immediately appointed by the government to proceed to the southward, in order to collect all the disposable force south of the Coleroon; whilst Col. Baillie, from the northern provinces, was ordered to proceed south, in order that their respective detachments should join at Conjeveram, the appointed rendezvous of the whole, about fifty miles west of Madras, where Sir Hector Munro was to take the command: the troops in the vicinity of the presidency of Madras, under Lord Mac Leod, and those at Pondicherry, under Col. Braithwaite, being ordered to proceed to the same point. Col. Cosby was also provided with a large sum of money to discharge arrears due to the cavalry in the southern provinces; without which, it was apprehended, they could not move from their cantonments.

The colonel, with only a few attendants, succeeded, at very considerable risk, in getting to Tanjore,—the country being by this time overrun by the enemy's cavalry and light troops,—and from that garrison, and the garrison of Trichinopoly, and the Tinnevelly country, collected two regiments of cavalry, and about 2000 infantry, with six light guns; and, with this force, lost no time in repassing the rivers Coleroon and Covery, which, at this period, were at their greatest height and rapidity; and having, with much fatigue and difficulty, accomplished that object, chiefly by the means of basket boats covered with leather, and the indefatigable industry of the officers and troops under his command, proceeded, with the greatest expedition, northward for Conjeveram, the place appointed, as before-mentioned, by the Commander-in-Chief, Sir Hector Munro, for the general rendezvous of the whole.

The colonel's orders being discretionary, he, on his route, attempted to carry by assault the strong fort of Chitteput, having a fausse bray, wall, and wet ditch, of which the enemy had just got possession; and in this hazardous undertaking, he succeeded so far as to cross the ditch, enter the fausse bray, and even plant his ladders against the inner ramparts, and would certainly have accomplished his object, had not the garrison been prepared, by the treachery of one of the Nabob's Subadahs, who accompanied him as a guide from Gingee, and by whom Hyder's commander in the fort was informed of the meditated attack, as was afterwards proved by various circumstances, and the desertion of the guide, who suddenly disappeared, just as the attack began. The consequence was, the ramparts were completely manned; but notwithstanding this, and a heavy flank fire, it was not relinquished till several of the ladders were broken, and two officers, Capt. Billcliff and Lieut. Eastland, and a number of men, were killed and wounded between the walls; and day-break rendering a further perseverance no longer prudent, the wounded were withdrawn, and the retreat effected in the best possible order.

The colonel, after allowing a few hours repose to his men, marched for Wandiwash, a fort belonging to the Company he had to pass, and on the glacis of which he ordered his tents to be pitched and left standing, in the care of the garrison, as a blind to the enemy, who he knew watched his motions, and gave notice of them to Hyder; and having heard a heavy firing, though at the distance of near forty miles, in the direction of Conjeveram, moved as soon as it was dark, and marched the whole of that night for the general rendezvous. This firing afterwards proved to be the action between the detachment under Col. Baillie, and Hyder, in which the former was completely defeated, the whole being either killed, wounded, or taken prisoners; and, in consequence, Sir Hector Munro, not thinking it prudent, after such a loss, to risk an action with Hyder, destroyed his heavy guns, and retreated from Conjeveram the same evening, to Chingleput, followed by large bodies of the enemy.

Such was the melancholy and unpromising state of affairs when Col. Cosby arrived within ten miles of the rendezvous, and was met by a large detachment of the enemy's cavalry, &c. flushed with their late success over Col. Baillie, and by Sir Hector Munro's retreat, and on the lookout for him, as they supposed, an easy prey; and at the same moment, and not till then, he, by the greatest good fortune, learnt from a wounded Sepoy, who had escaped from the fatal action, what had happened, and thus found himself placed in one of those critical and trying situations which do not often occur.

There was but a choice of two measures to adopt: The first, and which seemed to promise most safety, was to retreat southwards towards Cudalore; the other, to effect, if yet possible, a junction with Sir Hector Munro, to whom such a force as the colonel had was now of the greatest consequence. He adopted the latter, concealing from all but a few of his officers the alarming news he had just received; and to do this and assign a reason for changing his line of march, gave out that he had received instructions to move on Chingleput, in order to bring up provisions and stores placed there for the army; and, countermarching his line, now formed in column, with a regiment of cavalry in front and one in rear; ordering his cannon, in the first instance, to the head of the line, with directions not to open till it should become absolutely necessary, and then by a successive and regular discharge down the right flank of the column, the left being covered by the river Palar, till the rear of it came up to them, then to relimber, and, by a rapid movement, to regain the front: repeating this manœuvre without intermission, the column moved progressively on, at a steady pace, whilst skirmishing parties of the rear regiment of cavalry, commanded by Major Jourdan, kept at bay the most daring of the enemy, who continued to increase in numbers during the whole march, being joined by those who had pursued our army the night before, and were now returning, and at times pressed hard on the rear and right flank; but the disposition already mentioned, and the effect produced by the almost constant fire of the field pieces, effectually drove the enemy back, and Col. Cosby reached the ford of the river, about a mile from Chingleput, with inconsiderable loss on his side, whilst the enemy suffered severely.

When within about three miles of Chingleput, this detachment was discovered on the plain by some officers, from the top of a high building in that place, and at first taken for Hyder's regular troops, till the firing of the field pieces, and the enemy's rockets, and ultimately by means of glasses, the English standards were discovered, and proved to be Col. Cosby's division; and being reported to Sir Hector Munro, he ordered such troops as could be immediately collected to move down to cover his crossing the river; but before the first party could reach him, the enemy, thinking further attempts fruitless, had retired. " The joy which the main army felt on this occasion was heightened by surprise, as Col. Cosby had marched nearly 200 miles in a very short space of time, though great part of the country through which he came from Trichinopoly, was overrun by the enemy*."

Previous to Col. Cosby's junction, Sir Hector Munro had thoughts of moving the army direct to the Dutch settlement of Sadras, on the sea coast, about ten miles off, as the most secure position for ensuring the receipt of supplies by sea from Madras; and for finally embarking the European part of the army, if such should be found at last necessary. Col. Cosby's arrival, however, occasioned an immediate change in these measures, it being then determined to march directly for Madras; and he was appointed to lead the line with his own division. The army, accordingly, moved from Chingleput the same evening, and reached St. Thomas's Mount, a strong position nine miles west of Madras, by noon the next day, a few only of the enemy's irregular cavalry having been seen during the march, although there was every reason to suppose that Hyder would have followed up his late success, by attempting to prevent its reaching Madras; which, had he succeeded in doing, there is no saying what the consequences might have been†.

Soon after this, Sir Eyre Coote, then Commander-in-Chief in India,

* History of the War in India, from 1780 to 1784.

† It may here be observed, that Sir Hector Munro was a most excellent and well-meaning character, but unfortunately too easily guided; and that, at this period, he had about him those who had little experience.—Colonel Cosby's junction was of the greatest consequence, and was so acknowledged by the whole army. The fate of the Carnatic depended upon it, and the Company's army reaching Madras before the enemy's.

arrived from Bengal, bringing with him a reinforcement of 500 Europeans, and a large sum of money, then much wanted by the presidency of Madras. Nor was this the only want; Hyder's troops being so spread over the whole country, and a strong corps of his, under one of his best generals, named Lawlah, posted thirty miles to the northward of Madras, that all supplies coming from that quarter were instantly cut off. Sir Eyre Coote, in consequence of these circumstances, detached Col. Cosby, with three regiments of Native infantry, a regiment of cavalry, and light guns, to dislodge the above force.

This service was performed with such secrecy and skill, that every one of the enemy's videttes were taken; and had not a delay been occasioned by being obliged to wait the fall of the tide of a river that lay in the road, few of the enemy, it is supposed, could have escaped, it being intended to surprise them before day-light; but as the dawn broke when within a short distance, Col. Cosby's approach was prematurely descried, and the enemy had more time for preparation than was intended them. They, however, were soon defeated, and fled in confusion, leaving their camp, some horses, arms, and a quantity of provisions, cattle, &c. &c. to the captors; and Col. Cosby returned to head-quarters in the course of twenty-four hours, having in that time marched sixty miles, bringing in with him, besides what he had taken from the enemy, a further supply of provisions, collected on his route; and, on his arrival, received the following note from Sir Eyre Coote :—

"*December* 14, 1780.

"My dear Colonel,—I am sorry for your disappointment: however, you have done more than could have been expected, after the unfortunate detention you met with. You do very well to refresh your men at Motoo Kistna's Choultry. I march to-morrow to the Mount.   (Signed)   "Eyre Coote, Commander-in-Chief.
"*Lieut.-Col. Cosby.*"

Sir Eyre Coote soon after having assembled the army, in order to raise the siege of Arcot, then besieged by the enemy, Col. Cosby was honoured with the command of the advanced corps of the army during the remainder of that campaign, which (Arcot having surrendered) was chiefly consumed in watching Hyder's motions; until news arriving that a large French fleet was on the coast, and apprehending they might effect a landing of troops at Pondicherry, which, although it had been dismantled after our taking it, might still afford them a position, and facilitate a junction with Hyder, Sir Eyre Coote marched for that place with all possible expedition, and encamped on the Red Hills, about three miles from thence, on the 7th of February 1781.

The next morning, under the persuasion, from the various intelligence he had received, that Hyder was still at or near Arcot, at least eighty miles off, he took three battalions with him from the line of encampment into Pondicherry, for the purpose of destroying all the boats, which might otherwise be employed in disembarking any troops the French might have on board. Sir Eyre Coote had scarcely left the encampment, with Col. Owen, who commanded the detachment before mentioned, when Col. Cosby's duty, as commandant of the cavalry, having led him to visit the grand guard, about two miles distant, no sooner arrived there, than he perceived, from a rising ground, the whole of Hyder's army, in full march, on the Permacoil road, towards the Red Hills, on which the English army was encamped. He immediately dispatched one of his dragoon orderlies, with a penciled note, after Sir Eyre Coote, towards Pondicherry, informing him of this circumstance; and returning directly to the line of encampment, took upon himself the responsibility of ordering the drums to beat to arms, as he gallopped along the front, as the surest and most expeditious method of calling in stragglers, many being out foraging, and preparing the army against an attack; the line of encampment being at this time open in parts by the departure of the three battalions.

Sir Eyre Coote, on receiving Col. Cosby's note, immediately returned, and soon after put the army in motion towards Cudalore, apprehensive that Hyder might get there before him, and possess himself of that place, containing the only supply of provisions the English then had to look to. But Hyder, fortunately not knowing of the state of the English army, as above-mentioned, and having that morning made a very long march, instead of pushing for the Red Hills, deliberately took up his ground about five miles distance, on the opposite side of a large tank, where he remained till the British army was on the march for Cudalore in the evening, when he again put his in motion, and soon getting on the right flank of ours, cannonaded and annoyed us with flights of rockets during the greater part of the night, and till within a few miles of the Bound's Hedge of Cudalore, when he drew off, but not before his light troops had at one time penetrated between the rear of the English line and the rear guard, and carried off a considerable quantity of stores.

There were in camp two senior officers to Col. Cosby at the time he acted as before-mentioned, Lord M'Leod and Sir Hector Munro; he therefore felt it his duty first to inform the one on the left of the line, Lord M'Leod, of the enemy being in sight; but, as he declined giving any orders, referring Col. Cosby to his senior, who was at least two miles off on the right, the colonel conceived himself justified in adopting the measure he did, and which Sir Eyre Coote was pleased highly to approve of. This circumstance is mentioned to shew there are critical times, when a deviation from strict military etiquette may be excused.

The army being now placed in a temporary cantonment, within the Bound's Hedge of Cudalore, and Col. Cosby's health having for a considerable time been in a dangerous state, he was strenuously advised by the faculty to proceed to Europe as the only means of recovery*, and was charged with the confidential despatches of govern-

---

* Extract of a letter from the right honourable the president and select committee of Fort St. George to the honourable court of directors, dated Oct. 1782.

"Lieut.-Col. Henry Augustus Montague Cosby having for many months laboured under a severe indisposition, without any prospect of relief in this country, has at length been obliged to proceed to Europe for his recovery. The absence of an officer of his

ment and the Nabob of Arcot. But the English being then at war both with the French and Dutch, he was unfortunately made prisoner on his way, at the Cape of Good Hope; he however had the address to preserve his despatches, and being soon after allowed to proceed to England, had on his arrival the honour of knighthood conferred upon him by his late Majesty George the Third.

Sir Henry returned to his duty in India in 1784, and was shortly after, in the following year, appointed by Lord Macartney the Governor of Madras, successively to the commands of Trichinopoly and the Tinnevelly district. The Poligars of the latter country having fallen under the displeasure of the Nabob of Arcot, our ally, Sir Henry was directed to take the field against them with three regiments of Native infantry, a corps of European grenadiers, a regiment of cavalry, and field train of artillery, and was so fortunate as to bring them to terms in a short time.

In 1786 Sir Henry was promoted to the colonelcy of the 4th regiment of Madras European infantry, and to the command of a brigade, consisting of the above regiment and six regiments of Native infantry; and at the close of the same year returned to his native country; upon which occasion the government of Madras were pleased, in their despatch to the court of directors, by the ship in which Sir Henry came home, to write as follows:—

"*Madras, Dec. 23, 1786.*

"In the 80th paragraph of our address, under date the 14th of Oct. last, we informed your honourable court that we had permitted Col. Sir Henry Cosby to proceed to Europe; we have now to acquaint you that he embarks on board the Man-ship. It is not here necessary to dwell upon the character of Col. Sir Henry Cosby, of whose zeal

character and abilities is a real loss to the service, and we hope that the re-establishment of his health will soon permit him to return to it.

(Signed) "MACARTNEY, Gov. &c. &c.
"ALEXANDER DAVISON.
"J. HENRY CASAMAIJOR."

and service repeated testimonials are to be found upon our records; we shall therefore content ourselves with repeating to your honourable court, that he has uniformly maintained the military reputation which he long since acquired, and that we consider him as one of the most valuable officers in your service.

 (Signed)   " ARCHIBALD CAMPBELL, Gov. and Com.-in-Chief.
      " ALEXANDER DAVISON, Council.
      " JAMES HENRY CASAMAIJOR, Council."

In 1796, Sir Henry obtained the rank of major-general in his Majesty's army in the East Indies, with some other of the East India Company's officers, promoted to rank as such from 1793, in consequence of a new regulation made for the East India Company's army, in the settling of which Sir Henry having, at the request of the officers in India, been placed at the head of the committee in England for conducting the business, had the good fortune, not only to have his conduct highly approved of by the late Lord Melville, then Mr. Dundas, one of his Majesty's ministers, and at the head of the Board of Controul for India Affairs, but also by his brother officers in general, Mr. Dundas observing to the committee, on their taking leave at their last meeting, that his (Sir Henry Cosby's) disinterested zeal in behalf of his brother officers, and his unwearied exertions, entitled him to participate in the benefits to be derived from the arrangements, and that he thought he merited an exception to be made in his favor to the regulation, prohibiting an officer's return after five years' absence. Mr. Dundas, at the same time, appealed to the members of the committee for their sentiments on this proposition in favour of Sir Henry, " who unanimously bore testimony to the merits and virtues of their president, from whose unremitting attention, conciliating manners, and professional knowledge, they had on various occasions experienced the most important advantages; nor could a doubt exist that their brother-officers in India would with the utmost cordiality receive Sir Henry among them, and rejoice to see him in the station due to his long and distinguished services, and in the enjoyment of those honours and advantages, for the acquisition of which he had so strenuously and disinterestedly exerted himself in their behalf." It is necessary to observe, that this alluded to the circumstance of Sir Henry Cosby having been upwards of five years in England, and was by the act of parliament precluded from returning to India but under certain rules. The committee of officers were also pleased, at a subsequent meeting, after Sir Henry had withdrawn, to resolve on writing the following letter to the Company's army in India.

" *To the Officers of the Establishments of Bengal, Madras, & Bombay.*

" GENTLEMEN,—In our general letter by the " Dart," which will convey this despatch, we have, as far as the very short interval that has occurred between the final settlement and her departure would permit, explained every particular relative to the new arrangement.

" But our despatches would be materially defective, did we omit to express to you at this interesting period, when we are on the point of closing our proceedings, the impression we have received, and shall ever retain, of our respectable president's disinterested zeal, and unwearied exertions in your cause: these have commanded our esteem and gratitude through every stage of the negociation, and must render his name dear to every officer in the Honourable Company's service, whilst a trace of their military establishment in Asia shall exist.

   (Signed)   " J. PECHE, Maj.-Gen.—R. SCOTT, Lieut-Col.
           J. BRUNETT, Major.—J. TAYLOR, Capt.
           J. BAIRD, Lieut.—J. ASHWORTH, Lieut.
           and Sec.—J. SALMOND, Lieut. & Sec.

" *Berner's Street, Oct.* 13, 1795.

This was followed by a flattering mark of esteem of the coast-army in particular, evinced by a handsome service of plate, which they were pleased to order to be presented to Sir Henry.

A depot in England, for the training and disciplining 2000 recruits for the East India Company's service, forming part of the new regulation, Sir Henry was appointed to the command of that situation, intended to have been in the Isle of Wight; but, from a difference of opinion between the East India Company and the Board of Control, this measure was ultimately abandoned. He was afterwards promoted to the rank of lieutenant-general, in common with other major-generals of his standing in the East India service; and, at his death (17th January, 1822), was senior of that rank on the local list.

THE LATE MAJ.-GEN. SIR HENRY WHITE, K.C.B.

(Bengal Establishment.)

This officer commenced his military career the 1st of August 1772, as a cadet on the Bengal establishment. He was appointed ensign 14th N. I. 25th July 1776; lieutenant, 12th July 1778; captain, 21st March 1793; major, 31st August 1798; lieutenant-colonel, 21st February 1801; colonel, 25th July 1810; and major-general, 4th June 1813.

He served in the year 1773 under General Sir Robert Barker, and was present when the combined Mahratta army, under Madajee, Scindia, and Tykojee Holkar, were driven across the Ganges at Ramgaut. He was at that time in a distinguished corps, called the "Select Picket*," consisting of a body of gentlemen cadets, who were formed into a company, and carried arms, until vacancies occurred for their receiving commissions: this picket was always posted on the right of the advanced guard of the army in the field.

In 1774, Mr White served in the expedition against the Rohillas

---

* Of the officers composing this corps, only three are now living, and they are knights commanders of the order of the Bath.

under Col. Champion, who then commanded the Bengal army. He was present at the battle of Cutra, or St. George, where the enemy were defeated with great loss: their Com.-in-Chief was amongst the slain; and the existence of the Rohillas terminated as a nation :— that country, the finest in India, now forms one of the most valuable provinces of the British empire in Asia.

In 1776 he was appointed to the 2nd European regiment, being then an ensign: with this corps he served as adjutant, in Fort-William, upwards of twelve months; when, at his own request, he was removed to the 26th battalion, then in the field.

In 1778 he was promoted to the rank of lieutenant, and detached with artillery, 300 infantry, and 100 Rohilla horse, to fortify and defend the Ghauts (passes), near Hurdwar, against the incursions of the Sikhs, which service he accomplished, though the enemy made several attempts to cross the river at his post.

In the years 1780 and 1781, Lieut. White served with the grenadier corps then formed on the frontiers to act against the Mahrattas; and in 1782 he commanded the flank companies of the 18th regiment of Sepoys, with which he crossed the Jumna, near Culpee, and was present at the capture of that fort. He subsequently commanded the first battalion of the same regiment, and was employed with it for fifteen months in repelling the incursions of the Mahrattas from Culpee, and the neighbouring districts; after which it was marched to the lower provinces, on the occasion of Cheyt Sing's rebellion.

The peace of 1782, with the Mahrattas, leaving no prospect of service in the upper provinces of India, Lieut. White was removed, at his own request, to the 12th regiment N. I. then in the Carnatic. In the battle of Cudalore against the French army, in 1783, he commanded the first battalion of the 12th regiment, one of those corps from northern India which closed with, and astonished by their bravery, the oldest and best regiments from France.

The general peace in Europe and in Asia terminated the operations against Cudalore, into which the French retired; and Lieut.

White returned with his regiment to Caunpoor, a march of near 2000 miles.

On the breaking out of the war with Tippoo Sultaun in 1790, Lieut. White again marched from Bengal to the Carnatic, as senior subaltern of the 14th battalion of Sepoys, being one of the six battalions which marched under the command of Lieut.-Col. Cockerell, in aid of the forces employed against the Sultaun of Mysore.

In 1791 he was present with his corps at the siege and capture, by storm, of Bangalore; and also at the battle fought near Seringapatam, on the 15th of May in that year, when Tippoo's forces were defeated by the British army under the command of Lord Cornwallis.

After this the army retired, but continued in the field; and towards the close of the year operations being resumed with vigour, the important hill-forts of Savendroog, Nundydroog, Outradroog, Ramgurry, &c. fell to the British arms. At the storming of Savendroog*, Lieut. White led the 14th battalion.

* It may not be considered as uninteresting to furnish an account of that stupendous rock and its surrounding scenery :—The fortress of Savendroog is situated on one of the largest rocks in Mysore, rising above half a mile in perpendicular height, and extending at its base many miles in circumference; every part of it presenting a surface, black, steril, and unfriendly, communicating to the mind an idea of an exertion of nature, when in her most sullen mood.—The noxious vapours of the atmosphere descend, and collect around its summit in the night, and continue till dissipated by the rising sun, when the same dreary and unfruitful rock returns to the view. The ascent is difficult, and in most parts inaccessible; abrupt sallies of the rock oppose the approach and form innumerable precipices towering above each other in rugged majesty till by their aspiring height they are almost among the clouds. This inhospitable rock is surrounded by a country in strict concordance with itself, every where broken into ravines and frightful chasms, offering to the eye huge unconnected masses of matter, that seem to have been hurled from the hand of Omnipotence, to manifest on earth the power and activity of Celestial wrath. The thick and impenetrable jungle which covers the surface, as far as the eye can reach, except where the view is broken by the intervention of barren rocks, appears to have remained undisturbed since the earliest period of creation. The exertions necessary to form gun-roads through those pathless jungles, are inconceivable.

Savendroog is embraced on every side by thick belts of bamboo forests :—on entering these wilds, the appearance is picturesque and romantic; the branches issuing from the clumps of bamboo trees run in different directions, and form elliptical arcades of various heights and magnitudes, which recal to memory the structure so remarkable in the aisles of

Early in the following year, 1792, the army under Lord Cornwallis again advanced upon the capital of Mysore. On the night of the 6th of February, Tippoo Sultaun's entrenched camp, under the walls of Seringapatam, which was strengthened by several enclosed redoubts, well furnished with artillery, was stormed by the British troops under the personal command of Lord Cornwallis; on which occasion Lieut.

Gothic cathedrals. The heavens are completely shut out from the eye in these gloomy recesses, which are but faintly illumined by gleams of light, that here and there force a passage through the foliage. On penetrating into one of these wildernesses, a volunteer subaltern who had at this period joined the army, aptly applied to it the lines of Lucan, descriptive of the Massilian Grove; and he sometime afterwards related what he felt and saw in a different situation near Savendroog in the following words:—

" A few days preceding that fixed for the assault of Savendroog, I was stationed, early in the morning, with a company of Sepoys on the pinnacle of a rock, proudly eminent, and towering above the neighbouring heights. Here I was destined to behold a scene, exceeding in sublimity the powers of description. I gained the summit just as the approach of day was announced by the crimson rays that yet faintly gleamed across the east; but quickly the sun ascending above the horizon, shot his brighter rays on the surrounding objects, and disclosed to my astonished view the altitude of the rock on which I stood, and the extent of the prospect it commanded. I beheld myself elevated to the region of the clouds, which, now and then, in detached masses, rolled beneath me on either side of the precipice, intercepting from my view the scenes below; and now dispersing, my eye was left to range to the full extent of vision; beneath were collected the armies of the chief powers of the Peninsula—the British army, that of the Mahrattas, and of the Nizam, were all within my view: when I turned my eye to the rock of Savendroog, I beheld the garrison actively employed, and their besiegers not less so. I was musing on the scene, when I was suddenly aroused by the fire from the British batteries, which now began to play upon the fort, and which were immediately answered by the besieged garrison. The peal of cannon succeeded too rapidly to allow me to distinguish for an instant the absence of the roar, which was again repeated by reverberating through the vallies and rocky chasms, and rendered still more awful by the fall of immense masses of rock, which, rolling from precipice to precipice, seemed by their fall to shake the foundations of the heights from which they tumbled. The effect of such a scene can be better conceived than expressed. On the first opening of the fire my imagination was filled with the idea of the sound that at the awful day of trial shall summon the dead from the recesses of the grave; and, passing from one thought to another, I felt moved, like Xerxes, with sorrow, when he surveyed his mighty host, and reflected in how short a period the whole should be no more.

" After a few transitions from thought to thought, I fell into a profound reverie, and (if I can form any idea of what then passed in my mind) I fancied myself something more than mortal, and that I was elevated into the region of spirits; nor was I awoke from my dream, till a keen sensation of hunger afforded me an infallible symptom of my being still mortal."

White led the right wing of his battalion, the 14th N. I.; his commanding officer, Capt. Archdeacon, was on the right of the left wing; the column marched by the right: in the darkness of the night the wings of the battalion separated, and Capt. Archdeacon* was killed.

In all night operations some confusion or mistakes are inevitable, and the Com.-in-Chief, Lord Cornwallis, before day-break chanced to be in a very critical situation; which occasioned Lieut. White to move to his assistance, without delay, with the right wing of his battalion, and which suffered considerably in the charge made against the left wing of the Sultaun's army, then advancing to the spot where the Com.-in-Chief was but slenderly guarded. On the following day, Lord Cornwallis was pleased to signify, through Lieut.-Col. Cockerell, who commanded the division of the Bengal army serving in Mysore, his applause and approbation of the conduct of the detachment under Lieut. White, and ordered a letter to that effect to be read in front of the corps. The last of the above operations is admirably detailed in one of a series of admirable letters, written in 1793 and 1794, and from which the following is an extract:—

"I left the seven companies of the 52d regiment, and three companies of the 14th Bengal battalion (commanded by Lieut. White) on the inside of the Bound hedge, where after dispersing the enemy by their charge, they resumed their order of march by half companies, and pursued the fugitive enemy through their camp, which remained covered with elephants, cattle, guns, tents, and other equipage.—This disposition, which had been formed without halting, occasioned an interval between the front and some of the rear divisions of Europeans; a separation that was of but short duration, for the palace in the Deriah Dowlat Baugh, pointed out the direct line to the island, to which those divisions of Europeans with the companies of the 14th battalion, pushed on. Approaching within thirty or forty yards of the river they per-

* This worthy and esteemed character, whose social and other virtues won the respect and affection of his brother-officers, had laboured under an impaired state of health during the greater part of the war; and, from indisposition, he was but ill suited to undergo the fatigues of the 6th of February; but he would not repress a desire of sharing in what was expected to be the closing service of a long and arduous scene of uncommon difficulties.

ceived a body of the enemy's cavalry on its verge; they immediately formed and gave them a volley, which routed and dispersed them. The divisions now continued their march, and fording the river, joined those that had preceded them. While in the act of escalading the garden wall of Dowlat Baugh, Capt. Hunter, who commanded these seven companies of the 52d regiment, resolved to remain in the Dowlat Baugh till circumstances should point out where his co-operation might be necessary to any other attack. Here some diversity of opinion of his senior occurred between Capt. Hunter and the officer commanding the companies of the 14th battalion (Lieut. White), relative to the further progress of the Sepoys. The deference due to the opinion of his senior officer readily induced the latter to wave the suggestion of his own judgment. He, therefore, as soon as his grenadiers, and a party of pioneers, that joined him in the march through the enemy's camp, had forced open the exterior entrance to the palace, communicated his intention to Capt. Hunter of drawing up his party in the large saloon that they had just entered, and where he would be in readiness to receive his orders.

" While the grenadiers of the 14th battalion and the pioneers were employed in forcing their way into the palace, a party was discovered approaching the large flight of steps that led to it; on which the rear division was ordered to face, and wait their near approach. The party at first was so indistinctly seen, that it could not be ascertained who they were; but on advancing they proved to be of the enemy, who, ignorant that any part of our army had reached the Dowlat Baugh, were marching thither to take post. They approached so unguardedly, that their front rank was received on the points of the Sepoys' bayonets before they were aware of their danger, which as soon as they had thus fatally experienced, the surviving few precipitately fled.

"The party was now drawn up in a spacious hall, where they remained about an hour and a half. During this time the garden was reconnoitred by an officer and party of Sepoys. In its centre there was a square hall fitted up with great pomp and elegance: this was Tippoo's favourite place of retirement; but was chiefly distinguished for a much-admired painting, by a European artist, representing the defeat of Col. Baillie's army.

" In the course of reconnoitring the garden two men belonging to the enemy were seized—the intelligence received from them was alarming: they stated that the Sultaun's army was again rallying—that the fugitives were joining their left wing, which had not as yet been engaged. This information, together with the non-arrival of any other corps of the centre column, and the unaccountable silence that now began to prevail, and want of information relative to the operations or success of every other part of the army, naturally excited much anxiety. In this situation Lieut. Dowse, of the Madras Engineers, came down to the place in which the Sepoys had taken post, and expressed his willingness to go in quest of the centre column. The officer commanding embraced the offer, and sent a Jemadar's party of his men to accompany him on that perilous service. Two or three other of Havildar's parties were also ordered to proceed by different routes, in the hopes of collecting information: but this intention was defeated, for the enemy's cavalry soon obliged them to return; and soon afterwards a party of the enemy, with some guns, were observed in motion on the opposite side of the river; on which Capt. Hunter sent an officer to request Lieut. White to recross the river with his party, to charge, and seize the guns. For this purpose the three companies of N. I. instantly moved out; and at the same time the companies of the 52nd descended the garden-wall. Scarcely had they gained the river before the enemy, who had rushed into the Dowlat Baugh from the right and left, in considerable force, began to pour their musquetry on the party recrossing it: however, the men were so defended by the water, that the enemy's fire had little or no effect. Having gained the opposite bank of the river, they proceeded to the Sultaun's redoubt, now commanded by Capt. Sibbald, which they reached without interruption: but still they could obtain no information respecting the other parts of the army, nor of the situation of Lord Cornwallis. Here, therefore, it was determined to halt, and await the occurrence of any event that might direct them where their co-operation could be advantageously employed. It was soon discovered that the enemy were coming down in force: the men immediately got under arms; but, as their ammunition had been destroyed in crossing the river, the Sepoys expressed some uneasiness on that account. They were exhorted by their officers to disregard the want of ammunition, and to confide in their bayonets: they were desired to recollect the inefficiency of the enemy's musquetry, which they had so often experienced in the day, and that now, in the darkness of the night, it ought to be considered as utterly useless. To these arguments they listened, though without entire satisfaction: luckily, at that instant, the people in charge of the magazine of the 28th battalion having been accidentally separated from their corps, came up and afforded an abundant supply of ammunition. The serjeant in charge of it was ordered to supply the 52nd, and to carry the remaining part of it into Sibbald's redoubt, where it proved of the most essential use in the sequel of the day.

"Captain Madan, one of Lord Cornwallis's Aide-de-Camps, now came up, and informed Lieut. White of his Lordship's situation, and of his want of assistance. The party, on this intelligence, immediately moved off towards the ground which it was known his Lordship occupied: the Sepoys had quickly regained their wonted spirits, and now loudly vociferated thanks to their guardian Saint Hussian, for the supply of ammunition which he had so auspiciously sent them. The moon had already set, and the irregular flashes of musquetry that shot across the gloom afforded the only guide for their course; at length, amidst a confusion of noise, the sound of Highland bagpipes was heard, which indicated the 74th regiment, the principal corps of Lord Cornwallis's reserve, was near at hand: but, as some of the pipes used by the enemy had a similar sound, when distantly heard, Ensign (now Lieut.-Col. Sir Thomas) Ramsay, of the 14th battalion, the better to ascertain the body to whom they were advancing, was directed to run forward; and, if the conjecture of its being the 74th regiment was verified, to request the commanding officer to desire his men to hollo " Bangalore." " Bangalore!"

re-echoed through the air, from the men of the 52nd and those of the 14th, who were advancing in parallel lines.

" The enemy at this moment, with their fresh cushoons, were closing upon the 74th ; but, mistaking the party that was coming up for the advance of the columns of the army, they suddenly halted: Capt. Dugald Campbell, commanding the 74th regiment, availed himself with admirable promptitude of this circumstance ; and as soon as these companies of the 52nd and 14th battalion had joined him, he charged the enemy, though both Europeans and Sepoys did not amount to one battalion."

Lieut. White was, for his distinguished conduct on this occasion, allowed to continue in command of the battalion, 14th N. I., till its return to its own presidency in 1793, which, being an exception to the general rules of appointment that prevailed in the service at that time, was felt by Lieut. White and the whole army as a highly honourable distinction and reward, well calculated to excite professional emulation.

Having succeeded to the rank of captain in March 1799, he was appointed to the 2nd European regiment ; and, in 1794 and 1795, he was actively employed in raising a large body of recruits in the provinces under the presidency of Bengal, for filling up the corps on the Madras establishment.

In 1798, having attained the rank of Major, he proceeded to England to recover a constitution injured by so long a course of field-service.

It should here be noticed, that this officer had served nearly twenty-six years, almost always in the field, previous to his attaining the rank of field officer; that prior to the regulations of 1796 no regimental rank being known in the Company's army, captains commanding battalions were virtually in the situation of colonels; and their senior lieutenants in that of lieutenant-colonels or majors: moreover, that during the above-mentioned period, there were but few intervals of precarious peace ; and that, besides the more important services which have been particularized, Maj. White had largely partaken of the enterprising and partizan warfare constantly occurring in India, particularly in the Vizier's (now king of Oude) dominions, in quelling insurrection, subduing refractory Zeemindars, capturing mud forts, and repelling the incursions of freebooters, or insurgents, from neighbouring states.

After remaining a short time in England, Major White returned (August 1801) to his duty in Bengal; and having been promoted to the rank of Lieut.-Col., he was appointed to the command of the Company's 2nd European regiment.

At this period, Lieut.-Col. White suggested to the Com.-in-Chief the expediency of forming a strong corps of marine Sepoys, to serve by sea and land, and was ordered soon after to raise a regiment of two battalions, of 1000 men each: this object he successfully accomplished; and the 20th, or marine regiment, now forms one of the most valuable and distinguished corps in the East India Company's service.

The Mahratta war promising an active scene for military operations, Lieut.-Col. White applied to be removed from the command of the marine regiment, then at the presidency of Fort William, to a battalion in the field; and, in consequence, in September 1803, he joined the army, under the personal command of Gen. Lake, on its march to Agra.

The division of the army to which his battalion (the 1st of the 16th Bengal N. Reg.) belonged, was commanded by Brig.-Gen. Clarke, who was ordered to take the city of Agra by assault. The general forced the outward barriers at day-break, on the 10th of Oct.; and Lieut.-Col. White being on that occasion second in command, was detached to get possession of one quarter of the city, while the general pushed on to storm the Jumna Musjeed, or Great Mosque, which was strongly fortified, and defended by six battalions, with twenty-eight pieces of artillery. Gen. Clarke being, after a spirited attack, repulsed with considerable loss, retired from the town, and sent to Lieut.-Col. White to do the same, and join him without delay; but, conscious that the animation and confidence the enemy would derive by regaining the city, would be attended with the most fatal consequences, he, Lieut.-Col. White, took upon himself the dangerous responsibility of postponing a compliance with the orders of his superior officer, seized upon a strong position in the centre of the city, and entrenched his column in it, sending immediate information to Gen. Clarke, and suggesting his return; which the general accordingly did in the evening. On the following morning, the general proceeded to head-quarters, and Lieut.-Col. White was left to carry on the operations against the Jumna Musjeed.

Having discovered a favourable point from which to throw shells into the area of the Mosque, where the enemy's battalions were placed, stinted in room, Lieut.-Col. White counted upon the dismay and confusion that would be produced among such numbers by the bursting of some of his shells; and, accordingly, held his column in readiness to proceed to the assault the moment that should be the case. Such, however, was the effect produced by these measures, that two officers were sent out by the enemy, with proposals to capitulate; and the six battalions were permitted to march out in silence at nine o'clock at night, and the Jumna Musjeed commanding the principal gate of the fort, was taken possession of by Lieut.-Col. White, and his little band, who on this occasion covered themselves with glory, and greatly contributed, by their firmness and gallantry, to accelerate the fall of Agra, which surrendered by capitulation on the 18th of the month.

The Com.-in-Chief, Gen. Lake, in his despatch to government, dated 10th Oct. 1803, made the following observation:—

" I feel myself under particular obligations to Lieut.-Col. White, who commanded five companies of the 16th reg. N. I., for his judicious and gallant conduct on this day."

The following extract, from general orders, will also shew the sense entertained of Lieut.-Col. White's services on this occasion:—

" Head-Quarters, Camp before Agra, 13th *October* 1803.

" The Com.-in-Chief is happy in expressing his approbation of the behaviour of the officers and troops employed in seizing the city of Agra, on the 10th instant.

"His excellency feels particularly indebted to Lieut.-Col.-White, for the judgment and gallantry he displayed on that occasion; and to the officers and men of that detachment of the 16th regiment under his command."

In November 1803 he was appointed a brig.-gen., and was successfully engaged in the action of Laswarree, where a grape shot struck him in the breast. From the plan of attack adopted on this occasion, it necessarily followed, that the corps which were more immediately engaged, and suffered most in the battle of Laswarree, were those whose situation in the column of march brought them first in contact with that point of the enemy's position against which the attack was directed; and in the Com.-in-Chief's orders of thanks on the occasion, the six companies of the 1st battalion 16th regiment, commanded by this officer, and the 2nd battalion of the 12th, under Major (now Maj.-Gen. and C. B.) R. Gregory, were the corps of N. I. specially noticed, for their timely and gallant advance to the support of His Majesty's 76th regiment, which, being at the head of the column, was the corps to commence the attack, and close with the enemy. Our loss in the battle of Laswarree was very considerable, but it was decisive, and terminated the campaign in that part of India, by the defeat, capture, and dispersion of all the corps and field equipments in the service of Dowlut Rao Scindia in Hindostan.

In Dec. following this officer was employed by Lord Lake to command the forces detached from the main army, to get possession of the province of Gohud, then in the hands of the Mahrattas; and in prosecution of this service the capture of the important fortress of Gualior, often called the Gibraltar of the East, which, from its natural strength, was for ages considered secure against any open attack, became the object of primary attention; Lieut.-Col.-White, conscious that if Gualior fell, all the subordinate fortresses would speedily surrender, determined to strike at the point at once, from the fixed and general persuasion that the guns from the upper fort would speedily dislodge or destroy any that should be so desperate as to lodge themselves in the town, which went round the rock. No enemy had ever attempted the enterprise; the experience, however, which the lieut.-col. had had in the sieges of droog, or hill-forts, in the former Carnatic and Mysore wars, convincing him that this apprehension was ill-founded, he determined to attack the city by surprise, and was so fortunate as to get possession of it by a night assault. He then applied to Lord Lake for a strong battering train, and for additional Native troops. These being promptly supplied, breaching batteries were erected, and a practicable breach being made, in the only part of the fortress that was not impregnable, the place surrendered on the 4th of February 1804.

The success of this arduous undertaking was speedily followed by the surrender of the forts of Gohud and Doudpoor, and of all the numerous subordinate forts, and the retreat of the Mahrattas from every part of the province. The following extract from General Orders will shew the sense entertained by the Com.-in-Chief of this service:

"*Head Quarters, near Surate*, 10*th Feb.* 1804.

" The Com.-in-Chief has great satisfaction in publishing his high sense of the distinguished services of the detachment employed in the reduction of the fortress of Gualior under Lieut.-Col. White, throughout the whole of this arduous and important service, which claims his Excellency's best thanks and warmest acknowledgments."

After the fall of Gualior Lieut.-Col. White was appointed to the command of that place, in which he continued during the remainder of the war, until it was restored to Dowlut Rao Scindia in 1806. In the following year Lieut.-Col. White, finding his health greatly impaired, embarked for the Cape of Good Hope, and eventually proceeded to Europe.

On the augmentation of the Order of the Bath this officer, then a maj.-gen. in the army, was one of the first advanced to the dignity of Knight Commander.

The character of Sir Henry White, as drawn by an old brother officer, is so just that the Editor, who was personally attached to the general, cannot avoid here inserting it.

" Maj.-Gen. Sir Henry White was a real soldier; enamoured of danger and the active habits of the field, and contemning luxury and repose, he courted service wherever it was to be found; and when he arrived at rank and command, he scorned to seek popularity at the expense of his public duty, but sedulously endeavoured to call forth in every one under his authority the same ardent spirit of professional devotion in the discharge of their several duties, of which it was at once his pride and practice to set them an animating example.—The last moments of this officer were characteristic of that highly-gifted mind and spirit which distinguished him through life. His constitution, which was uncommonly good, gradually yielded to the decay of nature. Twelve or fourteen hours before his death, he ordered himself to be put on horseback, having always been enthusiastically fond of taking exercise in that way; and the following morning at two o'clock, in possession of all his faculties, he expired in his chair, with the serenity of a christian and the firmness of a hero.

" Thus departed this life, full of years and of honour, on the 7th of Nov. 1822, at Bath, Maj.-Gen. Sir Henry White, eighty years of age, nearly forty of which were passed in the active scenes of military life, in the service of the East India Company, and the subsequent period in the enjoyment of the well-earned honours which his Sovereign was pleased to bestow, and of a large circle of kindred friends who duly appreciated his professional and social virtues."

In addition to his valuable suggestion for forming a corps of Sepoy Marines, Sir Henry White submitted at different periods of his military career, a variety of plans for the improvement and benefit of the forces of the Honourable East India Company.

LIEUTENANT-GENERAL ROBERT MACKAY.

(Madras Establishment.)

THIS officer obtained an ensign's commission in the native infantry of the Madras establishment in 1775, after having served eleven months as a volunteer in the artillery. In 1778 he marched with a party from Madras to join the army assembling for the investment of Pondicherry under the command of Sir Hector Munro. Shortly after the army had broke ground before the place, the government of Madras ordered two additional battalions of native infantry to be raised; to one of which Mr. Mackay was appointed adjutant, but not being able to obtain permission to remain with the army till the capture of the fort, he proceeded to join the head quarters of the corps. On the fall of Pondicherry the battalions were reduced, and six months after he was re-appointed adjutant of the 4th battalion, native infantry.

This battalion early in Dec. 1780, formed part of the detachment sent from Madras, under the command of the late Lieut.-Gen. Sir Henry Cosby, to surprise a large body of the enemy's marauding horse, about thirty miles north of Madras, which by marching all night was partly effected, (see page 18.)

The 4th battalion joined the army commanded by Lieut.-Gen. Sir Eyre Coote,, encamped at St. Thomas' Mount, the latter part of December, 1780, and marched on the 1st of January, 1781, in order to relieve Wandiwash, then closely besieged by Hyder's son, Tippoo Saib, and on the route took the fort of Carangooly by a coup-de-main. After relieving Wandiwash, the army moved towards Pondicherry, and encamped on the red hills near it, while the Com.-in-Chief went into the place, and ordered the destruction of all the boats along the beach, and at the ford of the river Ariancoopan. Whilst this was executing, from the commanding ground on which the English were encamped Hyder's army was seen approaching at a considerable distance. The drums were immediately ordered to beat to arms, the tents struck, and information sent to the Com.-in-Chief, who directed that the army should march by the right forthwith, on the road to Cudalore, (as already stated in the narrative of Sir Henry Cosby's services, p. 19).

The army remained encamped at Cudalore near six months, that town forming a convenient depôt, whilst detachments were continually sent out to beat up the enemy's parties, and to collect cattle and grain. In June, the Com.-in-Chief having received information that a Braminick pagoda (or place of worship) called Chillimbrum, had been strongly fortified, and converted into a magazine of provisions, by order of Hyder, he determined to endeavour to take it by assault, and the army in consequence moved from Cudalore to Portonova, within a few miles from Chillimbrum. A detachment was then formed (of which the 4th battalion was a part) and marched to the village. On arriving at the main street, which led to the pagoda, it was warmly saluted by showers of ball from wall-pieces, &c. that scoured the street; however, a party with two twelve-pounders dashed through, and firing one of the guns against the gate, so shattered it, that the garrison called for quarter; but some of the English being overheard declaring that their ammunition was expended, the enemy returned to the works, and drove them from the gateway with considerable loss. Hyder, who, on the army reaching Cudalore, had marched south to plunder Tanjore and Tinnevelly, received so exaggerated an account of the defeat of the English upon this occasion, and so earnest a petition from the reporter to come, and by his presence complete their destruction, that he returned from the southern districts by very extraordinary forced marches, and his encampment was discovered before there was an idea of his being in the neighbourhood.

On the 1st July, 1781, Sir Eyre Coote moved out to meet the enemy, throwing all his baggage towards the beach, having been promised by Admiral Hughes all the protection his light vessels could afford. Before the action commenced, a masked battery was discovered, and avoided by a judicious counter-march. The battle began at seven in the morning. The English army, not 7000 strong, were opposed to a body of 100,000 regulars and irregulars. The numbers of the enemy enabling him to take possession of a range of sand hills, that rendered the situation of the English baggage very perilous, Sir Eyre Coote, who deemed it indispensable to dislodge him, ordered the 2nd line to attack and drive him from his position. The English charged twice with great spirit, but without success: the third time, however, they carried their point; and, on this being reported to the Com.-in-Chief, the first line was ordered to advance on the enemy, which it did at four in the afternoon, driving him before it until two o'clock the following morning.

After halting the next day, Sir Eyre Coote moved to the north-west, and captured the fort of Tripassoor, thirty miles west of Madras, a position of consequence, principally as a key to the pollams, or hilly country, governed by many petty chieftians, tributaries to the Nabob of the Carnatic, from whom were derived considerable supplies for the army. All the open country had been despoiled and ravaged by hordes of irregular horse, who burnt the villages, plundered and massacred the inhabitants, and drove all sorts of cattle off to the Mysore country. Arrangements being made for a field-hospital at this place, the Com.-in-Chief marched towards the enemy, who was strongly posted at Perambancum, on the same ground where Col. Baillie's detachment had been defeated the year before, having formed powerful batteries of heavy ordnance with the walls of the ruined houses; and having a deep and broad ravine covering the whole of these works, and a great part of the infantry of his army; several heavy batteries enfilading at many points the road by which the English approached the position.

A firing was commenced by the enemy on the advanced guard, from some guns of a small calibre, about eight in the morning, (27th Aug. 1781), but the action did not become general until near eleven. While the general was reconnoitring, the enemy's batteries caused severe havoc, but after a long struggle and sanguinary contest, they were obliged to yield. The 2nd line, commanded by Col. Pearce, (to which the 4th battalion was called from the baggage guard, during the battle) was skirmishing with the enemy all night, and at day-break next morning was near a very large force of horse and foot, commanded by Tippoo Saib, but who, on its advancing, precipitately retreated.

On the 28th the English halted, and marched the next day in the direction of Velore, a hundred miles west of Madras. On the 29th

Sir Eyre Coote having intelligence that the enemy was near, strengthened his body guard with the picquets in waiting, and went out to reconnoitre, shortly after sending orders for the army to join him. The detail of the day having again placed the 4th battalion on the baggage guard, in marching to the position pointed out by the field officers of the day, it was attacked by a party under the command of Hyder's son, Tippoo Saib, who with considerable address endeavoured to flank it with ten field pieces; this attempt being defeated, he made an effort to prevent it, taking post in a choice situation against horse that had been selected; in this he was also foiled: he nevertheless attacked, but the broken rocky ground proved an obstacle to his success. The general engagement began immediately after this battalion was left in quiet possession of its post. The first observation of the battalion on its commencement created considerable alarm: an immense body of cavalry was seen moving down in a solid column upon the 2d line, but it was soon perceived that the English troops wheeled right and left, from the centre backwards, and let them pass, paying them well for their temerity. As soon as the rear of the column had cleared the English army, the enemy returned in the same manner, and were received as on the first time: their number were supposed to be ten thousand: of their horse they lost nine hundred: an officer and a standard were also taken.

Sir Eyre Coote, solicitous to maintain his army without looking to Madras for supplies, where a great scarcity prevailed, encamped in the Pollams, and in furtherance of his object of providing his army during the rainy season, formed a detachment of three native corps, the 4th, 8th, and 16th, under the command of Lieut.-Col. Owen, to provide and send into camp rice and cattle for the army. This detachment marched in October and encamped near the mouth of a pass, being almost centrically situated between its own army and that of Hyder's, cantoned at Arcot. The 16th battalion was immediately detached with all the tent bullocks of the three corps into the interior of the Pollams, to procure and dispatch provisions to the army, and from the head-quarters of the detachment, parties were constantly sent out to endeavour to intercept convoys going to Hyder's camp, and to surprise the enemy's horse in the neighbourhood, but whose intelligence was so superior that the parties seldom succeeded. They were upon the whole, however, such an annoyance to Hyder, that he sent a numerous and select corps of horse and foot to surprise and cut them off. This force, after marching all night, arrived at the English outposts at day-break, drove them in, and followed them so rapidly, that there was scarcely time to blow the tents up with the spare ammunition, and reach the pass, before the enemy arrived in great force. Fortunately the evening before this attack a company of European grenadiers, two six-pounders, and three two-pound gallopers, with a small party of pioneers, had joined the detachment from the army, with a view to an attack by a coup-de-main on a small fort. This reinforcement proved highly serviceable, as without the guns the detachment could not have defended the mouth of the pass, from whence the enemy was driven repeatedly, and great havoc made in his columns of horse. Whilst this took place in the rear, the enemy endeavoured to establish himself in our front, but failed and were driven back. Thus a small detachment of not 1500 firelocks, successfully defended themselves against 30,000 picked men. The loss it sustained was considerable, but by no means in proportion to that of the enemy. In the evening the detachment joined the army, which was marching to its succour. Shortly after the army was cantoned for the remainder of the rainy season, within twenty miles round Madras.

The beginning of Jan. 1782, the army marched with a considerable supply of grain and provisions, for the relief of the garrison of Velore, embracing a range of hills all the way on its baggage flank, until within a short march of the place. When within a few miles of Arcot, Hyder's head-quarters at this time, and capital of the Carnatic, an attack was expected from his army on the following morning, but during the night he employed a party of pioneers to inundate a large track of low ground that the English were obliged to pass in their march, by cutting the banks of a large reservoir for watering the rice fields in the dry season.

The English proceeded on their march the next day (11th Jan.) with no other than the usual attendance of irregular horse, until the European brigade of the army got entangled in the slough, when the horse dispersed, and a furious cannonade commenced, but which slackened on some guns being opened by the English; and the officer commanding the 2nd having halted, and advanced towards the enemy, he retired.

On the 13th the English returned by the same route, menaced by a considerable body of horse, which, being dispersed by a few rounds from the twelve-pounders, Hyder's army was discovered drawn up in line at a short distance. Sir Eyre Coote immediately advanced, but the enemy retired precipitately, keeping up a fire of heavy artillery from a great distance.

After various marches and counter-marches, and several feints to alarm the enemy for some of his principal posts, the English by a forced march got between Hyder and one of his chief depôts, called Arnee: to save this place he now advanced, and it was expected that he would hazard an action; but in this the English were disappointed, for as they moved forward he retreated, and by the superiority of his draught cattle, left them as distant as he pleased. Sir Eyre Coote, annoyed at not being able to get near enough, ordered all the flank companies of the army to be formed in front of the line, and to push on at charging pace until they came up with the enemy's rear, supporting the flank companies by an advance of the rest of the troops: they overtook the enemy in the bed of a river, and captured a number of ammunition carts and several tumbrils.

Tippoo dying the latter end of this year (1782,) his son was obliged by this event to appear in the Mysore to establish his authority, leaving the English to cope with the French only, and detachments of Tippoo's troops left with them. The celebrated Marquis de Bussy commanded them in Cudalore, a place taken from the English, and the fortifications of which he had much improved. No further operations of importance occurred in this war.

Lieut. Mackay was appointed aid-de-camp to Col. Reinbold, of the

Hanoverians, who had two regiments under his orders in India, and in 1783 took the field under the command of Gen. Stuart, then commanding the troops of the Madras establishment.

The army was encamped on the south-west bank of the river Cavery, near the fort of Chingleput, and while there, Sir Eyre Coote died*, having returned to Madras from Calcutta. The loss of this general was unfeignedly lamented by the whole army, natives as well as Europeans, by all of whom he was sincerely beloved.

About the middle of May the army moved from the banks of the Cavery southward towards Cudalore, where the tents were pitched south of the bound-hedge, and lay encamped inactive for many days, till the field-officers of the army obtained (at their unanimous request) a council of war, when it was determined to attack the French lines, which they had thrown up along the whole front of the English army. In pursuance of this plan, a field-officer was detached in the night of the 12th of June, with a force to drive the enemy from a post they had on a hill commanding our left flank: if the attack succeeded, he was directed to hoist a flag on the point of the hill at day-break, when a battalion of European grenadiers (to which Lieut. Mackay belonged) it was agreed, should immediately march, and attack a grand battery that terminated their lines. The signal being hoisted, this body of 330 choice veterans moved on to the berme of the ditch, but found it so deep and well stoccadoed at bottom, that it was utterly im-

---

* Sir Eyre Coote was not less a fortunate than an heroic soldier. In his mind military glory and the honour of his country superseded every personal consideration. To firmness and intrepidity of character he united the most tender sensibility: the pleadings of distress never reached his ear in vain—the voice of sorrow was the eloquence that overwhelmed him; to that his heart, too tender for the keenness of its feelings, melted into tears of pity and benevolence.—It may here be observed, that the foundation of our empire in Asia was laid, and its subsequent aggrandizement effected, by an handful of men surrounded by hostile myriads. A constellation of extraordinary characters (amongst whom stood prominent, Clive, Lawrence, Ford, and Coote,) appeared in the earlier periods of the extension of our Asiatic dominions, as if decreed by fate to erect the British standard in the East— to establish it on a firm and permanent basis, from whence its conquests were destined to extend beyond the banks of the Brahmapootra on the east, to the Indus on the west—to aspire to the Indian Caucasus on the north, and on the south to be bounded only by the shores of the ocean.

possible to succeed: on retiring, the corps suffered severely from the repeated discharges of cannister grape from four 26-pounders. Another mode of attack was then resolved on, which was, that the grenadiers should endeavour to turn the flank, and get in the rear of this powerful battery, whilst the first and second lines attacked generally in front. This was carried into execution; but the enemy having laid the ground the English had to pass under water; they were obliged to wade through mud and water for nearly half an hour, by which means they were so much retarded that their first line, headed by a young corps that had never before been in action, were so roughly treated by the fire of grape from the grand battery, that they were panic-struck, and retired. Possession of this battery being however obtained, by an officer's party of N. I., the army proceeded, and took all the small works along the line. It appeared that the French on seeing that the havoc made on the head of the English column (almost every officer in the front divisions being killed or wounded) caused the men to waver, sallied out of the battery, and attacked the first line with irresistible impetuosity. The grenadiers had not been many minutes in possession of the enemy's lines, when four regiments were seen approaching from the direction of the English camp, and which being recognised as French, the English were compelled to retreat, with some loss, to the grand battery, which they retained. The number of killed and wounded on both sides in this battle (called Cudalore) was great. The English had 1500 killed and wounded; the French lost full as many.

On the 20th of the same month, the enemy, in three columns, made a sally on the English trenches. One column succeeded in getting between the trenches and the supporting picquets in waiting, whilst the other two attacked the right and left of the trenches. The darkness of the night, and the turning of the English flank, rendered their situation extremely difficult; but the Bengal native troops behaved with undaunted gallantry, the rear rank opposing in the rear, and the front rank over the parapet: at the same time, a wing of the grenadier battalion arriving from camp, immediately stood to their arms, and closed the interval through which one of the columns entered; and, by some accident, some drummers beat the grenadier's march, which accelerated the retreat of the enemy: a Count Dumas, who led the left column, was taken prisoner; the right-hand column was dreadfully raked by a small battery of six-pounders, whilst striving to escalade; and the one that entered by the right, lost above 100 in prisoners, besides killed and wounded: the English also suffered considerably.

At this period a great scarcity of provisions began to prevail, so that the cattle for the carriage of the tents, &c. were dying in the lines, and the army were unable to move for want of means to convey guns, tents, or ammunition; thus every thing wore a most gloomy and unpromising aspect, when most unexpectedly a flag of truce arrived from the enemy, announcing a peace in Europe between France and England, which was confirmed from Madras next day, and a cessation of hostilities took place, at a time when the ruin of this army seemed inevitable.

Lieut. Mackay immediately obtained permission to proceed to Madras, where he was appointed to a native corps in one of the northern provinces. In the year 1785 he was made capt.-lieut. to a corps doing duty at Madras; and in the year 1789 promoted to a company, and appointed to a regiment of European infantry at Velore; on joining which, he obtained the grenadier company, with which he had served in the field nearly two years as first lieutenant.

A few months after, Captain Mackay was appointed by the government of Madras to the command of the fort of Arnee, of which it had been determined to make a grand depôt during the war just then recommenced with Tippoo Sultaun. He accordingly took charge of the garrison of Arnee in May 1789, where he remained during the war, and at its close was relieved, and joined his regiment at Velore.

War with France having succeeded the short peace, an attack on Pondicherry was resolved on, and the corps to which Captain Mackay then belonged not being one of those selected to form the siege, he got appointed to one that was; and when the place fell, had the temporary command of a corps that formed part of the garrison.

Early in the year 1793 he was appointed to command a native corps in the subsidiary force of the Nizam of the Deccan, which he joined immediately. The next year the detachment, consisting of two native battalions, a company of artillery, and six six-pounders, were ordered to proceed against some refractory subjects of the Nizam's; whom, after beating in the field, and taking all their guns, he was directed, the next evening, to take the pettah, or town. On getting over the mud wall that surrounded it, he found that a party, twice the amount of the number under his command, were in possession of a high hill, of difficult access, in the middle of the place, which he was obliged to storm, and was so fortunate as to succeed, with the loss of only one man, taking a standard, and killing and wounding several. Captain Mackay next besieged, with only two breaching guns, a strong fort called Rachare, and took it by assault on the second day.

In the year 1797 he left the subsidiary force, and was appointed major to a regiment, named in the arrangements for forming an army to attack the Spanish settlement of Manilla: the 1st division of transports with troops arrived at the Prince of Wales's Island, the rendezvous, but the expedition being countermanded, Major Mackay was directed, with four companies of the regiment to which he belonged, to reinforce the officer commanding the troops at Amboyna; and had permission to return to the coast in 1799, on account of ill health. In 1800 he was made commandant of Ryacottah, on the frontiers of Mysore: in six months afterwards he was directed to complete his battalion to 1200 firelocks, and to march, agreeable to instructions sent him, to watch the motions of some plunderers that, during harvest time, frequently descended from the hills, and pillaged the neighbouring villages. A short time after, he was ordered by the commanding officer of the troops in Mysore (Col. Wellesley, now Duke of Wellington,) to march to Bangalore, there to await the arrival of a field officer of His Majesty's service, marching with troops and recruits for the regiments of the line in the Mysore country, and with that party to proceed to Seringapatam.

On the day of his arrival, Major Mackay received the commands of the governor in council of Madras to move immediately to take possession of a large tract of country ceded to the Madras government by his highness the Nizam of the Deccan: this accomplished, he was ordered to join a division of the army under the command of Maj.-Gen. Dugald Campbell; by whom he was almost immediately after detached with his own corps, and a brigade of guns, to take possession of the capital of a petty hill Rajah, and secure him as refractory and disobedient. The Rajah escaped, but made his peace soon after. Maj. Mackay was next detached with a troop of cavalry, and an officer of artillery, with a brigade of guns added to his corps, on a hill and jungle service; on which occasion he was obliged to conceal his corps in the woods by day, and march all night. He was three weeks occupied on this tiresome expedition, taking one of the petty chieftains prisoner, burning the gates, and destroying the little fort of another, and forcing a third to make his submission.

In 1802 he went on furlough to Madras, and while there on private business, an application was received by the governor from the commanding officer in Mysore, requesting that two experienced field officers might be sent up to him, to command two corps that he thought required older officers at their head than they had, as he was going on service; and the subject of this memoir was directed by the Com.-in-Chief to hold himself in readiness to proceed to Seringapatam, as the exigencies of the service required it. He begged leave to set off immediately, as the distance was great, and it was the hottest season of the year; but was assured, that he should be informed in due time to enable him to join: he repeated his application without effect; and when ultimately he obtained permission to march, though he used every effort, by travelling day and night, he arrived too late. He did duty at Seringapatam until Sept., when he applied for leave to go to England, after above twenty-nine year's service. In Oct. 1802 he left Madras, and arrived in England March 1803.

The 21st September 1804 he obtained the rank of lieut.-col. commandant; 25th April 1808, that of colonel; 4th of June 1811, that of maj.-gen.; and the 19th July 1821, of lieut.-gen.

THE LATE LIEUT.-GEN. VERE WARNER HUSSEY.

(Bengal Establishment.)

THIS officer was appointed to the artillery on the Bengal establishment in 1769; arrived 6th Oct. 1770; lieutenant fireworker, 12th March 1771; lieutenant, 10th Jan. 1773; captain, 28th Feb. 1777; major, 17th April 1786; lieut.-col., 14th Sept. 1790; colonel, 8th Jan. 1796; maj.-gen., 1st Jan. 1798; and lieut.-gen., 1st Jan. 1805.

He embarked for Bengal in 1770, where he engaged in arduous service in common with his contemporaries. Whilst in the Carnatic, under the command of Gen. Sir Eyre Coote, and on actual service, he received a severe wound. After three years confinement, the Gov.-Gen., Mr Hastings, appointed him commissary of ordnance and stores out of the provinces, and to the command of the artillery in the province of Benares, and in the garrison of Chunar, where all the military boats at that station were placed under his charge.

In 1785 he proceeded to Europe on furlough, and returned to India in 1788; in 1797 he succeeded to the command of the Bengal artillery; in 1799 he returned to Europe; and in 1803 was transferred to the retired list.

Owing to the wound above-mentioned, Lieut.-Gen. Hussey continued very lame till his death, which took place in 1823.

LIEUTENANT-GENERAL WILLIAM NEVIL CAMERON.

(Bengal Establishment.)

THIS officer was appointed a cadet on the Bengal establishment in Feb. 1772, and having some knowledge of mathematics, was nominated an assistant engineer, and employed at the fort of Buxar till 1774, when he joined the cadet corps serving with the army in the Rohilla campaign, and was employed under the field engineer in throwing up some temporary works. In May 1775 he obtained a commission in the corps of engineers, and joined at Fort William; shortly after which he was appointed deputy to the field engineer with the army in the Vizier's country, where he was engaged in active service. In 1777 he rejoined the head-quarters of his corps at Fort William; in July 1778 he was promoted to the rank of lieutenant; and about the end of that year was ordered to proceed with a detachment under Maj. Camac, intended to join Gen. Goddard in the Mahratta country; but after having moved to the Company's western frontier, and halted for some weeks, the detachment was recalled, and cantoned at Dinapore. In 1779 he joined a detachment under Maj. Popham, as field engineer, which crossed the Jumna to assist the Rannah of Gohud in opposing the Mahrattas, and was engaged in the operations terminating with the escalade of the fortress of Gualior, which was effected by surprise just before the dawn of the 3d of August 1780. About this period government deemed it advisable to threaten Scindia's northern frontier, and a strong force, commanded by Col. Camac (added to the detachment serving in the Gohud country,) was appointed for this service; to which this officer was attached, and saw some active service; as well as with a superior force under Col. Muir, who succeeded Col. Camac. About this period (June 1781) he was promoted to the rank of captain. In 1782 arrangements being made with the Mahrattas, the army went into cantonments, and Capt. Cameron proceeded to Calcutta.

In 1784 he was appointed field.engineer to the army serving in the Vizier's country; and in 1787 obtained the situation of commanding engineer in the fortress of Chunar. The 15th Nov. 1788 he was promoted to the rank of major; and the 24th Feb. 1793 to the rank of lieut.-col. and chief engineer at Fort William, where he continued to fill the duties of that office, with a seat at the military board, till 1804, and then was brought on the general staff of the army as maj.-gen. Early in the following year, finding his constitution much impaired, he was obliged, against his inclination, to return to Europe, after a continued absence of thirty-three years. He obtained the rank of colonel 3d May 1796; of maj.-gen. 1st Jan. 1801; and of lieut.-gen. 25th April 1808.

LIEUTENANT-COLONEL HENRY A. O'DONNELL, C. B.

(Bengal Establishment.)

THIS officer arrived at Madras as a Bengal cadet in January 1781, and served in a corps of cadets, when Hyder Ally threatened that fortress. In May of the same year, he was appointed, as lieutenant, to the detachment of Bengal troops, serving in the west of India, under Gen. Goddard; and on his way to join that army at Bombay by sea, volunteered to serve at the sieges of Nagapatam and Trincamale, and was wounded in the head at the storm of fort Osnaburg, at the latter place. On his recovery he joined Gen. Goddard's army, and partook of the services performed by it. In 1791 he volunteered, and served in the Carnatic, in the war against Tippoo Sultaun, under Lord Cornwallis, until the storming of Tippoo's lines, on the 6th of Feb. 1792, at Seringapatam, put an end to that war. In 1793 he was employed in quelling an insurrection of Rajah Damoodah Bunga in the Midnapore district, pursuant to the instructions of Mr. Dowdeswell, the judge and magistrate of that district; upon which occasion he received a letter expressing the approbation of that gentleman for the promptness and decision with which he executed that duty. The 7th of January 1796, he obtained the rank of captain. In the latter end of 1802 he served under the late Lord Lake at the sieges of Sasnee and Bidzergur, at the siege of Agra in 1803, and at the battle of Laswarree on the 1st Nov. in that year. In 1804 Capt. O'Donnell commanded the 12th regiment of Bengal N. I. under Brig.-Gen. Monson, in the disastrous retreats to and from Rampoorah. The grenadier companies of that detachment were formed into a body, which he commanded in a night attack, on the south bank of the Chumbul river; upon which occasion he succeeded in completely routing the enemy, and taking a considerable number of horses and camels. He was promoted to the rank of major 21st Sept. 1804, and commanded a battalion of the 12th regiment N. I. under Lord Lake, in his extraordinary forced marches from Delhi to Furruckabad, with the reserve of the army, where Holkar's army was surprised and routed. He served at the siege of Deeg in command of the same corps, and was wounded in the right hip at the first storm of Burtpoor, in Jan. 1805. In March 1807 he commanded a force sent against the fort of Ackbarpoor in the Vizier's dominions, which he took by storm, and received the thanks of the resident at Lucknow on that occasion. In April 1808 his battalion formed part of a detachment, under the command of Lieut.-Col. (now Maj.-Gen.) R. Gregory, employed in reducing the forts of Buddree and Gowrah, in the dominions of the Newaub Vizier. In Oct. of the same year he commanded a force employed against some refractory Zemindars, who, possessing nineteen mud forts in the Vizier's dominions, set his government at defiance: having succeeded in taking the principal fort by storm, the others speedily surrendered, and Major O'Donnell got possession of the whole in a few days; upon which occasion he received letters, expressive of the high approbation of his Excellency the Com.-in-Chief, the commander of the forces, Capt. Baillie, resident at Lucknow, and of his Highness the Newaub Vizer—and of which the following are extracts. He was promoted to lieut.-col. 8th Sept. 1809, and removed to the command of the 2nd battalion 4th N. I.

Lieut.-Col. O'Donnell was appointed June 4, 1815, a knight companion of the order of the Bath.

Extracts of Letters referred to in the preceding Service.

" To Major O'Donnell, Commanding at Purtaub Ghur.

" Sir,—Having submitted your letters of 1st, 2nd, and 3rd instant to Maj.-Gen. St. Leger, commanding in the field, I am directed to convey to you his sincere congratulation upon the success resulting from your gallantry and decision in the attack of the fortress of Peter Serai. (Signed) " Wm. Casement, A. D. A. G."

" D. A. G. Office, Head-quarters in the Field,
    Caunpoor, Nov. 8, 1808."

" To Major O'Donnell, Commanding at Purtaub Ghur.

" Sir,—I am directed by Maj.-Gen. St. Leger, commanding the army in the field, to acknowledge the receipt of your despatch of the 5th inst. and to express to you his warm acknowledgments and congratulations upon the very merited success so honourably obtained by the detachment under your command. The Maj.-Gen. refrains from saying more upon what so soon must be made known to the Com.-in-Chief, but desires me to assure you, he anticipates with heartfelt satisfaction a communication of his Excellency's sentiments upon the result of a very short but honourable warfare, so entirely to be attributed to your personal decision, with the gallantry of the officers and troops under your command.

(Signed) " Wm. Casement, A. D. A. G.

" D. A. G. Office, Head-quarters in the Field,
    Caunpoor, Nov. 12, 1808."

" To Major O'Donnell, Commanding at Purtaub Ghur.

" Sir,—I am directed by Maj.-Gen. St. Leger, commanding in the field, to communicate to you the very great satisfaction he derives in conveying to the officers and soldiers under your command the very merited and high approbation of the Com.-in-Chief, which the Maj.-Gen. cannot perform in a manner more satisfactory to himself and to them, than in the expression of his desire that the acting Adjut.-General's letter, a copy of which is hereunto annexed, may be read and explained to the Native soldiers, at the head of the detachment that was employed so honourably to themselves, and beneficially to the service.   (Signed)   " WM. CASEMENT, A. D. A. G.

" *D. A. G. Office, Caunpoor, Nov. 27, 1808.*"

" *To* MAJOR-GENERAL ST. LEGER, Commanding in the Field.

" SIR,—I have had the honour to lay before the Com.-in-Chief your letter of the 7th inst. referring to Maj. O'Donnell's despatch of the 1st to my address, giving an account, for his Excellency's information, of the success of his operations against the refractory Zemindars of the Nawaub Vizier in the district of Purtaub Ghur.

The Com.-in-Chief requests you will signify to Maj. O'Donnell his Excellency's best thanks for the promptitude, judgment, and decision, with which he conducted the service recently entrusted to him; and that the same be communicated to Major Knox, and the whole of the officers and men composing Maj. O'Donnell's detachment, by whose gallant exertions the authority of the Vizier has been so speedily re-established, and the detachment so soon enabled to return to its cantonments.   (Signed)   " G. F. FAGAN, Acting Adj.-Gen.

" *Head-quarters, Camp Hoorall, Nov. 16, 1808.*"

" *To* MAJOR O'DONNELL, Commanding the Detachment in Kewaee.

" SIR,—I have the honour to acknowledge the receipt of your letter under date the 1st inst., conveying the satisfactory and important intelligence of the success of the troops under your command against the fortress of Peter Serai, and the entire destruction of the rebellious garrison of that fortress. The extraordinary rapidity and success of your operations against Peter Serai are highly creditable to your zeal and judgment in conducting them, and to the gallantry of the

troops under your command; and I anticipate the speedy surrender of all the remaining fortresses, as the effect of the severe but salutary example which you have afforded in the reduction of Peter Serai." (Signed) " J. BAILLIE, Resident.
"*Lucknow, 5th Nov.* 1808."

" *To* MAJ. O'DONNELL, Commanding the Troops at Purtaub Ghur.

SIR,—I have the honour to acknowledge the receipt of your several despatches.

" The rapidity and complete success of your operations in the district of Kewaee have already obtained, as they merited, the expressions of my admiration and respect, and have been communicated in suitable terms for the notice of the Gov.-Gen. in council. His Exc. the Vizier has also desired me to convey to you his sentiments of approbation and applause. (Signed) " J. BAILLIE, Resident.
"*Lucknow, 12th Nov.* 1808."

LIEUTENANT-COLONEL GEORGE CONSTABLE.

(*Bengal Establishment.*)

THIS officer joined the reg. of Bengal art. in Fort William, as a cadet, the 5th Nov. 1781; he was promoted to lieutenant fireworker 26th July 1782; to lieutenant, 26th June 1788; to capt.-lieut. 8th Jan. 1796; to captain, 18th Feb. 1802; to major, 28th Feb. 1806; and to lieut.-col. 5th Dec. 1809.

In 1781 he was employed in garrison duties, and the practice of artillery in its various branches; in 1782 in arrangement and exercise of the camp at Dum Dum, in the vicinity of Calcutta; and in 1783 he embarked on board ship for Madras, and joined the Bengal army in the Carnatic under the command of the late Gen. Sir Eyre Coote. On peace being established with the Mysore chief, the artillery returned by sea to Bengal. In 1784 he was ordered on garrison duty at Fort William, and employed in regimental exercise and practice of artillery in the camp at Dum Dum.

In 1785 he was detached to the powder works for proof and examination of gunpowder, on removal of the contractor, Capt. Stewart, Edward Hay, Esq. in charge. At the end of this year he was ordered to join the Gholundauz N. Art. at Chunar cantonments, where he remained until the reduction and distribution of that corps, as ordered by government, the men being transferred to the N. I. battalions.

In 1786 he was ordered to join by water the artillery at Dinapore, and was employed in the practice of artillery on the banks of the Soane river, constructing mud redoubts, mining and blowing them up, and in surveying Patna magazine. At the annual relief of the troops at the close of 1787 he was ordered to Caunpoor with the Dinapore division, consisting of the King's and Company's troops, under the command of Col. N. Macleod, and put on field-roaster duty.

In June 1788, orders being issued for his promotion and removal from the field, he proceeded by water to the presidency, and was posted to a company of artillery at Dum Dum. In Jan. 1789 he was ordered to march from the presidency, with two companies of artillery, for Burhampoor and Dinapore, accompanied by two new constructed six-pounder carriages for experiment: they were reported after trial unserviceable. In Nov. he was directed to proceed from Dinapore, with one company of artillery, to Caunpoor, where he cantoned. In 1790 and 1791 he was employed in regimental duties, and frequently detached to Lucknow. In 1792 he had orders to bivouac on the flank of cantonments with a company of artillery; and in Nov. he marched and entered Futtehgurh. In 1793 general orders were issued for the station troops to retrograde to the presidency, infantry for Barrackpoor, artillery for Dum Dum, where he joined the head-quarters of the regiment, and after practice with the corps moved into Fort William. In 1794 he was directed, with three companies of European artillery, with their gun lascars, staff, and establishment complete, to embark on board the ship Fort William for Madras. The artillery detachment was destined to accompany a chosen division of the army assembled in the vicinity of Madras, and intended for foreign service; but on Lord Hobart's arrival from England to relieve Sir Charles Oakley, the governor of Madras, the design was abandoned. It was then considered unadvisable to embark so large a European force from the Coromandel coast: the artillery re-embarked for Bengal, and landed in Fort William. In 1795 he was employed on the garrison duties; in 1796 he received orders to embark on board of boats, with a detachment of artillerymen and guns, to proceed by the Sundyabunds for Chittagong, where he landed, and commanded the artillery in that province to the close of 1797. From thence he was directed to proceed by water alone to join the army in the field under Gen. Sir James Craig: he embarked in the river Ganges, and landed at Caunpoor in Dec. In 1798 he was detached with men and guns to the residency at Lucknow, where he remained three months on command, and then fell back to Caunpoor. In Dec. he accompanied the field army for Anoopshire, to give check (as published in general orders by Gen. Sir James Craig) to Zeman Shaw, the king of Cabul's advancement in favour of Tippoo Sultaun.

Shortly after the army had reached its destination at Anoopshire, intelligence being received of Vizier Ally's rebellion at Benares, the field army quickly retrogaded, and encamped at Lucknow; from which capital this officer was detached, under command of the late Gen. Robert Stuart, with a well-equipped artillery, in pursuit of Vizier Ally and his adherents, at the foot of the Nepaul mountains: he came up with the rebels at the village of Toolsepore, where they dispersed and fled in every direction. The assassin rebel, Newaub Vizier Ally, disguised as a fakeer, made his escape to the Rajah Jeypore, but was afterwards delivered up by the Rajah to Col. Collins, and died a prisoner in the garrison of Fort William.

This service accomplished, the army returned to Caunpoor, from whence this officer was detached with men and guns for Lucknow residency, and remained on command till the close of 1799, when he fell back with his division to Caunpoor cantonments. In Jan. 1800 he was ordered by Gen. Sir James Craig to Futtehgurh, under the command of Gen. R. Stuart.

In May 1800 he was detached with artillery, and a battalion, 7th N. I., Col. James Morris commanding, for the reduction of Distempore fort; which was captured, after a gallant defence, dismantled, mined, and blown up. He returned to Futtehgurh, and from thence in 1801, under command of Gen. R. Stuart, marched to Barrelie, for the reduction of the Nabob of Lucknow's refractory corps. They were reduced, disbanded, and the Nabob's ordnance sent to Lucknow; and this service effected, the troops fell back to Futtehgurh.

Early in 1803 the fort of Sasnee was besieged by the troops from Caunpoor: an attempt to storm having failed, the Com.-in-Chief, Lord Lake, went to the siege to view and conduct the operations; and the artillery, with this officer, were then ordered to join from Futtehgurh. Batteries were opened against the fortress, and Sasnee was taken with the loss of a few artillery men. He next marched against Bidzergur, a fortress of great strength and respectability, which fell after a severe loss (including Col. Gordon, who was killed.) Lieut.-Col. Constable was here wounded in the belly by a cannon shot in the grand battery, when besieging the place at noon-day, and in the presence of the Com.-in-Chief. The fortress taken and garrisoned, the army marched against Catchoura, which surrendered on a battery being constructed: the enemy evacuated the fort at night. The Com.-in-Chief then ordered the Caunpoor and Futtehgurh divisions to return to their respective stations, preparatory to more extensive operations—the conquest of the Dooaub, and the famed empire of Delhi, the capital of Hindostan.

At Futtehgurh Lieut.-Col. Constable, judging himself sufficiently recovered from the effects of his wound to take the field again, he, in the month of August 1803, with the artillery, left the station, and joined the English army assembled under command of Gen. Lord Lake at Mindy Ghaut, on the banks of the Ganges. The army marched against the Mahratta and French forces assembled under Gen. Perron, their Com.-in-Chief, in the pay of Dowlut Rao Scindia, and defeated them on the 29th of Aug. near Coil: on the 4th of Sept. 1803 attacked and blue open the gates of the hitherto considered impregnable fort of Allygurh stormed and captured the fortress, with Gen. Pedrong commandant, 281 pieces of ordnance, and a numerous garrison. Upwards of 2000 of the enemy were killed. The British loss was considerable: 228 officers and privates of the artillery and infantry were killed and wounded. The French Com.-in-Chief in the field, Gen. Perron, at the same time came in and surrendered himself.

After garrisoning Allygurh the army marched towards Delhi, and on the 11th of Sept. defeated the enemy, consisting of cavalry, infantry, and a large train of ordnance, under Gen. Louis Bourguien. The loss of the enemy amounted to 3000 men, with sixty-eight pieces of cannon, whilst that of the British in killed and wounded did not exceed 400. On the 14th the army crossed the river Jumna, entered Delhi, and on the same day Gen. Bourguien surrendered himself with four of his officers. On the 24th of Sept. the army marched from Delhi; on the 2nd Oct. arrived at Mutra; and on the 4th encamped before Agra. On the morning of the 10th the Com.-in-Chief ordered an attack on seven battalions of the enemy's infantry, encamped with a considerable number of guns on the glacis. The enemy were defeated with the loss of 600 men and 26 pieces, brass guns, with their tumbrils. The British loss amounted to 228 killed and wounded. After this obstinate defence, operations for the siege commenced; the grand breaching battery was constructed within 350 yards of the fort, near the river, and completed with eight eighteen-pounders and four howitzers, an enfilading battery of four twelve-pounders to the left of the breaching battery, and to the right two twelve-pounders.

At break of day of the 17th the fire from the batteries commenced, and was ably directed to breach, and bring the bastion into the ditch, which the enemy perceiving, sent out next morning to capitulate, and the garrison, amounting to 6000, surrendered.

The fruits of this glorious conquest were from twenty-two to twenty-four lacs of rupees, seventy-six brass guns, and eighty-six iron guns of different calibres, mortars, howitzers, carronades, and gallopers:—total 164, with their tumbrils. One of their guns, surveyed by Lieut.-Col. Constable, was of a most extraordinary nature, *viz.* brass of one cylinder, calibre twenty-three inches, metal at the muzzle eleven and a half inches, diameter of the trunnions eleven inches, length fourteen feet two inches, length of the bore eight feet eight inches, of the chamber four feet four inches, diameter of ditto ten inches, length of the cascabel one foot two inches, weight of the gun $1207\frac{1}{2}$ maunds, equal to 96,600 pounds. The ball, made of cast-iron, weighed 1500 pounds, and 108 pounds of gunpowder were requisite to fill the chamber. The enemy shot balls of stone. The gun was valued at 100,000 rupees.

After garrisoning Agra, the army marched on the 27th Oct. in pursuit of the enemy from the Deccan, the last of the French organized corps, to which was attached a formidable field artillery. On the morning of the 1st of Nov. 1803, Lord Lake gallantly advanced with the cavalry and galloper guns, and came up with the enemy at the village of Laswarree, and, in order to detain them till the artillery and infantry were up, his lordship engaged. The struggle was severe, and the loss of men on both sides very great; but the object was accomplished: the artillery and infantry got up with the advance by eleven o'clock, A. M. after an hour's halt, and march of twenty-five miles under a burning sun. The army formed, attacked, and by four o'clock in the afternoon victory declared for the English. The loss sustained by the British accomplishing this decisive victory was great, 800 killed and wounded; that of the enemy 7000. The whole of their seventeen battalions of infantry were annihilated, except about 2000 prisoners: seventy-two pieces of artillery were captured, 5000 stand of arms, forty-four stand of colours, sixty-four ammunition tumbrils, three with money, the bazars, camp equipage and baggage, elephants, camels, and above 1600 bullocks---their cavalry cut up and broken. On the 8th of Nov. the English left the bloody field, the stench of which was intolerable;—a bed of honour to the conqueror and vanquished, and to Asia repose.

On the 16th of April 1804, Col. Monson was detached from the line with a company of artillery, ten guns, and three battalions of Sepoys: he was afterwards joined by a corps of N. C. Col. Monson's division was attacked and defeated by Holkar. The health of Lieut.-Col. Constable being much injured, he was compelled, in May 1804, to obtain leave from Lord Lake to quit the field, and proceed to Agra and Futtehgurh, where he arrived in June. From thence he embarked in the Ganges for Calcutta, and landed in August, preparatory to a European voyage for the benefit of his health; and, in Sept. 1805, he arrived in England, on furlough, after an absence of twenty-five years.

In 1806 Lieut.-Col. Constable obtained permission of the court of directors to put himself under the control of the board of ordnance, (the Marquess of Hastings then Master-Gen.) to forge and cast ordnance on the same principle as manufactured in Asia, and taken at Allygurh, Delhi, Agra, and Laswarree. From having been a member of a committee for the survey of all the captured guns and stores, &c. he obtained a thorough knowledge of the enemy's brass ordnance with iron cylinders, their nature, properties, and formation, possessing advantages and superiority over the guns of Europe. In this object he succeeded, after experiencing innumerable difficulties, but which he was enabled to surmount through the assistance of the board of ordnance, and under the auspices of Gen. Sir Thomas Blomfield, who furnished him with materials from Woolwich. The guns were cast by Lieut.-Col. Constable in London, put to proof, and surveyed by a committee of artillery field-officers at Woolwich, and the thanks of the honourable board of ordnance were conveyed to him for his trouble.

In March 1808 Lieut.-Col. Constable again embarked for India, and landing on the 22nd August, was put on field-officer's duty in Fort William garrison. In Feb. 1809 he received orders to proceed by water to Allahabad, to command the artillery in that fortress, where he practiced and exercised the artillery corps in Col. Shrapnell's experimental shot and shells, the principles of which he had acquired of that judicious and scientific officer whilst in England. At the expiration of two years' command, Lieut.-Col. Constable's health declining, he was reluctantly compelled to give up the command, and shortly after returned to England.

In the year 1816, and in conformity with the East India Company's regulations, Lieut.-Col. Constable forwarded to the secretary at the East India-House (most unwillingly, it being his ambition to die in the service) certificates of his state of health, requesting permission to retire from the service on the pay of his rank, which was granted; " the reward of thirty-five years foreign service."

The following is an extract of a letter from the court of directors, dated the 29th April, 1808, to Lord Minto, then Gov.-Gen. in Bengal, in reference to Lieut.-Col. Constable's introduction at Woolwich of the Asiatic mode of casting brass ordnance with iron cylinders.

" In our letter of the 2nd of May, 1806, you were informed that we had shipped for your presidency a quantity of shells of a new and improved construction, for the use of field artillery; and as we conceive that the effect of these shells would be better appreciated were there an officer on the spot experimentally acquainted with their construction, to be occasionally advised with and consulted, and who would also be able to instruct others in their use, we recommend to your notice Major Constable, belonging to the corps of artillery on your establishment, who, during his stay in England, has been employed under the orders of his Majesty's board of ordnance, and has therefore acquired such a knowledge of the principles of the construction of these shells, and of the improvements lately introduced into the Royal Arsenal at Woolwich, as to render him well qualified for the purpose above-mentioned. Major Constable has also evinced a laudable zeal in having successfully introduced into the Royal Arsenal the Asiatic mode of casting brass ordnance, and we direct that you communicate to him our approbation of his conduct in this respect. Major Constable proceeded to Bengal in the Hugh Inglis."

Description of Brass Guns with iron cylinders, as manufactured in Asia, and cast in England in 1806, under the direction of Lieut.-Col. George Constable, of the Regiment of Bengal Artillery, by order of the Honourable the Board of Ordnance, the Marquess of Hastings then Master-General.

The gun metal is a composition of brass and iron: the cylinder smooth as glass, and formed of metal of a distinct quality: vent of solid iron, and gun made after the English model.

The advantages of the Asiatic ordnance are strength and lightness. In strength equal to iron ordnance; in lightness less than brass. In proof of the latter position, a three-pounder of the above consistency, proved at Woolwich, weighed 2 cwts. 3 qrs. and 1 lb.: an English three-pounder weighs 3 cwts. being a difference in metal of 27 lbs. The advantages in respect to weight are of the greatest importance; *viz.* facility of movement, light and easy exercise in the field and in garrison, and a consequent saving both in men and horses. On ship-board a reduction of one-fourth or one-fifth in weight of metal must be of incalculable service.

It is notorious to officers who have seen much service, that brass guns are, owing to their fusibility, often rendered in the field and in batteries totally unserviceable. From the running and melting of the guns, increase of windage, &c. the shot is fired without a certainty of direction or distance; and hence it is evident that a brass train of artillery at sieges can never be relied on[*].

[*] The necessity of resorting to brass guns with iron cylinders, for all services by sea and land, as recommended by Lieut.-Col. Constable, appears deserving the serious attention of the British government.—J. P.

LIEUTENANT-COLONEL JOHN BAILLIE.

(Bengal Establishment.)

This officer was appointed a cadet on the Bengal establishment in 1790; ensign, the 15th March 1773; lieutenant, 17th Nov. 1794; captain, 30th Sept. 1803; major, 2nd Jan. 1811; and lieut.-col. 14th July 1815.

In Nov. 1791 he arrived in India, and in 1797 he was employed by Lord Teignmouth to translate from the Arabic language an eminent work on the Mahomedan law, compiled by Sir William Jones. On the first formation of the college of Fort William, about 1800, he was appointed professor of the Arabic and Persian languages, and of Mahomedan law in that institution. From 1803 to 1807 he served as political agent of the Gov.-Gen. in Bundlecund; and on the death of Col. Collins, in 1807, he was appointed resident at Lucknow, where he remained till the end of 1815; and in June 1818 he was placed on the retired list.

Lieut.-Col. Baillie was elected 28th May 1823, to a seat in the direction of the affairs of the East India Company, vacated by the retirement of Mr. Cotton.

The following extract of a letter to the Court of Directors from the Gov.-Gen. in Council of Bengal, descriptive of Lieut.-Col. Baillie's services in India during the eventful period of the Mahratta war, which commenced in 1803, with an extract from the answer to that letter by the Court of Directors; and another extract from a minute of the Gov.-Gen., Lord Minto, expressive of the opinion entertained by that nobleman of the Lieut.-Col.'s services, under his immediate authority, and as his representative at the court of Lucknow—are inserted as honourable testimonials of this officer's public career:—

Extract of a Letter from the Hon. the Gov.-Gen. in Council, to the Hon. the Court of Directors, under date the 1st of May 1807.

" Your Hon. Court will observe, that on this occasion the Gov.-

Gen. deemed it his duty to record the high sense which he entertained of the distinguished merits and exertions of Capt. Baillie, in the execution of the arduous duties committed to his charge, during his two missions to Bundlecund, and to propose, that the public thanks of this government should be given to Capt. Baillie for the great and important services which he had rendered, and for the zeal and ability which he had exerted in the successful accomplishment of the views of the British government in Bundlecund: suggesting at the same time that our opinion of Capt. Baillie's merits and claims should be stated to your Hon. Court, with a recommendation that such reward be granted to that deserving public officer, as on a review of his important services your Hon. Court might consider him to merit.

" Concurring entirely in the justice of this honourable testimony of applause and approbation, and in the propriety of the Hon. Gov.-Gen.'s suggestion, we consider it to be our duty to enable your Hon. Court justly to appreciate the value of Capt. Baillie's services, by a succinct review of his conduct in the execution of the arduous duties committed to his charge; although the general nature of them, as recorded on the proceedings of this government, and from time to time reported in our despatches to your Hon. Court, or to the Hon. the Secret Committee, must already have attracted your attention.

" With a degree of public spirit highly honourable to his character as an officer, Capt. Baillie, soon after the commencement of the war with the confederated Mahratta chieftains, although engaged in the duties of professor of Arabic and Persian in the college of Fort William, offered his services as a volunteer in the field, and proceeded to join the army then employed in the siege of Agra. At that time the precarious situation of affairs in the province of Bundlecund, requiring the superintendence of an officer qualified by talents and abilities to conduct the various important and difficult political negociations, on which depended the establishment of the British authority in that province, His Excellency the Com.-in-Chief, with the approbation of government, selected Capt. Baillie for the conduct of that arduous duty.

" The original object of the British government, as connected with the general operations of the war, was to establish its authority, in the name of the Peishwa, over that portion of the province of Bundlecund, the command of which was necessary for the protection of our own territories against the hostile attempts of the enemy, who at an early period of time projected the invasion of our western provinces, by the aid of the chieftains possessing military power in Bundlecund.

" The prosecution of this object placed the Nabob Shumshere Behader (who, under a commission issued by Amrut Rao, when seated on the Musnud of Poona by Jeswunt Rao Holkar, had proceeded to occupy the province of Bundlecund) in a state of enmity to the British power. The cause of Shumshere Behader was supported by the Rana of Culpee, and other chieftains of the province, whilst, with a view to counteract this combination, the descendants of the ancient chiefs of Bundlecund were encouraged to employ their exertions in recovering the possessions wrested from them by the arms of Allee Behader, the father and predecessor of Shumshere Behader.

" The latter chieftain had been defeated, but not subdued, and it was deemed expedient, with a view to the accomplishment of our political objects in Bundlecund, to establish the influence of the British government by conciliation rather than by hostility. The transfer of a large proportion of the Peishwa's nominal possessions in Bundlecund, which occurred shortly after Capt. Baillie's mission, gave us a more direct interest in the province, and rendered necessary the occupation of most of the territories which the Boondelah chiefs had been encouraged to seize.

" To combine with the establishment of our authority over the lands ceded by the Peishwa, the conciliation of the chiefs who were to be deprived of them, at a time when the British government was engaged in a contest with the Mahratta power, and when the province of Bundlecund was menaced with foreign invasion and disturbed by internal commotion, became a duty of the most arduous and difficult nature, requiring the exertion of eminent talents, firmness, temper, and address. It was connected also with the duty of superintending and directing the operations both of the troops of the British government, and of the auxiliaries, under the command of Rajah Himmut Behader, for the support of which, lands of the estimated produce of twenty lacks of rupees per annum had been assigned. It embraced the reduction of the power and influence of Himmut Behader and the Native chiefs of Bundlecund, without weakening their attachment or hazarding their revolt, and the establishment of the British civil power and the collection of revenue in the province, under all the disadvantages of impending invasion, and the desultory operations of numerous bands of predatory troops.

" Within the short space of three months, these objects were accomplished by the zeal and ability of Capt. Baillie; and we have reason to believe, that in the months of May and June 1804, when the regular force retreated on the invasion of the province by the troops of Ameer Khan, and when the utmost disorder was apprehended in consequence of the decease of Himmut Behader, the British authority in Bundlecund was alone preserved by the fortitude, ability, and influence of Capt. Baillie. Even at that crisis of distress and danger, Capt. Baillie was enabled to frame an arrangement with regard to the lands granted in Jaidad for the support of the late Himmut Behader's troops, which laid the foundation of their ultimate transfer to the possession of the British government. Ample testimony to the merits and services of Capt. Baillie on this occasion is borne by the Supreme government in its despatch to the Hon. the Secret Committee of the 15th of June 1804. The record of Capt. Baillie's correspondence, however, testifies more demonstratively than the preceding statement, the arduous, laborious, and responsible nature of the duties committed to his charge, the zeal and ability with which he fulfilled them, and the importance of his services to the interests of the Company, during the eventful period of the last war.

" The services of Capt. Baillie were subsequently continued in his capacity of a member of the commission appointed in July 1804, for the administration of the affairs of Bundlecund: and the introduction of the regular civil and judicial system into that portion of the province, which had been subjected to the British authority principally by the means of Capt. Baillie's ability and exertions, admitted of his return to the presidency in the month of July 1805.

" Notwithstanding, however, the various arrangements concluded by Capt. Baillie with the Nabob Shumshere Behader, and other chieftains of rank and power in Bundlecund, by which their interests were connected with those of the British government, much remained to be accomplished for the complete establishment of our rights and interests in that province.—Of the territory ceded by the Peishwa, under the additional articles to the treaty of Bassien, to the extent of 3,616,000 rupees annual produce, lands of the value of twelve lacks of rupees per annnm only, had been acquired. The Jaidad of the late Himmut Behader yet remained to be resumed. The situation of the numerous chiefs in Bundlecund relatively to the British government, their claims and pretensions, together with various other important questions connected with the establishment of the British authority in the province, continued unadjusted.

" The objects to be accomplished are accurately detailed in Capt. Baillie's able report of the affairs of Bundlecund, to which we have frequently had occasion to refer in our despatches of the past year to the Hon. the Secret Committee. Those objects were, in our decided judgment, alone susceptible of attainment by the aid of Capt. Baillie's personal exertions, knowledge, influence, and abilities; and this conviction occasioned Capt. Baillie's second mission to Bundlecund in Dec. 1805; the arduous duties of which, Capt. Baillie with his characteristic spirit of public zeal undertook, without the prospect of any other immediate profit than that which was annexed to his actual situation in the college of Fort William.

" Our successive despatches to the Hon. the Secret Committee, and to your Hon. Court, commencing with the month of March 1806, contain a regular narrative of Capt. Baillie's proceedings during his second mission, under the instructions from time to time issued for the guidance of his conduct. The first success of his exertions was manifested in the peaceable dismission of the turbulent and ferocious body of Nangahs, the continuance of which in the service of government opposed a material obstacle to every salutary arrangement. The next and most important object accomplished by Capt. Baillie, was the complete resumption of the Jaidad lands of the late Himmut Behader, without the slightest commotion, although opposed by the powerful influence of the family, and a numerous body of military chieftains, in command of large bodies of troops, and in possession of numerous forts; thus effecting the peaceable transfer to the British dominions of a territory yielding an annual revenue of eighteen lacks of rupees (225,000*l.* sterling), with the sacrifice only of a Jaghire of little more than one lack of rupees per annum. The services of Capt. Baillie were further enhanced on this occasion, by the successful manner in which he resisted the extensive claims of the manager of the Jaidad, for arrears of pay to the troops, and balance of revenue. These objects were not accomplished by the presence of troops, but by the personal influence and address of Capt. Baillie, which enabled him to controul the impulse of the strongest interest supported by local power, and to subvert the efforts of combination and intrigue, by which the progress of his measures in the establishment of the British authority within the Jaidad, in the occupation of the forts, the discharge of the troops, and the final settlement of the lands, were embarrassed and impeded.

" Capt. Baillie's arduous exertions in the completion of those important arrangements, were not restrained by the repeated reports of external and internal confederacies. The same firmness of character and maturity of judgment, which had formerly distinguished his conduct amidst scenes of turbulence, disorder, and rapine, enabled Capt. Baillie to resist the influence of these interested reports, and to prosecute to a successful issue the important objects committed to his charge.

" With a similar spirit of energy and zeal, aided by the exertion of his political talents and address, Capt. Baillie succeeded in accomplishing those arrangements with the principal chieftains in Bundlecund, which were prescribed by our instructions, and which have produced a degree of tranquillity and security hitherto unknown within the limits of that turbulent province; and has finally placed the authority and relations of the British government in Bundlecund in a condition to admit of our conducting the affairs of the province under the ordinary system of administration established in other parts of the Hon. Company's dominions. These services have been rendered peculiarly important and meritorious, by the extraordinary local and incidental difficulties which opposed the execution of them, as well as by the advantages, political, territorial, and pecuniary, which government has derived from them.

" Under such circumstances, we cannot doubt your honourable court's concurrence in our opinion, that Capt. Baillie has established a peculiar claim to distinguished reward."

Extract of a Letter from the Hon. the Court of Directors to the Gov.-Gen. in Council in the Political Department, dated Sept. 14, 1808.

" With respect to the strong recommendation contained in your last-mentioned despatch, that an adequate reward might be conferred on Capt. Baillie for the services rendered by that officer whilst he acted as political agent to the Gov.-Gen. in the province of Bundlecund; we observe by your letter in the political department of the 31st July, 1807, that your government has itself had an opportunity of rewarding those services, of the importance of which we are fully sensible, by the appointment of Capt. Baillie to the office of resident at Lucknow, on the demise of Col. Collins, which appointment, for the reasons stated in Sir George Barlow's minute of the 22nd June 1807, we hereby confirm."

Extract of a Minute of the late Right Hon. the Earl of Minto, Gov.-Gen. of Bengal, nominating Mr. George Baillie to the office of Assistant to the Resident at Lucknow, under date the 5th of March 1813.

" I will confess that a very powerful motive with me in proposing this appointment is an earnest desire to promote the personal and official comfort of Maj. Baillie, and to meet his wishes on a point in which I know them to be warmly engaged. This arises solely from the high sense which I entertain of his great public merits, and if it partakes of the nature of a personal feeling, it is one which has its origin in public motives alone. Maj. Baillie is entirely unknown to me, except through the medium of his official correspondence and proceedings, and the high character which he bears for honour, integrity, learning, and talent. The sentiments of public respect, esteem, and applause, which a candid and impartial observation of his conduct has impressed on my mind, are known to the Board, and the proceedings bear testimony to the sense entertained by the present and former governments, of the ability, zeal, perseverance, and fortitude, displayed by Maj. Baillie, on various occasions of uncommon difficulty and delicacy, and by which he has resisted and overcome obstacles not to be surmounted by one possessing those qualities in an inferior degree.

"It is therefore with a high degree of satisfaction, in which I am persuaded I shall be joined by my colleagues, that I find myself able to propose an arrangement, which will combine with the indulgence of my cordial disposition to gratify Maj. Baillie, an effectual provision for the necessities of the public service in the instance under consideration."

THE LATE COLONEL THOMAS WELSH.

(Bengal Establishment.)

THIS officer was appointed on the Bengal establishment in 1769; cornet, 12th Sept. 1769; lieutenant, 2nd Feb. 1773; captain, 18th Jan. 1781; major, 1st March, 1794; lieutenant-colonel, 1st Jan. 1798; colonel, 29th May, 1800; and in August following placed on the retired list.

In 1806 Col. Welsh was a candidate for a seat in the East India direction. He died 11th April, 1822.

The following extracts, from public documents and letters, shew the services of this officer, and are honourable testimonials of his military career.

Extract of Gen. Goddard's Letter, May 27, 1780, *to the Bengal Govt.*

" It is with the greatest pleasure I can communicate to you two successful enterprises, which closed the scene of our operations in the field, and have been attended by the most beneficial consequences to the Company; particularly the latter, both by the splendour of the action, and the peaceful security it has given to the new-acquired Pergunnahs, &c.—The second action, above alluded to, was performed by Lieut. Welsh, who, on the 17th inst. I detached from this place, &c.—This action has been as decisive as it was possible to be; and I beg to express my entire satisfaction with, and approbation of, the spirited and well-judged conduct of Lieut. Welsh."

Extract of Gen. Goddard's letter, June 20, 1780, *to the Bengal Govt.*

" Since my arrival at this place, the detachment under Lieut. Welsh, with whose success against Gunnesse Punt, one of the Mahratta leaders, I have already made you acquainted, has effected a very material piece of service, and completely eradicated every trace of the Mahratta power in this neighbourhood, and destroyed even the most distant hope he could have of giving farther disturbance to our new possessions, &c.—The enterprise I allude to is the taking of Parneiro, a fort situated on a high hill, &c.—It was defended, for two days, by a garrison consisting of about 400 men; who, finding Lieut. Welsh had, with immense difficulty and perseverance, and by his steady and good conduct, &c. &c. thought proper to surrender into the hands of the English. Lieut. Welsh has since made himself master of two inferior forts, Arzin Ghur and Under Ghur. The former has a district of one lack of rupees, lying around and dependent on it, &c.—These acquisitions have put the English in entire possession of the sea-coast from Cambait to Dumaun, comprehending a tract of near 150 miles."

Extract of a Letter from the Bombay Govt. to the Court of Directors, July 25, 1780.

" After the separation of the armies, a detachment was employed with much success and advantage, under the command of Lieut. Welsh. He surprised and totally routed a body of the Poonah forces," &c.

Extract of a Letter from the Gov.-Gen. in Council to Gen. Goddard, dated Oct. 9, 1780.

" The successful enterprises, of which you have advised us, of detachments under the command of Maj. Forbes and Lieut. Welsh, and particularly those under the latter, did not come to our knowledge without heightening the favourable opinion which we before entertained of the merits of these gentlemen, and have not passed without leaving the impression which they deserve with us," &c.

Letter from the Gov.-Gen. to Capt. Welsh, Lucknow, June 10, 1784.

" As it is much my wish that you may receive and keep some lasting testimony of the esteem which I entertain for your merit, I request your acceptance of the accompanying sword. It is not in itself of any value; but I may flatter myself that there are many to whom such a pledge of the estimation in which I hold your character will at least prove of no disservice to it; especially if it is understood that you are known to me by no personal recommendation, nor by the habits of society, but only by public service.

" *Captain Welsh.*" (Signed) " WARREN HASTINGS."

Extract of a general Letter from the Hon. the Court of Directors to the Bengal Government, April 28, 1790.

" As it appears, from the Company's records, that the gallantry and good conduct of Captain Welsh entitle him to our favourable notice," &c.

Extract of a Letter to Capt. Welsh from the Dep.-Adj.-Gen. to the Army in Mysore.

" The different measures you have pursued so successfully, on the late service, his Lordship has particularly expressed his approbation of," &c.

" GENERAL ORDERS, *Camp, Dec.* 27, 1791.

" Lord Cornwallis has been highly satisfied with the report that Capt. Welsh, of the Bengal infantry, has made of the reduction of the important forts of Ram Gurry and Sherie Gurry, by the detachment under his command," &c.—" His Lordship is sensible that the complete success of the plan is principally to be attributed to Capt. Welsh's judicious conduct, for which he desires that he will accept of his warmest acknowledgments."

Extract of a Letter, dated Fort-William, Dec. 23, 1792, from Lord Cornwallis to Capt. Welsh, when on service in Assam.

" The complete success which has attended your judicious and spirited exertions affords me the greatest satisfaction, and your conduct in every particular claims my warmest approbation."

Extract of Station-Orders, by Maj.-Gen. Sir James Craig, Sept. 10, 1798, on the review of the 2nd regt. of Native cavalry, previous to Lieut.-Col. Welsh's departure for Europe.

" Sir James Craig joins in the general sentiments of the regiment on the approaching departure of their Lieut.-Col. His unremitting attention to the regiment, the effects of which were so well displayed this morning, has added to the regret of being deprived of his farther exertions as an officer, to that which, in common with all, he feels at the loss of his society as a gentleman."

Extract of Militia-Orders, dated Fort-William, Dec. 21, 1798, by Lord Mornington.

" The Gov.-Gen. will not attempt to discriminate the merits of individuals belonging to the corps; but it is his duty to express a particular sense of the service rendered by Lieut.-Col. Welsh, of the 2nd regiment of Native Cavalry, in forming the corps of Militia Cavalry, which has derived great advantage from the valuable instructions of that respectable officer."

On Lieut.-Col. Welsh's departure from Calcutta for Europe, he received a valuable sword from the gentlemen of the corps, with the following inscription:—

" January, 1799,
" Presented to Lieut.-Col. Welsh, by the corps of Calcutta Militia Cavalry, in grateful remembrance of the benefits they received from his attention to their discipline on their first formation."

LIEUTENANT-COLONEL JAMES PEARSON.

(Bengal Establishment.)

This officer was appointed a cadet on the Bengal Establishment in 1768; he arrived in Bengal in 1769; was a few months afterwards promoted to the rank of ensign, and to that of lieutenant in 1773. At the commencement of 1781 he was promoted to the rank of captain, and appointed to the command of the 2nd battalion of the 25th regiment of N. I.—one of the five corps ordered from Bengal to Madras, to form a junction with the army there, under the orders of Sir Eyre Coote, who had taken the command of the forces of that establishment, after the annihilation of Col. Baillie's detachment, and Sir Hector Munro's disastrous retreat before Hyder Ally's superior numbers. The Bengal detachment marched from Midnapore in Jan. 1781, and joined Sir Eyre in August.

The command of the 25th regiment devolved on Capt. Pearson, in

June 1781, and he continued at the head of it until its return to Bengal in 1785. He served with it during the campaigns of 1781-2, and 3; was present in all the actions with Hyder Ally; *viz.* the battle of Perambancum, Aug. 27, 1781, which immediately followed the capture of the fort of Tripassoor; battle of Shulingur, 27th Sept. following; siege and capture of the fort of Chittore, Nov. 1781; action near Velore, 10th Jan. 1782; second action near Velore, 13th Jan.; battle of Arnee, June 2, 1782; and with the French, when joined by Tippoo's troops, in the engagement of the 13th June, 1783, at Cudalore.

Capt. Pearson returned to Madras upon the cessation of hostilities; marched from thence to Bengal in the beginning of 1784, and arrived there in Jan. 1785, when the detachment was broke up. In 1788 he was appointed to the command of the 20th battalion of N. I., which corps he commanded, in 1794, in the Rohilla action. In 1795 he was promoted to a majority; in 1797, to the rank of lieutenant-colonel; and in June of that year terminated his military career in India, after near twenty-eight years of active service in that climate. He left Calcutta upon his first furlough in June 1797; arrived in England in Dec. of that year; and in the same month of the year 1798, resigned the military service of the Hon. East India Company, and was placed on the retired list.

LIEUTENANT-COLONEL GEORGE RABAN, C. B.

(Bengal Establishment.)

This officer arrived in India in May 1782, and joined the Bengal army, under the command of Gen. Goddard, at Surat, and served with it till its arrival and dissolution at Caunpoor, in 1784. In 1786 he was ordered to Prince of Wales's Island, in command of a company of Gholundauz, and remained on that island till 1794, holding also the appointment of garrison store-keeper. He was present at two engagements with the Malay forces, belonging to the King of Quedah, in which they were defeated. He served during the Mahratta war with the grand army, under Lord Lake; was present at the battle and capture of Allygurh; at the battle of Delhi; at the siege and capture of Agra; at the siege and capture of Deeg; and at the siege of Burtpoor. He commanded the artillery with Col. Don's detachment at the capture of Rampoorah in Holkar's country; also with Col. Bowie's detachment, at the capture of the fort of Turcela in the Gohud country; at the siege and capture of the city and fort of Gohud; and in two campaigns in the Rewah country. He received public thanks in general orders from Lord Lake, the Com.-in-Chief, for his conduct at the storming of the fort of Deeg, and the capture of Rampoorah; also from Col. Don, commanding the detachment at that capture; and from Col. Bowie, commanding in Gohud, at the capture of the city and fort of that name.

Lieut.-Col. Raban was appointed, June 4, 1815, a knight companion of the order of the Bath; and the 6th May 1817, retired from the East India Company's service.

The following are the dates of Lieut.-Col. Raban's commissions:— cadet of artillery, 1782; lieut. fire-worker, April 26, 1783; lieut. Nov. 25, 1790; capt. Jan. 8, 1798; maj. Sept. 16, 1807; brevet lieut.-col. June 4, 1813.

LIEUTENANT-COLONEL JABEZ MACKENZIE.

(Bengal Establishment.)

THIS officer was appointed to an ensigncy in the East India Company's service (Bengal Establishment) Sept. 27, 1769; lieut. Dec. 1, 1772; capt. Jan. 1, 1781; ditto in the " King's army," *(East*

Indies only) July 9, 1783; maj. Jan. 8, 1796; ditto in the "King's army" *(East Indies only)* March 1, 1794; lieut.-col. Oct. 30, 1797; ditto in the "King's army" *(East Indies only)* Jan. 1, 1798.

In the early part of 1778 he was appointed on the staff, as adjut. of the N. I.; and subsequently maj. of brigade to the Bengal detachment, sent by the supreme government of India to Bombay, under the command of Gen. Goddard; and served under that commander until the middle of the year 1784, when he returned to Bengal, and was appointed to the command of the 2nd batt. 36th regt. of N. I.

In June 1801, he received permission from the hon. the court of directors to retire from the service on the full pay of lieut.-col.

MAJOR-GENERAL THE HON. ARTHUR SENTLEGER.

(Madras Establishment.)

This officer was appointed cornet in the 2nd grenadier troop of the 1st regiment of Native cavalry the 12th Jan. 1781; and in Feb. of that year served with the army under Sir Eyre Coote, and in the rear regiment of the rear guard, when it was attacked by Hyder Ally's whole force on the march from Pondicherry to Cudalore. In July following, he succeeded to the command of the troop, and with it led the army into action at the battle of Portonovo, where he had a horse killed, and another wounded under him. He served at the battle of Perambancum, 27th August, and at that of Shulingur, 27th Sept. following; at the battle of the Swamp near Velore, 10th Jan. 1782; second battle of the Swamp, 13th Jan.; and at the battle near Arnee, 2nd June in the same year. In 1783 he served with the army under Gen. Stuart, and was present at the siege of Cudalore. In this year he was promoted to the rank of lieutenant, and employed by Col. Macartney to endeavour to bring the mutineers of the cavalry to a sense of their duty.

In 1790, Lieut. Sentleger was sent by his majesty's ministers over land to India with despatches. He joined the army in the field under Gen. Medows, and was ordered to re-inforce his body guard the day he drove Tippoo Sultaun's army down the Tappore pass. In 1791, he served in the army under Lord Cornwallis, and was in the 3rd regiment of cavalry, commanded by Col. Stevenson, which corps led the charge on the day Gen. Floyd charged the whole of the enemy's army with the cavalry. He served also at the siege of Bangalore; in pursuit of Tippoo's army after the siege; and at the battle of the Black Rocks, near Seringapatam. He was present at the siege of Seringapatam in 1792, and served under Col. Maxwell against the southern Poligars. In 1793 he was present at the attack of Shevagurry and Pandellumchorchy. In 1796 he obtained the rank of captain, and was employed with two squadrons under his command, to keep the southern Poligars in check during the siege of Pondicherry. In 1798 he was promoted to the rank of major, and took the field in command of the 3d regiment of cavalry in the army under Gen. now Lord Harris. From the 3d he was removed to the command of the 4th regiment, with which he was present at the battle of Mallavelly and siege of Seringapatam. He next served under Col. Stevenson, and commanded 10 companies of infantry at the storming of Semogah; he was also present at the storming of Shekarpore, after which he was appointed by Col. Stevenson to command a brigade of cavalry and infantry, employed in the pursuit of Dundiah, who was driven into the Mahratta country. He next seized the fort of Mundanagore; was then ordered, by Gen. Wellesley, now Duke of Wellington, to advance, and his force augmented to three battalions with the fourth regiment of cavalry, with which he defeated the Mahratta's at Sambranee.

The 4th of Sept. 1799, he obtained the rank of lieut.-col. and was appointed in this year commandant of the 6th regiment of cavalry. His next service was the seizure of the fort of Hurrcall, for which he received the thanks of Gen. Wellesley, and the gov.-gen. At the latter place he was severely wounded.

In 1800 Lieut.-Col. Sentleger had the command of the cavalry cantonment of Arcot, including his majesty's 19th, 6th, and 8th regiments of cavalry.—In 1801 he served under Gen. Campbell, and was ordered to take the field in command of his majesty's 25th, 1st, 4th, and 6th regiments of cavalry; with these corps he made a forced march of sixty-three miles, and surrounded a fort until the infantry came up, which prevented a war.—In 1803 he was ordered to Hyderabad to command the cavalry, with the Nizam's subsidiary force: and on the 10th Sept. he marched through the enemy's cavalry to the relief of Col. Stevenson, then formed with the infantry in a hollow square, the enemy's cavalry trying to break it. He was next present at the siege of Asseergur.

At the battle of Argaum, under Gen. Wellesley, Lieut.-Col. Sentleger commanded his majesty's 19th, 3rd, 4th, 5th, and 6th, and 8th regiments of cavalry, and for his conduct was thanked by Gen. Wellesley, and in public orders.—He afterwards commanded the army covering the siege of Gawelgur, 14,000 horse, 8,000 infantry, and thirty-six guns.

In 1804 he was honoured with a gold medal: in 1808 he commanded the fort and cantonment of Trichinopoly, having under him the 6th regiment of cavalry, his majesty's 69th foot, one company of artillery, and three battalions of Sepoys.

In 1809 Lieut.-Col. Sentleger was ordered to take the field, with the southern division, against Travancore, with an army of between 6 and 7000 men, consisting of the 6th regiment of cavalry, his majesty's 64th and 3rd Ceylon regiments, a company of royal artillery, a company of coast artillery, four battalions of Sepoys, and one company of pioneers. On the 10th of Feb. he stormed the Arumboolee lines; and on the 17th fought the battle of Cotart Negra Coil. On the 19th of the same month he took the forts of Oudagurry and Pulpanaveram, for which he received the most ample and repeated thanks from the Madras government; and which put an end to the Travancore war, as the Rajah immediately submitted to the authority of the Madras government.

In this year, 1809, Col. Sentleger was ordered to Europe, and suspended the service, in consequence of false representations to Sir George Barlow, that it was his intention to make war on the government. After an investigation of his conduct, both at Madras, before the Supreme Court of Judicature, when he was not present, and by the Court of Directors, he was restored in 1813 to his rank and situation in the service—was appointed Col. of the 4th brigade of cavalry at Madras—received 2000*l.* as a reward for services—and was brevetted by his present Majesty, then Prince Regent, as Maj.-Gen. from the 1st Jan. 1812.

The following are honourable testimonials of Maj.-Gen. Sentleger's services:—

" *To the Honourable Lieutenant-Colonel Sentleger.*

" SIR,—You were informed, by a letter addressed to you yesterday, that the Hon. the Gov. in council has been pleased to appoint you to the command of the troops proceeding from Trichinopoly to Travancore. His Exc. the Com.-in-Chief having, since the dispatch of that letter, communcated to the Gov. in council a representation of circumstances connected with your claims, and the Gov. in council deeming it material that you should be distinctly informed of his sentiments on that subject—I am directed to transmit to you the enclosed copy of the Com.-in-Chief's letter, and of the reply addressed in consequence to his excellency.

(Signed) " G. BUCHAN, Chief Sec.
" *Fort St. George, Jan.* 17, 1809."

" *To George Buchan, Esq. Chief Secretary.*

" SIR,—I hasten to state to the Hon. the Gov. in council, that from an omission on my part, in not representing in terms sufficiently strong the loyal and decisive spirit which marked the conduct of the men of the 6th Reg. of N. C. when recently called upon to form a detachment for foreign service, the feelings of a brave and respectable officer have been severely wounded; and it is a duty I owe to him and to his corps to bring to the notice of government the prompt and active manner in which the troop was formed, in the hope that the Hon. the Gov. in council will be pleased to extend such marks of its approbation as the case may seem to require. I think the 6th regiment is as much entitled to honourable distinction as those corps which have already been commended by government. The enclosed letter from the Hon. Lieut.-Col. Sentleger will point out more forcibly how much he has been hurt by this neglect of mine. The second part of the letter now alluded to, is written under the most painful sensations. The pride and honourable ambition of a gallant officer, whose abilities and exploits have frequently been acknowledged, and whose name stands on the records of government, the testimony of his signal services, is deeply affected, and the candid and moderate appeal he has conveyed to me, I have the honour to lay before the Hon. the President in council; and while I sympathize with Col. Sentleger in being separated from his regiment, and placed in a most cruel predicament, yet, aware of the power and patronage of the Hon. the Governor, I can only lament that the selection did not fall upon a man for whose zeal, energy, and military talents, I will safely pledge myself.

(Signed) " HAY MACDOWALL, Com.-in-Chief.
" *Madras, Jan.* 13, 1809."

" *To Lieutenant-General Macdowall, Commander-in-Chief.*

" SIR,—I am directed by the Hon. the Gov. in council to acknowledge the receipt of your Excellency's letter of the 13th inst. received yesterday.

" The Gov. in council has thought it proper, under the explanation conveyed in your letter, to express in general orders his strong approbation of the good conduct of the 6th Reg. N. Cav. It is, at the same time, the duty of the Gov. in council to observe, that Lieut.-Col. Sentleger should have been aware, that it is at all times the desire of the Gov. in council to signalize merit by every means in his power, and the expressions conveyed in the letter of that officer cannot be approved. Previously to the receipt of your letter, your Exc. was informed of the intention of the Hon. the Gov. in council to appoint the Hon. Lieut.-Col. Sentleger to the command of the troops now proceeding from Trichinopoly. Your Exc. will be aware, that it is inconsistent with the usual course of the public service, that an explanation should be assigned of the motives which may regulate the selection of officers for particular commands. It is sufficient to observe, that the selection of Lieut.-Col. Sentleger for his present command, must evince that the Gov. in council has full confidence in the qualifications of that officer for the execution of the important duties now confided to him, and has no doubt but those duties will be carried into effect with zeal and judgment. It is probable that your Exc., in adverting to these circumstances, might not have considered the statement, alluded to in the concluding part of your Excellency's letter, to be essential on a point already decided.

     (Signed) " G. Buchan, Chief Sec.
" Fort St. George, Jan. 17, 1809."

" *To the Honourable Lieutenant Colonel Sentleger.*

" Sir,—I am directed by the Hon. the Gov. in council to acknowledge the receipt of your two letters of the 10th inst. received to-day, which convey the satisfactory information of the storming of the lines of Travancore, in a manner highly honourable to yourself, and to the officers and troops under your command.

The Gov. in council has expressed his further sense of the distinguished service in general orders of this date, but I have been directed to take this occasion of conveying to you the Gov. in council's approbation of your conduct. (Signed) " G. Buchan.
" Fort St. George, Feb. 15, 1809."

Extract of a letter from Lieut-Col. Macaulay, Resident at Travancore, to the Hon. Lieut.-Col. Sentleger.

" Sir,—I have been honoured by the receipt of your letter of the 20th inst., and I feel myself, in common with every well-wisher to the interests and glory of our country, indebted to you for the active and masterly manner in which you have overcome the serious obstacles that were opposed to the progress of the forces under your command. In the short space of ten days the enemy's lines and position have been rapidly carried, the forts of Oudagurry and Pulpanaveram occupied, and the detachment encamped within a few miles of the Rajah's capital.

" *Quilon, Feb.* 22, 1809."

From General Wellesley, (now Duke of Wellington.)

" *Seringapatam, March* 12, 1800.

" MY DEAR COLONEL,—I have the pleasure to inclose the extract of a letter which I have received from government, by which you will perceive that the Supreme government are not unmindful of your services; I conclude, that you will receive a copy of this letter.

(Signed) " ARTHUR WELLESLEY.

" *To the Hon. Lieut.-Col. Sentleger.*"

Extract of a Letter from the Right Hon. the Gov.-Gen. in Council, Feb. 4, 1800.

" We were highly pleased with the decision and vigour of the Hon. Lieut.-Col. Sentleger's conduct, in driving the Mahrattas from the village of Hulliall, of which they had taken possession in violation of the rights of the company, and of the Nizam, under the treaty of Mysore: we request our sentiments on this occasion to be communicated to Lieut.-Col. Sentleger."

MAJOR-GENERAL JOHN HILLY SYMONS.

(Madras Establishment.)

THIS officer was appointed, Feb. 14, 1780, a cadet of infantry; and arrived at Madras on the 10th Oct. following, when he joined a party of cadets attached to a Madras battalion of European infantry, serving with the army, then encamped near Madras, commanded by Maj.-Gen. Sir Hector Munro. In Nov. he was appointed to an ensigncy, and joined the 21st battalion of Sepoys. He served with the 21st battalion of Sepoys at the siege and capture, Aug. 2, 1781, of the fort of Tripassoor, the army commanded by Sir Eyre Coote, then Com.-in-Chief in India. He was present, 27th Aug. following, in a battle with the army of the Nabob Hyder Ally Cawn at Tracollom; and on the 27th Sept. in a battle with the same chieftain on the plains of Shulingur. On the 23rd Oct. he was present with his regiment, the 21st battalion of Sepoys, which formed part of a detachment of one company of European grenadiers, two hundred horse, six battalions of Sepoys, with twelve field-pieces, under the command of Col. Owen, which detachment was defeated by Hyder Ally Cawn.

In the latter affair, Ensign Symons being wounded in the leg, was sent to the fort of Tripassoor, the army depôt, with the sick and wounded of the army. On the 15th Nov. this fort was besieged by Tippoo Saib, son of Hyder Ally Cawn: a breach was practicable for three days and nights, and Ensign Symons, unrecovered of the wound in his leg, was carried up and placed on the works at night, in order to give confidence to the Sepoys. The approach of Sir Eyre Coote's army relieved the fort.

In June 1782, he was present with the 21st battalion of Sepoys in a battle with the Nabob Hyder Ally Cawn on the plains of Arnee: he commanded the grenadiers of the 21st battalion of Sepoys at the attack of the French lines at Cudalore, June 13, 1783, and was in the column led by the late Col. Kelly, which at day-break turned the right of the enemy. On the 23rd July following, he served with the 21st battalion of Sepoys, which marched with a strong detachment from Cudalore, and joined the army under the command of Col. Fullarton, at Dundigull, in the southern part of India. He was then detached from the battalion with a grenadier company, which formed part of a grenadier corps, under the immediate command of the Hon.

Capt. (now Lieut.-Gen. Sir Thomas) Maitland, of the 78th foot. He served at the storm of the covered way and capture of the fort of Palicaudcherry; also at the taking of Coimbetoor. The 11th May, 1786, he was promoted to the rank of lieut., and appointed to the 17th battalion of Sepoys; and on the commencement of hostilities by Tippoo Sultaun in 1790, he was appointed adjut. to a revenue corps, to render it fit for field service. In 1793 he accompanied Capt. Gabriel (now Maj.-Gen.) Doveton, with a grenadier company of the 4th battalion of Sepoys, which formed part of an escort to the camp of the late Tippoo Sultaun with the hostage princes. The 8th Jan. 1796, he was promoted to the rank of captain of infantry, and stationed with the Poligar of Congoondy. In 1799 he was appointed quartermaster of brigade to a detachment under the command of the late Col. Alexander Read, forming part of the grand army which took the field against Tippoo Sultaun.

During the campaign, Capt. Symons was appointed superintendent of Bringanes; in 1800 he was employed by government on a mission to the Chittoor Pollams in settling disputes among the Poligars; and in 1801 in adjusting the supply accounts, and the accounts of the bullock department of the army. He was next appointed judge and magistrate of a civil and criminal court, established at Seringapatam, for the good order and civil government of the fort and island, under the superintendence of the present Duke of Wellington, at that time commanding the forces in Mysore and Malabar, and by whom he was subsequently appointed superintendent of police and the bazars in the fort and on the island. He was promoted, April 14, 1802, to the rank of major, and proceeded to the field with the grand army in the Mahratta war, as agent for draft and carriage cattle. The 14th Dec. 1804 he was promoted to the rank of lieut.-col.; and in 1808 appointed by government superintendent of police at Madras; the 4th June 1813 he obtained the brevet of colonel, and on the 11th March 1819 left Madras for Europe on furlough on sick certificate, for the re-establishment of his health. On the 20th Sept. 1818 he was promoted to the rank of colonel in the regular course of the service, and succeeded to a regiment; and on the 12th Aug. 1819 obtained the brevet of major-general.

LIEUT.-COL. SIR JOHN KENNAWAY, Bart.

(Bengal Establishment.)

This officer was appointed a cadet on the Bengal establishment in the year 1772; ensign in 1773; capt. in 1783; maj. in 1795; brevet lieut.-col. in 1796; col. of the East Devon legion, yeomanry cavalry in 1805; and of the 7th or East Devon local militia in 1808; the command of both which regiments he still holds.

In the year 1788 he was appointed adjut. to the infantry of the Futtehgurh brigade (consisting of eight battalions of Sepoys, three regiments of native cavalry, four companies of artillery,) commanded by Col. M. Leslie; in the year 1781 Persian secretary to Col. J. D. Pearse, commanding the army that was sent from Bengal to the relief of the Carnatic*; and in 1786 aid-de-camp to the late Marquess Corn-

---

* " The force detached to the Carnatic in 1781 was commanded by Col. Pearse. It consisted of four regiments of two small battalions (500 men each) of N. I. some N. Cav. and a proportion of artillery. This corps, which marched about 1100 miles along the sea-coast, through the province of Cuttack and the northern Circars, to Madras, arrived at that presidency at a most eventful period, and their services were eminently useful to the preservation of our power in that quarter. Among the many occasions which this detachment had of distinguishing itself, the attack on the French lines at Cudalore in 1783 was the most remarkable. The Bengal Sepoys that were engaged on that occasion behaved nobly. It was, we believe, one of the first times that European troops and the disciplined natives of India had met at the bayonet. The high spirit and bodily vigour of the Rajpoots of the provinces of Bahar and Benares (the class of which three-fourths of the army was then composed) proved fully equal to the contest. In a partial action, which took place in a sortie made by the French, they were defeated with severe loss; and the memory of this event still continues to be cherished with just pride both by the officers and men of the Bengal Native army. When Col. Pearse's detachment, which had been reduced by ser-

wallis. From the latter office he was removed to the diplomatic situation of resident at Hyderabad in 1788; which he was obliged to relinquish through ill health, and returned to England in 1794, and ultimately to retire from the East India Company's service, on half-pay, in 1801.

For his military services he had the honour of having his name enrolled, " for future marks of the esteem and favour of government," among those officers of the Bengal army, who served against Hyder Ally and the French, commanded by the celebrated Mons. Bussy, in the campaigns of 1781, 2, 3, and 4, under the late Lieut.-Gen. Sir Eyre Coote, as appears from the following copy of a minute of the late Right Hon. Warren Hastings, Gov.-Gen. of India; and for his civil services he was rewarded with a baronetcy in the year 1791, and a pension, by the annexed resolution of the court of directors of the East India Company, in 1796.

" MINUTES OF COUNCIL, *Jan.* 26, 1785.
" The following Minute, by the Gov.-Gen. being so consonant to the ideas of the other members, and so creditable to himself, they requested and obtained his permission for the publication of it at length in General Orders.

" The detachment sent from this presidency to the relief of the Carnatic consisted, in its original formation, of about 5000 men, and is now reduced, by the service it has seen, to less than 2000. These small remains being returned to Ghysetty, the Gov.-Gen yesterday visited their encampment; and he hopes that the Board will allow that indulgence to his feelings, excited by the mixed sentiments of gratitude and regret which were impressed by the occasion, as to

vice from 5000 to 2000 men, returned to Bengal after an absence of four years, the policy of Mr. Hastings heaped every distinction upon them that he thought calculated to reward their merits, or to stimulate others to future exertion of a similar nature. He visited the corps, and his personal conduct towards both the European officers and Natives gave grace to his public measures. A lasting impression was made on the minds of all, and every favour was doubled by the manner in which it was conferred.

(See an admirably written Article in the Quarterly Review of May 1818, *attributed to the pen of a distinguished Officer of the Madras Army.)*

accept with candour the following remuneration which it has induced him to make in their behalf. The board have liberally rewarded the services of the Native officers and privates of the detachment, and afforded such testimonies of those which have been rendered by the European officers, as will be felt by men professing the spirit of honour which they have so signally displayed, with sentiments superior to such as are excited by the pledges of substantial bounty; neither is it easy to devise others. Such additional honours as may be bestowed, the Gov.-Gen. now begs leave to recommend; and these are as follows:—

" 1st, That a sword be given to Col. Pearse, the commanding officer of the corps, and one to each of the Lieut.-Col.'s, his second and third in command, Lieut.-Col. Edmonstone, and Lieut.-Col. Blane, both as a testimony of their faithful and meritorious services, and for the incitement of example to others their juniors.

" 2dly, That the officers who are now attached to the corps, in whatever degree of command, may be confirmed in their stations and commands, notwithstanding the general rules of appointment. Such an indulgence will be equally grateful to the officers themselves and to the men who have served with them, as the removal of the former for the sake of a literal adherence to general rule, would appear like the privation of the right which the chance of hard and severe service has given to the surviving officers of the detachment, in favour of others who have enjoyed a long season of repose, and would be a severe separation of the Sepoys from the officers to whom they are endeared by their common sufferings, and operate as a more cruel hardship by placing them under strangers, to whom their merits will be unknown or unfelt.

" 3dly, That the names of the officers be entered on record, for such future marks of the favour and esteem of government as the rules of the service may admit; and to this list may be joined, on the same principle, that of the officers who have lately served with the other great detachment returned from the other side of India.

" This is the last appeal which I shall make to my present colleagues in the administration; and I venture to declare, without consulting them, that the sentiments of every one are similar to my own, from the same impulse, excited by the personal meeting with men so deserving, and among them some veterans who were once his associates in the same career of military enterprise, and that those of my successor* will be not less favourable, when to the spirit of liberal discernment he shall have joined the same personal motives as those which I have ascribed to myself and Mr. Stables†.

(Signed) " WARREN HASTINGS.

" *To Sir John Kennaway, Bart.*

" *East-India House, Nov. 29, 1796.*

" Resolved,—That in consideration of the important services rendered to the Company by Sir J. Kennaway, he be granted an annuity of 500*l*. per annum, for the term of seventeen years and a half‡ from Michaelmas last, if he shall so long live."

LIEUTENANT-COLONEL WILLIAM RABAN.

(Bengal Establishment.)

THIS officer was appointed a cadet in the East India Company's service in Dec. 1780, and joined his regiment in Bengal, as a lieut. in May 1782. He served as a subaltern under Sir Robert Abercromby during the Rohilla campaign in 1794. In 1802 he was promoted to the rank of capt.; and at this period there being no active service in India, he obtained a furlough for three years to England, and

---

* Sir John M'Pherson, Bart.

† John Stables, Esq. formerly in the army, and commanded a battalion at the battle of Buxar.

‡ The then unexpired term of the Company's charter, which, with the annuity, have been since renewed.

returned to India in 1805; at the latter end of which year he was promoted to the rank of major, and joined his regiment.

In 1811 Maj. Raban volunteered to serve with the expedition about to proceed on foreign service, and was appointed to command the 6th battalion of Bengal volunteers: he was engaged in the different affairs of Weltervreede, Maisur, Cornelis, &c. &c.; and for his services in Java received, along with the other commanding officers, the medal conferred for the attack and capture of that place.

Maj. Raban next volunteered his services under Maj.-Gen. Gillespie in the expedition to Palambang, and commanded the N. Brig. When the army was formed and arranged for service, he was appointed to command the reserve; and on the Maj.-Gen. proceeding to Palambang, this officer was directed to march with the reserve to take possession of the island of Banca, and to hold it in the name of His Majesty: which service he performed, remaining in the island one month.

On the operations at Palambang being concluded, the troops this officer had commanded were left at Banca, and he volunteered to accompany Maj.-Gen. Gillespie to the attack of the Sultaun of Jogocarta, and being unattached, he was invited by the Maj.-Gen. to be placed on his staff; unfortunately the ship in which he embarked made a tedious passage to Java, and the unsuccessful attack on the fortress of the Sultaun took place the very evening Maj. Raban arrived at Samarang; intelligence of which he received on his way to join the General.

Active service being at an end, Maj. Raban was shortly after, with the consent of the Maj.-Gen., appointed by the Gov. in council resident of Cheribon, and at the same time to hold the military command of the district.

The 11th Sept. 1811 he was promoted to the rank of Lieut.-Col.; and after remaining two years at Cheribon, his affairs calling him to Europe, he obtained a furlough to offer his resignation of the service, and sailed from Java in July 1814.

MAJOR ARCHIBALD DOUGLAS MONTEATH.

(Madras Establishment.)

This officer was appointed to a cadetship in 1795, and as such served with the 4th regiment of light cavalry at the siege and capture of Pondicherry; on the 1st June he was appointed cornet in the 1st regiment light cavalry; adj. of the same regiment in 1797; in 1799 he was promoted to the rank of lieut., and appointed quarter-master to the 2nd regiment light cavalry; with which corps he served in the campaign against Tippoo Saib and Doondia Waugh.

In 1800, on the 7st regiment light cavalry being raised, Lieut. Monteath was removed to that corps as lieutenant and quarter-master; and in 1803 he was appointed agent for cavalry supplies to the army under the orders of Maj.-Gen. Sir Arthur Wellesley, and as such served in the Mahratta campaigns of 1803 and 1804. He was promoted to the rank of captain in the 7th regiment of light cavalry on the 1st May 1804, and appointed secretary to the officer commanding the northern division of the army; but owing to bad health was forced to quit the army in the field, and proceed to Bombay. In Sept. 1805 he embarked for Europe on sick certificate. On the 11th March 1809 he was promoted to the rank of major in the 7th regiment light cavalry; and in 1811 retired on the half-pay list.

MAJOR-GENERAL HENRY WEBBER.

(Madras Establishment.)

This officer was appointed to a cadetship, on the Madras establishment, 6th May 1780; ensign, Aug. 13, 1780; lieut. March 17,

1786; capt. July 1, 1796; maj. Dec. 24, 1800; lieut.-col. Sept. 21, 1804; col. June 4, 1814; and maj.-gen. Aug. 12, 1819.

He arrived at Madras in Jan. 1781, and in July volunteered to join the army under Sir Eyre Coote, and was present at the battle of the 27th Aug. fought at Polylore, and where he received a severe contusion in his thigh from a cannon-shot. Officers being required to serve in the army formed in the Tanjore country, under Lieut.-Gen. Sir Hector Munro, Ensign Webber again volunteered his services, and was present at the attack of the lines, and at the siege of Negapatam. He afterwards joined the field force under Col. Braithwaite, and escaped the fate of that officer by being compelled from severe indisposition to go into sick quarters. He joined the force subsequently formed at Trichinopoly under Col. Lang, and was slightly wounded in the head at the taking of Caroor. He was next attached to Col. Fullarton's army, and served under that officer until the peace concluded with Tippoo Sultaun in 1784; after which he did duty with various corps in different parts of the coast of Coromandel, agreeably to the usages of the service at that period. He assisted in subduing the rebellious Rajahs in the northern Circars until 1792, when he joined the army under Lord Cornwallis, and was present at the attack of the lines of Seringapatam on the 6th of Feb. In 1801, being promoted to the rank of major, he joined the head-quarters of the Madras European Reg. at Amboyna, and was immediately appointed to command at Banda, from which he was shortly relieved, being selected by Col. Oliver, Com.-in-Chief in the Moluccas, to command at Ternate, which place had been recently taken from the enemy by Gen. Burr, and was in an unorganized state. He held the appointments of civil resident and commanding officer at fort Orange for nearly two years, and repeatedly received the thanks of Col. Oliver for his conduct in reconciling the discordant interests of the Malay princes of Ternate, Tidore, and Bachian; and on his being ordered to deliver over the island to the Dutch, he received the public thanks of the Dutch governor who relieved him, in the name of the Sultaun and inhabitants of Ternate, for his attention to their welfare during the period of his administration.

Maj. Webber returned to the coast of Coromandel with the remains of the Madras European Reg. and was sent to join the force under the command of Col. Harcourt at Cuttack.

In 1804, being promoted to the rank of lieut.-col. he was nominated to command the 2nd batt. 22nd N. I.; and in 1807, after an absence of twenty-seven years, obtained a furlough to visit his native country. He returned to Madras in 1809, and was ordered to join his corps at Cananore, and where he was employed in reducing to obedience the rebellious Poligars in the Wynaad, for which service he received the thanks of government. He was subsequently appointed by Gen. Abercromby to command Chitteldroog. In 1815 he was nominated by government to command the Mysore division, and in 1816 the ceded districts, head-quarters at Belpary, which station he quitted in 1819, on being promoted to the rank of colonel, and returned to England.

MAJOR JAMES DERMISTOUN BROWN.

(Madras Establishment.)

THIS officer served in India from Jan. 1797 till Oct. 1814 without a furlough; he was compelled to leave India on sick certificate, and from continued ill health, to retire from the service in 1819, on the half-pay of capt. only. He served with the army under Gen. (now Lord) Harris in Mysore in 1799; and with the army under Gen. Dugald Campbell, in the ceded districts, in 1801; and with that under Gen. Sir Arthur Wellesley, in the Mahratta country, in 1803 and 1804.

He was appointed to command the flying artillery of the 25th, late

22nd light dragoons, in 1799; appointed quarter-master of artillery in 1801; and in 1803 to the temporary charge of ordnance and military stores, proceeding under the orders of Sir A. Wellesley, by whom he was appointed to the charge and direction of an establishment at Poonah, for the construction and repair of the field ordnance carriages. In 1805 and 1806 he served as acting major of brigade, and acting commissary of ordnance, at the Mount: in Sept. of the latter year he was appointed commissary of ordnance at Seringapatam; he was present at the siege and storm of that place, and received the medal given on that occasion.

The following are the dates of this officer's commissions:—lieut. fireworker, April 1796; lieut. Feb. 1800; capt.-lieut. Oct. 1801; capt. Nov. 1806; brevet-maj. June 1813; and major of artillery, Sept. 1, 1818.

MAJOR FRANCIS F. STAUNTON.

(Bombay Establishment.)

This officer commenced his military career at the early age of sixteen, as a lieut. in the Cheshire fencible infantry, raised by Col. Courtenay, joined that corps at Chester in 1795, and did duty with it in England, and in Jersey, until April 1798, when he obtained a cadetship on the Bombay establishment; and arriving at Bombay on the 21st Sept. in that year, was immediately appointed ensign in the 1st or grenadier battalion of Bombay Native infantry.

At that period regimental rank had not taken place in the Company's army, and it was then considered desirable in many respects to be posted to that distinguished corps, always the first ordered on service—a compliment paid to this officer by the late Gen. James Stuart, then Com.-in-Chief at that presidency, on the plea of his having served at home, as a lieut. in his Majesty's army; further assuring him that as soon as the prescribed documents (which he directed him to write for) reached Bombay, he should be placed at the head of the list of cadets of his season, a precedence he was entitled to by the Company's regulations. Gen. Stuart resigned the command of the Bombay army, and returned to England before the documents arrived; and Ensign Staunton's applications for the precedency of rank, to which he considered himself entitled in the Company's army, failed of success[*]. The war with Tippoo Sultaun immediately followed, and Ensign Staunton served with the grenadiers during that eventful period; he accompanied them to the siege, and was at the storm of Jemaulabad in the Canara country, in 1799.

Regimental rank having taken place, this officer was removed to the 4th N. I. then serving against Doondia Cawn, in the Scindia country. He joined and did duty with that corps, until an alteration in regimental rank removed him to the 2nd battalion of his former regiment, the grenadiers. He joined at Surat, and proceeded with the corps on the expedition to Egypt. A brother of this officer was at this period serving as capt.-lieut. in the 13th foot, then before Alexandria, and in consequence Ensign Staunton obtained leave to precede the Indian army, and arrived at Alexandria some days before it surrendered, in the expectation of serving with his brother's regiment; but in this he was disappointed, by the capitulation of Gen. Menou. He then rejoined the Indian army, and continued with it during its stay in Egypt, where his regiment suffered much from the plague and ophthalmia. On the return of this corps to India, it immediately

---

[*] There are three instances in which the claim for precedence has been admitted in this officer's own regiment on similar grounds, *viz.* Capt. Montresor obtained it from having held a commission in the Suffolk Fencibles; Capt. Brown on a like plea; and Capt. Morin for having been in the Jersey Militia. The loss of military rank is peculiarly unfortunate in the present case. At the battle of Corygaum, one of the most **distinguished** affairs in Indian History, this officer commanded with the rank of captain only, although he had then been twenty years in the service, and received the Seringapatam and **Egyptian** medals: from not being a field-officer, he was, by the regulations, excluded from the **honours of the Bath.**

took the field in Guzerat. Ensign Staunton served at the siege of Baroda, the capital of that province, and in various parts of that country, until ill health compelled him to return to England for his recovery. On that object being accomplished, he rejoined his corps at Poonah, and served with it during the late Mahratta war: he was present at the battle of Kirkee, under the command of the late Lieut.-Col. Burr; and commanded a detachment, consisting of his corps, the 2nd battalion of grenadiers, 300 irregular horse, and an officer and twenty-six European artillerymen, with two six-pounders, that defeated the Peishwa's army at Corygaum*, on the 1st Jan. 1818; on

---

* It is but just to the services of this officer to record in this place the sentiments of the late President of the board of controul, Mr. Canning, on this brilliant affair:—

"The combined courage and attachment of the Native and British troops were never more conspicuous than on one occasion, which I will take the liberty to particularize, for the purpose of paying a just tribute, as well to the Native troops as to the talents of an officer commanding them. It is an instance which I may select without invidiousness, as the rank of the officer does not allow of his name being mentioned in a vote of thanks. A body of between 8 and 900 men, all natives, except the artillery, the proportion of which to a force of this strength many gentlemen present can estimate more correctly than myself, was on its march from a distant part of the Peishwa's territories to Poonah, soon after the denunciation of hostilities, and unexpectedly found itself in presence of the whole Mahratta army. What was the exact amount of the Peishwa's force I am not able to state with precision, but the cavalry alone was not less than 20,000. The small band which I have described, hemmed in on all sides by this overwhelming superiority of numbers, maintained through a long day an obstinate and victorious resistance: victorious—for they repelled on every point the furious attacks of the enemy. The chief suffering of which they complained during this singular and most unequal contest was intolerable thirst, which they could not procure the means of slaking until the action was over. In the end they not only secured an unmolested retreat, but they carried off their wounded! In such a waste and wilderness of space and of glories, distracting the sight and perplexing the judgment, it is satisfactory thus to select some small insulated field of action, which one can comprehend at a single glance, and of which (as of some green and sunny spot in a far-stretching and diversified landscape) one can attach and delineate all the characteristic features. From this one small achievement, small as to extent, but mighty with reference to the qualities in it, the spirit which pervaded and animated the whole Indian army may be inferred. The officer who commanded this gallant little force was Capt. Staunton: his rank does not entitle him to be recorded in our votes, but the House will be glad to learn that his merits and services have not been overlooked by his immediate employers, the court of directors."

(*See Mr. Canning's Speech, March 4, 1819, on moving the thanks of the House of Commons to the Marquess of Hastings and the army in India.*)

which occasion the annexed orders were published by the Governor-General and Sir T. Hislop.

The following are the dates of this Officer's commissions—Ensign, 21 Sept. 1798; Lieutenant, 6 March, 1800; Captain, 23 April, 1807; and Major, 16 April, 1819.

"GENERAL ORDERS, *Bombay Castle, 7th Feb.* 1818.

" Although the 2d battalion of the 1st regiment N. I. is at present detached from the immediate controul of this government, yet as it forms a part of the Bombay army, the Rt. Hon. the Gov. in Council feels it a most gratifying duty to publish the following divisional orders issued by Brig. Gen. Smith, with Capt. Staunton's report of the gallant defence made on the 1st inst. at Corygaum, against the army of the Peishwa in the presence of his Highness, by the detachment under Capt. Staunton's command.

" *Division Orders by Brig. Gen. Smith, C. B.*
Camp near Seroor, 7th Jan. 1818.

" The commanding officer having received the official accounts of an attack made by the Peishwa's army on a small detachment commanded by Capt. Staunton, of the 2d batt. 1st reg. Bombay N. I. at the village of Corygaum, has great satisfaction in publishing the particulars for general information, and in holding it up to the force, as one of the most brilliant examples of gallantry and perseverance recorded in our Indian annals. This detachment, consisting of a detail of Madras Art. and two 6-pounders, 1st batt. N. I. about 600 strong, and about 300 auxiliary horse, the whole under Capt. Staunton, marched from Seroor for Poonah, at 8 P. M. on the 31st Dec. and reached the heights overlooking Corygaum about ten in the forenoon, 1st Jan. from whence the whole of the Peishwa's army, estimated 20,000 horse, and several thousand infantry, were discovered in the plain south of the Beemah river. Capt. Staunton immediately moved upon the village of Corygaum with the intention of occupying it, and had scarcely succeeded in reaching it with his detachment, when he was attacked in the most determined manner by three divisions of the Peishwa's choicest infantry, supported by immense bodies of horse and the fire of two pieces of artillery; the enemy's troops were stimulated to their utmost exertions by the presence of the Peishwa on a distant height, attended by the principal Mahratta chiefs, who flattered his Highness with the prospect of witnessing the destruction of this gallant handful of British troops. The enemy obtained immediate possession of the strongest posts of the village, from which it was found impossible to dislodge them, and possession of the remaining part was most obstinately contested from noon till 9 P. M. during which time almost every pagoda and house had been repeatedly taken and retaken, and one of the guns at one time was in possession of the enemy. Towards the close of the evening, the detachment was placed in the most trying situation; at this period nearly the whole of the artillery men were killed or wounded, and about one-third of the infantry and auxiliary horse. The exertions which the European officers had been called upon to make in leading their men to frequent charges with the bayonet had diminished their numbers: Lieut. Chisholm of the artillery, and Mr. Assist. Surg. Wingate, 2d battalion 1st regiment, were killed, and Lieut. Swanston, Pattinson, and Connellon wounded, leaving only Capt. Staunton, and Lieut. Jones and Mr. Assist. Surg. Wyldie, nearly exhausted, to direct the efforts of the remaining part of the detachment, who were nearly frantic from the want of water, and the almost unparalleled exertions they had made throughout the day without any sort of refreshment, after a fatiguing march of twenty-eight miles. Under cover of the night they were enabled to procure a supply of water, and at 9 P. M. the enemy were forced to abandon the village, after sustaining an immense loss in killed and wounded.

" The British character was nobly supported throughout the whole of this arduous contest, by the European officers, and a small detail of Madras Art. The Medical officers also led on the sepoys to charges with the bayonet, the nature of the contest not admitting of their attending to their professional duties; and in such a struggle, the presence of a single European was of the utmost consequence, and seemed to inspire the native soldiers with the usual confidence of success. At day light on the 2d the enemy were still in sight, but did not renew the attack, although it prevented the troops, whose ammunition was nearly expended, from procuring any supply of provisions. Capt. Staunton however made preparations for moving according to circumstances; and the manner in which that officer availed himself of the few resources which remained to him after such a conflict, to prosecute his march, and bring away the numerous wounded of his detachment, is highly praiseworthy. The detachment moved during the night of the 2d upon Seroor, which they reached at nine o'clock on the forenoon of the 3d, having had no refreshment from the 31st Dec.—Capt. Staunton brought in nearly the whole of the wounded, and both the guns and colours of the regiment, which the enemy had vainly hoped to present as trophies to the Peishwa.

"In concluding these details the Com. Officer begs to offer to Capt. Staunton and the whole of the European and Native commissioned, and non-commissioned officers and privates engaged at Corygaum, his best thanks for their noble exertions, and exemplary patience under every species of privation; which he will not fail to bring to the notice of Government and his Exc. the Com.-in-Chief. The Commanding Officer deems it proper to record the names of the officers engaged in this brilliant affair.

"Madras art. Lieut. Chisholm, (killed); Assist. Surg. Wyldie. 2d batt. 1st reg. Capt. Staunton, commanding detachment; Lieut. and Adj. Pattinson, (wounded, since dead); Lieut. Connellon, (wounded); Lieut. Jones, 10th reg. doing duty 2d batt. 1st reg.; Assist. Surg. Wingate, (killed). Auxiliary horse, Lieut. Swanston, Madras establishment, (wounded.)

"The Gov. in Council entirely concurs in the opinions expressed by the Brig.-Gen. in these general orders, and he cannot in better terms convey his sense of the intrepidity displayed by this detachment, than by reciting the observation of the Brig.-Gen. in his official report to the Resident at Poonah, that the action of Corygaum was one ' of the most brilliant affairs ever achieved by any army, in which the European and Native soldiers displayed the most noble devotion and most romantic bravery under the pressure of thirst and hunger, almost beyond human endurance.'

" His Exc. the Com.-in-Chief is requested to convey to Capt. Staunton, commanding the detachment, to Lieuts. Jones and Connellon, of the 2d batt. 1st reg. and to the Native commissioned and non-commissioned officers, and privates who survived the late arduous and glorious contest, the thanks of Government for their distinguished services on that occasion. The Gov.-in-Council laments that so splendid a triumph should have been attended with so severe a loss as that shewn in the return of the killed and wounded;* though, considering the great disparity of numbers, the length of the contest, the fatigues and privations of the detachment, it is to be wondered the loss was not more severe. The Gov.-in-Council, desirous of conferring on this corps some signal mark of the favour and approbation of the Government, directs that the 2d batt. of the first reg. be placed on the same distinguished footing as the 1st batt. which has, for many years, in consideration of its gallant services, been designated the Grenadier Battalion, and that the two battalions be henceforth called the 1st or Grenadier Regiment.

" Corygaum, the scene of its late exploit, is to be incribed on the colours of the 2d batt. of the Grenadiers, and on the appointments of the officers and men, in addition to any other which may have been heretofore granted. The Com.-in-Chief is requested to obtain correct returns of the widows and children of the several Native officers and soldiers killed in action, or who have since died of their wounds, in order that they may be provided for under the established regulations of Government."

" *By the Commander in Chief, Bombay, Feb. 9th*, 1818.

" In publishing to the army the foregoing Government general orders of the 7th inst. detailing the battle of Corygaum, His Exc. the Com.-in-Chief cannot deny himself the gratification of adding his ap-

---

* Sixty-two killed, and 113 wounded, exclusive of auxiliary horse.

plause and admiration of the brave conduct of Capt. Staunton and the whole of the detachment engaged in that glorious contest. The well-established fame and former services of the 2d batt. 1st reg. N. I. were alone sufficient proofs of what might be expected from such a corps even under the most trying circumstances, but the noble devotion displayed at Corygaum places in the most flattering point of view the character of the Bombay infantry. The Com.-in-Chief feels more than ordinary satisfaction in performing the pleasing duty assigned to him by government of conveying to Capt. Staunton, Lieuts. Jones and Connellon, the Native commissioned, non-commissioned officers and privates of the 2nd batt. 1st or grenadier reg., the sentiments of high approbation and thanks which the Right Hon. the Gov. in council has been pleased to express, and in which the Lieut.-Gen. most cordially and perfectly concurs, whilst he congratulates them most sincerely on the distinguished honours conferred on the battalion, in commemoration of their heroic bravery at Corygaum. His Exc. Sir M. Nightingall cannot conclude this public expression of his sentiments without paying a well-merited tribute of applause to the memory of Lieut. and Adj. Pattinson, and Assist.-Surg. Wingate, in whom the service has sustained a severe public loss.

" The officer commanding the 2nd batt. 1st or grenadier reg., will be pleased to transmit to the Adj.-Gen.'s office, without delay, a correct return of the widows and children of the several native officers and soldiers killed in the action, or who may have to be provided for as directed by the regulation of government. A correct nominal return of the Native commissioned and non-commissioned officers, drummers and privates, who were present at Corygaum, and survived the action, to be likewise transmitted without delay to the Adj.-Gen. of the army."

" *By the Honourable the Vice-President in Council.*
" *Fort William, March* 19, 1818.
" The despatch, of which the following is a copy, addressed by his Exc. Sir T. Hislop, to his Exc. the most noble the Gov.-Gen., on

the subject of the brilliant exploit achieved by the detachment under the command of Capt. Staunton of the 2nd batt. of the 1st reg. Bombay N. I. at Corygaum, on the 1st Jan. last, having been received at the presidency since the date of the government gazette of the 5th inst., in which the details of that memorable victory were inserted, is now ordered by the Hon. the Vice-President in council to be published for general information, together with the general orders issued under the authority of his Exc. Sir T. Hislop on the occasion, omitting such parts as have already been officially communicated to the public."

" *To his Excellency the Marquess of Hastings, Governor-General, &c.*

" *Head-Quarters, Army of the Deccan.*

" My Lord,—I have extraordinary satisfaction in transmitting, for the information of your Lordship, the official details of one of the most heroic* actions which has ever been fought and gained by a handful of men over a large army. The accompanying transcript of Brig.-Gen. Smith's despatch, and of the general order which I yesterday published to the army on this brilliant occasion, will place your Lordship in full possession of the particulars of the battle, in which the 2nd batt. of the 1st reg. of Bombay N. I., aided by a small party of Madras artil.-men, with two six-pounders, and about three hundred auxiliary horse, have nobly sustained, during a whole day, and finally repulsed, the unceasing and vigorous efforts of the Peishwa's army, under circumstances of peculiar difficulty and privation, which render the exploit altogether unparalleled. I need not again in this place recapitulate the names of the officers who have aided the intrepid Capt. Staunton in gaining the victory of Cory-

---

* The foundation-stone of a monument, destined to perpetuate the defence of Corygaum, was laid on the 26th March 1821. A brass-plate, with the following inscription—" This Foundation-Stone was laid, Anno Domini 1821, by the Most Noble the Marquess of Hastings, Governor-General of India, and the Honourable Mountstuart Elphinstone, Governor of Bombay,"—was deposited in the foundation-stone, with a few British coins, and a scroll of parchment containing the names of the persons present at the ceremony.

gaum; their individual merits are brought to your Lordship's notice in the accompanying documents, and they will be certain to receive from their government and their country, that admiration of, and gratitude for their devoted gallantry, to which they are so highly entitled. I most sincerely congratulate your Lordship on an event which has, if possible, heightened the renown of the Indian army, and from which I cannot but anticipate results of the highest political importance, since such a defeat must inevitably tend to paralyse the future exertions of the enemy, and prove to him the hopelessness of continuing a war with any success against a power which has such troops to oppose to him. (Signed) " T. HISLOP, Lieut.-Gen.
" *Camp at Mehidpoor, Jan. 23, 1818.*"

" *By the Commander-in-Chief.*
" *Head-Quarters of the Army of the Deccan.*
" It is with feelings of inexpressible gratification, that the Com.-in-Chief has to announce one of the most heroic and brilliant achievements ever recorded in the annals of the army, which took place at Corygaum, between Seroor and Poonah, on the 1st inst. The official details of this glorious affair reached the Com.-in-Chief yesterday, in a despatch from Brig.-Gen. Lionel Smith, C. B. commanding the 2nd or Poonah division of the army of the Deccan; and his Exc. is pleased to publish the Brig.-Gen.'s orders issued on the occasion, that the army may be placed in full possession of every particular of an event displaying so bright and distinguished an example of devoted courage and admirable constancy.

" The Com.-in-Chief having published the foregoing order, in the sentiments of which he most cordially participates, feels unable to do greater justice to Capt. Staunton and his gallant detachment; but in conveying to that officer and his brave troops the expression of his thanks and highest admiration, his Exc. entreats them to believe, that the distinguished intrepidity and enduring fortitude they have so nobly shewn, under circumstances of the most trying privation, will for ever remain deeply impressed upon his heart, and be recorded as one of the brightest deeds in the annals of our Indian history. It will be his Exc.'s most gratifying duty immediately to bring to the special notice of his Exc. the most noble the Gov.-Gen., and Com.-in-Chief in India, the particulars of this brilliant and glorious event.

  (Signed) " T. H. S. CONWAY, Adj.-Gen. of the Army.
" *Camp near Mehidpoor, Wed. Jan.* 21, 1818."

  " *By the Most Noble the Marquess of Hastings.*

  " *Head-Quarters, Camp Byramghout,* 13*th March* 1818.
" The Com.-in-Chief of all the forces in India, having received the official details of the action at Corygaum, is pleased to direct that they shall be entered into every orderly-book of the Bengal army, to remain a recorded proof of what may be achieved by disciplined intrepidity against even the persevering courage of immensely superior numbers. His Lordship offers his applause and thanks to Capt. Staunton, and Lieuts. Connellon, Jones (10th reg.), and Swanson, and Assist.-Surg. Wylie of the Madras establishment, and to the native officers, non-commissioned officers, and men, of the several corps which participated in the glorious defence of the village against the Peishwa's army.

  (Signed) " J. NICOLL, Adjut.-Gen."

  " *Head-Quarters, Goruckpore,* May 21, 1818.
" SIR,—I am instructed by the Marquess of Hastings to apprize you of your having been nominated an honorary aid-de-camp to the Gov.-Gen. as a mark of his lordship's high approbation of the undaunted gallantry, steady perseverance, and cool judgment, which so eminently distinguished your conduct, in the memorable action of the 1st Jan. last, at Corygaum. This appointment will neither interfere with your present duties, or entail the necessity of your joining his lordship's head-quarters; it is meant as purely honorary, and will give you no other privilege but that of being considered as a detached

branch of his lordship's family, and of wearing the uniform of his Excellency's staff, when not on duty with your regiment.

    (Signed) "C. H. DOYLE, Lieut.-Col. & Mil. Sec.
" *To Capt. Staunton, 2nd B. 1st Reg. Bombay N. I.*"

LIEUT.-COL. SIR THOMAS RAMSAY, BART.

(Bengal Establishment.)

IN 1782 this officer served as a volunteer in the 6th batt. of Bengal N. I. then forming part of the Bengal detachment, on actual service in the west of India, under the command of Lieut.-Col. Charles Morgan, successor to Gen. Goddard, with which he remained until 1786, when he became a supernumerary on the reduced establishment introduced by Lord Cornwallis, under whose government he served upwards of four years on the reduced pay of his rank. The above detachment, which left the Bengal provinces in 1778, consisted of six battalions of N. I. two of N. C. and a field train: they quitted their temporary cantonments in the vicinity of Surat on the 3rd Nov. 1783, marched through the Mahratta country, and encamped on the banks of the Jumna, near Etya, on the 10th March following, when the several corps were ordered to their destination. The 6th batt. to which Sir Thomas was attached, commanded by Capt. Archdeacon, was immediately ordered on actual service to Kyrabad in the Vizier's provinces, at that time in a state of rebellion; but it proceeded no further than Lucknow, from whence it shortly after returned to the cantonments at Caunpoor.

In 1790 he volunteered to serve with the late Col. Cockerell's detachment, which marched by land from Bengal to the Carnatic, and partook of the whole of Lord Cornwallis and Gen. Medow's cam-pains in Mysore: Sir Thomas was present at the night attack of Feb. 6, 1792, on Tippoo's lines: he served in the Bengal detachment, and was attached to the battalion commanded by Capt. Archdeacon, and, on the fall of that officer, by Capt. (the late Maj.-Gen. Sir Henry) White, he had the honour of receiving, in common with the detachment that was engaged in the morning attack, the thanks of Lord Cornwallis for his conduct on that occasion. He was immediately after detached with an escort from Sibbald's redoubt in quest of Capt. Dugald Campbell, in command of his Majesty's 74th Reg. with the parole of Bangalore, by order of Capt. White, to obviate any mistake from the darkness of the night in forming a junction, Tippoo's troops having reassembled. To accomplish this service Sir Thomas had to pass through the enemy's encampments, and having discovered the 74th, he immediately gave the signal word, "Bangalore," which being shouted by the regiment, it was shortly after joined by three companies of the 6th N. I. under Capt. White, and a detachment of the 52nd regiment.

Sir Thomas continued to serve with Col. Cockerell's detachment until the peace of Seringapatam, when he returned by land with the detachment, after three years' absence from Bengal. On his promotion to the rank of lieut. Lord Cornwallis was pleased to order him to proceed to the Andaman islands, in command of the troops of that settlement, where he remained two years. He returned to Bengal in 1796 in a bad state of health, and in Sept. 1799 was removed from the native branch of the service to the Bengal European Reg. and performed the duties of adjut. to that corps, until he obtained the rank of capt. regimentally, in Sept. 1804, when he marched with his corps from Dinapore to the province of Bundlecund, then suffering from the depredations of Holkar and his followers.

Sir Thomas was in actual service in Bundlecund, under the command of Col. Peregrine Powell and Lieut.-Col. Fawcit, from Dec. 1803 until June 1804, when his corps was ordered into cantonments at Allahabad. In Nov. 1804 he marched with the European Reg. from Allahabad to Muttra, and from thence proceeded with the army under Lord Lake to Burtpore. He was wounded in the trenches before that place on the 7th Jan. 1805, and was incapacitated from further duty until the 20th of the following month. On the fourth and last fruitless attack on the above fortress, commanded by Col. Monson, of his Majesty's 76th Reg. Sir Thomas commanded the light company of the European Reg. during the storm, and was again severely wounded in the face by a musket-ball; on which account he received no remuneration from the East-India Company, although usual on similar occasions.

Sir Thomas, from the nature of his wounds, was, in this year, under the necessity of leaving India for Great-Britain: in 1809 he returned to Bengal; and in Nov. of the following year, was detached to the Molucca islands, then commanded by Lieut.-Col. S. Kelly, who dying in Dec. 1811, the command devolved upon Sir Thomas: he remained there until the arrival of the Dutch troops at Amboyna early in April 1817, at which period the Spice islands were delivered over to the Dutch authorities.

In July 1817 Sir Thomas obtained permission to return to Europe on furlough; he arrived in this country on the 2nd March in the following year; and in May 1821 again returned to India.

The following are the dates of this officer's commissions:—cadet, June 23, 1783; ensign, April 13, 1785; lieut. Oct. 28, 1793; capt. Jan. 8, 1798; maj. July 25, 1810; and lieut.-col. June 1, 1818.

MAJOR-GENERAL GEORGE DICK.

(Bengal Establishment.)

In 1779 this officer proceeded to India as a cadet on the Bengal establishment. He was appointed ensign Feb. 27, 1780; lieut. March 27, 1781; brevet-capt. Jan. 7, 1796; capt.-lieut. in 1797, and subsequently regimental capt.; maj. March 5, 1814; lieut.-col. Nov. 22, 1807; brevet-col. June 1, 1814; regimental col. Dec. 1819; and maj.-gen. July 10, 1821.

In 1790 he was employed on service in the district of Silhet; in the latter end of 1792, the whole of 1793, and part of 1794, in Assam; in the latter end of 1794 he was appointed adjut. to the 12th battalion of N. I. and joined that corps whilst it was serving with the army in Rohilcund, under Sir Robert Abercromby: in 1796 he was appointed adjut. and quart.-mast. to the 4th reg. of N. I.: in 1803 he proceeded on foreign service, in command of a battalion of Native volunteers, and was absent at Ceylon and Penang until the latter end of 1805. In 1814 he was nominated a brigadier, and served as second in command to Maj.-Gen. Marley, with the division that was commanded by that officer during the first campaign against Nepaul. In 1816 he was again nominated a brigadier, and served as second in command with the division under the immediate and personal command of Sir David Ochterlony, in the second campaign against Nepaul. The Gov.-Gen. and Com.-in-Chief, the Marquess of Hastings, appointed him in the latter end of 1817 to command the 2d brigade of the centre division of the grand army that served under his lordship's personal command, and on the breaking up of the army in the early part of 1818 this officer was sent to command the troops in Bundlecund, as a brigadier, in which situation he continued until the beginning of 1819, when he was compelled, by sickness, to leave it in progress for England for the recovery of his health.

LIEUTENANT COLONEL JOHN TOMKYNS.

(Bengal Establishment.)

This officer was appointed a Cadet of artillery in 1778; admitted 14 Sept. 1778; Lieut. fireworker, 6 Nov. 1778; Lieut. 17 Feb.

1784; Capt. 27 Oct. 1794; Major, 12 Nov. 1804; and Lieut.-Col. 15 May, 1804.

In 1780 this officer accompanied the detachment, consisting of five regiments of Native infantry and a company of artillery, which marched from Calcutta to Madras, under the command of Col. Pearse, to join the army commanded by Sir Eyre Coote. He was present at the storming of the fort of Tripasoor; in the engagement of 27 Aug. 1781, with Hyder Ally at Pollilore; at Sholinghur in Sept. following; and in that of 22 Jan. 1782, when Hyder Ally attacked the rear of the British army on its march to the relief of Velore. He was also present at the action near Mimundrum, 13 Jan. 1782; at that of the 16th of the same month; and at that near Arnee 2d June following.

In 1783 he served under Gen. Stuart, and was present at the storming of the French lines at Cudalore 13th June, 1783; and at the affair of the 25th June, when the French made a sally to regain their lines, but were defeated. In 1786 he was present at the capture of a strong fort, north-west of Furruckabad; in 1790 he served under Gen. Sir Wm. Medows, and was present at the capture of some forts. He served at the capture of Dindigul 22 Aug. 1790; and at that of Palicaudcherry 22 Sept. following. In 1791 he served under Lord Cornwallis; and was employed, 2d March, with a party to blow open the gates of Oscotta. He was at the capture of Bangalore, 21st March, 1791; and in the engagement with Tippoo, near Seringapatam, 15th May, 1791; at the capture of Outradroog, Nundydroog, and Savandroog; and at the storming of Tippoo's lines near Seringapatam, 6 Feb. 1792. In the following year he was employed to the eastward of Chittagong, under the command of Col. Erskine, and took possession of many of the enemy's forts, which were evacuated as soon as the British came in sight. In 1799 he served under Lord Harris, and was at the capture of Seringapatam, Chitteldroog, and some other forts. In 1800 he served under Col. Wellesley, (now Duke Wellington,) and commanded the artillery at the capture of several forts in the Mahratta country.

In 1803 this officer proceeded to Europe, and in May 1805 retired from the service.

MAJOR JOHN HICKS.
(Bengal Establishment.)

This officer was appointed a Cadet on the Bombay establishment in 1797; Ens. 21 Sept. 1798; Lieut. March 6, 1800; Capt.-Lieut. Oct. 1, 1809; Capt. Nov. 18, 1809; and Maj. May 4, 1820.

On his arrival in Bombay in 1798, he was first posted to the 2d batt. 3d reg. N. I.: he joined at head quarters at Tellichery in charge of recruits, and was present with the battalion in 1799, in the campaign against Tippoo Sultaun, and at the siege of Seringapatam, taken by storm 4th May, 1799. On his promotion to lieut. he was removed to the 2d reg. N. I. which corps he joined at Goa in May 1800, and marched with it to the army under Col. Wellesley, against Doondia Waugh. He was present at the storm of Ranahednore, Damul, and Seronge. He served as quart.-mast. of brig. to Col. Capper, afterwards to Col. Spry, whose brigade, when the above service was over, by the defeat and death of Doondia Waugh, formed part of the force under Col. Stevenson, which marched into Wynaad, against the Cotiote Rajah in 1801; he was present with the advanced guard under Col. Spry, at the skirmish near Manantadoy. On the field force being broken up, this officer joined his batt. stationed at Pullinyau, in Wynaad. In 1802 the batt. marched to Montaga, afterwards to Cananore: in 1803 he marched with a detachment of his battalion of 300 men under Capt. Mealy, into Cotiote, to scour the jingles after the enemy: in the same year the battalion left Malabar for Goa; in April 1804 embarked for Surat, marched to Cappermanjee, and joined the army assembling under Col. (now Lieut.-Gen. Sir John) Murray, who was replaced by Maj.-Gen. Jones. This officer proceeded with the above force to Burtpore, where it formed a junction with the grand army, under Lord Lake. He served with the batt. when it formed part of the storming party on the 21st Feb. 1805, which was beat back with considerable loss. In March 1806 the Bombay div. reached Baroda, where it was broken up, and the batts. ordered to different stations.

The 2nd batt. 2nd reg. began its march for the Deccan, and reached Ahmednugger in May; in Jan. 1807 it was ordered to Bombay, and on the 5th Feb. marched again for Baroda, remained only a short time, and proceeded into Kuttywar to join the field force under Col. Walker. As soon as the service was over, the batt. began its march back towards Bombay, and reached Tannah in April 1808, when this officer was transferred to the 1st batt., which he immediately proceeded to join at Seroor. In Dec. 1808 part of the Seroor force took the field, and this officer served as cantonment Adj. to Col. Cooke till its return in Feb. 1809, when he marched with the batt. to Bombay; and on promotion to a company was again transferred to the 2nd batt.; with which, in Nov. 1810, he marched to Poonah; accompanied the flank companies in May 1812, which joined the field force under Col. Montresor at Punderpoor, and returned to Poonah in December.

In Feb. 1813 he was appointed by the resident at Poonah (Mr. Elphinstone) to command a battalion of the Peishwa's regular brigade, then about to be formed. In Sept. 1815 he marched in command of a detachment from the brigade to receive charge of a state prisoner (Trimburja Dinglea) from the Killedar of Wussunda Ghur, who was delivered over to the British government. In March 1817 he marched in command of part of the brigade, and joined the force under Col. (now Maj.-Gen.) Smith in the field; returned to Dapoone cantonment in July 1817; in October proceeded to Bombay on sick certificate; and in August 1818 to sea, for the recovery of his health. He reached Bombay in Jan. 1819; again took the command of the battalion, and in Dec. 1819 marched with it to Poonah.

The 12th reg. was in orders to be raised on the 1st June 1820, and the 1st batt. at Poonah, by volunteers from the auxiliaries (late Peishwa's brig.), to which this officer was placed in the command by

Maj.-Gen. Smith, and continued by the Com.-in-Chief, Sir C. Colville.

In Oct. he left the batt. for Bombay, and in Nov. embarked for Malwah, to take the command of the 2nd bat. 2nd reg.; with which he remained till April 1821, when he embarked with it for Bombay; and in May following returned to England, in consequence of his health having severely suffered from a service in India of nearly twenty-three years.

COLONEL SIR MARK WOOD, BART.

(Bengal Establishment.)

ENTERED the corps of engineers in the East India Company's service, Bengal establishment, in 1770; in 1778 attained the rank of capt.; in 1786, on the arrival of the late Marquess Cornwallis in India, he attained the rank of maj. of engin. and surv.-gen.; in 1787 that of col. and chief engin., in which situation he continued till 1793, when ill health obliged him to return to England. The 16th Feb. 1795 he was promoted to the rank of col. in His Majesty's service*.

* It may here be observed, that our late august sovereign George III. arranged a list of the army, including the officers of His Majesty's army and those of the East India Company, at a time when that excellent monarch had much at heart the union of both services. Sir Mark Wood presented to His Majesty in 1795 a model in ivory of Fort William, Bengal, one of the most complete fortresses in the world; and on that occasion the King produced the above-mentioned list.

THE LATE COLONEL JOHN COCKERELL.

(Bengal Establishment.)

THIS much-distinguished officer went to India in 1763 under the immediate protection, and in the family, of Gen. Caillaud, appointed Com.-in-Chief at Madras. Col. Cockerell, then scarcely fourteen years of age, and a cadet in the East India Company's service, was received into the family of Gen. Sir Robert Barker, Com.-in-Chief at Bengal, to whose staff, young as he was, he was immediately attached. At the age of eighteen he became military sec. to Sir Robert; an appointment in which he continued until Sir Robert returned to England in 1774, when Col. Cockerell, then a capt. in the army, accompanied him. In the spring of 1776 he again went out to India; and in the following year Mr. Hastings (then Gov.-Gen.) appointed him to his military staff, intending that he should succeed to the situation of military sec.; but it being found expedient in 1799 to send an expedition from the upper provinces to Bombay, across the peninsula, Capt. Cockerell was fixed upon to accompany it as quart.-mast.-gen., and in that capacity displayed talents of the highest order. The detachment* was commanded by Col. Leslie, who was succeeded in

---

* At the commencement of the year 1778 the presidency of Bombay having been seriously embarrassed by the pressure of the Mahratta war which then prevailed, the Gov.-Gen. felt the necessity for effectual succour, both in specie and troops, being afforded to that quarter of the Hon. Company's possessions, with as little delay as possible. Supplies of the former had been, and would again be sent by sea, in the course of a six weeks or two months voyage (as well as by bills through the native bankers of Benares), but no such resource presented itself with regard to troops. On this emergency the comprehensive mind of Warren Hastings formed the resolution (on his own responsibility, when opposed, as it was understood, by a majority of his colleagues in the government) to order a compact, yet efficient detachment, of Native troops from the Bengal army, to march across the continent of India, " through the hostile and unknown regions from the banks of the Ganges to the western coast of India," to create a division in the councils and operations of the

the command by Col., afterwards Gen. Goddard. The detachment marched across the peninsula to Poonah and Bombay, where this part of the Bengal army remained, and Col., then Maj. Cockerell, was present at several sieges, and of some of which he had the conduct. On the termination of the war he marched back with the army to Bengal. Subsequent to his return, Lord Cornwallis, on his arrival to take charge of the supreme government of India, had appointed Maj. Cockerell to his staff; and upon it being found necessary to augment the army of the Carnatic, on the first Mysore war against Tippoo Saib, by a very strong reinforcement, Lord Cornwallis appointed Col. Cockerell to the command of the troops sent from Bengal in this year; and which marching through the Nizam's country, joined that part of the Madras army under the command of Col. Maxwell, and subsequently joined the grand army under Lord Cornwallis. Col. Cockerell was present at the siege and capture of Bangalore, the siege of Seringapatam, and, preparatory thereto, attached to, and second in command of, that part of the army which was ordered to the attack and capture of a strong fort, preparatory to the night attack against Tippoo himself, with his army under the walls and in front of Seringapatam. After the peace with Tippoo, Col. Cockerell marched back with the Bengal detachment to Calcutta, and immediately on his arrival embarked for Europe: he had not been in England more than two years when his health began to decline,

enemy, and eventually to co-operate with the Bombay government and forces in the prosecution of the war in which they were involved.

Its first rendezvous was Culpee, a town on the right bank of the Jumna, near Caunpoor, whence it commenced its march on the 12th June 1778. It reached Rajgurh, a town in Bundlecund, on the 17th Aug.; where it halted so much longer than Mr. Hastings thought necessary, that he removed Col. Leslie, the commanding officer, and appointed Lieut.-Col. Goddard to that charge. Under this active and enterprising officer it continued its route through Malwah and Candesh to Surat; presenting the extraordinary spectacle of a corps of the natives of Hindostan, under the guidance of a few English officers, marching from the banks of the Ganges to the westernmost shores of India. During the five years that they were absent from their home, the men of this detachment conducted themselves in the most exemplary manner, and acquired distinction in every service in which they were employed. *(See Williams's Historical Account of the Bengal Native Infantry.)*

and after having gone to Lisbon, at the advice of his physicians, and returned to London, he died in July 1798.

Col. Cockerell was a Persian scholar, profoundly versed in all the politics of India; a good man, and an excellent officer.

LIEUTENANT-COLONEL DONALD MACLEOD, C. B.

(Bengal Establishment.)

This officer joined as a cadet the 1st Europ. reg. in 1781; was appointed ensign in the 3d Europ. reg. on the 13th March in the same year; lieut., on the 9th July 1783; removed to the 29th reg. N. I. in 1785; and, on being supernumerary, to the 6th Europ. reg. in 1786; appointed to the 13th batt. N. I. in 1790, on its march to Madras; adj. to the 25th bat. N. I. in 1796; adj. to the 2d bat. 11th N. I. in 1799; brevet capt. in 1795, and capt. in the reg. in Aug. 1800; appointed to the 1st batt. of the 11th in May 1807 (which corps he commanded until he went on furlough to Europe in 1810); brev.-maj. in 1808; maj. in the reg. in 1810; returned to India in 1813, and joined the 2d batt. 11th reg. N. I. which corps he commanded until July 1819, when he was appointed commandant to the garrison of Agra; brev. lieut.-col. 4th June 1814; lieut.-col. in the reg. 15th May 1815.

On the commencement of hostilities with Tippoo Sultaun in 1789-90, a detachment, as stated in previous services, marched from Bengal to Madras, to form part of the army to be employed against the enemy. Lieut. Macleod joined the 15th batt. which corps formed part of this detachment, and remained with it during the whole of the war. However actively the troops were employed after the campaign begun, nothing decisive was effected until Lord Cornwallis joined and assumed the command in person. The successful operations that followed, until the conclusion of the peace at Seringapatam in March 1792, have been already stated. Lieut. Macleod met the approbation of his superiors on every occasion.

On the return of the detachment to Bengal in 1793, the 13th batt. was ordered to the upper provinces, and were stationed at Caunpoor in 1794: in this year the Rohilla chieftain Tyzoolah Khan died, leaving his eldest son, Mahomed Ally, heir to the Musnud, under the protection of the British government. Golaum Mahomed, another son of Tyzoolah Khan, found means to confine his eldest brother in prison, where he afterwards died. He then seized the treasure, which had been accumulating for many years, and being very active, assembled in a short time an army.

All the Company's troops at the stations of Caunpoor and Futtehgurh formed immediately under the personal command of Gen. Sir Rob. Abercromby, Com.-in-Chief in India, and on the general's arrival on the borders of their country, the Rohillas were prepared to meet him in great force. A battle took place on Oct. 26, 1794, in which the British troops were ultimately victorious, but with very great loss. The 13th batt. from its situation in the reserve, and other causes, suffered more than any other corps. Of eight officers, including the commandant, present with the corps, five were killed, and one wounded; Lieut. Macleod, the officer wounded, had four sabre-cuts, three of which were slight and one severe. The casualties among the native officers and Sepoys were in equal proportion.

The Rohillas were followed to the foot of the hills, or as far as they could go, without any attempt being made by them to oppose the Com.-in-Chief, after that action: they submitted in the end to such terms as were dictated to them, and which deprived them of the power of again opposing the British government.

In Aug. 1800, Lieut. Macleod, after serving twenty years and four months, was promoted to the rank of capt.-lieut. and to that of capt.; and a new arrangement took place in the Bengal army, by which he was appointed to the 2nd batt. 11th N. I.

On war being declared against the Mahratta states in 1803, the 2nd batt. 11th reg. joined a detachment sent into the Bundlecund country. The troops that were prepared to resist this detachment, when drawn out for action, made no stand; they contented themselves with a distant cannonade before they went off the field. The service was next confined to the reduction of mud forts, of which there were many; but few of them gave much trouble before they surrendered. The detachment proceeded thence to Culpee, where, on the day of its arrival, a wing of the 2nd batt. was sent with a detachment of artillery, to prepare and open a battery on the fort. Capt. Macleod received a severe wound from a matchlock shot on the same evening; and the battery having opened early next morning, the fort was given up before noon.

Immediately after this occurrence, the 2nd batt. was removed from the Bundlecund detachment, and ordered to join another detachment, then on its march with a battering train to besiege Gualior. On arriving before that place, the siege was carried on regularly, and with so much success, that a breach was at last supposed to be practicable, notwithstanding the elevation of the rock. The besieged were of this opinion, and capitulated. The 2nd batt. formed part of the garrison placed in the fort.

From various successes of the British troops over those of the Mahrattas in every quarter, the war was now considered to be at an end; and all the troops, with the exception of one detachment, returned into cantonments. Capt. Macleod obtained permission to repair to Europe on furlough; but accounts having been afterwards received that the detachment left in the field was retreating before Holkar with his whole force, he withdrew his application, and obtained permission to rejoin his corps. On his return he found that the corps had unfortunately left the garrison of Gualior too early in the rainy season, for the purpose of bringing to obedience some refractory Zemindars, who did not submit to the Rannah of that country. They had been, for some time before, in a fort in a very unhealthy situation, and most of the officers and of the European artillerymen were laid up with fevers;

the Sepoys also were in a deplorable state from the same cause. They had however made progress in breaching the fort; and it being nearly practicable, that evening the place surrendered. On the same evening also, orders arrived for the battalion to join the army forming under the Com.-in-Chief; but on its sickly state being discovered, it was ordered into cantonments. The men who were able to perform their duty, and could be spared, were however required to join a detachment employed in suppressing insurgents within the provinces, who began to rebel when the army crossed the Jumna river. Two companies had marched for this service, and Capt. Macleod obtained the Com.-in-Chief's permission to join them. He found the detachment before a fort, with very little equipment for a siege. One or two mines were sprung; and after some days the fort was evacuated at night, although a very strong place. The next fort, to which the detachment marched, was not so easily taken: no impression was made on it during a month, and it held out until Meer Khan, with all his force, crossed the Jumna river, on his way towards his native country Rohilcund. Commonah, the fort that was besieged, being on his route, the commanding-officer of the detachment thought proper to raise the siege, and retire under the walls of Allygurh, a distance of about seven coss. Maj.-Gen. Smith, with all the cavalry, was in pursuit of Meer Khan, and arrived on the next morning at Allygurh: he ordered the infantry detachment to cross the Ganges into Rohilcund, to co-operate in protecting the principal places from the depredations of the enemy, and also to prevent insurrection in his favour. Meer Khan was however too quick. He was a whole day at Meradabad before Maj.-Gen. Smith came up, as he had to take the ammunition out of the tumbrils in crossing the Ganges, and the enemy had no incumbrance of the kind. The infantry came up at last, and were ordered to Bareilly. Soon after arriving at this last place Capt. Macleod was ordered with a small detachment, against insurgents that had assembled in the western part of these districts. He had the good fortune to reach their vicinity before they were aware that any troops were nearer to them than Bareilly, but the sudden alarm caused an immediate dispersion, which prevented his being able to come up with any of the rebels afterwards. One chieftain of another party at some distance from this place made a stand, but when the detachment came up to them, they gave way and fled.

Maj.-Gen. Smith had now forced Meer Khan to recross the Ganges and Jumna; and the country being in a state of tranquillity, Capt. Macleod rejoined his corps in cantonments, where he arrived in May 1805, and found it recruited and fit for the service that was required of it in Dec. following.

To conclude a peace with the Mahratta states, became the next object, and to this end it was stipulated, that all the Rannah of Gohud's country, should be again delivered over to Scindia. Gualior was still garrisoned by the British troops, but Gohud the capital was, from the time it was taken possession of, delivered over to the Rannah. He lost no time in repairing the works, and putting it in a proper state of defence, with a sufficient number of troops, under the direction of his own adherents. The Ranny and his son, a young boy, took up their residence in the palace. Having made these preparations, he represented to the officer commanding at Gualior, that he had no authority over the Ranny or the garrison of Gohud, nor could they be prevailed upon to give up the place. A siege became necessary, and the 2d batt. 11th reg. was ordered to join the detachment intended for that service. On forming this detachment five companies of Native grenadiers, being one from each batt. were placed as a reserve under the command of Capt. Macleod. The siege was carried on until the engineers reported the breach practicable. Towards the evening of that day the other five grenadier companies were ordered to join the reserve, making it ten companies of 800 privates, with their proportion of European and Native officers. Capt. Macleod was to attack the place with them on the same evening. Accordingly as soon as it was sufficiently dark the party was put in motion, and it arrived near the edge of the ditch in perfect silence, before any challenge was made. The immediate discharge from the whole face of the works, however, was a convincing proof that the attack was expected, and that they were prepared for it.

The Havildar and twelve sepoys, who volunteered to precede the head of the reserve, rushed forward, but Capt. Macleod observing that they were retarded by turning out of their way to return the fire that was upon them, he ran to the Havildar and succeeded in wheeling them round, and leading them up the breach. The officer of the leading company followed, but only one or two sections of that company would come up the breach. The Native officers, instead of preventing the company from breaking, made themselves busy among the men who carried ladders, and before Capt. Macleod could attend to them, they had got the ladders so as to obstruct the passage. He exerted himself in throwing down the ladders, and expostulated with those who were backward, but which had no effect for a long interval, during which the troops were exposed to a destructive fire from under cover of the works. At length, by reminding them of the stigma their conduct would stamp upon them for ever, one man moved up first, then two and three followed together, until a path was clear for the head of the column. He then gave the signal for the breach being carried, and the sections moved rapidly, but in good order up to the breach. A very considerable extent of ruins and broken ground lay between this place and the town, which by the difficulty of getting over it caused heavy loss to the Rannah's troops, as the sepoys were able to come up with them in their retreat. The reserve had, out of the officers, two killed and three wounded, and of 800 privates about 100 killed and wounded. A breach was soon made in the inner walls of the town, and the whole capitulated.

LIEUTENANT-COLONEL JAMES NAGLE.

(*Madras Establishment.*)

THIS officer sailed from England early in 1781, in the fleet commanded by Commodore Johnstone, and was in the engagement at

Port Praya with the French fleet: shortly after his arrival in India he was made a prisoner, when under the command of Sir Eyre Coote, and remained such until 1784. In 1789 he served under Lieut.-Col. James Stuart in subduing the Colingoody Poligars; in 1790, under Gen. Medows, in the reduction of the strong forts of Dindigul and Palicaudcherry, the districts of Coimbetoor, Caroor, Errode, and all the other strong places below the Ghauts; in 1791 he entered the Mysore country, under Lord Cornwallis, and was present at the siege of Bangalore, battle of Seringapatam, and every other service the army was employed on. In the latter part of 1792 he was employed under Lieut. Col. Maxwell in the Tinnevelly district, against the Shevegurry and Chocumpetty Poligars; in 1793 at the siege of Pondicherry, under Gen. Braithwaite; in 1794 he was stationed by Col. Dugald Campbell in the Nagpoor district, to check the predatory spirit of the Poligars, in the vicinity of his post. In the same year an expedition was fitting out at Madras to attack the Isle of France, and this officer volunteered his services, which being accepted, he joined Maj. Urban Vigors's flank corps of Europeans. The expedition was countermanded, and he returned to his corps in the Tinnevelly country. Early in 1795, his corps, with the 3d reg. of N. Cav. under Maj. Stevenson, were ordered to surprise the Ramnad Rajah; which they effected by severe night marches. In Oct. of the same year, he embarked at Ramisseram, under Col. Dugald Campbell, to attack Menar, and subdue the western posts of Ceylon, belonging to the Dutch. In Nov. he embarked at Menar, with three companies, for the reduction of Calpentine and Putelang, and to garrison these two posts, being the most advanced towards Columbo. In Jan. 1796, a division of the army for the attack of Columbo, consisting of the 7th, 9th, and 35th batts. embarked at Menar with the flank companies of the 73d reg. under Maj. Barbet, and proceeded to the rendezvous of Niagumbo, where they were joined by the other troops, destined for the same service. After disembarking, the whole proceeded by land to Columbo; the corps to which this officer belonged formed part of the advance under Maj. Petre: during the whole march they were constantly skirmishing with the enemy.

On the 14th Nov. this officer received instructions from Col. Stuart to proceed back to Niagumbo with the force to command that post, for the purpose of covering the disembarkation of stores, ammunition, and provisions, that were coming from the coast for the use of the army; also to receive supplies of provisions from the king of Candy for the same purpose, and furnish guards for the convoy of them to the army.

After the fall of Columbo, he was ordered to proceed to Trincomale by land, with a small reinforcement for that garrison; he was sixteen days performing the march, without a single tent for the detachment, during almost incessant rains, and often obliged to make rafts of the branches of the trees for conveying the detachment across the rivers.

In 1797 he received orders from Col. Champagné, 80th reg., then commanding Trincomale, to proceed to Batticoloa, and take upon himself the command of the fort and its dependencies. In July 1797 he quitted Ceylon with his corps for Pondicherry. An expedition was then embarking at Madras and Pondicherry for the attack of Manilla, and this officer applied to Gen Braithwaite to be employed: the General appointed him to his own reg., the 3d Europ.; he embarked with it at Pondicherry, and sailed with the first division of the fleet for Prince of Wales's island, where the remaining part of the expedition, under the command of Adm. Renier, arrived: in a few days after orders arrived from Madras countermanding the expedition, and the troops returned to their respective destinations, except the 3d reg., which was ordered to the Moluccas and Malacca, where this officer remained until 1800, when he returned to Madras, and found himself appointed to the 1st bat. of the 4th reg., doing duty at Madras. Early in 1801 he was ordered, with five companies, to proceed to the Tinnevelly country, and to place himself under Maj. Macauley, who was appointed to command the force against Pandellumcouchy: on which occasion he received the following letter:—

"Sir,—I am directed by Maj.-Gen. Bridges to signify to you, that the celerity in the movement of the detachment under your command from Madras to Trichinopoly, is considered by the officer commanding the army in chief as a strong proof of your zeal and activity, and which he shall keep in his remembrance.

<p style="text-align:center">(Signed) " MONTAGUE COSBY, M. B.
" <i>Head-Quarters, Trichinopoly, March 22, 1801.</i>"</p>

After the fall of Pandellumcouchy, he was employed, in July 1801, with his detachment, under Col. Agnew, in the reduction of Colangodu, Callacoil, and Sheraville; during this service he was detached to Dindegul, with a large force under his command, consisting of five companies of the 1st bat. 7th N. I., a troop of cavalry, his own corps, and two six-pounders, to bring money and provisions to camp, and the garrison of Madura. On the reduction of the aforesaid places, and the seizure of the chief and principal men of the district, he was ordered to escort the heavy guns, stores, and elephants, to Madura; and on his arrival there, received the following order from Col. Agnew: " Oct. 12, 1801.—The flight of a large body of rebels toward the Vierapatchy hills renders it expedient to reinforce Lieut.-Col. Innis's detachment, now on its march to Dindigul: you will therefore proceed and join that officer."

On the 18th Oct. the rebels were dislodged from their strong barriers in the Vierapatchy mountains, and on the next day this officer received the following instructions from Col. Innis:—" You will proceed, with all convenient expedition, to the Dindigul Valley; and you will use your utmost exertions in preserving that district from depredation, and in apprehending or destroying the fugitive rebels, or their adherents." The detachment under his command fortunately apprehended the chief of the remaining Poligars who were still in arms, and lodged him safe in the garrison of Dindigul; and peace being restored in the disturbed provinces, he returned to Madras in Jan. 1802. Out of six European officers belonging to the five companies that left Madras, two were killed, two dangerously wounded, and the subject of this memoir received a severe contusion on his right shoulder. Shortly after he was ordered, with the corps he commanded, to form part of the garrison of Velore: a few weeks subsequent to his arrival there, the corps was reviewed by the commanding officer, Sir T. Dallas. Nothwithstanding five companies of the bat. had been separated from the other five companies, and employed nearly twelve months in constant Poligar service, Sir T. Dallas was pleased to express, in garrison orders, his entire approbation of the discipline and appearance of the corps, and reported the same to head-quarters. In Nov. following, the corps was ordered on field service, with directions to march for Bangalore; and this officer was ordered to place himself under Maj.-Gen. Wellesley.

In 1803 the army entered the Mahratta country, and this officer commanded the corps in the battle of Assaye, 23d Sept., and he received thanks, in brigade orders, from Col. Wallace, for his conduct in the action. On the 26th he was detached with the corps, 500 Mysore horse, and two guns, for the purpose of overtaking a supply of grain, reported to be at the distance of about twenty-five miles from camp: two dealers in that article were sent with a detachment to prevail on the owners of the grain to bring it into camp; at his arrival at the place where the grain was reported to be, he was informed that the convoy had moved off early in the morning; he detached small parties of horse to gain intelligence where they were; at three in the morning of the 27th an account was brought in, that the bullocks were about ten miles further from camp than at first supposed: to pursue them beyond the place of his instructions, had any unfortunate accident happened, he was aware might be attended with serious consequence to himself; whilst, on the other hand, the loss of 1000 bullocks laden with grain, as mentioned by Sir Robert Barclay, would have been severely felt by the army, being at a great distance from supplies, and might retard his operations; he therefore, after placing his tents and baggage in a place of security, moved off at four A. M., and was fortunate in finding the bullocks loaded, and on their march to a still greater distance; he prevailed on the owners of the grain to return with him to the place where he left his tents, dispatching an account of his proceedings to head-quarters, as appears from the following answer.

"I have communicated your letter of this date from Sepperat to the Hon. Maj.-Gen. Wellesley, who is glad that you have found so many bullocks loaded with grain; he depends on your bringing them safe into camp to-morrow.

(Signed)   " R. BARCLAY, Dep. Adj.-Gen. in Mysore.
"*Camp at Assaye, Sept.* 27, 1803, 10 *o'Clock, P.M.*"

Whilst the army was on its route from Assaye to besiege Gawelgur, this officer was detached from the line of march with his corps, 500 Mysore horse, an engineer officer, four guns, and escalading ladders, to attack a fortified town that lay at the distance of about six miles from the line of march: having effected this object without occasioning a halt to the army, he joined it at the end of three days; and Maj.-Gen. Wellesley was pleased to express his approbation of his conduct.

On the 29th Nov. the battle of Argaum was fought; and after the peace in 1804, the army being on its return to Poonah, Maj.-Gen. Wellesley formed a light corps, consisting of all the British cavalry, the Mysore horse, the 74th reg., 8th bat. N. I., and a detailed corps, consisting of one hundred picked men from each corps in camp, with a proportion of European officers, and two iron twelve-pounders; the command of which was given to Capt. Nagle. This detachment was commanded in person by Maj.-Gen. Wellesley: it marched day and night, the greater part without tents, in pursuit of a large body of Pindarry horse, which it surprised, capturing four guns, and all its plunder. After joining the army, Capt. Nagle was taken very ill, and obliged to go to Bombay on sick certificate, quite a cripple, and in so debilitated a state, that he was put on board ship in the accommodation chair: on his arrival at Madras he obtained a sick certificate, declaring that to save his life it was necessary for him to proceed to Europe. He arrived in England in March 1805, and in Jan. 1808 was placed on the retired list.

During the twenty-four years' service of this officer in India, sixteen of which were in the field and foreign service, he was employed at seven sieges, and in five engagements, exclusive of a variety of Poligar and jungle fighting, and he is now totally deprived of sight. An addition to his arms was granted him, in consequence of his services at the battle of Assaye, &c. with the motto, " On with you."

LIEUTENANT-COLONEL JOHN NELLY.

(Bengal Establishment.)

APPOINTED a cadet in 1781; lieut. fireworker, July 29, 1782; lieut. Dec. 28, 1788; capt.-lieut. Jan. 7, 1796; capt. June 1802; maj. Sept. 5, 1806, and lieut.-col. Dec. 8, 1810.

This officer arrived in Bengal in Nov. 1781. In 1784 he left the presidency, being appointed adjut. to a division of artillery proceeding to the upper provinces; and in 1788 returned to Calcutta. In Feb. 1790 he embarked for Madras with the 2nd battalion of artillery, under Lieut.-Col. Deare, and served under Gen. Medows and Lord Cornwallis during their campaigns in the Coimbetoor and Mysore countries. He was present at the capture of Bangalore and several other forts, and the different attacks on the lines before Seringapatam. In June 1792 he returned to Fort William, after an absence of two years and four months; during which time he never missed a day's duty, nor experienced an hour's illness.

In Jan. 1794 he again embarked for Madras with a detachment of artillery, commanded by Col. (the late Lieut.-Gen.) Hussey, and destined for an attack on the French islands. On the arrival of the detachment, the expedition was countermanded, and it returned to Fort William.

In 1801 this officer was detached with his company, and commanded the artillery at Dinapore and Allahabad in succession, until Jan. 1803, when he joined the head-quarters of the army at Caunpoor. In Aug. 1803, his company composed part of the army led by Gen.

Lake against the Mahrattas: he was present at the battle of Coil; storming the fort of Allyghur; battle of Delhi; capture of Agra, and battle of Laswarree. On the arrival of the army at Delhi, he was elected by his brother-officers prize agent.

After the battle of Laswarree, this officer was directed by the Com.-in-Chief to entertain as many of the enemy's Gholundauz and Lascars as were desirous of entering the Company's service. Numbers came in, who, during the ensuing campaign, gave proofs of their attachment, and performed many acts of bravery.

In Sept. 1804 the army again took the field, under the command of Lord Lake, and this officer commanded the artillery in the memorable pursuit of Holkar from Delhi to Futtehghur: he was present and took an active part in the siege of Deeg, and in the three different attacks on Burtpore, in the last of which he received a ball in his right eye, whilst in command of the batteries, which is still lodged in his head. He was shortly after appointed commissary of ordnance, and to the charge of the arsenal at Allahabad, where he remained till the end of 1809, when, in consequence of the suffering from his wound, he resigned the situation, and joined the artillery at the presidency.

In Jan. 1811 Lieut.-Col. Nelly embarked for Europe; and finding, at the expiration of his furlough, that the weakness of sight had increased, and that he could not perform the duties of an artillery officer to his own satisfaction, he retired on full pay.

LIEUTENANT-GENERAL ROBERT BELL.

(Madras Establishment.)

APPOINTED cadet of artillery Jan. 1799; lieut. fireworker, Sept. 1799; lieut. Sept. 1781; capt. April 1788; maj. Dec. 1800; lieut.-

col. Sept. 1801; col. April 1804; maj.-gen. July 1810; and lieut.-gen. 12 Aug. 1819.

This officer served as adjut. to the corps of artillery; as commissary of stores at Trichinopoly, and on field service in the southern division of the army; with the army under Gen. Medows; and with the army under Lord Cornwallis. He served as commandant of artillery with the Indian army in Egypt, composed of detachments of royal artillery and detachments from the several presidencies in India. He commanded the details of artillery at the storm of Seringapatam, May 4, 1799; and was commandant of artillery under the presidency of fort St. George, with a seat at the military board, from May 1805 to Jan. 1820.

On the 22d Jan. in the latter year, he embarked for Europe on board the Abberton, under the salute due to his rank, when the following farewell order to the corps of artillery was issued:—

"*Artillery Head-Quarters, St. Thomas's Mount, Jan. 22, 1820.*

" The period of Maj.-Gen. Bell's departure for England having arrived, he has much sincere gratification in offering his assurances of high consideration and regard to the corps of artillery. The valuable services of the coast artillery on every occasion where they have been employed, are strongly marked on the records of government, and by the several Commanders-in-Chief.

" The Maj.-Gen. has had the honour to belong to this excellent corps for upwards of forty-one years, of which period he has had the good fortune to have been at its head as commandant of artillery for fifteen years. The example of harmony, cordiality, and confidence, displayed by the officers during that period, and the social intercourse which has prevailed throughout, is to Maj.-Gen. Bell a most grateful recollection. The commandant of artillery has ever had the most satisfactory aid and support from the artillery staff, in conducting the extensive and important duties of the artillery brigade, and cantonment offices, the ordnance and laboratory department. Maj.-Gen. Bell takes this farewell occasion to offer his most unfeigned good wishes for the continued high character of the corps of artillery."

The merits of Lieut.-Gen. Bell were recorded in general orders by the governor in council on his proceeding to Europe. The Lieut.-Gen. is the author of a work containing rules and instructions for the guidance of officers respecting the management of guns.

COLONEL HENRY WORSLEY, C. B.

(Bengal Establishment.)

IN 1780 this officer embarked for India as a cadet on the Bengal establishment; he arrived at Madras in Jan. 1781, in which month he attained the 13th year of his age.

The presidency of fort St. George having been at that time threatened both by land and sea, consequent to the recent defeat of Col. Baillie's detachment, which spread consternation throughout the settlements on the coast of Coromandel, the government of that presidency had recourse even to the juvenile services of the cadets; those of the season destined for Bengal, as well as those for Madras, were ordered to land, formed into a company, and trained to the use of arms. The army in Bengal having been considerably augmented about the same period, in consequence of the general war which then prevailed in Europe and in Asia, this company was ordered round to Bengal, and where this officer landed in April 1781, having been already promoted to the rank of ensign, and in the course of the same year, in common with the cadets of the season, amounting to nearly 100, to that of lieut. Proceeding 1000 miles up the Ganges, he joined the 2nd European reg.; and shortly afterwards the 30th reg. of Sepoys, to which he was posted, and was employed with that corps on service during 1781-2, in reducing several strong mud forts in the Zemidary of Benares, which were in a state of resistance, owing to the insurrection excited by the revolt of Rajah Cheyt Sing. In 1783 he was appointed adjut. to his reg., and was employed with the 1st batt. on service in the Kymoor hills towards the close of that year.

In 1785, the 30th, then become the 33rd reg., fell under the extensive reduction of the army, consequent to the general peace of 1783-4; and this officer was posted to the 8th N. I. In 1786 he was on service with that corps at the siege and capture of the fort of Bujerah, in the province of Furruckabad; and at the close of the year he was removed, on a new arrangement of the corps of the army, to the 32nd battalion of Native infantry.

In 1787, under the auspices of Lord Cornwallis, then Gov.-Gen. and Com.-in-Chief, this officer, in common with the officers of the "Company's army," was admitted to an equality of rank with the officers of the "King's army," with date of rank from the cessation of hostilities at Cudalore in June 1783, and commissions on behalf of his Majesty were issued accordingly by his Lordship.

Early in 1788 Lieut. W. embarked with a detachment of volunteer Sepoys on service to the island of Sumatra, whence the detachment returned to Bengal at the end of the year.

In 1790 he embarked with 1000 volunteer Sepoys, and a proportionate number of officers, to supply the war casualties in the eight battalions of Bengal Sepoys engaged in the Mysore war, under the Gov.-Gen. and Com.-in-Chief, Lord Cornwallis.

He joined the 7th batt. of Bengal Sepoys on that service, in Oct. 1790, and was engaged with it, in the centre column, at the night attack of Tippoo's fortified camp under the walls of Seringapatam, on the 6th Feb. 1791, and the subsequent operations against that place, which led to the cession of half the dominions of the Sultaun, and the payment by him of the expences of the war, according to the treaty concluded on the occasion.

After the return to Bengal of the troops of that presidency, which had been engaged in the Mysore war*, Lieut. W. was reappointed, in 1794, to the batt. (the 32nd,) from which he had volunteered for that service. An interval followed, during which no actual service fell to the lot of this officer; he continued with his corps, zealously devoted to the duties of the profession, and cultivating the attachment of the native soldiery, whose behaviour and conduct justifies a motto† applied to them at an early period, and which has in many instances been verified, to the mutual honour of the European officers‡, and that of the Asiatic troops.

---

* On this occasion some of the corps performed a march of 2000 miles from their cantonment in the Carnatic (during the rains) to the frontier stations in Oude.

† " Command our lives through the medium of our affections."
Vide Williams's History of the Bengal Native Infantry.

‡ A brief description of the composition of the native armies of the three presidencies, founded on the observations referred to in a preceding note (p. 88) cannot be irrelevant in a work of this nature.

BENGAL ARMY.—The native cavalry of Bengal, consisting of eight regiments, forms a most efficient and distinguished branch of the army to which they belong. The men are rather shorter than those in the same corps at Madras. The latter are almost all Mahomedans, and three-fourths of the Bengal cavalry are of the same race. The fact is, that with the exception of the Mahratta tribe, the Hindoos are not, generally speaking, so much disposed as Mahomedans to the duties of a trooper; and though the Mahomedans may be more dissipated and less moral in their private conduct than the Hindoos, they are zealous and high-spirited soldiers, and it is excellent policy to have a considerable portion of them in the service, to which experience has shewn they often become very warmly attached.

In the Native infantry of Bengal the Hindoos are in the full proportion of three-fourths to the Mahomedans. They consist chiefly of Rajpoots, who are a distinguished race among the Khiteree or military tribe. The standard, below which no recruit is taken, is five feet six inches: the great proportion of the grenadiers is six feet and upwards. The Rajpoot is born a soldier: the mother speaks nothing to her infant but deeds of arms, and every sentiment and action of the future man is marked by the first impressions that he has received. If he tills the ground (which is the common occupation of this class,) his sword and shield are placed near the furrow, and moved as his labour advances. The frame of the Rajpoot is almost always improved (even if his pursuits are those of civil life) by martial exercises. He is from habit temperate in his diet, of a generous though warm temper, and of good moral conduct. He is, when well treated, obedient, zealous, and faithful. Neither the Hindoo nor the Mahomedan soldier of India can be termed revengeful, though both are prone to extreme violence in points where they deem their honour, of which they have a very nice sense, to be slighted or insulted. The Rajpoot sometimes wants energy, but seldom, if ever, courage. It is remarkable in this class, that even when their animal

By the regulations of 1796-7, this officer was posted, on the introduction of regimental rank, as lieut. to the 1st reg. of N. I.; and furlough to Europe, with pay, for three years, having then been granted

spirits have been subdued so as to cause a cessation of exertion, they shew no fear of death, which they meet in every form it can present itself with surprising fortitude and resignation. Such is the general character of a race of men, whose numbers in the Bengal army amount to between thirty and forty thousand, and of whom we can recruit in our own provinces to any amount. But this instrument of power must be managed with care and wisdom, or that which is our strength may become our danger.

MADRAS ARMY.—There cannot be men more suited, from their frame and disposition, for the duty of light cavalry, than those of which the Madras corps is composed. They are, generally speaking, from five feet five to five feet ten inches in height, of light but active make. Their strength is preserved and improved by moderation in their diet, and by exercises common to the military tribe, and which are calculated to increase the muscular force.

The Native infantry of Madras is generally composed of Mahomedans and Hindoos of good cast: at its first establishment none were enlisted but men of high military tribes. In the progress of time a considerable change took place, and natives of every description were enrolled in the service. Though some corps, that were almost entirely formed of the lowest and most despicable races of men, obtained considerable reputation, it was feared that encouaagement might produce disgust, and particularly when they gained, as they frequently did, the rank of officers. Orders were in consequence given to recruit from none but the most respectable classes of society; and many consider the regular and orderly behaviour of these men as one of the benefits which have resulted from this system.

The infantry Sepoy of Madras is rather a small man, but he is of an active make, and capable of undergoing great fatigue upon a very slender diet. We find no man arrive at greater precision in all his military exercises; his moderation, his sobriety, his patience, give him a steadiness that is almost unknown to Europeans: but although there exists in this body of men a fitness to attain mechanical perfection as soldiers, there are no men whose mind it is of more consequence to study. The most marked general feature of the character of the natives of India, is a proneness to obedience, accompanied by a great susceptibility of good or bad usage; and there are few in that country who are more embued with these feelings than the Madras Sepoy.

BOMBAY ARMY.—It was at Bombay that the first Native corps were disciplined by the English. Of the exact date we are ignorant, but regular Sepoys are noticed in the account of the transactions of that part of India some time before they were embodied at either Madras or Bengal. A corps of 100 Sepoys from Bombay, and 400 from Tellichery, is mentioned as having joined the army at Madras in 1747; and a company of Bombay Sepoys, which had gone with troops from Madras to Bengal, were present at the victory of Plassey. The men of the infantry of Bombay are of a standard very near that of Madras. The

to the officers of the Company's service, he availed himself of it* in 1797, in consequence of a very impaired state of health. In 1800 he returned to Bengal.

By the regulations above quoted, this officer received the brevet of capt. from Jan. 1796, in common with all subalterns of the Company's service who had served fifteen years; and in 1798 he attained the rank of capt.-lieut. and also that of capt. regimentally; and was removed, on the augmentation of the army, to the newly-raised 15th reg. which he joined in 1801. Towards the close of that year he was ordered on service, in command of five companies of the batt. the 1st of the 15th, across the Jumna, to take possession of some wild and refractory districts between the Jumna and Taounse rivers, which were part of the territory ceded to the Company by the treaty of that year with the Newaub Vizier. Capt. Worsley was actively

---

lowest size taken is five feet three inches, and the average is five feet five; but they are robust and hardy, and capable of enduring great fatigue upon very slender diet.

This army has, from its origin to the present day, been indiscriminately composed of all classes—Mahomedans, Hindoos, Jews, and some few Christians. Among the Hindoos, those of the lowest tribes of Mahrattas, and the Purwarrie, Soortee, and Frost sects, are much more numerous than the Rajpoots and higher casts. Jews have always been favourite soldiers in this army, and great numbers of them attain the rank of commissioned officers. It is probably owing to the peculiar composition, and to the local situation of the territories in which they are employed, that the Sepoys at Bombay have at all periods been found ready to embark on foreign service. They are, in fact, familiar to the sea, and only a small proportion of them are incommoded in a voyage by those privations to which others are subject from prejudice of cast. But this is only one of the merits of the Bombay Native soldier; he is patient, faithful, and brave, and attached in a remarkable degree to his European officers. There cannot be a class of men more cheerful under privation and difficulties, and though desertion is very frequent among the recruits of this army, who, from the local situation of Bombay, can, on the first feeling of disgust at discipline, always in a few hours escape to the Mahratta territories, where they are safe from pursuit, there are no men, after they become soldiers, more attached to their colours.

* Capt. Worsley had repaired to Calcutta for the purpose of returning to Europe on furlough, when an invasion of the frontier provinces was threatened by Zemaun Shah, King of Cabul, who, having advanced with a large force as far as Lahore, the British army was ordered to take the field; and the regiment to which Capt. W. belonged being then on the frontiers, he travelled post 1000 miles to rejoin it. Zemaun Shah, however, retired, and Capt. W. returned to Calcutta, and embarked for Europe.

employed on that service till the close of 1802, when he joined the head-quarters of the reg. at Caunpoor.

Early in 1803 he was ordered in command of a detachment, consisting of the flank companies of the batt., and a squadron of cav., to escort supplies of stores, &c. to the army then in the field, under the Com.-in-Chief in person, to subdue the forts of Sasnee, Bidzergur, &c. situated in the Dooaub, and forming part of the cession of territory by the Newaub Vizier, but the chiefs of which resisted the authority of government. On that occasion Capt. Worsley was engaged in the sieges of Bidzergur and Cutchoura; and was afterwards ordered by the Com.-in Chief to take possession of and to dismantle the outer fort of the refractory chief of Tutteeah.

In Aug. 1803 a large portion of the army took the field against the confederated Mahratta chieftains, and a formidable French faction, which, grafted on the Mahratta power, had established itself in the centre of the Dooaub, and in possession of the capital and the royal family of Delhi.

The 15th reg. was one of the corps that moved out with the Com.-in-Chief in Aug.*, and though, by an augmentation then ordered, Capt. Worsley was transferred to the 21st reg., the Com.-in-Chief was pleased, in consequence of the scarcity of officers with the corps taking the field, to order him (as well as other officers similarly situated) to continue to serve with his previous corps, the 15th, during the arduous campaign, which witnessed the commencement and the close of the war with Dowlut Rao Scindia, by the end of the year: Capt. Worsley, accordingly, participated in the brilliant achievements under the personal command of Gen. Lake†, which occurred in the following order: Attack of the French-Mahratta army near the city of Coil, 29th Aug. 1803;—assault and capture of Alligurh, 4th Sept;—battle of Delhi, 11th Sept.;—attack of the enemy's infantry

---

* When the army was brigaded on that occasion, the Com.-in-Chief offered Capt. Worsley a brigade-majorship; but he preferred serving with his corps, in which he was second in command.

† Afterwards created, for his services, Lord Lake of Delhi and Laswarree.

and guns under the walls of Agra, 10th Oct.;—siege and surrender of that fortress on the 18th of the month;—and, lastly, the battle of Laswarree.

It fell to Capt. Worsley to have the casual command of the bat. (the 1st of the 15th) in the battle of Delhi, the lieut.-col. having been with the advanced picquets, as field officer of the day; as was likewise the case in the action of the 10th Oct.: the corps employed on that service marched on different points of attack, and the commanding officers and corps were severally thanked, in general orders, for their successful exertions on the occasion, by which the enemy's field force was completely defeated, and the siege of the fortress immediately commenced. It surrendered on the 18th of Oct., and the 1st of the 15th, which was on duty in the trenches, had the honour, with the col. of the reg., of planting the British colours on the ramparts of the " key of Hindostan," the important and favourite fortress of the renowned Akbur.

At the battle of Laswarree, 1st Nov. 1803, Capt. Worsley commanded the bat., the col. having been left sick with the battering train and heavy baggage. The bat. formed part of the right wing on that hard-fought day; and after the action, it was ordered to pass the night on the field of battle, collecting and succouring the wounded, and securing the captured guns and stores.

In Sept. 1804 this officer was promoted to the rank of Major. On the return of the army to cantonments for the rainy season of 1804, after watching the motions of Holkar during the hot winds on the sandy plains of Jushpoor, Maj. Worsley was ordered to join the 21st reg. N. I. The retreat of the division of the army left in advance under Col. Monson, did not allow the Com.-in-Chief, or the corps which had returned to cantonments, much time for repose. All were again called to the field to oppose the progress of Holkar and his forces, which, following up the flood-tide of their success against Col. Monson's detachment, established their head-quarters at Muttra in Sept., pushing their predatory incursions into the Dooaub, and, by their cruelty and rapine, spread dreadful consternation far and near.

On that occasion the Com.-in-Chief, on crossing the Jumna at Agra, appointed Maj. Worsley to the command of a detachment, hastily formed of some companies of infantry from the 11th and 23d regiments, with four field-pieces, and Skinner's corps of horse, with orders to drive the enemy out of the Dooaub, wherever they were to be found. That service having been speedily accomplished, he was ordered with the detachment to occupy the city of Muttra (retaining also the command of the contiguous troops, posts, and garrisons in the Dooaub), for the purpose of concentrating and forwarding supplies, and keeping open the communication with our own provinces and the grand army proceeding in pursuit of Holkar's infantry and guns, which, on the approach of the army under the Com.-in-Chief, had pushed off to lay siege to Delhi, whilst Holkar, with an immense body of horse, hung on the flank and rear of the British army, endeavouring to harass and impede its progress. In this arduous and laborious situation, surrounded by avowed and secret enemies, Maj. Worsley was employed during the period of the operations at Deeg, Burtpore, &c. until June of the following year (1805), when the army retired into cantonments on the western bank of the Jumna, and the Com.-in-Chief established his head-quarters at Muttra.

The services which Maj. Worsley rendered in that situation were duly appreciated, as may be inferred from the Com.-in-Chief's sense of them, which was expressed in the following manner:—On meeting his Excellency on his approach to Muttra, he addressed this officer by name, observing, " I hope you will not be offended at my having recommended you to government, for the appointment of Dep.-Adj.-Gen. to the army; I by no means consider that appointment as adequate to your deserts, nor is it all that I have in view for you. The Adj.-Gen. is about to depart for Europe, on account of ill health, and I intend you to be his successor in the office of Adj.-Gen. to the army." Maj. Worsley accordingly entered on the office of Dep.-Adj.-Gen. and proceeded with the Com.-in-Chief of the army, in pursuit of Holkar's forces, to the banks of the Hyphasis, which terminated the war by a treaty with that chieftain, near to the spot where Alexander erected his altars, at the close of his march towards India. Early in 1806 this officer was appointed Adj.-Gen. to the army, under the presidency of Bengal, with the rank of Lieut.-Col. in virtue of his office; and in 1809 he attained that rank on the establishment. He continued to perform the duties of the laborious office of Adj.-Gen. (with an interval of severe illness,) until the beginning of 1810, when his constitution had become so impaired that he felt it necessary to tender his resignation* of the office; and in 1811 he returned to Europe on furlough, for the benefit of his health.

Whilst in Europe he was applied to in 1813, by Lord Moira, (now Marquess of Hastings) to fill the office of principal private secretary to his lordship, then about to embark as Gov.-Gen. and Com.-in-Chief of India. Although his health was not restored, he accepted this flattering mark of distinction, and repaired to India in the course of that year. But his health was again so completely subdued by the effect of the tropical climates during the voyage, that he had no alternative on reaching Calcutta but to solicit permission to relinquish his appointment; and he returned to Europe in 1814.

In 1815, when the Prince Regent extended to the Company's army a participation in national honours, this officer was nominated one of the Companions of the Order of the Bath.

After a protracted residence in England, for the recovery of his health, in the spring of 1818, the period had arrived which rendered

* On this occasion the following General Orders were issued by the Vice President in Council:—

"*Fort William*, 16 *Jan.* 1810.

"Lieut.-Col. Worsley is permitted, at his own request, to resign the situation of Adj.-Gen. from the date of the arrival of his successor at the presidency. On this occasion the Vice President in council feels that it would be an act of injustice to that meritorious officer to omit the expression of his regret, at the loss which the service will sustain, by his resignation of the high and important situation on the general staff of this army, which he has filled with such distinguished ability, zeal, and advantage to the public interests; and His Exc. in council is happy to declare, in this public manner, his entire concurrence in the sentiments of cordial and unqualified approbation of Lieut.-Col. Worsley's conduct, in the discharge of the arduous duties of his office, which have been conveyed to government by the Commander-in-Chief.

it necessary, agreeably to the regulations of the service, to return to his duty, or to retire on the full pay of his rank; and accounts being received of armies from all the Presidencies in India being in the field, and of the confederacy of the Mahratta powers, with the Pindarry hordes, in hostility to the Company's government, Lieut.-Col. Worsley, desirous of participating in the honours of Lord Hastings' administration, embarked for India, and reached Calcutta in Sept. 1818.

Soon after his arrival the Marquess again honoured him with his gratuitous notice, and he was nominated to the important office of secretary to the government in the military department. The same misfortune in regard to health again attended him: his constitution could no longer endure the influence of a tropical climate; and after three or four months trial, feeling himself quite unequal to the laborious duties of the office, he voluntarily relinquished it,* and joined the corps to which he was posted, and did duty with it during the year 1819, in the hope, that with relief from the more arduous duties of office he might enjoy a better state of health. But the result proving otherwise, it only remained for him to adopt the alternative of embarking for Europe in Dec. 1819.

In Aug. 1819 he was promoted to the rank of Colonel by Brevet: and in 1822 he obtained the rank of Colonel, and the command of a regiment on the establishment of Bengal.

* Extract from a Minute, by the Governor-General, in the General Department, dated 30 Jan. 1819.

"It is impossible for me to assent to Lieut.-Col. Worsley's wish of being emancipated from the duties of the Secretary's department, without expressing my deep regret at the cause which compels his retirement. The benefit which the public service had to expect from the experienced talents of Lieut.-Col. Worsley would have made it a matter of concern that any motive should oblige him to relinquish a station in which his zeal, energy, and known impartiality, must have given satisfaction to every one. But our sensations on the subject must be painfully increased, when we learn that even his short application to the duties of his office, perhaps too intensely exerted, have increased those complaints which before constrained him to seek relief from another climate: while Lieut.-Col. Worsley is assured how much this consequence of his assiduity is lamented, he will have to reflect with gratification on the degree in which he possessed the esteem and confidence of government.

LIEUTENANT-COLONEL WILLIAM YOUNGSON.

(Madras Establishment.)

In April 1782 this officer landed at Madras, being one out of seventy cadets for that season on that establishment: he was promoted to the rank of ensign soon after landing, and in June joined the army in the field under Lieut.-Gen. Sir Eyre Coote. In Dec. of the same year he was appointed to a Native corps in the Circars; and in Nov. 1788, upon the raising of two new regiments, to one of which he was appointed, he obtained the rank of lieut. In 1790 he was nominated to the brigade staff of the army in the field under Gen. Sir. W. Medows, and subsequently under Lord Cornwallis; and from that period until 1802 (with the exception of about six months) he was either employed on the staff or on detached command. In June 1802 he joined his corps, the 14th N. I., as senior capt. upon the abolition of the office of quarter-master; in March 1804 he was promoted to the rank of major, and in July 1805 to that of lieut.-col.; and on the 26th Aug. 1807, in consequence of ill health, he was placed on the retired list.

COLONEL MARK WILKS.

(Madras Establishment.)

In 1782 this officer was appointed a cadet; in 1786 dep.-sec. to the Military Board; in 1787 sec. to a diplomatic mission under Sir Barry Close; in 1788 fort-adj. at Fort St. George; in 1789 aid-de-camp to the gov.; from 1790 to 1792 brig.-maj. and aid-de-camp to Gen. James Stuart, and served in the campaigns of that period; in 1793 assist. adj.-gen.; and in 1794 mil.-sec. to Gen. James Stuart.

From 1795 to 1799 this officer was on furlough from ill health; and from the latter year to 1803 he served successively as mil.-sec. and private sec. to the Gov. and Town-Major of Fort St. George; in 1803 as mil.-sec. to the Com.-in-Chief; major, 21st Sept. 1804; from 1803 to 1808 he served as political resident at the court of Mysore; the 4th April 1808 he obtained the rank of lieut.-col., and was obliged in this year, from ill health, again to go on furlough; 20th Nov. 1812 he was appointed gov. of the island of St. Helena; the 4th June 1814, col. by brevet; and in 1816 he returned from St. Helena to England. The 15th Oct. 1818, he was placed on the retired list.

LIEUTENANT-COLONEL GEORGE MACMORINE.

(Bengal Establishment.)

This officer joined the army at Fort William 1st Nov. 1781, as a cadet of inf.; was promoted to the rank of ensign 23d July 1782; to lieut. 19th Jan. 1785; to capt. by brevet, 7th Jan. 1796; to a comp. 3d Jan. 1802; to maj. by brevet, 25th April 1808, and regimentally, 13th Sept. 1809; to lieut.-col. by brevet, 4th June 1814, and regimentally, 16th Oct. 1814. After eighteen years' service in the campaigns of the period, in different corps, as change of regulations, &c. required, he was, when regimental rank took place, adj. of a batt. of grenadiers on service in Rohilcund, and being posted to the 1st batt. 10th reg. he joined it as brevet capt. and adj. in June 1800. In 1805-6, he held the office of commissary of supplies, &c. and the pay department, with Gen. Dowdeswell's division of Lord Lake's army; in 1807-8, he was Brig.-Maj. to the division of the field army on the north frontier at Meerat; which situation he resigned in Jan. 1809, to take the command, as Brev.-Maj. 1st batt. 10th reg. then preparing for service; but though much in camp and marching on the frontiers, no affair of great importance occurred under his command until the end of 1816, when a subsidiary force was ordered, under Col. Adams, C. B. for Nagpore, and of which Lieut.-Col. Macmorine's battalion formed a part; and as the Pindarries were then plundering the Rajah's country, he was ordered in advance with the 1st batt. 10th and 1st batt. 23d regts. four six-pounders, and two squadrons of the 6th Bengal cavalry; and having assembled this force at Lohargong from different posts in Bundlecund, he marched on the 19th Dec. for the Nerbuddah, through a difficult country, and where there was no regular road, and the British troops had not been before, but without delay, or meeting any of the enemy, who had passed far to the southward.

On the 1st Jan. 1817, he established a post of five companies at Jubblepore, and moved forward and to the south of the Nerbuddah, to relieve a brigade of Madras troops, under Col. Scott, at Garrerwara, who were dispersed at different places for the defence of that part of the country and line of the river. The main body of the Bengal force, under Col. Adams, passed Lieut.-Col. Macmorine's position in Feb., and relieved the remainder of the Madras army at Husseinabad, 110 miles more to the westward, the whole force being disposed along the line of the river, from east to west, about 200 miles, in small parties, supported by others in the rear, to guard the country from the Pindarries, and to attack them whenever opportunity offered, and which proved a fatiguing duty, until the river became impassable by the setting-in of the rainy season, when the British obtained some rest in temporary cantonments. After the rains the troops of the different presidencies made combined movements against the Pindarries into Malwah, and Col. Adams having moved with the head-quarters of his division, Lieut.-Col. Macmorine was left in command with the 1st brigade of the 5th division of the army of the Deccan, for the defence of the whole line of the river to the northward.

It shortly appeared to Lieut.-Col. Macmorine, that instead of serving as a protecting force to the Rajah's country, it would be necessary to concentrate his corps to act as circumstances might require, or according to the orders he might receive. He consequently made all due reports of what was going forward, and formed arrangements for bringing together small parties at different points, who might join him as soon as required. The plan was not long arranged till it became necessary to execute it: while in progress, he also received intelligence through his spies (for all other communication was cut off) that the Rajah's troops had attacked the British at Nagpore; and two days after, when he was concentrated, and considering what steps would be proper, in the absence of any orders, to pursue with respect to the Rajah's troops, who had committed no act of aggression in his quarter, he received a letter, *Via* Husseinabad, from the resident, acquainting him that the Rajah's troops had been repulsed, and a cessation of hostilities agreed upon; but that, upon the arrival of reinforcements, the terms of peace would be settled, or hostilities recommence.

Lieut.-Col. Macmorine had but just assembled his force in time to prevent being attacked in detail; and having a large quantity of military stores, cattle, and grain, passing for Husseinabad, and no place of security near, he embraced the interval to move rapidly to that quarter, and having lodged all with the baggage and sick in the fort there, where a battalion was stationed, again hastened back to a centrical position with his disposable force, 14 companies, 4 guns, and 300 irregular horse, having received orders from the resident to attack any body of troops assembled with hostile intentions.

Lieut.-Col. Macmorine continued moving rapidly eastward towards Serinagur, where a large force was collected; and on arriving at Garrerwara, he dispatched messengers with a letter to ascertain their intentions, and inviting to a friendly communication, &c., but that otherwise he should consider them as rebels to the Rajah and enemies of the English government; and having previously some knowledge of the place and environs, and adopting measures to obtain more, he resolved to attack them (if hostile) upon the north side, there being a deep rugged river on his side (the west,) and the other sides being more difficult than the north; he had also called on Gen. Hardyman by express to aid him with a squadron of the 8th N. C. to join about six miles north of the enemy, all being arranged to move to that point in the morning, to act as required, on receipt of an answer to his letter. In the meantime, however, he obtained intelligence of another body of 5 or 6000 men intending to cross the Nerbuddah, and join those at Serinagur, which induced him to move off immediately, and continue his march till midnight, when he arrived at the place fixed upon for the junction, sending expresses for the squadron to do the same, and join him, which was also executed during the night of the 3rd Jan. 1818.

On the following day, having obtained a hostile or evasive answer, Lieut.-Col. Macmorine resolved to attack on the 5th: he made arrangements and moved accordingly. When within about a mile of the walled town and fort and their position on a height joining to the N. E., he placed all articles of baggage in a bend of the hills, formed in mass of columns, and advanced in that order, in some degree covered by high fields of grain till within 5 or 600 yards of the enemy, who opened a smart fire from his guns, both on the heights and in the town and fort. Lieut.-Col. Macmorine then formed line, his guns opening on the enemy with good effect, and observing their cavalry indicate a movement as to attack the left flank, he immediately ordered his cavalry then on his left, the town being on his right, and the height in his front, to gain their right flank, and immediately charge, while the infantry charged the height and the town. The whole moved in the most gallant and rapid stile and best order, driving the enemy from their position and the town with great slaughter, capturing their guns, military stores, baggage, elephants, camels, &c. and the cavalry continuing in pursuit till the whole were dispersed and lost in the thickets and hills, which prevented vast numbers being killed and taken. The loss of the enemy was not less than 400 men, and their force was 3 or 4000 infantry, and about the same of cavalry; while in Lieut.-Col. Macmorine's 14 companies of infantry, squad. of cavalry, and 300 irregular horse, the loss was eight or nine men, and seventeen horses, killed, wounded, and missing. This body of the enemy did not again re-assemble, but dispersed to their abodes, and the force north of the Nerbuddah did not attempt to cross.

Lieut.-Col. Macmorine had received orders to take civil charge of the country, south of the river where he commanded, and having settled matters, and placed authorities in the place, and hearing the enemy north of the river were moving west, intending to cross and join the people in the hills south of the valley, he moved rapidly to prevent it; and on their finding themselves frustrated they dispersed, and several strong forts and the whole country submitted to the British authority, with the exception of one very strong hill fortress, which overlooked the valley, had a very strong garrison, and numerous artillery of large calibre, and being secretly supported by the Rajah, and having an army in the adjoining hills, it continued hostile. It became an arduous task to guard the newly-ceded country from the plunder of this garrison, which however this officer had the good fortune entirely to prevent, and the enemy suffered severely in every attempt they made, and when circumstances permitted, a battering train being sent, and it was within a few days' march, the place was surrendered to Lieut.-Col. Macmorine, with all the guns, &c. and taken possession of on the 13th May, 1818; soon after which, and on the approach of the rains, his force again went into temporary cantonments.

In the beginning of 1819 Lieut.-Col. Macmorine conducted a column (one of the three) for invading the Goandwana territory, and bringing that lawless tribe into subjection, as well as to obtain possession of the Ex-Rajah of Nagpore, who had taken refuge in that wild and strong country; but as he made his escape in disguise as a religious mendicant, there was not much difficulty to contend with, beyond what the mountains and forests presented to regular troops; and all being settled, they again returned to their former cantonment in April; and when the strong hill fortress of Assurghur, in Candesh, the last object of the war, was captured, and a relief of the troops effected, Lieut.-Col. Macmorine marched in the beginning of May, with the two battalions of the 10th regiment, retracing the same route by which he came three years before, and now become a high road, until the route for Benares branched off to the eastward; and on the 10th June took up his station within the provinces, after having been twenty-four years on field duty and frontier posts.

During the time of the services above recited, Lieut.-Col. Macmorine received high commendation in orders from his superiors; and on the occasion of the victory at Serinagur, the Com.-in-Chief sent him personally a copy of the general orders issued to the army, as annexed.

In Feb. 1820 Lieut.-Col. Macmorine proceeded to Europe on furlough, and in 1822 returned to India.

" *To Lieut.-Col. Macmorine, commanding Detachment.*

" Sir,—I had the honour to receive and submit to the most noble the Com.-in-chief your letters of the 5th and 6th Jan., giving the details of your spirited and well-conducted attack on the enemy's troops in their position at Serinagur, which the Com.-in-Chief has deemed worthy of commendation in general orders of this date, a copy of which I have the pleasure of enclosing.

   (Signed)   " James Nicol, Adjut.-Gen."
" *Camp Oochar, Jan. 16, 1818.*"

" General Orders, by the Commander-in-Chief.
   " *Head-Quarters, Camp Oochar, Jan.* 16, 1818.

" The official details of the late proceedings of a detachment of the Nagpore subsidiary force, under the command of Lieut.-Col. Macmorine, of the 10th N. I., having reached the Com.-in-Chief, his lordship has much pleasure in announcing to the army another instance of successful gallantry on the part of our troops, in the total defeat and dispersion of a large body of the Nagpore Rajah's troops, strongly posted at Serinagur, having their left flank covered by the fort and tower of that name. The troops engaged on this occasion were, the 1st batt. 10th N. I. and 2nd batt. 23rd N. I.*, a squadron

---

* Fourteen companies of those corps only were present or in that quarter.

of the 8th N. C., and a division of the 2nd Rohilla horse, with a small detachment of artillery. The capture of the enemy's five guns, together with their camp and baggage, and their total defeat with considerable slaughter, attests the good conduct of the troops; to whom, as well as to their leader, the Com.-in-Chief desires that his approbation and thanks may be communicated, particularly to Lieut. Chambers, commanding the squadron of the 8th N. C. and Lieut. Martindell, in command of the division of the 2nd Rohilla cavalry, who are noticed with much commendation for their gallantry by Lieut.-Col. Macmorine.

(Signed) " JAMES NICOL, Adjutant-General."

LIEUTENANT-COLONEL ALEXANDER WALKER.

(Bombay Establishment.)

THIS officer was appointed, in 1780, a cadet on the establishment of Bombay; on Nov. 24, 1782, ensign, and posted to the Bombay European Reg.; and on the 12th Dec. following he embarked with his corps, which formed part of the field force under Gen. Mathews, to act against the possessions of Hyder Ally on the coasts of Canara and Malabar. In the course of this service Ensign Walker was present at the attack and assault of the forts of Rajahmundry, Onore, Cundapore, the Hussorn Ghurry, or Bednore Ghaut, of Mangalore, and at various engagements or skirmishes which occurred during that campaign. In the course of it also he was removed to the 8th batt. of Sepoys, a distinguished corps, which was afterwards, for its valour and fidelity, appointed " The grenadier battalion."

With this batt. he was present at the attack of some batteries which enfiladed the encampment near Mangalore, and which were carried by the bayonet. He also led the attack at the head of the grenadier company of this batt., and carried a fort* or redoubt, of which it was necessary to dispossess the enemy previously to the formation of the siege of Mangalore. At the attack of the Ram Tower, a strong and commanding out-work, Ensign Walker was severely wounded; and although not quite recovered of this wound when Tippoo appeared before Mangalore, he joined his corps, which was posted with some other troops on an eminence, a short distance from the fort, to prevent its close investiture by the enemy. This force, however, overpowered by numbers, was compelled to retreat.

In the course of the remarkable siege which followed, Ensign Walker was again wounded, and received repeated marks of approbation from Col. Campbell, a distinguished and eminent officer, who commanded the garrison. When a cessation of hostilities was concluded with the enemy, Ensign Walker was one of the two hostages who were delivered on the part of the British troops, as a security for the conditions of the truce. For his " spirited and zealous†" conduct on this occasion, the government of Bombay bestowed on Ensign Walker the pay and allowances of captain for the period that he was in the hands of the enemy, and a donation of 2000 rupees from the treasury.

In Dec. 1785 Ens. Walker joined and sailed with an expedition to the north-west coast of America: the object was to collect furs, and to establish a military post at Nootka Sound, which it was intended Ens. Walker should command. The expedition proceeded to Nootka Sound, and explored the coast as far as lat. 62 north; but the scheme of establishing a post was abandoned: and in Jan. 1787 Ens. Walker

---

* This was a small fort of four bastions, originally built by the Portuguese, but of which they had been deprived by Hyder.

† The words of Brigade-Major Wolsely's letter. Ensign Walker remained as a hostage in Tippoo's camp from the beginning of August until the 25th November, nearly four months.

rejoined the grenadier batt. which was in garrison at Bombay. On the 9th Jan. 1788, he was appointed lieut.

On the renewal of hostilities with Tippoo in 1790, this officer embarked with his batt. which formed part of a detachment under the command of Lieut.-Col. Hartley, intended for the relief of the Rajah of Travancore. Lieut. Walker served in the campaign that followed, and was appointed Adj. of the line to the detachment. He was present at the battle of Tiroovanangary, and at the attack of the fort of Trincalore, which was carried by escalade. The next service in which Lieut. Walker was employed was the campaign of 1791, under Sir Robert Abercromby, against Tippoo Sultaun: he was appointed by the com.-in-chief adj. to the 10th batt. of Sepoys, and in this capacity he made a second campaign against Tippoo in 1792, which terminated in the treaty of peace, dictated by Lord Cornwallis before Seringapatam. On this event Lieut. Walker was re-appointed to his former corps, the grenadier batt., but soon afterwards he was appointed Military Sec. to Lieut.-Col. Don, the officer commanding in Malabar. In 1795 Lieut. Walker was appointed quart.-mast. of brig. but he relinquished this situation, and joined his regiment, to be present at the siege of Cochin. He was also at the taking of Columbo in 1796, when he was appointed military secretary to Col. Petrie, who commanded the Bombay division of the army.

On the expiration of this service Lieut. Walker was appointed an assistant to the commissioners for administering the affairs of Malabar. In the same year, 1796, he was appointed military secretary to Gen. Jas. Stuart, and held that confidential situation during the whole period that general was com.-in-chief of the army at Bombay. On the 8th Jan. 1796, Lieut. Walker was promoted Capt. by Brevet. On the 6th Sept. 1797, he was appointed capt.-lieut. and on the same day full captain; but his commission from his Majesty for the latter rank was dated 1st Jan. 1796. In 1797 he was appointed dep.-quar.-mast.-gen. to the Bombay army, which was some time afterward followed by the official rank of maj. In 1798 he was appointed dep. mil.

aud.-gen., and the Court of Directors nominated him to succeed to the office of auditor-general on the first vacancy.

In 1799, on the breaking out of the war with Tippoo, Maj. W. was appointed quart.-mast.-gen. to the Bombay army in the field: he was at the battle of Seedasere, and at the siege of Seringapatam, which terminated the career of Tippoo. Maj. Walker received one of the honorary gold medals conferred for this service. In 1800 Gen. Stuart returned to Europe, and Maj. W. received the instructions of government to proceed to Cochin ; and, on the Gen.'s departure, he investigated some complicated but important affairs with that Rajah. At this period Lord Wellesley, the Gov.-Gen., expressed his approbation of Maj. Walker's services and character, by offering to appoint him one of his extra aid-de-camps. In the same year Maj. W. was appointed a member of the commission for the administration of the government of Malabar. In Dec. Col Wellesley applied for one of the commission to attend the operations of the army preparing from Mysore to reduce the districts of Wynaad and Cotiote, at that time in a state of rebellion ; and Maj. W. was selected by his colleagues for this service. On its termination he received the thanks of the government of Madras. These were repeated by the same government on the dissolution of the commission.

The arms and political views of the Company were about this time directed to Guzerat, and Maj. W. was appointed to command the troops, and to conduct the negociations, which were to establish our influence in that part of India. He marched with a considerable detachment, and joined the Guicawar troops before Kurree, the chieftain of which was in rebellion against the superior government. Whilst negociations were going forward, the rebels treacherously attacked the British, with a force calculated at 25,000 men. An action ensued, and, after an obstinate conflict, the enemy were repulsed with great loss. On the part of the British a considerable loss was also sustained. A large reinforcement arrived under the command of Sir William Clarke, when the fort of Kurree was breached, and carried by assault. On this occasion the Gov.-Gen. in council desired his " thanks to be signified to Maj. W. for the judgment and address which he manifested in the conduct of the negociations, and for his distinguished exertions of military talents in the conflict in which he was unavoidably engaged with the rebels."

On the 7th June 1802 Maj. W. was appointed political resident at the court of his highness the Guicawar Rajah, and a subsidiary force was stationed at Baroda; which place, in the same year, was besieged, and the Arabs expelled. The collection of the revenues of the districts which were ceded from the Peishwa and the Guciawar were placed under the administration of Maj. W. On the 1st Dec 1803, he was appointed Maj. in the army. In 1803-4 Maj. W. was appointed to the charge of the district of the Punch Mehals, of the city and Pergannah of Broach, and other districts which were conquered from Scindia and the Peishwa. On 23d April 1805 a definitive treaty of alliance was concluded by Maj. W. and His Highness the Guicawar Rajah, which received the unqualified approbation of the Gov.-Gen. in council, and the Court of Directors. In 1807 Maj. W. was appointed to command an expedition into Kattywar. His instructions were prefaced in the following terms :—" I am directed to inform you, that as no officer on this establishment equally unites with yourself the essential qualifications of the requisite information, and local influence, for the purpose of conducting the objects of the projected expedition into Kattywar to their desired issue, the Hon. the Gov. in council is pleased to vest the command of the detachment to be employed on this especial service in you."

On the 27th Nov. 1807, after a practicable breach was effected, the fortress of Kundorna Ranaca surrendered to the detachment. The Gov.-Gen., the Gov. in council of Bombay, and the Com.-in-Chief, expressed in their general orders " their thanks to Maj. W. and their approbation of the judicious mode of attack of Kundorna Ranaca, the spirit, vigour, and effect, with which it was conducted."

In the course of this expedition Maj. W. effected the abolition of the revolting practice of infanticide, which had prevailed from time immemorial among the Jahrejah Rajapoots; and a deed of the most solemn nature was executed by the Jahrejah chieftains, renouncing for ever this unnatural crime*. The natives also agreed to abstain

---

* It is however with serious concern that we have to state that the promising and flattering expectation of the removal of infanticide (a crime originating in family pride, in an unwillingness to communicate the blood of the Rajahpoots through the marriages of their daughters) has been attended with limited success. But Lieut.-Col. Walker cannot be held responsible for any events which may have prolonged or retarded the abolition of this revolting crime, since his departure from India. He left it under the most promising circumstances. He obtained from each of the Jahrejah chiefs, in the name of themselves and their dependents, who alone practise infanticide, unequivocal and positive agreements to abstain in future from the crime of putting their infant daughters to death. They separately and voluntarily entered into a most binding engagement, by which they became liable to a severe pecuniary penalty in case of the violation of their contract. They made a solemn acknowledgment that it was contrary to their own religion, and that whoever should be guilty of the repetition of the crime, should be branded with all the infamy, disgrace, and privation of privileges involved in the loss of cast.

Under the influence of these engagements many of the Jahrejahs actually saved their children, and presented them to Lieut.-Col. Walker, with all the feeling and affection natural to parents. As this happened a year after they had bound themselves to preserve their daughters, it afforded a strong proof that they were at that time sincere in their intentions, and meant to perform their engagements. All their conduct and actions were in favour of this conclusion. A favourable change was produced, and the foundation of reform was evidently laid. It was proved to the natives, that the practice was against their sacred institutions, and that it was revolting to the best feelings of the human heart. It appeared only necessary to watch long enough over the system, until the subject and the habit should be forgotten. We had only to convince them that the vigilant eye of the government, like that of the Deity, does not turn away from the view of crimes, and that it is always on the watch for their detection. It would appear that the number saved in the course of ten years has been about 100, and perhaps a third part of these were preserved in the first two years after the agreements were concluded. But even from this statement we may expect that the humane endeavours of the British government will ultimately be crowned with success. The number saved, small as it may be to the whole who have suffered, is equal probably to that which would have been saved in a 100 years, under the usual state of the Jahrejah mind. The present able and enlightened Governor of Bombay has directed the attention of the local authorities to the subject, and by blending it with our policy will effectually ensure for ever the abolition of infanticide. He expects to eradicate this crime, against the first principles of our nature, by attending to the erudition of the lower classes, and by improving the state of society. It will yield, he justly imagines, to civilization and more improved views of social life.

Mr. Elphinstone instructed the political agent in Kattywar, under date 9th Jan. 1821, to adopt the most vigilant and unceasing measures to detect and to punish the commission of the crime. He is directed not only to remonstrate with the chieftain who commits the offence, but to exact from him the penalty of his guilt, and to reward those who are atten-

from the practice of Tragga, a species of suicide, ; and Maj. W. effected agreements with the piratical states in this part of India, not

tive to their engagements. The following are extracts from those instructions, addressed to Captain Barnewell, the political agent.

"Though the Hon. the Gov. does not think that it would be prudent to authorize the employment of regular informers for the purpose of detecting instances of this atrocity (the commission of infanticide) he feels the greatest anxiety to employ every practicable means for its suppression; and, considering that the practice is entirely unconnected with religion, and unsupported by the opinion of the bulk of the community, even in the countries where it exists, he cannot but entertain a hope that more effectual means of extirpating it may yet be devised. It is to be hoped, that from the direct communication which now subsists between you and the inhabitants, you will be able in the course of your circuits to obtain information in some of the many instances of this crime, which must occur. It will then be in your power to visit the offence, not only on the person who has committed it, but on the head of the village, or the chief who shall appear to have connived at it. Your influence ought likewise to be always employed in discountenancing this atrocity, and in encouraging an opposite course. When remissions (of tribute or revenue) are refused to a chief, it may be noticed as one reason for rejecting his request, that he has not been zealous in suppressing infanticide: on the other hand, when an abatement is granted, it may perhaps be possible to reserve to government the right to recover the amount after a certain period, unless the chief and his byaud can prove their attention to the rule in question by the production of a certain number of female children of their cast. The proportion must of course be much smaller than a calculation of the births in so many families would authorize us to expect. With a view to encourage parents in sparing their female children, you are authorized to throw all fines levied on chiefs for other offences, as well as for infanticide, (after indemnifying the sufferers by each,) into a fund to be distributed in portions to children so preserved."

We may now indulge a reasonable expectation, that these renewed exertions of the British government will put a stop to the crime of infanticide. We may entertain even sanguine hopes that this blot on human nature will be utterly eradicated. Nature herself is working in our favour. The Jahrejahs, we may expect, will again move within the range in which nature acts: they express no pride, as they did at first, in the destruction of their offspring, and feel no shame in rearing them. All the infants they have saved have been the consequence of their own choice, and natural affection may produce its effect. By the force of frequent admonition, and the influence of rewards and punishments which have been instituted by Mr. Elphinstone, we may confidently predict the triumph of nature and humanity over a guilty habit, sanctioned by the culpable impunity of ages.

An account of the measures adopted for the suppression of infanticide, with remarks on other customs peculiar to India, has been published by an intelligent officer (Major Moor,) of the Bombay army, whose literary researches on this and other occasions cannot be too highly appreciated.—J. P.

only to renounce the practice of piracy, and all right to wrecks, but to pay a considerable sum to the merchants who had suffered from their depredations. A compromise and settlement was at the same time made with the Rajahs and petty chiefs of Kattywar, for the regular payment of their respective revenues and tributes, without requiring that this should be annually enforced by a military expedition. All these missions, in favour of humanity and the public interest, received the strongest approbation from the governments of India and the Court of Directors. The Gov.-Gen. writes—" We discharge a satisfactory obligation of our public duty in expressing the high sense we entertain of the great zeal, prudence, and ability which have distinguished the conduct of Maj. W. in the execution of the important and arduous service in which he has been employed in the districts of Kattywar. The singular judgment and discretion which regulated the whole of that able officer's proceedings, the perseverance and activity which have animated his endeavours to promote the objects of the expedition, and have enabled him to surmount the great embarrassments and difficulties which opposed their accomplishment, entitle Maj. W. to the highest approbation and applause."

On the 21st Oct. 1808 Maj. W. was promoted to the rank of lieut.-col.; and the state of his health obliging him to solicit a furlough to Europe, the request was complied with, and the following orders issued:

" GENERAL-ORDERS, by the Hon. the Gov. in Council.

" *Bombay Castle, Jan.* 19, 1809.
" THE Hon. the Gov. in council is pleased to permit Lieut.-Col. A. Walker of the 1st reg. N. I. to proceed to England, with the option of returning to, or retiring from, the service, at the expiration of his furlough. In thus announcing the departure of Lieut.-Col. Walker, the Gov. in council discharges one of the most gratifying obligations of his public duty in recording, in concurrence with the sentiments of the commanding officer of the forces, his unreserved testimony to the distinguished merits of an officer, whose progress throughout the service has uniformly reflected the highest credit on the profession of

which he has proved himself so respectable a member. The character of Lieut.-Col. Walker first attracted the notice of this government in the confidential situation which he held of sec. to Lieut.-Gen. Stuart, as Com.-in-Chief of the forces under the presidency, and who having moreover appointed him to the office of dep. quart.-mast.-gen. in Jan. 1799, the Lieut.-Col. subsequently accompanied that experienced officer in charge of the arduous duties of quart.-mast.-gen. to the Bombay army that co-operated in the reduction of the fortress of Seringapatam in the memorable campaign of that year. The selection of the Lieut.-Col. to fill eventually the appointment of the assist. to the aud.-gen. having been communicated to the Hon. the Court of Directors, they were pleased to direct in 1801 that he should succeed to the responsible situation of aud.-gen. to this presidency, on the occurrence of any vacancy in the department. The several occasions, however, which the administration of this presidency has had to avail itself of the experienced talents and acquirements of that officer, have interrupted his succession to the principal charge of either of the two above-mentioned offices in the immediate line of his profession,— in view to which he had thus successively been selected,—and in both of which he was eminently qualified to promote the public service. Having accompanied the committee of government that proceeded to Malabar in the year 1797, the knowledge which Col. W. thence acquired of the state of affairs in that province, joined to his conciliatory character, led to his being nominated a member of the commission that was formed for regulating the affairs of Malabar, at a crisis which demanded the selection of servants of approved judgment and talents. On the abolition of the commission, Lieut. Col. W. returned to this presidency, and would have succeeded to the office of aud.-gen., pursuant to his nomination to that situation by the Hon. Court, had not the course of events called for the exercise of his tried abilities in promoting the national interests in a more active and delicate scene of operation. The Baroda state having solicited the interposition of the Hon. Company's favour and authority in extricating the government from the various difficulties and distresses under which it then laboured, this officer proceeded to the northward in 1802; and in the short warfare which ensued, Lieut.-Col. W.'s services attracted the thanks of his Exc. the most noble the Gov.-Gen. in council, " for the judgment and address which he manifested in the conduct of the negociations with the minister Rourba, and for Maj. Walker's distinguished exertion of military talents in the contest in which he was unavoidably engaged with the superior force of Mulbar Rao Guicow." Having successively engaged in the reduction of the active and dangerous opposition that immediately distracted the Guicawar state, the attention of Lieut.-Col. W. has for these last seven years been sedulously devoted, in his capacity of resident at Baroda, in co-operating with the administration of the Guicawar government towards the restoration of its affairs; after the attainment of which important object, he is now returning to his native country, with the regret of his own government at the loss of his able assistance, with the distinguished approbation of the Gov.-Gen. of India for the eminent services he has rendered, and the general good wishes of his sovereign and subjects in the Company of the Hon. Company's ally, at the court of which he had thus long and usefully resided."

In the beginning of the year 1809 Lieut.-Col. W. embarked in the Earl St. Vincent, and proceeded as far as Point de Galle on his passage, from which he was induced to return to Bombay in consequence of a requisition from the Gov.-Gen. Lieut.-Col. W. again entered Kattywar at the head of a British force of more magnitude than the former, and was joined, as he had been on the first occasion, by the Guicawar army. On the 17th June the detachment took the fort of Kandader. On the 7th July, a practicable breach having been effected, the fort of Mallia was carried by assault, after an obstinate resistance.

The general orders by the Com.-in-Chief on this occasion expressed the " highest gratification, and congratulated the army on an achievement so distinguished by judgment, decision, zeal, and intrepidity, and so highly creditable to the troops engaged. The Com.-in-Chief begs to distribute his praise and gratitude to Lieut.-Col. Walker, Maj. Mahony, and the officers and men, for their spirited, gallant, and energetic conduct on this arduous enterprise."—The following is an extract from the government orders on the same event:—" In thus narrating the circumstances that attended the reduction of the fort of Mallia, the Gov. in council affords the most satisfactory testimony to the able disposition that had been planned by that judicious and experienced officer Lieut.-Col. Walker, and to the promptitude, vigour, and bravery by which that plan was carried into effect by that gallant detachment under that officer's command, which has added another conspicuous exploit to those which have already distinguished the zeal and intrepidity of the Bombay army."

Negociations ensued with the state of Kutch, which were ably conducted and concluded by Capt. Greenwood, who was deputed by Lieut.-Col. W. for this purpose. On the 1st Oct. the piratical fort of Positra surrendered to the detachment.

After having accomplished all the objects of government, and tranquillity being completely re-established, Lieut.-Col. W. obtained leave to return to his native country. The following orders were issued by the Governor in council:—

"*Bombay Castle, Jan.* 23, 1810.

" The Hon. the Gov. in council is pleased to permit Lieut.-Col. Walker to proceed to England, with the option of retiring from, or returning to, the service at the expiration of his furlough. The sentiments of government on the high professional character and distinguished merits of Lieut.-Col. Walker were expressed in the orders dated the 19th Jan. 1809, on the occasion of that officer's former embarkation for Europe. The communication of the wishes of the Rt. Hon. the Gov. Gen. that the residence of Col. Walker in this country might be prolonged, for the purpose of carrying into effect an arrangement of great political importance, determined the Lieut.-Col. to return to his station, and to reassume the functions of his office. Having immediately entered upon the delicate duties committed to his able management, the progress of his negociations, and the success of his measures, have been marked by that judgment, ability and address, of which he has afforded so many decided proofs, at the same time that the reputation of the British arms has been maintained and extended under his approved military talents and skill, in a degree that has already attracted the distinguished approbation of the Right Hon. the Gov.-Gen. The Gov. in council, therefore, in announcing Lieut.-Col. Walker's ultimate return to his native country, embraces the opportunity of renewing the expression of the obligations of the government for the important services which have already received its cordial and unqualified testimony, and which have been enhanced by the eminent and substantial benefits that this presidency has derived from his protracted residence in India."

Lieut.-Col. Walker arrived in England 9th July 1810, and on the 24th June 1812 he retired from the service. In 1822 he was appointed, by the Court of Directors, Gov. of St. Helena, with the rank of Brigadier-General.

LIEUTENANT-COLONEL GERVASE PENNINGTON.

(Bengal Establishment.)

THIS officer was appointed a cadet on the Bengal establishment in 1782, and arriving in India in July following, commenced his military career in the artillery at the practice-ground at Dum Dum. In 1784, he served under Col. Sir John Cummings, then in command of the temporary brigade, so called on account of having been formed, in addition to the fixed subsidiary force provided according to treaty with the Newaub, for the express purpose of protecting the N. W. frontier of the Newaub's dominions from the predatory incursions of the Siks, who, annually, with large bodies of horse, levied contributions or laid waste the country. In this brigade Mr. Pennington continued to serve until early in 1786, when, in consequence of a new organization and partial reduction of the army, he was struck off, with many others of all ranks, to the half-pay list, on which he remained till 1788, when being brought on the effective strength, he rejoined the reg. of artillery, then on its practice-ground at Dum Dum. In 1791 he was again appointed to the army of observation on the Newaub's frontier, with which he served until the close of 1793, and was in that year promoted to lieut. In 1794, having volunteered his services, he embarked with the force furnished from the Bengal army for the reduction of the isles of France and Bourbon.

In 1796, the government of Bengal having found it expedient to relieve the subsidiary force, then composed of troops from the Madras presidency in the Nizam's dominions, a brigade of the Bengal troops, with the artillery in which Lieut. Pennington served, assembled at Midnapore, the rendezvous, in December, whence it marched in the following Feb., and arrived at its ground of encampment, near Hyderabad, the capital of the Nizam's dominions, in June, after a march of between nine hundred and a thousand miles. The Bengal subsidiary force was commanded by the late Col. H. Hyndman, of the Bengal service, who so effectually directed its operations in the reduction of Perron's army, near that capital, when eleven thousand men laid down their arms, surrendering fifty-five pieces of field-ordnance, and seventy-four European officers, prisoners of war, to a force under six thousand.

At the close of 1798, the health of Lieut. P. being much impaired, he, by the advice of his medical friends, left Hyderabad, and proceeding to the sea-side, availed himself of an opportunity, which then offered, of visiting Bengal, where intelligence having arrived of the war with Tippoo, in which the Bengal brigade, then at Hyderabad, was to be employed, he re-embarked in a merchant-ship for Madras; but which ship being captured by the French frigate La Forte, he became a prisoner, with the loss of his baggage. From this situation being released by Capt. Cooke, of the Sybelle, who captured the La Forte, he arrived at Madras in time to join Col. Reade's division on its march to Seringapatam.

After the fall of that capital, the army was broken up in divisions, when Capt. P., having been promoted by brevet in the preceding January, served with that division, which, under the command of Col. Dalrymple, pursued Doondia Cawn, and attacked the hill fortress of Chitteldroog, at that time supposed by the natives to be impregnable. Doondia was twice over taken, suffering each time considerable loss, and Chitteldroog surrendered.

Capt. P. having returned to Bengal at the close of the Mysore war, he was appointed aid-de-camp to Maj.-Gen. G. Deare, whom he joined while in command of a division of the army, for the expulsion of the Arracanese, who had made an irruption into Bengal on its S. E. frontier.

In 1802 this officer was promoted to capt.-lieut. in the art., and the following year, continuing in his capacity of aid-de-camp, he served with Maj.-Gen. Deare, who was charged during that campaign of the Mahratta war, with the defence of the frontier lying between the Soane and the Jumna.

In 1804, Maj.-Gen. Deare having retired from the army, Capt. Pennington was permitted, on his own request, to join the grand army, then under Lord Lake, and at the siege of Burtpore, when covering the retreat of a column, after the last assault of that place, he was severely wounded by grape-shot in the head and shoulder.

In 1805, this officer, though not yet promoted to full captain, was nominated by Lord Lake to the command of the art. with the grand army, then under his Lordship's personal command, with permission to select from the art. those officers he preferred to serve under him. In this situation he remained till the termination of the war in Feb. 1806, when he was appointed to the command of the experimental troop of horse art., and in the same month was also promoted to the rank of capt. of art. In 1809 Capt. Pennington commanded the horse art. with the army serving on the Settledge or Hesudrus, under the command of the late Lieut.-Gen. St. Leger, and at the close of that year, it having been deemed expedient to increase the horse art. to three troops, Capt. Pennington was, by a special order of government, appointed to the command of that corps, on its augmented establishment.

In 1810 Capt. Pennington was promoted to the rank of Maj. by brevet. In 1814 he was appointed to the command of all the art. in the division serving under Maj.-Gen. Gillespie, in the mountain war with the Ghoorkas, and at the siege of Callinger,* where the maj.-gen. was killed. After the reduction of Callinger, Maj. Pennington was withdrawn from the mountains, to join with his horse art. the army of observation, formed on the Jumna, under Maj.-Gen. Sir W. G. Kier. In 1817 he commanded the horse art. at the siege of Hattrass, which was taken possession of, with thirteen other forts of no inconsiderable strength, in the course of that year; and in Oct. following he joined, with his whole corps, after a march of twenty days, the grand army, formed at Secundra, for the Pindarry war, under the personal command of Lord Hastings, with which he served to the termination of that campaign in 1818.

In Sept. 1818, government having deemed it expedient to augment the horse art. to a brigade, composed of six troops, with one rocket troop, Maj. Pennington was promoted to the rank of Lieut.-Col. and appointed to the command of that corps. In 1819, finding his con-

---

* On this occasion Major Pennington received the following letter :—

" SIR,—The zealous, able, and most useful assistance afforded by you, to the late and ever-to-be lamented Maj.-Gen. Gillespie, both prior to and at the attack of Callinger, having been made fully known to the Right Hon. the Com.-in-Chief, I have great pleasure in obeying his Exc.'s commands, to convey to you his particular thanks for your voluntary and highly meritorious services, in superintending and directing an arduous department to which you was not publicly or regularly attached, in addition to the duties of your own more immediate and important command; and to acquaint you that the proofs afforded on this occasion of your talents, gallantry, and exemplary zeal, are duly appreciated, and will not fail to be held in recollection by the Right Hon. the Com.-in-Chief. It is his Exc.'s wish, that as long as you remain in Col. Mawby's camp you will retain the general command of the whole artillery in it, which will be communicated to Col. Mawby.

(Signed) G. H. FAGAN, Adj.-Gen."

stitution much impaired, by an uninterrupted service of more than thirty-six years, and having also suffered from three wounds, he proceeded on furlough to England. In 1823 he returned to India. In the course of his service Lieut.-Col. Pennington was twice appointed to the office of paymaster, once to that of commissary of supplies, and once to that of commissary of ordnance; but while holding these offices he continued to perform his duty in the line.

LIEUTENANT COLONEL WILLIAM THOMAS.

(Bengal Establishment.)

THIS officer commenced his military career in 1795, at the age of fifteen, having been appointed to a lieutenantcy in a reg. of foot, commanded by Col. (afterwards Gen.) Sir Robert Stuart, Bart., and was subsequently removed to the Northumberland reg. of fencible inf., which he joined in 1796 at Jersey. In Aug. of the same year he sailed for India, having been appointed a cadet, and reached Calcutta 16 Mar. 1797. He was immediately appointed ens. in the 2d batt. 5th reg. N. I., which corps he joined at Caunpoor in Aug. In Oct. he was promoted to lieut. in the 2d batt. 1st reg. N. I. which he joined at Futtehgurh, and immediately took the field with that division of the army, under the late Lieut.-Gen. R. Stuart, in order to form a junction with the Caunpoor division, under the late Gen. Sir Jas. Craig, with the view of deposing Vizier Ally, and of placing the legitimate heir, Newaub Sandut Ally, on the throne of Oude, in pursuance of that chief's treaty with the British government. This service having been accomplished, the division returned to their cantonments. In Sept. 1798, the 1st reg. again took the field, and proceeded to Bareilly in Rohilcund, to afford assistance to the governor of that province. The reg. marched from thence, and joined the remainder of the Futtehgurh division at the city of Caunpoor. The political objects having been peaceably accomplished, the division proceeded to form a junction with the field army, assembled at Anopsheher, under Sir J. Craig, with the view of opposing Zemaun Shaw, the king of Cabul's threatened invasion of Hindostan. The grenadier companies of the army having been formed into two batts. Lieut. Thomas was appointed by Sir James adj. to the 1st batt. Zemaun Shaw having retreated from the Attock, (to which river he had advanced in prosecution of his project) in consequence of disturbances in his own dominions, the field army broke up, and Lieut. Thomas proceeded to join the 13th reg. at Benares. The 23d batt. having been ordered to Azimghur, for the purpose of disarming and disbanding some refractory batts. of the Oude government, Lieut. Thomas applied and obtained permission to join it. In the early part of 1801 the batt. was actively employed in the field against a refractory Zemindar, named Ataur Sing, who, in his principal strong hold, Autroliah, maintained an obstinate siege of several weeks. The Pettah was at length carried by assault on the 1st April, and Lieut. Thomas had the honour of being one of the first to enter the place with the centre column of attack. The enemy were closely pursued through the town to the ditch of the fort, which they evacuated during the night, having suffered severely in their defence. The troops immediately moved against the fort of Hurrain, the next in consequence to Autroliah, but the enemy were so thoroughly disheartened that they only stood one day's open batteries, and evacuated the place. In this manner twenty-two strong holds were gained possession of, and delivered over to the Newaub's officers. In 1803 Lieut. Thomas was detached from Purtaub Ghur, with two companies, across the Jumna into the Bogalkund district, to repress some marauders in that quarter. From this duty he was called upon to join a force, collecting for the siege of the fort of Chowkundic; a breach having been effected, orders were given for the assault, and Lieut. Thomas's detachment proceeded with the storming column; but the ditch presented such formidable obstacles, and the men, carrying the scaling ladders, having been all killed or wounded by the heavy fire kept up from the garrison, the signal was given to retreat; and the storming party received the commanding officer's thanks, " for their gallant though unsuccessful exertions at the breach." Capt. Graham, who led the party, fell pierced with nine balls! The place was subsequently evacuated during the night.

The 23d Sept. 1804, this officer was promoted to a company, and nominated about the same time by the Com.-in-Chief, the late Lord Lake, to form levies of recruits for the general service of the army. In 1808 Capt. Thomas took his furlough to Europe; and in July 1812 embarked on board the Hon. Company's ship, Euphrates, on his return to Bengal, the Court of Directors having conferred upon him the command of the troops on board. The voyage proved propitious to Columbo in the island of Ceylon; but leaving that port in prosecution of the voyage to Calcutta, the ship was wrecked in the night of 1st Jan. 1813, on the ridge of rocks extending from Dindia Head, and totally lost. The night being calm, the passengers and troops were landed with but one casualty among the latter; but the greater part of the baggage was lost. The passengers experienced the kindest treatment from the British residents at the port of Matura, who promptly came to their aid, while sitting round fires kindled by the natives on the beach, and conveyed them to their houses. Capt. Thomas marched the troops to Matura, and subsequently to Point de Galle, where he embarked on board the Hon. Company's ship, Northampton, and landed at Calcutta 15th March. He was immediately appointed by the Com.-in-Chief, to take charge of, and discipline, 500 recruits for the European reg. in fort William, and afterwards proceeded with them to Burhampoor. In June 1814, this officer was promoted to Maj. by Brevet, and obtained the regimental step 16th Dec. following; and, having commanded the left wing of his batt. for some months at Etaweh, he proceeded to the head-quarters at Agra.

The Nepaul war not having been brought to a conclusion, the 2nd batt. 13th N. I. was ordered to march from Agra for the province of Kamaoon in Nov., and early in Dec. arrived at Champownt, the ancient capital of the province, and relieved the batt. 11th N. I. which had been much reduced by sickness. Maj. T. was soon afterwards detached with the left wing of his batt. to the advanced post of Chowpakiah, on the right bank of the Kali, and relieved a grenadier batt. put *hors de combat* by sickness. Here Maj. T. remained till the signature of the Ghoorka peace, when, having succeeded to the command of his batt., he returned to join the head-quarters at Champownt, where the right wing remained cantoned till Nov. 1816, when the corps descended the hills, and occupied the post of Meradabad in Rohilcund.

The 2nd batt. 13th reg. having been selected to form part of the centre division of the grand army, under the immediate command of Lord Hastings, Maj. T. commenced his march from Meradabad the latter end of Sept. 1817, and reached the general rendezvous at Secundra, on the banks of the Jumna, on the 20th Oct., the day appointed, when upwards of 14,000 troops were at once assembled. The division crossed the Jumna on a bridge of boats a few days afterwards; and while it advanced towards the Scind river, Maj. T.'s batt. was left to cover the construction of a *tête de pont* by the principal field-engineer, on the completion of which the batt. proceeded to join the head-quarters, escorting treasure and grain for the army, with which the detachment arrived on the 9th Nov. On the 18th of the same month a detachment was formed, designated the advanced guard of the army, under Brig. Philpot, consisting of a troop of horse art., H. M. 24th dragoons, the 3d reg. light cavalry, four fort art. guns, and the 2nd batt. 13th reg. This detachment marched immediately *via* Sumptur and Jhansi to Burwa Sangur, where it halted from 24th Nov. till 3rd Dec., observing the motions of Kurreem Khans Dhurrah of Pindarries. These pursuing a rapid course towards Narwar, the detachment proceeded by forced marches to the Scind *via* Datteeuh, and reached Sonari Ghaut on the 7th. Here the baggage, with the left wing of the 2nd batt. 13th reg., was left, while the remainder of the detachment crossed the river, and proceeded rapidly to Cheemuck, a position commanding the only road from Narwar to Gwalior. The detachment proceeded onward to Narwar, the infantry keeping pace with the cavalry: when arriving within a few miles of the place, it was discovered that Kurreem Khan had fled; and as that chief was more closely pursued by the left division, the detachment countermarched by Mustoorah to Cheemuck, where it remained till recalled to head-quarters on 24th Dec. The latter end of the following month this officer was again detached with his batt. to cover a grand foraging party from camp, and to overawe some forts from whence opposition had been experienced. This service having been satisfactorily accomplished, the corps proceeded to Sumptur, and relieved the batt. in charge of the battering train at that place, agreeably to orders received from head-quarters. Brig.-Gen. Watson soon afterwards followed with two more native batts. and a reg. of light cavalry, and on the 15th Feb. the whole marched *via* Traree and the Malown Ghaut, in order to effect a junction with the left division of the grand army under Sir D. Marshall at Kimlassa. This having been effected, the division moved on the town of Sangur; and a political agent having arrived in camp, the whole district quietly submitted to the British government by negociation. The division next marched to reduce the fort of Dhamornie, garrisoned by the troops of the Nagpore Rajah. The Killadar having rejected terms of capitulation, the batteries were opened, and six hours battering and bombardment compelled him to surrender at discretion. From Dhamornie the division commenced a tedious and harassing march, dragging the guns through jungles and over roads where no wheeled carriages had ever been before, towards the Nerbuddah river, for the reduction of the fortified town and citadel of Mundlah, likewise belonging to the Rajah of Nagpore. The division, after encountering great difficulties from the almost-impassable state of the roads, came before the place on the 18th April, and a breach having been effected, it was carrried by assault on the 26th, the enemy suffering a loss of between 5 and 600 men. Eight companies of the

2nd batt. 13th reg., under Maj. T., formed part of the storming column, and his name was noticed with applause in the general orders issued by Lord Hastings on the occasion of the capture of this important fortress. Chowra Ghur, another fort belonging to the Nagpore Rajah, having for some time resisted a British force that had invested it, the division immediately moved in that direction, and on the approach of the advance the place surrendered. The division then recrossed the Nerbuddah, and returned to canton for the rainy season, at Sangur; and thus terminated the campaigns of 1817-18.

Government having determined to form the siege of the stupendous fortress of Asseerghur, the Sangur train was put in requisition, and commenced its march under the escort of the 2d batt. 13th reg. on the 3d March 1819. Gen. Watson soon followed with another batt., and the detachment joined the besieging force under Gens. Sir John Doveton and Sir John Malcolm, on the 1st of April. At this siege were assembled the troops of the three presidencies; and after an incessant bombardment and battering, during which the heavy guns were nearly rendered unserviceable, in consequence of the great elevation at which they had to fire at the breach, the place surrendered on the 9th April. At this memorable siege there were present three British ladies, one of whom was the wife of the subject of our memoir.

The combined army having received the thanks of the commanding general, broke up on the 15th of the same month, and the Sangur division returned to its cantonment on the 20th of May, having marched a distance of nearly 600 miles, encumbered by a large battering train, at the most inclement season of the year, the thermometer being higher than 110 degrees in the tents.

On the 6th July 1820 this officer was promoted to the rank of lieut.-col., and appointed to the command of the 1st batt. 22d reg., which he immediately proceeded to join at Secrora in Oude. From this post he was removed with his batt. to Kurnaul. Lieut.-Col. Thomas was subsequently appointed to the 2d batt. 7th. reg. and to the command of Seetapore in Oude.

LIEUT.-COL. MARMADUKE WILLIAMSON BROWNE.

(Bengal Establishment.)

THIS officer was appointed a cadet in 1790, and went out to India at a very early period of life: on the 17th June 1792 he was promoted to lieut.-fireworker in the Bengal art.; lieut. 21st Feb. 1801; capt.-lieut. 24th Sept. 1804; capt. 20th Feb. 1808; maj. by brevet, 4th June 1814.; in the reg. 1st Sept. 1818; and lieut.-col. 7th Aug. 1821.

In 1797-8 he was appointed adj. and quart.-mast. to the art. with the army assembled at Lucknow, under the personal command of the Com.-in-Chief, Sir A. Clarke; in 1798-9, maj. of brig. to the art. with the army under Sir James Craig, assembled on the N. W. frontier at Anopsheher, to oppose the incursion of Zemaun Shaw; in 1799, in command of a detachment of artillery sent out against several refractory forts in the Benares district; in Nov. 1800, quart.-mast. to the 2d batt. of art., which he held until appointed maj. of brig. to the reg. in March 1806; this he resigned in Jan. 1809, on being appointed principal deputy commissary of ordnance; and on the 1st Nov. 1821, to the highest and most honourable staff situation held by officers of artillery—that of principal commissary of ordnance commissariat.

This officer was selected by the Gov.-Gen. the Marquess of Wellesley, and appointed to the charge of the experimental horse art., which he held from Feb. to Nov. 1801, when he resigned to take his tour of the field duties; he was also in Nov. 1809 selected by the Com.-in-Chief, without any application of his own, to be one of the agents for army clothing; and which he held till Jan. 1822, when he was removed by an order from the Court of Directors, after having held the situation for twelve years, to the entire satisfaction of the government, and the colonels of regiments, who were more immediately concerned: the reason assigned for removing this officer was, that his holding two appointments was contrary to a late regulation of the Court regarding pluralities.

He served during the whole of the campaigns against the Mahrattas from Aug. 1803 to July 1805, and held the situation of quart.-mast. to the art. with the army under the personal command of the Com.-in Chief, Lord Lake; during which period he was present and engaged in the attack of Gen. Perron's troops, under the walls of Allygurh, 29th Aug. 1800; the battle of Delhi, 11th Sept; attack on the troops under the walls of Agra; battle of Deeg; the sieges of Allygurh, Agra, Deeg, and the four attacks on Burtpore; also, at the relief of Delhi.

Lieut.-Col. Brown, after serving thirty and a half years in the East Indies without visiting Europe, and having been absent from his duty only nineteen months on account of his health during that period, was obliged in Jan. 1822 to resign his staff situation, and avail himself of the indulgence of the service, by proceeding to Europe on furlough, for the recovery of an impaired constitution.

LIEUT-COL. THOMAS DUER BROUGHTON.

(Bengal Establishment.)

In March 1797 this officer arrived in India, as a cadet on the Bengal establishment, and was posted as ensign to the 2d batt. 9th N. I. stationed at Burgam. Towards the end of this year the 13th and 14th regs. N. I. were raised, and this officer was promoted to lieut. in the latter, and directed to join the 2d batt. about to be raised at Buxar. In the formation of this corps under Maj. (late Maj.-Gen.) Cunningham, Lieut. B. applied himself diligently to acquire a knowledge of his parade duties; and in the autumn of the following year he and the late Lieut.-Col. Ludlow, C. B a few years his senior, offered their services to command two companies of volunteers from the batt. intended to form part of the three corps raised in the same manner throughout the army, and destined to join the Madras army about to take the field against Tippoo. Lieut. Ludlow being soon after appointed adj. to a regular batt. returned to take charge of his appointment; and his companion embarked for Madras with the 1st batt. of volunteers, under Capt. John Malcolm, in Dec. 1798. A voyage of five days landed them at the place of their destination; and being joined by the other two batts. they marched, after a short stay at the Mount, under the command of Maj.-Gen. Popham, who had been sent round from Bengal to command the troops of that presidency, to join the army assembling in the neighbourhood of Ryacotta, under the personal command of Gen. Harris. Lieut. Broughton was present at the whole of the operations of the campaign of 1799, including the march to Periapatam, under Gen. Floyd, for the purpose of forming a junction with Gen. Stuart and the Bombay army, which ended in the capture of Seringapatam; and subsequently at the first pursuit of Doondia, under the Duke of Wellington, (then Col. Wellesley.) At the conclusion of this service, the Bengal brigade formed part of the troops selected to garrison Seringapatam, where they remained till Dec.; when they were ordered to Madras with as little delay as possible, for the purpose of being re-embarked for Bengal. Upon their arrival, however, the intentions of government were changed, and the three batts. of volunteers were directed to commence a long, though not uninteresting, march through the northern Sircars, towards their own presidency. On reaching Masulipatam their services were required to reduce a refractory Zemindar in the neighbouring hills; and they were accordingly detained for that purpose. This measure, however, was not approved of by the gov.-gen., who required their immediate return; and accordingly, as soon as steps could be taken to relieve them they resumed their march, and reached Midnapoor, the frontier station of Bengal in that quarter, in July, 1800. Here they found orders for the formation of the three volunteer batts. into the 18th and 19th regs. of the line, the 15th, 16th, and 17th, having been raised during their absence from Bengal. Previously to their departure, in Dec. 1798, the system of rising by regimental promotion had been established; and Lieut. Broughton had been appointed to the first European reg.; which corps he proceeded to join at Dinapoor, as soon as he was released from his duties with the volunteers. In the following year the Marquess Wellesley made his progress through the extended provinces of the governments committed to his immediate care; and Lieut. Broughton accompanied the flank companies of his reg., which formed his Lordship's guard during his residence at Patna. At the express desire of the gov.-gen., he was afterwards appointed to the command of a guard of thirty men from his corps, intended to form part of his Lordship's personal escort throughout the remainder of his tour. In the discharge of this agreeable duty, Lieut. Broughton acquitted himself so much to the satisfaction of his Excellency, that he nominated him adj. and assist. teacher of Hindostan, to the Cadet company, upon its institution at Barasett in the following year. The trouble and vexation, however, attendant upon teaching grown-up boys their exercise, and instructing them in the rudiments of a new language, soon disgusted him with this situation: and accordingly, upon the breaking out of the Mahratta war in 1803, when two volunteer batts. were raised, he again offered his services; they were accepted, and he was appointed quart.-mast. of the 1st batt., which he joined with half a dozen of his young pupils, who had passed their examinations, and were declared qualified to join regiments. The two wings of this batt. were destined for different services. The first which sailed went to Ceylon; and the other, which Lieut. Broughton accompanied as staff, formed part of the expedition under the late Lieut.-Col. (then Capt.) Morgan, which took possession of the town and district of Balasore, in Aug. 1803.

In the course of the following year, Capt. Morgan being removed to the command of a provincial batt. about to be raised at Culpee, that of Balasore, together with the whole of the civil authorities, devolved upon Lieut. Broughton. In the discharge of the several functions of magistrate, collector, and secret agent, he obtained repeated testimonies of approbation from Lieut.-Col. Harcourt, first commissioner, and commanding in the province: he retained these situations till the arrival of Mr. Kerr, of the civil service, who had been permanently appointed to the superintendance of the district.

Early in 1805, the wing of the batt. under Lieut. B.'s command was ordered to Barrackpoor: and on the 14th Nov. following he was promoted to the rank of capt.-lieut.: he remained at Barrackpoor till Feb. 1806, when he was appointed to command the escort, consisting of two companies, about to proceed with Mr. Mercer, the resident, to the camp of Dowlut Rao Scindia.* He set off immediately by Dawk, to take charge of his new appointment; and joined Mr. Mercer at Agra, where he was making preparations for the march. About this period this officer's commission as capt.-lieut. in the army, was antidated to 29 Dec. 1804, in consequence of the resignation of a lieut. of the reg. in Europe, of which due information had, from some cause or other, not been transmitted to India. In this responsible situation Capt. B. continued till the close of 1811, when he took his furlough, and returned to his native country.

Capt. B. was included in the brevet which took place at the peace, and obtained his rank in the army as Major from the 4th June, 1814. In the following year he returned to India, and landed in Calcutta in Aug.; when, his reg. having been for some years at the eastern islands, he was directed to assume the command of a large body of recruits assembled at Burhampoor, and formed into a temporary corps of eight companies. As the choice of recruits had become much more extended since the peace, this division, as it was termed, of the European reg. exhibited the finest body

* During his residence in Scindia's camp, this officer obtained that information respecting the customs and manners of that singular people, which he has given to the world in the "Mahratta Letters:" and it was there too he profited by his proficiency in Oriental languages, acquired at Barasett, in collecting, arranging, and translating his "Specimens of the Popular Poetry of the Hindoos' country."

of European inf. that had probably ever been seen in the Company's service; and Maj. Broughton's exertions to do it justice, in disciplining and training, were cheerfully and ably seconded by half a dozen officers, who had on various occasions returned from the reg., and were directed to join and do duty with this division. At the commencement of 1816 Maj. B. was ordered with four of these companies to Java, where they arrived in Apr.; and the maj. was appointed to the command of Weltevreden, having, on the 4th of the preceding month, been promoted to a regimental majority.

Expectations seem to have been entertained by the Indian govt. that that valuable and beautiful island would not have been so speedily given over to the Netherlanders, and a new government and fresh troops had accordingly been sent from Bengal. They had, however, scarcely reached their destination, when news of the arrival of the Dutch fleet, with the authorities and troops on board, was received. Arrangements were speedily commenced for the delivery of the island to its old sovereigns, and the departure of the British troops. Maj. B.'s detachment was among the first to embark for Bengal, where it arrived at the end of Sept.; and the division was once more united under his command, and stationed at Burhampoor. It was there inspected in Feb. 1817, by Lord Hastings, who expressed his approbation and thanks to Major Broughton and his officers, in the most flattering terms; and soon after, upon the arrival of the head-quarters of the reg. from Macassar, directed him, in General Orders, to assume the command, and consolidate the whole into one corps, upon one system of internal arrangement; an effective lieut.-col. being, in the same orders, posted to the corps, but instructed to confine his duties to the command of the station. The reg. was soon after joined by another detachment, consisting originally of three strong companies, which had been for many years at Amboyna; and in amalgamating these several bodies, who viewed each other with the most jealous eye, and in the introduction of many new regulations and habits, as well as eradicating some old ones, Maj. B. found ample calls for his unremitting attention, as well as for the exertions of every officer of the corps. His success, however, was complete; and it is to him, that the reg. is indebted for the formation of the rifle company; which, under the immediate care of its commandant, Capt. Wood, attained to a state of perfection, both in discipline and appearance, in the highest degree creditable: the establishment of the regimental school; the distribution of the men into messes; the appointment of color serjeants, the first in the Company's army, and which led to the extension of that rank throughout the army of Bengal: and finally, for the organization and establishment of the regimental savings' bank; an establishment which has opened to the sober and steady soldier the means of securing a supply for the future comforts of his family, or his own old age; and to the more thoughtless, a temptation to throw into another channel the rupee, which was destined for the canteen or the gaming table. To the usual and anxious labours of such a command was soon added, that of his old employment, the instruction of young officers. A regulation was made for all the infantry cadets to join, in the first instance, the European reg. where they were to continue, till reported by the Com. officer qualified to join Native corps. A memorial pointing out the additional and troublesome duties thus devolved upon the Com.-officer of the European reg., while his allowances and emoluments were much inferior to those of officers commanding Native corps; together with the disadvantages under which the officers in general of the former laboured, when compared with their brethren in the latter service, was delivered by Maj. Broughton into the hands of the Marquess of Hastings, on Christmas day, 1818; and some months after, an additional salary was attached to the command of the European reg., as a compensation for the extra duties of the situation. Maj. Broughton, however, who had then held that command for four years, and under whose care nearly two hundred young men had been prepared to join the different corps of the army, was not allowed to benefit by this regulation. It was now directed, that the Europ. reg. should not be left without the presence of a lieut.-col., though that want had not been felt during the long period it had been absent on service to the eastward. The enjoyment of the additional salary was also limited to that rank: an effective lieut.-col. was again appointed; and in Feb. 1820 Major Broughton delivered up his anxious charge to his successor.

This officer was promoted to lieut.-col. Sept. 1, 1822.

MAJOR-GENERAL W. H. BLACHFORD.

(Bombay Establishment.)

This officer arrived in Bombay in Aug. 1777; the 7th March 1779 he was appointed a cadet in the engineers, Bombay establishment; the 1st Jan. 1780 he was promoted to an ensigncy, and served at the siege of Bassien, with the army commanded by Gen. Goddard. After the storm of that fortress, he was one of the sub-engineers employed to survey that territory, and to establish a chain of field-works for the security of the environs against Mahratta horse. On the 20th Feb. 1783 he was promoted to lieut. He served in the memorable campaign commanded by the unfortunate Gen. Matthews, from the first landing of the army on taking of Rajamundroog on the Canara coast, to the conclusion of peace that followed in 1785. During this long and trying campaign, Lieut. B. served at the siege and storm of Onore. He was entrusted with repairing the breaches, and making other improvements in that fortress; and ultimately he had the honour of being the only engineer officer belonging to that garrison during the successful defence it made under the command of Maj. Torriano. The siege and blockade of Onore lasted eight months under the most pressing events, arising from famine, sickness, and desertion; the garrison were at length relieved by a peace, which returned them to Bombay, reduced from their original strength of 1200 to about 250, for embarkation to the Presidency. The want of provisions was at one time so seriously felt, that a number of horses were killed and salted as a last resource, rather than surrender to Tippoo's forces. After this service Lieut. B. was appointed senior engineer to the garrison of Surat.

The 27th Sept. 1785 Lieut. B. was promoted to the rank of a capt. In 1785-6 he was ordered to Tellichery, where he suggested various plans, which ultimately led to a curtailment of the original lines to a more limited system of defence. In Jan. 1787 he returned to the presidency, to the ordinary duties of his department. In April 1790 he was ordered, as senior field-engineer, with a detachment under Gen. James Hartley, for the relief of the King of Travancore, attacked by Tippoo. Gen. Hartley landed, and cantoned near Cochin. Tippoo had made a successful attack on the Travancore lines, but the timely arrival of the Bombay detachment saved the interior of the territory from further depredation. Capt. B. was detached to ascertain whether the fort of Cranganore (belonging to the King of Travancore) could be defended against Tippoo, who was preparing to attack it. Its local position was very tenable and strong; but the total want of supplies of every kind for its defence induced Gen. Hartley to give up the idea of defending it. The Travancore garrison was withdrawn, and the fortress was blown up by Tippoo's troops the next day. On the opening of the season, Gen. Hartley's army, joined by the Travancorians, marched to Palicaudcherry, encamped there some time, and relieved Madras garrison at Paulghaut, where Capt. B. succeeded to the duties of engineer, which he held until Gen. Hartley's division was directed to return to the coast of Malabar. On the 10th Dec. 1790 the detachment came up with the enemy, strongly posted for defence near Trevanagary; after a severe action, Tippoo's forces were completely defeated. In this engagement Capt. B. received a severe wound on the side of his head—a musket-ball passed through his hat, and lodged near his temple; the ball was immediately extracted, but the wound was very obstinate in healing.

In Jan. 1791 Gen. Hartley's detachment formed a junction with the Bombay army assembled at Cananore, under Sir Robert Abercromby. Capt. B. joined it, and was attached to the van with some pioneers to clear the road for its march up the Ghauts. In the execution of this fatiguing duty, with an impaired state of health (his wound not having healed,) he was attacked on reaching the head of the Ghauts, with a violent fever and delirium, that threatened his existence. In this despairing condition he remained a long time too ill to be moved: the surgeon at length laid open his wound, conceiving some splintry adhesion of the skull prevented its healing, when a piece of Capt. B.'s hat was found buried in it. This discovery effected a favourable change for removing him to Tellichery, where he arrived with total loss of memory; and from thence embarked, and arrived in Bombay in May 1791. On recovering from that illness, he rejoined the army at Cananore in Oct. 1791, and resumed his duties in the field during that service, and siege of Seringapatam by Lord Cornwallis, which campaign terminated in a peace with Tippoo. From this period (20th May 1792) he returned to the ordinary duties of his department at the presidency, and was employed on a particular survey of the town of Bombay, to ascertain the superficial measurement each house occupied within the garrison.

In 1794-5 he succeeded to the appointment of superintending engineer at Bombay, which he held until he was compelled to seek a furlough to Europe for the benefit of his health. Capt. B. quitted India 17th Jan. 1796, and arrived in England 4th Aug. following. He returned to India 17th Feb. 1798, and arrived in Bombay 4th June following. He was then ordered to Cananore, as superintending engineer to the works carrying on to a great extent. About this period the Bombay army, under Gen. James Stuart, assembled at Cananore, to proceed a third time up the Ghauts, to co-operate against Tippoo's capital. On the army quitting Cananore, Capt. B. was appointed to the command of the garrison. The duties of it became important to exercise, as the place formed a centrical depôt for forwarding and receiving supplies for the armies besieging Seringapatam. He held the command of Cananore until the conclusion of that campaign, and then returned to Bombay.

He was promoted to the rank of maj. 11th Dec. 1801, and resumed the duties of superintending engineer at the presidency, which he continued to discharge until Sept. 1803; when finding the state of his health on the decline, he yielded to the necessity of proceeding to Europe on furlough. He quitted India 14th Sept. 1803, and arrived in England 2nd Feb. 1804. He succceded to the rank of lieut.-col. 1st May 1804; and on the 6th March 1805 he obtained, by succession, the rank of full col. of engineers.

Previous to M.-Gen. Blachford's leaving Bombay he had passed more than twenty-two years in actual service in India, independent of his furlough. He addressed the court of directors, representing the impaired state of his health, arising from a bad wound, and various trying duties he had undergone in India, requesting their permission to remain in England as a full colonel, with the advantage of sharing in the offreckoning fund as chief engineer of Bombay; which request they were pleased to accede to.

MAJOR-GENERAL THOMAS HARDWICKE.

(Bengal Establishment.)

This officer was appoined lieut. fire-worker in the artillery, Bengal establishment, Sept. 10, 1778; lieut. Feb. 16, 1784; capt. Aug. 20, 1794; maj. July 26, 1804; col. Sept. 25, following; col., by brevet, June 4, 1813; col. in the reg. April 21, 1817; and maj.-gen. Aug. 12, 1819.

In Sept. 1781 he marched with the detachment from Bengal, under the command of Col. Pearse, to join the army at Madras, commanded by Sir Eyre Coote; he was present, in Aug. 1781, at the siege and capture of Tripasore; and in the battle of Perambancum, against the army of Hyder Ally; in Sept. he was in the action with the same army on the plains of Sholinghur; in Nov. at the capture of Chitore in the Pollams; in the cannonade, Jan. 10, 1782, of the swamps, on the march to relieve Velore; and in the cannonade at crossing the same swamp, when returning towards Madras; in June 1783 he was at the assault on the French lines at Cudalore, and engaged in the trenches when attacked, on the 25th of that month, by the garrison of Cudalore. In 1790 he proceeded with a detachment of Bengal artillery to join the army at Madras, under Sir W. Medows; was present at the capture of the several forts of Caroor, Deraporum, Arivacoochy, Erouad, Coimbetoor, and Settimungalum. He was with Col. Floyd's detachment in the cannonade of the 13th Sept. against the army of Tippoo Sultaun; and at the action of the following day, near Shaoor, on the march to form a rejunction with Gen. Medows. He was in the attack of the 15th May 1791 on Tippoo's lines before Seringapatam; and at the taking of Outradroog on the 18th June.

In Dec. 1795 he was at the investiture of Savandroog; and in the same month appointed commissary of ordnance by Lord Cornwallis, and put in charge of the magazines of Bangalore; in 1793 he returned to Bengal, and was, by Lord Cornwallis, appointed adjutant and quarter-master of artillery. He was present, Oct. 26, 1794, in the Rohilla battles in Rohilcund, near Bettoriah, then holding the rank of capt. The 15th Sept. 1797 he was appointed commissary of ordnance, in which situation he continued till declining health obliged him, in 1803, to proceed on furlough to Europe. In 1806 he returned to Bengal: on the 5th July 1816 he was appointed acting commandant of the regiment of Bengal artillery, and he has continued to serve in India till the present time.

MAJOR-GENERAL ARCHIBALD FERGUSSON.

(Bengal Establishment.)

This officer was appointed a cadet on the Bengal establishment in 1776; ensign, Dec. 25, 1777; lieut. Sept. 5, 1778; capt. July 11, 1795; maj. July 31, 1799; lieut.-col. Dec. 26, 1802; col. June 4, 1811; col. 4th N. I. Nov. 5, 1812; and maj.-gen. June 4, 1814.

He served in the 3rd N. I. until promoted to a company, and fourteen years as adjut. He commanded the 2d batt. 7th N. I. for several years; and from 1812 commanded the 18th reg. and station of Barrackpoor, which he left in Dec. 1814, on his return to Great-Britain. Few corps in the Bengal army were more employed on field service, on frontier duty, and in command of different posts, than the above, during the periods of this officer's command.

LIEUTENANT-COLONEL THOMAS M. WEGUELIN.

(Bengal Establishment.)

This officer was appointed a cadet on the Bengal establishment in March 1781: he arrived in Calcutta in April 1782, and was promoted to ensign; and to lieut. on the 1st Aug. following, having previously joined the 3d European reg., then in quarters at Burhampoor. In Nov. of the same year, he was removed to the 1st batt. 22d reg. N. I. at the frontier station of Futtehgurh, in the dominions of the Newaub of Oude; and in March 1783, proceeded with the batt. on the collections in the Furruckabad district, in the course of which the mud-fort of Kersanna was reduced by force, after four or five days open trenches.

In this reg., which, in 1785, was incorporated into one batt., and denominated the 28th, Lieut. W. continued to serve for thirteen years, when it was drafted, in 1796, into the 2d reg. N. I., on the new organization of the army; on which occasion he was promoted to capt., by brevet, and attached to the 1st batt. In Dec. 1797 he was removed to the 1st batt. 13th reg. N. I., then forming at Chunargur; and again to the 1st European reg., to which he became permanently posted, on the introduction (in 1799) of regimental rank into the Company's army.

Capt. W. partook of the various services on which the several corps, to which he was successively attached, were employed; in the course of which he proceeded, on the breaking-out of the war with Tippoo Sultaun in 1790, with the 28th batt., which formed part of Lieut.-Col. Cockerell's detachment, and which served with the British armies in Mysore, during the campaigns of 1790, 91, and 92. He was present in the battle of Seringapatam, May 15, 1791; in the assault of the enemy's entrenched camp and lines before that capital, on the night of the 6th Feb. 1792; and at the siege of the city which followed: also at the reduction of several forts in Mysore, which had previously fallen in the course of the war. On the night of the 6th Feb. the 28th Bengal batt. formed part of the centre column, under the personal command of Lord Cornwallis; and on penetrating the enemy's lines, Lieut. W. was placed with his company in one of the captured redoubts (the Sultaun's,) which was afterwards known by the name of Sibbald, in compliment to the gallant Capt. Sibbald, of H. M. 74th foot, who, with a company from that reg., commanded in the redoubt, and was killed in one of the repeated attacks which it sustained and repulsed during the remainder of that night and the following day. The defence of this redoubt, against which the enemy brought up in succession his best troops, headed by Lally's reg. of Europeans, became an object of interest and solicitude to the whole army; it was left to its own means, and could not have held out but for the fortuitous circumstance of the ammunition of the 28th batt. which had fallen in the rear, having been brought for security under the protection of the redoubt: as it was, the casualties both in killed and wounded were numerous, and bore a large proportion to the defenders.

Capt W. returned with the detachment, on the termination of the war, to Bengal. In the affair with the Newaub Vizier Ally at Benares, in 1799, he commanded the 1st batt. 13th N. I., and shortly after joined the 1st European reg. at Caunpoor, and moved with it to Dinapore at the close of that year. In Sept. 1803, having then attained the rank of capt. regimentally, he proceeded, in command of the flank companies of his reg., to join the army under Lord Lake, then conducting the war in the north-west provinces against the Mahratta states; and in progress commanded a considerable detachment from Caunpoor with stores and supplies. On joining the army, the flank companies of H. M.'s 22d foot, and those of the Company's European reg. were formed into a flank batt., under the command of a field officer; but shortly after Capt. W., with the latter companies, joined a detachment proceeding for the siege of the strong hill fort of Gualior, conducted under the command of Col. (the late Maj.-Gen. Sir H.) White, and which terminated in the surrender of that celebrated fortress, after a practicable breach had been effected, and preparations made for carrying it by assault.

In Sept. 1804 Capt. W. was nominated to the situation of dep. judge-adv.-gen. in the field or provinces northward and westward of Allahabad, and in that capacity accompanied the army under the Com.-in-Chief, and was present at the siege of Burtpore: he continued to hold that appointment until March 1808, when he became ineligible on his promotion to a majority; and in June of the same year he was selected by Lord Minto, then Gov.-Gen. of India, to command an expedition preparing for the defence of the Portuguese settlement of Macao, against any premeditated attack from the French. On this occasion the local rank of col. was conferred on Maj. W. to ensure him the command of the combined troops, in case any officer of the Portuguese service at Macao should have been of senior rank to his regimental commission.

The expedition* sailed from Bengal in Aug., and anchoring in Macao Roads on the 20th Oct. following, landed without delay, and occupied, with the division from Fort St. George, which had previously arrived, the defences of the settlement, with the exception of the fort called the Monte, and two batteries, which it was deemed expedient should remain in charge of the Portuguese troops.

The alarm and jealousy of the Chinese government (which could not be made to comprehend, or at least to admit, the necessity of such precautionary measure) at the proximity of a British force in possession of Macao, were soon found to be insurmountable; the troops had landed without the consent of the local authorities, while a general feeling of enmity on the part of the Chinese inhabitants was manifested in repeated affrays and assaults, particularly on the Sepoys, whenever opportunity presented; and it became necessary, to prevent further acts of aggression, as well as those of retaliation, to restrict the troops to their respective quarters as much as possible. In this state affairs remained for some time, pending, it was understood, a reference to the Emperor; in the mean while the trade was stopped, and every endeavour at negociation, or even at explanation, equally rejected, though personally attempted by Admiral Drury and the president of the select committee of Supercargoes: the reply invariably was—" Put your troops on board, and then we will hear you." Under these untoward circumstances, the British property at Canton was claimed, and the Company's servants withdrew from the factory; while the Chinese, on their part, placed a line of armed junks across the river, to intercept the communication, leaving space for only one boat to pass. The time at length arriving in which a reply might be expected from Pekin, a rumour prevailed, and was corroborated in a letter from the president, that a numerous armed force had moved from Canton to expel the British troops; and shortly after two small

---

* The troops forming the expedition consisted of 200 rank and file of the Company's European reg. and a volunteer batt. of 650 firelocks from Bengal, 100 Europ. art. (with a train of 8 eighteen and 4 twelve-pounders, 2 eight inch mortars) and 2 field pieces, and 2 companies of His Majesty's 30th foot from Madras.

encampments were observed on the main island opposite to Macao, from which a party crossed over, and took possession of the jos-house at the Portuguese extremity of the isthmus. All supplies to the troops were at the same time prohibited on pain of death; the Chinese inhabitants ordered to remove from the city, and the Portuguese to keep within their houses, preparatory to the actual commencement of hostilities. These strong indications on the part of the Chinese precluding further prospect of reconciling them to the continuance of the troops at Macao, as was also declared in several despatches received from the viceroy at Canton, it became necessary to determine on the line of conduct expedient to be adopted under these unexpected proceedings. The question was accordingly taken into consideration, and in the then state of affairs, and declared opposition of the Chinese government, it was finally judged most advisable to abandon the intention of occupying Macao, and, in order to the re-establishment of our commercial relations with that nation, to re-embark the troops. That measure was accordingly adopted, and the expedition returned to India; the division from Bengal arriving at that presidency about the middle of Feb. 1809.

While these measures were in progress, the city of Macao being open and exposed on all sides, and filled, it might be presumed, with internal enemies, every requisite precaution was taken to guard against surprize or insurrection, as well as to repel attack; at the same time cautiously avoiding the appearance of alarm. With this view, the troops being unequal to the general protection of the whole city, the line of defence was confined principally to the Monte, and upper parts of the town, in its vicinity, and the guns, camp equipage, and stores, removed to within the proposed limits. Signals, also, were concerted for assembling the troops at the several posts appointed for them, in the event of any sudden movement being necessary; while every attention was directed to the preservation of order and tranquillity in the town, which, from the irritated state of feeling of all parties, required constant care and vigilance to effect. The sense entertained by the Supreme government of the conduct of Maj. W., under such unusual circumstances, as well as in the general command of the expedition, will be seen from the following extracts of letters, and general-orders issued upon the return of the detachment to Bengal :—

"*Council-Chamber, Feb.* 27, 1809.

" Your despatches, of the dates mentioned in the margin*, containing a detailed report of your proceedings in China, and of transactions in that quarter, having been submitted to the consideration of the Rt. Hon. the Gov.-Gen. in council, I am directed to communicate to you the sentiments of government on the tenor of your conduct, in the execution of the arduous and important service on which you have been employed. His Lordship in council discharges a satisfactory obligation of his public duty, in recording the high sense which he entertains of the great prudence, discretion, vigilance, and activity manifested by you throughout the whole course of your proceedings, in a situation of perhaps unprecedented delicacy and embarrassment, in which the most important interests of the Hon. Company and the British station in China materially depended upon the exercise of those qualities. The Gov.-Gen. in council considers you entitled to the expression of his distinguished approbation for your uniform and successful attention to the maintenance of discipline and subordination among the troops, at a time when their patience and forbearance were put to the severest trials, by repeated insults and provocations on the part of the Chinese inhabitants of Macao. All the measures and arrangements you adopted for the accommodation and relief of the troops, and for the regulation of the staff, are entirely approved; as also the able narrative of political transactions contained in your despatches of the 5th and 21st Dec. The Gov.-Gen. in council also highly approves the professional judgment displayed by you in the defensive arrangements which you adopted to provide against the contingency of an attack on the part of the Chinese. The whole tenor of your proceedings, indeed, fully justifies the high opinion of

---

* 15th and 24th Nov., 5th, 21st, and 22d Dec. 1808; and 14th and 16th Feb. 1809.

your judgment, temper, and ability, which induced his Lordship in council to select you for the command of the troops in a situation of such peculiar delicacy and importance; and his Lordship in council will have great pleasure in conveying to the notice of the Hon. the Court of Directors the distinguished merit of your conduct and services on the occasion.

   (Signed)   " N. B. EDMONSTONE, Chief-Sec.
" *Major Weguelin.*"

   " *Head-Quarters at Kurnaul, March* 7, 1809.

" I am directed by the Com.-in-Chief to acknowledge the receipt of your letter of the 21st Dec. 1808, from Macao Roads, with the enclosures referred to; and that of the 18th ult., reporting the return to Bengal of the detachment under your command. His Exc. directs me to convey to you the expression of his best thanks for the judgment, prudence, and discretion with which you have exercised and fulfilled the duties of the command for which you were selected. To the zeal and attention manifested by you in the arduous and trying situation in which you were placed, his Exc. primarily ascribes the praiseworthy conduct, by which the whole of the officers and troops have been distinguished during the expedition.

   (Signed)   " H. WORSLEY, Adj.-Gen.
" *Major Weguelin.*"

  Extract of General Orders, Fort William, Bengal, 27 *Feb.* 1809.

" The detachment of the Hon. Company's European reg., and the corps of Native volunteers, which proceeded to Macao, under the command of Maj. Weguelin, having returned to the presidency, the Right Hon. the Gov.-Gen., in council, deems it proper to direct a public communication of his sentiments, regarding the meritorious conduct of Maj. Weguelin, and of the officers and men under his command, during the period of their employment in China. The highest applause is due to Maj. Weguelin, for the judgment and ability manifested by him, in the precautionary measures which he adopted, to prevent the evil consequences of irritation so justly excited amongst the European and Native troops under his command, by the unfriendly and often injurious conduct of the native inhabitants; for his uniform vigilance, attention, and exertion, to which is materially to be ascribed the preservation of tranquillity at Macao; for his indefatigable endeavours to promote the comfort, and relieve the wants, of the troops, in a situation in which they were exposed to all the inconveniences of restraint and privation; and for the professional skill which he displayed in the defensive arrangements which it was judged necessary to adopt.

(Signed)   " N. B. EDMONSTONE, Chief Sec."

The detachment being broken up on its return to Bengal, Maj. W. shortly after joined the European reg., to which he was attached, at Dinapore, and remained at that station in the command of the corps, until Dec. of that year (1809), when he returned to the presidency, on leave. On the establishment of the commissariat, (1st Feb. 1810,) in Bengal, Maj. W. was appointed dep. commissary gen. at that presidency; and in that capacity proceeded in Sept. following, in charge of the department, with the expedition against the Isle of France and dependencies. On the landing of the troops he was placed by his Exc. the Hon. Gen. Abercromby, Com.-in-Chief of the expedition, at the head of the commissariat, for the supply of the forces from the three presidencies of India, and from the Cape of Good Hope; and on the surrender of the island, was finally appointed by his Exc. Gov. Farquhar, Commissary Gen. of the Isles of France, (Mauritius), Bourbon and dependencies. He continued to hold that situation for twelve months, when the Isle of Mauritius and dependencies being annexed to his Majesty's government, from the 1st Dec. 1811, the Company's troops and public authorities returned to their respective presidencies in India, where Maj. W. arrived (in Bengal) the latter end of March 1812; and had the honour to present to the

Gov.-Gen. a letter from Gov. Farquhar, addressed to his Lordship in council, expressive of his Exc.'s approbation of his conduct, at the head of the commissariat in those islands, as will be seen by the following extract:—

"I avail myself of the departure of Maj. Weguelin for Calcutta, to return your Lordship the best thanks of this government, for having allowed us to benefit so long from the services of that valuable officer. The indefatigable zeal, regularity, prudence, ability, and vigilance, of the Dep. Commissary Gen., have afforded essential aid, in the management of public affairs in a newly conquered colony, when the objects and duties of that department have been of primary importance, and could have been effectually accomplished by such peculiar qualifications only as Maj. Weguelin possesses; and which has so fully realized the highly distinguished recommendation, with which his appointment, by your Lordship, to these islands, was accompanied.

(Signed) "R. T. FARQUHAR.
"*Port Louis, 20 Jan.* 1812."

The commissariat accounts of the expedition were brought up, and completed by Maj. W., and submitted to audit, in the course of six months after his return to Bengal; on which occasion the approbation of the Gov.-Gen. in council, and also of the Court of Directors, was conveyed to him.

On the 1st July, 1812, Maj. Weguelin was appointed commissary gen. of Bengal, with the official rank of lieut.-col.; which rank he also attained regimentally, on the 16th March, 1814. However important the duties* of commissary-gen. may be, they afford little

---

* These duties embraced many branches of military supply, in addition to the victualling of the troops, to which, in Europe, the commissariat is generally confined, viz.—the supply of and feeding elephants, camels, and bullocks; also of horses, for the cavalry and horse artillery. The supply of military stores, and timber for the arsenal and maga-

matter of a nature to be recorded in a military memoir; suffice it therefore to say, that Lieut.-Col. Weguelin continued to discharge those duties for the period of eight years and a half, in the course of which they were nearly doubled; and in which also occurred the two extensive wars with the government of Nepaul, and for the suppression of the Pendarries, involving hostilities with the whole of the Mahratta states, that of Scindia only excepted: the extra expences of these wars in the commissariat department did not exceed 200,000l. in the former; and not more than double that amount in the latter; though embracing the supply of several divisions upon an extensive and distant scale of operations. The general efficiency and success of the commissariat department, while under Lieut.-Col. W.'s direction, as well as on those more momentous occasions, may be seen in the following extract of general orders by government, issued at Fort William, 2d Feb. 1816:—

" The Gov.-Gen. in council, has had occasion repeatedly to notice, in terms of the highest commendation, the very exemplary conduct of the officers of the commissariat department, and the satisfactory and œconomical results of their zeal, industry, good management, and exertions; qualifications which have not failed to call forth the strongest expressions of approbation and applause from the Hon. the Court of Directors: but these encomiums were bestowed on the commissariat, with reference to its operations, either in time of tranquillity or of inconsiderable warfare. Seasons not favourable to the vast resources of the department, and of the more active energies of its officers, which could alone be thoroughly developed in the arduous and trying scenes of an extensive campaign. The period has at

zines; of half-wrought ordnance materials for the gun-carriage agencies; of infantry accoutrements, galloper harness, and cavalry saddles; of the camp equipage of the army; of diet, clothing, and necessaries, for the European and general hospitals; of boats for transportation of troops and stores; of barrack cots and quilts for the troops; also the providing hired camels and bullocks for the transport of grain; of draft and carriage bullocks and carts for the ordnance; park and hospital stores; and carriers for the sick with troops actually in the field; supplies for the islands, &c.

length arrived, in which the powers of the commissariat have been put to the severest trials; the result has exceeded the most sanguine expectation of his Exc. the Com.-in-Chief, and of the Government; and his Lordship in council has now no hesitation in pronouncing the commissariat department to be equally efficient in all its branches in time of war, as it has proved itself to be in time of peace. The result of the exertions of the commissariat during the last campaign, has left to his Exc. the Right Hon. the Gov.-Gen. in council, nothing to be expected, or even to be desired, which could add to the efficiency or reputation of the department; while the unprecedented œconomy with which supplies of every description were procured and transported, notwithstanding the difficulties opposed to their transit, reflects unbounded credit on the officers of the department. To Lieut.-Col. Weguelin, commissary-gen., and to Maj. Lumsdaine, dep.-com.-gen., the warmest acknowledgments of the government are eminently due, for the wisdom, zeal, and unremitting attention, with which they have so successfully discharged the duties of their high and important situations, under circumstances peculiarly trying."

Lieut.-Col. W. being obliged, by private affairs, to return to Europe on furlough, obtained leave to resign his appointment of commissary-gen. on the 31st Dec. 1820, that measure being necessary, according to the rules of the service, which do not admit of a staff-officer retaining his appointment, while absent on furlough. He embarked on his return to England, in Jan. 1822, having been detained to the end of the preceding year, for the purpose of bringing up and closing the accounts of the department, which he reported completed and to have passed audit, on the 29th Dec. 1821: the total expenditure in the commissariat department, during the period he was commissary-gen., exceeded six millions sterling, the whole accounts of which were brought forward in his office, under his personal superintendence and responsibility. The opinion and sentiments entertained by the supreme government of Lieut.-Col.

Weguelin's public conduct, not only in his late responsible situation, but generally during a service of forty years, are expressed in the subjoined extracts of letters, addressed to him by order of the Gov.-Gen. in council, on the occasion of his departure for Europe: he had also the honour of bearing a letter from the Gov.-Gen. to the Chairman of the East India Company, in which his Lordship observes, " that in enabling Lieut.-Col. Weguelin to offer his personal respects, he feels justified in affording him the facilitation for that honour, by the zeal and attention which he has ever manifested in your service. The comparatively moderate expence attending the extensive military operations of 1817 and 1818, will be the best proof of the order established in his department, and will not fail to make him appear deserving of being favoured with your countenance."

Extract of Letters, dated 3d and 11th Jan. 1822, from the Mil.-Sec. to Government, addressed to Lieut.-Col. Weguelin.

" Your letter of the 29th ult., adverting to your approaching departure for Europe, has been duly submitted to the most noble the Gov.-Gen. in Council. Your zealous and indefatigable services in the commissariat, from its first establishment until the present time, the last eight years and a half at the head of the department, embracing a series of military operations on a scale of magnitude not before that period witnessed in India, have been equally creditable to yourself and beneficial to the public interests. His lordship in council considers it but an act of justice to record the expression of this sentiment, and to add, that the attention and careful fidelity with which you have unceasingly endeavoured to promote the efficiency of the department entrusted to your charge, and to œconomise the public funds of the state, under circumstances which demanded unremitting regularity and exertion in the important duties of your office, entitle you to the acknowledgments of government. The closing of your accounts will necessarily be brought before the Hon. the Court of Directors, when the Gov.-Gen. in Council will derive considerable gratification in offering to the notice of the court the name of an officer, who, whether in his reg. or on the general staff of the army, has invariably merited the approbation of his superiors. Recent circumstances, I am commanded to observe, have induced government to establish it as a rule, not to publish in general orders the merits of officers when not decidedly of a military nature, otherwise the approbation of his lordship in council of your acknowledged services in the commissariat would have been conveyed to you through that medium.

(Signed)   " W. CASEMENT, Sec. Mil. Depart."

LIEUT.-COL. GABRIEL RICHARD PENNY.

(Bengal Establishment.)

THIS officer was appointed a cadet on the Bengal establishment in 1798; ensign, Nov. 1, 1799; lieut. Nov. 17, 1799; capt. Jan. 2, 1806; maj. Jan. 25, 1815; and lieut.-col. Nov. 12, 1820. He was present at the three memorable actions of Delhi, Laswarree, and Deeg; at the sieges of Sasnee, Bidzergur, Cutchoura, Allygurh, Agra, Deeg, Burtpore, Hattrass, and Asseerghur. He was severely wounded at Burtpore. In 1808 he volunteered on foreign service, and was present at both campaigns against the power of Nepaul.

LIEUTENANT-COLONEL THOMAS GARNER.

(Bengal Establishment.)

This officer was appointed a cadet in 1795. In July 1796 he volunteered his services for the taking of the Dutch fleet at Saldanah Bay, Cape of Good Hope; on which occasion he, with others, received the thanks of Maj.-Gen. Sir James Craig, K. B. In 1798 Lieut. Garner proceeded with his reg. (the 1st European on the Bengal establishment,) which formed part of the army under Sir James Craig, employed to check the expected invasion of Zemaun Shaw, King of Cabul. In 1799, having been posted to the 16th reg. N. I., Lieut. G. was employed with a detachment under Maj. Lally, in escorting the assassin Mirza Vizier Ally (Ex-Nabob of Oude) to Calcutta, when he, with others, received the thanks of the Gov.-Gen., Marquess Wellesley. In 1801 Lieut. G. was appointed assist. regulating officer at Bhajepoor, a station of trust and importance; in which he, on different occasions, obtained the approbation of his superiors. In Sept. 1805, having been previously posted to the 22d reg. N. I., he obtained the rank of capt. and in 1815 that of maj., when he joined the army under Sir David Ochterlony, destined for the subjection of the Nepaulese: on this occasion Maj. G. had the honour to command the advance guard of the army through the Saul Forest, in Feb. 1816.

Peace being concluded by Sir David Ochterlony at Muckwanpoor, the thanks of government, as also of the British parliament, were voted to the army; and Maj. G. was soon after appointed to command the 1st batt. 22d reg., ordered to check the Pindarries with the Nerbudda field force. In Nov. 1817, this batt. under Maj. G., after a long and severe march of sixty miles in thirty hours, arrived in company with a detachment of the 6th N. C. at Nagpore, in time to prevent a second attack on the gallant remains of Col. Scott's small force. On the 16th Dec. following, at the memorable attack of the enemy's batteries near the town of Nagpore, in which upwards of eighty pieces of cannon were taken, the corps under Maj. G. bore a conspicuous part, and received the warm thanks of the officer commanding the force. Maj. G. was afterwards named in terms of high approbation in the orders issued by the Com.-in-Chief, and published by government.

Whilst on this service, the corps which Maj. G. commanded had in killed and wounded upwards of ninety officers and men.

In 1820 this officer proceeded to Europe on furlough for the benefit of his health; and early in the year 1821, after a service of twenty-four years, he was promoted to the rank of lieut.-col.

MAJOR JAMES ATKINSON.

(Bengal Establishment.)

This officer was appointed a cadet on the Bengal establishment in 1780; he arrived at Madras 5th Jan. 1781, and joined the army, then taking the field, under Sir Eyre Coote, against Hyder Ally. He served as a volunteer to the end of the first campaign, and then sailed for Calcutta, where, on his arrival, he found he had been promoted lieut. 25th July 1781, (H. M.'s corresponding commission, 9th July 1783.) He was posted to the 11th N. I. then in the field, and six months after appointed adjut., in which capacity he served fifteen years. He commanded the above corps for nine months, every officer above him being killed in an action with the Rohillas in 1794. He obtained the brevet of capt. Jan. 7, 1796; a capt. lieutenantcy, Sept. 10, 1798; capt. by brevet, Jan. 7, 1796, and regimentally, July 31, 1799.

On the army being new modelled, he was appointed adjut. and quart.-mast. to the 10th N. I., which composed part of a subsidiary force sent to Hyderabad. After reducing the fourteen batts. in the service of the Nizam, commanded and officered by Frenchmen, the reg. joined the forces proceeding to Seringapatam, under the command of Gen. Harris; and Capt. Atkinson served as dep. quar.-mast.-gen. in the division commanded by Col. Wellesley; and at the storming of Seringapatam, 4th May 1799, he commanded a flank company.

Capt. Atkinson commanded the escort of the late Admiral Sir Home Popham's embassy to the Arab states in 1801-2: he continued in that situation eleven months, and then returned to Bengal. In 1803, his health being seriously injured, he repaired to England on a furlough of three years. He was promoted to a majority Sept. 21, 1804.

In Aug. 1803 Maj. Atkinson offered his services, through the Court of Directors, for any situation in which government might think proper to employ him, wherein he might be serviceable to the state, then threatened with invasion by Buonaparte.

Maj. Atkinson retired from the Company's service Aug. 16, 1805, his constitution being too much impaired to admit of his returning to India.

MAJOR JAMES EYLES.

(Bombay Establishment.)

THIS officer was appointed a cadet on the Bombay establishment in 1788: he arrived in India 1st Sept. 1799, and 31st Dec. following received a commission as lieut.-fireworker in the Bombay art.; he attained the rank of capt. 6th Sept. 1797, and of maj. in 1811.

In Jan. 1791 Lieut. Eyles accompanied the army under Sir Robert Abercromby to the reduction of Cananore; from thence through the Coorg Ghauts and country to Periapatam, and in the subsequent retreat to Malabar. Continuing with Sir Robert's army, he was at the junctions with the grand army at Seringapatam, and in the action fought with the Bombay troops, (better known by the name of the duck fight.) From this period he remained in Malabar, and was employed with the field brigade under Col. Crawfurd, 75th, stationed for the protection of the Dutch settlement of Cochin. He was subsequently appointed adjut. of the batt. of art. at the presidency, which situation having held for about a year, he relinquished for the command of the art. at Palicaudcherry; but he was almost immediately recalled from that station to accompany the art. with the Bombay division, against Columbo, and to which art. he was appointed adjut. He was present at the reduction of Columbo and Point de Galle; and remained nearly a year in Ceylon with this detachment, when it returned to Malabar.

This officer was immediately after sent on the Cotiote service, under Maj. Anderson, in command of the art.; and on Col. Dow assuming the command, with an increased force, this officer was appointed dep. com. of stores, and subsequently held the additional staff situation of sec. to the commanding officer. On the termination of this service he was recalled to the command of the art. at Palicaudcherry; from whence he was withdrawn to join the army under Gen. Stuart in the Mysore war, and again appointed adj. to the art. in the field. He was present at the siege and reduction of Seringapatam, and returned with the Bombay army to Malabar. In the following season he accompanied the division under Col. Sartorius, which marched to take possession of Mangalore and Canara, but Jemaulabad, or Jemaulghur, holding out, he was employed in the batteries to reduce it. This place was subsequently taken by a rebel named Timnaick, and the subject of this memoir was at its second reduction employed in command of the art. On that army returning to garrison and cantonment, he was appointed dep. com. of stores in Canara; but on that province passing under the government of Fort St. George, the appointment was abolished, and this officer succeeded to the command of the art. both in Malabar and Canara. From this situation he was removed to Bombay, and embarked on board one of the Company's ships, with a detachment of art. as a reinforcement, employed to protect the Peishwa on his flight from Poonah, when he proceeded by water from Bancoot to Bassien. Shortly after this officer joined the troops under Col. Murray to the northward, and after serving two campaigns he returned to Bombay, on being appointed commissary of ordnance and stores under that presidency.

The state of Maj. Eyles's health did not allow of his completing the full period of twenty-two years service, when he was compelled to quit on sick certificate. The 6th Feb. 1812 he was placed on the retired list.

LIEUTENANT-COLONEL THOMAS GIBSON.

(Bombay Establishment.)

APPOINTED a cadet on the Bombay establishment 13th March 1781, and sailed from England in the Nassau in June following, but the ship being driven back by stress of weather, this officer did not arrive in Bombay till the 5th Sept. 1782; from which date he became an ensign. By the system then existing, he was led to expect the rank of lieut., but the low state of the Company's finances obliged the government to reduce the lieuts. in each batt. of N. I. from eleven to six, making the total number of lieuts. seventy-five less than the former complement; by which means there were many supernumeraries, and the promotion of Ens. Gibson was retarded more than five years. In 1793 he returned to England, for the benefit of his health; and his constitution being much impaired, he did not arrive in India the second time till March 1797. In 1796 he was promoted to the rank of capt. by brevet, having served fifteen years, which commission was consequently dated 13th March in that year; he was appointed capt.-lieut. in 1797; regimental capt. early in 1798; maj. in 1803;

and lieut.-col. 25th Feb. 1807. He retired from the service, on the full pay of his rank, 5th July 1811.

Lieut.-Col. Gibson's services in the field are—three campaigns against the Nairs, in the woody countries Cotiote and Wynaad; the first in 1797, the second in 1803.

LIEUTENANT-COLONEL HENRY H. PEPPER.

(Madras Establishment.)

In 1797 this officer was appointed to the Madras establishment; he arrived in India in 1799, and joined the 1st batt. 13th reg. at Trichinopoly; he was removed to the 1st batt. 3d reg. in the following year, and which formed part of the southern field detachment; he was present at the repulse and storm of the fort of Pandellumchorchy, and at each of the affairs which took place in that campaign; he served under Maj.-Gen. Wellesley, and Col. Wallace, the whole of the Mahratta campaigns of 1802, 3, and 4; in the latter he was promoted to capt., and was present at the various battles and storms, with the exception of the battle of Assaye, at which period he was detached with three companies of the batt., and formed part of Capt. Baynes's detachment, employed in escorting supplies from Ahmednuggur to the general's camp. In 1804-5 he was attached to the British resident's escort, with Dowlut Rao Scindia; in 1806-7 he was appointed inspector of Poligar forts in the southern division, and in 1808 returned to his corps: he was on field service, and in command of five companies of the corps, during the Travancore war in 1809, and present at the storming of the lines, and battles of Negra Coil; in 1810 and 1811 he was quartered at Bangalore and Seringapatam; in 1812 on field service, and in command of the flank companies of the corps during the disturbance in the province of Wynaad, and present at the relief of the Sultaun battery. Towards the close of 1812, and until 1814, the light troops were formed and drilled at Bangalore; in the latter year the batt. was removed to Wallajahbad. This officer embarked with his corps at Madras towards the close of 1814, and landed near Genjam, to be employed on a particular service in that district, but which terminated the day the corps landed. In 1815 he joined, with his regiment, the army under the Com.-in-Chief on the banks of the Toombuddra river, after a march of 800 miles; ten days after its joining the army it was broken up, but at which period this officer was promoted to the rank of maj. and removed to the 2d batt. of the reg.; he joined it on its march to Madras, where the corps remained till towards the close of 1816, when it left the presidency for field service in the Guntoor districts, and performed a march of sixty-eight miles within thirty hours, after making ten days marches at the rate of twenty-miles per day; and succeeded in arriving at a populous village two hours before 5000 Pindarries made their appearance, whose scouts, after reconnoitering the place, returned to the body of Pindarries: they immediately moved off, and were pursued for two days, when they quitted the Company's territories, and entered the Nizam's country.

In 1817 Maj. Pepper obtained the command of the troops in the Guntoor and Paulnaud districts, and had a line of 130 miles to protect, in order to prevent the Pindarries entering this part of the Company's dominions. In 1818 he made forced marches with the troops, in order to join Gen. Lang's division, encamped on the banks of the Toombuddra river, a distance of 500 miles. On the monsoon setting in the principal part of the troops returned to cantonment, and Maj. Pepper was left in command of a detachment on the banks of that river. When the detachment was ordered into quarters, he was removed to the command of the 1st batt. 3d reg. stationed at Jaulnah, and forming part of the Hyderabad subsidiary force, which suddenly moved from Jaulnah; he joined it near Ellichpoor, and shortly afterwards was placed in command of a brigade, with instructions to push on to Nagpoor, and place himself under the orders of the British

Resident, who directed him to serve under Col. Scott, C. B. commanding the Nagpoor subsidiary force, which force moved early in 1819, in order to co-operate with the Bengal divisions, under Col. Adams, C. B., for the purpose of attacking the Ex-Rajah of Nagpoor, who had taken up a position at Putchamarry; and on moving the divisions towards him he fled for the Hill fort of Asseerghur. Maj. Pepper was put in command of a detachment, with orders to pursue and destroy any of his followers, or Arabs, that he might fall in with: the force returned to Nagpoor in 1820, and this officer was directed to proceed with his corps to the Powny districts, about 50 miles east of Nagpoor, in order to attack and disperse the Goonds, who had assembled in that district, and where he remained three months and then returned to Nagpoor. The rebel chief shortly afterwards gave himself up to the civil power.

Maj. Pepper being at this period attacked with fever, he proceeded on a sick certificate for six months to Masulipatam, from thence by sea to Madras, and from thence returned to Nagpoor: this was the first time he was absent from his corps or duty. In 1821 he was promoted to the rank of Lieut.-Col. and the batt. was relieved, and ordered to proceed to Pallamcottah, a distance of 1100 miles, and from thence to Wallajahbad.

MAJOR CHARLES STEWART.

(Bengal Establishment.)

THIS officer commenced his military career in the Warwickshire militia, in which reg. he was appointed an ensign, 1st Sept. 1779, and immediately joined it at Coxheath camp. In Nov. he marched with the corps to Lincoln, and in the following summer was again encamped on Triptree heath, in Essex; at the end of the summer the reg. was ordered to Chelmsford, where Ensign Stewart acted for some time as adjutant.

On the 4th Jan. 1801 he was appointed, through the interest of Lord Hertford, a cadet for Bengal, and on the 13th March he left England, in the fleet under the command of Commodore Johnstone; the ship in which he embarked, (the Hinchinbrooke) after being severely injured, and a fourth of the crew killed or wounded, was taken by the French fleet in Porto Praya bay, island of St. Jago; but was retaken on the following day by the English fleet.

On passing the Cape of Good Hope, the Hinchinbrooke parted from the fleet in a gale of wind, and owing to several adverse circumstances did not reach her destination till May 1782, when Mr. Stewart was immediately appointed to an ensigncy in the 2d European reg. stationed at Caunpoor, and during her voyage up the Ganges was promoted to the rank of lieut. In 1783 he was removed to the 34th batt. N. I.; and upon the reduction of that corps was, at the recommendation of his commanding officer, Maj. Wm. Macleary, appointed adj. of the 4th reg. N. I., just then arrived from Bombay. He shortly after joined at Futtehgurh, and in the cold weather of the year 1784 marched with the army, under the command of Sir John Cummings, to Anopsheher, to prevent the Mahrattas from crossing the Ganges. In the end of 1785 the 4th reg. marched from Futtehgurh to Dacca, and in consequence of the great reduction of the army, was reduced to the 4th batt.

After a residence of two years at Dacca, the 4th batt. marched to Dinapore, and in the subsequent years to the stations of Jionpoor, Chunar, Benares, Caunpoor, Lucknow, Futtehgurh; and in the early part of 1794 reached the Presidency.

On the 8th Jan. 1796, he was promoted to the brevet rank of capt.: he some months after resigned the adjutantcy, which he had held for twelve years, and was removed to the 2d batt. 5th reg. N. I. commanded by his brother-in-law, Lieut.-Col. J. Mackenzie, then stationed at Caunpoor.

In the end of 1797 he was appointed adjut. and quart.-mast. to the

6th reg. N. I. at Futtehgurh, and acted for some time as dep.-quart.-mast.-gen. at that station. In the early part of the following year he marched with the army, under Sir James Craig, to Lucknow, for the purpose of deposing Vizier Ally, and of placing the Nabob Saadet Ally on the Musnud. In the end of the year 1798 he marched under the command of Maj.-Gen. Robert Stuart, to Rampoora in Rohilcund, for the purpose of settling the affairs of that district. In 1799, in consequence of the levelling of the Bengal army, Capt. Stewart was transferred to the 11th reg. quartered at Midnapore, and on 31st July promoted to the regimental rank of capt. in the 1st batt. In 1800 he proceeded with the above-mentioned corps to Sultanpoor, in the province of Oude. In 1801 the 11th reg. was stationed at Caunpoor, and in the end of that year he marched with the 1st batt. to Etaweh, on the banks of the Jumna, which was then ceded by the Nabob to the British.

In the beginning of 1802 Lieut.-Col. M. Symes, of H. M. 76 reg. joined the army at Caunpoor, and was very shortly after appointed by the Gov.-Gen., ambassador to the court of Ava. On this occasion the Col. requested that Capt. Stewart might be appointed to the command of the escort, to consist of two companies from the Native corps, at the Presidency. He was also nominated second member of the embassy, and in case of accident, to succeed Col. Symes. The embassy sailed from Calcutta, in May 1802, and after a stormy voyage reached Rangoon in June, and from thence proceeded to the capital, Ummerapoor. In Feb. 1803 the embassy returned to Calcutta, and in the following month Capt. Stewart was appointed, by the Marquess Wellesley, assist. professor of the Persian language, in the college of Fort William. During part of the time he was attached to the college, he was also aid-de-camp to Maj.-Gen. Cameron, commanding at the Presidency, and subsequently aid-de-camp to Mr. Udny, who for some months acted as Governor. Capt. Stewart continued in the college till Feb. 1806, when he embarked for Europe; and immediately on his arrival in London was appointed Professor of Oriental Languages, in the

East India College, Hertfordshire. On the 12th of June 1807, he was promoted to a majority, and in Aug. of the following year retired upon the pension of his rank, having served the East India Company twenty-six years and a half.

LIEUTENANT-COLONEL SAMUEL WOOD, C. B.

(Bengal Establishment.)

This officer was appointed a cadet of infantry, on the Bengal establishment, the latter end of 1780: he sailed from England with Commodore Johnstone's fleet, 13th March 1781, and was in the engagement between the French and English fleets at Porto Praya, and formed part of the forces under Gen. Medows, for the attack of the Cape of Good Hope, which was afterwards abandoned by that officer. He arrived in India in March 1782, was then promoted to ensign, and immediately joined Gen. Goddard's detachment, at that time on actual service on the western coasts. He was promoted lieut. in July 1782, and served with the above detachment till the peace with the Mahrattas, in Nov. 1783, when he marched with the army across the peninsula to Bengal, where on its arrival the whole of the troops composing it received the particular thanks of the Gov.-Gen. in council, and Com.-in-Chief, and the commissioned officers were assured of a prior claim to the favour and patronage of Government. In Jan. 1796 he was promoted to capt. In 1799 he served with the force assembled at Goorackpoor, under Gen. Stuart, for the purpose of proceeding against Vizier Ally, who had collected a large body near Betool, which, after two slight attacks, was completely dispersed, and Vizier Ally obliged to fly with a few horsemen for refuge to the fort of Jeypoor.

Capt. Wood commanded the 1st batt. 12th reg. N. I. at the assault of the town of Agra, 11th Oct. 1803, when the place was carried; he also commanded the batt. in the trenches, during the siege of the fortress of Agra, until that place capitulated. On both occasions the whole of the troops employed, received the thanks of Lord Lake, the Com.-in-Chief. He commanded the same batt. at the battle of Laswarree, 1st Nov. 1803, when the enemy were completely defeated, and the whole of their artillery, 75 pieces of cannon, captured; and which this officer had the honour to escort in safety from the field of battle, a distance of 65 miles, through the enemy's country, and deposit in the fort of Agra. In Dec. 1803 he was appointed to a new-raised reg. the 22d N. I., and ordered by the Com.-in-Chief to discipline and bring it forward as speedily as possible; and he had the honour to report the whole reg. fit for any service, in less than six months from the time the men first had a musket put into their hands. In Aug. 1804 he was ordered to proceed with the 1st batt. 22d reg., and take the command of the fort of Allygurh, in which station he continued upwards of twelve months, and preserved that important place, under circumstances of extreme difficulty and impending danger, the fort being, when he took the responsibility of it, entirely unprovided with provision, the whole district in a state of rebellion, and the city of Coel, from whence supplies for the garrison had always been obtained, shortly afterwards given up by its rebellious inhabitants to the enemy, and taken possession of by the troops of Jeswunt Rao Holkar. Thus circumstanced, and with a force not amounting to 400 rank and file, (having been obliged to detach four companies of his batt. on another service) and unprovided with public money, he retained possession of the fort, having, by the greatest exertions, and by making use of private money, procured supplies for the garrison.

With a force not exceeding in rank and file 400, and a small detachment of art., he stormed and carried the city of Coel, when opposed by a body of 2000 horse and foot of Holkar's, and its rebellious inhabitants. This event took place 22d Sept. 1804, when the town was declared subject to military law, and, as well as the fort, placed under Capt. Wood's jurisdiction; and although the district was twice invaded, once by Holkar, and once by Ameer Khan, during the time he held these posts, which was more than twelve months after he retook the town, he was so fortunate as to retain them till there was no longer any apprehension for their safety.

On the 5th June 1805 he was promoted to a majority; and the latter end of that year, having been relieved from the charge of Allygurh, was ordered with his batt. to join the force assembled under Gen. Dowdeswell, for the purpose of proceeding to take a position on the northern frontier of the Dooaub, to intercept Jeswunt Rao Holkar, should he endeavour to escape with his army by that way. Upon the breaking-up of Gen. Dowdeswell's detachment, he was ordered with the 1st reg. N. C. and 1st batt. 22d N. I., to occupy the frontier station of Saharunpoor; and, in addition to this force, had two batts. of the Begum Sumroo's, with their artillery, placed under his immediate command. Here he remained till Sept. following; and, on quitting the command, received the following letter from the officers of the detachment:—

" SIR,—About to leave Saharunpoor, you are not permitted to depart without a recorded testimony of our extreme satisfaction with your public conduct whilst in command of the detachment, and of our deep regret at the loss of your society. The expression of sentiments we all so sensibly feel, it would be unjust to withhold; to yourself the conveyance of them, we hope, will be a source of some little gratification. We offer you our ardent wishes for honour and happiness, in compliance with the dictates of sincerity; and remain, Sir,
" Your most obliged and faithful servants,
(Signed by every Officer of the Detachment.)
" *Saharunpoor, Sept. 29, 1806.*"

On the 29th Aug. 1809 Maj. Wood commanded the 1st batt. 22d

reg. at the storming of Bohwanny. Shortly after this he was ordered to join the force under the present Sir Gabriel Martindell, assembled in Bundlecund the latter end of 1809, to oppose Ameer Khan, which advanced into Malwah in Jan. 1810, and co-operated with a large force from Madras under, the late Sir Barry, Col. Close. For this service the whole of the troops received the thanks of Sir George Hewett, then Com.-in-Chief in India. On the 11th March 1811 this officer was promoted to lieut.-col. He continued to serve with the army in the field until the bad state of his health, and a lameness which rendered him incapable of mounting his horse, obliged him to return to England, where he arrived the beginning of Aug. 1814; and in Sept. 1816 he retired from the service on the full-pay of his rank.

Lieut.-Col. Wood was appointed a Companion of the Bath on the extension of that Order.

MAJOR PATRICK CAMERON.

(Madras Establishment.)

This officer was appointed a cadet in 1802, and cornet April 27, 1803: he arrived in India 2d Jan. 1804, and was promoted to lieut. 28th Oct. of the same year; quart.-mast. in Feb. 1809; capt. Nov. 4, 1814; and maj. Sept. 1, 1818. He served in the campaigns of 1805, 6, 7, 8, 9, and 10, under the late Cols. Wallace and Close, and in the Mahratta war of 1817-18 with Maj.-Gen. Sir Lionel Smith's division of the Deccan army, in pursuit of his highness the late Peishwa, and subsequently with Sir John Doveton's division, which terminated the campaign. He was present at the cavalry affair with Sookareem, near Pepulgaum in Berar, in Dec. 1805, and at the battle of Ashtee, Feb. 20, 1818.

MAJOR-GENERAL MALCOLM GRANT.

(Bombay Establishment.)

In 1776, at a very early age, this officer was appointed a cadet on the Bombay establishment. In 1779 he served with a corps opposed to the Mahrattas during the war in support of Ragonath Rao. In 1780 and 1781 he served at the siege of Bassien, and with the Bengal army under Gen. Goddard. From 1781 to the conclusion of the Mahratta war he was employed in the enemy's districts of Bassien, and at Terrapore, Maughaum, Mandeire, Danoo, Omerghaum, Belalghur, Underghur, &c., and afterwards under Gen. Macleod in Malabar. In 1788 he repaired on furlough to England. On his return to India he was employed from 1792 to 1798 in Malabar, at that period in a very disturbed and unsettled state. In 1799, on breaking out of the war with Tippoo Sultaun, he commanded the Bombay grenadier batt., forming part of the force sent from Bombay, under Col. Little, to co-operate with the Mahrattas. This force being ultimately obliged to retire from the Mahratta territories, Maj.-Gen. Grant's (then Maj. Grant) corps embarked at Jayghur, and pushed forward by sea, by way of Cananore and the Poodycherum Ghauts, to join the grand army under Gen. (now Lord) Harris; and having reached Sidapoor on the river Cavery in the Coorgah country, returned, on the capture of Seringapatam, to Malabar, with the army under Gen. James Stuart, and was immediately employed in taking possession of Mangalore and the province of Canara, and at the siege of the fortress of Jemaulabad. In 1800 he returned to Malabar, then in rebellion: in 1804 he suceeeded Col. John Montresor in the command of Malabar and Canara, the former province being still in open rebellion. In Dec. 1804, Madras troops from Mysore were ordered to relieve the Bombay troops in Malabar and Canara; this relief having taken place, Maj.-Gen. (then Col.) Grant, on his passage to Bombay, having received reinforcements of a detachment of art. battering cannon, howitzers, and stores from the presidency, landed on the coast of Concan, with about 3000 men under his immediate command, and, in pursuance to orders from government, reduced the important fortress of Savendroog, and its dependencies, then held, as Gen. Sir Barry Close expressed himself, by " the wily and atrocious rebel Hurry Bellal." For this service Maj.-Gen. Grant received the entire approbation of government, of Lieut.-Gen. Oliver Nicolls, Com.-in-Chief, of the late Gen. Sir Barry Close, British minister at the court of Poonah, and of his highness the Peishwa. In 1807, this officer being in extreme ill health, and his constitution greatly impaired, returned to England.

The following are the dates of this officer's commissions: Ens. 20th Nov. 1777; lieut., 1st May 1780; capt., 1st Dec. 1790; major, 15th Jan. 1796; lieut.-col., 6th March 1800; lieut.-col. commandant of a reg. of N. I. 1st. Oct. 1809; col., 25th July 1810; and maj.-gen., 4th June 1813.

MAJOR MICHAEL RIDDELL.

(Madras Establishment.)

THIS officer commenced his career in India in 1804; he was present at the suppression of the mutiny at Velore in July 1806; and at the commencement of 1809 was ordered to Bombay, and joined a detachment of cavalry destined (with about 2000 other troops) for Persia, under the orders of Maj.-Gen. Sir John Malcolm: circumstances, however, occurring to render the expedition unnecessary, it was broken up, and the Madras troops sent back to their own presidency. As soon as this measure was determined on, Maj. Riddell sailed from Bombay to England for the recovery of his health: in 1812 he returned to Madras, and from that period until the fall of the fortress of Asseerghur in 1819, he was either actually in the field, or on a frontier station, liable to move at a moment's notice. The 7th reg. of cavalry, to which he belonged, was with Sir John Doveton, who commanded the Hyderabad subsidiary force, in all the excursions and harassing movements after the Pindarries in 1815-16.

An idea of the fatigue the troops underwent in this desultory warfare, may be formed by the description of a march executed by a squadron of cavalry under Maj. Riddell's command in April 1816. He received orders from Gen. Doveton to make for a certain point, distant about thirty miles from the camp, and to endeavour to obtain information of a body of Pindarries, expected in the direction of the Adjuntah pass, near to which the British were encamped: he marched at seven o'clock at night, and on the road received various reports of their approach, which he transmitted to the Gen.; but on reaching the point to which he was ordered, all traces of them were lost; for, in fact, they had passed on some miles distant from the camp before this officer received instructions to quit it. In about half an hour a trooper made his appearance, with an order for his immediate return; the squadron accordingly retraced its steps, and found the force had moved six miles beyond its former ground. On approaching the camp, about ten in the morning, Maj. Riddell received directions to remain two miles from camp, as an outlying squadron: in a short time after he was desired to join the force; and on his arrival, at two o'clock in the afternoon, he found the whole cavalry mounted, and had only time to take up his position in the line, when this force moved off, marched twenty-five miles, found the enemy gone, rested two hours, and came back to their original ground, twenty-five miles more, by ten next morning,—making a distance of 116 miles in 39 hours. When the Mahratta war broke out in 1817, the 7th reg. was ordered to Maj.-Gen. Pritzler's division, and Maj. Riddell was present at the different affairs with the enemy's cavalry, until the junction of the division with that of the Bombay army commanded by Maj.-Gen. Lionel Smith. The cavalry of both divisions being placed under the latter officer, it encountered and defeated the whole of the Peishwa's force at Ashtey, which occasioned the surrender of the Sattarah Rajah and family. A short time afterwards, a distribution of the cavalry between Maj.-Gens. Doveton and Smith, placed the 7th reg. under the command of the former officer, with whom Maj. Riddell continued until the fall of Asseerghur, in April 1819.

The following are the dates of this officer's commissions: Cornet, 18th July 1804; lieut., 21st Feb. 1808; capt. 7th Sept. 1811; and major, 15th July 1819.

MAJOR G. J. GILLESPIE.

(Madras Establishment.)

This officer was appointed a cadet in Feb. 1797, and arriving at Madras in Aug. 1798, was promoted to an ensigncy, and appointed to the 2d batt. 11th reg. N. I. then ordered on field service, and forming a part of the force assembled at Begoarah, on the banks of the Kistna, under Col. (now L.-Gen.) Roberts, for the purpose of destroying the French force and influence at Hyderabad; which being effected in Oct. and every thing adjusted, the Hyderabad detachment, as it was then called, received orders to march to the Carnatic, to join the army under Gen. (now Lord) Harris, which was then forming for the siege of Seringapatam; that object having been attained, Ensign Gillespie (who was removed to the cavalry during the march of the army to Seringapatam, but who continued to do duty with the 11th N. I. during the siege) joined the 2d reg. of cav., then composing part of the detachments under Cols. Stevenson and James Dalrymple, employed against the noted freebooter Doondia. On the 10th of Sept. the latter officer, after some hard marching, came up with, and attacked the whole of Doondia's force, with the 1st and 2d regs. of cav., and succeeded in defeating him with great loss. Doondia, however, continued to collect the remains of his army, which obliged Col. S., who joined after the action on the 10th, with the 4th cav., to push after him again; and Doondia was compelled to take refuge in the Mahratta country. Col. S., although within a few hundred yards of the enemy's army, declined then attacking it, and returned to the Mysore country. All prospect of further active service in the field being at an end, Ens. Gillespie was ordered to proceed to Bangalore to join the 4th reg. cav., to which he had been removed in Sept. 1799, and promoted to a lieutenantcy. He was employed on detached duty till May 1800, when the 4th reg. was again ordered on field service against Doondia, which terminated in Sept. following by the defeat of the enemy, and death of the freebooter.

Lieut. Gillespie next accompanied the 4th reg. into the ceded districts, first composing part of a detachment under Col. Monnypenny, and afterwards with the force under Gen. D. Campbell. This force was actively employed till the beginning of 1803 in attacking many Poligar forts, &c. in these districts; and in Feb. of that year the 4th was ordered to form part of the army under the present Duke of Wellington, for the purpose of attacking Scindia, who then meditated the subversion of the Peishwa. The battles of Assaye and Argaum followed, in which the Madras troops were engaged. Lieut. Gillespie, however, had the misfortune, from a very severe kick from a horse, to be with the rear-guard of the army on the day of the former battle.

Peace having been concluded with the Mahrattas in the end of 1803, the 4th cav., in Sept. 1804, returned to the Carnatic, when it was again ordered on field service, with a detachment under Col. Monnypenny, against the Chitore Poligars. This service closed in March 1805, by the capture of the Rajah, and his execution put a period to the troubles in that part of the country.

The 4th now went into cantonments at Conatore, near Arnee, to refit in men, horses, and appointments. In July 1806 the 4th were employed in the suppression of the mutiny at Velore; and in Dec. it was again ordered to march, and early in 1807 formed part of a light detachment under Col. Bowness, employed to escort the Peishwa on a pilgrimage to Sundoor, but the real object was to attack, if necessary, the numerous rabble of horse and foot who accompanied his highness, and whose licentious habits could only be kept in check by the dread of punishment.

Early in 1808 the 4th again took the field, and joined the Bombay army in the Deccan under Col. Wallace, employed against Mayputram and Sookah Roodur; that service detained the reg. in the field till June 1808, when it went into cantonment at Jalnah. A marauder, by name Wyud Ally Cawn Bunguish, started up in Nov. of that year, and after a short but active service, the detachment under Col. Doveton, of which the 4th composed a part, succeeded in destroying his whole party, and, aided by the people of the country, in taking him prisoner: his force was surprised by the 4th and 8th cav., and a corps of flankers from the infantry, after a march of 120 miles. In March 1809 the troops returned into cantonment at Jalnah, and at the end of the year again took the field with the army under Gen. Close, against Meer Cawn, who then plundered the Peishwa's territories in the neighbourhood of Bundlecund. No event of any consequence occurred in this service, and matters being adjusted with the chieftains, the 4th went into quarters at Hyderabad in June 1810; where it remained till Oct. 1812, when it marched for Cuttack, to cover that and the Gauzam provinces from an expected visit from the Pindarries, but as they did not make their appearance, the 4th were ordered to Arcot, where they arrived in July 1313. The remainder of the latter, and part of the following year, were passed in recruiting and refitting the reg.; and in Aug. 1814 Maj. G. was appointed paymaster of Trichinopoly, where he continued till Oct. 1819, when he was, for the second* time, promoted to the rank of maj., and rejoining the 4th

---

* In consequence of casualties in the army, and the dismissal of the present Lieut.-Col. Lushington from the service during the disturbances in the Madras army in 1809, Major G. was promoted to the rank of Major in April 1812; but on the restoration of Lieut.-Col.

cav. at Bangalore, commanded it from Feb. 1820, till he left India, in consequence of ill health, in Jan. 1822.

During the above period of service Maj. G. was occasionally employed in leading attacking parties against small forts, and selected for the command of light detachments in the field; he was adj. to the 4th cav. from Sept. 1802 till Aug. 1805; he held the temporary command of a cav. brig. both in the field and in cantonment, and obtained the thanks of Sir S. Achmuty and Sir John Abercrombie, Coms.-in-Chief, and of Gen. Hare, as well as the approbation of other officers, under whose command he served. Maj. Gillespie has received the Seringapatam medal.

MAJOR HORACE DURAND.

(Madras Establishment.)

This officer entered the service of the East India Company in 1793; he served at the last siege of Pondicherry, in 1795-6; and was present at the capture of Malacca, Amboyna, Banda, and their dependencies. In 1811 he accompanied the expedition under Sir Samuel Achmuty, and was at the reduction of the Dutch settlements in the island of Java.

The dates of Maj. Durand's commissions are—Ens. 1793; lieut. 29th Nov. 1797; capt.-lieut., 27th June 1804; capt., 21st. Sept. 1804; brev.-maj. 4th June 1814; maj., 19th July 1817.

Lushington to the service by the Court of Directors, the local government of Madras thought fit to cancel Maj. Gillespie's commission, after his having held it nearly for a year and a half, and during that time in the command of the reg. on active service against the Pindarries.

LIEUTENANT-COLONEL ARTHUR GIBBINGS.

(Madras Establishment.)

This officer, after passing through the different gradations of military rank, attained that of Lieut.-Col. in the army, 10th Dec. 1800; and was appointed Lieut.-Col. 3d Native Infantry, 13th Jan. 1801. His services commenced in India, in the year 1777, and terminated after the Mysore campaign, in 1800, in which latter year he was compelled to return to Europe for the re-establishment of a constitution impaired to excess, the natural consequence of severe trials encountered during a period of thirteen years' service in the field, and various parts of India; and which finally obliged him, in May 1803, to retire from the service.

LIEUTENANT-GENERAL CHARLES BOYÉ.

(Bombay Establishment.)

This officer was appointed a cadet 4th May 1776; ensign 4th Aug. following; and lieut. 4th Dec. 1779. He was actively employed three campaigns, under Gen. Goddard, Maj. Forbes, and Brig. M'Cloud; at Mangalore, and present at the assault of Cananore. The 18th June 1784 he was promoted to capt.-lieut., and appointed to the command of several Native corps. With this rank he served as Commandant of Tellichery and Surat station. The 8th Sept. 1788 he was promoted to capt., and appointed to the European reg. proceeded to Darwar, and was present at the assault of that fortress in 1793, under Col. Frederick. The 4th June 1793, he was appointed to the command of a local batt. of Sepoys at Surat. The 9th July 1796 he was promoted to maj., and appointed to the command of the 2d batt. 4th reg. N. I. at Bombay. The 28th Dec. 1798 he attained the rank of lieut.-col., and proceeded in command of the 2d batt. 4th reg. N. I. on field service, under Lieut.-Col. John Little, to Jygur, to co-operate with the Mahrattas against Tippoo Sultaun. In April following he was appointed to command a detachment of two batts. of Sepoys; he proceeded to the Malabar coast, and joined Col. Wiseman's brigade in May 1799, and was actively engaged in taking possession of the lower country, and forts on the sea coast, in Canara, from Neelsaram to Sadishgure; he was also employed against Doondia Waugh; and took possession of Hydergur Ghaut. In July following he was appointed to command the district of Cundapoor: in Jan. 1800 he was removed, and appointed to raise the 2d batt. 6th reg. N. I. at Surat, and commanded that garrison. In 1802 he was transferred to the 1st batt. 3d reg. N. I.: he proceeded to Bombay, and obtained the command of a field force, consisting of detachments of H. M. 84th and 88th regts., a company of art., complete field train, 1st batt. 3d reg., and the 1st batt. 7th reg. N.I.; and marched with it to Bassien, under the orders of the late Sir Barry Close, resident with his highness the late Peishwa, Badjee Row. In April following, Col. Murray, H. M.'s 84th reg., succeeded, as senior officer, Lieut.-Col. Boyé in command of the field detachments; with this force Lieut.-Col. B. proceeded to Poonah. He commanded a brigade of N. I. and joined the grand army, under Maj.-Gen. Sir A. Wellesley. At the conclusion of the war with Scindia, and other refractory Mahratta chieftains, Lieut.-Col. Boyé was removed to the 2d batt. 4th reg. N. I.: he proceeded to Goa, and commanded a brigade in the Portuguese dictrict of Salsette. He was removed from the 2d batt. 4th, to the 1st batt. 8th reg., joined that corps at Ahmednuggur, and commanded that district; afterwards proceeded to Poonah, and commanded that station; proceeded with his corps, the 1st batt. 8th reg. N. I. to Surat, and commanded that garrison, till promoted to col. 25 April 1808, when he was appointed Commandant of the 9th reg. N. I. and the garrison of Tanna.

"*G. O. Bombay Castle, 14th Jan.* 1810.

" Col. Charles Boyé, 9th reg. N. I. has the permission of the Gov. in council, to proceed to Europe, on furlough, under the existing regulations. The Gov. in council will have much pleasure in noticing, to the Hon. the Court of Directors, Col. Boyé's long services, in this country; and the zeal and attention with which he has discharged his duties as an officer, in the Hon. Company's employ.

(Signed) " F. WARDEN, Chief Sec·, R. GORDON, Adj.-Gen."

The 4th June 1811 he was promoted to the rank of maj-gen., and on the 4th March 1812 appointed to the staff; in Jan. 1815 he obtained the command of the army at the Presidency of Bombay, with a seat as President of the Military board; and on the 6th Feb. 1816, Lieut.-Gen. Sir M. Nightingall relieved him from the command of the army, agreeably to his appointment from the Court of Directors.

Extract of a Letter from the Gov. in Council, the Rt. Hon. Sir Evan Nepean, Bt. to Maj.-Gen. Boyé.

" SIR,—I have had to repeat more than once, that while you held the command of the army under this Presidency, the duties were performed to my entire satisfaction."

Maj.-Gen. Boyé's limited time of four years on the staff expired on the 6th March 1816; and he was relieved by Maj.-Gen. Lawrence. In Jan. 1820 he proceeded to England on furlough, and the 3d Aug. 1821 was promoted to the rank of lieut.-gen.

LIEUT.-COL. NATHANIEL CUMBERLEGE.

(Bengal Establishment.)

THIS officer entered the service of the East-India Company, before the age of fourteen, in Oct. 1783, just after the peace; and many batts. having been reduced on that occasion, he was not promoted, but remained as a cadet and supernumerary ensign upwards of six years: on coming on the effective strength he was appointed to an European corps, with which he remained for some years. On his promotion to lieut. he joined the 19th batt. N. I., and marched with it to Dacca. In 1797 he applied to be moved into the field, and joined the 7th reg. N. I. at Lucknow. Soon after his arrival he was ordered with two companies to escort treasure to Sir James Craig's army, which was then assembling at Midny Gunje, for the purpose of proceeding to Anopsheher, to arrest the progress of Zemaun Shaw, who was advancing towards Lahore with the avowed intention of restoring the Mussulman government, and extirpating the English. On delivering over the treasure, he was ordered to Caunpoor, to escort art. and stores to the army. On joining Sir James at Anopsheher, news arrived of the massacre at Benares, and the return of Zemaun Shaw to Cabul, which occasioned the breaking-up of the army; and this officer marched down again with Gen. Stuart, under whom a detachment assembled at Gooracpoor, for the purpose of proceeding against Vizier Ally, who had collected a large body near Betool. After some hard marches, and two slight attacks, the body with Vizier Ally dispersed, and he was obliged to fly with a few horsemen towards Jeypoor; on which the detachment returned to cantonments. Immediately after this he was ordered to join the 2d batt. 2d reg. N. I. at Chunar, to which, owing to the new regulations, he had been appointed some time; he accordingly joined the corps early in 1799, and marched with it to Juanpoor, and was appointed acting adjutant. Early in 1800 he was ordered to Sultanpoor, in the Vizier's country, to disband his batts., which having effected, the corps returned, and cantoned at that station. In Oct. 1800 he was appointed adjut. and quart.-mast. to the reg., and directed to join the 1st batt. On his arrival the corps was ordered to proceed to Futtehgurh; and on the march an express arrived to move towards Dalmow Bareily, against an impostor, who had assumed the name of Vizier Ally, and was plundering the country in conjunction with some disaffected Zemindars: after two attacks in the jungles, and the destruction of a fortified village, the enemy were dispersed, and the impostor fled to Lucknow. where he was discovered and taken, having had his thigh broken in the last action. The corps then moved to Futtehgurh. It 1801 it was ordered to the frontier, to a place called Shekoabad, where it was cantoned. In 1802 it was ordered out with a detachment under Col. Blair, to attack some strong forts in the Dooaub, when this officer was appointed brig.-maj. to the detachment, and was the acting staff at the siege of Sarsnee, Bidzergur, Cutchoura, and Tutteah; after the reduction of these forts the detachment broke up, and returned to their respective cantonments. In 1803 he was ordered out with the corps to join Lord Lake, at the commencement of the Mahratta war, and immediately on joining the grand army was again appointed maj. of brigade. He was at the battle of Coil, the storming of Allyghur, the battle of Delhi, the battle of Agra, and the siege of that fortress. On the reduction of the latter, he was ordered in with his corps as quart.-mast. and act. fort adjut., which appointments he held until promoted to capt. in 1804, having been twenty-one years a subaltern. For his services Capt. Cumberlege was repeatedly thanked in public orders by Lord Lake. On his promotion he was appointed by his lordship to the staff, at Dinapore, which appointment he held until 1811, when he was promoted to maj., and again joined his old corps, the 2d batt. 2d reg. N. I. In 1812 he was ordered into Bundlecund, and was employed at the siege of Callinger. At the storming of that fort he had the command of the column of light inf., and was thanked in public orders for his conduct on that day and during the siege; he also received the thanks of the Court of Directors. On the fall of that fortress he returned with his corps to Dinapore. In the latter end of the same year he was again ordered to Bundlecund; and in 1813 he joined Col. Adams, by whom he was ordered up the third range of hills near Chundeeah, to guard the passes against the Pindarries, with a detachment of eleven companies of N. I., art., and pioneers. In May 1813 he returned to Kietah in Bundlecund, having received the thanks of Col. Adams, and a letter from the adj.-

gen., by order of the Com.-in-Chief, approving highly of his conduct in every respect during the period of that command.

The latter end of 1813 he was ordered to Purtabghur, which station he commanded for eighteen months, consisting of his own corps and a reg. of cavalry. In 1814 he was promoted to lieut.-col., and obtained the permanent command of the 2d batt. 2d reg. N. I. In 1816 he was ordered to Muttra, to proceed to Jeypoor, but circumstances prevented the detachment moving to that place; in 1817 he was ordered to Agra: in 1818 he marched to Dhoolpoor, to guard the fords of the Chumbul against the Pindarries.

When the grand army broke up, Lieut.-Col. Cumberlege applied for leave of absence to return home on furlough, having been thirty-five years employed without asking leave of absence. He arrived in England in May 1819. The following letter was addressed to him by the officers of his corps, on his giving up the command:—

"Sir,—On the occasion of our approaching separation, we beg leave to convey to you a testimony of the high estimation in which we have regarded your character, both in public and private life, during the long period you have held the command of the corps to which we belong; and, to commemorate the sentiments of esteem we entertain towards you, we have respectfully to request your acceptance of a sword, to be presented in our name by Capt. John Duncan, in London. To our unfeigned feelings of regret at your departure, we beg leave to add our earnest wishes for your happiness; and bidding you farewell, &c. &c.

(*Signed by every Officer present in the Corps.*)

"*Agra, Aug.* 28, 1818."

LIEUTENANT-COLONEL JOHN JOHNSON, C. B.

(Bombay Establishment.)

On 26th Aug. 1784 this officer arrived at Bombay; and the 31st May 1785 was appointed to an ensigncy in the engineers; in 1790 he joined the Mahratta army, and served at the siege of Darwar; in 1792 he served with the Madras engineers at the siege of Seringapatam, and returned thence as surveyor with the Mahratta army to Poonah. Malabar being given up in 1793, he surveyed the southern half of that province: in 1796 he served at the siege of Cochin, under Col. Petrie; in 1797 he served as senior engineer with the detachments under Cols. Dow and Anderson, in Cotiote; in 1799 he served with the Madras engineers at the siege and storm of Seringapatam, and accompanied the detachment to take possession of the Canara districts, and was at the taking of Aukola and Sadasewghur. In 1800 he acted as engineer and surveyor with the detachments at Goa; and in 1802 he joined Sir A. Wellesley; he was left in charge of the repairs of the fort of Hullihall, and appointed to the command of the pioneers. In 1803 he joined Sir A. Wellesley on his entering the Mahratta country, and acted with his army as senior engineer, surveyor, and in charge of the guides at the attack and capitulation of Ahmednuggur, and storm of Gawelgur: he attended Sir A. Wellesley at the battles of Assaye and Argaum, and the defeat of the Pindarries, Maunkaisur, &c. In 1804 he was attached to the Poonah subsidiary force as dep. quart.-mast.-gen., senior engineer, surveyor, and in charge of the guides, and as such served at the sieges of Chandore and Gaulna. In 1805 he was appointed conservator and surveyor of the timber forests of Canara, which duty he continued till its completion (two years and a half) on crutches, having been severely cut while felling teak timber, and was consequently, in 1808, obliged to proceed to Europe for recovery. The 25th April in this year he obtained the rank of maj., and that of lieut.-col. 4th June 1814. In June 1812 he returned to Bombay, and held the situation of superintending military and civil engineer at the presidency until 1815, when he was appointed quart.-mast.-gen. to the field force under Col. W. East, C. B., with whom he served at the sieges of Aukola, the city and fortress of Booj, and Kutcote. He thence accompanied the force into Okamundel to besiege Dwarka, Bate, and several other fortified places. In the same year he was nominated a Companion of the Bath. In 1816 appointed quart.-mast.-gen. of the Bombay army, and surveyed the mountainous passes of the Deccan.

In 1817 he obtained a furlough, and returned over-land through Persia, Georgia, Russia, Prussia, &c. to England.

The services of Lieut.-Col. Johnson have on several occasions been approved in public orders, of the last of which is the following:—

Extract of a Letter from Colonel Sir A. Wellesley to His Excellency the Governor-General.

"*Camp at Deagaum, Dec. 15, 1803.*

" Capt. Burke, who commanded the art. with the subsidiary force, and Capt. Heilland of the pioneers, and Capt. Johnson of the Bombay engineers, are also entitled to my acknowledgments. The two latter were sent from my division to assist Col. Stevenson. Upon the occasion of mentioning the name of Capt. Johnson, I cannot omit to inform your Excellency, that throughout this campaign that officer has performed the most important service in the department of the guides entrusted to his charge; and I have no doubt but that his surveys will be a valuable public acquisition."

LIEUTENANT COLONEL DAVID FOULIS.

(Madras Establishment.)

THIS officer arrived in India in 1789: he was appointed to an ensigncy 5th Oct. 1790, and attached to the flank company of the 15th batt. N. I., and in the same year entered the enemy's country (Mysore), under the command of Capt. Alex. Phaor, and took possession of several hill forts above the Ghauts. He was appointed cornet in the 3d reg. cav., commanded by Maj. James Stevenson, 23d Sept. 1791, and served under Lord Cornwallis during the whole of the Mysore war. He was present at the siege of Bangalore; at the attack of Tippoo's army, under Lieut.-Col. Floyd, with six regts. of cav., under the walls and guns of Bangalore, on the 6th March 1791; at the siege of Savendroog; at the battle of the Carrygaut hills near Seringapatam, on the 15th of May 1791; and at the blowing-up of the battering train, and retreat of Lord Cornwallis in that year; at the storming of Tippoo's lines and army before Seringapatam, 6th and 7th Feb. 1792, and at the first siege of Seringapatam, and its capitulation. He served in the same reg. in subduing the southern Poligars, with the army under Lieut.-Col. Maxwell, in 1793; was present at the siege of Pondicherry, as a volunteer, in 1794; and made a forced march of 120 miles in two nights and two days, with little intermission, under the command of Maj. Stevenson, who surprised and seized the Rajah of Ramnad in his strong fortress and palace in 1794. In the same year, under Maj. Stevenson, he marched with his corps, dismounted, at night, and seized three of the principal Poligar Rajahs in their beds.

He was promoted to lieut. in the 1st reg. cav. 1st Nov. 1798. He served the whole of the Mysore war, under Gen. Harris, in 1798 and 1799; he was present at the battle of Malavilly, at the 2d siege of Seringapatam, capture and death of Tippoo Sultaun. Lieut. F. received the Seringapatam medal, after the fall of Seringapatam;

Lieut. F. served under Lieut.-Cols. Stevenson and Dalrymple, in several actions and skirmishes with the Mahratta Doondia, who they attacked with 500 cavalry, 3000 stable horse, and drove into the Shekarpoor Nullah, afterwards into the Wurda river, and captured his guns. In this service Lieut. F. was wounded. He was appointed brig.-maj. to the 2d brig. of cav. 26 April 1800, and subsequently aid-de-camp to Col. Stevenson. In 1801 Doondia having again assembled a large force, the British took the field, under the command of Lieut.-Col. Wellesley, and Lieut. F. was at the taking by storm of the forts of Ranny Bednore, Coongul, and Dummel, and at the different affairs and severe marches during that campaign.

He was promoted to capt.-lieut. in the 1st reg. cav. 30th July 1800, and to full capt. in the same reg. 2d Sept. 1801, which rapid promotion was occasioned by the numerous deaths at the unhealthy station of Chitteldroog.

The health of Capt. F. being much impaired, he, in July 1803, sailed for England: and in July 1805 returned to India over land, arriving at Bombay in Oct., by the way of Hussam in Denmark, Lubec, Berlin, Dresden, Prague, Vienna, Buda, Temiswar, Hermanstadt, Buckerest, Verna, embarking on the black sea to Constantinople, cross the Bossphorus to Sentara in Turkey, by Boli, Amaria, Mardin, Drarbekeir, Mosul, and Bagdad; sailing down the Tigris to Bussorah; down the Euphrates to Bashier; down the Persian gulf to Murcatt, and crossing the Arabian sea to Bombay. He was twice cast on shore on the Persian side by a leaky Arab ship.

In April 1807 Capt. F. was appointed general agent for the purchase of remount horses for the Madras cavalry. In Aug. 1809 he again returned to England in bad health, by the way of China, Brazil, and the United States of America. He was promoted to maj. in the 1st reg. light cav. 1st Jan. 1812, and returned to India in Oct. 1813, by Ceylon.

In Nov. 1814, he marched in command of the 1st reg. light cav. to escort his Highness the Peishwa through a part of the Company's dominions, to visit some of the principal places of worship. In

Jan. 1815 he took the field in command of the 1st light cav., under Col. Doveton, and from that time till Nov. 1817 was in constant and harassing marches after the Pindarries in Berar, Candesh, &c.

In 1818 he commanded the Ellore and Masulipatam districts, and a detachment of H. M.'s 86th reg. flank companies, and Native flank, on the frontiers of Palnaud, for the protection of the districts against the Pindarries. In Sept. 1818 he marched with the 1st light cav. to the Carnatic to refit, and commanded Arnee. In the beginning of 1819 he was appointed to the command of the cav. cantonment of Arcot.

He was promoted to lieut.-col. in the 1st light cav. 26th July 1819; and appointed to the command of the 6th light cav. in July 1821.

LIEUTENANT-COLONEL JACOB THOMPSON.

(Bombay Establishment.)

THIS officer was appointed a cadet in Feb. 1777; he arrived at Bombay in Aug. following, and was posted to the art. as a lieut. fireworker 8th Dec. in the same year. In 1778-9 he served with the army which marched into the Deccan, under Brig.-Gen. Egerton, to support the pretensions of Raysbah to the dignity of Peishwa. In March 1779 he was appointed lieut., and shortly after was ordered to Broach, where he did garrison duty till near the end of 1782, when he joined the army which was then formed to act under Brig.-Gen. Matthews, against the dominions of Hyder Ally on the Malabar coast. He was present at all the sieges and engagements which occurred in that campaign, from its commencement with the siege of Onore, till the capture of Mangalore. At the latter place he was left with the command of the art., with instructions to place it, as far as depended upon that department, in a state of defence; and he did duty there during the time it was besieged by Tippoo Sultaun; on which occasion Lieut. T. was wounded. The 24th May 1785 he was appointed capt. In May 1790 he went in command of the art. with Capt. Little's detachment, which served with the army under Parasu Ram Bhow, and was present at all the operations of that army during the war. At the conclusion of the peace, in 1792, he was appointed to the command of the art. on the Malabar coast; and in 1794 removed to Bombay. The 23d June 1794 he was promoted to a majority; at the end of 1798 he was appointed com.-gen. of stores to the army which proceeded from the Malabar coast under Lieut.-Gen. Stuart, to co-operate with that which marched from Madras under Lord Harris, against Seringapatam. Before the army marched, he succeeded to the command of the art. of the Bombay army, and in that capacity served at the siege of that place, and subsequently at the reduction of Jemaulabad, the last fortress in the dominions of Tippoo Sultaun which held out against the English authority. On the breaking up of the army he returned to Bombay, and shortly after left India for Europe on a sick certificate. The 1st of Jan. 1800 he had the brevet of lieut.-col.; and at the end of 1802 he retired from the service.

The approbation of this officer's services by the Gov. and Com.-in-Chief in Bombay, will be seen from the following extract from the minutes of council, dated 16th Jan. 1800:—

"The application from Maj. Thompson of the corps of art., for permission to proceed to Europe with leave, and with the choice of eventually retiring on the pay of his rank, being supported by the prescribed medical and pay certificates, is acquiesced in by the Gov. in council. The Gov. in council on this occasion very willingly subscribes to the Com.-in-Chief's testimony on the professional merits of this officer, whose skill and judgment have been in various circumstances conspicuously and advantageously displayed during the long period he has been employed in the Company's service; and the Board will not fail to notice him to the Court of Directors, as a person deservedly entitled to the public commendation of his superiors."

LIEUTENANT-COLONEL ALEXANDER LAURISTON.

(Bombay Establishment.)

This officer arrived at Bombay 18th Oct. 1778; was appointed to an ensigncy in Dec. 1779; and promoted to lieut. 1st May 1780. He was present at the capture of Porsuk and Calliun; and in 1783 accompanied the troops sent by sea for the relief of Mangalore, a strong fort on the coast of Malabar. That object being accomplished, they were ordered back to Tellichery, and the flank companies of the 6th, 10th, 13th, and 14th batts. formed into one batt., the command of which was given to Maj. Frederick: Lieut. L., who belonged to the 6th batt., continued with this force all the campaigns under Gen. Macleod. He next served against the Biby, or Queen, of Cananore, an ally of Tippoo's; her subjects, the Moplays, had never been conquered, and were a brave and hardy race: much hard fighting ensued before they were subdued, and a peace concluded. Lieut. L. had been appointed adj. to the grenadier batt., but the service being now over, his batt. was reduced, and the officers ordered to the presidency. On arriving at Bombay Lieut. L. did duty with the European infantry, until he was transferred to the 2d batt. Sepoys, and ordered to proceed to Surat. In 1788 the establishment being augmented, Lieut. L. was transferred to the 11th batt., which, with the 8th batt., and a company of art. and gun Lascars, with six six-pounder field-pieces, were in orders, in May 1789, to join the Mahrattas, and co-operate with them against Tippoo Saib. This detachment, commanded by Capt. John Little of the 8th batt. N. I., left Bombay 20th May 1790, sailed down the coast, and joined the Mahratta army, commanded by Parasu Ram Bhow, amounting to from 10,000 to 15,000 men of all descriptions. During this service, which lasted two years, the detachment was under canvass, (the first, and perhaps the only instance, of an Indian army being out two rainy seasons) and actively employed. The detachment being entirely under the controul of Bhow, was subjected to his caprice and whims; on some days it was ordered on a long march, and countermanded the same night to the ground it had left, without any reason being assigned; and whenever a place refused his summons, and would not yield to his troops, the detachment was instantly employed to compel it. He was at last so convinced of the use of the detachment, of their moderation and good behaviour, that he applied to the Mahratta government for a sum of money, as a gratuity, or honorary distinction, for their conduct. The detachment captured several forts. In Jan. 1791 Lieut. L. commanded a grenadier company, and being the senior lieut. in the detachment, he was much employed in the reduction of Darwar. (See Lieut. (now Maj.) Moor's narrative of Capt. Little's detachment.) In March 1792 the detachment quitted the Mahratta army, recrossed the Cavery, and joining Gen. Abercromby's army, accompanied it back to Cananore, and thence embarked for Bombay. Lieut. L. was promoted to capt. 22d Aug. 1794, and transferred from the 11th batt. N. I. to the 2d batt. European infantry, and obtained the command of the 1st grenadier company. This reg. being ordered down to the Malabar coast to relieve the 1st European reg. at Cananore, embarked from Bombay 24th Dec. 1794, and arrived at its destination on the 29th. The English being then at war with the Dutch, the two flank companies were ordered to Cochin to join the forces assembling there under Col. Petrie; Capt. L. arrived at camp before Cochin 17th Sept., and joined Maj. Wiseman, who commanded the Bombay troops. The enemy made little resistance, and did not stand the storm: when the British batteries had opened, and destroyed most of their defences, after firing one day and night, they capitulated, and peace was concluded 19th Oct. 1795. The flank companies of this officer's reg. were now relieved by two of the same regiment, and ordered back to Cananore.

Soon after war having commenced with the Cotiote Rajah, three companies of this reg., under Maj. Anderson, were ordered into his country. In this service, principally bush-fighting, the British proceeded through the enemy's country, took possession of all his strong holds, and obliged him to make peace. In Sept. 1797 another Native reg., the 5th or Travancore reg., was raised; Maj. Anderson, Capt. L., and a few other officers, were transferred to it, and ordered to Calicut, where it was raised. In April 1800 it was sent from Calicut into the Pynaad country, to quell some disturbances amongst the inhabitants; but towards the end of that month Capt. L. was relieved, and ordered to proceed to the presidency to join another corps, having been promoted to a majority in Jan. 1799, and transferred to the 1st batt. of the 7th reg. Native infantry.

In March 1801 Maj. L. embarked, in command of his reg., for the Red Sea, arrived at Cossier, in Upper Egypt, disembarked the 21st May, and continued encamped till about 18th June. During this period the batt. suffered so severely from drilling and working parties, that nearly half of the corps, including Maj. L., were sick, and in the hospital; and, in consequence thereof, the batt. returned to Bombay. Finding his constitution considerably impaired, and being strongly recommended by medical friends to return to Europe, Maj. L. sailed from Bombay 16th Nov. 1801. He was promoted to lieut.-col. 3d July 1802, and retired from the service in Aug. 1804.

LIEUTENANT-COLONEL THOMAS SHAW.

(Bengal Establishment.)

This officer was appointed a cadet in 1777: he arrived in Bengal in Oct. 1778; and after doing duty three months in the 3d European reg. as ensign, volunteered for field service, to proceed with drafts to reinforce the army under Col. Goddard in the Mahratta country.

The defeat of the Bombay army in 1779, and Col. Goddard's consequent spirited march to the west of India, prevented the junction.

The drafts, and two battalions of the line, proceeded to Dinapoor cantonments, whence they were ordered in Aug. to Caunpoor, and in 1780 were augmented and formed into four batts., for the purpose of forcing their way across the Deccan, to accomplish their original destination, the reinforcement of Col. Goddard's army: but a treaty with the Rannah of Gohud affording full employment for these four batts. (in the 2d of which this officer was first lieut.,) a troop of cavalry, and a small park of field-pieces, under Capt. William Popham, in a short, active, and successful campaign, expelled the Mahrattas from Gohud, and removed the seat of war into the enemy's country. Lieut. S. led the grenadiers of the 2d batt., which, with the 4th batt., commanded by the gallant and enterprising Captain William Bruce, surprised the Mahratta camp, (then three miles distant from the English and Rannah's camps,) in a night attack, in which the enemy lost some hundreds of horses, most of their equipments, and were so completely discomfited that they did not again encamp near the English. The 2d batt., with the grenadier company of the 1st, formed the storming party for the capture of the fort of Lohar, and Lieut. S. led the grenadiers of the 2d in the assault. He volunteered to serve with the detachment which took Gualior by escalade in 1780; but as the 2d batt., commanded by the veteran Capt. Wm. M'Clary, formed the covering party, his services were declined; and on the success of the attack, the 2d batt. promptly gained possession of the Shaher Punnah.

In 1781 Lieut. S. was appointed adjut. to a detachment of from 5 to 6000 men, commanded by Lieut.-Col. Jacob Camac, for the invasion of Malwah, to withdraw Mahajee Scindia from the Mahratta confederacy at Poonah, and was soon after appointed quart.-mast. to it: the detachment advanced to Seronge, and after retiring several marches, turned back, completely surprised Scindia's camp, captured all his guns, ammunition, &c.; and on this occasion the Mahratta forces, horse and foot, were so totally dispersed, that Lieut. S. fortunately saw the standard elephant separated from the army, and with an orderly trooper, crossed the river Scind and took it. This little army was reinforced by some regs. of cav. and inf., and Col. Muir appointed to command. In 1781-2, peace being concluded with Scindia, Col. Muir's detachment was broken up, and the several corps ordered to the cantonments of Furruckabad and Caunpoor: at the latter station, and at Lucknow, Lieut. S. held the command for several months of the 2d batt. 34th reg. of Sepoys.

In 1785 Lieut. S. was appointed to discipline the corps of Hill Rangers, stationed at Bhaugulpoor, being the first military officer attached to them, the corps being under the judge and magistrate. In 1786 he was appointed adjut. to it by Lord Cornwallis, and in 1793 his lordship appointed him to command the corps. During his command, the Rangers were inspected by Gen. Sir A. Clarke and Sir David Baird, who both expressed their approbation of the high state of discipline which the corps had attained, as being very creditable to the commanding officer.

This officer continued to command this little corps as lieut., capt., maj., and lieut.-col., till the end of 1804, when the impaired state of his health compelled him to return to Europe, after twenty-six years and three months service in India. The 22d Feb. 1809 he was placed on the retired list.

The following are the dates of this officer's commissions: ensign, Oct. 1778; lieut. Oct. 19, 1778; capt. Jan. 7, 1796; maj. May 29, 1800; lieut.-col. July 13, 1803.

MAJOR-GENERAL JAMES GEORGE SCOTT.

(Madras Establishment.)

In July 1781 this officer was appointed a cadet; and in Nov. ens. 1st Circar batt., from which he was removed to the art., and joined the army, then under Lieut.-Gen. Sir Eyre Coote. He was present at the battle of

Cudalore*, 13th June 1783, and at every intermediate service in the Peninsula until 1787, when he was appointed inspector of stores at Masulipatam. The 22d July 1788 he was promoted to lieut. In 1790, in command of the art., and in charge of the engineer and store departments, he joined the Nizam's first subsidiary force, and was present at the reduction of the whole eastern division of the Dooaub. In 1791 he was at the taking of the strong hill-forts of Kopaul, Behader, Bundah, and Gandicottah; he commanded the European artillerymen that led the storm of the lower fort of Gurramcondah, on which occasion he received the thanks of Lord Cornwallis. In 1792 he joined the grand army at Seringapatam, and served with it until the conclusion of the peace.

In 1793 Lieut. S. was appointed dep.-commissary gen. of stores, and was at the head of that department at the siege and capture of Pondicherry. In 1794 he was nominated to the same station in the intended expedition to the Mauritius, but which did not take place. In 1795 he was appointed commissary of stores to the forces employed under Col. (late Gen.) James Stuart, against the Dutch settlements in Ceylon, and was present at the siege of Trincomale, the capture of Columbo, and until the final reduction of the island. The 7th Jan.

---

* The following curious anecdote is from Wilks's Sketches of the South of India:—

"Among the wounded prisoners was a young French sergeant, who so particularly attracted the notice of Colonel Wangenheim, commandant of the Hanoverian troops in the English service, by his interesting appearance and manners, that he ordered the young man to be conveyed to his own tents, where he was treated with attention and kindness until his recovery and release. Many years afterwards, when the French army, under Bernadotte, entered Hanover, General Wangenheim, among others, attended the levee of the conqueror. 'You have served a great deal,' said Bernadotte, on his being presented, 'and, as I understand, in India?'—'I have served there.'—'At Cudalore?'—'I was there.'—'Have you any recollection of a wounded sergeant, whom you took under your protection in the course of that service?' The circumstance was not immediately present to the general's mind; but on recollection, he resumed, 'I do indeed remember the circumstance, and a very fine young man he was; I have entirely lost sight of him ever since, but it would give me pleasure to hear of his welfare.'—'That young sergeant,' said Bernadotte, 'was the person who has now the honour to address you; who is happy in the public opportunity of acknowledging the obligation, and will omit no means within his power of testifying his gratitude to Gen. Wangenheim."—Vol. ii. pp. 442-3.

1796 he obtained the brevet of capt. In 1797 he was nominated commissary to the forces, under Sir James Craig, intended against Manilla, but which did not take place; and in Sept. of the same year, on the death of Lieut.-Col. George Hall, he was appointed commissary in charge of the arsenal and laboratory of Fort St George.

In 1798, from extreme ill health, Capt. S. was forced to embark for England. In 1799 he was appointed to a company. On the first dawn of recovery he returned to India, and in Nov. 1800 was appointed commissary of stores to the forces in the field, under the Hon. Col. Wellesley, against the rebel Doondia Waugh. Capt. S. was present the whole of that successful campaign; and at the close of the same year was nominated commissary to the Indian army, ordered to Egypt, and finally put under the orders of Sir David Baird. He remained in Egypt until the surrender of the French at Alexandria.

In 1801 Capt. S. was entrusted by Sir David Baird with despatches for Lord Wellesley, and directed to proceed over-land, *via* Aleppo, Bagdad, and Bussorah; in which service he acquitted himself to the satisfaction of the Gov.-Gen. In 1802 he was appointed public agent of the government, to found and establish the gun-carriage manufactory at Seringapatam. He was promoted to the rank of maj. Sept. 21, 1804; and to that of lieut.-col. July 4, 1807. In 1809 the gun-carriage manufactory was brought to maturity, under the immediate superintendence of Lieut.-Col. S.; and in the course of seven years' management of the institution, he received numerous testimonials of the unqualified approbation of the Court of Directors and the local government, through the military board; and on his resignation, to proceed to England to repair a shaken constitution, and on private affairs, he again received testimonials of approbation of conduct, &c.

In 1813 Lieut.-Col. S. returned to India, with orders from the Court of Directors to resume the office of public agent, but with which the government did not comply. On the 5th March 1814 he was appointed to command the fort and garrison of Seringapatam. The 4th June following he received the brevet of col. In 1818 he returned to England, and the 26th Jan. 1822 obtained the rank of major-general.

LIEUT.-COL. GEORGE B. BELLASSIS.

(Bombay Establishment.)

This officer was appointed a cadet in the East India Company's service in 1791; he arrived in India in 1792, and joined the artillery in 1793. The first service in which he was engaged was the siege of Seringapatam: he was in the action of the 6th March at Saidasur, where Tippoo Sultaun commanded in person, and lost a very large portion of his picked troops. In the following year he commanded a large detachment in the field, under Col. Dunlop, at Mangalore; and was at the siege of Jemaulabad in the same year: in the following he commanded the art. at Goa, under Sir Wm. Clarke; he subsequently, in the same year, commanded two companies of art., with the ircomplete field equipments, in Canara, under Col. Mignan, from which command he was appointed a dep.-commissary of stores. In 1809 he was ordered from Poonah, to command the art. with the field force, under Col. Walker, in Kattywar: he was present at the siege of Malwah, which place was taken by storm; in the same year he returned to a command of art. at Surat, from which place he was ordered, in the following year, to command the art. in the Deccan, under Col. Montresor: he took the field with that officer, in command of the art., and as field commissary of stores. He next served under Brig.-Gen. Smith, when the war with the Peishwa broke out, as brigadier of artillery, in the Deccan, commanding the horse and foot artillery; and was at the capture of Poonah. He attained the rank of brevet maj. Jan. 4, 1814; was appointed capt. in the art. June 22, 1814; and lieut.-col. Sept. 1, 1818.

The following are honourable testimonials of the services of Lieut.-Col. Bellassis.

" Mallia, 5th Sept. 1809.

" Lieut.-Col. Walker begs to return his best thanks to Capt. Bellassis, for the success and zeal with which he has prosecuted the destruction of the works and fortifications of Mallia, and the accuracy and complete effect of the mines afford sufficient proof of the skill exhibited in its construction. The commanding officer is also much indebted to Capt. Bellassis for the attention with which he superintended this troublesome duty."

" Bombay, 3d March, 1813.

" Sir,—In reply to your reference, I beg leave to inform you, that Lieut.-Gen. Stuart, who commanded the Bombay army in Mysore in the campaign of 1799, and which terminated in the capture of Seringapatam, frequently expressed to me, as adj.-gen. of the army, his approbation of your conduct during that service; and some time after, in a letter to me from Fort St. George, while com.-in-chief of that army, he expressed himself much obliged to Mr. Duncan, for having appointed you a dep.-commissary of stores in the arsenal at the Presidency, as he was determined to provide for you had he remained on the Bombay establishment, for your spirited and gallant conduct at the siege of Seringapatam.

(Signed) " Robert Gordon, Adj.-Gen.

" To Capt. Bellassis."

LIEUT.-COL. COM. ALEXANDER CALDWELL, C. B.

(Bengal Establishment.)

APPOINTED to the art. on the Bengal establishment in 1782; lieut.-fireworker, 3d April 1783; lieut. 26th Nov. 1790; capt. 7th Jan. 1796; maj. 15th May 1807; lieut.-col. 1st Mar. 1812; and lieut.-col. commandant 4th May 1820. This officer arrived from Europe at Madras in April 1783, and joined the reg. of art. in Fort William in July.

When on command at Midnapore in 1793, he volunteered his services, and accompanied the art. to the coast of Coromandel, with the army under Lord Cornwallis. In 1796 this officer, then capt., marched with his company from Bengal, with a detachment under Col. Hyndman, to Hyderabad, for the purpose of subjugating a French force in the territories of the Nizam. This service being effected, at the close of the year 1798 Capt. C. joined the grand army under Gen. Harris, and served with it the whole of the war in Mysore. In March 1799, at the battle of Malavilly, he commanded a brigade of six guns, on the left wing of the grand army, in that action with Tippoo Sultaun. In April he commanded the art. at the attack of the intrenched tope near Seringapatam, on the morning the present Duke of Wellington succeeded against that post, and received his thanks. He accompanied Col. (now Gen. Sir Alex.) Campbell, H. M. 74th reg. the evening he attacked the enemy on the glacis of Seringapatam, spiking some of their guns. He served in the batteries the whole of the siege of Seringapatam, and until the assault and surrender of that fortress. He also served with the Bombay army, commanded by Gen. Stuart; after which he proceeded with Col. Bowser to the reduction of Gurrumcondah, Gooty, and Hurrial, in the command of the art., and acted as field-engineer at the sieges and captures of those forts: he commanded the storming party at the taking of the pettah of Gooty, where he had the sole charge of constructing the batteries and other works; and for which service he received the thanks of the officer commanding, in general orders, dated 12th Aug. 1799. His conduct was also particularly noticed in a public despatch from Col. Bowser of the same date, addressed to Col. Close, Adj.-Gen.; and Gen. Harris's approbation thereof, conveyed through the Adj.-Gen. to Col. Bowser, dated Fort St. George, 2d Nov. 1799. In Sept. 1799 Capt. C. was detached under the command of Col. Desse to the attack of two Poligar forts, Cuptal and another fort; on one of which occasions he led the European art.-men up to the breach with a loaded 6-pounder, and from the arduous nature of the service sustained a great loss in killed and wounded, and received a contusion on his right shoulder.

In 1800, war being over, Capt. C. returned to Bengal. In 1805 he was appointed aid-de-camp to Gen. Green, then on the staff at the Presidency of Fort William. In Feb. 1810, this officer, then Maj. Caldwell, was sent by Gen. Hewitt, Com.-in-Chief, on the expedition to Java, and commanded the whole of the art. during the reduction of that colony. He received Sir S. Achmuty's thanks in general orders, dated 17th Sept. 1811, on behalf of himself, and the detachments of royal and Bengal art. under his command. On his return from Java to Bengal, the Gov.-Gen. in council was pleased to publish a gazette extraordinary, dated 27th June 1812, expressive of approbation of Maj. Caldwell's conduct, and the art. under his command; he also received a letter from Sir S. Achmuty, dated 3d July 1812, expressive of his approbation of his zeal and ability while serving under his command; and the approbation and thanks of Lieut.-Gen. Sir George Nugent, Com.-in-Chief, while in command of the 2d division of field art., dated Agra, 19th Nov. 1812.

Lieut.-Col. Caldwell is a Companion of the Bath: he has received the Seringapatam and Java medals. He returned to this country in 1821.

MAJOR MAJOR H. COURT.

(Madras Establishment.)

This officer entered as a cadet at the Royal Military Academy, Woolwich, in April 1799; received certificates of qualification in Dec. following, and was appointed lieut. of art., Madras establishment, 7th March 1800.

Lieut. C. was employed with the field detachment under Lieut.-Col. Jas. Innes, which marched from Dindigul in Feb. 1801, to co-operate with Col. Stevenson's detachment in the Wynaad country. Returning from thence the force was employed subduing the Poligar chieftains of three refractory Pollams, amongst the hills adjoining the western Ghauts, during the execution of which service the troops suffered severely from the hill fever, but met with little opposition from the people. The detachment afterwards joined the field force under Col. Agnew, with which it co-operated in subduing of an extensive opposition of the Poligar chiefs, adjoining to the Madura and Tinnevelly districts, who had risen in arms against the government. This service terminated at the close of 1801.

Lieut. C. was promoted to capt. 17th Aug. 1804. In Oct. 1807 he commanded a detail of art., employed with a detachment embarked under the command of Col. Lockhart, of H. M.'s 30th reg. on board of ships of war, which proceeded under the orders of Sir E. Pellew, (now Visc. Exmouth), to the harbour of Sourabaya, at the eastern end of the island of Java, for the purpose of destroying the Dutch line of battle ships lying there: the batteries which commanded the passage were taken and destroyed, and the ships burnt, with little opposition from the enemy.

In Oct. 1809, Capt. C. was appointed by the government of Madras to the command of 200 European art. and inf., then embarked on board of H. M.'s ships Dover and Cornwallis, which sailed from Madras Roads, under Capts. Sir E. Tucker and W. A. Montague. Being joined off Batavia Roads by H. M.'s sloop Samarang, the force proceeded, under the orders and directions of Sir E. Tucker, against the island of Amboyna, which was attacked on the 16th, and surrendered on the 19th Feb. 1810. Capt. C. held the civil and military command of this place until Feb. 1811, at which period, by arrangements from Bengal, the command of the island of Banda was entrusted to him until April 1812, when he returned to British India. In July 1813 he received the civil and military command of the island of Banca, and the office of Resident at the court of Palembang, where he remained until the transfer of the island of Banca to the Dutch in Dec. 1816. The 4th June 1814 he obtained the brevet of major.

LIEUTENANT-COLONEL GEORGE WILTON.

(Bengal Establishment.)

This officer went out to India in 1777, and was appointed a cadet on the Bengal establishment 29th Sept. 1778, and ensign 17th batt. N. I. 14th Sept. 1779; with this corps he marched in the same year into the Khyrabad country, against some refractory Zemindars. This object accomplished, the batt. was ordered back to join the detachment then forming, under the command of Col. Muir, to march to Etaweh, cross the Jumna into the Mahratta country, against Scindia. Ensign Wilton served this campaign, and returned to Caunpoor with the army, when he was appointed adj. to the 23d N. I. With this corps he marched to the relief of Lucknow during the disturbances at that place, and from thence into the Gorackpoor country, to relieve Col. Hannay, and also to Fyzabad. In 1782 the Gov.-Gen., (Warren Hastings), appointed this officer, who had been promoted to lieut. 3d Jan. 1781, to be one of his aid-de-camps, in which situation he continued until that most eminent statesman* returned to England in 1786, when Sir John Macpherson succeeding to the government, he also appointed Lieut. W. to be one of his aid-de-camps; and on the arrival of Lord Cornwallis as Gov.-Gen. his Lordship directed Lieut. W. to remain in his family as acting aid-de-camp, which office he held until nominated adj. of the 10th N. I., but shortly after joining that corps Lord Cornwallis appointed him adj. and quart.-mast. to the 2d brigade, commanded by Col. James Nicol, and which appointment he held till 1795, when he was nominated assistant to the regulating officer, Capt. John Hutchinson, of the Jaghurdar institution. The 7th Jan. 1796, he was promoted to capt., and on the death of the regulating officer in 1801, the Gov.-Gen., Lord Wellesley, appointed Capt. Wilton to be his successor. On the 30th Sept. 1803 he was promoted to maj.; and on the 27th Nov. 1805 to lieut.-col. In Feb. 1807, in consequence of declining health, Lieut.-Col. W. was compelled to return to England on furlough, and from the same cause obliged, in Oct. 1809, to retire from the service.

* " When the standards of Hyder Ally floated over the desolated fields of the Carnatic, which the inert rulers of Madras had left exposed at every point to invasion; when a league of Mahratta leaders brought combined disgrace and discomfiture on the immature efforts of the government of Bombay; when internal rebellion threatened the peace of Bengal; and the opposition and violence of his colleagues embarrassed and impeded all his measures; the mind of Hastings derived energy from misfortune, and fire from collision, and no one, we are convinced, can dispassionately read the history of the period to which we allude, without being satisfied that, to his intimate knowledge of the interests of the government which he administered, to his perfect acquaintance with the characters of every class of the natives, and to his singular power of kindling the zeal and securing the affections of those he employed, we owe the preservation of the British power in India."

Quart. Rev. Vol. XVIII. page 409.

COLONEL ARTHUR DISNEY.

(Bombay Establishment.)

This officer was appointed a cadet in Dec. 1776, and arrived at Bombay in Aug. following. In 1777 he was nominated to act as adj. to the 1st batt. N. I., being qualified by having passed an examination, speaking and writing the Hindostan language. In Dec. he volunteered his services, and commanded a company of Sepoys, with Maj. Eames's detachment, to cover the retreat of the Bombay army, under Gens. Carnac, Egerton, and Cockburn, from Tullagaum on the Poonah expedition, to proclaim Ragunoth Rao as Peishwa. In 1778 he resumed his duties in garrison at Bombay: in 1780 this officer, then a lieut., joined, with the 1st batt. N. I. commanded by Maj. Abington, the Bengal army, under Gen. Goddard, at Comrandge, in the Guzerat country, and was present at the taking of Dubboi, Brodera, and Pitlad. In Feb. he led the storm of the left wing of grenadiers, at Almadabad, under the command of the present Maj.-Gen. Anderson. In April he accompanied the force under Gen. Goddard, that stormed Scindia's camp six miles from the encampment at Camboale, and shared the glory of the day, with the thanks of both Houses of Parliament to him and the troops. In May Lieut. D. returned to Bombay, and was immediately ordered to Callian to oppose the enemy encamped on the river Arless; the British routed and dispersed the Mahratta force, under Obazie Gunness, in three several engagements, and burnt his camp: after which, the force under Gen. Hartley returned to Bombay for the monsoon or rainy season in June, and the 1st batt. of Sepoys garrisoned Callian, under the command of Maj. Abington. In 1781 Lieut. D. commanded several detachments, employed to blockade the impregnable fortress of Bowa Mullen, about fourteen miles from Callian in the Concan. In Oct. he accompanied Maj. Abington with his batt., and ascended the woody hill of Bowa Mullen, taking a position at the foot of the staircase, and perpendicular face of the hill, to form a blockade. In Dec. he erected a battery of two six-pounders to batter the gateway, about 200 feet perpendicular height: he was appointed to command the grenadiers that attempted the storm with ladders, when the forlorn hope was completely destroyed, with many others, and swept down the precipices, by huge masses of stone rolled down the staircase by the enemy; which obliged the party to be withdrawn, by order of Maj. Abington. Lieut. D. was wounded in the back by a blow from a stone, descending the hill to the encampment. In May a second unsuccessful attempt being made to storm, the ladders were found short, and broken; the blockade was abandoned, and the 1st batt., which was reduced from 1200 to 347 men, was recalled to Bombay.

In 1781 Lieut D. was appoinied by Gen. Goddard adj. and quart.-mast. to the marine batt. of Sepoys. In 1782 he was removed by Gen. Mathews to be adj. of the European reg., and to accompany the expedition which that officer commanded to the Canara coast and Bednore. In 1783 Lieut. D. led the storm of Onore, with the European grenadiers, and captured the fort. In March he was appointed aid-de-camp to Gen. Mathews, and sent on an embassy to the king of Travancore, and to command his troops, which were to join the British force in Malabar. He was recalled in April 1783 to Mangalore, and commanded a corps, being one-third of the garrison of Europeans and Sepoys that escaped from Bednore when Gen. Mathews was taken prisoner. In May he was at the storm of the enemy's camp at Mangalore, commanded by Gunness Punt, one of Hyder's generals. Four large guns, with their tumbrils, bullocks, and ammunition, were captured. On the 18th of the same month, the British being driven into the fort by Tippoo's and the French troops, commanded by Col. Cosigney, making a force of nearly 80,000 men, Lieut. D. was appointed to command, with his corps, the cask battery outside the fort; which was kept possession of during a nine months' siege. Lieut. D., on this occasion, was severely wounded in the head by a musket ball.

On the British evacuating Mangalore, and arriving at Tellichery, in Feb. 1784, Lieut. D. was appointed by Gen. Macleod brig.-maj. to the Bombay army in the field. In 1785 he returned to Bombay, and was appointed by the Bombay government adj. and quart.-mast. 7th batt. N. I. In March 1786 he was selected to command the inf. and afterwards the troops, at Diego Garcia, in the Indian Archipelago, near the Mauritius. In May 1787 he returned to Bombay, and was appointed fort adj. in the island of Salsette. In 1788 he was nominated, by Gen. Medows, fort adj. and quart.-mast. at Surat. The 11th Jan. 1790 he was promoted to capt., and appointed by Col. Frederick to the grenadiers, previous to the capture of Darwar.

In 1791 Capt. D. having burst an abscess on his liver, he was compelled to return to Europe for the reinstatement of his health. In 1793 he offered his services to the Court of Directors to be employed at home in their regiments, and offered, through the Duke of York, to raise a reg. for the line at his own expence, which the adoption of the veteran batt. prevented being accepted. In 1796 Capt. D. returned to India; in Jan. 1797 he was ordered to the Malabar coast, and took post in the Wynaad district, on the top of the Poodiacherrum Ghaut, previous to the arrival of Col. Dow's detachment. In March he was employed by Gen. Stuart commanding escorts from Callicut to Tellichery, preparatory to the army taking the field against the Pychee or Cotiote Rajah. He commanded the detachment of the 4th reg. on the 19th March, at its retreat down the Eleacherrum Ghaut (from want of provisions); in which retreat Maj. Cameron and his batt., with four officers, were cut to pieces, and the greater number of the force wounded, by the Pychee's troops. In May Capt. D. commanded a wing of the army under Col. Dow, at the attack of the Canonte Newaub's palace, at Tutucullum, in Cotiote. In June he was ordered to the command of the 1st batt. of the 4th reg. in Cotiote: in Oct. he was nominated to the command of the troops in Cotiote; and in Dec. he received the thanks of Gov. Duncan, and Gen. Stuart, for his conduct in Cotiote. On the 20th of the latter month Capt. D. was ordered from the cantonment in Cotiote into the Coorga country, above the Ghauts, to protect the Poodiacherrum pass, and the depôt of grain collecting by the Coorga Rajah for the Bombay and Madras troops destined for the reduction of Seringapatam. The 26th Jan. 1797 he attained the rank of maj. In March following, on the arrival of the Bombay army, commanded by Gen. Stuart, above the Ghauts, Maj. D. was ordered in advance with Col. Montresor's brigade to within six miles of Periapatam, Tippoo's boundary. On the 5th of that month he was ordered in advance of the brigade to the hill of Seedaseer, to take post, Tippoo having appeared in great force at Periapatam; and on the 6th he commanded the 1st batt. 4th reg. N. I., and repelled the renewed and strengthened attacks of the enemy from daylight till five in the afternoon, being constantly engaged, several of the muskets having melted, and burst in the muzzle and touch-holes, from the heat of firing. Maj. D. in April commanded the batt. in the attack on Tippoo's outworks, and in making a lodgment for the enfilading batteries of the Bombay army before Seringapatam. He was on duty in the trenches during the storm of the 22d at Seringapatam; and on the 25th returned to Cotiote, and resumed his command on the Malabar coast. In Aug. he was ordered into the Canara country with the Bombay army; in Sept. to proceed up the Ghauts, and to take the command of Bednore; and in Nov. appointed, by Col. Wellesley, to the command of the province and fort of Bednore.

The 6th March 1800 this officer obtained the rank of lieut.-col.; and in this month he was obliged to relinquish his command, and decline the offer of the collections in the Soonda country, owing to a debilitated constitution, and a relapse of the liver complaint, occasioned by a dysentery acquired before Seringapatam: he consequently embarked for Europe. In 1804 he returned to India; and in 1805 he was appointed to command the 1st batt. of the 5th reg. at Goa, under Gen. Sir William Clark. In 1806 he was appointed by his exc. the viceroy of Goa to command the Algoada fort and reg. of European Portuguese grenadiers, joined by H. M.'s 86th reg. and two batts. of Bombay Sepoys, with a competent force of art., making on the whole above 4000 men. In 1807 he was ordered from Goa to Poonah in the Mahratta dominions, and commanded the cantonment. Lieut.-Col. D. in this year received " a coup-de-soleil" whilst attending the Peishwa, and was obliged to repair to Europe. The 25th July 1810 he attained the rank of col. Being unable to return to India, he was compelled in 1813 to retire from the service, and thus lost his promotion to maj.-gen. by a few weeks.

The following is an extract from the general letter from Bombay to the Court of Directors, dated 29th Nov. 1800, in reference to Colonel Disney's services:—

" Lieut.-Col. Disney has our permission to return to Europe for the recovery of his health. We have great pleasure in adding, at this officer's request, our testimony of his services in India, of which, as our proceedings of the 26th April contain a full statement, we have only to refer your Hon. Court to the detail of facts therein related."---*Paragraph* 32.

        (Signed)   " R. RICHARDS, Sec. to Govt."

MAJOR-GENERAL JOHN BAILLIE.

(Bombay Establishment.)

THIS officer was appointed a cadet in March 1777; he arrived at Madras in Feb. 1778, and in May obtained the commission of lieut. fireworker; and in Nov. of the same year accompanied the expedition which invaded the Deccan, for the purpose of placing Ragonath Rao Dada Saib on the Musnud of the Mahratta empire. The then commander of art., Col. Degen, third in command of that army, nominated him his aid-de-camp. This small force, consisting of but 3000 men, traversed the Concan, and ascended the difficult pass of the Bhore Ghaut without opposition, but had scarce entered the Deccan, when it was opposed by an army at least thirty times its number. Surmounting every obstacle opposed to its progress, the army at last arrived at the town of Tilligom, eighteen miles from Poonah, where it encamped, within about a mile and a half of this predatory host. Confident of superiority in disciplined valour, and little regarding the hostile demonstrations of so disorganised a mass, the British were in anxious expectation that the expedition would be, during the night, crowned with success, by the storm of the enemy's encampment, the dispersion of his army, and consequent fall of his capital, when, at 10 P.M. of Jan. 11, 1779, an order was issued to march; but it was not of a complexion to sustain confidence or inspire hope, for the traces were soon discovered of the former route, and the army learned that the destruction of the greater part of the camp equipage and stores, in flames, previous to their departure, had been expressly ordered to facilitate their retreat*. The Mahrattas

* The campaign of 1779, disastrous and disgraceful as it was to us, afforded many brilliant examples of genius and gallantry, on the part of the subaltern officers, in the command of posts. The following eulogium on one of them, Lieut. Flint, is extracted from "Wilks's Sketches of the South of India:"—

"Strange as in these days the proposition may sound, this lieut. was an officer of very considerable experience: to a scientific knowledge of the theory, he added some practical acquaintance with the business of a siege; and to military talents of no ordinary rank, a mind fertile in resources, and a mild confidence of manner, which, as his troops were wont to say, rendered it impossible to feel alarm in his presence. He found the place (Wandiwash) in a ruinous state, furnished with abundance of cannon, but no carriages, and little powder: he repaired the works, constructed carriages, and manufactured powder. He had not one artilleryman; but he prevailed on the silversmiths, who, according to the routine of Hindoo warfare, are the apology for cannoneers, not only to attend regularly to be instructed in the exercise, but, in the subsequent siege, to perform their duties in a respectable manner. From the 12th of Aug. 1780 until the 12th of Feb. 1783,—an eventful period, during which the flower of Hyder's army were before the place seventy-eight days of open trenches, and, after being foiled in open force, made repeated attempts to seize it by stratagem, or starve it into surrender,—this officer, never once casting off his clothes at the uncertain periods of repose, not only provided the means of internal defence, but raised a little corps of cavalry, for exterior enterprise; and during a protracted period of famine and diversified misery elsewhere, not only fed his own garrison, but procured important supplies for the use of the main army; for which he was justly deemed to be the centre of all

thus relieved from apprehension of further offensive operations, issued like a torrent from their camp, hung on our rear, and pressed hard upon our flanks, and so completely embarrassed the march, that it was day-break ere the army reached near to Worgaum, a village five miles distant, which had been previously burnt by the enemy. In this position their reiterated attacks were repulsed for three days, with some loss on the side of the British; but the enemy suffered so severely, that the British might have effected a retreat to Bombay in the face of an enemy, whose energies, by whatever cause excited, were never yet known to survive a succession of defeats, had not the procrastinating pusillanimity of the diplomatic field deputies, unfortunately attached to the army, arrested its career in the moment of victory, and disgracefully compromised the honour and interests of the nation, by a capitulation which had no other ostensible object in view than their own personal safety. Had the surprise of the enemy's camp been attended with but partial success,—of which there can be no doubt in the mind of any one in the least conversant with Indian warfare,—the attendant panic must have completely opened the road to Poonah, and prefaced, perhaps invited, the proposal of an advantageous peace; whilst that military anomaly, the precipitate retreat of a gallant army, uncrippled by loss in action, and abundant in every description of equipment, in the face of an enemy it despised, was indicative of nothing less than terror in the controlling authorities. And that such was the opinion of their superiors, both at home and abroad, is evinced by the pointed disapprobation of the Hon. Company, and the refusal of the Bombay government, hampered as it was with financial difficulties, to ratify this degrading treaty, at that eventful period when an universal confederacy of the

correct intelligence. The model proposed by the experienced for the imitation of the young and aspiring; the theme of general applause; honourable in private life as he was distinguished in public conduct,—the barren glory remained to him of preserving the letters on service, written in Sir Eyre Coote's own hand, full of affectionate attachment and admiration. Col. Flint is living*, and in London. Fancy would associate with the retirement of such a man marks of public approbation, and dignified competency; but human affairs too often reflect an inverted copy of the pictures of the imagination!"—Vol. II. pp. 264-5.

* Died in 1820.—J. P.

Native and European powers threatened the subversion of our eastern empire. These are decisive proofs of the imbecility that gave it birth; and at the very time, too, when the Mahratta sceptre was almost within the grasp of our ally Ragonath, and his numerous secret partizans only awaited his arrival at the capital to join the British standard, and hail him chief of the empire;---a consummation which must have instantly dissolved the Native league against us, and rendered England mistress of the destiny of India.

The Bengal detachment, under the command of Brig.-Gen. Thos. Goddard, having completed its arduous march across the Peninsula, reached Surat in Feb. 1779. Ens. Baillie was in April attached to a company of art., ordered to reinforce that army, which, the war being again renewed, took the field Jan. 1, 1780. He accompanied it as aid-de-camp to Col. W. A. Baillie, commanding the art. and a brigade. He was present at the siege and storm of Ahmedabad, and all the other operations, which produced the conquest of the rich and extensive province of Guzerat. In the following campaign he was present at the sieges and surrender of Bassein and Arnaul, two strong fortresses of the Northern Concan; and with the army, when, after the reduction of these and other places of inferior moment, Gen. Goddard pushed on to the foot of the Bhore Ghaut, carried the pass by a coup-de-main on the night of his arrival, though it had been strongly fortified since the former ascent of the Bombay army. Arrived at Condola, a short distance beyond the summit of the Ghaut, the general determined on the occupation of this formidable position, as a secure depôt, whence to draw his supplies, if necessary, in the progress of his operations, and a point *d'appui* in the event of disaster: and to strengthen it still further, the enemy being in great force, immediately threw a redan across a rocky projection, skirted by a thick jungle, in his front;—a precaution justified by the incessant exertions of the enemy for six weeks to dislodge him, though weakened by the frequent absence of large detachments requisite to ensure the safety of the Bangaries between Panwell and the Ghaut. The overwhelming superiority of the Mahratta cavalry, which amounted to three-fifths of their army, consisting of above 100,000 men, and opposed to but 200 Bengal and 500 Khundahur horse, was however fatal to this project; and the loss of two large convoys of grain bullocks, below the Ghauts, from the British weakness in that essential arm, reduced the general to the necessity of repassing the Ghaut, before the approaching monsoon should render the roads impassable.

The retreat was commenced at night; and the enemy, from their more intimate knowledge of the various collateral passes of the mountains, were enabled, on its discovery, to anticipate the arrival of the British in the Concan. The general deliberately continued his march upon Panwell, constantly harassed by large bodies of Arabs, who availed themselves of the numerous difficulties of a road encumbered with rocks, gullies, and jungles, to annoy him, by which he lost a considerable number of men, and some valuable officers; but having passed this intricate tract, the enemy refused the plain, and, disabled by their efforts, left the general to pursue his route to Panwell, whence he proceeded to Callian, and cantoned for the monsoon.

On the 10th May 1780 Ens. Baillie was promoted to a lieutenantcy, and to the rank of capt. July 22, 1787. In 1790 he served as aid-de-camp to Col. Charles Frederick, who commanded the Bombay force attached to a division of the Mahratta army under Purseram Bhow, in the reduction of Darwar, a strong fortress, belonging to Tippoo Saib, in the province of Gunduck, which was long and gallantly defended by the veteran Killedar, Budder Alzemen Cawn, a Surdhur high in the confidence of the Sultaun, and at length surrendered in March 1791. The protraction of this siege must be, however, in a great measure, attributed to the parsimony with which the Bhow, (upon whom the British were entirely dependent for the battering train,) supplied the British batteries with ammunition. The loss upon this service was considerable; but that of our accomplished and indefatigable commander, Col. Chas. Frederick, who, previous to the capitulation, died of a dysentery, occasioned by excess of zealous exertion, oppressed his brother-soldiers of all ranks with the deepest sorrow.

In 1792 Capt. Baillie was in command of the art. of Col. Jas. Balfour's brigade, with the Bombay force, under Maj.-Gen. Sir Robert Abercromby, which joined the army of Lord Cornwallis before Seringapatam, when Tippoo was compelled to surrender half his territory, and to defray the expense of the war. In 1795 he commanded the art. under Col. Petrie, in command of the force at the siege and surrender of Cochin. On the 6th May 1795 he received the brevet of maj. He commanded the art. of the line of the army under Lieut.-Gen. James Stuart, at the siege and capture of Seringapatam, by the combined armies of the three presidencies, under the command of Gen. Harris, in 1799. He obtained the brevet of lieut.-col. Jan. 1, 1800; the majority of the corps of art. Oct. 18, 1803; the lieut.-colonelcy, Sept. 21, 1804; the brevet of col. July 25, 1810; the colonelcy of artillery, Sept. 8, 1812; and the brevet of maj.-gen. June 4, 1813. He returned to India in May 1818, in command of the art. of the Bombay establishment, agreeably to the new arrangement; and, as senior officer, succeeded Lieut.-Gen. Sir M. Nightingall in command of the army, Jan. 7, 1819, which situation he held until the arrival of the present Com.-in-Chief, the Hon. Sir Charles Colville, on the 9th Oct. 1819.

In May 1822, the period of Maj.-Gen. Baillie's nomination to the command of the art. having, under the operation of the orders from the Court of Directors of April 23, 1817, expired, his services were acknowledged in general orders, of which the following is an extract:—

" The Gov.-in-Council has great pleasure in acknowledging the private worth and professional merits of Maj.-Gen. Baillie, the highly creditable state of efficiency in which he has left the reg. of artillery, and during the period he exercised the chief command of the army of this establishment, the satisfactory manner in which he conducted the duties of that important station. The Gov.-in-Council will not fail to bring the testimonials, which have been borne to the merits of Maj.-Gen. Baillie, to the notice of the Hon. the Court of Directors, and to point out to them the long and highly-respectable course of service which he has gone through in this army."

MAJOR-GENERAL TREDWAY CLARKE.

(Madras Establishment.)

This officer embarked as a cadet for India in Jan. 1780; he arrived at Madras in July following, and was soon after promoted to lieut. fire-worker in the corps of artillery.

Upon the army taking the field, under the command of Gen. Sir Hector Munro, on the invasion of the Carnatic by Hyder Ally Cawn, in Aug. 1780, Lieut. C. was appointed aid-de-camp to Col. James, the commandant of artillery; and on the 10th Sept., upon the advance of the army from the village of Conjeveram to form a junction with the detachment commanded by Lieut.-Col. Baillie, Lieut. C. had been ordered forward early that morning with a party of pioneers, to make a road over a swamp for the crossing of the art. of the army, when two wounded Sepoys belonging to the detachment came in to him, and communicated the fatal intelligence of the defeat*

---

* Repeated reference to this defeat occurring in these services, the following paragraph, extracted from Col. Wilks's Sketches of the South of India, cannot be regarded as irrelevant :—

" Col. Baillie, after ordering his fire to cease, went forwards to ask for quarter, by waving his handkerchief; and, supposing acquiescence to be signified, he ordered the Europeans, who to the last moment preserved an undaunted aspect and compact order, to lay down their arms. The enemy, although they at first paused, and received him as a prisoner, after being slightly wounded, perceiving the same unauthorized straggling fire to continue, rushed forwards to an unresisted slaughter of eighty-six officers—thirty-six were killed, or died of their wounds, thirty-four were wounded and taken, and sixteen were taken not wounded; the carnage among the soldiers being much in the same proportion. Hyder's young soldiers in particular amused themselves with fleshing their swords, and ex-

and capture of the whole of that force by the main body of Hyder's army, under the command of his son, then Tippoo Saib. This event Lt. C. felt it to be his duty to return immediately, and report personally to the Com.-in-Chief, who, upon receiving it, gave orders forthwith for the army to fall back to the village of Conjeveram, and subsequently to the neighbourhood of Madras.

Col. James, the commandant of artillery, having been obliged from ill health to retire from the army at the close of that year, Lieut. C. joined his own corps, and moved in the succeeding campaign with the army under the command of Gen. Sir Eyre Coote; and at the attack made by storm upon the fortified pagoda of Chillambrum, in June 1781, he was so severely wounded as to be compelled in consequence to leave the army and return to Madras, where, in 1783, not being sufficiently recovered for field-service, he was appointed by the Gov., Lord Macartney, to the command of the artillery in Fort St. George.

Upon the raising of a second batt. of art. in the year 1786, Lieut. C. was appointed quart.-mast. to it: he served in that capacity until July 1788, when he was removed by his promotion to the rank of captain.

hibiting their skill on men already most inhumanly mangled, on the sick and wounded in the doolies, and even on women and children; and the lower order of horsemen plundered their victims of the last remnant of their clothing: none escaped this brutal treatment, excepting the few who were saved by the humane interposition of the French officers, and particularly Mons. Pimorin, of the regular French line, who had joined with a small detachment from Mâhê, a short time previous to its capture in 1779; and Mons. Lally, who has already been introduced to the reader's notice. It is scarcely necessary to add, that the whole corps, with all its equipments of every description, was irretrievably and totally lost."—Vol. II. pp. 277-8.

Lally, who had first served with Basalut Jung, then with Nizam Ally, was disposed, about 1778, to try his fortunes with Hyder, who stipulated, for a certain amount of force, to pay him 5000 rupees a month. The Frenchman, not being able to bring the precise number, received only, as the first month's pay, 2000 rupees. He demanded an audience, talked loud, and gasconaded.—" Be quiet," said Hyder, " and be grateful for getting so much; you have not fulfilled your stipulation, and I have overpaid you in proportion to your numbers: I do not give an officer 5000 rupees a month for the beauty of his single nose."

Upon the breaking out of the war with Tippoo Sultaun, the beginning of 1790, Capt. C. was present with his corps, which continued in the field the whole of the campaign of that year, under the command of Gen. Sir William Medows; and in the subsequent campaigns of 1791 and 92 with the same army, under the command of Lord Cornwallis, until the peace made by his lordship with Tippoo Sultaun under the walls of Seringapatam.

Capt. C. commanded the art. of the brigade of inf., headed by Maj. Gowdie, on the 6th March 1791, which fortunately advanced in time to rescue the whole of the British cav. from destruction, when thrown into disorder and retreat, by having made an imprudent dash at the camp of Tippoo's army under the walls of the fortress of Bangalore.

Capt. C. was also present at the sieges of Bangalore, Seringapatam, and most of the principal hill forts which were captured during the active campaigns of 1791 and 92 in the Mysore country. In 1793 he was present and assisted at the siege and capture of the French settlement at Pondicherry. In May 1796 he attained the brevet of maj. in H. M.'s army in India; and in 1797 he was selected by the then Com.-in-Chief at Madras, Gen. Sir Alured Clarke, for the command of the art. in the southern division of the army, commanded by Gen. (afterwards Sir John) Floyd.

In Feb. 1798 Maj. C. had the appointment of head commissary of ordnance and stores at the presidency of Fort St. George, conferred upon him by Lord Hobart (since Earl of Buckinghamshire,) then Gov. of Madras, which very responsible situation he continued to hold under the Lords Wellesley, Powis, and Wm. Bentinck, until the end of the year 1804, when he was permitted, upon his own application, to resign and to return to England.

In June 1801 Maj. C. was promoted to a regimental majority, and in the month of Oct. following he was further advanced to a lieut.-colonelcy in the corps of art. In 1808, in consequence of losses which he had sustained in his private fortune by the failure of his agents at Madras, he applied to, and was allowed by the Hon. Court of Directors to return to Madras, and with an order from the court to be reappointed, on the first vacancy after his arrival out, to the office he had retired from in 1804, and in Jan. 1809 he was accordingly reinstated therein: in May of the same year he was removed by the government of Madras, and appointed commandant of the corps of art.; in July following he succeeded to a reg. as lieut.-col. commandant; and in July 1810, having been advanced by brevet in H. M.'s army to the rank of col., he at the same time received the like rank in the Company's service.

In March 1811 Col. C. was compelled, by very severe illness, to request the permission of the government of Madras to resign his official situation and to revisit England. In June 1813 he obtained the rank of major-general.

Within the last three years a communication was made to this officer, by the desire of the chairman of the Court of Directors, that if he felt disposed to return to Madras, for the purpose of assuming the command of the art. of that presidency, the chairman would have much pleasure in proposing him to the court for that office. This handsome and gratifying offer, as evincing the favourable sentiments entertained of his character by his honourable employers, Maj.-Gen. Clarke was under the necessity of declining, being assured by his medical advisers, that it was their decided opinion, a very short residence at Madras would place his health, from the state of debility his constitution had been reduced to in India, beyond the controul of medical relief.

MAJOR-GENERAL THOMAS BROWN.

(Bengal Establishment.)

ENS. in Sept. 1779; lieut. in 1783; capt.-lieut. Nov. 1, 1798; capt. June 23, 1799; maj. June 16, 1800; lieut.-col. Jan. 22, 1802: col. June 4, 1811; and maj.-gen. June 4, 1814.

This officer entered the Hon. Company's service as ensign in the infantry in Sept. 1779, and was removed to the cavalry in March 1797, and appointed to the 4th reg., in which branch of the service he has since remained.

He went as a volunteer to Bencoolen in 1789, and succeeded to the command of the troops at Fort Marlborough, with local rank, in 1793. In the following year, when a French squadron of four ships of war appeared off the place, and threatened to destroy and plunder it unless it was ransomed for three lacks of dollars, Capt. Brown, on whom the charge of the place devolved when martial law was proclaimed, refused to listen to any proposals, and resolved to defend the fort to the utmost with twenty Bengal artillerymen and 300 Sepoys. Every exertion was made to repair the sea defences, which were in a bad state, and Capt. B. assisted by Lieut. Macdonald, then of the Bengal engineers, and the late Capt. Hutchinson, of the Bengal art., prepared batteries and furnaces for hot shot. The French commodore finding his menaces had no effect, sheered off, after capturing an Indiaman that lay at anchor.

Capt. B. was removed to the 4th reg. of cav. soon after his return to Bengal, and was with it when it was sent to Benares, in the tumult excited by Vizier Ally. In 1798 he was removed to the 1st reg. of cav., and was employed in Oude against the rebels whom Vizier Ally had stirred up.

In Oct. 1799 Col. Collins, then the British Resident at Scindia's court, was sent by Lord Wellesley to Jeypoor, to obtain the person of Vizier Ally, who had taken refuge there, on account of his infamous treachery, in murdering Mr. Cherry, in contempt of the law of nations. Lord Wellesley was anxious to have him seized, and made an example of the extent of our power to punish, when thus insulted. Col. Collins selected Capt. Brown for the command of his escort, and the charge of this state prisoner. He had two 6-pounders, a squadron of cav. and two companies of Sepoys for the escort; and Vizier Ally was put under his charge as soon as he was brought into the British camp. Great apprehensions were entertained of an attempt at rescue by his friends; but by firmness, and the most vigilant precautions, Capt. B. brought him safely through the Jeypoor and Mahratta territory, and delivered him over at Futtehgurh. For his conduct on this service he was publicly thanked by Marquess Wellesley. On his promotion to lieut.-col. in 1802 this officer was posted to the 2d cav., which he commanded under Lord Lake at the sieges of Sasnee, Bejighur, and Cutchoura, in that year. He served under his Lordship during the whole of the Mahratta war, and commanded his reg. during the first campaign, at the sieges of Allygurh and Agra, the action at Coil, the battles of Delhi and Laswarree. In the second campaign he commanded a brigade of cav. at the sieges of Deeg and Burtpore, and the action of Afzulgurh. On Lord Lake marching in pursuit of Holkar into the Douab, Lieut.-Col. B. was left in command of the brigade of cav. with Maj.-Gen. Fraser; and when the maj.-gen. defeated Holkar's inf., and captured his heavy guns under the walls of Deeg, Lieut.-Col. B. had to oppose the Mahratta cav., and cover the line as it advanced to carry the batteries, with his weak brigade: (he had only 484 men in the field mounted). This service was effectually performed; and the line was not once charged by the enemy's horse. Maj.-Gen. Fraser was mortally wounded in the action.

In 1807 Lieut.-Col. B. was removed to the command of his old reg. of cav. (the 1st), and sent to Bundlecund in 1809, to join a force assembled in the end of that year to oppose Meer Khan, under (the present) Sir Gabriel Martindell. This force advanced into Malwah in Jan. 1810, and acted in co-operation with a very large Madras force, under the late Sir Barry Close. In the meantime Gopal Sing, an able, bold, and popular chief, who had been dispossessed of some districts a short time before by the British government, invaded the rich province of Bundlecund, from which nearly the whole troops had been withdrawn to form the force under Col. Martindell. Descending into the level province at the head of a large body of horse, he easily eluded the pursuit of infantry by the length and rapidity of his marches; and proceeded coolly to collect the revenues, and to burn wherever payment was refused. In consequence of this, Lieut.-Col. Brown was detached into Bundlecund with the 1st reg. of cav., and directed to take command of all the detachments he found, against Gopal Sing. By a succession of rapid marches he unexpectedly came up to the marauding force, with four squadrons of cav.; attacked them instantly, though posted in difficult ground, dispersed them with great loss, and drove Gopal Sing up the Ghauts, with only six horsemen in his company. The high sense entertained by government of this service was communicated to Lieut.-Col. B. in public orders by the Commander of the forces. In Oct. 1810 Lieut.-Col. Brown was sent up the Ghauts, and placed in command of the different detachments employed there against Gopal Sing; instead of merely repelling his incursions he obtained permission to pursue him through the Jungles, where he took shelter, and to destroy his strong holds. The whole of 1811 was occupied in pursuing and harassing this marauding chief, whose force, whenever he attempted to draw it together, was dispersed. At last Gopal Sing was so wearied out with this incessant pursuit, that he came in and surrendered himself to the Gov.-Gen.'s agent; this restored quiet to the province. Col. Brown received repeatedly the thanks of government for his judgment and exertions in this very fatiguing and harassing service; and the Court of Directors afterwards expressed their high approbation, in a letter which was published in general orders.

At the siege of Callinger, in Jan. 1812, Col. B. commanded a covering force, employed to intercept reinforcements going to the garrison from Rewah. After the place surrendered the 1st cav. were sent to Muttra, where Col. B. commanded, and in the same year was appointed to the government command of the Muttra and Agra frontier, which he held until his embarkation for Europe in the end of 1814. During this time a force was assembled, in Nov. 1813, under Maj.-Gen. Marshall, against the Rajah of Alwarand; Col. B. was appointed second in command, and to the immediate command of the cav. and horse art. employed.

Upon his obtaining leave to proceed to Europe, the government expressed in public orders, " The high sense entertained of the zeal, ability, and devotion to the public interests, which had so uniformly and conspicuously marked his course through the different gradations of the army, and the entire satisfaction which the government and the officers, who had successively held the chief command of the army, had derived from the very able and exemplary manner in which he had exercised, for a considerable period, the duties of a very important and extensive command."

Maj.-Gen. B. returned to Bengal in May 1816, and was immediately placed on the staff, and appointed to command a division of the army in the field. At the siege of Hatras in Feb. 1817 he commanded the cav. and in Oct. 1817, when Lord Hastings took the field against the Pindarries, Maj.-Gen. B. was appointed to command the centre division of the grand army, with which his Lordship fixed his head-quarters. From this situation he was selected to command a light force, chiefly of cav., with which he was detached to the westward, with authority to attack the Pindarries and their abettors, wherever he found them. Upon reaching the Chumbul he found that war with Holkar had broken out, and that after the overthrow at Mehidpore some chiefs had occupied Rampoorah, his ancient capital, and were levying contributions for themselves. Some of the rich inhabitants of Rampoorah sent to inform him of this, and beg his aid. He crossed the Chumbul, after a forced march by night, surprised the city, and carried it by assault, took one of the rebel leaders prisoner, and cut up the force they had collected. Their train of eleven fine brass cannon fell into the hands of the victors. In the same month, (Jan. 1818), in consequence of Scindia's governor at Jawnd having refused to give up some Pindarry leaders, and even opened his guns upon a squadron of the 3d cav., Maj.-Gen. Brown assaulted the town in open day, blew open one of the gates, and took the place by storm. At the same moment Capt. E. Ridge, whom he had sent with the 4th cav. to the other side of the town, carried the Bhow's camp, took his field guns, and dispersed his inf. This action occurred at a moment when it was of material service to the object of the war, for many were inclined to follow the Bhow's plan of making zealous professions to the British, and secretly assisting the Pindarries in concealing themselves, but this signal blow struck a terror through Malwah and Meywar, and made all such trimmers take warning by the fate of Jawnd.

Lord Hastings thanked Gen. Brown in public orders, for his services in this detached command, and soon after the campaign in that quarter being over, the centre division of the grand army was broken up, and Maj.-Gen. B. returned to command the Caunpoor division of the army. He subsequently commanded the Dinapoor division. In 1822 Maj.-Gen. Brown returned to England.

LIEUTENANT-COLONEL THOMAS POGSON.

(Madras Establishment.)

This officer arrived at Fort St. George as a cadet in 1780, a short time prior to the army taking the field, under Sir Hector Monro, which he joined and proceeded with, for the purpose of effecting a junction with Col. Baillie's division, but who was totally defeated by Hyder Ally before this object could be accomplished. Sir Hector consequently retreated to the neighbourhood of Madras, (see p. 17.)

Shortly after this event Mr. Pogson obtained an ensigncy. In Jan. 1781 he again proceeded with the army, under the command of Gen. Sir Eyre Coote, and was present at the different engagements of that campaign. The batt. to which he belonged formed part of a division detached by Sir Eyre under Col. Owen to the Pollams. The division was attacked by the enemy, and after a hard battle to gain a pass it effected a retreat, with considerable casualties, loss of camp equipage, and private baggage, and rejoined. It again proceeded to the ground from which it had retreated, and in a few days attacked the fort of Chittore; at the capture of which Ens. Pogson was posted in a battery with a covering party, and received a wound in his hip, by the graze of a gun-shot, which lamed and confined him for near five months. Upon his recovery, Lord Macartney, then Gov. of Madras, ordered him to do duty with his body guard, and with which he served for some time, and the Nabob's cav. being taken into the Company's service, he received his first cav.-commission. On his promotion to a lieutenantcy he was removed from the body guard, and appointed to the 2d reg. of cav. then in the neighbourhood of Trichinopoly, commanded by Capt. (afterwards Gen.) Stevenson, and with which he was at different periods on service, against refractory Poligars. In 1786, whilst still in the same reg., his horse fell with him, when at full speed, by which his skull was so much fractured in several places, that it was deemed expedient by the faculty that he should proceed to England, as the only chance he had of recovery. In 1789, on his return to India, he took the field with his corps, the 3d cav., in the army under the command of Gen. Sir W. Medows. In this campaign the 3d reg. formed part of a division of the army, detached by Gen. Medows, under Col. Floyd, in the Coimbetoor country, to the neighbourhood of Suttamungulum. The division was attacked by Tippoo Saib, and after a severe action, which, at intervals, continued for two days, it beat off the enemy, and made good its retreat to the main army, but with the loss of camp equipage, and baggage of every description. At the conclusion of this campaign Lord Cornwallis joined from Bengal, and soon after proceeded towards Seringapatam.

On reaching Bangalore Tippoo's line of march was seen moving from the immediate neighbourhood of that place, and Col. Floyd,* commanding the reserve of the army, beng about to take up his ground, pushed on with the cav. to attack. The subject of this memoir was on this service detached from his regt. with two troops

* At an early part of the advance Col. Floyd received a bullet through his cheek, which brought him to the ground.

under the immediate command of Brig.-Maj. (now Maj.-Gen. Sir Thomas) Dallas, in pursuit of the enemy, and several guns, elephants, baggage, &c. were taken. The army shortly after laid siege to, and captured Bangalore, and some other forts. This officer was next present at the battle of Seringapatam. At the conclusion of the war his regt., under the command of Major Stevenson, proceeded to the Tinnevelly country, and while on service in that country, it was employed in subduing refractory Poligars. In 1801 this officer joined, and took the command of the 4th regt. of cav., then in a division of the army, in the ceded districts of the Nizam, commanded by Gen. Dugald Campbell, with which he served about a twelvemonth. He was then appointed lieut.-col., and to the command of the 7th reg. cav., and the fort and cantonments of Sera in the Mysore, where he remained until the Mahratta war broke out. At this period an efficient officer of rank being deemed necessary to take the command of the 3d reg. of cav., it being a part of the subsidiary force, serving with his highness the Nizam at Hyderabad, and commanded by Col. Stevenson, Lieut.-Col. Pogson received the appointment, and succeeded to the command of the cav. brigade of that force on Col. Sentleger leaving it; he continued to serve with it, acting in concert with Gen. Wellesley, and he led a brigade of cav. at the battle of Argaum, where the latter officer commanded in person, and Lieut.-Col. P.'s conduct was approved in general orders.

In the latter war the health of Lieut.-Col. P. suffered exceedingly; and he was at length compelled, in 1804, after a period of nearly five-and-twenty years' service, to retire on the half-pay of his rank, and proceed to England.

LIEUTENANT-COLONEL KINGSTON EGAN.

(Bombay Establishment.)

THIS officer was appointed cornet in H. M. 21st light dragoons, 14th Dec. 1796; at the age of fifteen he was nominated a cadet on the Bombay establishment, where he arrived 21st Sept. 1798, and was promoted to ens. 2 batt. 4th N. I. In Feb. 1799 he proceeded on service with Col. Little's detachment to the Mahratta country, from thence to the Malabar coast, and accompanied the force which took possession of Mangalore. In the same year he was employed with a detachment under the late Maj.-Gen. Sir George Holmes, in the taking of Aukola and Sidathegur in Canara. The 16th Jan. 1799 he was promoted to lieut. and posted to the 1st batt. 3d N. I., from which corps he was removed to the marine batt. on the augmentation of the army. In May 1802 Lieut. E. joined with the flank companies of the fencible reg. of N. I. the force under the command of the late Col. Sir Wm. Clarke, and proceeded to the reduction of the forts of Kurree in Guzerat. In 1803 he joined the 1st batt. 3d N. I. then with the force at Bassien, for the protection of the Peishwa, from whence he proceeded with that chief to Poonah. In the same year he did duty with the 1st batt. 3d reg. Madras N. I. in the army under Maj.-Gen. Sir A. Wellesley, and continued with it till the termination of the war with Scindia. In 1804 he was appointed fort-adj. at Surat, and in the same and early part of the following year employed in escorting supplies of provisions and military stores from Surat, for the army in the field in Candeish. The 13th March 1808 he was promoted to captain. In 1809, in command of a detachment from the 2d batt. 2d reg. and marine batt., formed into a batt., Capt. E. proceeded with Lieut.-Col. (now Maj.-Gen.) Lionel Smith, to the Persian Gulph, to act against the Juassarnee pirates. In 1817 he was appointed to the command of Anjur in Cutch. The 1st Nov. in that year he was promoted to maj., and obtained the command of the marine batt. The 4th July 1821 he was promoted to lieut.-col.; and in April 1822 transferred to the 2d batt. 6th reg. N. I. at Ahmedabad, Guzerat.

LIEUTENANT-COLONEL WILLIAM FARQUHAR.

(Madras Establishment.)

APPOINTED a cadet Feb. 1791; ensign, 22d July 1791; lieut., 16th Aug. 1793; capt., 29th May 1798; major, 25th July 1810; and lieut.-col., 12th Aug. 1819.

This officer arrived at Fort St. George 19th June 1791, and was appointed to do duty with the corps of engineers. He joined the grand army under Lord Cornwallis in the Mysore country 16th Aug., and served with it until the conclusion of peace with Tippoo Sultaun; during which period he was present and assisted at the sieges and storming of the hill forts of Nundydroog, Savendroog, and the taking of Outradroog; he was present on the night of the 6th Feb. 1792, when Tippoo's fortified camp, under the walls of Seringapatam, was stormed and taken; he assisted during the whole progress of the subsequent siege of that capital. In Aug. 1793 he was at the capture of the French settlement of Pondicherry; during which service he officiated as adj. to the corps of engineers. In July 1795 he was appointed principal engineer to the expedition proceeding against Malacca, under the command of Maj. Archibald Brown; and was present at the surrender of that colony, 18th Aug. following. In 1797 he was appointed to proceed with the expedition destined against the Spanish settlement of Manilla, which was subsequently countermanded. The 12th July 1803 he succeeded Lieut.-Col. Taylor in the chief civil and military authority at Malacca.

In 1811 Maj. F. was appointed, by the government of Madras, to join the expedition under Sir S. Achmuty, destined to reduce the Dutch settlements on the island of Java. On the 8th June of that year he was placed, by Sir S. Achmuty, in charge of the departments of intelligence and guides; he proceeded with the expedition, and landed at Chillingching, in the vicinity of Batavia, 4th Aug.; and was present on the morning of the 10th, when the advance, under Maj.-Gen. Gillespie, engaged the enemy near the cantonment of Weltervreeden. Maj. F. assisted in constructing the batteries, &c. against the enemy's works of Cornelis, and was present at their storm and capture, Aug. 26. He commanded a division of the British troops at the surrender of Gressei, Sourabaya, and Fort Lodouyk, 22d Sept. He was appointed *pro tempore* to the chief civil and military authority in the district of Sourabaya; the exercise of which authority he merely assumed for a few days, when he delivered it over to Col. Gibbs, and returned to Batavia, where he was offered, by Lord Minto, the situation of British resident at the court of Djocdjocarta; but which appointment, with his Lordship's concurrence, he declined, in order to return to his former command at Malacca, which he resumed the latter end of October 1811.

In July 1818 Maj. F. was employed, by the government of Prince of Wales' island, on a political mission to the eastern Malay states of Poutiana, Lingen, Rehio, and Siak, for the purpose of forming commercial treaties with those powers. Subsequently he officiated as British commissioner in restoring Malacca to the king of the Netherlands; which was amicably effected on the 21st Sept. 1818.

Maj. F. finally quitted Malacca for Penang, Dec. 23, where, soon after his arrival, he received an order from the Supreme government, appointing him to take charge of such new establishment as might be formed to the eastward of Malacca. On the 19th Jan. 1819 he sailed from Penang, with a detachment of troops under his command, destined to garrison such new settlement as might be eventually fixed on in the straits of Malacca. He visited the Carimon islands and Singepoor on the 29th Jan.; and proceeded from the latter place on a second mission to Rehio, and returned again to Singepoor on the 4th

Feb.; immediately after which arrangements were made, in concert with Sir T. S. Raffles, for founding the new establishment; which was done accordingly on the 6th of the above month, when the British flag was formally hoisted. From this date Lieut.-Col. F. assumed the civil and military charge of the new factory, and has ever since been uninterruptedly employed in superintending the foundation and advancement of the establishment.

LIEUTENANT-COLONEL ANDREW AITCHISON.

(Bomaby Establishment.)

This officer was appointed a cadet on the Bombay establishment at the age of fifteen, and arrived in India 3d Sept. 1796; he was promoted to ensign 22d March 1797; lieut., 6th Sept. following; capt.-lieut., 3d July 1804; capt., 28th April 1805; brevet maj., 4th June 1814; maj. by regimental succession, 1st Nov. 1817; and lieut.-col. 4th May 1820.

In 1799 he served in the field as lieut. with Col. Little's expedition in the Concan during the Mysore war; under Col. Wiseman, in taking possession of the province of Canara, consequent to the fall of Seringapatam; and at Goa, under Col. Sir Wm. Clarke, in the same year; as lieut. and adj. he served under Col. Sir A. Wellesley, in the campaign against the rebel chief Doondia Waugh, in the Deccan, 1800 and 1801; under Col. Stevenson, in the conquest and occupation of the district of Wynaad, and in Cotiote, during the rebellion of 1801 and 1802; and with a corps of observation in Canara, under Lieut.-Col. Spry, during the Bullem war, and at Goa in 1802 and 1803. He served in 1803, 4, and 5, as capt., with the field army in Guzerat and Malwah, in the successive campaigns under Col. Murray, and Maj.-Gen. Jones; and with the combined armies in Hindostan, under the personal command of Lord Lake.

Whilst a subaltern this officer performed the duties of adjut. to a batt. upwards of five years; as capt. he held the following staff appointments in the field army in Hindostan, commanded by Lord Lake; the two latter until the breaking up of the forces, on the general termination of hostilities, in 1806:—*viz.* brig.-maj. to a brigade; dep. judge-advocate-gen. to the Bombay division; and dep. adjut.-gen. in charge of the department at head-quarters.

Early in 1807 Capt. A. went to England, on medical certificate, to re-establish his health, much impaired by the above course of active field service. In 1811 he returned to India from furlough; since which period he has filled the under-mentioned military appointments at the presidency, and on the general staff at head-quarters:—mil.-sec. to the Gov. of Bombay; town-maj. at the presidency; adjut.-gen. of the army, (with the official rank of lieut.-col.); military auditor gen., and member of the military board.

On attaining the latter appointment, (which he continues to hold,) and which is considered the next military nomination to that of general officer on the staff, the Com.-in-Chief, Sir Miles Nightingall, expressed in a general order, published to the army, his Excellency's " entire satisfaction at the zeal and ability with which this officer had conducted the important duties of adjut.-gen."

LIEUTENANT-COLONEL DAVID NEWALL.

(Madras Establishment.)

This officer was appointed ens. in Ap. 1796; he landed in India in Jan. 1797, joined his reg. at Pondicherry, and embarked with it in Aug. on the expedition intended for the reduction of Manilla, which expedition was abandoned after a considerable part of the troops had assembled at Penang. In Nov. following Ens. N. was promoted to lieut. He was stationed at the Moluccas, until those islands were restored to the Dutch in 1803; during which period he was employed as adjut. of a Malay reg., as fort adjut. of Fort Victoria, acting muster-master, &c.; and was present, under the command of Col. Burr, at the capture, in June 1801, of the Dutch island of Ternate. In 1803 Lieut. N. returned to the continent of India, and joined Sir A. Wellesley's army in the Deccan, but too late to share in the campaign of that year. He was promoted to capt. in Sept. 1803, returned with his reg. to the south of India, and was appointed, in 1807, inspector of Poligar forts in the district of Tinnevelly.

Capt. N. commanded the 1st batt. 4th reg. in action with the troops of the Rajah of Travancore, on the 15th Jan. 1809. The 1st batt. 4th reg. formed a part of the brigade under the command of Colonel Picton, of H. M.'s 12th foot, and during the action was detached from the brigade, to attack the advance of four batts. of Travancore troops, who were advancing with four six-pounders, for the purpose of turning the right of the British line. Capt. N., with the batt. under his command, charged the enemy's batts., completely routed them, and captured all their guns. On this occasion Capt. N. received a severe wound in the arm. He was honoured with the thanks of Colonel Chalmers, the officer commanding the division, and of the Hon. the Gov. in Council of Madras, in general orders.

Capt. N. embarked with the expedition, which was fitted out at Madras, for the reduction of the island of Bourbon, and was present at its capture, July 8, 1810, under the command of Col. Keating. He was next employed at Bourbon, under the immediate orders of Gov. Farquhar, in the civil department; and in Dec. 1810 did duty with a batt. of flank companies at the reduction of the Isle of France, under the command of Maj.-Gen. the Hon. John Abercromby. Capt. N. was promoted to the rank of maj. in Nov. of this year, and employed at the Isle of France, under Gov. Farquhar, in situations of confidence and trust, until 1812; at which period he was obliged to repair to England in a bad state of health. He returned to India in 1814.

In 1815 Maj. N. commanded a batt. of the army, formed in the ceded districts, under Lieut.-Gen. Sir T. Hislop. He was employed in 1816 in command of a batt. in the Commin district, which he successfully protected from the incursions of a body of Pindarries, who had made depredations, and been guilty of great cruelties in the neighbouring district of Guntoor. In July 1817 he was selected, by the Com.-in-Chief, for the command of a detachment from the division of Col. Pritzler, and was sent in advance into the south Mahratta country, on the delicate and important duty of recovering from the Peishwa's authorities the fortresses of Koorhgul and Darwar, which duty was conducted to the complete satisfaction of government.

He was next appointed to the command of the garrison and fortress of Darwar. In Dec. 1817 he was promoted to lieut.-col., and employed in the command of a brigade, in the division under Maj.-Gen. Munro, without prejudice to his command of the garrison of Darwar. He commanded the right division in the attack and escalade of the Pettah of Sholapoor; and was present at the sieges and capture of Guduck, Dumul, Budumy, Belgum, and Sholapoor—at each of which places he received the thanks of Maj.-Gen. Sir T. Munro, in division orders, for his energy and good conduct in the field, and also those of Sir T. Hislop, Com.-in-Chief of the Madras army, and of the Marquess of Hastings.

Lieut.-Col. N. was appointed British Resident at the courts of the Rajahs of Travancore and Cochin in the end of 1820.

MAJOR WILLIAM HENLEY.

(Bengal Establishment.)

APPOINTED a cadet in 1798; ens. and lieut. Oct. 30, 1799; capt. Jan. 26, 1807; and maj. June 30, 1819.

In April 1800 he joined the 1st batt. 7th N. I. and in July 1801 the 2d batt. 6th N. I., then employed on field service in a detachment of five batts., under Col. Marley, against refractory Zemindars in the northern Circars. In Sept. 1802 he was appointed adjut. to the 2d batt. 6th N. I., and in Nov. 1803 employed with it in the reduction of a fort in the Allahabad district (Chowkundie,) in which service the casualties of the batt. amounted to about 100, including two officers. In Jan. 1804 he was appointed adjut. and quart.-mast. to his reg. (6th N. I.,) and in Feb. 1805 adjut. and quart.-mast. to the 24th N. I., then newly raised. He joined the 2d batt. in March 1805, and commanded the corps from that time until Oct. 1806, discharging also the duties of brig.-maj. and pay-mast. to the Gohud subsidiary force, composed of three batts. under Lieut.-Col. Bowie, with which the 2d batt. 24th N. I. was employed in the field from Ap. 1805 to Ap. 1806. In Nov. 1808 he was employed with the 2d light inf. batt. in a division of the army, under Lieut.-Gen. St. Leger, which was embodied for the occupation of the territory of the independent Seik chiefs, situated between Delhi and the Sutuleje. He was appointed to the command of the batt. in Feb. 1809, which he held until its reduction in May ensuing. From Dec. 1809 to June 1812 he was occupied in the preparation of a code of the standing orders and regulations of the Bengal army; from July 1812 to Jan. 1813, in command of 1st batt. 24th N. I.; from Jan. to June 1813, in command of a detachment of flank companies, employed in field service, under Maj.-Gen. Wood and Col. Martindell, on the southern frontier and in Rewah. From Nov. 1813 to Dec. 1815 he was on furlough to Europe; and in Jan. 1816 appointed to officiate as an assistant to the adjut.-gen. of the army. From May to Nov. following he was in command of the 1st batt. 24th N. I.; and in the latter month appointed assist.-adjut.-gen. to the Nagpore subsidiary force, with which he served in the Pindarry campaign of 1817-18, being nominated also to the superintendence of the contingent of troops furnished by the Newaub of Bopal, in Dec. 1817. In Feb. 1818 he was appointed political agent to the Gov.-Gen. at Bopal.

MAJOR DANIEL MITCHELL.

(Bombay Establishment.)

This officer served with the Bombay army during the campaign against the late Sultaun of Mysore, and afterwards at the blockade and subsequent capture of the strong and most remarkable fort of Jemaulabad. He was employed at two different periods in the Cotiote and Wynaad jungles, services as trying and unhealthy as any in India. He rose to the rank of capt. in 1803, and to that of maj. Sept. 18, 1809. In the following year he was compelled to retire from the service, the climate of India having proved most destructive of his constitution.

The following are honourable testimonials of Major Mitchell's services:—

Certificate from Major-General Wiseman.

" I do hereby certify, that Capt. D. Mitchell served under my command in the Bombay Europ. reg. highly to my satisfaction, both as an officer and a gentleman; and I had so good an opinion of his abilities as an officer, that I more than once selected him for services of some importance, and which he performed to my satisfaction. I must add, that he volunteered for active service in the Cotiote, in the province of Malabar, during the monsoon, at a very perilous time, when officers were much wanted on that arduous service; and I am much concerned that his ill health deprives the service of so meritorious an officer.

(Signed) " J. Wiseman, Bombay Establishment.
" *London, Feb. 3, 1809.*"

Certificate from Lieutenant-Colonel Howden.

" I do hereby certify, that Capt. D. Mitchell, of the East India

Company's service, did duty in the field with the 1st batt. 5th Bombay Native reg. in the late campaign, against the Sultaun of Mysore; during the whole of which arduous service he conducted himself as an active, spirited, and zealous officer. As a proof of this officer's zeal for the service, I conceive it an act of justice to state, that on the commencement of the war in India in 1799, he joined the 5th reg. in the field as a volunteer from the 4th reg., then stationary in Bombay. On this occasion I have to regret the loss the public service will sustain in an officer of his merit and experience, and to express my concern that Capt. Mitchell's ill-health should oblige him to relinquish it.

(Signed)   " A. HOWDEN, Lieut.-Col. late 1st batt. 5th reg.
" *Malvern Wells,* 17*th June,* 1809.   Bombay Estab."

LIEUTENANT-COLONEL EDWIN CHITTY.

(Madras Establishment.)

THIS officer entered the army in 1796: on his arrival in India in the same year he was ordered to join the 2d batt. 8th reg. N. I., then at Veeragottum, a field-station, from whence he was detached on several very fatiguing and harassing detachment services, until promoted to lieut., when he was removed to the 1st batt. of the same corps. He proceeded soon afterwards to join the grand army assembling in the neighbourhood of Wallajabad, and marched into the Mysore country. Lieut. C. was present with his corps the whole campaign, and received the silver medal to commemorate the fall of Seringapatam, after which the corps proceeded to many parts of the Mysore country, when Lieut. C. experienced much hard marching and severe duty, until the augmentation of the army in 1800, when he was removed and ordered to join the 2d batt. 16th reg. N. I., under the present Maj.-

Gen. Dyce, who nominated him his acting adj., and which appointment, together with the acting fort-adj. of Palamcotta, and acting maj. of brigade to the Tinnevelly district, he held until promoted to a company. From the loss of health in 1812 Capt. C. was obliged to proceed to Europe on furlough; and on returning to his duty was detached after the Pindarries to Hanyhar, and several places on the banks of the Toombuddra, and to Harponelly. When at the latter place Sir Thomas Hislop, the Com.-in-Chief, appointed him to the command of a flank batt., with the field force under Maj.-Gen. Pritzler, with whom he continued until that force was broken up; after which he was continually detached on a variety of duties, and encountered many very hard marches, until promoted, 1st Sept. 1818, to lieut.-col., when he was appointed to the 1st batt. 24th reg. N. I., a new corps ordered to be raised at Ellore. This object Lieut.-Col. C. accomplished at an early period, and obtained the approbation of the reviewing officer, who was pleased to express his entire satisfaction of the state of discipline, and the equipment of the corps. Lieut.-Col. C. effected a march of 560 miles to the northward with this newly-raised corps, it being its first movement, without the loss of a man, for which service the corps received the approbation of the Com.-in-Chief.

LIEUTENANT-GENERAL GEORGE HARDYMAN.

(Bengal Establishment.)

In 1771 this officer was appointed a cadet: in Oct. 1772 he arrived in India, at which period the cadet corps was 100 strong. No promotion took place for the cadets of that season, until 1776, when this officer was appointed ensign. He was promoted to lieutenant in June 1778, and to capt. 1st April 1793. He subsequently obtained the latter rank in the " King's army," was appointed to a majority in the cav. 1st April 1798; lieut.-col. 29th May 1800; col. 17th July 1801; maj.-gen. 25th April 1808; and lieut.-gen. 4th June 1813.

Lieut.-Gen. Hardyman returned to England in 1803, after having served thirty years in India, twenty of which were passed on actual service or under canvas.

LIEUTENANT-GENERAL JOHN ORR.

(*Madras Establishment.*)

In 1777 this officer was appointed a cadet, and promoted to an ensigncy in the 21st batt. N. I. Madras army, early in 1778. He served with that corps in the same year at the siege of Pondicherry; during which service he was appointed adj. to the 2d batt. 2d reg. of European inf. in the room of Lieut. Thompson killed. After the siege he served as maj. of brig. to a detachment under Col. Hopkins.

After the unfortunate defeat of the army under Col. Baillie, when the Carnatic was almost entirely in possession of Hyder Ally's army, whose cav. had penetrated to the gates of Madras, this officer was appointed by the Gov. and Com.-in-Chief, Lord Macartney, and Sir Eyre Coote, to the command of a small partisan corps of one troop of cav. two companies of inf. and 300 Poligars, to which two gallopper guns were attached. This detachment was formed for the purpose of escorting treasure, provisions, and stores, to the army then in the field, under Sir Eyre Coote, and for the supply of different forts in the Carnatic, some of which were at the time invested by the enemy. He commanded this corps until the end of the war, and was honoured with the approbation and public thanks of those distinguished characters, with whom he had kept up a constant confidential correspondence. During this service the corps was frequently attacked by the enemy, but particularly on one occasion, when it was repeatedly charged by a body of between two and three thousand horse, and in great danger of being cut off for several hours, being ten miles distant from the army. The nature of the service on which this detachment was employed precluded the possibility of having tents either for officers or men, which, added to the excessive fatigue by day and night, deprived him of health.

The detachment having been broken up, this officer was appointed to the cav., and the command of the Gov.'s body-guard was conferred upon him, in which situation he continued until the year 1787, when ill health obliged him to return to England. In 1789 he returned to India, and finding the army in the field, he joined it without delay as capt. and second officer in the 1st reg. of Native cav. commanded by Maj. Tonyn. This corps was shortly afterwards detached in pursuit of a body of horse hovering about the camp, by which it was led into an ambuscade composed of a strong force of cav., inf., and guns, but after a gallant resistance it made good its retreat, although severely suffering to the extent of one-third of officers, men, and horses. He served with the cav. under Gen. Floyd, when that officer charged Tippoo Sultaun's army, on the line of march near Bangalore, when the cav. suffered very severely. He was appointed maj.-commandant of the 5th reg. of cav. during the first campaign of Lord Cornwallis, in the Mysore country, and at the head of that reg. he had the good fortune to capture two standards in the general action before Seringapatam, when the cav. under Gen. Floyd charged Tippoo Sultaun's line. The cav., after this being much reduced, were ordered into the Carnatic for a supply of horses, and fresh field equipments, in preparation for the next campaign; but as horses could not be procured in sufficient number, to remount all the corps, a selection was made of the 19th dragoons, the 3d and 5th regts. of cav., whereby he had the honour of serving to the end of the war. He was promoted to col. in 1802, and got a reg. in 1805.: he obtained the rank of maj.-gen. in 1809, and that of lieut.-gen. in 1814.

MAJOR SAMUEL CLEAVELAND.

(Madras Establishment.)

This officer obtained an ensigncy in H. M.'s 12th foot in 1798, and was transferred to the Company's service in 1799; at the latter end of which year he arrived in India, and was promoted to lieut. in the 16th N. I. In March 1800 he was transferred to the art., and in Dec. following embarked with a company of art. on the expedition to Egypt under Sir David Baird; and in May 1802 re-embarked at Suez for Madras. In Jan. 1803 he joined the grand army assembled under the orders of the Com.-in-Chief, Gen. Stuart. In Sept. 1804 he was promoted to capt.; and in April 1805 commanded the art. in Travancore. At the latter end of 1806 he went to England on sick certificate, and returned to Madras in Jan. 1810. In May following he embarked with his company on the expedition to Bourbon, and was present at the capture of that island, and the isle of France. In Jan 1811 he returned to Madras, and in May following joined a company of art. at Hyderabad. In Dec. 1814 he was appointed commissary of ordnance, and to the command of the art. ordered on the expedition to Ceylon; and in Feb. 1815 appointed assist. com.-gen. of ordnance to the army assembled on the Toombuddra, under Lieut.-Gen. Sir T. Hislop. In June 1817 he was appointed com. of ord. to the reserve division of the army, and served with it during the whole of its operations in the Mahratta campaigns; and succeeded to the command of the art. with the division in June 1818. In May 1819 he was present at the siege and capture of the hill fort of Copauldroog; on which occasion, in common with other officers commanding corps, he received the thanks of Lord Hastings. He was promoted to the brevet of major in June 1814, and obtained that rank regimentally in Oct. 1821, when he was posted to the horse art. In March 1822 he was appointed to the command of the art. with the light field division of the Hyderabad subsidiary force.

MAJOR JOHN STAPLES HARRIOTT.

(Bengal Establishment.)

APPOINTED a cadet in 1796; ensign, 13th Oct. 1797; lieut., 10th Sept. 1798; capt., 22d Oct. 1805; and maj., 1st Aug. 1818.

This officer did duty with the 8th N. I. from March to Sept. 1798, at Chunar; and with the 9th N. I., at Caunpoor and Lucknow, from Dec. following to April 1799, when he was finally posted to, and joined the 2d N. I. In Feb. and March 1803 he served with the army under Lord Lake, besieging the strong forts of Catchoura, &c. in the Dooaub; and in Aug. of the same year accompanied his reg. into the field, upon the breaking out of the war with the Mahrattas. He was at the capture of Coil, the storm of Allygurh, the battle of Delhi, 11th Sept.; in which, whilst storming a very strong and well-served battery, constructed by French officers, of 62 pieces of cannon, he lost his right leg. In 1804 he was nominated to the general staff of the army, as Persian interpreter to general courts martial: and in 1806 appointed to the barrack and executive departments; in which situation (occasionally officiating as dep. judge-advocate, &c.) he remained until March 1817.

LIEUTENANT-COLONEL ARTHUR MOLESWORTH.

(Madras Establishment.)

THIS officer entered the service of the East India Company (after graduating as A. B. at Cambridge) in 1794. He served as lieut. during the siege of Columbo in 1796, in the 35th (now 1st batt. 13th) Madras N. I.; afterwards, in quelling the rebellion of the Cingalese, for about six months, in the interior of Ceylon. He returned to the coast in 1798; and, with the 2d batt. 3d Native reg. served during the whole campaign against Tippoo Sultaun. He was present at the battle of Malavilly, under Gen. Harris; served during the whole siege, and was in command of the light companies of the 2d batt. 3d N. I. on the storming party of Seringapatam, 4th May 1799, and had the honour of receiving the medal presented to commemorate that day. Soon after the conquest of Mysore he was appointed adj. to the 2d. batt. 3d N. I. He was removed in 1800 to the 2d batt. 5th reg., as lieut. and adj.; and served with the latter corps against some refractory Poligars in the ceded districts. In 1801 he was promoted to capt.-lieut.; and in Sept. appointed sec. to Col. Oliver in his civil and military command of the Moluccas; from whence he returned to Madras on the restitution of those islands to the Dutch. In 1805 he went home on furlough, according to the regulations of the service, and revisited India in 1807.

Capt. M. was promoted to major in Dec. 1809; and commanded the 2d batt. 5th N. I. from 1811 to 1817. He received the brevet of lieut.-col. 4th June 1814, and was appointed lieut.-col. in the Company's service 14th April 1817. He was removed to the 2d batt. 22d, in April 1818; and soon after to the 2d batt. 18th, then about to depart on foreign service to the island of Ceylon. Lieut.-Col. M. was appointed, by government, to command the coast auxiliary troops sent to that island: the rebellion therein being crushed, he returned to the coast in Dec. 1818.

MAJOR GEORGE POLLOCK.

(Bengal Establishment.)

In 1803 this officer was appointed a cadet, and lieut. 3d Sept. in the same year. He arrived in India in Dec. following, proceeded to the field in Sept. 1804, and joined the army under Gen. Fraser. He was present at the battle of Deeg, 13th Nov. 1804, and at the siege and capture of that place in Dec. following. He next served at the siege of Burtpoor, Jan. and Feb. 1805; and joined the art. with Col. Bowie's detachment near Gualior in April 1805. He commanded the art. with Col. Ball's detachment in the Rewarrie country in 1805-6; and at Meerut in 1806. He was promoted to capt.-lieut. 17th Sept. 1805; appointed quart.-mast. to the 2d batt. of art. 14th Oct. 1806; adj. and quart.-mast. to the artillery in the field in Aug. 1808; adj. and quart.-mast. to the 1st batt. of art. 4th Oct. 1809; promoted to capt. 1st March 1812; and in the latter year commanded the art. at Futtehgurh. Capt. P. next commanded the art. under Gen. S. Wood, in Jan. and Feb. 1816, in the Nepaul war. He was appointed brig.-maj. to the reg. of art. 15th Aug. 1818; assistant adj.-gen. of the Bengal art. 13th Feb. 1819; brev.-maj., 12th Aug. 1819; and regimental major 3d May 1820.

LIEUTENANT-COLONEL RICHARD DOOLAN

(Bombay Establishment.)

This officer was appointed a cadet in 1780; he sailed for India in the Godfrey, and was captured by the combined fleets of France and Spain, under Don Juan de Langara. Returning to England, Mr.

D. obtained a passage in H. M.'s ship Hero, and again sailed for India in March 1781. He was at Port Praya, under Commodore Johnson, when our fleet was attacked there by Suffrein; and at the Cape of Good Hope, when the homeward-bound Dutch East India ships were captured in Saldanha bay. He arrived in Bombay 5th Jan. 1782, having previously gained the rank of lieut.; he was posted to the Bombay European reg., commanded by Lieut.-Col. Jackson, then serving in the army under Brig.-Gen. Mathews, and was in the grenadier company which led the storming party at the capture of Onore in Jan. 1783. He was then attached with part of his company to the grenadier batt., commanded by Capt. Dunn, which proceeded to Cundapoor, taking many hill-forts and fortified places in its way.

Lieut. D. was appointed to act as adj to a small detachment sent towards Travancore, which carried by storm the Ghaut, or pass of Hydernugger, and marched into the province of Bednal. He was present at several severe affairs; in one of which he was shot through both thighs. Gen. Mathews' army being taken prisoners by Tippoo Sultaun, Lieut D., with many other officers, was sent into rigid confinement at Chittledroog; but he was, owing to his disabled state, the only officer not subjected to the ignominy of being put in irons. On the peace with Tippoo in 1783, Lieut. D., with many other officers, was released, and proceeded to the Carnatic. He returned to Bombay in Oct. 1784; himself, Capt. Facey, and about sixty rank and file, being the only survivors of the Bombay European regiment.

Lieut. D. was soon after transferred to the 7th batt. of Sepoys, commanded by Capt Sparks, stationed at Tanna. This corps was reduced in 1785, and Lieut. D. was then posted to the 6th, under Capt. Dow. He joined it at Tellichery, and did duty in Malabar, till compelled by a violent fever to return to the presidency. On his recovery he again joined his corps in Malabar, and continued there till 1788, when ill health compelled him to come to England*.

---

* It is gratifying to record acts of liberality on the part of those in power; and under that feeling it may here be stated, that the Court of Directors of that day, viewing Lieut.

Having recovered his health, he returned to India, and arrived at Bombay in Oct. 1789; he was posted to the 2d batt. of the European reg., commanded by Col. Frederick, and proceeded with this corps in Dec. to Darwar, then closely besieged by the Mahratta army under Purseram Bhow. This was a service of some severity; and Lieut. D. commanded the forlorn hope at the unsuccessful attempt* to carry that formidable fort by assault in Feb. 1791.

After the fall of the fort, Lieut. D. was removed to the 8th batt. N. I., under Capt. Little, who commanded a brigade of the Bombay army which served several years with that of the Mahrattas under Purseram Bhow. Battalions were then commanded by captains, and companies by lieutenants. Lieut. Doolan being senior lieut. of the 8th, Capt. Little's, commanded it during the remainder of the brilliant campaigns of that detachment†.

At the storm of Tippoo's entrenched camp near Simoga in Dec. 1791, Lieut. D. was again severely wounded; and after the restoration of peace with Tippoo, he was again compelled to repair to England‡ for the recovery of his health. Having effected this object, he returned to Bombay in 1795, and was posted, as a capt., to the 2d batt. 3d N. I., and joined a force under Col. Dow, acting in Wynaad, and other perturbed districts in Malabar. This was a most disagreeable, trying, and fatal service, in which Capt. Doolan had a small

---

D.'s sufferings and his services in a meritorious light, ordered that his staff allowances, as adj. and quart.-mast., should be made good to him during the period of his imprisonment, and gave him a compensation for his loss when captured by the combined fleets in 1780.

* This failure broke the heart of the gallant Colonel Frederick.

† The operations of this detachment, and of Purseram Bhow's army, were published in a narrative, by Lieutenant (since Major) Moor, of the Bombay army.

‡ The following extract of a letter from the government of Bombay to the Court of Directors, dated 21st Dec. 1792, marks the sense entertained by that government of Lieut. Doolan's services:—

" Lieutenants Richard Doolan and Edward Moor having been severely wounded in the late war while serving with the detachment under Capt. Little, it was recommended to them, by the faculty, to proceed to Europe, as the only chance left to effect a cure. They accordingly applied to us for permission, and to make such mention of their services to your Hon. Court as would ensure them the means of subsistence during the period they might be ne-

separate command, and several opportunities of distinguishing himself.

Subsequently Capt. Doolan was in the 1st of the 5th N. I., and in charge of a post superintending the transmission of supplies for the army under Sir Arthur Wellesley, then in close pursuit of Doondia; in the duties of which service Capt. D. gave entire satisfaction to Sir Arthur.

Capt. D. was afterwards engaged with his corps in a series of services and affairs in Wynaad and Cotiote, against the Pyche Rajah, and other refractory chiefs, in Malabar, and about that time was promoted to a majority. He was again attacked by the fever, then so common with those serving in Malabar, under which he suffered for nearly a year. In 1805 he obtained the rank of lieut.-col; and in Feb. 1807 retired from the service.

MAJOR-GENERAL GEORGE HANBURY PINE.

(Bengal Establishment.)

APPOINTED a cadet on the Bengal establisment in 1780; ensign, 27th April 1781; lieut., 19th June 1781; capt., 7th Jan. 1796;

cessitated to remain at home; and further stated, that, being in very straitened circumstances, it would be impossible for them to put their intentions into execution without some assistance from government. From the very honourable testimonies which they produced from the several officers under whom they served, of their uniform good conduct on every occasion, and the Com.-in-Chief having also expressed the high sense he entertains of those officers' zeal and merit, we considered them as deserving some assistance; but as it never had been usual to pay the passage of wounded officers, we could not undertake to do it. Yet, in consideration of their inability to defray the same themselves, and being under the necessity of proceeding to Europe as the only chance they have for the recovery of their wounds, which they have received in the service, we have consented to make them an allowance of ———, &c. &c. The several testimonials, and the surgeons' certificate, are transmitted; and from our experience of your Hon. Court's munificence, and readiness to distinguish any of your servants who, by particular zeal to recommend themselves, have suffered so severely, we indulge the hope that the gentlemen in question will be judged proper objects of your liberality."

major, 30th Sept. 1803; lieut.-col., 12th June 1807; col., 4th June 1814; and maj.-gen., 19th July 1821.

On his arrival at Madras in Jan. 1781, this officer offered his services as a volunteer to serve with the army then at the Mount under Sir E. Coote, in the war with Hyder Ally, but which, in consequence of his extreme youth, were not accepted. After doing duty for two months at Fort St. George, he embarked in March for Bengal, where, on his arrival in Fort William, he found himself promoted to lieut. in the 3d European reg.; with which corps he did duty at Burhampoor till Sept., when he was appointed to the 2d batt. 32d reg., and ordered to March for Dinapore, and was employed in quelling some commotions in the interior of the country near Gyah, and afterwards at Buragong. In 1783 he was ordered with his corps for Caunpoor, where it was stationed till 1785, when peace being restored, and being a supernumerary in the reg., he embarked for Europe for the recovery of his health.

In 1790 he returned to India, and in 1791 joined the grand army under Lord Cornwallis, as a volunteer. He was attached to the 2d batt. of volunteers, and accompanied the army to Seringapatam; was at the storming the enemy's lines, 6th Feb. 1792; and continued his services with the corps in prosecuting the siege till peace was concluded. He then marched back to Bengal, and on the dissolution of the volunteers, he was transferred to the 32d batt.; with which corps he engaged in the Rohilla war, in Oct. 1794, under Sir Robert Abercromby; and since that period was actively employed in various parts of the provinces, in disbanding the Newaub's troops, and restoring order. In 1803, it being a time of peace in India, he obtained a furlough to Europe, for the benefit of his health, and was captured by a French privateer in the channel, and detained a prisoner of war till 1814. He returned to India in 1817; was appointed to command at Cuttack in March 1820; and in the following year arrived in England.

MAJOR DAVID PRICE.

(Bombay Establishment.)

This officer quitted England in the Company's ship, Essex, in March 1781, on his way to India, having obtained the appointment of a cadet on the Bombay establishment; and after being present in the action with De Suffrein's squadron in Porto Praya bay, reached Madras on the 24th Aug. of the same year.

Proceeding down the Coromandel coast towards his ultimate destination, he solicited, and obtained permission, to serve as an acting ensign with the troops employed under Sir Hector Munro, for the reduction of the Dutch settlement of Negapatam; and on the capture of that place he proceeded further with the British squadron, under Sir Edw. Hughes, towards Trincomale, in the island of Ceylon; where he again served in the same capacity of acting ensign, with the detachment of volunteer Sepoys, employed with the seamen and marines, in storming the works of Fort Ostenburg, at the entrance of the inner harbour of Trincomale.

He then rejoined the ship, in which he prosecuted his voyage towards Bombay; where, after having repulsed an attack from some piratical cruisers, and being subsequently dismasted in a tremendous hurricane, and after a variety of contingencies, some of them of a perilous description, he finally arrived on the 31st April 1782. The 21st Nov. following he obtained an ensigncy, and accompanied the division proceeding to the Malabar coast, under Gen. Mathews; landed under the guns of Rajahmundroog in Canara, and being ordered to join the 2nd batt. N. I., then under the command of Capt. Carpenter, served under that veteran and able officer in a variety of detached operations, which effectually secured the northern district of Sadashengurr, or Carwar, against all the attempts of the enemy to repossess it, until the pacification with Tippoo towards the commencement of 1783; in consequence of which, the whole of Canara being re-ceded to the Sultaun, the batt. returned to the Presidency.

From that period to the year 1790, the British possessions in India being, with little interruption, permitted to cultivate the arts of peace, nothing occurred of moment for military record. But on the 24th of May in that year, in consequence of the attack on the Rajah of Travancore by Tippoo Sultaun, this officer, who had been promoted 2d Feb. 1788, left the Presidency, with the detachment of troops, under Capt. (afterwards Col.) Little, destined to co-operate with the Mahrattas, against the Mysore territory. Having joined the allies under Purseram Bhow, the combined troops appeared, on the 14th Sept., before Darwar, a fortress then of considerable importance in the northern frontier of the Sultaun's dominions.

Having subsequently served in the siege of that place, and a practicable breach being reported, on 7th Feb. 1791, Lieut. P. was employed with a grenadier company to attack a half-moon in the covert way of the fort, and under fire of the principal tower he received two musket wounds, one in the arm and the other in the leg, in consequence of which, on the 2d March following, the latter was amputated.

On the 12th April ensuing, after the surrender of Darwar, Lieut. P. was obliged to quit the troops then on their march to the southward, and proceed to the Mahratta capital of Poonah, where he remained attached to Sir Charles Malet's escort (then the Resident) until the treaty of peace concluded by Lord Cornwallis, before the metropolis of Seringapatam, again deprived the soldier of his occupation. He was then removed to a staff appointment at Surat.

In 1795 he received the appointment of judge-advocate to the army under the Presidency of Bombay, being then a capt. by brevet. This appointment he continued to hold until his departure from India. In 1797-8 Capt. P. accompanied Col. Dow, as secretary, on an expedition into the district of Wynaad, above the Malabar Ghauts; on his return from which, he twice narrowly escaped being cut off by the enemy.

In the early part of 1799 he proceeded, as judge-advocate and

Persian translator to Lieut.-Gen. Stuart, the Com.-in-Chief, with the Bombay division destined to co-operate in the siege of Seringapatam ; was present at the memorable repulse of the Sultaun's troops at Seediveir hill, on the 6th of March, and during the siege and final reduction of the capital of Mysore, which took place on the 4th of May. Capt. P. remained at Seringapatam until the succeeding month of Oct., when he returned to the Malabar coast, and finally to the Presidency of Bombay.

The 25th June 1804, he attained the rank of maj.; and in Feb. 1805, after a continual service approaching to twenty-four years, Maj. P. received the permission of government to return to Europe on furlough. On the 8th Sept. following he arrived in England, and in Oct. 1807 retired from the service.

MAJOR-GENERAL EDWARD SWIFT BROUGHTON.

(Bengal Establishment.)

This officer was appointed a cadet in 1777: he arrived in Calcutta, and was promoted to ensign in July 1778; in Oct. following to lieut., and appointed to the 1st European reg. in the field. In 1780 he was removed to the 3d batt. N. I., which corps formed part of the detachment of batts. under Lieut.-Col. Cockerell, which, as before stated, marched to Madras, joined the grand army, and served with it during the whole war in Mysore.

In 1796 Lieut. B. was promoted to capt., and in 1798 his batt. formed part of Sir Jas. Craig's army assembled at Anopsheher, to oppose Zemaun Shaw, who threatened the invasion of Hindostan, but a rebellion in his own country obliged him to return. In 1800 Capt. B. was promoted to maj., and posted to the 2d European reg. In Oct. Lord Wellesley appointed him to the command of a volunteer batt. of

Sepoys, 1100 strong, which embarked on a secret expedition, rendezvoused at Trincomale, and was joined by several corps under Gen. Baird, and sailed in Feb. for the Red Sea; six companies reached their destination, but the transports, with the other four companies and staff, and part of H. M.'s 80th reg., under Col. Champagné, the second in command, were obliged to bear up for Bombay, being in want of water and provisions, having been seventeen weeks at sea.

In Jan. 1802 Maj. B. embarked with the four companies for a Portuguese settlement in the gulph of Cambay, and was afterwards employed in the Guzerat, under Gov. Duncan, who expressed his approbation in general orders of the good conduct of the corps. In July he embarked and returned to Calcutta, where, on his arrival in Aug., Lord Wellesley appointed him to the command of the Ramghur batt. In July 1803 he was promoted to lieut.-col., and war breaking out with the Mahrattas he was appointed to command a detachment, consisting of about 3000 men. Lt.-Col. B. entered Sumbhulpoor, belonging to the Nagpore Rajah, and reduced the whole province, which was ceded to the Hon. Company at the peace, and for this service he received the annexed thanks of the Gov.-Gen. in council. In 1806 he obtained permission to return to England on furlough, and in 1808 the Court of Directors appointed him Lieut.-Gov. of their island of St. Helena. The 1st Jan. 1812, he was promoted, by brevet, to Col., and in 1813 solicited and obtained the Court of Directors' permission to resign and return to England on furlough, having been five years Lieut.-Gov. The 4th June 1814 he was promoted to the rank of Maj.-Gen.

"*To Lieutenant-Colonel Broughton.*

" I am directed to take this opportunity of signifying to you, that his Excellency in council has remarked, with sentiments of the highest approbation, the zeal, activity, judgment, fortitude, and ability, which have distinguished your conduct, both during the continuance of the war, and since the conclusion of peace; and his Excellency in council has great satisfaction in recording this public acknowledgment of the services rendered to the Hon. Company by your zealous, able, and judicious exertions, in the execution of the important duties committed to your charge.

(Signed) " N. B. EDMONSTONE, Sec. to Govt.
" *Fort William, Aug.* 10, 1804."

LIEUTENANT-COLONEL JAMES SMITH.

(Bombay Establishment.)

THIS officer was appointed a cadet in 1791; and in March of the same year embarked for India. On his arrival, in July following, he was commissioned with retrospective effect, and posted to the 2d Bombay European reg., quartered at Bombay; and on the breaking up of the monsoon, in Sept., he was removed and posted permanently to the old 7th batt., which corps he joined on the coast of Malabar. The army, under Gen. Sir Robert Abercromby, was then about to break ground from Cananore, preparatory to the second campaign against Tippoo Sultaun; the 7th batt. belonged to this army, and with it this officer proceeded to Seringapatam, where he participated in the various services which fell to the lot of the Bombay army, under its distinguished general. On the conclusion of hostilities with Tippoo in 1792, the army retraced its steps to Cananore, and was broken up, the brigades and corps belonging to it moving to their respective destinations. The 7th batt. next proceeded with the grenadier batt. and a company of art., the whole placed under the late Lieut.-Gen. R. Gore, to Calicut. The cession of Malabar to the Company placing the civil and military controul of that fine province under the government of Lord Cornwallis, rendered Calicut, from its centrical situation, a position of considerable importance, and it consequently became the head-quarters of the commanding-officer in the province, the late Maj.-Gen. Hartley.

From the end of 1792 to 1795, the subject of this memoir was actively employed with his corps in different parts of the southern province of Malabar, more particularly in the pursuit and ultimate dispersion of the force under that active and enterprizing rebel, Oona Moota. On the commencement of the dry season, in Sept. 1795, his corps was suddenly ordered up to the presidency, to reinforce the garrison of Bombay; more as a precautionary measure than arising from any actual necessity, to guard against any hostile attempt on the part of the French fleet, then in the Indian seas. About this time he succeeded to the adjutantcy, and he was engaged in the duties of that appointment till the end of 1798, the corps to which he belonged having become in the interim the 2d batt. 4th reg.; the new regimental system which took place in 1796 throughout India occasioning an alteration in the numbers of regiments.

At the commencement of 1799 this officer accompanied Colonel Little's brigade into the Mahratta country, to join and co-operate with the Mahratta army against Tippoo Sultaun, and ultimately to act in concert with the grand army, under Gen. Harris, in the operations before Seringapatam. The expectation entertained of joining the army in Mysore was however frustrated by the duplicity of the Mahrattas, who kept the brigade in a state of inactivity under one pretext or another, until the end of the dry season, when it was deemed advisable to quit Sungumsen, the point of rendezvous, and to march the British detachment back to Zyghur, where it embarked on board boats the end of April, with the exception of the art., and sailed for Cananore on the coast of Malabar, to assist in preserving the peace and quiet of that province against the restless spirit of its inhabitants, rendered bold and daring by the absence of most of the troops at Seringapatam. The capture of that place and the death of Tippoo soon followed; and the brigade, reinforced by the 1st batt. 3d reg., the whole under Col. (now Maj.-Gen.) Grant, were ordered into Canara, to obtain possession of the forts and strong holds belonging to the late Sultaun in that province, which service, under very trying circumstances, was performed during the monsoon in 1799.

In Dec. following this officer proceeded with his corps to Goa, to join the British troops at that station, under the late Sir William Clarke, H. M.'s 84th foot. In March 1800 he was promoted, and removed, by a new regimental distribution, to capt.-lieut. and adj. of the 1st batt. 6th reg. In March 1801 he was promoted to a company, and at the beginning of the following year selected by his commanding officer to proceed, in command of 400 men, on service to Kurree, with a field force placed under the command of Col. Walker, to act against the enterprising chieftain, Mulhar Rao, who was then opposed to the government of his highness the Guicawar at Baroda. At Cambay this force was joined by 1000 troops belonging to the Guicawar, and arriving at its destination in March, found Mulhar Rao strongly entrenched and fortified, at the head of 30,000 troops, in front of the town and citadel of Kurree. On the 17th of that month the British engaged the enemy under the guns of his entrenched batteries; on which occasion Capt. Smith lost the services of 150 men out of 600, having been previously joined by two companies of fencibles, under the late Capt. Wilkinson. The British force, owing to its great exertions on that day in favour of the Guicawar dynasty, became so crippled, as to be under the necessity of retiring to a position immediately in the rear of the field of battle, where it entrenched itself, and awaited a reinforcement of 4000 men, under Sir William Clarke: the arrival of that formidable corps put an end to field operations in this quarter.

About this period Capt. Smith was compelled by severe illness to quit the army, and return to Surat, from whence he proceeded to Bombay after the rains, for the purpose of taking a furlough for three years to England; but, before the expiration of his time, the pressing demand for officers, in 1805, to meet the exigencies of the service, under Lord Lake, induced Capt. Smith to hasten his return to India, and accordingly he embarked on board the Sir William Pultney in July of the same year; by which means he was fortunate enough to join the Cape expedition, under Sir David Baird and Sir Home Popham; and was present at the attack and capture of that place---a corps, in which he had a company, having been previously formed at St. Salvador, on the coast of Bengal, by order of Gen. Baird, composed of cadets and soldiers intended for the three presidencies of India.

After the capture of the Cape, Capt. Smith proceeded on to Bombay, where he arrived in May 1806. Whilst at Bombay, he was selected, by the acting commanding-officer of the forces, Gen. Jones, to officiate as exercising officer of the 1st batt. 6th reg., its commanding-officer being incapacitated from the loss of a leg. Capt. Smith joined with his corps the Goa force, under Col. Adams, 78th reg., at the latter end of 1807. During his stay at Goa, he succeeded, in 1808, to the junior majority of the reg., and was appointed to command the corps to which he belonged. At the latter end of 1809 he was ordered to join the Poonah force, under Maj.-Gen. Champagné, by the route of Merritch and Tasgom, through the southern parts of the Deccan: with this force he remained on service till the end of 1810, his batt. being then ordered down to Bombay, where it was stationed for two years, when Maj. Smith was again ordered to the Deccan, to join the field force then under Maj.-Gen. Montresor; with which he continued till the middle of 1814, having been promoted in the interim to a lieut.-colonelcy.

In consequence of an arrangement to give another officer the command of a batt., Lieut.-Col. Smith joined the 2d batt. of his reg. at Baroda in April of the latter year, and with it marched with the field force under Maj.-Gen. Sir George Holmes, to watch the motions of Scindia's army on the banks of the Myhee; he continued with this force till the middle of 1815, when extreme ill health compelled him to go to Bombay. Before he was sufficiently recovered to encounter fatigue, he was ordered to Poonah, to assume the command of the 1st batt. 9th reg., owing to the absence of its commanding officer, on sick leave to Bassora; and immediately waved all personal consideration to meet the urgency of the case, though the order was afterwards rescinded. At the end of 1815 he joined his own batt. in Guzerat;

and in April 1816 left Baroda to join the field force at Poonah, by the route of Bensder Ghaut, being the first corps that ever marched through that pass. From that period till the end of 1817, Lieut.-Col. S. continued in the Deccan, participating in all the duties of that service, besides the occasional responsibility of arduous separate commands. Having suffered throughout the latter period of a service of twenty-seven years a train of diseases that nearly proved fatal, he complied with the recommendation of his medical advisers, and returned to England in 1818. Remaining under the severe influence of the before-mentioned diseases, the consequence of his protracted service in India, and of fatigue and anxiety in the execution of his duties, he was induced to prolong his stay in England till the latter end of 1821; at which time he was preparing to return to his duty, when he succeeded to the command of a regiment.

The following are the dates of this officer's commissions: ensign, 17th March 1791; lieut., 16th July 1794; capt.-lieut., 6th March 1800; capt., 21st March 1801; maj., 4th Feb. 1808; lieut.-col., 2d Oct. 1813; lieut.-col. commandant, 16th Nov. 1821.

MAJOR-GENERAL ST. GEORGE ASHE.

(Bengal Establishment.)

APPOINTED a cadet in 1778; ensign, 5th N. I., in Oct.; lieut., 3d Nov. in the same year; capt., 7th Jan. 1796; maj., 4th March 1800; lieut.-col., 1st Jan. 1803; col., 1st Jan. 1812; and maj.-gen. 4th June 1814.

This officer served in the field through the course of the Mahratta war, under the government of Warren Hastings, and was dangerously wounded on that service; he was also in a state of active service during the whole of Lord Lake's campaigns. His corps formed part of the division of the army under the immediate command of the late Maj.-Gen. Sir. H. White, against Agra in 1803, and his cooperation was in a superior degree conducive to the success of the operations on that occasion. In the latter end of the same year Sir H. White was detached, with a force from the grand army, to drive the Mahrattas from the province of Gohud, and, if possible, to obtain possession of the very strong and important fortress of Gualior. On the arrival of Sir Henry at the fortress, he found it necessary to apply for a reinforcement; and, in consequence thereof, Lord Lake detached 2000 Native troops, the European flank companies, a strong battering train, with the pioneers of the army, under the command of Lieut.-Col. Ashe, to join Sir Henry before Gualior (which at that time was deemed impregnable); and during the siege Lieut.-Col. A., in the words of Sir Henry, " displayed the most enthusiastic bravery and devotion."

The fort was situated on a rock, and the part that had been breached was difficult of access, and though the field officer whose turn it was to command the storming party had all the requisites of the most ardent zeal and courage, it appeared to Sir Henry that he did not possess that bodily activity which was so especially necessary on such a service. Sir Henry naturally felt the delicacy of his situation, in being obliged to order an officer out of his turn on such a perilous duty, when Lieut.-Col. Ashe relieved him from his perplexity, by volunteering his services to lead the storming party. Fortunately, however, a few hours before the columns were ordered from the trenches to the assault, the garrison most unexpectedly capitulated. Sir Henry was no sooner master of the fortress, than he dispatched Lieut.-Col. A., with a force, to get possession of the fort of Gohud; which duty was promptly performed, and his services acknowledged by Lord Lake in public orders. Lieut.-Col. A.'s corps afterwards formed part of the force under Col. Monson, who found himself under the painful necessity of retreating from Jeswunt Rao Holkar's army. Having sustained a considerable loss in passing the Banass nullah, or river, he (Col. Monson) announced to the troops that they should endeavour to reach Agra,—distant about 100 miles,—in the best way circumstances would allow, as they could not continue their march in a body with sufficient rapidity to escape the overwhelming force of their pursuers. "On that occasion Lieut.-Col. Ashe dismounted from his horse, animated his men to stand by their colours to the last, and promised to lead them to Agra :—which he accomplished*."

Ill health, the consequence of a long series of service in India, obliged Lieut.-Col. A. to seek the climate of Europe; but, after a short stay, he returned to his duty in India. He was subsequently appointed by Lord Hastings a commissioner to settle the affairs in Rohilcund, with the command of all the troops in that province. In 1821 he returned to England.

MAJOR CHARLES STUART*.

(*Bengal Establishment.*)

In 1796 this officer was appointed a cadet of infantry, of the season 1795, on the Bengal establishment; he embarked for India 12th Aug. 1796, but the ship having been detained several weeks at the Cape of Good Hope, he did not arrive at Fort William till March 1797. He was very shortly after promoted to the rank of ensign, and posted to the 3d N. I., but did not receive a commission, or join that corps, having been transferred‡ to the cavalry, and directed to join the 2d reg. Bengal light cav., then stationed at Caunpoor: his commission dated 13th Nov. 1796. Different circumstances having delayed his departure from Calcutta, this officer did not join his reg. till Dec. 1797; and early in Jan. following, the squadron to which he

---

* Letter of Sir Henry White.

† Lieut.-Col. John Stuart, who commanded His Majesty's 9th foot, and died of wounds received at the battle of Roleia, in Portugal, in 1808, was brother to this officer.

‡ This was the last year in which transfers from the infantry to the cavalry were permitted by the Court of Directors to be made by the local authorities in India.

was posted, formed part of a detachment which marched from Caunpoor to escort the late Newaub of Oude to Lucknow, the supreme government having determined to place him on the Musnud, in room of Vizier Ally, deposed. As resistance was expected, an army of about 12,000 men was assembled at Lucknow, under the Com.-in-Chief, Gen. Sir A. Clarke; but no opposition was made, and the force gradually dispersed. In 1798 the 2d reg. formed part of an army, consisting of from 12 to 14,000 men, collected at Anoopsheher, under Gen. Sir James Craig, to repel the threatened invasion of Zemaun Shaw, king of Cabul; but dissensions in his own country prevented the execution of his plan. In Jan. 1799 Vizier Ally, the deposed Newaub of Oude, having fled from Benares, after murdering several British subjects, it was apprehended he would raise commotions in Oude; in consequence of which, the greater part of the army marched from Anoopsheher to Lucknow, in the vicinity of which it remained some time, and then broke up; the corps to which this officer belonged returning to Caunpoor about June 1799. Under the new arrangement of regimental rank at this period, this officer was posted to the 3d light cav., and two regts. of cav. being added to the establishment, he was promoted, 29th May 1800, to lieut., and, at the same time, appointed adj. to the corps.

In 1800 Lieut. S. was employed with part of the reg. in pursuit of a person, who, in the name of Vizier Ally, endeavoured to raise commotions in the vicinity of Lucknow. Favoured by the nature of the country, which is covered with trees and underwood, he for some time evaded the different parties sent against him, and was at last apprehended in the town of Lucknow. In 1801 the 3d light cav. was reviewed by Gen. Lake, Com.-in-Chief, and Lord Cornwallis, Gov.-Gen., who were so pleased at the state of discipline in which they found the corps, that they bestowed the highest encomiums on it in the general orders of the day, and presented Maj. C. Middleton, who commanded it, with a sword, having an inscription on it expressive of their sense of his professional merits. Shortly afterwards, the reg. marched to the vicinity of Juanpoor, as part of the Gov.-Gen.'s escort, and when relieved from that duty marched to Bans-Bareily, the new station assigned to it, which it reached in April 1802. From thence it proceeded on service, and after the fall of Sasnee it was left there, whilst the army undertook the siege of Bejighur, on the capture of which this corps was directed to join, and the army marched on to the fort of Catchoura. In a few days this place yielded, and, nothing more remaining to be done, the different corps were ordered back to their respective stations. Early in Aug. 1803 the 3d cav. was ordered to join the army, then assembling for the war with the Mahrattas.

In the course of the campaigns that followed, viz. from 1803 to early in 1806, this officer was present at the attack of the enemy's horse in the vicinity of Coil, the capture of Allygurh, the siege and capture of the fort of Agra, the battle of Laswarree, the capture of Rampoorah, the battle of Deeg, the siege and capture of Deeg, the siege of Burtpoor, and the pursuit of Ameer Khan, with various skirmishes and incidental services of minor importance. On the restoration of peace the 3d cav. was ordered to Muttra; and in the cold season of 1807-8 this corps, in which this officer had now attained the rank of capt.-lieut., (commission dated 11th March 1805) and the situation of quart.-mast., marched from Muttra, forming part of a detachment assembled under Maj.-Gen. Dickens, of H. M.'s service, to chastise a refractory Zemindar, who had refused obedience to the civil power. During this service two forts, Cumoonah and Gounowree, and a small intermediate Gushee, were taken. This service completed, the 3d cav. was sent into cantonments at Cutch in Bundlecund, about which time Capt. S. resigned the quarter-mastership; and soon after, 4th April 1807, was promoted to the regimental rank of capt. In 1808-9 Capt. S. commanded a squadron of his corps, constituting part of a detachment under Maj. Cuppage, employed above the Ghauts, in the southern part of Bundlecund, to reduce several petty chiefs to the obedience due to the Rajah of Punnah, which service was effected without difficulty, only one Gushee making any opposition. The detachment then joined a force under Col. Martindell, destined to act against the hill fort of Adjeegurh; which place yielded after a slight resistance. In March 1809 the corps returned to quarters; and in April Capt. S. received intimation of the intention of the Gov.-Gen., Lord Minto, to appoint him to the charge of the Cadet Institution at Barrasett, near Calcutta, and was directed to proceed to the Presidency, where he arrived in Aug., and immediately assumed the command of the Cadet Company, and which he retained until Aug. 1811, when the institution was abolished. The conduct of Capt. S., whilst in that command, received, as shewn by the annexed general orders, the approbation of the supreme Gov.; and the Com.-in-Chief, Gen. Hewett, then Vice-President, during the absence of Lord Minto at Madras, was also pleased to approve of the manner in which Capt. S. had conducted the duties of the institution, and offered to appoint him his aid-de-camp, as a public testimony of the favourable opinion he entertained of his services.—(See the accompanying letter.)

Gen. Hewett left India at the commencement of 1812, having previously appointed this officer to act as assistant adj.-gen. to the army, in which situation he was confirmed by government, at the recommendation of Gen. Sir George Nugent, Com.-in-Chief, successor to Gen. Hewett. The 16th May 1816 he attained the rank of maj.; and on the first vacancy which occurred in the adj.-gen.'s office, he was appointed, March 1817, second dep.-adj.-gen. of the army, and in May following first dep. This latter situation he held till the commencement of 1820, when he was compelled by ill-health to solicit leave of absence, and to proceed to the Cape of Good Hope, having nearly completed twenty-three years service in India. Not finding his health re-established by a residence at the Cape, he obtained a furlough to England, where he arrived in 1822.

Extract from General Orders by his Excellency the Vice-President in Council.

"*Fort William, 27th Aug.* 1811.

" Orders having been issued for the abolition of the military Institution at Barrasett, on the 1st of Sept. next, under instructions to that effect, received from the Hon. the Court of Directors, his Exc. the Vice-President in Council, deems it an act of justice publicly to record his high sense of the valuable services of Captain Charles Stuart, and the other officers attached to the Cadet Institution, and of the zeal and unremitting attention which has so uniformly marked their conduct in the exercise of the peculiar duties of their different departments.

" To Capt. Stuart in particular the warmest approbation is due, for the firmness and decision which he has so frequently displayed in many trying and delicate situations since his appointment to the command of the Cadet Company."

Letter from Lieut.-Col. Carey, Secretary to Gen. Hewett.

" Head-Quarters, 5th Sept. 1811.

" My dear Sir,—The departure for England of Capt. Sharp, the Vice President's aid-de-camp, affording Gen. Hewett an opportunity of further testifying to you and to the world the approbation with which he has viewed your conduct in the arduous situation, from which the recent orders of the Court of Directors have relieved you, I am desired by his Exc. to say, that, if to be announced in public orders as his aid-de-camp, in the room of Capt. Sharp, would be at all gratifying to your feelings, he will be most happy to nominate you to the situation. Circumstanced as the general now is, his sole motive is a compliment to your character and merits; for, under the expectation of Lord Minto's early return, and, at any rate, of his own embarkation for England in Nov. or Dec. next, the appointment, in a pecuniary point of view, is undeserving of a moment's attention, and on this account the gen. is particularly anxious, that in the event of your accepting it you do not put yourself to any expense for dress, or to inconvenience, in attendance upon him, as he has literally no duty for you to perform. Allow me to express the satisfaction I derive in being the channel of this communication.

(Signed) " P. Carey.

" *To Captain Stuart.*"

COLONEL ANDREW M'DOWALL, C. B.

(Madras Establishment.)

This officer entered the East India Company's service in 1783, and immediately after his arrival at Madras, was ordered to march and join the army under Col. Fullarton to the southward, and in the same year was at the siege and capture of Palicaudcherry, and the reduction of the principal part of Tippoo Sultaun's forts in that tract of country. In 1789 he served with one of two corps that were sent to Travancore to defend the Rajah's lines; also with the grand army, under Sir W. Medows and Lord Cornwallis, in 1790, 91, and 92. He was present at the storming of the pettah of Bangalore; at the siege and taking of that fortress, and in the action of the 15th May 1791, under Lord Cornwallis, with Tippoo's army, at the Carri Ghaut Hills. On the 6th Feb. 1792 he served under the same com. at the storming of Tippoo's redoubts before Seringapatam; also with the grand army, under Lord Harris, at the battle of Malavilly, and the siege and taking of Seringapatam in 1799. In 1801, 2, and 3, he served under Maj.-Gen. Dugald Campbell, in settling the country ceded to the Company. In 1817 he again took the field under Lieut.-Gen. Sir T. Hislop, Com.-in-Chief of the Madras army, and commanded a brigade at the battle of Mehidpore. In 1818 he was selected to command a detachment to act against Bajee Rao's hill forts, in the provinces of Gungtory and Candeish, and after taking Unki-Tunki, Rajdair, Trimbuck, and Malligaum, twenty-five other forts, surrendered, and both provinces were subdued. Lt.-Col. M'Dowall's small detachment suffered severely on this service, but not so much as might have been expected, from the extraordinary strength of the hill forts he had to attack. Lieut.-Col. M'Dowall is a Companion of the Order of the Bath.

LIEUTENANT-COLONEL ARCHIBALD SPENS.

(Bombay Establishment.)

This officer was appointed a cadet of the season 1780, and embarked in the following year; but, owing to various detentions of the ship, did not reach India until Sept. 1782. In Nov. of the same year he obtained an ensigncy, and was posted to a corps of grenadiers. In Dec. he proceeded with the army under Gen. Mathews, which landed in Canara: he was at the storming of Onore, taken in Jan. 1783; at the attack of Cundapore, and of the Hussanghurry Ghaut, leading to the capture of Bednore. His corps took possession of the fort of Bednore, and was soon afterwards ordered to join the troops forming the siege of Mangalore, which it was also ordered to take possession of on its surrender. Tippoo, after the re-capture of Bednore, proceeded to lay siege to Mangalore; and a large body of his troops being considerably in advance, were attacked by Col. Campbell, and beaten, with the loss of their guns. Ens. S. was engaged in this affair; and in the subsequent attack of the Eadgaw hill by the whole of Tippoo's army, when the British were driven back to the fortifications. Mangalore was then invested, to which garrison Ens. S. belonged, during the whole of that memorable siege.

In May 1787 he obtained the rank of lieut. In 1790 he accompanied the same grenadier corps, with the detachment under Colonel Hartley, from Bombay, which landed in the Rajah of Travancore's country, near Cranganore, and was with it at the battle of Travenan Gurry and capture of Ferokabad. Lieut. S. remained with the detachment until it joined the army, under Gen. Abercromby, at Cananore, preparing to co-operate with Lord Cornwallis at Seringapatam. He continued with this army during all its operations in 1791 and 1792, until the peace of Seringapatam. While employed on these services, Lieut. S. held the situation of baggage-master to the force under Col. Hartley; quarter-master of brigade, under Gen. Abercromby; and adj. of a batt.; which last appointment he held until 1795, when he obtained leave of absence to Europe. In Jan. 1796 he was promoted to capt., by brevet; in March 1797, to capt.-lieut; and in July following to capt. In 1798 he returned to Bombay, and was appointed to the command of a provincial batt. at Surat; and on the disbanding of this corps, in Dec. 1799, joined his reg. at Goa. In 1800 he received the government appointment of major of brigade in the provinces of Malabar and Canara, to which he immediately proceeded; and in this situation, and as secretary to the commanding-officer, he was present during the warfare in Cotiote.

In 1802 Capt. S. was appointed aid-de-camp to the Gov. of Bombay, and, in that year, dep.-quart.-mast.-gen. to the army. In the latter situation he accompanied a detachment, sent to Basseen for the protection of the Peishwa, to which he was also appointed commissary. This detachment was considerably reinforced, and subsequently escorted the Peishwa to Poonah, where it joined Sir A. Wellesley.

When Sir Arthur marched from Poonah, he placed Capt. Spens in the important charge of a large depôt of provisions, with instructions for receiving grain and provisions from Bombay, and forwarding them to his army in advance. This depôt soon became of the utmost consequence, and encreasing quantities of provisions of all kinds poured into it, while the country around was in a state of famine. His conduct in the management of this complicated department met with Gen. Wellesley's marked approbation, of which he had the satisfaction of receiving a gratuitous testimony conveyed to him, with his thanks, through the Com.-in-Chief at the presidency. He received the same personally from Sir Barry Close, the resident at the Poonah durbar; and, previously to his being relieved from that charge and leaving Poonah, he was appointed quart.-mast.-gen. of the army, with the rank of lieut.-col., having, in Jan. 1803, been promoted to major.

In 1804, on his appointment of quart.-mast.-gen., he proceeded to the presidency, to take charge of that office, and took his seat at the military board. In May 1807 he was promoted to lieut.-col. In 1808 he obtained permission to return to Europe for the benefit of his health; and on his leaving Bombay, the following general order was issued by government :—

"*Bombay Castle, July 5,* 1818.

"Lieut.-Col. Spens, quart.-mast.-gen. under this presidency, having produced the prescribed certificates, has the permission of the Hon. the Gov. in Council to proceed to Europe for the benefit of his health, with the option of retiring from the service in England, agreeably to the regulations.

"In granting this permission, the Hon. the Gov. in Council joins in the regret, expressed by the commanding-officer of the forces, at the departure of an officer of Lieut.-Col. Spens' experience and abilities, whose zealous exertions have contributed so successfully to place the important department of quart.-mast.-gen. on the most extensive scale of utility."

Lieut.-Col. Spens ultimately requested permission to retire from the service, which was granted in Nov. 1809.

LIEUTENANT-COLONEL MICHAEL KENNEDY.

(Bombay Establishment.)

THIS officer commenced his service as a volunteer in the Company's army, having been invited to India by a relation, who commanded the Madras artillery; his death, whilst this officer was on his passage out, in 1781, left him many years unprovided for, and deprived him of the advantages he had expected from raising nearly half a company of recruits, and bringing them almost at his own expense to

Portsmouth. He was present as a volunteer at the siege of Cananore in 1783, and saw some of the roughest service about that period. His commission as ensign was dated in 1791, shortly subsequent to the battle of Travenan Gurry, under Col. Hartley, than which few actions have been fought more desperately, or decided more important consequences. He was present and actively employed during the first Seringapatam campaign, and was wounded before that place in Feb. 1792; on which occasion his services were publicly acknowledged. He was a second time wounded in the Surat river in 1795, under circumstances which gained him some credit: a body of pirates having captured a ship of about 600 tons, belonging to a merchant in Surat, were prevented by the ebb tide from carrying her out of the river, the water on the bar being too shallow; he was ordered to retake the vessel with a detachment of thirty Sepoys; he laid his boats alongside, under a very heavy fire; boarded, and carried the ship. The loss of the enemy was very severe, while the casualties in the detachment were trifling, only a few killed and wounded; this officer was among the latter; he received two wounds, one a pistol-ball and the other a sword wound in the arm. He volunteered his services, but was refused permission, by Gen. Stuart, to join the army which took Seringapatam in 1799. In 1802 he was ordered to join the army under Sir Wm. Clarke, and commanded a separate detachment, the flank companies of 1st batt. 3d reg. N. I. He had charge of it at Kurree, and maintained rather a perilous position for several days. After the surrender of the fort, he was appointed by Sir William to escort the chieftain, Mulhar Rao, to Cambay. On delivering him up to the late J. Duncan, this officer was appointed to the command of Fort Victoria, and ordered to proceed to that station without delay. Shortly after his arrival, the Mahratta war of 1802 having driven the late Peishwa from his capital, he fled to the town of Mahr, twenty-five miles east of Fort Victoria; and this officer was ordered, by the government of Bombay, to join him there in capacity of agent. On Holkar's troops descending the Ghauts in pursuit of him (the Peishwa,) his highness and his brother, Chimnajee Appa, proceeded overland to Savendroog; while his minsters and his treasure, under charge of this officer, were conveyed to the same place by water. At Savendroog, this officer received an order from government to enforce the acceptance of the subsidiary force; he succeeded in this object, and, in conformity to the orders of government, attended his highness to Basseen. There being joined by Col. Close, and every thing being arranged, he obtained permission from the Gov. to return to Fort Victoria, where he was ordered to raise a local batt. for the protection of the Company's territory in that quarter from the ravages of Holkar's troops, who were scattered through the Concan. The Gov. was pleased to order a letter to be addressed to this officer, intimating his approbation of his conduct during the time he was employed with his highness: his services in the political department, in attendance on the prince, and in the guardianship of his person, until he parted from him at Basseen, are recorded in the papers published by order of parliament at that period.

He next acted as the Gov.'s agent, and superintended the proceedings which took place when the Bombay army, on its removal from Malabar, was employed in the reduction of the island fort of Savendroog, then in rebellion against his highness's authority. He was appointed shortly after town-maj. of Bombay, and private sec. to the Gov., which duties he discharged until the death of the Gov., when he joined his batt.

In 1815 he commanded a brigade for the protection of the Attavesy from the Pindarries, a labour which, however, only occasioned him anxiety of arrangement and preparation, as the banditti* never ad-

* The Pindarries are a singular race; singular in their formation, in their habits, in their physical qualities, in their moral attributes, and in their social system. Chance made them a people; plunder and robbery constitute the bonds of their union; cunning and courage are the patents of their nobility; and superior talent for intrigue and military skill the sole title to command. In the rapidity of their movements, their endurance of fatigue, their attachment to their horses, their want of discipline, and their predatory mode of warfare, the Pindarries strikingly resemble the least civilized of the Cossacks: their number is stated to amount to between thirty and forty thousand; but in a community liable to such fluctuations, it is not easy to form any accurate idea of their real strength. A year of plenty reconciles many to peaceful habits, and a season of scarcity multiplies the horde of free-

vanced in his direction. In Jan. 1818 he was ordered with his batt. into the Concan; the batt. consisted of recruits, having been only embodied a few days, and the old soldiers, intended to form the basis of its discipline, &c. having never been able to join, from the alarm and preparation following the breaking out of the Mahratta war. With these recruits, assisted by a detachment of 180 men from the 1st batt. 11th reg. N. I., and the crews of two cruisers, which contrived to work up the Bankoot river, and two twelve-pounders from the Prince of Wales' Island, brought up a steep mountain, seven miles in length, on men's shoulders, this officer attacked and took Mundenghur, on the 15th Feb. 1818; the garrison was triple his force, and the fort one of the strongest hill forts in the Concan: the enemy stockaded the whole line of approach, and defended every irregularity which a most rugged ascent of more than a mile from this officer's position enabled him to avail himself of. The stockades were stormed in succession, the Killedar and most of the garrison killed, and the place finally carried by assault.

Being obliged to leave a large garrison in Mundenghur, this officer returned, after making some arrangements for its defence, to Savendroog, to recruit and drill the batt. On the 2d March he mustered upwards of 250 volunteers, and marched to the attack of the hill forts of Paulghur and Ramghur. He arrived before them on the evening of the 3d, and the next morning attacked and took the forts by assault, without the loss of a man, though they were prepared to offer a warm reception; but the British, by not mounting the hill the way the enemy expected, avoided their stockades. From this time until the 4th June, this officer took the whole country between the 17th and 18th deg. of north latitude, from the sea to the Ghauts, closing the campaign by

booters beyond the powers of common calculation. But whatever may be their force, they chiefly inhabit the country north of the Nerbuddah, round Nimbawar, Kautapore, Goomass, Beresha, and part of the Bilsa and Bopal territory. Unless when united on an excursion, they live together in societies of one or two hundred; which, as is the case in most irregular combinations, are governed by him who possesses the greatest personal influence.

See Quarterly Review, May 1818.

the capture of Rutna-Gurry*. Since that time he commanded, in 1819, the southern division of Guzerat; and upon the formation of a force for the Gulph, he volunteered his services, which were accepted, to proceed with Sir Wm. Keir against Rasal Khyma; but his batt., 1st. 3d reg. N. I., being withdrawn from the expedition, he was deprived of the honour he had anticipated. Upon the formation of the south Concan into a division command, the services of this officer were acknowledged by his being appointed to it.

LIEUTENANT-COLONEL DAVID PROTHER, C. B.

(*Bombay Establishment.*)

THIS officer was appointed to an ensigncy on the Bombay establishment in Sept. 1796; lieut., 6th Sept. 1797; and actively employed on the coast of Malabar from 1798 to 1800. In Feb. 1802 he embarked for Guzerat, and joined the force at Cambay under Lieut.-Col. Alex. Walker†, destined for the reduction of Kurree. He was appointed to command the pioneers, and acted as aid-de-camp at the battle of Kurree, 17th March. On the 16th April he was appointed capt. of Guides, and was present at the storming the enemy's lines, and surrender of the fortress of Kurree, under the command of Gen. Sir W. Clarke. He was appointed in Feb. 1803 fort-adj. and garrison quart.-mast. of Surat; and the same year promoted to a company. In 1806 he was appointed barrack-master of Surat; on the 23d July 1810 promoted to a majority, and assumed the command of the 1st

---

* A decision of government on prize-money states, that the places were, for the most part, peaceably surrendered, because the Killedars had orders to surrender their forts to this officer from certain chieftains in the Deccan. It is however notorious, that they frequently had secret orders to resist to the utmost.

† Vide services, p. 147.

batt. 9th N. I., at Baroda. In Dec. 1814 he accompanied the force under Gen. Sir W. Holmes, and was present at the siege and capture of Palhaunpoor; and in 1815 marched to the Deccan, and was actively employed under Brig.-Gen. Smith, till 1816. He was promoted lieut.-col. 28th Oct. 1816, and appointed to the command of the Concan field force, 9th Nov. 1817. On the 26th, at the head of five companies of Native troops, and a detachment of H. M.'s 17th dragoons, and 47th reg., he attacked and drove the Peishwa's troops from the stockades established in the difficult fastness' of the Bhore Ghaut; by the maintenance of which position the supplies of the army had been a considerable time detained, and the communication obstructed between Poonah and Bombay, to the exclusion of intelligence, so mutually desirable to the authorities of the presidency and the Deccan. On the 31st Dec. 1817 he captured the Fort of Kotelaghur, in the northern Concan; 20th Jan. 1818, the fort of Kurnella, or Funnell hill, which surrendered by capitulation after three days' siege. The latter fort is so narrow as almost to have baffled the ability of the professional officers engaged, who nevertheless twice set the funnel in a blaze, thereby inducing the enemy to come to terms. On the 4th Feb. he captured the fort of Owchetghur; on the 5th, Soorghur; 8th, Pallee, or Purusghur; 13th, Meaghur; 15th, Boorup, or Soodaghur,—all in the southern Concan. On the 27th the force and battering train ascended the Bhore Ghaut into the Deccan; and on the 2d March defeated and drove the garrison of Loghur, or Iron Rock, from their strong positions and outworks, which, with Issapour and Toong, were taken on the 7th. On the 11th defeated a large body of the enemy before the walls of Koarre, which surrendered at discretion on the 14th, after several hours bombardment; on the 12th, Ragh and Mutchey. On the 20th the force quitted the Deccan, and returned to the Concan; and on the 16th April, on its route to invest Rhyghur, attacked and defeated a large force of the enemy posted in stockade, consisting of the garrisons of Tulla and Gonzella, both of which surrendered on the 18th; on the 20th, Manghur; and on the 11th May the important fortress of Rhyghur. A more vigorous or active siege, for the inadequacy of the force and means, was never attempted against a fort near 2500 feet from its base: it was carrying war against a mountain. The measures taken are marks of prodigious labour; 2 thirteen-inch brass mortars, 1 iron thirteen-inch, and iron bed (which required the utmost exertion of 1200 men for four days to place it in the battery), 1 ten-inch, 2 eight-inch—4 five-inch howitzers—4 twelve-pounders, and 6 sixpounders, were carried up three hills, exposed to the enemy's fire, before the battery could be laid for effect. An action had previously occurred, in which Col. Hall, of H. M.'s 89th reg., surprised and defeated a large body of the enemy with considerable loss, drove them into the Khoob Larri bastion (a very formidable position), which was subsequently carried. The siege lasted fourteen days, pushed with extraordinary fatigue and endurance; at last the enemy submitted to terms, and one of the strongest forts in India became the conquest of this force. The garrison, consisting of near 3000 men, with their families, were permitted to retain all their private property; but the Killedar broke the treaty, and embezzled public treasure to a large amount—near 10 lacks of rupees, or 120,000*l.* sterling. The consequence was, the subjection of the whole country, and the forts specified, besides several others to the southward of the Bancoot river. The Peishwa's wife was in the fort, and was permitted to retain all her property, which was considerable. On the 13th May the fort of Lingana was captured by the troops under Lieut.-Col. Prother's command; on the 16th, Kangoory; 17th, Myputtghur; 18th, Chunderghur; 21st, Koordew; 31st, Reodunda and Beewarree. He continued actively employed till Oct. 1818; and on the 3d Jan. 1819 embarked for England, on account of ill health, having completed an actual service of twenty-two years and three months. He has since returned to India.

The following extracts from official communications shew the sense entertained by government of this officer's services:—

From the Honourable Mountstuart Elphinstone, 12th *May* 1818.
" Our guns are just announcing the fall of Rhygur; I wish you joy

of this great event, which crowns all your former successes with the capture of the strongest fort in India."

From General Orders of the Governor General.

" The rapid succession of fortresses, including many of high reputation and remarkable strength, subdued by Lieut.-Col. Prother in the Concan, with an inconsiderable force, sufficiently testifies the eminent exertions of that officer."

From General Orders of the Right Honourable the Governor in Council.

" The Right Hon. the Gov. in council will have much pleasure in bringing to the notice of the Hon. the Court of Directors the prominent activity, perseverance, and valuable services performed by Lieut.-Col. Prother, during the late war, in command of a field detachment employed in subduing numerous fortresses in the Concan."

Lieutenant-Colonel Prother is a companion of the Bath.

MAJOR GEORGE HERBERT GALL.

(Bengal Establishment.)

This officer was appointed to the Company's service in 1794-5; he sailed for Bengal in 1796, and was posted to the 3d reg. light cav. 9th Oct. in that year; and in 1798 marched with the corps from its cantonment at Moneah, in Bahar, to join the grand army formed on the frontiers of the British possessions, under Gen. Sir James Craig, who advanced to Anoopsheher; from whence the army returned in several columns into cantonments, Zemaun Shaw, king of Cabul, having declined the contest. Cornet Gall, at the conclusion of the campaign, was promoted (23d June 1799) to lieut. in the 1st. reg. N. cav., stationed at Futtehgurh. This corps was ordered, in 1799, to cross the Ganges, and formed part of Maj.-Gen. R. Stuart's division in Rohilcund, subsequently commanded by Col. (now Lieut.-Gen.) Russell. On the return of the 1st reg. to the cantonment of Futtehgurh, Lieut. Gall's troop, and another from the 1st, were selected to accompany Col. Collins, Resident at the court of Dowlut Rao Scindia, to the court of the Rajah of Jeypoor; and Lieut. G., being the senior officer, commanded the squadron of cav., which, with some inf., and a detachment of art., was placed under the general controul of Capt., now Maj.-Gen., Thos. Brown.* This service, which bore a political as well as a military character, terminated in the seizure of the notorious Ex-Newaub, Vizier Ally, in spite of a numerous force of Scindia's troops, encamped under the walls of a city, and commanded by the French Gen. Perron. The thanks of the Resident, and subsequently of the Gov.-Gen., Lord Wellesley, were conveyed to Lieut. Gall, in common with his brother officers, for his conduct on that occasion, which ultimately led to Lieut. G's appointment to the Gov.-Gen.'s bodyguard.

After joining that distinguished corps, Lieut. G. obtained leave from his lordship, to serve with the army under Gen. Lake, who was then besieging Sasnee: he was present at the capture of Bejighur, and the fall of Catchoura, and at the latter place had one horse shot dead under him, and another severely wounded.

On returning from this service, Lieut. G. was the bearer of a letter from Gen. Lake to Lord Wellesley, expressive of the Gen.'s approbation of Lieut. G.'s conduct.

During the Mahratta campaign, Lieut. G., being then adj. to the body-guard, formed part of Lieut.-Gen. Martindell's army of observation, which covered the operations of the grand army, during the siege of Burtpoor. The Gov.-Gen., Lord Minto, having occasion to proceed to Madras, Lieut. G., who had been promoted to capt. 11th March 1805, proceeded by sea with the whole of the body-guard, to the command of which he had succeeded, to Fort St. George, the

* Vide Services, page 253.

officers and men acting as marines on board the Company's ship,* General Stuart, which sailed in company with the Dover frigate, having on board the Gov.-Gen., Lord Minto. His Lordship having accomplished his objects, Capt. G. returned by land to Bengal, about the time that the expedition against Java was preparing, upon which occasion he volunteered his services, and they were accepted; and his example was followed by every individual officer, non-commisssioned officer, and private trooper of the body-guard. This corps landed with the first division of Sir S. Auchmuty's army, at Chillingching in Java, and being immediately attached to the advance, under Maj.-Gen. Gillespie, marched to Tanjan Priok, where the troops bivouacked, and the next day took possession of Batavia, the French and Dutch retreating as the British troops advanced. In the warm engagement, which ended with the forcible possession of the enemy's lines at Weltevreeden, Lieut. G., who commanded a reserve, consisting of the body-guard, dismounted men of H. M.'s 22d dragoons, and a brigade of art., received the public expression of the Com.-in-Chief's approbation of the conduct of those troops. After the assault of the redoubts at Cornelis, Capt. G., still attached to Maj.-Gen. Gillespie's brigade, obtained the thanks of that officer, of the Com.-in-Chief, and of the Gov.-Gen. of India, and was one of the officers on whom a medal was bestowed by the Prince Regent. Immediately after the fall of Cornelis, Capt. G. was ordered to place himself under the orders of the late Maj.-Gen. Gibbs, who marched all night to surprise Buitenzorg, which, by direction of the Maj.-Gen., Capt. Gall summoned to surrender, and it was accordingly delivered up. During this campaign Capt. G. received a slight contusion on the right side, and a severe wound in one of his eyes.

Lord Hastings having succeeded Lord Minto in the government of India, was pleased to continue Capt. Gall in command of the body-guard, to which his lordship added a squadron, which, with the rest

* French frigates sailing in couples at that time in the bay of Bengal, rendered it necessary to have an armed ship in company with the frigate.

of the corps, accompanied his lordship on his grand military tour, in the upper provinces of Hindostan, in 1814-15, during which the Gov.-Gen. terminated with signal success the Nepaul war.

At the expiration of upwards of twenty years actual residence in India, Capt. G. was compelled, by ill health, to return to England on furlough. In Sept. 1818 he was promoted to the rank of field-officer.

Maj. Gall, during his residence in India, held the following situations:—aid-de-camp and private secretary to the Vice-President in council, Peter Speke, Esq.; aid-de-camp and private secretary to Sir G. Barlow; aid-de-camp to, and commanding the Gov.-Gen.'s body-guard; secretary to the Board of Superintendence for the improvement of cattle in India; second Member of that Board; and superintending officer of Calcutta militia.

MAJOR R. H. CUNLIFFE.

(Bengal Establishment.)

This officer arrived in India in Dec. 1800, having obtained permission from the Court of Directors to remain in England, for the purpose of completing his military education, one year after his nomination to a cadetship, and he in consequence joined the 1st reg. N. I., then stationed at Dacca, in Aug. 1801, with the rank of lieut. He had previously been directed to do duty in the 9th reg., stationed at Shahabad, in Rohilcund, which corps he actually joined, and thus had an opportunity of visiting all the principal military stations, then occupying the line of the river Ganges, and of obtaining, at this early period, a degree of topograpical and local knowledge of a country in which he was destined to serve, that under other circumstances he could not have acquired for years. In 1804 he was, at the recommendation of his commanding officer, appointed adj. to the 2d batt., and in 1806 adj. and quart.-mast. to the reg.

During the campaign of 1803-4 the situation of his corps precluded its participation in that war, and though in the subsequent year it had approached nearer to the scene of active operations, it was employed in the less conspicuous, though not less honourable or dangerous duty, of reducing fortresses in the Dooaub; which were occupied and resolutely defended by the former possessors of the adjacent lands. On the 1st Jan. 1807 Lieut. C. obtained his company; and in June 1811 he was nominated sub-assist. commissary-gen., in which capacity he accompanied the force, under Maj.-Gen. Sir G. Martindell, employed in the reduction of Callinger, a hill fortress in Bundlecund. In March 1813 Capt. C. was appointed an assist.-commissary-gen.

The general calm which followed the cessation of hostilities in 1805, was not disturbed till the rupture with the Nepaulese in 1814, on which occasion Capt. C. was selected for the charge of the commissariat department, attached to the forces destined to penetrate to the centre of the enemy's territory, and to obtain possession of their capital. He was present under Maj.-Gen. Sir D. Ochterlony, at the attack and defence of the heights near Muckwanpore, which led to the immediate subjection of the Nepaulese by their ratification of the treaty of peace previously proposed.

In Feb. 1817 Capt. C. accompanied the army, under Maj.-Gen. Sir D. Marshall, during the siege of Hattrass: in Oct. following he was attached to, and accompanied, as chief of his department, the right division of the grand army, under Lieut.-Gen. Sir Rufane Donkin. He obtained his majority in Oct. 1818, and was appointed dep.-commis.-gen. of the Bengal army, in July 1821.

MAJOR HENRY HODSON.

(Bengal Establishment.)

This officer was appointed a cadet in 1798, promoted to ensign in Sept. 1799, and joined the 2d batt. 9th N. I. at Caunpoor, in Dec. following. After visiting Agra, in company with Sir James Craig, in the early part of 1800, the first duty he was ordered on was that of forming part of a detachment, under Maj. Lally, that escorted Vizier Ally by water from Caunpoor to Allahabad, in progress to Fort William. In May 1800 he was promoted to lieut., and was employed with the above corps the greatest part of that year, and the succeeding one, in quelling different disturbances in the dominions of the Nabob of Oude. In 1802 he was permanently posted to the 2d batt. 12th N. I., which was selected the same year by Lord Wellesley, to form his personal escort to Lucknow. Early in 1803 the batt. joined the force under Lord Lake, then employed against the refractory Killedars of Sasnee and Bejighur, two mud-forts, situated in the Dooaub, between Furruckabad and Agra; they were reduced after some difficulty and no inconsiderable loss of lives, particularly in the beating back of the storming party at the former, and the blowing up of a powder-magazine in taking possession of the latter, by which a distinguished officer of the art. (Lieut.-Col. Gordon) lost his life.

After this service the batt. remained some months in garrison at Bejighur, and Lieut. H. proceeded thence on sick leave to the presidency, from thence to Bombay, afterwards to Madras, and eventually, in 1804, to England. On his return to Bengal, in 1808, he joined his batt., then at Purtaub Ghur, in Oude; and in the close of that year, and beginning of the succeeding one, it was employed in very active service in the reduction of a string of mud-forts in the Handeea district, bordering on the Company's provinces of Benares and Juanpore. In Sept. 1809 he was promoted to capt., and in Dec. marched with the batt. to the cantonment of Dinapore. In Aug. 1810 he volunteered, with two junior officers and 200 men of his corps, for the expedition against the Isle of France, and was at the capture of that colony in Dec. following. Capt. H. remained thirteen months in garrison on the island, and returned to Bengal in Jan. 1811; three months after he embarked with the batt. in boats at Calcutta for Chittagong, to co-operate in the campaign against the Birmans. Early in 1813 the corps returned to Calcutta, and in July of the same year, Capt. H. was obliged, from ill health, to proceed to the late French islands; from thence he continued his voyage to the Cape of Good Hope, St. Helena, and Europe, and returned to India again in May 1818. In Aug. following he obtained his majority, joined his corps at Muttra in December, and in February 1819 succeeded to the command of it. In Feb. 1820 he was appointed, with the left wing of the corps, to the command of the fort and station of Allyghur, in the Dooaub, where he remained till Oct. of that year, when the whole batt. (united again) removed to the station of Etaweh, and of which post and corps Maj. H. was appointed commandant.

LIEUT.-COL.-COM. HUGH S. OSBORNE.

(*Bombay Establishment.*)

In May 1790 this officer joined the Bombay Europ. reg. as ensign; was present with it at the storm of Tippoo's battery on the heights near Cananore, the capture of several small redoubts, and the surrender of the enemy's army, under Hussan Ally Cawn, in 1791; during the early part of the campaign he served with the army under Maj.-Gen. Robert Abercromby. As lieut., he was employed partly with the 2d and partly with the 3d batt. N. I. on field service, from

June 1792 to Oct. 1794, against the Mopla rebels in the south of Malabar.

Preferment being held out to such of the Company's officers as made themselves acquainted with the Malabar language, Lieut. O., in 1796, obtained the situation of translator, to which was afterwards added registrar to a civil court in the northern division of the province, and in which he continued until 1799, when he joined his corps, the 1st batt. 2d reg. N. I.; was employed with it during the siege of Seringapatam, and commanded a flank company of Sepoys on the 4th May 1799, the day of the storm.

As capt., this officer was appointed, in 1800, collector, judge, and magistrate of three districts below the Ghauts, and subsequently of Wynaad in the upper country; from which he was removed, on the transfer of the Malabar province to the Madras government, in Oct. 1801. He then rejoined his corps; and early in 1802 was appointed brig.-maj., afterwards altered to that of mil. sec., and Malabar translator to the commanding-officer of the province, which situation he held until May 1805, being most of that time employed in Cotiote and Wynaad, with the troops commanded by Col. John Montresor, of H. M.'s 80th reg., and latterly with Col. Alex. Macleod, of the Madras establishment. In 1805, on the restoration of tranquillity, Captain O. returned to England; on which occasion the following general order was issued:—

"*General Orders, Bombay Castle, Dec. 13, 1805.*
" The Hon. the Gov. in Council is pleased to permit Capt. Osborne, of the Bombay European reg., to proceed to Europe on furlough, on his private affairs, agreeably to the regulations. Capt. Osborne's services in Malabar, as well in the civil line as in his own professional capacity, have merited the approbation of the Hon. the Gov. in Council, and will be brought to the favourable notice of the Hon. the Court of Directors."

In 1806 Capt. O. returned to India, and 25th Feb. 1807 was

promoted to major. In the latter year he was appointed to the command of Broach; and resigning that situation, as lieut.-colonel, in 1814, he obtained the command of a native corps until June 1815, when he proceeded in command of a brigade on field service to Cutch, with the force commanded by Colonel East, of the Company's service, and returned to Baroda in April 1816. In Jan. 1817 he was appointed to the command of Tannah, and in Nov. of the same year, by desire of Lieut.-Gen. Nightingall, proceeded to take the command of the troops at Poonah, but lost the opportunity of commanding the line against the Peishwa's army on the memorable 5th of Nov., having arrived an hour too late; but the credit of the Bombay army was nobly sustained by the late gallant and excellent officer Lieut.-Col. Burr*.

Lieut.-Col. Osborne was next appointed, by Maj.-Gen. Smith, to the command of a brigade, and employed with it in a smart action, opposed to the whole of the Peishwa's troops, in crossing a place called the Jellua Ford, at four o'clock in the afternoon of the 16th November, when the enemy being driven off, and their camp found deserted on Gen. Smith's arrival on the following morning, with the principal part of his force, Lieut.-Col. O. continued in command of his brigade on field service against the Mahrattas until 1818, when he obtained the command of the Guicawar subsidiary force, and which he held until 1821, and then returned to Europe.

LIEUTENANT-COLONEL RICHARD SCOTT.

(*Bengal Establishment.*)

APPOINTED a cadet on the Bengal Establishment in 1768; ens. Feb. 18, 1769; lieut. June 16, 1770; capt. Aug. 26, 1779; maj. March 1,

* *Vide* Lieut.-Col. Burr's services.

1794; and lieut.-col. June 1, 1796. This officer, in 1778, was appointed brig.-maj. under that excellent disciplinarian, the late Col. Ironside, then commanding the third brigade: this appointment Capt. Scott held till the year 1781, when the Bengal army being reformed into thirty-six regiments of two battalions, he was nominated to the 1st batt. 26th reg., then under orders to the coast, which, with four other native regs., composed a part of Col. Pearce's detachment; and, upon the death of its commanding-officer, Capt. Scott succeeded to the command of the reg., which he retained during the arduous campaigns of Sir Eyre Coote against Hyder and Tippoo Sultaun; and at the close of the war the Bengal force returned to the presidency, when the Gov. Gen. in Council conferred the command of the 26th reg. upon Capt. Scott, as a reward for his services, although from his army rank he was not eligible to such command by seniority.

In the year 1790, war again breaking out with Tippoo Sultaun, the 26th reg. was selected, with some other distinguished corps, by Lord Cornwallis, to serve under his personal command on the coast: accordingly a large detachment proceeded to the coast, under Lt.-Col. John Cockerell*, whose merits, from having served under Gen. Goddard, were fully appreciated by the Bengal government. The 26th reg. distinguished itself at the capture of Bangalore, and the attack upon the entrenched lines before Seringapatam.

Some time after the return of the allied armies from Seringapatam, on the failure of the attempt against that capital, in May 1791, Capt. Scott was detached with the batt. he commanded, 26th Bengal N. I., to escort the convoy of stores, ammunition, &c., then on the way from the Carnatic to join the army, by the route of Amboor. This convoy was accompanied by the greater part of the Europeans landed that season, the recovered men, the recruits for the native corps with the army, and the Bombay volunteers; all of whom, together with the magazine, came up the Pednaigdurgum pass. As

* *Vide* Services, p. 114.

the magazine stores, carried by not fewer than 18 or 20,000 bullocks, was of more easy conveyance than the heavy train, it was sent on in advance from Amboor, with the Europeans and Natives, and joined the 26th Bengal batt., which awaited their arrival at the head of Pednaigdurgum pass. Capt. Scott, anxious to join the army, with the important convoy now under his direction, moved forward without delay. His escort consisted of the Europeans brought out in the ships of the season, amounting to 900; men for the native corps, 1000; Bombay volunteers, 500, (under their respective officers,) and two troops of cavalry, under the Hon. Lieut. Sentleger; all these added to Capt. Scott's own batt. of veterans, formed a body of upwards of 3000 soldiers, which in Europe would be considered as a command suited to the rank of a general officer.

The escort continued its march without any particular occurrence till it had gained a position to the westward of Colar. Here Capt. Scott received accounts from Capt. Read, an officer who was justly considered as the grand centre of intelligence, giving information of the enemy having unexpectedly appeared in great force; that the officer in command of Duanulla, which was not distant above 12 or 14 coss from Capt. Scott's position, had evacuated that fort, on the near approach of this body of the enemy, whose probable object, it was conceived, was to intercept and cut off the magazine, and advising Capt. Scott, in consequence, to make a forced march to the southward, through the jungle. This intelligence was in the highest degree alarming, and the situation not less critical. It is necessary to remark, that officers in command of escorts or detachments had orders to attend to the directions that should be communicated to them by Capt. Read, in consequence of any intelligence he might collect. Capt. Scott therefore would have been acting in literal obedience to his orders, and fully justified in his conduct, whatever might have been the result, had he followed the instructions of Capt. Read; but the ardent zeal of Capt. Scott, and his anxiety for the public good, was not confined by the narrow principle which does not extend the line of duty beyond the discharge of prescribed rule. In the critical situation in which he stood, he waved all attention to the feelings of personal interest, and wished not to shrink from the responsibility annexed to a deviation from orders, when he conceived that it was likely to promote the public good. Circumstanced as he then was he judiciously considered, that the safety of the essential supplies, under his convoy, was of more importance than that of the convoy itself, for the loss of these supplies must necessarily have protracted the duration of the war, not improbably to the extent of an additional campaign. He considered that a night march through the jungle, as advised, would expose the magazine to evident risk; for under such circumstances the incursion of a few Coolies, of whom there were always many hovering round, ready to take advantage of the least appearance of confusion, might have been sufficient to have driven off and dispersed the numerous train of bullocks conveying the magazine; and further, it was highly probable that the alarm created by a night march, occasioned by the dread of an enemy, would have made such an unfavourable impression on the bullock drivers, as to have induced them to consult their safety by flight. These and other considerations determined Capt. Scott to keep his ground till the morning; he did so; and the result fully vindicated the propriety of the measure. It was ascertained, that Capt. Read's intelligence, perhaps the only instance in the course of the war, was erroneous. The fort of Duanulla, it is true, had been evacuated from the belief of the intelligence of the enemy's advance; but on finding that the report originated in the appearance of a large body of Mahrattas, who were mistaken for the enemy, it was re-occupied by its former garrison. Capt. Scott, on determining to keep his ground, immediately dispatched an harcarrah to Lord Cornwallis, announcing the intelligence he had received, and stating the motives that induced him to decline the measure recommended, and his lordship expressed himself as highly pleased with the firm and judicious conduct of Capt. Scott. The escort, with its convoy, proceeded in perfect safety and good order, and after a few easy marches joined the encampment of the grand army. The junction of this convoy was of the highest importance: it had under its charge the magazine and military stores for the future prosecution of the war, and was the most important convoy and strongest detachment that joined the army during the campaign.*

A detachment under the command of Lieut.-Col. Robert, the late Gen., Stuart, marched against the strong hill-fort of Outradroog, on the 23d Dec.; and from the capability of its defence, and the reputation of its Killedar, an obstinate resistance was expected. The flag that was sent to summon being fired on, Lieut.-Col. Stuart, on the morning of the 24th, ordered Capt. Scott, with four companies of the 52d and 72d regts., and his own batt. of Sepoys, to escalade the lower fort; and on gaining possession of it, Capt. Scott had directions to remain until the necessary arrangements were made for the assault of the upper fort. Lieut.-Col. Stuart, who was well acquainted with the military ardour of Capt. Scott, perceived that he was proceeding to the assault of the upper fort, and expecting an obstinate defence, he sent an aid-de-camp to Capt. Scott, to enjoin the observance of the former order. But Capt. Scott, with a presence of mind almost peculiar to himself, and a promptitude to decide in the most difficult situations, saw clearly, that the favourable opportunity for assault that now presented would be speedily withdrawn, and that the moment then lost was irretrievable; for the enemy, astonished at the rapidity of the attack of the lower fort, and alarmed at the resolute approach of the assailants, became panic struck; fear succeeded astonishment, and presented a striking example of what Marshal Saxe terms *le cœur humain*; Capt. Scott aware that this infatuated state of the enemy would secure an easy victory, determined to rush on to the assault; he himself, with the greatest part of his men, were slung up the rocks and precipices, by ropes and turbans fastened on end; and having either escaladed or forced the gateways of the different walls, the fort was carried almost without any attempt at de-

* *Vide* Letters of Fabricius, 1793.

fence. Thus by the well-timed gallantry of Capt. Scott this important fortress was added to the list of our conquests, without the loss on our part of one single individual; and which, but for this spirited *coup de main*, might have stood a siege of some length*.

Capt. Scott remained at the head of the 26th reg. till the peace with Tippoo, when he resigned, owing to confirmed bad health, resulting from active service in the two wars.

In 1796, when the India service was reformed, and on which occasion Capt. Scott, as a member of a committee† of officers, was of signal service in obtaining the valuable concessions granted to the Company's army, by that liberal statesman, the late Viscount Melville, (whose memory should be held in grateful remembrance by every military servant of the East India Company), Capt. Scott thereby promoted to the rank of lieut.-col. was posted to the 4th reg., and proceeded to join his corps in Bengal, where, after remaining a short time, and finding the army of thirty-six batts. condensed into twelve unweildy regts.‡, and that there was little chance of obtaining a reg. in a reasonable period, he was constrained with other lieut.-cols. to retire, 9th Sept. 1797, on full pay, with his constitution so impaired as to leave no hopes of his being able to encounter further active service.

* Letters of Fabricius, 1793.   † Vide page 23.

‡ The impolicy of forming twelve heavy corps from thirty-six fine battalions, certainly was the only cause of depriving the Bengal army of many valuable officers, on which account it is to be regretted, that the honours of the Bath were not allowed to have a retrospective effect, so as to confer upon several retired officers of the three establishments, those rewards for services, which have been either overlooked or cast into oblivion; the only consolation they possess, is the gratification of seeing many of their juniors in the service obtaining those honours, and that promotion, which their services under a Wellesley, a Wellington, a Lake, and a Hastings, have been the means of drawing into action.

LIEUT.-COLONEL VALENTINE BLACKER, C. B.

(Madras Establishment.)

This officer served as a cornet during the Mysore campaign, with a troop of cav. of the Nizam's contingent, originally raised by the French at Hyderabad: he was present at the battle of Malavilly; joined in charge of a party of cav. the detachment of troops under Col. Stevenson in Dec. 1800, employed in Wynaad; and, when the cav., from the nature of the country, were sent back, he acted as aid-de-camp to Col. Stevenson during the remainder of the military operations. He next served with his own reg. in the operations to the southward, under Col. Agnew; he received a pike wound in a charge at Panjalumcourchy; had his horse piked under him; was thanked by Col. Agnew, commanding the force, for leading a company which surprised a party of the enemy near Calarcial, and for leading a successful charge of cav. against a party of inf. In 1802 he acted as secretary to Col. Pater, commanding the southern division, during eight months. In Nov. of the same year he was appointed assist.-quart.-mast.-gen. and capt. of guides; and marched in charge of the quart.-mast.-gen.'s department, with the troops assembled under Gen. Baird, at the opening of the Mahratta war, and returned from the field in Sept. 1803; he was eight months, from July 1804 to April 1805, in charge of the quart.-mast.-gen.'s department, with a body of troops assembled in the Chittoor Pollams, during which he led parties to the attack of two droogs (Nareul and Moogral), and was thanked by the officer commanding the force. In Aug. 1806 he was appointed dep.-quart.-mast.-gen. of the army, and was in charge of that department in 1809, during the military operations from Quilon, under Col. Chalmers. In July 1809 he took charge of the quart.-mast.-gen.'s department, with the troops assembled at St. Thomas's mount, and marched with the corps under Col. Close to Seronge, whence he was recalled to head-quarters, and in April 1810 appointed quart.-mast.-gen. of the army. In 1815 he took the field, at the head of the quart.-mast.-gen.'s department, with the army* of reserve assembled on the frontier, under the command of Sir T. Hislop; in 1817 he joined the army of the Deccan in the same official situation, and being constantly present with the Com.-in-Chief during the campaign, was at the battle of Mehidpoor, and the assault of Talneir.

Lieut.-Col. B. was subsequently appointed surveyor-gen. of India. In 1821 he returned to Europe on sick certificate; on which occasion the Gov. in council expressed, in general orders, " his high sense of the eminent and scientific services of Lieut.-Col. B., as quart.-mast.-gen. of the army of Fort St. George, during a period of ten years." Lieut.-Col. B. was appointed a companion of the Bath 14th October 1818.

The following are public testimonials of this officer's services :—

" *To his Exc. Lieut.-Gen. Sir J. F. Crodock, K. B. Com-in-Chief.*"

" SIR,—I consider it no less an act of justice than a duty incumbent on me, before I quit the station of quart.-mast.-gen., to state to your Exc. my opinion of the merits of Capt. Blacker, who, for a period of nearly four years, has been my assistant in office, and capt. of guides. In carrying on the duties of my department, I have ever found the utmost readiness in Capt. B. to afford me his assistance; which, from his active zeal, his general and local knowledge, and his professional talents, could not fail to be attended with beneficial consequences. His skill in regulating the marches of troops, in pointing out the most proper ground for encampments, and in providing for the supplies of an army, is well known to those officers who served with the army in the field under Gen. Stuart in 1803. I shall now beg leave to conclude, by assuring your Exc., that Capt. B. has been

---

* So denominated with reference to the operations of the Bengal army then carrying on in Nepaul.

indefatigable in instructing the Native guides in the principles of geometry and surveying; and he has brought that corps to a degree of perfection in their duties which was never before equalled.

   (Signed) " ALEXANDER ORR, Quart.-Mast.-Gen.
" *Fort St George, Aug.* 8, 1806."

Extract from a Minute of the Commander-in-Chief, 6*th July* 1812.

" Nor can I conclude this paragraph without recording my entire approbation of the zeal, ability, and general information, which prove the judicious selection of Lieut.-Col. Blacker for the office of quart.-mast.-gen. of the army, which he fills to my entire satisfaction, and with every advantage to the public services.

   (Signed) " S. AUCHMUTY, Lieut.-Gen.

Extract from the Minute, Nov. 22, 1814.

" I shall only trouble the government with one more enclosure, relating to the subject of this minute,—it is an extract from a secret minute of Lieut.-Gen. Hewitt, dated 27th Aug. 1810, and refers in the strongest terms of approbation to the conduct of Lieut.-Cols. Conway and Blacker. These officers have continued, since the date of Gen. Hewitt's minute, to evince the same qualifications which, at that period, so deservedly gained them his praise; they have invariably received the thanks of every general officer who has commanded the coast army since their appointments to their present offices; and I have sincere gratification in adding, that since that honour has been conferred upon myself, I have had the greatest reason to think myself fortunate in having such able and zealous assistants at the heads of the military departments as Lieut.-Cols. Conway, Blacker, and Morison.

   (Signed) " J. HISLOP, Lieut.-Gen."

Extract from Gen. Hewitt's secret Minute, Aug. 27, 1810.

" The evil of appointing officers deficient in rank, however eminently qualified by talent for these appointments, I have already noticed; but I hope it will not be supposed that I am casting the slighest reflection on the deserving officers now holding the appointments of adj.-gen. and quart.-mast.-gen., who, though but permanently captains, are yet, in zeal and talent, every way qualified to discharge the duties intrusted to them, with credit to themselves and benefit to the service; and I have therefore nothing further from my contemplation than the recommendation of any regulation which shall affect them or their deputies.

(Signed)   "H. Scott, Mil.-Sec."

Extract from a Minute of the Com.-in-Chief, Nov. 22, 1814.

" Lieut.-Col. Blacker is an officer of much experience in this country, having arrived at Madras in the year 1798. I am not aware that an officer better adapted than Lieut.-Col. Blacker for the situation of quart.-mast.-gen. can be found in this army; not one, certainly, who combines the same measure of professional science, with a correct, conscientious, and able system of conducting the complete details of which his department is composed.

(Signed)   "T. Hislop, Lieut.-Gen."

Extract from a Letter to the Marquess of Hastings, Gov.-Gen. and Com.-in-Chief, from Lieut.-Gen. Sir T. Hislop, Com.-in-Chief of the army of the Deccan, dated Camp on the Soopra, opposite Mehidpoor, Dec. 23, 1817.

" To Lieut.-Col. Blacker, quart.-mast.-gen. of the army, I feel it also particularly incumbent on me to express my best thanks, for the great aid I have received from him, not only through his personal exertions on the field of battle, but for the judicious reconnoissances made by him during our march, and before we engaged, by which I obtained the clearest information respecting the ford at which I subsequently crossed the Soopra; and the nature of the ground occupied by the enemy, by which I was enabled to make my dispositions for attacking them.

Extracts from a Letter to the Marquess of Hastings, from Lieut.-Gen. Sir T. Hislop, Camp at Talneir, Feb. 28, 1818.

" On this I directed a reconnoissance to be made by the Quart.-Mast.-Gen., Lieut.-Col. Blacker, and the officers of engineers, with a company of light inf., the deep ravines round the place preventing its accessibility on this service by the cav. picquets."—" A second reconnoissance having been made by Lieut.-Col. Blacker, who advanced to the outer gate for that purpose, I determined upon storming it, in the hope that, at all events, a lodgment might be made within."

Extract of General Orders by the Com.-in-Chief, Head-Quarters of the Deccan, Camp near Talneir, Feb. 28, 1818.

" The judicious and accurate reconnoissances made by Lieut.-Col. Blacker, Quart.-Mast.-Gen. of the army, and the ability and gallantry of that officer in conducting the important arrangements of his department during the operations of yesterday, were such also as to entitle him to his Exc.'s warmest thanks and acknowledgements."

LIEUTENANT-COLONEL C. S. FAGAN.

(Bengal Establishment.)

IN 1798 this officer went out to India as a cadet, and landing in Calcutta the beginning of Dec. 1800, was promoted to ensign in the 18th N. I. Sept. 28, 1799; and to lieut. 28th Oct. following. He joined the 2d batt. of the reg. in quarters at Dinapoor in May 1801; and in Nov. following marched with it* as part of the escort of the

* The 18th and 19th regs. were formed from the volunteers that had served with such distinction in the last Mysore war, and at the taking of Seringapatam; and this particular battalion was selected by Lord Wellesley for the duty, on account of its high character and state of discipline.

Capt.-Gen. and Com.-in-Chief, Lord Wellesley, on his tour through the upper provinces in 1801-2.

The Mahratta war, which broke out in 1803, calling nearly the whole of the Bengal army into the field, this officer's corps formed part of a detachment, commanded by Lieut.-Col. (now Lieut.-Gen.) Powell, destined for the conquest of the province of Bundlecund, and to cover the operations of the grand army, under Gen. Lake; on which occasion, the adj. of the corps being temporally removed to a superior staff situation in the detachment, Lieut. Fagan, although a very young officer, was selected by his commandant to officiate for him. He was present in the action with the enemy on the 12th Oct. 1803, and at the reduction immediately afterwards of many strong forts in that province. In Dec. following the corps, with another, was detached to aid a division of the grand army, under the late Maj.-Gen. Sir H. White, in the reduction of Gualior; in which arduous and interesting service he was appointed to act as an engineer. After the fall of that celebrated, and heretofore deemed impregnable fortress, he returned with the corps to his former detachment, the command of which, through the ill health of Col. Powell, and the death of his successor, Lieut.-Col. Pothill, had devolved on the present Maj.-Gen. W. D. Fawcett.

The irruption of a large Mahratta army into Bundlecund, under Ameer Khan, took place at this period, May 1804, and was the precursor of proceedings memorable for the judicial investigations they gave rise to; but far more so for the dreadful hardships, sickness, and mortality, to which the troops were subjected, and which will be long remembered by the survivors of that ill-fated detachment*. During the whole of the scenes here alluded to, this officer was present, on one occasion escaping most narrowly from falling into the hands of the enemy.

---

* It was the hottest season remembered for many years in India: officers and men fell daily, victims to heat and fatigue; and on the march to Kimchor Ghaut, on the Batwa river, 28th May, although partly effected at night, vast numbers of the troops and camp-followers perished from the want of water.

Lieut.-Col. (now Maj.-Gen. Sir G.) Martindell was nominated to the command of the detachment; and as soon as the state and reequipment of the troops permitted, he advanced to clear the province of the enemy. On the 2d of July this officer was present when Lieut. Col. M., with a select part of his force, attacked and routed a large body in their camp and formidable positions on the hills near Passwarree; and on the 28th of the same month, having had the adjutantcy of his batt. conferred on him by Lord Lake a few days before, he was severely wounded in an attempt to carry, by a *coup-de-main*, the strong hill-fort of Saitpoor. One of four attacking columns, composed of the batt. companies of his corps, was ordered to force, by blowing open the gates; and from particular circumstances, it fell to the lot of this officer to have the honour of rallying and leading the head of it in five or six different attempts on the main gate, close to which, from being exposed to the enfilade of some works in the rear, guns over the gateway, besides the musquetry from the whole garrison from all around, (after the failure of the other columns,) the entire front was at one time knocked down. After a month's siege, however, the place capitulated; but such service among hills in that climate and season, the periodical rains, was not to be carried on without severe sufferings, and accordingly on the day Saitpoor fell, a dreadful fever broke out among the troops, which, in its effects and consequences, was far more fatal than any thing before experienced; scarcely an officer or man escaped. Lieut. Fagan was attacked by it when just beginning to recover from his wound, and was one of two or three of his brother-officers given over by the surgeons at the same time.

The detachment returned to Culpee*, on the banks of the Jumna, and after a halt of two months, during which it was considerably reinforced and recruited, it was called to aid in the operations of the war

* On its arrival, there were only three officers, with a few men, around the colours of both batts. of the 18th reg.; the remainder were all in hospital, and casualties were hourly occurring. The other corps was nearly in the same state. The contagion quickly spread through the whole force; and the province altogether, from its unhealthiness at this period, was styled by the Europeans the " St. Domingo of the East."

against Holkar, which had broken out; as also to watch the movements of Dowlat Rao Scindia, who, in a suspicious manner, approached the grand army, then engaged in the siege of Burtpoor. After marching twice towards that celebrated fortress, and as often countermarching, according to the movements of that prince, the force halted in his vicinity; and the Com.-in-Chief, who, in the meantime, had concluded a treaty with the Burtpoor Rajah, effected a junction with it, upon which Dowlat Rao rapidly moved to the Deccan.

This officer had now attained the capt.-lieutenantcy of his reg., and he is, we believe, the first officer on the Bengal establishment who arrived at that rank within so short a period*.

Until May 1806 Capt. Fagan served with his corps in the same detachment, occasionally exercising the command of the former in the absence of the senior officers. The rains of this year were also passed under canvass at Jhansi, on the southern frontier of the province, and the season was nearly as fatal as the preceding one, from the general sickness and mortality that prevailed; added to which, officers and men suffered the greatest distress and privations from the circumstance of their being nine months in arrears.

The war with the Mahratta states was however now brought to a close, and Capt. Fagan obtained his first leave of absence to re-establish his health. At the end of six months he rejoined his batt., then relieved and in cantonments across the Ganges. To fill up its ranks, and restore its drill and discipline, (for he still held the adjutantcy,) became the duty of this officer, and he performed it to the entire satisfaction (as repeatedly acknowledged) of his commanding-officer. His promotion to a company, in 1808, deprived him of this situation. In Sept. 1809 the Com.-in-Chief, Lieut.-Gen. Hewitt, conferred on this officer the fort-adjutantcy and barrack-mastership of Chunar. His successor, Sir G. Nugent, removed him to the more important post of principal agent for army clothing, and he succeeded to a majority in his reg. in Oct. 1815.

* In the Hon. Company's army the officers rise by gradation to the rank of major in regiments or corps, and afterwards in a general list of field-officers of each branch respectively.

The removal of Maj. Fagan, by his staff appointment, from the regimental duties of his profession, did not prevent his being actively employed:---on the increase of the Bengal army, in 1814, he was selected to join two batts. of inf., one for local, the other for general service; this last, numbered the 1st batt. 29th*, was entirely disciplined by him, and he performed the duty so much to the satisfaction of Lord Hastings, whose head-quarters happened to be at the same station that year, that he was appointed, in 1817, to raise and discipline an infantry levy for the general service of the army. The 22d Sept. 1821 he obtained the rank of lieut.-col.

LIEUTENANT-COLONEL JAMES WELSH.

(Madras Establishment.)

At the close of 1789 this officer obtained a cadetship on the Madras establishment, and early in 1790 embarked for the East Indies; his first commission was dated 22d May of that year. He was stationed in garrison at Velore till 1791, when he joined a small party of Sepoys, under Lieuts. Mapother and Irton, detached against the irregular troops of Mysore, (who at that time infested and over-ran the Carnatic, even to the very gates of Madras,) and in Nov. of the same year he ascended the Ghauts with Col. Floyd's detachment, proceeding to join his new corps, the 10th batt., then serving in the grand army under Lord Cornwallis.

In Nov. 1792 he was promoted lieut., and removed to the 24th batt., with which corps he was present at the siege of Pondicherry, in July and Aug. 1793. In 1794 he was removed to the 9th batt.

---

* The Marquess of Hastings presented their colours to this corps; its uniform, and the dress of the European officers, are those of his lordship's regiment in the British service. It is also designated the " Moira-ka-Pulton," or Moira's Battalion.

In the end of 1795, and beginning of 1796, he was present at the capture of Ceylon; and remained on that island for three years, as dep. pay-master and fort-adjut. of Point de Galle. In Jan. 1799 he was removed to Masulipatam, as fort-adjut. and dep. post-master; on the 10th Dec. following he was promoted to capt.-lieut., and appointed adjut. and quart.-mast. of the 3d N. I., when joining the southern field detachment in the Tinnevelly district, he became quart.-mast. to that force.

Early in 1801, several Poligars, (of whom those of Pimgalumcoorchy and Murdoo were chief,) having thrown off the Company's yoke, this detachment was actively employed for eight months against 20,000 of the best and bravest soldiers in the East, and had actually one-third of its numbers killed and wounded on that service, including the two storms of Pimgalumcoorchy, &c.; during which period, though a staff-officer, Capt. Welsh was constantly personally engaged, either at the head of the flank or batt. companies of the 1st batt. 3d reg., or as a volunteer with other corps. On one occasion he was with a small party of native cavalry, which charged a body of pike and matchlock men of five times its own number, and the enemy, standing firm to receive it, were not dispersed and ultimately cut up without considerable loss, and extraordinary exertions of the assailants, among whom their gallant leader was piked through the lungs.

In 1803 Capt. W. was present with his corps during the whole Mahratta campaign, and personally engaged on the following occasions:—Storming the pettah of Ahmednugger; battle of Argaum; siege and assault of Gawilghur; and a volunteer with Maj.-Gen. Wellesley in the affair at Mahkerseer, (after a march of fifty-four miles). In 1804, when judge advocate and assistant surveyor to the Poonah subsidiary force in the field, Capt. W. commanded a party of 300 men, under Maj. James Campbell, of H. M.'s 94th reg., at the storming of the outworks of the hill-fort of Chandore; he took possession of the hill-fort of Dhoorp, commanded a select party of European and Native light inf., at the storming of the pettah and outworks of the hill-fort of Gallnah; was appointed a prize agent, (but the captured property was never given up to the army); and afterwards, at the head of a small body of cavalry and infantry, opened a communication between the army and Surat, through a country hitherto unknown, invested by Bheels (mountaineers armed with bows and arrows), and over a ghaut and jungle of thirty miles in extent. On this service Capt. W. caught a malignant fever, which several times reduced him to the brink of the grave, and which continued to oppress him for ten subsequent years.

In 1805 Capt. W. commanded his corps in the field, and also continued to perform the duties of his staff situation. Early in 1806 he resigned the judge-advocateship, and returned with his corps to the Carnatic; was promoted to major; and on the 19th Nov., when commanding Palamcotta, discovered a plot to murder all the Europeans, civil and military, at the station; and at the moment when his men (who were nearly related to many, and intimately connected with all the mutineers of Velore) were assembling at the barrack, with arms in their hands (suspecting the knowledge he had obtained), he collected his six European officers, and dashed into the barracks, seized the ringleaders (disarming one of them, a Native officer, with his own hand, while loading a musket), and secured the arms of the corps.

In the middle of 1807 Major W. proceeded from Bengal to England on sick certificate, distress of mind having increased his complaint to such a degree as to render it absolutely necessary, to save his life. Returning early in 1809 to Madras, he found that the corps to which he then stood appointed was taking the field; he set out post, and reached the force under Col. the Hon. A. Sentleger on the 6th Feb.; took the command of the 2nd batt. 3d reg. (five companies of the 1st batt. being also present), and was immediately detached about two miles in advance, to watch the enemy's motions, the force being encamped about five miles outside of the Travancore lines; here, on the 9th Feb., when no battering guns were within 200 miles, and a small subsidiary force in the interior was known to be surrounded, and in danger of being destroyed, by a whole population in arms, he volunteered his services, and planned an attack upon a fortified hill, which flanked and commanded the strong lines of Aramboolee, mounting fifty-two pieces of cannon, and defended by 9 or 10,000 men. The storming party, consisting of a few pioneers, with scaling ladders, a few European artillerymen, 150 men of his H. M.'s 69th reg., and nine companies selected from both batts. of the 3d Native reg., under twenty-five officers, assembled at his post, in advance, at 8 o'clock P. M.: he explained his plans to all the officers, and then set forward on an expedition, which appeared so rash even to those whom he was leading, that ere they had proceeded far he formed a forlorn hope of volunteer Europeans, and headed it himself. The night was extremely dark, and, though the total distance was within three miles, it took eight hours and a half to reach the works at the summit of the hill, scrambling through very thick jungles, into deep ravines, and over rugged rocks.

At half-past four A. M. the 10th Feb., Maj. W. found himself and Lieut. Bertram of the pioneers, with the forlorn hope alone, at the foot of a stone wall twelve feet high, having been directed to it by the enemy's patroles, who had just passed by with numerous lights; this was the moment for decision: he seized it, and with twenty resolute followers entered the place, climbing upon one another's shoulders, &c.: nearly at the same time the head of the storming party reached a part of the wall about 200 yards lower down; the ladders were applied, and the whole works carried before daylight, under a very heavy fire of cannon and musquetry, but which did little execution.

Major W. was publicly thanked in detachment and general orders, and the works named after him (though subsequently destroyed). The surviving officers of the storming party presented him with an address and piece of plate, on which is inscribed their admiration of his conduct. He was chosen a prize agent, but the appointment was afterwards annulled by government, and hopes were held out to him from head-quarters of more substantial benefits. In April 1812, when stationed at Seringapatam, in command of his old corps (the 1st batt. 3d reg.), he was detached in command of a flank corps, formed of Europeans and Natives, to quell a rebellion in Wynaad, and relieve the post of Manantoddy, besieged by the insurgents; this service was effected on his part by one march of 48 miles, and several of 20 and 30 per diem, through the deepest jungle; the insurgents were attacked and dispersed in all directions, and tranquillity restored within the month. On this occasion he received the thanks of Maj.-Gen. Wetherall, commanding the division, and of government through him, and Col. Webber, the senior officer, who had entered Wynaad from the opposite coast. The 20th Feb. 1813 he obtained the rank of lieut.-col., and was subsequently appointed dep. judg.-adv. at Bangalore.

LIEUTENANT-COLONEL CHRISTOPHER FAGAN.

(Bengal Establishment.)

This officer entered the service of the East India Company, as a cadet in the 19th reg. of N. I., in 1794; was promoted to ensign in 1795; lieut., in 1796; capt., in Feb. 1804; maj., 22d Feb. 1811; and lieut.-col., 14th July 1815. He was appointed in 1800 adj. to his batt.; which situation he voluntarily relinquished, to proceed with the expedition to Egypt in 1801, when he was appointed, by Gen. Sir D. Baird, agent for transports on the Nile,—a situation which he filled in such manner as to obtain him the most honourable recommendation from the Gen. to the Supreme government. He was subsequently nominated dep. judge-adv.-gen. on the junction of the Indian with the British army at Alexandria. From Egypt he obtained a year's furlough to England; and in Dec. 1803 was again in India, serving with his corps; with which he continued till Sept. 1810, when he relinquished the command of the batt., a post of advantage as well as honour, in order to proceed, as a volunteer, on the expedition against the French islands. After the conquest of the Mauritius, he solicited and obtained Maj.-Gen. Abercromby's permission to return to Bengal, to resume the command of his corps. On his arrival at Calcutta in Feb. 1811, the Gov.-Gen., in concurrence with the Com.-in-Chief, Sir G. Hewitt, appointed him dep.-judge-adv.-gen.; this appointment he lost on his promotion to a majority, through the operation of a rule which restricts that appointment to officers under the rank of maj.; on this change he rejoined his corps, and obtained the command of it, as well as of the military station of Lucknow.

In Oct. 1812, when Sir G. Nugent visited that post on his tour of inspection of the army, he reviewed the troops stationed there under Maj. F.'s command, and on that occasion issued the following general orders:—

"*Head Quarters, Lucknow,* 16*th Oct.* 1812.

"The review in brigade this morning of the 2d batt. 19th and 1st batt. 24th, under Maj. Fagan of the former corps, and at present in command of the troops at Lucknow, afforded the Com.-in-Chief high satisfaction, not only from the excellence of the performance of both batts., but from the successful example it exhibited, of the utility and benefit that must result to the service, from an assiduous and zealous attention on the part of officers in command, to the general orders which enjoin the exercise of troops in brigade, whenever circumstances admit of it. Those advantages were this morning very conspicuous in the different movements of the brigade, reviewed by his Exc.; admirably well selected with reference to practical utility in the field, and executed with a promptitude, regularity, and precision, highly creditable to Maj. Fagan, and the officers and men of both batts., that manœuvred under his directions on this occasion. Although the Com.-in-Chief had reason to be satisfied, in every respect, with the appearance and performance of both corps, justice to the 2d batt. 19th, and to Maj. Fagan, the officer who has so long held the executive command of it, requires that his Exc. should notice with peculiar approbation, and with his marked acknowledgment, the very high state of discipline in which he has found that fine corps."

In July 1813 Maj. F. was called from the active duties of his profession, and appointed judge-adv.-gen. The 14th of July 1815 he obtained the rank of lieut.-col.; and in Dec. 1816, declining health compelled him to quit India for his native country, on which occasion the Gov.-Gen. recorded his approbation of this officer's official conduct, in the following general orders to the army:—

"*Fort William, Jan.* 28, 1817.

" The Right Hon. the Gov.-Gen. in council, in communication with his Exc. the Com.-in-Chief, under whose immediate authority the administration of military law is conducted, performs a gratifying part of his public duty, in recording the high sense entertained by the government of Lieut.-Col. Fagan's eminent merit and zealous services, during the period that he has filled the distinguished office of judge-adv.-gen. in Bengal; and his lordship in council deeply regrets, that continued ill health should have compelled the lieut.-col. to return to Europe, and to relinquish the honourable employment, which he has filled with so much credit to himself and advantage to the state."

THE LATE LIEUT.-COL. CHARLES J. BOND.

(Bombay Establishment.)

THIS officer was appointed a cadet on the Bombay establishment in 1794, and entered the corps of art. in 1796. On the breaking out of the war in Mysore with Tippoo Sultaun in 1798, he was ordered to join the army under Gen. John Stewart, encamped on the heights of Cananore; he proceeded with the army, and was at the siege and capture of Seringapatam. During this service he was in the several attacks made by the enemy on the covering parties for the batteries, in one of which, when under the command of Lieut.-Col. Mignan, the enemy were repulsed with considerable loss in killed and wounded: at the close of the attack this officer was wounded. The following year he again took the field with a force under the command of Lieut.-Col. Sartorius, in the province of Canara, and was at the capture of the important fort of Jemaulabad, after an arduous and difficult siege. This fortress was in our possession a few months, when it was retaken by the enemy, and the commanding officer of the garrison killed. He again accompanied a force under Lieut.-Col. Cummings, of H. M.'s 75th reg., and was a second time at the siege and capture of this formidable fortress, which was again attended with considerable fatigue, and the loss of many men in killed and wounded. On his return from this service he was appointed adj. to the corps of art. When the expedition was ordered to proceed to Egypt under Lieut.-Gen. Sir D. Baird, this officer volunteered his services, and accompanied the army across the great desert, from Cossier to Gennah, on the banks of the Nile, and shortly after reached Grand Cairo, just as the French troops were about to evacuate that city. He was in Egypt the whole of the time the Indian army was there: in 1806, he again joined the field force under Col. Wallace in the Deccan, and remained till the latter end of 1807, when he was appointed to act as dep.-commissary of stores in Guzerat. From his services, and standing in the corps, he naturally looked forward to succeed to this office on a vacancy occurring; but was disappointed, and rejoined his corps, with which he remained till 1809, and was in that year ordered with the expedition under Commodore Ferrier to the Persian gulph. He commanded the whole of the art. on this service, and on his return was appointed to the command of the art. attached to the force under Lieut.-Col. Lionel Smith of H. M.'s 65th reg. in Kattywar; was at the siege and capture of the principal forts in that country; and received the thanks of that officer for his conduct. The following year he was ordered to join the field force, and take the command of the art. in the Deccan: he remained with this force till 1816, during which period the army was almost constantly under canvas, and marching in different directions. On the breaking out of the Mahratta war he was appointed to the command of a detachment of troops, for the attack of the important fort of Savendroog, conjointly with Capt. Hill, of H. M.'s ship, Tower: at the expiration of this service he was appointed to command the art., with the field force under Lieut.-Col. Prother, for the conquest of the territory in the south Concan, belonging to the Peishwa. In this laborious service he suffered more from fatigue than even in crossing the desert of Cossier; this country was never before visited by European troops, and is a continued chain of mountains, covered with impenetrable woods, numerous forts situated on stupendous heights, 2000 to 3000 feet above the level of the plain, with scarcely the appearance of a road leading to them. In this wild country the army was necessitated to carry with it almost every article of consumption, excepting grass. The art. branch, having a heavy train of ordnance and stores to transport over these unfrequented ghauts, at a dreadful season of the year, accomplished their labours, under circumstances of extraordinary difficulty, in the face of an enemy, and under the rays of a burning sun. The difficulty of taking position for batteries to bombard these heights, was no less arduous than dangerous, as it was impossible to march under cover to their forts, their extreme heights commanding every possible approach. Maj. Bond joined the army at Pallee, a strong and fortified hill fort, and was at its siege and capture. The army then proceeded to Boorup, situated more to the eastward, remarkably strong, and also a hill fort, about 2400 feet high. This fortress was reduced after a bombardment of three days, and the garrison surrendered. Maj. B then proceeded with the train of art. towards the important fortress of Loghur and Essapour, two forts of remarkable strength, situated above the Ghauts in the Deccan, both of which also surrendered. The army then proceeded to the fort of Koarre, a hill fort of the same description, commanding an important pass on the Swacy Ghaut: this fort sustained a siege of some length, and did not surrender till the principal buildings and one of the gates were burnt by the shells. Several other smaller forts were taken, which it is not important here to specify, as they were taken after slight skirmishing, and their out-works being carried by assault. The army then proceeded to the memorable fort of Ryghur, situated nearly on the same range of Ghauts, more to the south; this fort is at a greater height, and larger than any of the former; the labour of erecting batteries was very great, nor could a position be obtained till Maj. Hall, with a detachment of H. M.'s 89th reg., carried the enemy's extensive stockades by assault. The nature of ordnance for the reduction of so extensive a place, was necessarily of heavy calibre; it employed the whole army some days to get two 13-inch mortars to the situation required, the approach being so very steep and rugged; the light howitzers were carried on two elephants, taken from the enemy a few days before, and they considerably assisted in carrying up the heights the howitzers, carriages, and stores; but the heavy guns were dragged up by manual labour: the batteries all opened on the same day with considerable effect, several buildings were burnt, and in a few days the palace was fired, and every part destroyed. From the incessant fire kept up, and the large charges and great elevations, we were necessitated to use, the mortar beds were soon crippled, but by ropes and other means, we had the good fortune to keep them together, till the surrender of the place, which, in some measure, made up for the fatigues, as some treasures were found in the fort, with his highness the Peishwa's wife. The reduction of this fortress terminated the campaign. Maj. B. next accompanied the field force ordered, under the command of Maj.-Gen. Sir W. G. Keir, for the attack of the capital of Cutch, situated on the north side of the gulph of that name. The army assembled at Anjar on the 1st March, and were in readiness for movement on the 23d of that month, and on the 24th it marched. The force, consisting of 5000 men, with a handsome train of art., reached the vicinity of Booje on the 27th. At its approach to the enemy's principal works, a fire was opened on the lines, and their cav. appeared on the plain; but on a battery being formed of the field pieces, and after a smart fire, they were dispersed. On the following morning the enemy's works were carried by escalade, in a very gallant manner, by the flank companies of H. M.'s 65th reg., and those of the Sepoy corps; a battery on the height, in front of the lines, covered the attack, while the whole force made a movement towards the city. The enemy were driven from their works, with considerable loss in killed, wounded, and prisoners: this so much alarmed the Rajah, that in the course of the day he made an unconditional surrender of the town, which was taken possession of immediately: these operations completed the campaign. At the opening of the season of 1819, Maj. B. proceeded, again in command of the art., with the expedition under Maj.-Gen. Keir, to the Persian Gulph. In 1820 he obtained the rank of Lieut.-Col.; and in September of that year he died at Surat, deeply regretted.

MAJOR EDWARD MOOR.

(Bombay Establishment.)

This officer was appointed a cadet on the Bombay establishment in May 1782, and sailed for India, being then under twelve years of age, in Sept. of that year. Adverse winds, and the belligerent state of the European naval powers, caused the fleet in which he sailed to proceed to Madras, where he arrived in April 1783. In Aug. he was ordered by the government of Madras to proceed with a reinforcement to the relief of Mangalore, then closely besieged by Tippoo Sultaun. After a

southern passage of four months, no landing could be effected, and a general peace in Europe and in India was about that time concluded. In Sept. 1788 (after serving as ensign five years and ten months) he was promoted to lieut.; and in Dec. following, appointed by Gen. Sir William Medows (Gov. and Com.-in-Chief of Bombay) adj. and quart.-mast. of the 9th batt. N. I. On attaining the rank of lieut., he was eligible to the examination and allowance for speaking the country language; the certificate of the examining committee was as follows:—
" It would not be doing justice to this officer were we to omit noticing his very great proficiency; the more so, as he has not attained his eighteenth year."

War breaking out in 1790, Lieut. M. resigned his adjutantcy, and proceeded in command of a grenadier company of the 9th batt. to join the brigade under Capt. Little, serving with the Mahratta army, commanded by Purseram Bhow, then engaged in the siege of Darwar. Col. Frederick assumed the command of the brigade, and forming a grenadier corps of all the flank companies of the battalions of N. I. under his command, appointed Lieut. Moor adj. and quart.-mast. of it. With this corps, particularly formed for the more vigorously carrying on the operations of that memorable siege, he served before Darwar upwards of three months, until the surrender of the fort. In this time he was present at several affairs, usually attendant on a protracted siege, and in the assault of the fort, 7th Feb. 1791, he was on the storming party.

On the fall of the fort, the grenadier batt. was reduced, and Capt. Little again resumed the command of the Bombay brigade from Colonel Sartorius, who had succeeded on the death of Colonel Frederick; and it accompanied the Mahratta army to join Lord Cornwallis before Seringapatam. Proceeding with the grand army in its movements from Seringapatam to Bangalore, Purseram Bhow separated in the neighbourhood of the latter place, and marched northward. In an assault of the hill fort, Doridroug, near Bangalore, 13th June 1791, Lieut. Moor commanded the leading company, and was shot through the right shoulder. On recovering, he rejoined his corps, and was present at the siege, and on the storming party, at the capture of Hooly Honore, 21st Dec. 1791; and on the 29th following led the two flank companies of the 9th batt. at the battle of Gadjnoor, near Simoga. In this action all the attacks on the right, left, and centre of the enemy's position, having failed, Lieut. M. (the 9th batt. being in reserve) was ordered to renew the attack on the right, and to " penetrate the enemy's camp, if possible, and as far as possible :" he succeeded in reaching its centre, where he received a wound in his right knee, and a musket ball through his left elbow. The result of the affair was, the total route and dispersion of the enemy's army of 10,000 foot, and 1000 horse, most advantageously situated in a selected and strengthened position, and the capture of all his guns, baggage, and equipage. The commander narrowly escaped being taken. " The victory as it was," says Gen. Dirom, in his Narrative of this campaign, " did not require this circumstance to make it one of the most brilliant actions of the war."—p. 104. The British engaged were under 1000; every flank officer, except one, of the brigade, were killed or wounded in this action. At a visit which the commanding officer paid Lieut. Moor at night, after the battle, he expressly attributed the victory to him. He was the only European officer with the flank companies of the 9th, and had only one other European, a serjeant, with him.

On account of the severity of the wound through the elbow joint, which was and is wholly destroyed, Lieut. M. was compelled to quit the army, and eventually India, for the re-establishment of his health, much impaired by a continued campaign of upwards of eighteen months, attended by great exposure and privation, and marchings and journeys of more than 1500 miles; half of this, while suffering from his last wound.

The documents annexed (No. 1. to 15,) shew the sense entertained by the government of this officer's services. In consequence of the recommendations 1 to 4, strengthened by Lord Cornwallis, the Court of Directors were pleased to defray, at different times, Lieut. Moor's expences while in England* for the restoration of his health; which

* About this period (1794) Lt. Moor published a " Narrative of the operations of Capt.

being effected, he embarked again for India in April 1796, having now obtained the rank of capt. by brevet. In the beginning of 1797 he was appointed to the command of the honorary escort of two companies with the political resident at the court of Poonah, Sir Charles Malet; and during the time that this distinguished diplomatist was in the chair of government at Bombay, Capt. Moor officiated also, for about a year, as assistant or secretary to Mr. Uhthoff, who remained at the head of the embassy at Poonah. On the withdrawal of the Bombay embassy, Capt. Moor returned to Bombay; and on the breaking out of the last war with Tippoo Sultaun (having intermediately been on the garrison staff), he acted as Quart.-mast-gen. during Col. Little's absence in the field. On the Col.'s return, and resumption of his office, the general order, No. 5, was issued by the government of Bombay.

Capt. M. was appointed in July 1799 to an office, then first established, under the designation of Garrison Storekeeper, since and now called Commissary General. This he held until (Feb. 1805) his final departure from India, rendered necessary by the fatiguing duties of this office, superadded to those incident to various avocations, arising from a confidential agency with which he was honoured for several years by the Gov. of Bombay (Mr. Duncan), in periods requiring a great exertion of the resources of that settlement, which no ordinary means could have brought into such full operation. The outfit and supply of the expeditions to Egypt, under Gens. Sir John Murray and Sir David Baird, the latter under the arrangement and inspection of Gen. Wellesley—the campaigns of this officer against the Mahrattas, &c. being among the important operations that rested wholly on the supposed inefficient resources of Bombay.

The documents marked No. 5 to No. 12 refer to Capt. Moor's successful exertions in calling forth those resources, and creating new ones, far beyond what that fruitful island was known or imagined to possess.

Little's detachment, and of the Mahratta army, commanded by Purseram Bhow, against Tippoo Sultaun."

The military orders and regulations, bearing on the discipline and expenditure of the armies under the different presidencies in India, were found to have accumulated to a mass highly inconvenient, as regarded both the due comprehension of them by the superior authorities, and the requisite knowledge of them by those whose attention and obedience were essential. To remedy this inconvenience, as far as related to the Bombay army, Capt. Moor was requested by Gov. Duncan to make a Compilation or digest of the whole. This work was printed at the expence of government, and has been, and is, found very useful. On the occasion of its publication, and continuation, the letters No. 13 and 14 are recorded.

On Capt. Moor's applying for leave to vacate his office, and for a furlough to England, the general order No. 15 was issued by the Bombay government. He was soon after promoted to a majority; and finding, at the expiration of his furlough, in 1808, that the state of his health did not warrant his return to India, he applied to the Court of Directors for leave to retire on full pay. But, from the long voyage of the ship in which he went to India in 1782, her previous detention for convoy, and his absence from India for the recovery of wounds (one being, in fact, still unhealed, though received more than thirty years ago), he had not actually served the prescribed term of twenty-two years on the territory of India, and the rigidity of the regulation on this point admitting of no relaxation, he could retire only on the half pay of his rank; to which the Hon. Court, " being impressed with a very favourable opinion of his merits and services," as expressed in their letter, was pleased to add a pension, not large in amount, but acceptable from the flattering mode in which it was bestowed*.

* Since Major Moor's return to Europe, he has been distinguished by scientific and literary honours: he was elected a Fellow of the Royal Society in 1806, and he is also a Fellow of the Society of Antiquaries. In 1810 he published the " Hindoo Pantheon;" a work well received by the literary public in England and India, and now out of print. In 1811 he published a volume, in 4to. on " Hindoo Infanticide;" and in 1823, a work entitled " Suffolk Words and Phrases."

On returning to India in 1796, he was elected a member of the Asiatic Society of Cal-

No. 1.—*From Col. Little to the Gov. in Council, Bombay.*

"Hon. Sir,—Lieut. Moor having communicated to me the substance of a letter he is about to address to you, permit me to take this opportunity of bearing testimony to his uniform gallant conduct during his being under my command, while serving with the Mahrattas; where he was wounded two different times. It is with great regret I find he is under the necessity of proceeding to Europe, on account of his last wound, not only from what he has suffered from the wound itself, but the difficulties the expence must inevitably involve him in without some assistance from Government. I declare, that no instance has come within my knowledge, when the favour he requests could either be granted with more justice by government, or better merited on his part. (Signed) "John Little.

"Surat, 30th July, 1792."

No. 2.—*From Colonel Riddell to the same.*

"Hon. Sir,—It being the desire of Lieut. Moor that a letter from me should accompany his resignation,* I with great pleasure take the opportunity of bearing testimony to the invariable diligence and punctuality with which he has executed his duty while under my command, both as adj. to the 9th batt. in garrison, and the grenadier batt. at Darwar. His subsequent conduct, when in command of the grenadiers of my batt., during which time he was twice wounded, was not less zealous than spirited when called to exertion in the field; and I cannot but greatly regret the unfortunate cause that necessitates him to proceed to Europe, as well on his own account, as that it has deprived my batt. of his services. I deem his duty to have been uniformly executed in a manner highly satisfactory to me, serviceable to his employers, and honourable to himself.

(Signed) "John Riddell.

"Bombay, 10th Aug. 1792."

cutta; he is one of the original members of the Literary Society of Bombay, and of the Asiatic Society of Great Britain and Ireland. Having, since the peace of 1815, visited the continent, he has been elected member of the *Societé Asiatique* of Paris, and of the *Societé d'Emulation* of Cambrai.

Major Moor is now an acting magistrate in the commission of the peace, and a deputy-lieutenant for the county of Suffolk.

* At this period no furloughs were granted to officers of the Company's army. To come to England they were compelled to resign the service; and, of course, had no pay while absent. Leave to return to the service, without loss of rank, was applied for to the Court of Directors.

No. 3.—*From Colonel Sartorius to Lieutenant Moor.*

"Dear Sir,—In answer to your's of the 7th inst. I am happy to have it in my power to say, that during the service against Darwar your conduct has appeared to me very satisfactory, and if I may be permitted to add, the same sentiments were entertained of your merits by my predecessor, Col. Frederick, when he appointed you adj. and quart.-mast. of the then corps of grenadiers. You may, if you please, shew this letter to the general.

(Signed) "J. Sartorius.

"*Parell, Aug. 9th,* 1792."

No. 4. is the letter from the government of Bombay to the Court of Directors, dated 21st Dec. 1792, in favour of Lieuts. Doolan and Moor, and inserted with the services of the former, p. 279.

No. 5.—*Extract from General Orders, Bombay,* 11*th May,* 1799.

"Lieut.-Col. John Little having returned to the Presidency, will resume his office of Quart.-mast.-gen., of which he will receive charge from Capt. Moor, to whom it is only justice, on this occasion, to notice, that during this officer's temporary charge of this department, at a period when much business of detail has been transacted in it, requiring discretion and confidence, government have every reason to be gratified with Capt. Moor's execution of the duties that had thus devolved upon him.

No. 6.—*Extract from the Proceedings of the Bombay Government of the* 13*th Feb.* 1801.

"122.—A copy of this paragraph to be transmitted for the report of the Military Board; the Hon. Court being at the same time advised, that the office of Garrison Storekeeper has already received the confirmation of the Supreme Government, and been found by ourselves extremely useful on the occasion, more especially of the several maritime outfits, which we have recently been, and continue still, engaged in, by order of the Supreme Government, in which the zeal and honourable exertions of Capt. Moor, the storekeeper, have been very conspicuous, and are deserving of our sincere acknowledgments."

No. 7.—*From the Gov. in Council at Bombay, to the Supreme Government,* 6*th May,* 1803.

"We take this opportunity of advising your Exc. in Council, that in view to the expediency of keeping, as secret as possible, the objects of the extensive commissions we some time ago received, for supplies of provisions to the

Madras army, then preparing to march from the other coast into this vicinity, joined to our former experience of the ability, zeal, and energy, that Capt. Moor had so conspicuously displayed in the still larger supplies for the service above referred to, this officer was confidentially entrusted by this government, with the charge of collecting the several articles specified in the correspondence, between the Com.-in-Chief, at Fort St. George, the Hon. Maj.-Gen. Wellesley, and our President; and we have every reason to believe, that the diligence and economy which Capt. Moor has observed in the present instance, will entitle him to equal credit with that which he gained in respect to the equipments for the Red Sea, &c.

No. 8.—*Extract from the Secretary to Government, to Capt. Moor, Garrison Storekeeper.*

" IN reference to the latter part of the 4th paragraph, I am desired to intimate that the Hon. the Gov. in Council is fully satisfied with your zealous exertions in every instance, for the promotion of the public service at the present crisis; whether in the immediate discharge of your own official duties, or in such other instances of extra official duty as occasion has lately occurred of usefully employing you in.

(Signed) FRANCIS WARDEN, Sec. to Gov.
" *Bombay Castle*, 13*th May*, 1803."

No. 9.—*Captain Edward Moor, Garrison Storekeeper, &c. &c.*

" SIR,—I am directed, by the Military Board, to acknowledge receipt of your several letters, dated the 17th and 18th instant, and, in reference to that under the 17th, to intimate, that the Military Board will readily afford their testimony to the ability, fidelity, and uncommon exertions which you have evinced in the creditable discharge of those various and highly important duties, which have unceasingly engaged your attention since the establishment of the Garrison Storekeeper's office, and they have not a doubt but that the remuneration which you will receive on this occasion will be commensurate to your merits, and to the advantages which the public service has derived from your labours.

(Signed) " FRANCIS WARDEN, Sec.
" *Bombay Military Board Office, Aug.* 19, 1803."

No. 10.—*From the Hon. J. Duncan to Lord Wellesley, March* 14, 1801.

" I am almost sorry for the agency being ordered to be instituted here; for the provision department, I had, in Capt. Moor, so active, intelligent, honest, and zealous an assistant, in this important department, that I am persuaded it cannot be done better by any body. However, your lordship's commands must of course be obeyed, and I only postpone, &c. &c.

No. 11.—*From the Honourable Colonel Wellesley (now Duke of Wellington) to the Honourable the Governor of Bombay, April* 13, 1801.

" SIR,—I have the honour to inform you, that all the ships having troops on board, which I have expected at this place, have arrived, received their provisions, water, &c. and have sailed towards the place of their ultimate destination, excepting one ship, the Maria Louisa, from which the troops have been removed, and on which it is proposed to send to the Red Sea provisions and water, and forage for the cattle. She will be ready to sail in the course of a few days. As I commanded the expedition when it came here, and as all the ships have been re-victualled, in consequence of requisitions made by me, and I have had the best and most frequent opportunities of observing the manner in which the business was conducted by Capt. Moor, it is but justice to him to represent to you, that some of the ships were completely refitted, took in ballast, and received three months' water and provisions for their crews, and the troops embarked on them, and sailed in four days after they arrived; that five ships, which have been added to the armament from this post since my arrival, were equipped with six months provisions, &c. and the troops embarked in five days after the requisition was made for them; and that, in short, the whole business has been conducted with regularity, rapidity, and satisfaction to myself, and to all the parties concerned. As Capt. Moor was the only person concerned in making the arrangements, and conducting the details of the service, I cannot but attribute to him all the merit; and I therefore beg leave to recommend him to your notice, and to your favourable report of his exertions to the Governor-General."

No. 12.—*From the Marquess Wellesley, Governor-General, to the Honourable Jonathan Duncan, May* 5, 1801.

" I therefore entirely approve your appointment of Capt. Moor, whose zeal and ability in that department appear to render him particularly well qualified for the important and responsible charge which you have given him."

No. 13.—*From the Government of Bombay, to Major-General Bowles, Commanding Officer of the Forces.*

" SIR,—In acknowledgment of your letter of this date, I am directed to observe, that, sensible of the utility of the work undertaken by Capt. Moor, at the instance of the President, the Gov. in council has resolved, that it shall be sent to the press after it shall have undergone the suggested revision; for which purpose, you are desired to appoint a committee of qualified officers, who are, through you, to report such alterations as they deem eligible, for the purpose of compressing the whole into as convenient a size as possible, without omitting any thing really useful for the instruction or information of the army, under the respective heads into which the Compilation is divided; to each of which, the committee are also authorised to subjoin sufficient notices of such part of the military regulations as Capt. M. may possibly have omitted. I am farther instructed to observe, that the Gov. in council will hereafter decide on the reward which he may deem Capt. M. deserving of for the labour and attention he must have bestowed in collecting and arranging so comprehensive and useful a Code of information as he has now brought forward.

    (Signed)   " ROBERT RICKARDS, Secretary.
" August 22, 1800."

No. 14.—*To Captain Edward Moor.*

" SIR,—The Hon. the Gov. in council having taken into consideration the present improved state of your Compilation of military orders, and adverted also to the great labour, attention, and accuracy, which you appear to have bestowed on the original work, considers you to be justly entitled to remuneration on these accounts, and has accordingly been pleased to award to you, for the original work, the sum of 10,000 rupees, and for the additions since made to it, 2000, in full also of the expence you have incurred for copyists.

    (Signed)   " A. GRANT, Secretary.
" Bombay Castle, Sept. 14, 1804."

No. 15.—*Extract from General Orders, Bombay, Sunday, Nov.* 20, 1803.

" On the occasion of Capt. Moor's present application, eventually to vacate his office of Garrison Storekeeper during the course of the present season, and to return to England on furlough, Government have a pleasure in expressing the great and uniform satisfaction which that officer has afforded by the intelligent, zealous, and honourable discharge of the important trust and laborious duties of his department, enhanced, as both have been, by the circumstances of the extensive equipments by sea and land which it has been his duty to superintend, and of which he has acquitted himself so much to his own credit, and to the public advantage, as will, accordingly, be noticed to the Honourable the Court of Directors on his return."

LIEUTENANT-COLONEL ELLIOT VOYLE.

(Bengal Establishment.)

THIS officer was appointed a cadet in Dec. 1781; he arrived at Calcutta in Nov. following, and was promoted to an ensigncy in Feb. 1783; he became a supernumerary ensign, on reduced allowances, in 1785; and was promoted to lieutenant in Feb. 1790. In 1794 he marched with a detachment to drive the Burmahs out of the Chittagong district. In 1795 he was appointed aid-de-camp to Maj.-Gen. Morgan; in 1796, quart.-mast. of a European reg.; in 1797, adj. and quart.-mast. of a brigade, in a reg. of two battalions; and in Dec. 1802 promoted to capt. in the 10th N. I. In 1805 he went on furlough to England, after two-and-twenty years actual residence in Bengal. He returned to the service in 1809, and was appointed in 1811 aid-de-camp to Maj.-Gen. Stafford. He was promoted to maj. in Sept. 1813, and assumed the command of the 2d batt. of the 10th N. I.: in Oct. of the same year he was directed to join the Rewah field force under Col. Adams, and to take charge of the battering train and stores for that detachment: he served the campaign in that quarter till the corps was broken up in June 1814. In the latter service, one fort was stormed and taken, and 127 men killed; the rest of the service was mostly marching and countermarching, seldom seeing an enemy.

In Oct. 1814 he commanded the infantry of Lord Hastings' escort, as Gov.-Gen., in his tour of inspection through Oude, Bareilly, and Moradabad. In Dec. he was appointed to raise and discipline the 28th reg.; which service he performed to the entire satisfaction of the Com.-in-Chief, as published in general orders.

In July 1815 he returned to the command of his old batt. at Futtehgurh. In Oct. of that year he marched to join the force assembling at Seetapoor, for service in the Nepaul hills, but which was directed to return to cantonments the day it arrived at the place of rendezvous. He again marched, in Jan. 1816, with his batt., to join a force assembling a second time at Seetapoor, under Col. Nicholls. He proceeded with the detachment towards the Goorkah frontier; but after three days' march, an express arrived from Sir D. Ochterlony, that peace was concluded with the Goorkah government; on which the corps was broken up. In March following he applied to be placed on the invalid establishment, and the Gov.-Gen. appointed him to the command of the Benares provincial batt., where he continued until Nov. 1820, and then obtained leave to return to England, and retire from the service.

THE LATE LIEUT.-COL. CHARLES BARTON BURR, C. B.

(Bombay Establishment.)

LIEUT.-COL. BURR's father dying during the infancy of his son, the latter was appointed a minor cadet on the Bombay establishment, an institution then existing at all the British presidencies in India, and thus became provided for in the army. In consequence of this appointment, he was educated for the military profession, and after a few years instruction in England, soon after the conclusion of the American war, proceeded to the south of France, where he was placed at the Royal Military College of Soreze, in Languedoc; a noble institution, under the superintendence of the Benedictine order, situated at the foot of the Cevennes, and close to the famous basin of St. Ferriole, whence the great canal of Languedoc is supplied. At this princely institution, at which the then Prince Royal of Savoy and Carignan was at that time receiving his education, he remained till a few months before his return to England; some time after which, and at a moment when he was preparing to proceed to India, in virtue of his original military appointment, the whole of the minor cadets were struck off. This unexpected circumstance occasioned his purchasing a commission in H. M.'s 41st reg.; but the regency bill being then under discussion, a considerable delay took place in expediting the commission, during which, the Court of Directors having decided on sending out a number of cadets to India, he obtained a nomination in the list for Bombay, and, in consequence, withdrew the money which had been paid for a commission in His Majesty's service.

Early in April 1789 he sailed for India; and soon after his arrival at Bombay, an expedition being contemplated against the pirates of western India, who occupied the southern Concan in great force, he volunteered for that service. This expedition, however, was never sent, as about that time Tippoo Sultaun having made an attack on the lines of Travancore, a strong detachment of the Bombay army, under the late Maj.-Gen. Hartley, left the presidency for Cranganore, when he again volunteered with the grenadier batt.; but before the expedition sailed, he was promoted to an ensigncy in the 1st Europ. reg., which did not proceed on service till the end of the year, when being assembled at Tellicherry early in Dec., it composed a part of the field force then forming in Malabar, under the immediate orders of our then Gov. and Com.-in-Chief, Maj.-Gen. Sir Robert Abercromby, who immediately proceeded against, and reduced Cananore, then the head-quarters, and a principal station of the Sultaun's forces. On the storm and fall of the surrounding positions, the whole of the troops within the fortress laid down their arms, to the number of near 6000 men.

After this service, and the capture of some forts of minor importance to the southward, at which Ens. Burr had the good fortune to be employed, the whole army were occupied for a considerable time, in opening a communication with the Sultaun's capital, through the Coorga country. This, however, notwithstanding the extraordinary exertions they made, ultimately proved unavailing, as the retreat of Lord Cornwallis, with the combined Bengal and Madras army, from the enemy's capital, obliged the Bombay division to return to Malabar, after having reached Periapatam. As many of the sick and stores were left at that place, Ens. Burr, who was at the time ill with a violent fever, had a most narrow escape of falling into the hands of the enemy: he was left on the ground, and with great difficulty succeeded, on the ensuing day, by avoiding the route the army had taken, and going across, and through the jungly country, in overtaking it while in full retreat to its former positions in Malabar. He had, however, the satisfaction of saving the whole of his baggage, though most of that of the army was lost.

During the latter part of the campaign, this officer, having been intermediately promoted to a lieutenantcy, had the honour of being offered, though the junior officer of the corps, the command of the grenadier company of the 2d batt. N. I., to exchange from the 1st Bombay reg., in the light company of which corps he had been placed as an ensign; this compliment he accepted, and accompanied his new corps to Seringapatam the succeeding campaign, where it had the honour of supporting his former regt. in the distinguished part it bore in the action of the 22d Feb., exposed to the severe cannonade of the fort, and fire of the army to which it was opposed without. On the following morning hostilities were suspended, which led to the partition treaty of 1792, and the consequent evacuation of Mysore, and return of the Bombay army to Malabar, where Lieut. Burr's corps was immediately, after the monsoon, employed against the Noorganaad Rajah, who, falling into their hands, Lieut. Burr was selected to guard him; and, after his death, was appointed to accompany his successor in a tour he made to a neighbouring district, in the performance of some religious ceremonies rendered necessary by recent events. Some time after this his corps was again actively employed; and it continued till the conclusion of 1794, serving in the interior of Malabar against the disaffected Rajahs and Moplas, and fugitive Poligar chiefs, who had sought refuge from Tippoo's commanders, within the frontier of the Company's districts, in the Anamulla woods.

At the close of 1795 Lieut. Burr was appointed to the garrison staff of Palicaudcherry, in which situation he remained till his promotion to a company in 1800, ultimately succeeding to the command of that fortress. During the then recent hostilities with the Sultaun of Mysore, he had been entrusted with the negociations, which it was deemed advisable at that time to encourage with the Poligar princes on the Sultaun's frontiers, with whom he had the good fortune to establish the most amicable relations and co-operation, and a direct communication through the enemy's country, with our own districts in the Carnatic.

On his promotion to a company, being also honoured with the appointment of aid-de-camp to the com. of the forces, he hastened to the Presidency, but the monsoon having set in, and the ship on board of which he had embarked at Mangalore, being wrecked, after an ineffectual attempt to reach the Presidency, Capt. Burr was obliged to proceed to Goa, where an opportunity offering, he effected his passage to the Presidency at the end of Aug. Soon after his arrival, an expedition being in orders for Egypt, he obtained permission to accompany the 1st batt. of his reg., in command of its light company; but before it sailed he was nominated to an appointment on the staff of the expedition, in consequence, as he was given to understand, of the great interest he had taken in preparing his transport for that service. In the discharge of the duties of his new situation, Capt. Burr had the good fortune to be particularly selected by Lieut.-Gen. Sir John, then Col., Murray, to proceed in advance of the army, into the desert, in order to report as to the probable supply of water, and to direct the march of the army accordingly. This duty he executed to the Col.'s entire satisfaction, selecting a spot where he subsequently placed a detachment and working party, whose success in sinking several wells, which, at the present day, the Arabs call by his name, encouraged hopes, that similar success might attend their endeavours at other equally eligible distances, but which were not realized, as no further discoveries of the kind occurred, though strong detachments were afterwards sent in advance to accomplish this desirable object, as well as to improve those resting places that were already known to, and pointed out by, the Arabs. Capt. Burr subsequently superintended, and regulated the distribution of the water and forage to the division that accompanied the park, the strongest, and, from the number of draft cattle, the most difficult and embarrassing of all others, to cross this dreary and desert tract. He had the satisfaction to find, that not a single casualty occurred, either among the troops, followers, or cattle, throughout this arduous and interesting march of nine days, from the port of Cossier to the waters of the Nile, throughout which it had been necessary to provide, as on a voyage at sea, fuel and forage, and several days water to accompany the division.

The army, which had thus crossed the desert by divisions, being assembled at Gheena on the Nile, previous to its embarkation for Lower Egypt, Capt. Burr was sent in command of a convoy, that proceeded by land to Cairo; and though often beset and menaced by large bodies of Bedouins, reached that capital without loss, whence he accompanied the army to Rosetta by water, and subsequently to Alexandria, returning to Suez in the middle of 1802, and landing in Bombay early in July, when he lost no time in repairing to join his corps at Baroda in Guzerat, where affairs being in a most unsettled state, he had the honour of being appointed to command a select detachment of European and N. I., intended to take possession of one of the city gates, a project which was subsequently abandoned, and a strong detachment under his command placed for some weeks at the minister's, in the suburbs. The Arab mercenaries in the Guicawar service, however, refusing to evacuate the city, and having possessed themselves of a large portion of the pettah, the British line was ordered down, and a smart action took place in the streets, wherein we lost several officers and men. This rendered it necessary to open batteries against the fort; it sustained a regular siege for several days, during which Capt. Burr commanded the grenadier batt. and flank companies of his corps, embodied for that service; and subsequently took possession of, and commanded a position in the city, till Cannojee Row Guicawar, a natural brother of the reigning prince, having assembled a force in the neighbouring districts, rendered it necessary to reinforce the late Sir George, then Maj., Holmes's detachment. Capt. Burr proceeded with a strong division of his corps to join the field force, which was immediately after engaged with the enemy in a very severe conflict near Soulle, and ultimately succeeded in driving him from his position with great loss on both sides, capturing the whole of his camp, the chief himself narrowly escaping. Nevertheless, a few weeks afterwards, being joined by strong reinforcements, he again sustained an attack of several hours, at Chapria on the banks of the Watrook, which terminated in a second defeat: his minister, with whom Capt. Burr had a personal rencontre, and whose seal of state he obtained possession of, was killed with many of his followers.

These events, with some others of subordinate importance, afforded the field brigade ample occupation, till the approach of the monsoon, when the whole was broken up, and went into quarters for the rainy season, Capt. Burr's corps being stationed at Nerriaad.

On the breaking out of hostilities with Scindia, a force having proceeded against Broach, under Col. Woodington's command, Capt. B. applied for permission to attempt the surprise of the important and formidable fortress of Powaghur, an immense fastness of excessive elevation, and so difficult of access as to be regarded impregnable. Having, however, ascertained that the Bheels, in whose districts it was situated, occasionally scaled the mountain, and robbed the washermen of the garrison of their linen, Capt. Burr was sanguine of success, through the assistance of these people. It was, however, deemed too hazardous an enterprise, and on the fall of Broach the place was regularly besieged, and the lower works being partially breached, the garrison were intimidated into a surrender.

Col. J. Murray arrived soon after this event, and took the command of a field force ordered to be formed for the reduction of Scindia's districts within the province of Guzerat, and on its frontier, and immediately advanced on the enemy's capital, Oogein, in Malwa. Capt. Burr was appointed dep. quart.-mast.-gen. to this force. It forthwith took possession of the Panch Malls, districts belonging to Scindia, on the frontier, four of which are immediately within the province. The civil arrangements of these districts being confided to Capt. Burr, he had the good fortune of collecting and embodying, in a few days, a mass of information, which the Resident at Baroda, Lieut.-Colonel Walker, was pleased to acknowledge surpassed any thing he had been able to obtain regarding the Company's districts in that neighbourhood, of which he had for many months been in charge. This desirable point having been satisfactorily accomplished, the army proceeded to the northward, through the Pandawarra pass, in pursuit of Cannojee, who had, during the rains, assembled a large force on the north-eastern frontier, which retiring into Malwa as the British advanced, left them at liberty to direct their attention thither. Accordingly the army proceeded to Dohud, a fertile and interesting as well as locally important district of the enemy's, to which a division of the army, under Maj. Holmes, had been previously detached.

The rapid progress of the war in the Deccan, under the personal command of Col. Wellesley, had however led to a crisis, that disappointed the hopes entertained of penetrating Malwa, in co-operation with the army of the Deccan; and the peace which immediately ensued, obliged the force, to which Capt. Burr was attached, to retrace its steps to the districts in Guzerat, after replacing Scindia's officers in possession of the Dohud Purgunnah, the civil arrangements of which having been entrusted to Capt. Burr, constituted an object of his particular solicitude, and was regarded as a highly-honourable testimonial by Lord Wellesley and the supreme government, associated probably with some negociations of a political nature, wherein the confidence of his commander, Col. Murray, had afforded him an opportunity of rendering himself useful with Cannojee and the principalities on the frontier.

An interval of suspense succeeded the termination of this war, and occasioned the Guzerat field-army to be maintained in a state of efficiency, and soon after reinforced by corps withdrawn from Malabar and the Deccan, with which it again advanced to the confines of Malwa, and, after a short halt at Dohud, to Oogein, the capital of Scindia, now our ally, which had been menaced by Holkar, then in great force at Mundessor, an important position, well chosen by that able and enterprizing chieftain, as it equally menaced the capitals of our allies in Guzerat and Malwa, and both the British divisions then in the field, under the command of Cols. Monson and Murray.

As it would be irrelevant to enter into the detail of far the greater portion of the movements of the army, to which Capt. Burr was attached, it is sufficient to observe, that he was principally, if not wholly, entrusted with the conduct of a variety of political negociations and communications, which were discharged in a manner that left him nothing to regret, and probably occasioned the order which Lord Wellesley, then Gov. Gen., did him the honour soon after to forward, directing, that whatever Native auxiliary troops were subsidized in Malwa, to act with our force, should be placed under this officer's immediate charge; a compliment peculiarly honourable to Capt. Burr, who was personally unknown to his lordship.

The conduct of the Guzerat field force in Malwa not having proved satisfactory to the supreme government, occasioned Maj. Gen., now Sir Richard, Jones, to be appointed to its command, but produced no alteration in the general staff of the army, with which Capt. Burr continued serving throughout the campaigns in Hindostan and Sekkawatty; in the former of which he was entrusted with different confidential negociations by the Com.-in-Chief, Lord Lake; one of which, for the surrender of one of the city gates, during the siege of Burtpoor, he brought to a successful issue. His Lordship, however, for reasons unknown, determined on postponing occupation at the time it was offered, and this important and interesting negociation was ultimately abandoned.

In the succeeding campaign, whilst co-operating with the Bengal army, then on its march to Patteculla, with which view the Bombay division advanced to Kanoon, near Rewarree, within a few miles of Delhi, this officer, through the friendly prepossessions in his favour, and confidential intercourse he had established with Rychund, the able but ill-fated minister of the Jeypoor state, and acting under the sanction and authority of his immediate commander, Maj.-Gen. Jones, he was occupied in preliminary discussions with that minister on the subject of a pacification with Holkar, who had at that time retired into the Panjab. These produced a most conciliatory communication direct to the General; it was immediately followed up by a negociation with the Com.-in-Chief, which terminated in a peace with that chieftain, and put an end to the most protracted and, probably, most expensive war the East India Company had been for some time involved in; an event that might be said to consolidate the peace of India for a period far exceeding any thing that could have been reasonably anticipated.

On the return of the Bombay Guzerat army, the field force being broken up, this officer was appointed to the command of the 1st batt. 7th reg. then in the Deccan; and soon after sent to Goa, where he commanded at the fortress of the Aguada during the whole of the discussions with that government; in the execution of which duty he possessed the confidence, and acquitted himself to the entire satisfaction, of Col. (now Maj.-Gen.) Adams, who commanded the British force within the Portuguese territories; to whose talents, as a statesman and an officer, may be justly attributed the discomfiture of every hostile machination; with which view, his Exc. the Count de Sarceedos had been appointed, with a special commission and extraordinary powers, through the then powerful influence and ascendancy of the French cabinet at Lisbon.

An expedition into Kattywar being deemed necessary before the monsoon of 1809, this officer's corps was called to Bombay for that purpose, but, owing to the impediments it met with on its passage, was unavoidably detained at Bombay to replace the grenadier batt. of the 1st reg., which was, in consequence, substituted. On the termination of the monsoon, it was, however, again ordered to join that force, then destined for Cutch, but, in consequence of the irruption of Ameer Khan into Berar, directed immediately to join the force in the Deccan, with which it soon after took the field. This officer (then major in the army, which rank he attained 8th Oct. 1807,) commanded the right brigade during that campaign, which, however, the division being merely advanced for the eventual support of Gen. Close, was unattended with any active operation. The remainder of that, and the succeeding year, being passed in cantonments at Serroor, afforded him an opportunity of devoting his best endeavours to the improvement of his corps; which were rewarded by its attaining a high degree of professional reputation.

In Dec. 1811 Maj. Burr's batt. was relieved by the grenadier batt., from Kaira, in Guzerat, whose position it was ordered to occupy; in pursuance of which, the batt. had reached Panwell, when an express was received for its proceeding to Bombay, for the purpose of being embarked for Porebunder, in Kattywar, to form part of a field force there assembled, for the attack of the Newanugger Rajah, a powerful tributary of the Guicawar state. In obedience to this order, the whole corps proceeded to the presidency, and a few days after embarked, for what was considered a novel service, 1240 strong, without a single casualty from the day of the receipt of the order for its march; an instance of honourable devotion to the officers and the service, and which, it is much to be regretted, was attended with a very severe loss to the corps, several of the boats in which it was embarked being dismasted, and driven back in a storm, and one, on board of which were two European officers, the assistant surgeon, and upwards of 100 men and followers, foundering at sea, of whom only two were saved.

The service at Newanugger having honourably terminated, and added to the credit the corps had previously attained, this officer was ordered with it, and a troop of Bombay cavalry, to Guzerat, where fresh intrigues at Baroda rendered it probable their presence would be required; every thing, however, was restored to tranquillity before their arrival on the frontier, where, leaving the cavalry to cantoon at Runpoor, he proceeded on to Kaira, and cantoned the corps. It remained there till June 1815, part having been intermediately employed on the northern frontier of the province, and part of it latterly with the field force assembled on the Mayhe, under the command of Col. George Holmes, in which this officer (who had arrived at the rank of lieut.-col. 21st Jan. 1813) commanded the 1st brigade.

This force being broken up in May, Lieut.-Col. Burr's corps was immediately after directed to form a part of the field force, then ordered to be assembled in Kattywar, under Col. East, with which it continued during the whole of that service, and the succeeding campaign in Cutch, where he commanded the attack against the important city and fortress of Anjar, which terminated in its breach and reduction, its chief deeming it most prudent to surrender unconditionally at a moment the arrangements for the immediate storm were making, a powerful battery of five 18-pounders, erected during the preceding night, having effected a practicable breach, and destroyed the principal defences during the course of the day.

From Anjar the force proceeded to Booj; when negociations, succeeded by a peace taking place, the ulterior objects of the campaign were directed to the subjugation of the insubordinate districts of Cutch, and reduction of the remaining fastnesses occupied by the pirates of Oakamandal in that segregated peninsula. A most violent and severe fit of sickness obliged Lieut.-Col. Burr, in the midst of these operations, to quit the army with very faint hopes of a recovery; nor could he rejoin his corps till fourteen months after, when he proceeded with it to the Deccan, in April 1817; immediately after which, some unpleasant discussions occurring between the Company and the Peishwa's government, the brigade at Poonah was reinforced by a division of the field army, under the personal command of Col., now Maj.-Gen. Smith, which surrounding Poonah, led to the renovation of the treaties with the late Peishwa, on terms that were expected to produce a permanent pacification; an idea so deeply impressed on the mind of the government, that the cautionary fortresses that had been placed in their hands by the Peishwa's government, were faithfully restored, and a degree of confidence evinced towards him, that ill accorded with his sentiments. These were soon after obvious, his highness having assembled an immense army of 30,000 chosen troops of the empire at Poonah, while the Company's brigade at that station scarcely paraded 2000, one batt. having been sometime before withdrawn to complete the arrangements then in progress for the formation of the army of the Deccan, under the personal command of Lieut.-Gen. Sir Thomas Hislop, for the extirpation of the Pindarry hordes, to co-operate with which the Peishwa had been requested to furnish a body of 10,000 horse to join Col. Smith's force, consisting of the remainder of his highness's subsidiary, then advanced some marches beyond the Godavery.

At this interesting moment, the officer who commanded the Poonah brigade being appointed to the staff of the presidency of Bombay, the command of this division of the British force in India devolved on Lieut.-Col. Burr, under circumstances of peculiar difficulty, as although he had for a considerable time anterior thereto been sufficiently recovered to mount his horse, and undergo all ordinary exertions, the period had arrived when more than usual efforts, both of body and mind, might be expected to be required; as the brigade under his command occupied a position so completely identified with the capital, Poonah, that the magazine, in which were concentrated all its resources and means of defence, was not 100 yards from the suburbs of the city, within which and the adjacent camps his highness's army occupied the most favourable and proximate quarters, seating themselves within a few yards of the brigade's depôt of stores, which had been unfortunately placed at one extremity of the camp, while the treasury, in which there were several lacs of rupees, occupied the opposite flank of its straggling cantonment. The din and clamour of their troops and naggaras throughout the night, the momentary expectation of their sallying from their positions, which in a manner embraced the whole extent of that occupied by the brigade; and the general report existing at the time of the Native troops having been tampered with, and seduced from their allegiance by the Peishwa, rendered the situation of Lieut.-Col. Burr at that moment extremely critical and precarious, particularly as the very scite of his cantonment was so unfortunately contiguous to the plantations and enclosures of the suburbs as to afford ample cover to their infantry, even on the verge of the cantonment.

Under these circumstances, it became necessary for Lieut.-Col. Burr to abandon his position, and take up new ground at Kirkee, about three miles north, it being evident he could no longer, with common prudence or safety, remain where he was, menaced with an attack both day and night. The Peishwa had assumed a dissatisfied tone; and his troops, animated by the politics of the day, and gaining confidence from their numbers, evinced a most hostile disposition. Lieut.-Col. Burr being now joined by the Bombay European reg., which the aspect of affairs had occasioned being ordered from the presidency, he quitted, on the 2d Nov. 1817, the cantonment he had long and honourably maintained, and took up his ground on an acclivity, which afforded as favourable a position as circumstances admitted. The 3d and 4th were occupied in removing every thing that had not been entirely brought away, not omitting the flag-staff at head-quarters, which was dug up on the occasion, lest a trophy of that nature, falling into the hands of the Peishwa's troops, should be regarded as an auspicious omen.

Though his highness had permitted of this movement, and of the removal of the whole of the stores and provisions, without any molestation, (it had been necessary, however, to leave a strong detachment on the old ground till every thing was brought away,) there could be little doubt the die was cast, and that a few days, if not hours, would present the denouement of his policy. The Company's Resident, however, determined to postpone, to the last moment, adopting any further steps that might either be construed into fear or concession, and continued at his post till the Residency being nearly surrounded by the Peishwa's troops, in the afternoon of the 5th of Nov., on their moving out to commence hostilities, left him no other course to pursue than an immediate abandonment of the Residency, and every thing it contained, and retreat to camp; meantime the movements of the enemy had rendered it necessary to fall in the brigade, which, in consequence of a communication from the Resident, placing Lieut.-Col. Burr at liberty to act, hostilities were immediately commenced, with the view, in the first instance, of securing his retreat from the Sungum, which having been anticipated, induced him to occupy an intermediate position, to cover the brigade of his highness's regular infantry at Dapooree, thereby affording them an opportunity, which they fortunately embraced, of joining him, taking up their position in line, with three field-pieces as the action began. This was commenced by his highness's army opening a cannonade on Lieut.-Col. Burr's line, which, after assuring himself of the co-operation of the Peishwa's brigade, he had put in motion with a view of attacking the enemy's position.

As the details of this glorious and memorable event are to be found in the official report of that important day, which, to say the least of it, gave a tone to the events and politics of the war, it is not necessary to recapitulate them here; suffice it to observe, that on Lieut.-Col. B.'s victorious return to camp, he delivered over the command of the brigade to Lieut.-Col. Osborne, who had had the good fortune to join the post at Kirkee during the action, having been appointed to one of the corps under the command of Lieut.-Col. Burr.

It is unnecessary to dwell on the events which intervened till the arrival and junction of Brig.-Gen. Smith's army, as they are devoid of general interest; nor is it requisite to recapitulate those which followed on the junction of the head-quarters of the force, which soon after marched from Poonah in pursuit of his highness's army, leaving Lieut.-Col. B. again in command of the brigade and position, occupied at the enemy's capital; neither is it necessary to detail the unpleasant discussions* which occurred between Lieut.-Col. Burr and Brig.-Gen. Smith, and which occasioned the Lieut.-Col. to resign his command.

On his arrival at the Presidency, in March 1818, he was appointed to the divisional command of the southern district of Guzerat, which he held till Jan. 1819, when the Gov., Sir Evan Nepean, having in contemplation the military organization of the conquered districts in the Concan, removed him to the southward, as a preliminary measure to nominating him to a more extensive command, but an opportunity intermediately offering of placing him on the staff at the Presidency, he succeeded to a situation in Bombay, (agent for clothing the army,) which he retained until his death. No particular opportunities having offered of rendering himself professionally useful since quitting the Deccan, he endeavoured to establish his claims to the further acknowledgment of his superiors, by different interesting political communications and memoirs, which an extensive local information admitted of his submitting for the consideration of the government, whose thanks he had the honour of receiving, for the zeal and public spirit he manifested on these occasions.

The services of Lieut.-Col. Burr were further acknowledged by his being appointed a Companion of the order of the Bath. He died 20th May 1821, (aged 49) after a short but severe illness. His character is thus delineated by a friend.—" Nature had endowed him with talents of a superior order, which he rendered conspicuous by an unceasing and successful display of them, in the discharge of the many important duties connected with his professional character. This appears from his having been selected at an early period of his military career, to act in stations of high trust and acknowledged consequence, whose duties he discharged with great ability, and the most unblemished integrity. Nor would it be doing justice to his memory,

---

* See Lieut.-Col. Burr's " Appeal to the Marquess of Hastings."—Published by Hatchard, 1819.

if the warmth of his heart, the tenderness of his disposition, the generosity of his nature, were to be omitted, which, with all their confederate qualities, rendered him beloved through life, and lamented in death. He was interred with military honours, the soldiery of his batt. volunteering, from a general feeling of mournful respect and attachment, to attend his remains to the grave. The gentlemen resident at the station where he died, and its near vicinity, entered into a subscription to erect a sepulchral monument, as a memorial of their regard while he lived, as well as of the regret they felt for his loss, now he is no more."

THE LATE LIEUT.-COL. GEORGE HICKSON FAGAN.

(Bengal Establishment.)

This officer entered the Company's service, as a cadet, in 1794; was appointed ensign in the 1st European reg. 10th Oct. 1795; lieut., 18th reg., 6th Dec. 1796; capt., 25th reg., 22d March 1804; major, 7th April 1814; and lieut.-col., 1st batt. 22d reg., 1st Aug. 1818.

He embarked as a volunteer, for service on the Coromandel coast, in 1798, which was the first opportunity for proceeding on foreign service that presented itself after his entry into the Bengal army, and served the whole of the Mysore war of 1799 in command of a grenadier company; at the close of that war he lost his left arm, in endeavouring to render a voluntary personal service, which procured him, at the moment, the notice, and subsequently the substantial favour of, the Gov.-Gen., Lord Wellesley, in his appointment as assistant secretary to the Military Board in 1802, till which period he continued to do duty with his corps. In that situation his services were highly approved; in every beneficial arrangement connected with the equipment, the supply, the subsistence, the movement, and the general efficiency of the army, he participated much more than his ostensible situation required, and he received, more than once, the acknowledgments of the public officer, who bore the largest and most responsible share in those arrangements, as well as in the laborious revision of the whole of the military establishments under the presidency of Bengal, which took place during Lord Wellesley's administration. In June 1806 the additional situation of secretary to the Board of Superintendence, for improving the breed of cavalry horses, was conferred on Capt. Fagan; and, in this situation, though the abolition of that establishment had been determined on by Sir G. Barlow, soon after he became Gov.-Gen, he was the means of preserving it to the public, by the information he afforded, and the views he gave of that institution, and of the advantages that were, and the still greater ones that might be, derived from it. Both the preceding situations Capt. F. continued to fill till March 1808, when Lieut.-Gen. Sir G. Hewett, the Com.-in-Chief, and President of the Military Board, appointed him dep.-adj.-gen. of the Bengal army, with the official rank of major, and, at the same time, acting adj.-gen. during the absence, at the Cape of Good Hope, of the Adj.-Gen. This office Major Fagan continued to fill till the 3d of Jan. 1809, when he was relieved by the officer specially holding it. Maj. F. was next allotted as dep.-adj-gen. to the field army under Maj.-Gen. St. Leger, and accompanied that officer in his expedition against the Seiks, in 1809-10. Maj. F. continued as dep.-adj.-gen. in the field till the 11th Dec. 1811, when, on the demise of the Adj.-Gen., Col. Ball, he was appointed to that office, with the official rank of lieut.-col., though only a capt. in his reg. This appointment was confirmed by the Court of Directors, in consideration, as they expressly stated, of Maj. F.'s great merits as an officer, his having lost an arm on service, and officiated before as adj.-gen.; but they laid it down as a rule, in reference to the many instances that had lately occurred of officers of inferior rank, and short standing, being appointed to the highest and most distinguished offices in their military service, that no officer should, in future, hold the situation of adj.-gen., or quart.-mast.-gen., who had not attained the rank of major, either in his reg., or by the operation of H. M.'s brevet. This regulation of the Court was, agreeably to their orders, promulgated to the army; and the Supreme government, on that occasion, recorded their sense of the merits of Lieut.-Col. F. in the following general orders to the army :—

"*Fort William, Sept.* 23, 1814.

" His Exc. the Hon. the Vice-President in council most cordially participates in the satisfaction which his Exc. the Right Hon the Gov.-Gen·, and Com.-in-Chief, has derived, and expressed, in observing that the Hon. the Court of Directors, in prescribing a rule for the selection of officers to fill the office of adj.-gen. of the Bengal army, have been pleased to except from the operation of that rule the very meritorious officer who now holds that arduous and important situation. It is true, had it not been expressly declared by the Hon. Court, that the order was not to affect the appointment of Lieut.-Col. F., its scope would not necessarily have deprived the government, and the Com.-in-Chief, of that officer's highly valuable services, since his promotion to the rank of regimental major (subsequent to the date of the order) rendered him eligible to the office, according to the principle established by the Hon. Court, and published in general orders, under date the 13th ult.; still, it is most gratifying that a just sense of Lieut.-Col. Fagan's great merits should have determined the Hon. Court to exempt him from the operation of a rule which, at the time of its adoption, was supposed to include his case. Notwithstanding so public and so flattering a tribute to Lieut.-Col. F.'s character, the Vice-President in council, in concurrence with the Gov.-Gen., and Com.-in-Chief, cannot deem himself excused from discharging what he thinks an act of justice to that officer's reputation, by expressing his high opinion of Lieut.-Col. Fagan's particular qualifications for executing the office ably, and by declaring his own personal gratification in the power to avail himself of ' Lieut.-Col. Fagan's talents and indefatigable assiduity.' "

During the late arduous contest with the state of Nepaul, commenced and terminated by that great statesman and general, the Marquis of Hastings, Lieut.-Col. George Fagan was in the field with that illustrious commander, bearing the principal share in all the details and arrangements connected with the army, engaged in that memorable war; and his services were duly appreciated and acknowledged by the government, in their general orders of the 20th March 1816, announcing the triumphant close of that war, as the following relative extract from those orders will indicate:—" These acknowledgments ought not to be closed without an advertence to the claims of those who, though not actually serving with the divisions employed during the two campaigns, essentially promoted the success of the public efforts. To Lieut.-Col. F., and the officers under him, in the Adj.-Gen.'s department, on whom, in the execution of the Com.-in-Chief's orders, devolved the principal labour of detail in the preparation of the troops for the field, and in many subsequent provisions, the obligations of government are unfeignedly felt."

A few months preceding the termination of this war, Lieut.-Col. F. was compelled to withdraw from the labours of his office, and to solicit leave to proceed to the Cape of Good Hope, for the re-establishment of his health, which was seriously impaired by assiduous and indefatigable application to business. Permission was accordingly and immediately granted, and the same announced to him, in the following letter, from the Secretary to Government, in the military department:—

" Sir,—I am directed by the Right Hon. the Gov.-Gen. in Council, to acknowledge the receipt of your letter, No. 513 A. dated the 24th inst., with the medical certificate which accompanied it, and to acquaint you, that permission will be granted to you in general orders of this date, to make a voyage to sea for the recovery of your health, and to be absent, on that account, for ten months, on furnishing the prescribed certificate from the pay department. In making this communication, I am directed to signify to you the sincere regret of the Gov.-Gen. in Council, that ill health, acquired by an unwearied attention to the duties of the laborious and important department, of which you are the head, should, for a season, deprive the government of the benefit of your valuable services; and to express the anxious hope of his lordship in council, that temporary secession from your public avocations, and change of climate, may effectually restore you to the enjoyment of health.

 (Signed)   " C. W. GARDENER, Sec. to Government.
" *Council Chamber, 29th Dec.* 1815."

At the Cape of Good Hope, Lt.-Col. F. remained a twelvemonth without any decided amendment in his health, and his immediate return to England was in consequence deemed advisable; he accordingly embarked for that country in Nov. 1816, and thereby definitively vacated the office, which he had so long filled with acknowledged honour to himself and benefit to the state. The following general orders were issued by the Marquess of Hastings on the occasion of his retirement :—

       " *Fort William, April* 18, 1817.

" Lt.-Col. G. H. Fagan, late adj.-gen. of the army, having furnished a medical certificate from the Cape of Good Hope, the leave granted to him conditionally, in general orders of the 29th Dec. 1815, to proceed to sea for ten months for the benefit of his health, and confirmed in general orders of the 12th Jan. 1816, is altered to a furlough to Europe on the same account, commencing from the 14th Nov. last, the date of his quitting the Cape. While the Gov.-Gen. in Council indulges his regret at what the service has suffered in the relinquishment of the situation of adj.-gen. by Lt.-Col. G. Fagan, His Ex. must endeavour to diminish the effect of that loss by rendering the memory of Lt.-Col. Fagan's official exertions an example and incitement to the army. The universal tribute of acknowledgment paid to the ability and indefatigable zeal of Lt.-Col. F. ought to stimulate every officer to aim at attaining a similar character. This, however, is not to be acquired by order alone. Recollection of the tone of Lt.-Col. F.'s professional energy should impress this conclusion on every one disposed to strive for equal reputation,—that no talents, not even such as Lt.-Col. F. possessed, will carry an individual to proud distinction, unless he join to them habits of application, and a judicious direction of his genius. It is to the combination of these qualities that Lt.-Col. F. has owed the high estimation in which he is held, and the sorrow now expressed that the service has ceased to benefit by them."

Lieut.-Col. Fagan again returned to India about the end of 1820, and in a few months after closed his mortal career, May 25, 1821, at the age of forty-two.

THE LATE MAJOR GEORGE WILLIAMS.

(*Bombay Establishment.*)

THIS officer went to Bombay as a cadet in 1783, just after the cessation of a long war in India; a state of affairs which rendered promotion so slow, that he, in common with many of his contemporaries on that establishment, did not obtain his first commission as ensign earlier than 1788, when, on the reformation of the Bombay army in 1788, by Gen. Sir W. Medows, Gov. and Com.-in-Chief of that presidency, through the instrumentality of Major, now Lieut.-Gen., G. V. Hart, (then adj.-gen. of the Bombay army,) Mr. Williams obtained his commission. He was removed to Malabar, on promotion to lieut., early in 1789; where he remained several years, and served in those distinguished corps, the Bombay European reg., and the Bombay grenadier batt., in the campaigns in Mysore, under Gen. Sir Robert Abercromby, who commanded the field army employed against the dominions and capital of Tippoo Sultaun. After serving on the regimental staff of his corps, he was selected by Gen. Bowles, commanding officer in Malabar, as his mil. sec., which situation he continued to hold during that officer's subsequent command of the forces of Bombay. In 1798 he obtained the rank of capt.

A change in the command of the Bombay army removed this

officer from the general staff, and he proceeded to England on furlough for the benefit of his health. In 1801-2 he was again employed on the general staff of the Bombay army, as major of brigade to the contingent, then serving in Guzerat, under Lieut.-Col. A. Walker*, in co-operation with the government of his Highness the Guicawar. In the confidential discharge of a pacific and delicate mission to Mulhar Rao, on that chief's own invitation, Capt. Williams was treacherously detained in the fort of Kurree; while a furious attack was, with almost unexampled perfidy, impelled on the small body of troops under Col. Walker. The utter defeat and dispersion of the forces of Mulhar Rao, he being made a prisoner, effected the release of Capt. Williams. As a reward for his services and sufferings, he was appointed, by the Bombay government, dep. quart.-mast.-gen. to the subsidiary force in Guzerat.

The Guicawar ruler of Guzerat having ceded the important fort of Kaira to the East India Company, Capt. Williams was appointed to receive charge of, and command it. The cession was obtained under circumstances that made its surrender to the English a matter of uncertainty and anxiety; and it required much circumspection and management to ensure success to the enterprize, as it may be termed, of taking possession. This was effected, however, in the most complete and satisfactory manner; and Capt. Williams continued in the military command, charged also with the civil jurisdiction of the district, of which Kaira is the capital, until the general Mahratta war in 1803. He was then selected to direct the operations of a body of Guicawar cavalry, intended to act in co-operation with the Bombay army, under Maj.-Gen. (now Sir Richard) Jones, and the Bengal army, under Gen. Lord Lake, in the north of India. But, after proceeding some marches, this ill-organized body of horse, owing to the mismanagement or treachery of its immediate leader, Meyput Row, refused to advance any further, and returned into Guzerat. Capt. Williams, who was unable to prevent this defection, then joined the

* *Vide* statement of Services, p. 150.

army under Gen. Jones, advancing to the siege of Burtpoor, and was appointed commissary of provisions to that force, with which he returned, at the peace, to Bombay; and, in 1805, having been promoted to a majority, to England.

He retired from the service in 1807, and died at Bath 4th Jan. 18 19

MAJOR FREDERICK SACKVILLE.

(Bengal Establishment.)

This officer was appointed a cadet 20th Jan. 1801; ens. 1st Sept. following; lieut. 30th Sept. 1803; capt. 11th July 1811; and maj. (as dep.-quart.-mast.-gen.) 17th Feb. 1819. In April 1802 he joined the 2d batt. 18th N. I., under Maj. P. Don; and in July 1803 marched to Allahabad, and joined the division of the army destined to penetrate into Bundlecund, at the opening of Lord Lake's campaign, against the confederated Mahratta chieftains. In Oct. he crossed the Kane river, under the command of Col. (now Lieut.-Gen.) Powell, and attacked the confederated Bundela chieftains, drawn out in battle array, at Copsah, under the Newaub Shumcheer Behauder, routed them, and captured two guns and some tumbrils. On the 30th Oct. he was present at the siege and capture of forts Bursah and Chamonlie; and in Dec. at the siege and capture of Culpee.

In Feb. 1804, Lieut. S. marched to reinforce Col. (the late Maj.-Gen. Sir H.) White's division of the grand army, before Gualior*, which was reduced, after a severe and arduous siege of one month.

* The hill fort of Gualior stands unrivalled in India, for extent, importance, and natural strength. It is generally termed (as stated in page 35) the **Gibraltar of the East**, and is

Lieut. S. rejoined the division of the army in Bundlecund, in April, and was stationed at Kooneh, under the command of Col. Fawcitt. In May he was detached with the 1st batt. 18th reg., under Capt. J. N. Smith, to besiege the fort of Belah, belonging to a refractory chief, about eight miles from the head-quarters of the division. On arriving before the place, orders were given to detach three companies, under Capt. Watson, to protect the town of Kotrah from a body of Pindarries, reported to be in the neighbourhood, leaving for the siege one company of European art., one troop of cav., and seven companies of N. I. Lieut. S. was ordered with two companies, at 8 P. M., to precede the guns, and seize the village of Belah and outskirts of the fort, which, under favour of a bright full moon, were carried, a lodgment effected, and the guns advantageously posted, for commencing operations in the morning, under the command of Capt. Feade, of the art. In consequence of the harassing duty during the night, Capt. Smith deemed it proper to relieve the party in the trenches, by two companies under Lieut. Gillespie, leaving in camp (which, on account of water, was two miles distant from the fort) one troop and five companies of Sepoys, amounting altogether to nearly 450 men. At sun-rise, on an alarm being given, by the picquets, of a large enemy's force in sight, the drum beat to arms, and every preparation was made for defence: shortly after, numerous bodies of horse approached the camp, cut through it in various parties, burning the tents and carrying off cattle. At 8 A. M. this small corps found themselves hemmed in on all sides, whilst other bodies seemed engaged in surrounding the party in the trenches, where, unfortunately, the only 6-pounder had been sent to assist in expediting the siege. The enemy's force amounted to 22,000 men, under the command of the famous Mahratta chieftain, Ameer Khan. At 10 A. M. the report was heard of nine guns in the trenches, and

considered the key of Hindostan, by the commanding situation, in central India, which it possesses. The active and judicious measures adopted by Sir Henry, in his operations against this place, which, under the most common defence, is naturally impregnable, so astonished the garrison, as to lead to its surrender, after a close siege of little more than a month.—*Vide* also Sir Henry White's Services, page 24, *et seq.*

soon after the silence which followed, a summons was received to surrender, accompanied by the information of every individual in the trenches, having been overwhelmed and cut up. The corps immediately struck their camp, formed a square, and it was determined by Capt. (now Col.) John Nicolas Smith to fight their way to Kornah, where the head-quarters of the division lay, about eight miles distant. At 1 P.M. they rejoined the division, which had advanced two miles to meet the enemy, and to rescue the party now exhausted with heat and fatigue, in repulsing several attacks* of the enemy, in which they lost some men and the greater part of the baggage.

In Sept. 1804, Lieut. S. accompanied the division, under Col. (now Gen. Sir G.) Martindell, to take possession of the strong holds in Bundlecund, and to attack the enemy posted in the hills near Mahobah. On the 24th Sept. they attacked and routed the confederated Bundela chieftains, under Rajah Ram, at the lake, and on the heights of Mahobah, seized their camp, baggage, cattle, and supplies, and pursued them from hill to hill, driving them from a series of strong positions until the close of the evening.

In Sept. 1804, Lieut. S. was appointed, by Col. Martindell, to act as assist.-surveyor to the division, for the purpose of surveying the route of the troops over the unexplored country of Bundlecund. In Oct. he was present at the siege and capture of Jyhtpoor hill fort, 1300 yards in length, and well defended with art.: on the east face the fort is covered by a deep and extensive lake, and on the west side it is well supplied with strong flanking towers. The first assault, by escalade and a *coup-de-main*, at the gateway, was repulsed with a loss of nearly 500 men. The batteries were then opened in form, and the garrison reduced to a surrender, after a severe siege of one month, at a season the most unfavourable for military operations.

In Oct. Lieut. S. marched with the division to Culpee, on the

---

* At one time Lieut. S. had to defend himself against the combined attack of four horsemen, all of whom were shot dead on the spot; on this occasion he owed his life to the skill he had acquired in the art of fencing at the naval college at Portsmouth.

right banks of the Jumna river, to restore the health of the corps, nine-tenths being brought from Jyhtpoor in litters. In April 1805, the division being recruited and restored, marched, under Col. Martindell, to Hingoona, on the banks of the Chumbul, to observe Scindia's operations towards the relief of Burtpoor, besieged by Lord Lake. In May Lieut. S. was appointed by his lordship, surveyor to the Bundlecund division of the army, with an allowance of 1000*l.* per annum. In June he marched from the Chumbul, and took up a position of surveillance on the western frontier, near Ihansi, a rich and flourishing town, under an independent Mahratta chieftain, called the Bhow Rajah. In Nov. Lieut. S. was detached, by Col. Martindell, with a small escort, to survey some routes through the interior of the Bundela states, which he effected in rather more than a month, but with great difficulty, from the jealousy of the inhabitants, and suspicious character of his proceedings. In Dec. he accompanied the division through the Bundela states, and took up a position on the Banghem river, ten miles north of fort Callinger.*

In Feb. 1806 Lieut. S. was appointed by the Gov.-Gen., Lord Wellesley, surveyor of all the ceded and conquered countries south of the Jumna river, with authority to act and extend his surveys at discretion. In March he accompanied Capt. (now Lieut.-Col.) Baillie† on a tour of settlement. In April he proceeded with an escort, consisting of a complete company, to defend the British and Mahratta frontier on the right banks of the Jumna, especially the Talooks of Burdike and Joossepara; also to ascertain and lay down the confluence of the Chumbul, Sinde, and Pohoodge rivers, with the Jumna. Great difficulties and obstacles were opposed to this survey, in consequence of the jealousy and barbarism of the feudal tribes inhabiting the banks of the Chumbul and Sinde rivers; the company was ultimately threatened with attacks from parties of irregular troops; it was fired upon by the forts with which this country is covered, and expe-

---

* This hill fortress is of the same description as Gualior, containing in its interior a vast surface of table land, well cultivated, and supplied with springs of water.

† See his Services, page 64, *et seq.*

rienced every opposition to the obtaining of supplies. In June 1806 Lieut. S. returned to Bandah, in Bundelcund, for the rainy season, having succeeded in every point connected with his expedition. In Dec. he accompanied Mr. John Richardson, agent to the Gov.-Gen. in Bundlecund, and a strong detachment under Col. Arnold, with a battering-train, to reduce a variety of hill forts, above the second and third range of ghauts, subject to Gopal Sing, and situated along the southern frontier of the district.

In Jan. 1807 the detachment stormed a strong pass, numerously defended, leading up the second range, by a simultaneous attack of three divisions; two of which having, by a difficult and circuitous route, taken the enemy in the rear, produced an instantaneous panic, and their entire discomfiture. In Feb. they captured the fort of Salelchoo, and seized on two guns which the enemy, in withdrawing, had taken with them; reduced several forts and strong holds with ease and rapidity, arising from the skill and effects of Col. Arnold's attack on the main body at the pass of Mokundre. In March Lieut. S. proceeded, with a small detachment of thirty men, to penetrate and reconnoitre the country on the Boghela frontier, and to bring into his survey the Soane river: he found every place in arms at his approach, and was pursued by a large collected force for a considerable distance. In order to save his party, Lieut. S. galloped singly into the midst of them, at the moment they were aiming their pieces to fire, took them by surprise, and succeeded in gaining protection and supplies for the night. Similar proceedings occurred on the following day, when he received a note from Mr. Richardson, informing him of the rebel, Gopal Sing, having broken his faith, and who was supposed to be in pursuit of this little party. Lieut. S. marched immediately towards the head-quarters, sixty miles distant, passed during the night within hearing of the enemy, and arrived safely in camp on the following day.

In April he returned with the division towards Bandah, after a successful termination of the political intentions of government, as connected with the frontier tribes, and the wild and mountainous

Ghoonds. In Dec. 1807 he accompanied Mr. Richardson, with a strong detachment of art. and troops, to reduce several hill forts and refractory chiefs on the southern frontier of the district This force, under the command of Col. Cuppage, breached and captured Herapon fort, at the foot of the second range of hills, and commanding the pass; and in Jan. following it took possession of several strong holds and fastnesses in the wild and mountainous tracts inhabited by the Ghoonds.

Lieut. S. was appointed, in May 1808, by Lieut.-Gen. Hewitt, Com.-in-Chief, adj. to the 2d batt. 18th reg., with permission to continue his surveys: in July following he was appointed, by the Gov.-Gen. in council, surveyor in Bundlecund, with authority to act at discretion, and to prosecute his surveys *ad libitum*; under general instructions, however, from the Surveyor-Gen., Lt.-Col. Colebrooke. In Oct. 1809 he was appointed, by Lord Minto, Gov.-Gen. of India, surveyor in the ceded and conquered district of Cuttack, and to define the British and Mahratta boundaries in Orissa. In March 1813 he was appointed, by his lordship, superintendent of the new Juggernauth road, extending 300 miles from Juggernauth to Burdwan; and in Jan. 1817 Lord Hastings nominated him 1st assist.-quart.-mast.-gen. at the head of the topographical staff in Bengal. In March 1818 he was relieved, by Capt. E. R. Broughton, at his own express desire, from the duties of superintending the construction of the new road. A committee of survey was directed to inspect and report on the state of the road at the time of transfer; the concluding paragraph of whose report is as follows:—

" On consideration of the duty performed by Capt. Sackville, in the superintendence of works on a long extended line of 180 miles; both as it regards the labourers employed, organizing and controuling their numbers, supplies, and exertions; and with respect to the number and variety of bridges, in realizing materials, fixing their scites and dimensions, &c: and when the committee further consider the nature of the soils, rock, sand, and clay, over which the road is constructed and carried—the inclined plane over which it passes—

the deep flats which intersect it, and which must have impeded the work considerably—also the violence of the rainy seasons (particularly the last,) and the short intervals of dry weather and of dry ground for carrying on operations,—they (the committee) have no hesitation in declaring it as their opinion, that Capt. Sackville merits, and they hope he will be honoured with, some very satisfactory mark of the approbation of government, for zeal, activity, and ability displayed, which alone could have brought so difficult and arduous an undertaking to its present advanced state."

The previous opinion of the government in regard to this officer's exertions on the above duty, may be seen from the following extracts from Secretary Mackenzie's letter of 23d Aug. 1816.

"*Par.* 2.—The Gov. Gen. in Council has perused, with much satisfaction, the full and comprehensive report which you have furnished of your past operations, which has tended to confirm the very favourable opinion already entertained by government of the zealous and well-directed exertions which you have manifested in the performance of the important and arduous duty entrusted to you.—3. Your suggestions in respect to the future execution of the remaining portion of the work in question, likewise appear to his lordship in council calculated to be of great utility to the officer on whom that duty may devolve.—4. The Gov.-Gen. in Council received with concern the information that the state of your health rendered you desirous of being relieved from your present duty. His lordship in council must particularly regret that any thing should prevent you from completing the important work which you appear so successfully to have brought to its present stage; a service which need not be affected by any alteration likely to take place in the nature of your present appointment."

In May 1818 Capt. S. was appointed assist. quart.-mast.-gen. with Maj.-Gen. Sir G. Martindell's force, at Rhorrda, and to survey the country around it. In Feb. 1819 he was appointed, by Lord Hastings, dep. quart.-mast.-gen. of the Bengal army, with the official rank of major. In May 1819 he was appointed joint commissioner with Mr. Fleming, court of circuit judge, to investigate certain transactions at Malda of a civil and military nature; and in Feb. 1820 he returned to Europe on furlough.

In the course of his services, this officer has prepared for the government numerous plans and maps of Bundlecund, the district of Cuttack, &c. &c.

MAJ.-GEN. SIR DAVID OCHTERLONY, Bart. & G.C.B.

(Bengal Establishment.)

This officer was appointed a cadet in 1777; ensign, 7th Feb. 1778; lieut. 17th Sept. following; capt. 7th Jan. 1796; maj. 21st April 1800; lieut.-col. 18th March 1803; col. 1st Jan. 1812; and maj.-gen. 4th June 1814.

In 1781, this officer, then a lieut., belonged to the 24th Bengal N. I., which was one of the five regiments that marched from Bengal, under the command of Col. Pearse*, to aid the presidency of Madras, then engaged in war with Hyder Ally. The Bengal detachment joined the forces employed in that war, under the veteran Com.-in-Chief, Lieut.-Gen. Sir Eyre Coote, and partook of the very arduous and brilliant services of those campaigns. At the siege of Cudalore, in 1783, on an occasion in which the 24th reg. distinguished itself against the French European regiments, who, making a sally when this corps was in the trenches, were received on the points of their bayonets, and repulsed in a manner which will ever redound to the honour and glory of the Bengal army, Lieut. Ochterlony was wounded and taken prisoner.

* See p. 87.

On the close of the war in the Carnatic, Lieut. O. returned with his corps to Bengal, where his services were rewarded by the staff appointment of judge-adv.-gen. to one of the divisions of the army, in which situation he continued for many years.

In 1803, Lieut.-Col. Ochterlony was on service with the 12th N.I., under the personal command of the Com.-in-Chief, and present at the capture of the forts of Sasnee, Bejigurh, and Catchoura, in the Dooaub.

On the breaking out of the Mahratta war in 1803, Lieut.-Col. O. was appointed dep. adj.-gen. of the army; and, taking the field with the Com.-in-Chief, was present at the affair near Coel, on the 29th Aug., the assault of Allyghur on the 4th, and the battle of Delhi on the 11th Sept. of that year.

Immediately after the battle of Delhi, Lieut.-Col. O. was appointed Envoy or Resident at the Court of the Emperor Shaw Allum, in which situation he obtained the particular approbation and applause of the Com.-in-Chief and of government, for his judicious conduct during the siege of Delhi,* by the forces of Holkar, under Scindia.

After peace was completely restored in that quarter, a gentleman of the civil service was appointed to succeed Lieut.-Col. Ochterlony, at the court of Delhi, when he was nominated to command the fortress of Allahabad. From this inactive situation Lieut.-Col. O. was removed in 1809, to command a force, assembled on the north-west frontier, to oppose some hostile demonstrations of the Seiks. With that force he established a position on the banks of the Sutuleje, and continued in command in that quarter, until again called into the field during the Nepaul war.†

---

* Extract of a letter from a field-officer, dated Feb. 1805.—" Having received accounts from Col. Ochterlony, acting Resident at Delhi, that the whole of Holkar's infantry had invested that city, we marched to its relief, arrived there on 19th Oct., when the enemy moved off precipitately, after having battered the walls for eight days, which left the whole nearly in ruins; and although in the course of that time they made several assaults at different places, they were gloriously repulsed with great loss, on every occasion, by our gallant troops, not in number one hundredth part of the enemy; for which Col. O. has had the highest honours conferred on him, both by the Com.-in-Chief and Marq. Wellesley."

† Extract of a letter from a Staff-officer, explanatory of the origin of this war:—" For

The plan of the campaign was, by a variety of operations, undertaken at once, for the accomplishment indeed of separate objects,

a series of years the Nepaulese had been making encroachments on the British dominions, which, not being vigorously resisted at first, encouraged a continuance of the evil. At length a remonstrance was made to the court of Catmandoo on the subject, and commissioners were appointed on the part of both states, to examine jointly the pretended rights of the Nepaulese to the lands which they had acquired. The result of this enquiry was, a complete refutation of all their pretensions, and the production of the most satisfactory evidence of the artifice and violence with which their acquisitions had been obtained; but, notwithstanding this public exposure of their total want of right, they continued to evade, on various pretences, the demands of the British government for restitution. It was far, however, from the wish of the latter to engage in a war with Nepaul, if this extremity could have been avoided; and these measures of forbearance and conciliation were carried to the utmost extent compatible with the dignity of the English empire. In the course of these investigations it appeared, that the Nepaulese had occupied, about twenty-five years ago, a considerable part of the country, which has since been ceded to the Company, by the Newaub of Oude, and to which they had no better claim than they had to any other portion of the territory which they had seized. As this aggression, however, had not been made directly on the Company's dominions, it appeared possible to leave it in their hands, without injury to the credit of the British government; and it was, therefore, proposed to relinquish our right to it in their favour, on condition that they should peaceably restore the lands which they had usurped on the English territory. To this proposition an evasive reply was received, and it was found necessary to inform them, that we should insist on the resumption of this country, as well as of all the parts which they had acquired by direct aggression on the Company's dominions. In the meantime it was known, that they had for some time been laying up large stores of saltpetre, purchasing and fabricating arms, and organizing and disciplining their troops, under some European deserters in their service, after the model of the companies of our Sepoy battalions.

Under these circumstances, perceiving that there was no end to the evasions, that every effort at accommodation served only to augment their pretensions and their arrogance, and that longer delay would only render a contest more arduous, it was deemed indispensible, by the British General, to bring the question to immediate issue; and a portion of country in Goorackpoor, in which they had seized upwards of thirty villages, during the very progress of these discussions, was selected as a fit object to decide the point. Ample time was allowed for the progress of a messenger, from Calcutta to Catmandoo, for deliberation and decision on the subject there, and for despatch and execution of orders, by the Nepaulese authorities established in the territories in question; and they were distinctly informed, that if, at the conclusion of a specific period, determined by these considerations, this portion of country was not relinquished, the Company's officers should be replaced by force. A body of troops, adequate to the service, was at the same time held in readiness, and orders to carry the above resolution into effect, without reference to government, transmitted to the magistrates at Goorackpoor. At the conclusion of the appointed time, no steps whatsoever had been taken by the Nepaulese towards a compliance with this requi-

but these objects mutually facilitating each other, to wrest the country suddenly from the Nepaulese. With this view, it was intended that the principal division of the army, under Maj.-Gen. B. Marley, should move from Palna, on the capital, by the route of Etoude and Chusapanee, while a force, under Maj.-Gen. Sullivan Wood, should penetrate into Gorkah, by the route of Rootswild, and prevent the transfer of the war to the westward. The very same reasoning was applied in arranging the attack to be made on the troops serving in the western part of the enemy's dominions. A division under Maj.-Gen. Ochterlony, to advance from the Sutuleje, was directed against the force under Umar Sing, and Maj.-Gen. Gillespie, at the head of another, was to occupy the valley of the Dhoon, and the territory of Suenaghur, and cut off the communication with the capital, and the resources to the eastward. As soon as these operations were suffi-

sition, nor did they manifest the smallest symptom of any such intention. Accordingly Mr. Martin (the Judge) advanced with a small force, under Lieut.-Col. Richardson, and re-established the different Thannahs; the Nepaulese authorities, with what troops they had, retiring on his approach. For some time things went on in tranquillity; but when the troops had fallen back to avoid the unhealthy season, which, in that part of the country, is particularly fatal to any race of men but the natives of the province itself, a Nepaulese force descended from the hills, and surprised the Thannahs in the night-time, murdered and wounded a large proportion of the officers, the rest making their escape by flight. After all that had passed, an outrage of this sort might justly be considered as placing us at once in a state of actual war; but as no opposition had been made in the first instance to the establishment of the Thannahs, it was considered just possible that the peaceable execution of that measure might have been owing to orders transmitted from Catmandoo, and that the subsequent attack was the unauthorised act of the local authorities on the frontiers; and the British government, anxious to avoid involving the country in hostilities to the last, made one more application to the Rajah, to give him the option of disavowing this piece of violence, and of punishing the offenders: an application that proved as unavailing as the rest. It would be useless to add any comment to justify this war: it must be obvious, that it was necessary and unavoidable, and that the forbearance of the British government was carried to the very uttermost extent to which it was right that it should go. The security of the inhabitants, along the frontiers, had been destroyed; our territories usurped; our just demands, and our efforts at accommodation, alike treated with contempt; the aggressions continued during the very progress of the discussions entered into by both states, for the express purpose of investigating acts of the same unwarrantable violence; and finally, the British territory invaded by a military force, and the officers of the civil government murdered at their stations."

ciently advanced, another column was to possess itself of Almora and Keuraoon, and to open the routes between the different divisions.

The only part of this plan that can be considered as attended with complete success, was that entrusted to Maj.-Gen. Ochterlony; it is, however, unnecessary to enter into a review of the operations of the other divisions, and it will be sufficient, for the present purpose, briefly to sketch those of the western division, under the command of the subject of this memoir. Maj.-Gen. Ochterlony, who had to contend with a country of great difficulty, and with an enemy, who, throughout the campaign, displayed a degree of energy, of genius, and of resource, unprecedented in a native leader, by a series of operations, gradually forced him from post to post, and at length cooped him up, and compelled him to surrender, in the almost inaccessible fortress of Mallown. This success put us in possession of the more recent conquests of the Gorkahs, between the Ganges and the Sutuleje, and produced the immediate surrender of the fort of Jytuck, before which Maj.-Gen. Martindell (who, on the fall of Maj.-Gen. Gillespie, before Callinger, had succeeded to the command of his division,) had been long occupied, and with it the valley of the Dhoon, and the territory of Suenaghur.

Maj.-Gen. Ochterlony was one of the officers of the Hon. Company's service first selected for the honours of the Bath, and of which he was appointed Knight Commander. For his subsequent services in the Nepaul war of 1814, 15, and 16, he was created a baronet; a pension of 1000*l.* per annum was granted to him by* the East

---

* " At a Court of Directors, held on Wednesday, the 6th December 1815, a Report from the Committee of Correspondence, dated this day, being read, it was resolved unanimously, in consideration of the eminent and most beneficial services rendered to the Company by Maj.-Gen. Sir David Ochterlony, Bart. and K.C.B., in the war against the state of Nepaul, (by which the honour of the British arms was upheld, and the enemy, after the capture of extensive provinces, important to them, were obliged to sue for peace, on terms favourable to the Company,) a pension of 1000*l.* per annum be granted to him, to commence from the date of the victory over the Nepaulese army, the 16th of April 1815. The said grant being subject to the approbation of the Court of Directors."

India Company; and in December 1816 he was raised to the further dignity of Knight Grand Cross of the Order of the Bath; with which he was invested by the Gov.-Gen., the Marquess of Hastings.

The Chairman made the following address to the Court:—" The papers connected with this subject had been," he observed, "before the proprietors, and the most material of them were published in the newspapers; it therefore would not be necessary for him to take up much time in stating the merits of Sir David Ochterlony. They were of such a nature as not to need any laboured panegyric from him. They appeared so clear—they stood so completely by themselves, that they wanted not any adventitious assistance to support them. He should do no more than venture to state a brief outline of those services which the Company were now called on to reward. Gentlemen would be aware, that the enemy he had to cope with, in the Nepaulese, was one of a new description—one whom we never had to combat before. The Nepaulese were different in character from those Native forces with whom we had formerly to combat, and their country, almost inaccessible, was different from any into which our arms had previously penetrated. The war was, therefore, a very arduous undertaking from the beginning. A very great part of the enterprise rested with Sir David Ochterlony. It had happened that several of the operations conducted by other officers had failed; but Sir David was uniformly successful—his measures, in every instance, were judicious and proper—and they were crowned by a success continued and progressive. While other divisions of the army were repulsed, that commanded by him attained every object it sought to achieve, although opposed by a determined enemy, and having, at the same time, to contend with the disadvantages of a country most difficult of access. By his conduct he upheld the military character of this country, when reverses had taken place in almost every other quarter. ———— The great weight of the war rested on him; and the part he acted was of the utmost importance, both in its effects on the enemy, in its operation on the character of our own troops, and, above all, in its influence on the minds and feelings of the natives of India generally. Having supported the character and cause of his country in this manner, he compelled the enemy to have recourse to negociations, which he (the Chairman) trusted had ere this terminated in peace; but of this fact they had not yet received intelligence. The battles of the 14th, 15th, and 16th of April, on the Mallown hills, ended in the complete discomfiture of the Nepaulese forces. The principal officer of the enemy, Umar Sing Thappa, a brave and experienced man, was captured, the provinces of Gorkah fell into our hands, and a convention, leading to terms of peace, was entered into. These circumstances, and the recommendation of the government of India (for the Earl Moira himself, and the council of Calcutta, have given a particular prominence to the character and services of Sir David Ochterlony, and pointed him out to our earliest consideration), have induced the Court of Directors to accede, unanimously, to this resolution. But, if they wished to take a more general view of the subject, for the purpose of delaying the expression of their opinion on the conduct of Sir D. Ochterlony, they could hardly have done so with propriety, because the government of this country had already marked their high sense of his services, by conferring on him a very great honour. His pecuniary concerns were extremely moderate. Sir David was said to be a soldier who had literally lived on his pay, and had therefore saved nothing.

The following account thereof, is from the the Calcutta Government Gazette of 9th April 1818:—

"Maj.-Gen. Sir David Ochterlony having arrived at the head-quarters of his Ex. the most noble the Gov.-Gen. and Com.-in-Chief, his lordship availed himself of the Maj.-General's presence, to invest him with the insignia of the Grand Cross of the Order of the Bath, in pursuance of the authority and instructions of His Royal Highness the Prince Regent, signified to his lordship by Lord Viscount Sidmouth, one of his Majesty's principal secretaries of state. Friday, the 20th of March, on which day the camp was at Terwah, having been appointed for the performance of the ceremony, the civil officers in attendance on his Ex. the Gov.-Gen., the officers of the general staff of the army, and the officers of the body guard, and of the 2d batt. 25th reg. N. I., forming his Excellency's escort, were assembled at the Gov.-General's durbar tent on the occasion. The Newaub Ahmed Buksh Khan, and the Aumil of the district, with other local officers of the government of his Ex. the Vizier, as well as the native officers of the body guard and the escort, were also present. His Ex. the Gov.-Gen. entered the durbar tent at one o'clock, preceded by his secretary and the Persian secretary to the government, bearing respectively the badge and decorations, and the statutes of the order, and by the whole of his lordship's personal staff. His lordship having taken his seat, Sir David Ochterlony was introduced by Lieut.-Col. Doyle and Lieut.-Col. Young, with the usual forms; and having advanced to the edge of the carpet, on which the Gov.-Gen.'s chair was placed, his lordship rose and addressed him in the following terms:—

"SIR DAVID OCHTERLONY,—I cannot figure to myself any occasion on which the high honour of representing the Prince Regent could be equally flattering with this ceremony, in which he has deigned to order that I shall act for his Royal person. The instruction has communicated to me a portion of the warmth with which the generous mind of His Royal Highness glows at every opportunity of encouraging any effort that tends to promote the glory of the British nation, and I feel consciously elevated by the fulfilment of

Under these circumstances, the Court of Directors, to enable him to live in a style commensurate with the dignity bestowed on him by the Prince Regent, have passed the resolution now before the Proprietors. It was not necessary for him to take up their attention further; the motion was one that recommended itself. The Hon. Chairman concluded by proposing, 'That the Court do confirm the resolution.'—Agreed to unanimously."

such a duty. You are to receive the honourable badge with which I am commissioned to invest you, as a recognition of your admirable zeal, and of the advantages secured by that zeal to your country's interest. Such a public acknowledgment of your professional merit would alone be sufficient matter of pride; yet I have to congratulate you on what must be still more touching to your feelings. You have obliterated a distinction painful for the officers of the Hon. Company; and you have opened the door for your brothers in arms to a reward, which their recent display of exalted spirit and invincible intrepidity proves could not be more deservedly extended to the officers of any army on earth."

The Gov.-Gen. then invested Sir David Ochterlony with the insignia of the order, under a salute of thirteen guns.

As a further mark of distinction for this officer's services, an honourable augmentation to his arms was granted in Jan. 1817*; and in

---

* "*Whitehall, Jan.* 14, 1817.—His Royal Highness the Prince Regent, in the name and on the behalf of his Majesty, taking into consideration the highly-distinguished services rendered by Sir David Ochterlony, Bart., a major-general in the army in the East Indies, and knight grand cross of the most hon. military order of the bath, on divers important occasions during a period of thirty-nine years, particularly in the course of those arduous operations of the Mahratta war, which conduced to the decisive victory gained by the British forces under the command of the late Gen. Viscount Lake, in the memorable conflict before Delhi, on the 11th Sept. 1803; to the consequent surrender of that capital, and to the restoration of his majesty Shaw Alum to the throne of his ancestors; as also the proofs of wisdom and military talent afforded by this officer during the subsequent defence of the said city against the whole force of Jeswunt Rao Holkar; his prudent arrangement and disposition of the comparatively few troops under his orders; his judicious conduct, at so difficult a crisis, in the discharge of the high and important functions of British Resident at the court of Delhi, combined with his great energy and animated personal exertions, to which were chiefly attributed the safety of that capital and of the person of Shaw Alum, at a time when the loss of either might have proved highly prejudicial to the public interests in Hindostan; and further, the unremitting zeal, foresight, and decision, manifested by the said major-general, under circumstances of great difficulty, during the late contest with the state of Nepaul, especially in that series of combined movements, during the nights of the 14th and 15th of April 1815, against the fortified positions of the Gorkah army on the heights of Mallown, which led to the establishment of the British troops on that range of mountains, theretofore deemed to be impregnable; to the evacuation by the enemy of the fortresses of Mallown and Jytuck; to the defeat and surrender of Umar Sing Thappa, the chief commander of the hostile force; and to the successful and glorious termination of that campaign; and, lastly, the judgment, perseverance, and vigour, displayed by the said Maj.-Gen., as commander of the British forces,

Feb. following, the thanks of the British Parliament* were unanimously voted to him; and a beautiful piece of plate was presented to him by the officers who served in the division of the army under his command.

In 1822 Sir David Ochterlony was appointed Resident in Malwah and Rajpootana.

LIEUTENANT-COLONEL ARCHIBALD WATSON.

(Bengal Establishment.)

THIS officer was a cadet of 1794; he joined his reg., then serving on the frontier, early in 1797; and in 1798 marched with his reg., the 1st light cav., with the army under Maj.-Gen. Robert Stuart, into

upon the renewal of the contest with the aforesaid state, the happy and triumphant results of which have been consolidated by a treaty of peace between the East India Company and the Rajah of Nepaul, highly beneficial to the interests of the British empire in India;—His Royal Highness, desirous, in addition to other marks of his royal approbation, of commemorating the faithful and important services of the said Maj.-Gen., by granting unto him certain armorial augmentations, has been pleased to give and grant His Majesty's royal license and permission, that he, the said Sir David Ochterlony, and his descendants, may bear to the armorial ensigns of Ochterlony the honourable augmentations following, viz.— 'On an embattled chief two banners in saltire, the one of the Mahratta states, inscribed *Delhi*, the other of the state of Nepaul, inscribed *Nepaul*, the staves broken and encircled by a wreath of laurel,' with this motto to the arms, viz.—' *Prudentia et animo;*' and the crest of honourable augmentation following, viz.—' Out of an eastern crown, inscribed *Nepaul*, an arm issuant, the hand grasping a baton of command entwined by an olive branch;' provided the said armorial ensigns be first duly exemplified according to the laws of arms, otherwise the said Royal license to be void and of none effect."

* " *Jovis, 6 die Februarii,* 1817.—Resolved, That the thanks of this house be given to Major-General Sir David Ochterlony, Knt. Grand Cross of the Most Hon. Military Order of the Bath, for the skill, valour, and perseverance, displayed by him in the late war with Nepaul, to which the result of that contest is mainly to be ascribed; and also to the several officers of the army, both European and Native, for the bravery and discipline displayed by them in that arduous contest."

Rohilcund, to secure the family of Golaum Mahummud, Prince of the Rohillas. The same year he accompanied the army, under Sir A. Clarke, Com.-in-Chief, to depose Vizier Ally, the pretended Newaub of Oude. In 1799, he marched with the army, under Sir J. Craig, to meet the projected invasion of the Persian Zemaun Shaw. In Jan. 1802 he was selected for the command of a detachment against Toree Sing, a rebel Zemindar, in Rohilcund, on which occasion he had the good fortune to secure the person, and destroy the strong hold of that chief; for which service he received the thanks of the Lieut.-Gov. of the ceded and conquered provinces, the Hon. Henry Wellesley. Soon after, he commanded a squadron of his reg. at the siege, evacuation, and night affair with its garrison, of the fortress of Catchoura, under Lord Lake, when the enemy were entirely destroyed; and of the only two officers under him, on that occasion, one was killed and the other wounded—Cornets Pollock and Cornish.

Capt. Watson served in the first campaign under Lord Lake, and was present at the battle of Coel, Aug. 22, 1803; assault and capture of Allyghur; on which occasion he was capt. of the day. He accompanied Col. Macan's brigade (of which his reg. formed a part,) when detached from the army, in pursuit of the Mahratta force, under the French officer Fleury, when the Dooaub was cleared of the enemy. He was at the siege and surrender of Agra, and battle of Laswarree. He commanded the troops composing the foraging party of the army on the 11th Feb. 1804, when a body of hill-robbers, confiding in the security of their fastnesses, had carried off a number of the public camels, and other cattle of the army, baggage, &c.; and pursuing them through the passes of the mountains, attacked and destroyed their hill-forts and villages, killing a few and dispersing the remainder of the marauders, after having recovered the whole of the public camels and property. For the latter service he received the thanks of Lord Lake.

Capt. Watson was present throughout the second campaign under Lord Lake; he was detached from the line of march, by order of his lordship, with a squadron to protect and recover the public baggage, elephants, camels, &c. of the army, which Holkar's cav. were plundering, between Agra and Muttra, at the opening of the campaign. The numbers of the enemy's cav. frustrated this object; large reinforcements became absolutely necessary, and which at length joined Capt. Watson. He was present at the beating up of Holkar's camp, by the cav. under Lord Lake, in person, near Muttra; and Holkar, while the army was detained at Muttra, having marched and besieged Delhi, Capt. Watson was at the raising of the siege, and pursuit of Holkar down the Dooaub; the affair at Shamleh, where Col. Burns was shut up, 3d Nov.; action of Futtehgurh, 17th Nov.; the reconnoitring of Deig, by the cav. under Lord Lake, in the face of the combined cav. of Holkar and the Rajah of Burtpoor; on which latter occasion, Capt. Watson commanded the rear-guard, on returning to camp, extremely harassed by the enemy, a great number of whom were killed, though with a considerable loss on the side of the British. Capt. Watson served at the siege, assault, and capture of Deig; at the siege and four assaults of Burtpoor; and commanded the 1st reg. of cav., when in conjunction with a batt. of inf., (the whole under Capt. Geo. Welsh,) it sustained, by the occupation of a village, the united attacks of the combined armies of Holkar and Burtpoor until reinforced from Lord Lake's camp; when a general attack was made upon the enemy, who suffered severely, and lost many standards, &c. The detachment, on this occasion, received the particular acknowledgments of Lord Lake.

From this period till 1810, few opportunities offered for exertion, and Capt. Watson continued with his reg. for the most part in cantonments, and often in command of it.

In March 1810 he marched with his reg., and a batt. of inf., under Lieut.-Col. T. Brown*, against Gopal Sing; whose camp they beat up at Bechoun, on the 19th of that month. Capt. W. was some time after sent with a squadron up the first range of ghauts, in Bundlecund,

---

* Now Major-General—*vide* Services, p. 253.

to reinforce the troops employed against that chief and his allies. Having rendered himself thoroughly master of the nature and peculiarities of the country between the first and second ranges of hills (which formed the grand scene of the enemy's depredations), as well as of the principal haunts, secret connexions, family influence, &c. of the rebels, Capt. Watson projected an enterprise which, he hoped, might effectually destroy their power and resources, and put an end to that spirit of combination which their past successes in the province had of late given rise to. He observed that these successes had resulted chiefly from their superior knowledge, and our ignorance, of the country, the caution with which they had avoided encounters with our troops, excepting under circumstances of decided advantage; and that dispersion was the mode by which they had hitherto easily eluded the open approach or attack of our troops; re-assembling again, with the greatest ease, in any named quarter, in greater force than ever. Capt. Watson, accordingly, offered his services, and solicited the command of a detachment against them, with permission to move across the river Byarny, which lay between our troops and the enemy, then assembled in great force under the combined chiefs, Lutchman Sing, Himmut Sing, and Omrah Sing, the latter the nephew of Gopal Sing, the grand rebel and marauder, who himself at this time was absent. Capt. W., in the meanwhile, arranged a system of espionage, for the attainment of exact intelligence of the situation, force, haunts, and movements, as well as the individual character and interests of the enemy's chiefs and adherents: at the same time, he set on foot reports and stratagem, for deceiving the rebels as to the object of his detachment, in the event of its being formed, and passing the Byarny; of which he knew they would have immediate notice. Capt. Watson, on the 16th Nov., having obtained the command of a small detachment of observation, and the same day, quietly passing the river Byarny (about forty miles beyond which the enemy lay), and encamping a day on the opposite bank, he suddenly, by severe forced marches in the night, concealing his detachment during the day, and, by his patrols, intercepting all possibility of intelligence reaching the enemy, came upon them by surprise, a little before daybreak, on the morning of the 19th, at the village of Bhomory, and so entirely annihilated their force, that these chiefs never again made head; and the two former, after relinquishing their alliance with Gopal, were soon after slain, the first by his own, and the second by the country people.

The day after the affair of Bhomory, an order arrived from Maj.-Gen. Sir G. Martindell, commanding in the province, directing Capt. Watson's immediate recall, and ordering Col. Brown, commanding above the Ghauts, to proceed with his own force against the enemy. Had Capt. Watson, therefore, lost a few hours, or his plans been in the least immature, the opportunity would have been inevitably and for ever lost. His detachment thus recalled by Gen. Martindell, as too small to be hazarded, had been chiefly intended as a detachment of observation. The thanks of the Com.-in-Chief, and of the supreme government, to Capt. Watson, were, on this occasion, promulgated in general orders*.

In 1811 Capt. W. obtained the command of a detachment in subordinate co-operation with Col. Brown, against Gopal Sing in person; in the course of which, Capt. W. personally beat up the camp of that chief, at Chargong, and for a time dispersed his followers; but having been obliged to approach him in open daylight, the affair was not so decisive as he had hoped. Subsequently to this, that daring rebel, during the rainy season, had been for some time re-assembling troops, and was again in considerable force, preparing to pour into the British districts the moment the breaking up of the rains should permit him. At this period (the eve of the season of action) Capt. W.,

---

* *Extract from General Orders, Dec. 7, 1810.*—" The Gov.-Gen. in council has great pleasure in diffusing a knowledge of every transaction in which the officers and men of the military service of the Company have had an opportunity of manifesting their characteristic spirit of bravery and exertion; and on the present occasion, his Lordship in council discharges, with peculiar satisfaction, the duty of rendering justice to the skill and judgment displayed by Capt. Watson in planning the aattck of the enemy's force, and to his activity, zeal, and gallantry, and those of the officers and troops under his command, in carrying it into effect with such signal success."

by the temporary absence of Col. Brown, from illness, obtained the command of the troops above the Ghauts, and acquired such exact information of the situation and force of the enemy, as well as the perfect security he was in against all fear of attack in such a place as that he had chosen, and at such a time and season, that he planned, and submitted to Gen. Martindell, an attack on his camp and cantonment, with a view to destroy his hourly increasing force before it should arrive at maturity; and, above all, at that critical season of the year, when the breaking up of the rains, and the commencement of the cold weather, should enable him, as usual, in full strength, to inundate the districts under the British government or influence.

When Capt. W. marched against the enemy on this occasion, he had received an order from Gen. Martindell, in reply to his communication just mentioned, " not to pass the Keine, or any other river, till the enemy descended" (the second range of hills above which his camp and cantonments lay) into our districts. The Keine lay between Capt. W.'s camp and the second range of hills. The general, aware of the accumulating force of the enemy, his extreme caution, and the skill with which he always chose his ground, and seized every advantage where he himself personally commanded, was unwilling to hazard any detachments out of our own districts, or through the passes of the mountains, at such a season, and especially beyond the rivers, then swoln, and, for the most part, overflown by the rains, to a degree that rendered retreat difficult, if not, for a time, impracticable. But Capt. Watson being on the spot, and relying on the accuracy of his information, the tried fidelity of his spies, whom he had attached to his service by liberal rewards, together with his own knowledge of the passes of the mountains, the approaches to the enemy's camp, and the camp itself, with the ground in its vicinity, after assigning his reasons to Gen. Martindell, with his conviction that they would ultimately meet with his full approbation, which they accordingly did; and having previously formed several detachments, and directed their march upon different points, with a view to distract the attention of the enemy, he, by forced marches in the night, came upon him by surprise at day-break, on the morning of the 7th Sept., at the strong village of Chargong, drove him from his holds, and so totally defeated, dispersed, and destroyed his force, he himself escaping only by the swiftness of his horse, and his superior knowledge of the country, (which is every where full of rocky hills and ravines, deep, precipitous, rapid streams, thick jungles, impervious, but bye paths, known only to the enemy,) that that daring and formidable marauder no more attempted to make head; and, being further disheartened by the recent loss of his principal chiefs, hastily submitted to the British government. Capt. Watson again received the public acknowledgments of his superiors, the thanks of the Com.-in-Chief, and of the supreme government.

When the force was assembling against Java, Capt. Watson volunteered his services, with those of his whole troop; but at that period more cav. was not required. He was subsequently present at the siege of Callinger, in 1812, and was selected by Sir G. Martindell for partizan co-operation with his army, and for blockading the passes of the mountains, interception of reinforcements, as well as all egress from the garrison, &c. After having fully reconnoitred the place, and, through his spies, obtained accurate information regarding the interior, with the gates and wickets on that face of the fortress nearest to his detachment, and in other respects most eligible for such an attempt, Maj. Watson immediately planned, submitted to Gen. Martindell, and offered to conduct a party in disguise to enter the fortress, and seize one of the gates by stratagem. This enterprize depended on the circumstance of the enemy's soon expecting or not a reinforcement; the nature of the country making it almost impossible completely to blockade a place, which, on three sides, is surrounded by lofty mountains, terminating every where in steep precipices, and intersected by numerous, though very difficult passes, &c.; the fortress itself, situated on a high and extensive rock, bordered on all sides by craggy cliffs that overhang each other as they rise, even to the summit; the surrounding vales covered with thick woods and impenetrable jungles. Maj. Watson's party, lightly armed for the occasion, was to approach the fortress in disguise towards day-break, as such reinforcement, by paths he had discovered; fired upon with blank cartridges, and apparently pursued by the British picquets and out-posts, now become his supporters. Gen. Martindell's information, however, did not warrant him in accepting Maj. Watson's proposal, nor permit him to wait such contingency, though expected; and the assault, unhappily unsuccessful, and with very severe loss on our side, soon after took place.

He subsequently again volunteered for Java, where he understood a corps of light cav. was to be formed for that service. He next offered his services, through Gen. Champagné, to command a detachment for partizan co-operation with the corps assembling at that time, under Col. Prole, against the Bhattie country; and afterwards marched on that service with his reg., which he had now long commanded, with a division of the army under Brig.-Gen. Arnold. This expedition was attended with complete success.

He next offered his services, through Col. Bowie, commanding the Agra frontier, for clearing our borders in the river Chumbul, and the whole of Scindia's country, from the Pindarry banditti which infested them; and, finally, he commanded his reg., the 1st light cav., with Gen. Sir Rufane Donkin's division of the grand army, under the personal command of the Marquess of Hastings, during the late war with the Mahratta states, and in the complete extirpation of the Pindarry hordes, which had so long over-run some of the finest provinces of Hindostan. In Feb. 1820 Maj. Watson left India on furlough to Europe, since which he has attained the rank of lieut.-colonel.

The following are the dates of this officer's commissions: cadet, 8th Nov. 1795; lieut. 28th April 1797; capt. 22d Jan. 1802; major, 4th June 1803; and lieut.-col. in 1823.

LIEUT.-GEN. SIR DYSON MARSHALL, K.C.B.

(Bengal Establishment.)

This officer was appointed a cadet on the Bengal establishment in 1771; ensign, 8th Feb. 1773; lieut. 6th March 1778; captain, 4th Oct. 1781; major, 1st Jan. 1794; lieut.-col. 1st Jan. 1798; lieut.-col. commandant, 20th Oct. 1805; col. 25th April 1808; maj.-gen. 4th June 1811; and lieut.-gen. 19th July 1821.

In 1774 this officer served at the battle of Rohilla*; and in 1778-9, 80, and 81, in the campaigns in Malwa, in the war with Madajee Scindia, under Colonels Camac and Muir; and, in 1794, in Rohilcund. He subsequently, for several years, commanded the Ramgurh batt., a local corps, stationed on the south-west frontier of Bengal: he also commanded at Kurnaul.

At the attack and capture of the fortress and town of Hattrass†,

---

* " On St. George's day, 1774, the Rohilla battle was fought on the plains of Rohilcund, in which six Sepoy battalions were engaged, together with the 2d European regiment, under the command of Col. Champion, then the Commander-in-Chief in Bengal. They were opposed to a superior number of a very brave and hardy race of men, devoted to their leader, whose cause was their own, fighting for the country and home which he had established for them, in the fruitful province of Khuttair. Their gallant chief fell early in the action, when the discipline and valour of the British troops, and the execution of their artillery, soon spread terror and dismay among the Rohilla bands, and led to a prompt and decided victory."

Williams' Hist. Bengal N. I. p. 181.

† The following field army orders, by this officer, are inserted, as they particularly refer to the distinguished services of several officers :—

" *Camp before Hattrass, March 6.*—Maj.-Gen. Marshall congratulates the army he has the honour to command, on the successful termination of its services against the fortress and town of Hattrass ; which event has led to the surrender of Moorsaum and eleven other forts.

" To Maj.-Gens. Donkin, Sir J. Horsford, and Brown, and Maj. Anburey, General Marshal feels extremely indebted for the judgment, zeal, promptitude, and energy,

this officer had the command of the troops, and for his services was nominated a Knight Commander of the Bath. He also served during the Pindarry war.

which they invariably displayed in carrying into effect the operations devolving upon the several branches of the service to which they were attached.

" The science and skill displayed by the engineer and artillery departments were eminently conspicuous; and the bombardment and explosion of the enemy's principal magazine, which, without derogating from the merits of others, must be allowed to have given us almost immediate possession of the place, will long be regarded as the most memorable among the brilliant events of the last fortnight, and as demonstrative of the extent and soundness of that judgment and penetration, which, in the avowed anticipation of these very consequences, enabled the army, by the provision of adequate means, to ensure them. The practice of the artillery has answered the expectations of that high authority, to which the Major-General has ventured to allude in the foregoing observations. Another motive for them is to bring forward and illustrate the fact more closely, that where the means are equal to the science and practical knowledge known to pervade every branch of the army, the results must invariably be rapid and successful, even against such strong and formidable forts as Hattrass has proved to be.

" The infantry and cavalry on this occasion had abundant opportunities of showing their bravery, zeal, and devotion to the service.

" On one occasion, particularly, the Major-General was highly pleased with the alacrity and eagerness displayed by the infantry, who were formed in columns ready to storm the works of the town, holding out every expectation of success from men who evinced such resolution and desire of being led on.

" The duties of investing the fort latterly devolved on the cavalry, and their vigilance and constancy in maintaining the blockade entitle them to the Major-General's highest consideration. The loss sustained by the enemy in making their retreat from the fort reflects great credit on the two squadrons of his Majesty's 8th light dragoons, the 7th Native cavalry, and part of the 1st Rohilla cavalry, who entered ―――― and routed them.

" The pioneer corps has given another proof to the many already on record of their coolness in the most trying situations, and of their extraordinary skill and dispatch in the labours which belong to them in this particular species of warfare.

" Having thus noticed his high approval of the conduct of every branch of the army, Maj.-Gen. Marshall desires that the several officers employed on the general staff of the army will accept his warmest thanks for the able manner in which their several duties were conducted.

" The Major-General's personal staff, consisting of Capt. James, aid-de-camp, Major Cartwright, and Lieut. Sneyd, of the quart.-mast.-gen.'s department, who both volunteered their services on this occasion, and acted as aides-de-camp, are entitled to his best thanks for their ready assistance on all occasions.

Sir Dyson Marshall served his tour on the staff, in command of the field army, in which he was continued for a further period, during the absence of one of the staff generals on account of sickness.

COLONEL ALEXANDER HIND.

(Bengal Establishment.)

This officer was appointed a cadet of art. in 1779; promoted to lieut. fireworker 30th Sept. 1780; to lieut. 28th May 1786; to capt. 7th Jan. 1796; to maj. 12th Nov. 1804; to lieut.-col. 18th Sept. 1807; and to col., by brevet, 4th June 1814.

In 1781 he served at the rebellion of Rajah Cheyt Sing in Benares. He was present at the capture of the forts of Petitah Luçkypore, and Bejighur, at the time the Gov.-Gen., Warren Hastings, proceeded up the country, for the settlement of the Benares provinces. This officer was next ordered with a company of art. to join Lieut.-Col. Cockerell's* detachment, at Masulipatam, on its march to Madras in 1789, and which force joined the Madras army, under Col. Kellie, at Arnee. He was present during the whole of the operations that followed in the campaigns of Gens. Medows and Lord Cornwallis; at the siege and capture of Bangalore and Savendroog; and with Gen. Medows, when the army stormed Tippoo's lines, under the walls of Seringapatam, in 1792.

"The commissariat department, under Lieut.-Col. Stevenson and Capt. Cunliffe, answered the high expectations formed of it from past experience.

"Lt. Alpin's exertions as acting assist.-quart. mast.-gen. marked the zeal, intelligence, and ability of this deserving and promising officer; Capt. Watson, provincial assist. adj.-gen., and Brigade-Major Gough, had important and laborious details to conduct, which they performed to the entire satisfaction of the Major-General."

* See Services, page 114.

In 1793 he was detached with three companies of European art., under the command of Col. R. Bruce, and went by sea to Madras, to co-operate with the Madras troops, for the reduction of Pondicherry; but which capitulated, before the arrival of the detachments at that presidency. The art. returned by sea to Fort William. In 1794 he served on board the Britannia East Indiaman, armed as a ship of war, with a detachment of European artillerymen and inf., which vessel, in company with three others, viz. the Houton and William Pitt, and Company's frigate, Nonesuch, were employed in the protection of the India trade, against the French cruizers. He was at the capture of two French ships of war, with the Britannia and Nonesuch, in the streights of Sunday. The squadron was afterwards engaged by two French forty-gun frigates, a fifty-gun ship, and a brig, but which they beat off, at Hog Island, near Batavia. In 1801 he embarked by sea from Fort William, and served on an expedition to China. In 1805 he joined Lord Lake's army at Burtpoor, and served during that campaign.

In 1814 he returned to England; and the 15th Feb. 1818, obtained permission to be placed on the retired list, after a period of thirty-nine years service, thirty-five of which were passed in India without a furlough.

LIEUT.-GEN. SIR JOHN MACDONALD, K. C. B.

(Bengal Establishment.)

THIS officer was appointed a cadet on the Bengal establishment, in 1767; ens. 23d July, in the same year; lieut. 22d April 1769; capt. 7th May 1777; maj. 17th July 1781; lieut.-col. 1st March 1794;

col. 1st Jan. 1798; maj.-gen. 1st Jan. 1805; and lieut.-gen. 4th June 1813.

In 1781 this officer, then having the rank of maj., commanded a corps, in the service of the Newaub Vizier, in the province of Goorackpoor, contiguous to the Zemindary of Benares, at the time of Rajah Cheyt Sing's insurrection: on which occasion, by his influence and example, Maj. Macdonald materially contributed to check the spirit of rebellion, which spread over a large portion of the Vizier's dominions. He was subsequently Resident at the court of Scindia. In 1794 Maj. Macdonald belonged to the 2d European reg., and was engaged with it on the 26th Oct. in that year, in the hard fought battle of Betoorah,* on the plains of Rohilcund, (not far from the scene of the former Rohilla battle, on St. George's day, 1774,†) under the personal command of Lieut.-Gen. Sir Robert Abercromby, Com.-

* "*Camp Rampore, 26th Oct.* 1794.

" The whole line was ordered to be under arms this morning, an hour before daylight; the General and his Staff moved to reconnoitre some miles in front; they saw the enemy forming in full force; and after waiting some time to judge of the probable disposition they would take, rode back to camp to direct the arrangements for action. Our army moved forward in line, the art. in the intervals of corps, the cav. on the right flank; the charge of the enemy was most daring and gallant, and it is utterly impossible it could have been surpassed: both lines met, and intermingled. The bayonet at length prevailed, and our army pursued the enemy across the Doojoora rivulet. The enemy was said to have consisted of 25,000 men, of which 4,000 were cav., who directed all their efforts against the reserve, and made dreadful execution. The number of the enemy killed was great. Our loss in European officers was very afflicting. Maj. Bolton was shot, after having cut down several of the assailants. Maj. Bolton commanded the 18th batt. He was a remarkable large, powerful man. His batt. behaved with a degree of steadiness which would have done honour to the most disciplined corps in the world.

" The charge on the part of the enemy was particularly singular; they formed in line, infinitely beyond the extent of ours, in deep wedges, supposed of 50 deep. When the signal for our advancing was given, we moved in good order, slowly forward, at that time about 1200 yards from the enemy. They likewise moved towards us. When the lines were within 500 yards of each other, Gholam Mahomed's people scattered individually, approached in that extraordinary manner, and contested the point with our bayonets. They appeared to despise our musketry; and upon every discharge of art. embraced the ground, instantly rising again and advancing to the charge: their arms were spears, matchlocks, and swords; which latter, they employed with destructive effect, and their attack, as if by universal consent, was called the Highland Charge."—*Calcutta Gazette.*

† See Note, page 395.

in-Chief in India. Maj. Macdonald's reg. was one of the corps particularly engaged in this memorable battle. In consequence of the great extent of ground covered by the enemy, the Com.-in-Chief ordered the reserve, consisting of the 2d European reg., with two choice batts. of Sepoys, *viz.* the 13th on the right, and the 18th on the left, to be brought into the line, of which those corps became the right wing; and the cav. were also brought into line, forming on the right of the whole. Upon those chosen corps, composing the reserve, the enemy directed their principal attack, and were fast closing with them, when, by a lamentable fatality, the officer* commanding the cav. gave the word of command to wheel inwards, by quarter ranks, or such, at least, was the movement that took place; the consequence was, that they broke in headlong upon the 13th batt., the ranks of which became disordered, before the order of their gallant leader, Capt. Norman M'Leod, to fire upon the cav., could be executed: the enemy, for whom nothing could possibly have been more favourable, rushed in, sword in hand, and, in many instances, seized and turned aside the bayonets of the British troops with one hand, whilst they made use of their broad swords with the other; and following up the impression thus made, they penetrated, in like manner, Maj. Macdonald's reg., the 2d European, and the 16th batt., killing and wounding a great number of gallant officers and men of those three corps. The enemy were at length overcome, and compelled to retreat†.

When the 15th reg. was raised, in 1798, Col. Macdonald was appointed to the command of the corps, with which he served during the first campaign of the Mahratta war of 1803-4, and was wounded, in the command of a brigade, at the battle of Laswarree. In this engagement the right wing of the British army was under the command of Maj-Gen. Ware, and during the contest, in forcing the enemy's right, that veteran officer had his head carried off by a

---

* He absconded, to avoid being brought to trial.
† See Capt. Williams's account of the Bengal Native Infantry.

cannon ball, and was succeeded, in the command of the wing at this important crisis, by Col. Macdonald.

This officer was next appointed to the staff as col. there not being, at that period, sufficient maj.-gens. in India; and after his promotion to the rank of maj.-gen., he was nominated to the command of the Benares' division of the army, in which situation his personal influence and authority were particularly required to suppress a spirit of discontent, bordering on revolt, which occurred in the city of Benares, in consequence of some taxes ordered to be levied by the government.

For his conduct in the Mahratta war, this officer was one of the first, of the Hon. Company's service, admitted to the honours of the Military Order of the Bath, and of which he is a Knight Commander.

LIEUTENANT-COLONEL WILLIAM SANDYS.

(Bengal Establishment.)

IN 1779 this officer was appointed a cadet on the Bengal establishment: in 1780, when the belligerent fleets of France and Spain were off Plymouth, he lost his passage and passage money to India, by serving as a volunteer on board the Monarch, Capt. Adam Duncan, without pay or reward; and, in consequence thereof, he was allowed to proceed to India without prejudice to his rank. In Jan. 1781 he arrived at Fort St. George, and commanded a company of cadets, then embodied as part of that garrison, when Hyder Ally was in the vicinity. At the end of that year he applied to join Gen. Goddard's detachment, then serving at Bombay, and where he arrived in 1782, and was appointed to command a light inf. company, attached with guns to a body of cavalry, forming an advanced corps, the whole then being under the command of Col. Morgan. In 1788 he was appointed, by Lord Cornwallis, dep.-judge-adv.-gen.; and in 1790, in addition to the above appointment, he was made adj. and quart.-mast. to the two batts. of volunteers, then about to proceed with his lordship to Fort St. George, where he arrived in Jan 1791, and was immediately put in charge of all the extra cattle belonging to the East India Company. This charge increased during the war, and this officer became the agent for the carriage of the public camp equipage of the whole army; in which situation he continued until the termination of hostilities, by the peace of Seringapatam, in March 1792.

At the storming of Tippoo's lines, on the night of the 6th of Feb. 1792, this officer was one of those who conveyed the orders of Lord Cornwallis, principally to the 74th reg., within the bound hedge. On the morning of the 7th he was directed by his lordship to proceed cautiously towards the Carri Ghaut hill, to which his lordship meant to retire when the day broke, to ascertain whether it was in possession of the British or the enemy; for although the hill was not three-quarters of a mile in the rear of the centre column, no communication from it had been received: his lordship, at the same time, ordered him to take as many troopers of his body guard as he judged necessary. He was well mounted, but found much difficulty in tracing his way. From the flashes of the guns he could, at intervals, discover the hill: in crossing a ravine he lost the troopers, and halted a moment to listen; by this time the firing had ceased, and the grey of the morn appeared. Lieut Sandys cautiously advanced, but it was so dark that he got close to the hill before he well knew where he was. He heard a sentry cough, and immediately challenged three times; but no answer was returned: he now imagined that the hill was in possession of the enemy: all was still and quiet; but being unwilling to return without accomplishing the object for which he was sent, and having a little open space before him, which he remembered observing from the top of the hill the year before when foraging, he advanced, and asked, in a loud voice, "Who commands?" intending that his voice should reach the top of the hill; when, to his astonishment, a voice, which he knew to be that of Col. Close, the

Dep.-Adj.-Gen., replied, seizing the reins of his horse, at the same time, " General Medows." He found himself close upon the column, and saw the General, Col. Cockerell, and several other officers. Gen. Medows asked if Lord Cornwallis was well; and having answered a few more questions, he was impatient to get back to his lordship, and galloped away. At this time the day had so far advanced, that a person might be discovered at the distance of fifteen or twenty yards He soon met Lord Cornwallis, and the troops, retiring from under the cannon of the fort towards the hill, and astonished his lordship by reporting that he had found Gen. Medows'* army under the Carri Ghaut hill.

* In 1792, on the arrival of the British army in the vicinity of Seringapatam, a night attack of that formidable fortress was planned by his Exc. the Com.-in-Chief, Lord Cornwallis. As some errors and confusion generally attend night operations, it may here be presumed, that nothing but the peculiar situation of the enemy at this period could have induced his lordship to adopt this mode of attack; and unfortunately, on this occasion, a disaster occurred to Gen. Medows' column (alluded to in this service), which, from the possession it took of the General's feelings, nearly terminated his life.

The army moved in three columns; the right commanded by Gen. Medows, the centre by the Com.-in-Chief, Lord Cornwallis, and the left by Col. Maxwell. The centre entered the entrenchments, and a skirmish ensued, on which the enemy fled in consternation. In the meanwhile, the Native guide (furnished to Gen. Medows by Lord Cornwallis), either from error in judgment or design, led the right column wrong, and prevented its speedy junction and co-operation with the centre.

Gen. Medows marched along the Bound Hedge, and advanced on the Mosque redoubt, without a knowledge or suspicion of the fortification, until fired upon by the enemy. The General returned the fire of this formidable redoubt, gallantly defended by Gen. Lally's corps of Frenchmen, and the troops of Tippoo Sultaun, and finally stormed and carried it, after much bloodshed on both sides.

General Medows then proceeded to join the division under Lord Cornwallis. A swamp obstructed the march of his troops, and, in order to clear it, he took a circuitous route, by which he unknowingly entered the tract of the centre, and, to his great mortification, found himself at the Pagoda hill, where he was joined at day break by the Com.-in-Chief. These untoward events, which prevented the right column joining in time, disarranged the plan of the Com.-in-Chief, and most sensibly affected the mind of Gen. Medows. They were, however, no other than misfortunes incident to all night operations, on ground that was not familiar to any European.

The brave but sanguinary Tippoo made a powerful resistance, but his efforts were vain, and the British army, after driving him within the walls of his fortress, commenced a re-

The army got to the Carri Ghaut hill just before it was daylight, and before the enemy perceived that the centre column had retired. His lordship now gave orders for a relief of the troops on the island, and soon after the enemy commenced their attack upon Sibbald's redoubt.

With regard to the nature of the appointment held by this officer, it may be sufficient to observe, that the convenience of corps and individuals depending upon the exertions of the agent for the carriage of camp equipage, subjected him to almost constant personal exertions throughout the range of an extensive line, and to litigious and controversial correspondence; yet Lord Cornwallis acknowledged, that he had never received any complaints of partiality in allotment, or of a want of exertion to give immediate remedy or assistance when required by corps. In 1793 he returned to Bengal, having had under his charge, during sixteen months of the most active period of the war in Mysore, 102 elephants, 1000 head of other cattle, with about 700 people attached to them; and the whole of his salary (there were no emoluments) amounted to 2400 pagodas; and he was obliged to keep three horses to perform his duties, of which foraging was a principal one. In the active part of the campaign of 1792-3, he had 184 elephants under his charge.

The choice of the appointments at that time vacant was given, by Lord Cornwallis, to this officer, and he chose that of fort-ajdutant; to which afterwards was added the barrack-mastership of Fort William, which he held during the years 1794, 5, 6, and 7, acting as town-major frequently; and he was appointed aid-de-camp to the acting Governor General.

---

gular siege. A cessation of hostilities took place on the 24th Feb., and a pacification on the 19th March.

Lord Cornwallis gave every honourable testimony to the conduct of General Medows; and in his lordship's despatches to the Court of Directors, dated 4th March 1722, is the following encomium :—" No words can express the sense that I shall entertain through life of the ability, refined generosity, and friendship, with which General Medows has invariably given me his support and assistance."—J. P.

In 1798 he was appointed agent for the supply of military stores, which office he held until he was about embarking for Europe in Jan. 1803, when he was promoted to the rank of maj., having, in the intermediate time, been directed by Lord Wellesley, the Gov.-Gen., to act as adj.-gen. to the army in Bengal, still continuing to hold the appointment of agent of stores.

It should here be noticed, that shortly after the arrival of Lord Wellesley, in Bengal, in consequence of orders from the Court of Directors, his lordship canvassed and sifted, for six months, with singular scrutiny, and the unwearied application of the public officers, the appointment of this officer as agent of stores; and in May the Marquess rescinded the orders respecting his appointment, which he had peremptorily issued in Dec. preceding; and at his public levee, on the king's birth-day, in 1800, his lordship stated, that the investigation, although most severe, had done this officer much honour, and he congratulated him upon the result. Lord Wellesley further added, that he had, in consequence thereof, extended his appointment upon the old footing for six months; and it was renewed, from time to time, while he remained in India; his lordship declaring, that the gains were as exclusively and fairly this officer's own as much as any merchant's; the risks being his own, and the supplies, on urgent demands, particularly in the last Mysorean war, always readily furnished, and often upon his own advances and credit; that he saw not, how the public interests could be better promoted than by a continuation of the same system.

The following are the dates of this officer's commissions—ens. 29th July 1779; lieut. 21st March 1781; capt. 7th Jan. 1796; maj. 1st Jan. 1803; and lieut.-col. 21st Sept. 1804. He retired from the service 5th June 1805.

MAJOR-GEN. SIR GABRIEL MARTINDELL, K.C.B.

(Bengal Establishment.)

This officer was appointed a cadet in 1772; ens. 4th Aug. 1776; lieut. 21st July 1778; capt. 6th Aug. 1793; maj. 1st Nov. 1797; lieut.-col. 21st Feb. 1801; col. 25th July 1810; and maj.-gen. 4th June 1813.

This officer had the honour, with many other cadets, of the year 1772, to carry arms in a distinguished corps, already referred to, "The Select Picket."* They were early called into the field, and, in 1774, bore a distinguished part in the Rohilla battle of St. George. During several years of his service, as lieut., this officer was adj. to the corps of N. I. to which he belonged; and on his succeeding to the command of a batt., as lieut.-col., his corps was considered one of the best in the service.

The province of Bundlecund, and contiguous territories, continued, for some years, in a state of great anarchy and confusion, consequent to the Mahratta war of 1803-4 and 5; and Lieut.-Col. Martindell was twice selected, for the important command of the troops in that province, under circumstances of much embarrassment and difficulty. Hostilities and harassing warfare prevailed at all seasons of the year, so long as the malcontents held possession of many of the strong holds in that country, and it required both judgment and ability, in the commanding-gen., to oppose them with success, and bring that valuable territory to a complete settlement, and which was eventually accomplished.

In 1809 the strong fortress of Adjygurh surrendered to the troops under Lieut.-Col. Martindell's command; on which occasion the Gov.-Gen. expressed "the sentiments of approbation and applause, with which his Lordship, in council, contemplated the professional

---

* See page 24.

skill and ability displayed by Lieut.-Col. Martindell, in regulating the operations of the detachment." His lordship further recorded— " His public thanks generally, to the officers and men employed during the late campaign in Bundlecund, and especially to Lieut.-Col. Martindell, whose judgment and military skill, seconded by the courage and exertions of the gallant detachment, which he commanded, happily accomplished an undertaking, not less arduous in its nature than important in its effects, to the interest of the public service."

In 1812 the important fortress of Callinger, the capital, or headquarters of the province, surrendered to a large force, under Col. Martindell, after an attempt* to carry it by storm had been repelled by the garrison. The following paragraph is from the Gov.-Gen. in council's communication of this event to the Court of Directors—" We participate most cordially in the applause bestowed by his Exc. the Com.-in-Chief, and by Col. Martindell, on the exemplary, gallant, and persevering intrepidity manifested by the officers and men engaged in the assault; an assault, which, although it failed in the immediate attainment of its object, can scarce be deemed unsuccessful, since to the terror inspired by it must be ascribed the subsequent surrender of this almost impregnable fortress, on terms, and in a manner, which have maintained the credit of our arms, without any sacrifice of dignity, or any concessions of material importance, to our interests; we concur also entirely in the praise bestowed by the Com.-in-Chief, on the distinguished zeal, judgment, and exertions, of Col. Martindell, in conducting the arrangements and operations of the late service in Bundlecund."

* The western army, which stormed Callinger, was commanded by Maj.-Gen. Sir R. R. Gillespie, K. C. B. The gen. directed it to be stormed at all points at the same moment; unfortunately some of the divisions did not come up in time, and the others lost many men, and could make no impression. Gen. Gillespie, observing the disastrous state of things, flew to the head of the attacking column, but not being vigorously seconded, he failed, and lost his life in the attempt. Maj.-Gen. Martindell succeeded to the command of this army; another unsuccessful attempt was made to storm the place: the brave defenders, however, had suffered so much that they retired from the fort.

Maj.-Gen. Martindell was one of the officers of the Hon. Company's service, first selected for participating in the honours of the Order of the Bath, and of which he is a Knight Commander.

Maj.-Gen. Martindell held a distinguished command in the mountains, during the Nepaul war, and was subsequently occupied in restoring tranquillity to the province of Cuttack, disturbed by the incursions of a numerous banditti, connected with the predatory system of the Pindarries.

In April 1820, Sir G. Martindell received the command of the 1st division of the field army, and the general command of the field army, which appointment ceased in June 1822.

THE LATE MAJ.-GEN. SIR GEORGE HOLMES, K.C.B.

(*Bombay Establishment.*)

At an early age this officer left England as a cadet, on the Bombay establishment; in 1780, he obtained an ensigncy in the Bombay European reg., and was soon after promoted and removed to the 10th batt. N. I. With this corps, Lieut. Holmes was actively employed in the war against the Mahrattas, and was present, among other affairs, at the capture of Bellapore and Panwell, in 1780 and the following year. In 1781 and 1782, he was at the defence of Tellichery, so perseveringly besieged by the troops of Hyder Ally*,

---

* The character of this chieftain, whose name and actions have so repeatedly been referred to in this work, is thus pourtrayed by Col. Wilks, in his "Sketches of the South of India:"—

"In common with all sovereigns who have risen from obscurity to a throne, Hyder waded through crimes to his object; but they never exceeded the removal of real impediments, and he never achieved through blood what fraud was capable of effecting. He fixed his stedfast view upon the end, and considered simply the efficiency, and never the moral tendency of the means. If he was cruel and unfeeling, it was for the promotion of

under Serdar Khan. At the brilliant sally of the little garrison, under their gallant commander, Maj. Abington, Jan. 7, 1782, Lieut.

his objects, and never for the gratification of anger or revenge. If he was ever liberal, it was because liberality exalted his character, and augmented his power; if he was ever merciful, it was in those cases where the reputation of mercy promoted future submission. His European prisoners were in irons, because they were otherwise deemed unmanageable; they were scantily fed, because that was economical; there was little distinction of rank, because that would have been expensive; but, beyond these simply interested views, there was, by his authority, no wanton severity; there was no compassion, but there was no resentment; it was a political expenditure for a political purpose, and there was no passion, good or bad, to disturb the balance of the account. He carried merciless devastation into an enemy's country, and even to his own; but never beyond the reputed utility of the case: he sent the inhabitants into captivity, because it injured the enemy's country, and benefited his own. The misery of the individuals was no part of the consideration, and the death of the greater portion still left a residue to swell a scanty population. With an equal absence of feeling, he caused forcible emigrations from one province to another, because he deemed it the best cure for rebellion; and he converted the male children into military slaves, because he expected them to improve the quality of his army. He gave fair, and occasionally brilliant encouragement to the active and aspiring among his servants, so long as liberality proved an incitement to exertion, and he robbed and tortured them without gratitude or compensation, when no further services were expected; it was an account of profit and loss, and a calculation, whether it were more beneficial to employ or to plunder them. Those brilliant and equivocal virtues, which gild the crimes of other conquerors, were utterly unknown to the breast of Hyder. No admiration of bravery in resistance, or of fortitude in the fallen, ever excited sympathy or softened the cold calculating decision of their fate. No contempt for unmanly submission ever aggravated the treatment of the abject and mean. Every thing was weighed in the balance of utility, and no grain of human feeling, no breath of virtue or of vice, was permitted to incline the beam. There was one solitary example of feelings incident to our nature; affection for an unworthy son, whom he nominated to be his successor, while uniformly, earnestly, and broadly predicting, that this son would lose the empire which he himself had gained."

In the same work, Col. Wilks contrasts the characters of Hyder Ally and his son Tippoo:—

"Both sovereigns were equally unprincipled; but Hyder had a clear undisturbed view of the interests of ambition: in Tippoo, that view was incessantly obscured and perverted by the meanest passions. He murdered his English prisoners, by a selection of the best, beause he hated their valour; he oppressed and insulted his Hindoo subjects, because he hated a religion, which, if protected, would have been the best support of his throne; and he fawned, in his last extremity, on his injured people, when he vainly hoped that their incantations might influence his fate; he persecuted contrary to his interest; and hoped, in opposition to his belief. Hyder, with all his faults, might be deemed a model

Holmes was severely wounded. The lapse of years have caused almost a forgetfulness of such affairs as the sally in question; it was, however, very important at the time: it critically terminated the siege of a position of great military and political consequence, discomfited a large army, with vast loss to the besiegers, including guns, treasure, and prisoners, to a great amount. Among the latter were the person and family of the besieging general.

In 1783 Lieut. Holmes served under Gen. Macleod against Tippoo Sultaun: he was present at the storm and capture of Cananore; soon after which, the general peace in Europe led to similar tranquillity in India, which was not materially disturbed on the western side, until the confederacy of the English, the Mahrattas, and Nizam Ally Khan, against Tippoo in 1791. In that year and the following, Lieut. Holmes served with that distinguished corps, the Bombay grenadier batt., in Gen. Abercromby's army, at the siege of Seringapatam, and in the various services in Mysore and Malabar. In 1794 he was promoted to capt. in the Bombay European reg. In 1798 he was employed in Col. Little's detachment, which co-operated with the Mahratta army in the last war against Tippoo Sultaun. After the fall of Seringapatam, in the following year, many of Tippoo's forts in Canara refused to surrender to the English, and Capt. Holmes was selected to command a force to reduce them. Several of these forts resisted vigorously, but the service was very completely executed; and Captain Holmes received the particular

---

of toleration by the professor of any religion. Tippoo, in an age when persecution only survived in history, renewed its worst terrors; and was the last Mahommedan prince, after a long interval of better feeling, who propagated that religion by the edge of the sword. Hyder's vices invariably promoted his political interests; Tippoo's more frequently defeated them. If Hyder's punishments were barbarous, they were at least efficient to their purpose. Tippoo's court and army were one vast scene of unpunished peculation, notorious even to himself. He was barbarous where severity was vice, and indulgent where it was virtue. If he had qualities fitted for empire, they were strangely equivocal; the disqualifications were obvious and unquestionable; and the decision of history will not be far removed from the observation, almost proverbial in Mysore, " that Hyder was born to create an empire, Tippoo to lose one."

thanks of Maj.-Gen. Hartley, commanding-officer in Malabar and Canara.

The acquisition of Malabar by the English, however valuable, was a very troublesome one. Tippoo and his father had sacrificed army after army in the fruitless attempt to subjugate the Rajahs of that warlike country. The military tribe of Nair is very numerous; and such was their high spirit, that the idea of subjugation or dependance of any sort was indignantly spurned. The struggles of these desperate people evinced the military excellence of the material of which they were composed. It was a most harassing warfare; from its remoteness, carried on without eclat; from its nature, apparently without system; and from its results, long without much appearance of success. In this warfare, Capt. Holmes, who now commanded a batt. of Native inf., was foremost on all occasions. The Bombay army will long remember the spirit with which he at different times volunteered that most desperate and annoying service, the relief of Montana, and the perseverance and vigour with which he effected it. The annexed documents shew the sense entertained by his immediate superiors of Maj. Holmes' conduct in this trying service[*], as it was justly termed.

"*Provincial Orders, Cananore, Aug.* 8, 1800.

" Col. Sartorious requests Maj. Holmes will accept his warmest thanks for his zealous and active exertions in the relief of Montana. The commanding-officer's sincere thanks are also due to the whole of the officers and men employed, for their gallant and steady conduct, as reported by Maj. Holmes; without which, the obstacles they had to encounter could not have been overcome, in performing the services they have effected."

[*] It may here be remarked, that when, as in the contests at Seringapatam, Badajoz, Waterloo, &c., the eye of a whole army, and half the world, is on the deed, there are abundance of stimuli to professional exertion; but in such a service as the relief of Montana, carried on through trackless forests, where guns cannot move, in a pestiferous climate, at the worst season of the year, when, without seeing an enemy, your men drop every moment by your side, and combating almost every imaginable difficulty, except that stimulating one of a battle; there it is that the energy and perseverance of the soldier and the address of a commander are tried.

Brigade-Major Spens to Major Holmes.

"*Cananore, Oct.* 1, 1800.

"SIR,—I am directed by Col. Sartorious to acknowledge the receipt of your letter of the 29th ult., and to convey to you his most warm thanks for having, with so much judgment, with the detachment under your command, overcome every difficulty in executing the arduous and severe service of the last relief of Montana: and he begs you will make known, in the most public manner, to Captains Baird and Howden, and to all the officers and men of your detachment, his sense of their persevering exertions on this trying occasion, and which he will have great pleasure in reporting to the Hon. Colonel Wellesley.—I have," &c.

The Hon. Colonel Wellesley to Colonel Sartorious.

"*Camp,* 10 *miles south of Kopal, Nov.* 15, 1800.

"I also request that you will communicate to Maj. Holmes that paragraph in the inclosed extract, which relates to him. I am concerned that his health should oblige him to go to Bombay; and I request you will give the enclosed letter to the Gov. in Council of that settlement."

Extract (referred to above) of a Letter from the Chief Sec. to the Government of Madras to the Hon. Colonel Wellesley.

"*Fort St. George, Nov.* 7, 1800.

"I have had the honour of receiving your letter of the 13th ult. with its enclosures, and am directed to express to you the satisfaction of the Right Hon. the Gov. in Council at the conduct of Maj. Holmes, and of the troops under his command, in the last relief of the post of Montana."

The Hon. Colonel Wellesley to the Hon. the Gov. in Council of Bombay, (referred to above.)

"*Camp,* 10 *miles south of Kopal, Nov.* 15, 1800.

"SIR,—As I understand from Col. Sartorious that Maj. Holmes is about to leave Malabar, and to join his corps at Surat, I take this opportunity of expressing to you my high sense of the service which he has rendered to the public during the time that he has commanded the troops in the Cotiote districts. I have already taken an opportunity of mentioning, in favourable terms, his services to the government of Fort St. George;

but, as Major Holmes is about to be more immediately under your orders, I take the liberty of recommending him to your favourable notice.

(Signed) " ARTHUR WELLESLEY."

The Adjut.-General of the Bombay Army to Colonel Sartorius, commanding the troops in Malabar.

" SIR,—In reply to that paragraph of your letter of the 24th ult. on the subject of the zealous and active services of Maj. Holmes, which has been laid before government, I am directed, by the commanding-officer of the forces, to acquaint you that he embraces the earliest opportunity of signifying to that officer, together with his own, the very high sense which the Hon. the Gov. in Council entertains of Maj. Holmes's meritorious and gallant exertions in the arduous duties which he had to perform in the present Cotiote service, as well as of the conduct and persevering bravery of the officers and men who composed the detachment under his command, in the different operations which he was called on to execute; a declaration of well-earned praise, which the commanding-officer of the forces experiences great pleasure that it has fallen to his lot to communicate.

" The above you will be pleased to promulgate in such a way, as may make more generally known to the troops under your command, this public testimony of the merits of Maj. Holmes, and of the officers and men who lately served under him in the districts of Cotiote.

(Signed) " ROBERT GORDON, Adj.-Gen."

In 1801 and 1802, Maj. Holmes was employed under Gen. Sir D. Baird in Egypt, in command of the 2d batt. 1st N. I. Few or no opportunities occurred in that quarter for the Indian army to achieve any field laurels. The corps of Maj. Holmes, who was never an hour absent from it, was always in the most efficient state.

Immediately after the expulsion of the French from Egypt, and the return thence of the Indian army, Maj. Holmes' corps was sent into Guzerat. Our recent acquisitions in that quarter demanded very active military measures; and a series of very energetic service has almost ever since, that is, from 1802, been displayed on that belligerent arena. In that year, among other smart affairs, Maj. Holmes was present at the siege of Baroda. The following order was issued by the officer commanding the field force in Guzerat :—

"*Field Morning Orders, Baroda, Dec.* 27, 1802.

"Whilst Lieut.-Col. Woodington laments the loss of the gallant men who fell before Baroda, he congratulates the troops on the successful termination of hostilities, by compelling our enemies to evacuate the fort of Baroda, and accept the terms prescribed to them by government. He entreats the officers and men to accept his unfeigned thanks for the ready and willing support which he has received from them; and although the enemy gave the army in general but few opportunities of distinguishing themselves, still they did not fail to avail themselves of such as offered; as was instanced in the attack and defeat of a considerable body of Arabs by H. M.'s 86th reg. under Capt. Semple, on the 22d inst.; and also of Maj. Holmes, who, with his batt., repelled an attack of double his number, of Arabs, on the same day."

In 1803, Maj. Holmes commanded a field force operating against a rebellious member of the Guicawar government, and distinguished himself greatly on many occasions. The following are among the public testimonies of his services at this period :—

Mr. Grant, Secretary to the Bombay Government, to Lieut.-Col. Woodington, commanding the Subsidiary Force at Baroda.

"*Bombay Castle, Feb.* 14, 1803.

"SIR,—I am directed by the Hon. the Gov. in council to acknowledge the receipt of your letter of the 8th inst., with its enclosure, detailing the particulars of the attack of Canojee's camp, by the detachment under the command of Maj. Holmes. The Gov. in council cannot advert to the energy, intrepidity, and extraordinary exertions manifested by Major Holmes on that occasion, without expressing his highest approbation of the merits of that officer; and at the same time acknowledging, that to that officer's professional exertions and personal intrepidity, so conspicuously evinced at the crisis of this very serious attack, must be chiefly ascribed the complete overthrow of Canojee and his adherents, which government has no doubt will, under your instructions, be uninterruptedly followed up, till this war be brought to a happy termination."

Mr. Duncan, Governor of Bombay, to Major Holmes.

"Bombay, Feb. 14, 1803.

"MY DEAR SIR,—Although the official acknowledgment of your gallant conduct will reach you in due course, through Col. Woodington, yet I cannot refrain from separately expressing my own admiration of it. It seldom happens that a commanding officer has an opportunity to such a degree as circumstances led to in your case on the 6th, nor can any, I am persuaded, occur, where a better and more glorious use can be made of it: accept, then, of my sincerest congratulations and thanks, which I shall be happy, if the means should occur, of more substantially evincing my sense of, being, with sincere esteem, your faithful and obedient servant,

(Signed) "JOHN DUNCAN."

Major Holmes obtained a lieut.-colonelcy in 1803, and continued during that and the two following years on very active service, in command of a field detachment. He was at the siege and capture of Pawaghur, a service of considerable eclat, as this fortress was reckoned among the natives one of the most celebrated for strength in India. War was at this period extensively carried on against Scindia, Holkar, and other chieftains. On one occasion Lieut.-Col. Holmes' detachment escorted treasure, to a large amount, from Guzerat to the Bengal army under Lord Lake, besieging Burtpoor. On the march thither and returning, a line of about 600 miles through a hostile country, his detachment was smartly attacked by Holkar's active and annoying cavalry; but notwithstanding the notoriety of the nature of his charge, so inviting to the cupidity of the Mahrattas, he effected the service with the completest success. Until 1807 Col. H. was almost constantly employed in the field in Guzerat; he then succeeded to the temporary charge of the force subsidised by the Guicawar government, and in the following year that respectable command was conferred upon him by the government of Bombay, in approbation of his services, as appears by the two following extracts:—

Major Walker, Political Resident at Guzerat, to Francis Warden, Esq. Chief Secretary to the Government of Bombay.

" March 1, 1807.—Adverting to the absence of (on account of illness) Col. Woodington from the important duties of his command, it will not, I trust, be deemed improper, if I respectfully recal the attention of the Hon. the Gov. in council to the merits and services of Lieut.-Col. Holmes. The nature of these it may be unnecessary to detail, but they are warm in the recollection of this government (the Guicawar government of Guzerat), which would not only view with satisfaction, but conceive it peculiarly agreeable and acceptable, were these services noticed, by his being placed in Col. Woodington's situation during his absence. As an officer of great experience and reputation, Col. Holmes ranks high in the estimation of every military man; and the public service must continue to receive, from his well-known zeal, the same cordial co-operation and support, which is so necessary to its success."

Mr. Secretary Warden to Major Walker.

" Bombay, March 13, 1807.

" I am directed, by the Hon. the Gov. in council, to acknowledge the receipt of your letter of the 1st inst., and to intimate, that the eminent services rendered by Col. Holmes, in the successful resistance which that officer opposed to the inroads of Canojee, after his escape from confinement, in 1802-3, and to the party that adhered to him, give to that officer peculiar and appropriate claims to the command of the subsidiary force at Baroda, during the intended absence of Col. Woodington, and it is accordingly the intention of the Honourable the Governor in council to nominate him thereto."

The two following letters refer to operations of a detachment from the subsidiary force, with which Col. Holmes moved from Baroda (the Guicawar capital of Guzerat), in the rainy season of 1809, to repel an invasion of the frontier of the Guicawar territory.

The Adjutant-General of the Bombay Army to Lieutenant-Colonel Holmes, commanding in the Northern Division of Guzerat.

" Bombay, Sept. 19, 1809.

" SIR,—Your letters of the 3d and 5th insts., have been laid before the commanding officer of the forces, who directs me to inform you, that he has laid the subject before the Hon. the Gov. in council, who, he doubts not, will with him, be equally sensible of the zealous and active exertions of yourself, and the detachment under your command, on the service from which you have reported your return; and you will be advised of the sentiments of government thereon as soon as received.

(Signed) " ROBERT GORDON, Adj.-Gen."

Mr. Sec. Warden to Maj.-Gen. Richard Jones, Commanding Officer of the Forces at Bombay, 25th Sept. 1809.

" SIR,—In acknowledging the receipt of your letter of the 14th of this month, I have the honour to intimate to you, that the Hon. the Gov. in council has been pleased to grant field allowances to Lieut.-Col. Holmes, and the detachment under his command, whilst employed on the present service; and to signify to you, that the Hon. the Gov. in council concurs with you in opinion, and commends the ready zeal and promptitude with which Lieut.-Col. H. proceeded with the detachment on this service, at a season of the year the most inclement, with such equipments as were available, and which the aid of the Native government, and their own exertions, could furnish them with.

(Signed) " F. WARDEN, Chief Sec."

Lieut.-Col. Holmes continued in the command of the force in Guzerat, which was reviewed in 1812, by Gen. Abercromby, whose testimony to its state of efficiency and discipline was recorded in general orders.

Disturbances in Guzerat, and its neighbourhood, kept Col. Holmes's force in the field in 1813-14; but little opportunity offered for any distinguished service. There were some sharp affairs before the fort of Pulhunpoor. After the termination of one of the operations of this period, the following extract of a letter, from Mr. Sec. Warden, dated 6th Jan. 1814, to the political Resident at Baroda, was communicated to Col. Holmes:

" The regularity and good order with which the force under Col. Holmes has conducted itself, has not escaped the attention of government; and you will take an opportunity of conveying to that officer the sense which the Hon. the Gov. in council entertains of the conduct of the officers and men under his command during the course of the service, which has fortunately been brought to a termination without the necessity of having recourse to hostilities."

Early in 1815 it was deemed expedient to assemble a considerable army on the eastern frontier of the Guicawar territories, and the command was conferred on Col. Holmes; but in consequence of his obtaining the brevet of maj.-gen., the retention of that command was, it seems, incompatible with military etiquette; and his health having materially suffered by such an uninterrupted series of service, and the severity of much of it, he retired from the field. Guzerat had been particularly fatal and destructive, to the health of both Europeans and Natives, for two or three years preceding this period. The great satisfaction the services and conduct of Maj.-Gen. Holmes continued to the last to afford the governments under which he served, will be evinced by the two following public documents:

Extract of a Letter from Mr. Chief Secretary Warden to the Political Resident at Baroda, dated Bombay Castle, 23d March 1815.

"On the occasion of Maj.-Gen. Holmes's retiring from the command of the subsidiary force at Baroda, the Hon. the Gov. in council feels it due to the merits of that gallant officer, to express his entire satisfaction, with his conduct generally, as an officer on this establishment, and particularly during the period of his having exercised the functions of that important situation; and these sentiments the Gov. in council will have great satisfaction in communicating to the Hon. Court of Directors of the East India Company."

Translation of a Letter from His Highness Futteh Sing Row Guicawar, (Sovereign of Guzerat,) to Maj.-Gen. Holmes, dated Baroda, 20th April 1815.

"It has been communicated to me by Capt. Carnac, that, in consequence of your advancement to a superior rank, the command of the Hon. Company's troops subsidized by the Guicawar government, will devolve on another officer. In expressing my congratulations on your promotion, you must allow me to regret the unavoidable consequences of your relinquishing the command which you had held during many years. It is only an act of justice, on the eve of your departure, that I should render to you those sentiments which your conduct, during a period of nearly thirteen years, in the support chiefly of the interest of my government, have been so well calculated to excite. The important services performed by you, at the siege of Baroda, when in the hands of an Arab faction, and in the discomfiture of Canojee Row Guicawar, during his open rebellion against this state, are fresh in my recollection. The zeal, perseverance, and ability, with which the troops under your command destroyed the formidable resources of that misguided man, and the personal gallantry displayed by you at the moment which ensured victory, must always render your name highly distinguished in the estimation of myself and the government subject to my authority. While I return you my unqualified acknowledgments for your services on the occasion above stated, and in numerous other instances which the limits of a letter will not allow me to specify, it is with feelings also of considerable satisfaction that I am enabled to add, that the attentions and conciliatory demeanour which every servant of my government has experienced from you, in the progress of your long employment in Guzerat, will always ensure, from me and them, a lively interest in your future welfare and happiness.

"Accept my own best wishes, that in your native country every honour, due to your well-earned reputation, may attend you; and permit me to hope, that you will occasionally favour me with a letter, which may communicate glad tidings of yourself, and of those in whom you may be interested."

A cessation of field labours gave at first some hope that this gallant officer might recover sufficiently to enable him to accept a nomination on the general staff of the Indian army, but his constitution was too much broken to allow of any hope of restoration without a voyage to Europe, and he reluctantly resorted to this measure, at a moment when farther professional honours seemed to await him, in a rank that promised also a chance of making some provision for his family.

About this time the honours of the order of the bath were extended to the officers of the Company's army, and the Commander's Cross, apportioned to the Bombay establishment, was conferred on Major-General Holmes.

Towards the end of 1815, Sir George Holmes, confirmed in the opinion that his native climate alone could effect a restoration of his health, applied for a furlough, which was granted in general orders, of which the following is an extract:—

By the Right Honourable the Governor in Council.
"*Bombay Castle, Jan.* 19, 1816.
" Brevet Maj.-Gen. and Lieut.-Col. Sir George Holmes, K. C. B., is allowed a furlough to England, on his private concerns. The right Hon. the Gov. in council will perform a gratifying act of public duty in bringing to the notice of the Hon. the Court of Directors the many instances of meritorious conduct which Maj.-Gen. Holmes has evinced during a period of thirty-six years' service in India, the value and importance of which cannot be more forcibly exemplified than by the distinguished honour lately conferrred on him by His Royal Highness the Prince Regent."

When the Duke of York, as Com.-in-Chief, published to the British army a just eulogy on the character and services of the late Gen. Sir John Moore, H. R. H. laid particular stress on his being a " regimental officer ;" that is, one who was constantly with his regiment, especially in the earlier stages of his military career. This may be said of Sir George Holmes to as full an extent, perhaps, as of any officer in the army. In thirty-six years' service in India, his absence from his corps did not exceed six months, on account of his private concerns ; and such was the vigour of his frame, that in all this length of servitude, in such a climate, and at certain times, particularly in Malabar and Guzerat, in the most inclement seasons of sickly years, his total absence from his corps did not exceed five months. As a subaltern he served fifteen years ; as a captain, five ; as a field officer, sixteen. It may hence be readily concluded, that, from such a period of service in India, where, how little soever may be heard or thought in England of their operations, the troops are rarely idle, Sir George Holmes must have been a finished soldier: he truly was ; and to the last acted with the fire and zeal of a subaltern. His hardy and robust frame enabled him to bear up, until the last year or two, against every disadvantage of climate and privation. But no human stamina and zeal could support it longer; and it is to be deeply regretted that he persevered so long. But his services were wanted, and he did not allow himself a choice. With the hope of repairing his severely shattered constitution, he quitted India early in 1816. He would have had the first vacant regiment, which, with the pay of his rank, would have sufficed for a handsome maintenance to a man of his moderate habits and views; and he was not without hopes and expectations of recovering sufficiently to enable him to return to his duty on the staff of the Indian army, in further prosecution of his military career, and in the hope of making a suitable provision for his family. But it was otherwise ordained: his old friends, who saw him on his arrival in England, scarcely recognized the person of their former Herculean associate; and he survived but a few months. He died, universally respected, at Cheltenham, 29th Oct. 1816, being fifty-two years of age.

THE LATE MAJOR JAMES LUMSDAINE.

(Bengal Establishment.)

This officer was appointed a cadet on the Bengal establishment in 1800; he arrived in India in Oct. 1801, and immediately embarked with the expedition proceeding to Egypt. He was promoted to cornet in the 4th light cavalry, 3d Jan. 1802; and to lieut., 11th March 1805. In 1802, 3, 4, and 5, he participated in the whole of the brilliant and memorable campaigns of the late Lord Lake: in the course of the latter year he was nominated to the personal staff of the Gov.-Gen., and accompanied Maj.-Gen. Dowdeswell's division while on active service in 1805-6: he was present at the sieges of Kumona and Gunowa, under Maj.-Gen. Dickens, in 1807, at which period he was appointed agent for camels. In 1808-9 he attended Gen. St. Leger's army on the expedition to the banks of the Sutulege; and he continued actively employed up to 1812, when, as dep.-com.-gen., he obtained the official rank of major. In that situation his merits and conduct are recorded in the general orders issued by government on the termination of the Nepaul war[*], and subsequently on the occasion of his premature death, Sept. 14, 1816.

To the exertions of this officer, in conjunction with Lieut.-Col. Weguelin[†], may be ascribed the decided success of a department, which had many difficulties to encounter, and which has received the repeated and high commendation, both of the authorities in India and at home. The establishment at Hissar was suggested by Major Lumsdaine, and owed its flourishing condition to his management.

General Orders, by His Exc. the Right Hon. the Gov.-Gen. in Council, Oct. 4, 1816.

" The Gov.-Gen. in Council cannot omit the opportunity of expressing the deep regret with which government has received the melancholy event whence the vacancy arose: the death of Maj. Lumsdaine, whilst it must be a source of sorrow to all who enjoyed his acquaintance, and thence knew the solidity of his worth, as well as the amiable tone of his manner, is felt by government as a heavy public loss. The admirable order which he had introduced into the branches of the commissariat department, committed to his more immediate superintendence; the judicious energy through which he had matured establishments of important utility; and the skilful arrangements by which, during the Nepaul war, he provided the supply of the troops, under circumstances of unprecedented difficulty; have already been acknowledged by the Gov.-Gen. in Council in terms of high commendation, which they so justly merited; they will ever be remembered with grateful applause, and now unhappily call forth the testimony of poignant concern from the government at his premature decease. He has bequeathed to the service inappreciable benefits, for it is impossible that any one should contemplate his character and not be roused to emulate his generous and disinterested zeal: the consciousness of his having honourably and faithfully discharged all the duties that devolved on him through life, must have been the last glowing sentiment of his heart."

---

[*] See page 189.   [†] See Services, page 180.

MAJOR GEORGE STEVENSON MOUNSEY.

(Bengal Establishment.)

THIS officer was appointed a cadet on the Bengal establishment in 1781; and early in that year sailed for India in Commodore Johnston's fleet, and, after a twelvemonth's passage, landed at Bombay in March 1782. He joined, as ensign, the Bengal detachment, serving in the west of India, under Gen. Goddard, and was appointed to the 5th batt. N. I. At the end of that war, he returned with the detachment through the Mahratta country, to Futtehgur. In 1784, he was appointed to the 2d batt. 1st N. I., commanded by Major Duncan, then serving with Sir John Cummings' detachment in the field. He accompanied the regiment when it was detached to the Furruckabad district, to reduce the forts of Begarry, &c. In 1787, he was removed to the 32d N. I., with which he served in the Rohilla battle and campaign, under Gen. Sir Robert Abercromby. He was next sent on command from Burhampoor to Nattore, in the Ranjeshy district, and where he continued two years. Shortly after rejoining his corps, he applied for and obtained permission to accompany the volunteers proceeding by sea to join Lord Cornwallis's army in Mysore, and was appointed to the 2d batt., Capt. Hyndman's. At the end of the war, he returned with the army to Bengal, and rejoined the 32d. In the following year, he was appointed, as lieut., to the command of a troop in the 1st Native cav., but detached from that regiment at Mahoondy, after Vizier Ally's insurrection at Benares, in pursuit of a disaffected Rajah, who was surprised in his camp, and delivered up to the Nabob at Lucknow.

In May 1800, this officer attained the rank of capt., and was attached to the 6th Native cav. at Gazypoor. He had the honour to command Lord Wellesley's cav. escort in his lordship's tour up the country, until detached therefrom in command of a troop with Mr.

Routledge, sent to regulate the ceded districts of the Nabob Vizier, to Gooracpoor. At the expiration of a year he was recalled to join his regiment, then with the cavalry of the army, under the Com.-in-Chief, Lord Lake.

The 13th March 1803 he was promoted to the rank of major, and the command of the 6th reg. Native cav. on the death of Major Naire, killed at the taking of the fort of Catchoura. On the dispersion of the various corps, the 6th Native cav. was detached to the frontier station of Chandoorg. On the formation of the army, the same year, under the Com.-in-Chief, against Scindia, Maj. M. was ordered to march, and join the army before Delhi. He continued to serve in the command of the reg. till some time after the battle of Laswarree, when, from extreme ill health, and the advice of his medical friends, that (to save his life) it was necessary to go to Europe, he reluctantly quitted the army; and the 30th January 1807, retired from the service.

MAJOR WILLIAM LEONARD CARPENTER.

(Bombay Establishment.)

This officer did duty with the artillery for four years after his arrival in India, with the option of being permanently posted to that corps, but gave the preference to the infantry. He served on the expedition to the Red Sea in 1799, under Col., now Sir John, Murray; and was present in an affair at Suez with a detachment of the French army. He was permitted to proceed, as a volunteer, on the service to Egypt, under Maj.-Gen. Baird. He served in Cotiote during the rebellion of 1802, 3, and 4, and was present in many affairs with the rebels, and slightly wounded. He next served on an expedition against a body of Bheels, and was present in two affairs with them. He was selected to collect boats for the passage of the Poonah subsidiary force across the Godavery, on taking the field; on which occasion he received a letter, of which the following is an extract:—

" Colonel Wallace is sensible of the difficulties you have met with in the attempt to remove the boats by land, and is well pleased with your exertions."

He acted as adjut. to the 2d batt. 3d reg. for one year, during the absence of the adjut.; as recruiting-officer for eighteen months, during the absence of the officer holding that appointment; as assist.-adj.-gen. of the army six years and seven months; and as acting dep. adjut.-gen. from Dec. 1813 to Feb. 1816, when he was confirmed as dep.-adjutant.-general. In Dec. following, he was compelled to return to Europe on a sick certificate, after a service in India of eighteen years and two months. The 1st Nov. 1817 he was promoted to the rank of maj.; and the 8th Jan. 1821 retired from the service.

Maj. Carpenter served three months as ensign; seven years seven months as lieut.; one year as capt.-lieut.; and nine years as capt.

THE LATE COLONEL PATRICK WALKER.

(Madras Establishment.)

This officer was a native of Fifeshire: his family had been for many generations the proprietors of St. Fort in that county. He was born in 1766. In 1781 he obtained a cadetship in the East India Company's service; and in 1782 he embarked for India. His original appointment was for Madras; but, from a desire of accompanying his elder brother*, who had been appointed the preceding season a cadet for Bombay, he was removed to the same establishment. The fleet consisted of upwards of twenty Indiamen and transports, and was convoyed by seven sail of the line, under the command† of Sir R. Bickerton. It carried out a large body of troops, a vast quantity of military stores, and the first reg. of cav. sent from Europe to India.

The fleet, on its passage to India, was separated in a gale of wind off the Cape of Good Hope; and the Nottingham, on board of which ship this officer had embarked, arrived at Madras, instead of her original place of destination, Bombay. The reinforcements with Sir R. Bickerton anchored in the roads, at a time when the public affairs were in a desperate condition, when the declining state of Sir Eyre Coote's health disqualified him for the fatigues of the field, and when faction and cabal distracted the local government.

Some circumstances occurred before the arrival of the Nottingham at Madras, which it may not be superfluous to mention. On the 2d Sept. 1782, when off Ceylon, that ship fell in with the fleet under the command of Sir E. Hughes, which she joined, and on the next day saw the French fleet off Trincomale harbour. The French colours were at the same time seen flying on the forts, and left no doubt but that the place was in possession of the enemy. This was of course very unexpected and unwelcome intelligence, as our fleet was actually bound for Trincomale, to obtain a supply of water and provisions. This disappointment, however, produced the spectacle

* The present Lieut.-Col. Alexander Walker, whose services are introduced in this work, p. 147, et seq.

† The perilous situation of our affairs at that period, required this exertion; and the great body of European troops, as well as the new description of force which was introduced, changed, in a great degree, the nature and system of Indian warfare. The cavalry of the Native states have never been able to sustain the shock of the British horse, while the Native cavalry in the Company's service, under the instructions of their officers, have been made to rival, in discipline and efficiency, their European fellow-soldiers.

of a naval engagement; and Mr. Walker was present at this desperate but indecisive battle. Its consequences were nearly fatal to the ship in which he was a passenger. The British admiral, in order to repair the great loss he had sustained in the engagement, pressed every seaman on board the Nottingham, and left the officers to navigate the ship. The next night she was overtaken by a storm, and in the confusion of the fleet was run on board athwart the bows, by the Sceptre, a ship of the line. From the shock, the ship for a moment was under water; she lost in the concussion the figure at her head, and bowsprit, sprung all her masts, and a great part of her rigging was destroyed; but this misfortune was the means of saving the ship in the great storm which ensued in the roads of Madras. The day after that tempest, out of a numerous fleet, the Nottingham was seen alone in the roads: she had dragged with her last anchor close behind the surf, and expected every moment to be cast on shore; but, as she was without masts and unrigged, she was less exposed to the violence of the wind, and thus saved from destruction. The storm which had caused the encounter with the Sceptre ceased at daybreak.

Mr. Walker had now reason to regret that he had relinquished his first appointment, and was advised to get re-appointed to Madras. It was impossible to effect this with his original rank but by an order from home, and in the meantime he resolved to accept of an ensigncy in succession to the Madras cadets of the season. Having landed*, he offered his services as a volunteer; was appointed an ensign, and ordered to join the 16th batt. N. I., stationed at Trivatore.

* A short review of the state of affairs at the time of Ens. W.'s arrival at Madras in 1782, may contribute to explain the subsequent operations. For some years previous, Hyder Ally had carried on a successful war against the Company, and had collected almost the entire revenue of the Carnatic. The whole country was over-run by his cavalry, and, with the exception of Velore, Wandiwash, Carrangooly, and a few places on the sea-coast, every fort was occupied by detachments from his army. The Company's finances were at the lowest ebb, and their credit exhausted. The Madras army was paid and fed from Bengal. The calamities of war were at this time made more terrible by the effects of a dreadful famine, which depopulated the Carnatic. The streets of the

The principal exertions of the army were directed to provide for its subsistence; and the 16th was, in Dec., ordered to march to the northward on this service. It was joined at Pullicat by the 4th batt., and proceeded to Nelloor. It was appointed to escort thence a supply of cattle for the army, and soon afterwards joined it in the field for the campaign of 1783.

The spirits of the army were a little damped by the absence of their favourite general, Sir Eyre Coote, who was beloved by all classes of the military, but especially by the native troops, who almost adored him. The army marched from Tameran in the beginning of Feb. The first of its operations was of a singular nature: it was employed to demolish the forts of Wandiwash* and Carrangooly, by far the most

---

Fort, of the Black Town, and the esplanade of Madras, were covered with starved wretches, many of whom were dead and others dying. The vultures, the Paria dogs, jackals, and crows, were often seen eating the bodies before life was extinct. The general distress and calamity was aggravated by the destruction of a fleet of grain vessels, which had anchored in the roads with a supply of food. The inhabitants were in a moment deprived of the gleam of hope which this near approach of relief had inspired. On the 15th Oct., in the night-time, a monsoon gale set in, and almost all the ships in the roads were driven on shore and wrecked. The loss of the rice-ships at this late season was an irreparable misfortune. The famine encreased; and it was estimated, that, in consequence of this accident, upwards of ten thousand inhabitants perished.

At this period, Lord Macartney was governor of Madras, and Sir Eyre Coote commanded the army. The army had gone into cantonments, and the general had sailed for Bengal, to arrange with the supreme government the means and the plan for the ensuing campaign. Every resource was exhausted. It was necessary to obtain supplies of money, provisions, and equipage. Gen. Stuart held the temporary command during the absence of the Com.-in-Chief. The mode in which the army was cantoned, marked its inferiority and weakness; it was chiefly quartered in the environs of Madras, at the Mount, and in the garden-houses on Choultry Plain.

The country was abandoned to the undisturbed possession of the enemy. Hyder's army was principally stationed to the westward, about Arcot, Arnee, and other parts of the Carnatic. But before the close of this year Hyder Ally died, and was succeeded by his son Tippoo Saib. At this time Sir Eyre Coote's army was in a deplorable condition; its pay and batta in arrear six months. As nothing could be purchased, rice and provisions were issued to the troops. The officers were generally in great distress.

* It is said that Sir Eyre had disapproved of this measure, and had remonstrated against the destruction of those important posts. Wandiwash, in particular, he wished to preserve. While the enemy's army were ravaging the Carnatic, it afforded shelter and protection to the

important of the few fortified places that remained in our hands, which had so often and so successfully resisted the enemy, and which had repeatedly supplied the army with provisions, when not to be obtained elsewhere.

As the army approached near Wandiwash, it had an opportunity of offering battle to the united French and Mysorean armies. They were encamped at Nedingull. The enemy's horse, and their rocket-boys, had for some days harassed the line of march; Gen. Stuart threw his baggage into Wandiwash, and marched to give the enemy battle. The engagement was declined by Tippoo, notwithstanding his superiority in numbers, and other great advantages. As the British advanced, he retired across the river, and there was only an opportunity of firing a few guns at his rear. When, however, the army returned towards its baggage, it was again harassed and insulted by the enemy. Large bodies of their horse, rocket-men, and snipers, hung on every quarter, which the want of a sufficient body of cavalry rendered the British incapable of preventing. This caused a constant skirmish during the march*; and such was the character of every military movement in India, in the face of an enemy, at that period. The demolition of the ancient fort of Wandiwash was soon effected, but it was not accomplished without a very serious accident: the serjeant who had charge of the mines getting intoxicated, set fire to the train before the troops were called off, which blew up the magazine, killed and wounded an officer, and upwards of 100 men. The army next proceeded to Carrangooly, and destroyed that fort also.

inhabitants and moveable property of an extensive tract. It had recently been besieged, and its small garrison repulsed the army of Hyder. The fort was still commanded by Lieut. Flint †, who had performed this glorious service. It is further supposed, that Sir Eyre Coote had a soldier-like partiality for the place, as the scene where he had gained a decisive victory.

* At the end of one of these marches, the enemy's force attempted to carry off the head-quarters' flag after it was pitched, but the small body of British cavalry drove them away, and saved the standard. This circumstance is mentioned to shew the audacity of the enemy, and the defenceless state of an army without a sufficient force of cavalry.

† See a preceding note, p. 245.

Gen. Stuart then fell back to Vellout, near Poonamallee, for fresh supplies. The next service of the army, to which Ens. Walker's corps was attached, was to relieve and provision Velore. This place was surrounded by large bodies of the enemy's horse, and as the British approached Shoolingham, the enemy made a demonstration of opposing our march; but as we advanced, they moved of towards Arcot, and the relieving army arrived at Velore, with no other opposition than the usual skirmishes with the horse and rocket-men. The garrison of Velore were in high spirits. The northern Poligar chiefs, who border on that district, had thrown into the fort a partial supply of provisions.

After this service, Ens. W.'s batt. was employed on an enterprise, which, although it was not attended with success, may not be unworthy of notice, as it is characteristic of Indian warfare, and of the partisan duties by which it has always been accompanied. Moymangalam Durgam, a strong hill fort, about sixteen miles from Velore, and the key of those Poligar countries, had fallen into the hands of the enemy. Most of the families of the Native troops who had been taken at Arcot were there kept prisoners. These people contrived to hold a communication with their friends and relations in the army. By this means it was learnt that the garrison were usually off their guard at night, and it appeared very possible to surprise the place: it was also understood that Tippoo had here deposited a considerable treasure. The evening after the arrival of the army at Velore, the 16th batt., with its guns and some irregular horse, were detached on this service. A subadar of cavalry undertook to be the guide; but it happened that the family of this man was amongst the prisoners whom they were going to release, and he was apprehensive that they might suffer in the attack. With a view of providing for their security, he sent them a message, with advice to withdraw themselves from the danger, and to endeavour to leave the place. The females unto whom this intelligence was made had not the fortitude to keep it secret, and it was communicated to the enemy. As the detachment approached the fort, it was evident that the garrison were at their posts, from a blaze of blue lights, and a continued discharge of art. The pettah, however, was carried by storm, and the detachment returned to camp without any material loss. Feb. ended with these operations. Meanwhile the rapid success of Gen. Matthews in Canara, and his capture of Bednore, had alarmed Tippoo, who, early in March, suddenly evacuated Arcot, and marched his army with indescribable expedition out of the Carnatic. Syed Said was left with a large body of horse to levy contributions on the country, to intercept the supplies, and to watch the British operations. On receiving intelligence of this movement of the enemy, Gen. Stuart marched to Arcot, and took possession of that capital; thence the army returned to the Mount, in the vicinity of Madras, to be equipped for another expedition*.

The siege of Cudalore was the next operation of importance on which the 16th were employed. This service was the most severe and determined that a long war had produced in India. It was remarkable for the extent of the loss sustained on both sides, and for the distinguished share which the native corps of the British army bore in the various events of the siege; in the course of which, they met and charged the enemy with the bayonet†. On the 7th June 1783, the French outworks were stormed and carried after a desperate resistance. This siege was more a direct contest between the two nations, than the contemporary actions in the field, in which the forces engaged comprised a heterogeneous mass of native allies. The French force was large, and consisted almost entirely of Europeans. It was commanded by M. Bussy, a man of acknowledged talents and ability. The British government were desirous of opposing to him an officer of equal skill and experience. The army lingered between Permacoil and Chingleput, to wait the arrival of Sir Eyre, and to give the storeships time to rendezvous before Cudalore. At length that distinguished

* At this time a campaign consisted of a great number of short excursions, which lasted until the provisions were exhausted. The troops were obliged to return at intervals, which were never very long, to the source of their supplies on the sea-coast, and having provided for their wants up to a calculated period, they marched forth on a new enterprise.

† See pages 25, 87, and 379.

officer arrived at Madras, exhausted by anxiety and disease. He expired in two days afterwards, to the grief and affliction of the army: to his country, his loss was a misfortune ever to be lamented*.

Ens. Walker was present in many of the severest actions of the siege of Cudalore, and was employed with his corps on the grand attack which was made at day-break of the 13th on the French lines. The enemy, after having received a great reinforcement from the fleet, on the night of the 25th June, made a sally on the British lines, but were repulsed and driven back to the fort with great slaughter, having the colonel who commanded them made a prisoner. The 16th batt. was on this occasion in the trenches, and Ens. W. happening to be on the advanced picquet, sustained their first shock. The arrival of an English frigate with a flag of truce, brought a few days after this action intelligence of a peace in Europe, and probably saved the army from the necessity of a disgraceful retreat.

The war was still maintained against Tippoo, and the 16th batt., early in July, marched to the southward, where it joined what was called the southern army. The usual dissentions which prevailed among the ill-adjusted and incongruous authorities of the local and supreme government at that period, prevented this force from obtaining the full advantages which had been expected; but it performed, notwithstanding, many great and essential services, which depressed the enemy, and probably facilitated the peace which was soon after concluded. When this event took place, the forts of Palicaudcherry, Coimbatore, and Dindighul, with their respective territories, which were the fruits of this campaign, were restored to Tippoo, as a countercession, for rescinding the conquests made by the Mysorean power in the Carnatic from the nabob Mahommed Ali, the Company's ally; and for the restitution of Calicut, the district of Mount Delhi, the forts of Amboorgur and Sautgur, and other places to the English. This was the result of the war and of the campaign; but a few details of the previous operations may not be uninteresting, so far as they particularly relate to Ens. Walker's corps.

* See page 44.

When the siege of Cudalore was relinquished, it was judged necessary to reinforce the southern army under Col. Fullarton. Col. (the late Gen.) James Stuart, 72d reg., was appointed to command the detachment which was sent from the army before Cudalore, and he, an excellent judge of military merit, selected the 16th batt. as one of the corps which he wished to compose his force. The detachment marched for Trichinopoly about the 25th July; thence it proceeded by Caroor and Darmapooram to Dindigul, where it was soon afterwards joined by the troops under Col. Fullarton. This force now composed a strong and respectable army, but it was left to its own ways and means. As there was no money to pay the troops, it was necessary that they should derive their subsistence from the enemy's country, and this, it was evident, must depend upon the intelligence and activity of the departments of supply*.

Col. Fullarton arrived at the entrance of the Animallee forest without any material occurrence, and resolved on the arduous task of cutting a road through this immense wood to Palicaudcherry, which he intended to attack. Col. Kelly's brigade, of which the 16th composed a part, were employed as pioneers to cut a passage for the guns. This duty was of the most severe and disagreeable nature. It rained continually, the troops were constantly wet, the provisions were scarce and bad, and it often happened that the trees and jungle made it impracticable to pitch the tents. The troops, however, went cheerfully on, and the work was soon completed. Palicaudcherry was invested and regularly besieged. The rains were still incessant; the trenches were filled, and the water could not be drained off. The fall of the place was facilitated by one of those bold and decisive actions which have always been the subject of alternate praise and censure. The

* To these early difficulties, and the urgency of want, may be traced the progress and perfection of the Commissariat establishments in India, and of those excellent regulations which are now in force for the conveyance of provisions and stores. There is no school equal to that of necessity; and it is neither unamusing nor uninstructive, to look back on those infant institutions, and those abortive attempts, which it would be unfair to contrast with the success and vigour of subsequent transactions, which owe, in fact, their sustained and decisive tone to the feebleness and disappointment of former struggles.

Hon. Capt. Maitland had a corps of flank companies under his command, and occupied an important post in the investiture of the place. He seized the opportunity of a heavy fall of rain to surprise the garrison; he pushed forward his corps, and followed a party of fugitives through the first gate; the second he found shut against him; but the enemy lost their courage, a parley ensued, and a capitulation delivered the place into our hands. About 60,000 pagodas were found in this fort; and Col. Fullarton adopted the popular expedient of dividing this sum among the different ranks of the army on the drum-head. The share of a subaltern came to ninety pagodas; and in the scarcity of money at that time this was a great relief, to the subordinate officers especially. The next enterprise was directed against Coimbatore, which surrendered without resistance.

While the treaty which terminated hostilities was under discussion, but before any truce had been stipulated, a large body of horse under Rushan Khan made a full charge on the picquets of the British army, consisting of two batts., of which the 16th was one. The enemy were repulsed and driven off, but not without loss on both sides. After a cessation of arms had taken place, and we had evacuated the captured forts, the enemy were guilty of an act of great perfidy by attacking and cutting in pieces one of the advanced posts of this army. Col. Jas. Stuart, with a detachment, of which the 16th formed one of the corps, made a forced march in the night against this party who had violated the truce, but without being able to overtake them.

When the peace with Tippoo was concluded in 1784, the British troops were withdrawn from his country. The 16th, with a strong detachment, was for some time stationed in the Marwar country, near Shevagunga, to keep the Poligars in awe; but the 16th batt. was ultimately, in the same year, detached to Mellore, to make the Collery chiefs pay up their arrears of revenue. This was soon effected, rather by the judicious arrangements of Capt. Cox than by force. Every thing remained quiet, and the batt. continued stationary until near the end of 1785.*

* About this period the exhausted treasury of Madras was unable to meet the outstand-

On the conclusion of peace, the prospects of the officers in India were damped by the reductions to be expected in the army; and the promotion of the junior part of the service appeared so remote and uncertain, as almost to extinguish the hopes of attaining a respectable rank even in a long life. With this unpleasant view of futurity, Ens. Walker was induced to go on furlough to Bombay, with a design, should the circumstances of that presidency appear more encouraging, to claim his rank in that army. Finding, however, every thing more discouraging there, he soon afterwards returned to Madras, and rejoined the 16th batt., which was stationed in the southern provinces. In this situation he remained until the close of 1785, when he was removed to the cav. and appointed cornet in the 4th reg. His commission bore date 3d Dec. in the above year. The Native cav. were all in his Highness the Nabob of Arcot's service until 1784, when they were taken into the Company's. The corps at this time consisted only of four regs. Cornet W. joined the 4th at Arcot, where it was cantoned, and remained for several years. The interval of peace between 1783 and 1790 was employed in preparing for a war, which was to raise the character, and with that the power, of the British nation, to an elevation which it had never before attained in India. It was evident that an ill-observed peace could not be of long continuance. It was at the same time fortunate that Tippoo's wild aggression against

---

ing demands growing out of the war, and the local government resorted to the expedient of paying off the arrears of the army by promissory notes or draughts on Bengal. This was felt to be unjust; if the public distress allowed any alternative, it was impolitic. Some of the native corps were two years in arrear, and many of the European officers had more than twelve months pay due. The hardships inflicted by this measure are not to be described. It was at first impossible for the natives, and particularly for those who were to be disbanded, to convert their paper on any terms into cash. At length speculators appeared, and those poor men, who had supported the British government with unparalleled fidelity during the trying vicissitudes of a long war, were obliged to exchange their notes at a discount of 70 and 80 *per cent*. Some of the corps which were ordered to be disbanded, refused to give up their arms until they were paid their arrears in cash. Those who thus sought redress in mutiny were attacked and dispersed, without receiving any thing whatever. This happened to a batt. which was stationed near Madura, when the 16th and 20th batts. and a reg. of cav. marched against it. On the approach of this force, the corps threw away its arms, fled, and disbanded itself.

the Native powers of India had excited their alarm and resentment. The first act of injury was directed against an ally of the British government; but the flame of war was ready to kindle all around, and a general confederacy was formed under our auspices. The Company's army was in the highest state of efficiency, and their cav., in which they had heretofore been deficient, was of the due numerical strength, and in the finest order.*

The troops for field service in the Carnatic assembled at Wallajabad, and the 4th reg. of cav. joined this division. It proceeded in April to Trichinopoly, under Col. Musgrave, to join the main army, which was commanded by Gen. Medows. This campaign proved abortive; and on the 20th Jan. 1792 Lord Cornwallis assumed the command of the army. On the march of the army from Bangalore, two troops formed the advanced guard, under Cornets Deas and Walker. They were detached in front to secure some forage, but unexpectedly fell in with Tippoo's line of march crossing the front of our direction. Intelligence of this circumstance was immediately communicated to the field-officer, who was with the infantry of the advanced guard; and it appeared that neither his lordship nor Tippoo were aware of each other's movements. It was about two hours before any part of the line came up to the support of the advanced guard; and during all that time the enemy and our people continued looking at each other across a tank which was surrounded by a swamp. The enemy's cavalry formed, but merely to protect or cover his infantry, which retreated on various points, and were soon out of sight, their rear only receiving a few shots.

On the 27th Feb. about a thousand of the enemy's horse made their appearance, but soon went off: on the 28th the army reached Collar, which had only a small garrison of Europeans, and surrendered, on a

* This is to be ascribed in a great degree to the zeal and exertions of the late Sir John Floyd, at that time a lieut.-col., and who was indefatigable in disciplining the regts. The Company's cav. on the Madras establishment possessed probably some of the best officers that were ever seen in any army; and, under their direction, the squadrons attained a state of corresponding excellence. Cornet Walker, although he had yet acquired no higher rank, was numbered among those distinguished officers.

gun being run up to blow the gate open, without resistance: on the 2d March the British arrived at Ooscottah, which was garrisoned by Poligars and a few irregular infantry, who refused to give up the place; but when the first gate was forced, they surrendered at discretion. From the ramparts of Ooscottah large bodies of the enemy's horse were seen in motion; and it was certain that the army of Tippoo was near Bangalore. On the 4th the march was resumed: the enemy's horse were observed hovering in all directions, particularly in front and rear, and became extremely daring: they found means to interrupt a great part of the baggage; but while they were plundering it they were attacked by the cav., and every thing was recovered. On the 5th the enemy appeared in still greater numbers, both of horse and foot, but the day passed without an action, which Lord Cornwallis expected would have taken place, and the army encamped before Bangalore. On the forenoon of the 6th, at eleven o'clock, the enemy's army appeared in motion about three miles distant, and directing their march to the south face of the fort. The British cav. and the reserve, consisting of a brigade of inf., moved off at 3 P. M. to cover a reconnoitering party. This detachment, under the command of Col. Floyd, gained a height, from which the engineers could view the fort and make their observations. From this eminence the line of march of Tippoo's army, his guns and inf., were perceived moving on slowly and unconcernedly at no great distance, together with an immense quantity of baggage, which covered the plain to a great extent. It appeared that we had come upon them by surprise. Col. Floyd was a gallant and an unaffected soldier. The temptation was too great to be resisted; and he ordered the cav. to charge the enemy. The attack was instantly made; his batts. were dispersed; guns, stores, carriages, and baggage of every description were left in our possession. Here we ought to have stopped, and the success would have been complete; but, hurried on by the ardour of victory, the cav. continued to advance to the very head of Tippoo's line, and this handful of brave men soon found themselves beyond the reach of support. Col. Floyd was shot through the face and fell, but was removed by the care of his men. The wounds of the commanding officer deprived him of speech, and some unknown voice gave the word of retreat. The regts. were thrown into confusion, and the enemy pressed on their rear. The dragoons and Native troopers, however, displayed the most undaunted courage, and at length formed on an eminence which lay in their front. Capt. Dallas, now Sir Thomas, collected a small party, and went off full gallop to the eminence, where he halted and formed. Soon afterwards the whole cav. also formed at this spot, and stood fronting the enemy. About the same time the reserve under Col. Gowdie came up, and advanced in front of the height; whence a cannonade was opened on the enemy, which effectually checked them.*

In the first general action on the 13th May 1791, which Tippoo risked with the British army, the cav. were actively and gallantly employed. For some time the cav. of the enemy did not appear in any great numbers; but at last they were seen coming over the heights in considerable bodies, and threatened the left flank of our inf., having even made a charge upon a reg. of Europeans. The cav. under Col. Floyd immediately galloped through the intervals of the inf., and drove the enemy back so effectually, that they attempted nothing considerable afterwards. Again, after the enemy's line was broken, and they were drawing off their guns, (a constant practice of Tippoo, whenever the issue of a battle appeared dubious,) our cav. charged and rendered the victory complete. The ground was broken and full of defiles; but every obstacle was surmounted in the charge, which was made with spirit and execution.

The subsequent retreat of our army, and the circumstances attending it, belong to the general history of the war, and would be foreign

---

* Although this charge of the cav., having been made contrary to orders, was liable to blame, and was in fact censured by Lord Cornwallis, its gallantry excited the admiration of every soldier. There is also reason for concluding that the boldness of their attack prevented Tippoo from reinforcing the pettah or town of Bangalore, and by that means probably facilitated the capture of the place, which was carried the same morning by assault, after a defence of much resolution, which we may presume would have been still greater had they received the meditated succours.

to the purpose of this relation. The cav. were greatly reduced, and as they required rest, they were ordered into the Carnatic, to recruit their horses, and to repair their deficiencies. Lord Cornwallis in the interval employed himself in preparing for another campaign, and in reducing the hill forts contiguous to Bangalore and the Carnatic. The horses of the cav. being abundantly supplied with green forage and grain, soon recovered their condition; but there were no means of supplying their number, which was reduced to one half. It was therefore found impossible to mount more than two regts. and part of a third, for the next campaign. The 19th light dragoons and the 3d light cav. were accordingly ordered to be completed with horses, and the 5th light cav. to receive all that remained. Cornet Walker was appointed to do duty with the 3d reg., and joined that corps at Arcot, whence it marched to join the army in the field. In Jan. 1792, the army under Lord Cornwallis once more resumed its march towards Seringapatam. There was no general action in which the cav. had an opportunity of displaying their gallantry; but they were actively employed during the rest of the campaign in keeping the enemy's horse in check, and never failed to chastise whenever they could encounter them.

The third campaign of 1792, ended in the submission of Tippoo, the division of his treasure, and of a third part of his dominions, among the confederates. In the course of this brief but harassing war, which was a rapid series of privation and danger, victory and relief, Cornet Walker distinguished himself on many occasions, particularly in the severe cav. rencounter near Bangalore, which has been already related, and in all those active and useful duties which the cav. are peculiarly called upon to perform in the camp as well as on the march. On the 7th Jan. 1792 he was promoted to lieut., and removed to the 2d reg. Native cav. On the 24th Feb. Tippoo delivered his sons as hostages into the hands of Lord Cornwallis. Col. Stevenson* was appointed to

* Col. Stevenson was an officer of great honour and gallantry, activity and enterprise; his disposition was generous, his mind intelligent. He arrived afterwards at the rank of general, distinguished himself in that extended field for military talent, and acquired the friendship of the Duke of Wellington.

command the escort, consisting of his own reg. of cav. and several corps of inf., which accompanied the princes to Fort St. George. On the arrival of the hostages at Madras, the command of their guard of honour was conferred on Lieut. Walker. This was a delicate and important charge, which required the exercise of no small share of judgment, temper, and discretion. On the 24th Oct. Lieut. W. was appointed adjutant to the 4th cav. stationed at Arcot. The duties of this arduous appointment he was admirably qualified to perform. He was some time afterwards appointed grain agent to the same regt. The next staff appointment which Lieut. Walker held was that of brigade-maj. to the cav. employed at the siege of Pondicherry. He was appointed to this temporary service 6th Aug. 1793; when it was ended, he resumed his adjutantcy of the 4th reg. On the 9th Nov. the dep.-judge-adv. of the centre division of the army being indisposed, Lieut. W. was appointed to act as judge-adv. on the trial of Maj.-Gen. Geiles. The Com.-in-Chief expressed his approbation of the readiness with which he undertook, at so short a notice, this difficult duty, and of the attention which he had shewn in the execution of it. Lieut. and Adj. Walker was stationary at Arcot with the 4th reg. during 1794-5, and 6. On the 8th Jan. 1796, after a service of sixteen years, he obtained the rank of capt. by brevet. On the 23d Aug. 1797, he was appointed adj. and quart.-mast. to the details of cav. ordered on foreign service. This expedition was destined against Manilla, but was abandoned after some part of the force had embarked, from the apprehension of an attack by the French in India; and, when the service was countermanded, Capt. W. resumed the duties of adj. to his old regt. In the beginning of 1798 the regt. changed quarters to the cav. cantonment near Cudalore.

The decisive war which terminated the life and the government of Tippoo broke out in 1799. The corps to which Capt. Walker had been for many years attached, took the field with the army under the command of Gen., now Lord Harris. All our preparations on this occasion were equal to the magnitude of the stake at hazard. It was necessary to give more efficiency to the forces of our allies, and at the same time to conciliate their regard; two objects difficult to reconcile. It was requisite they should be in some state of discipline, to afford some ground for relying that they would obey the orders to be received; but, as this could only be effected by the instruction and agency of European officers, it became a matter of great moment to select for this trust men of approved judgment, temper, and experience.

Col. Wellesley was placed in the command of the Nizam's army, and, at his desire, Capt. Walker was appointed to serve with his highness's troops. This order was issued by the government of Madras on the 26th June. Soon afterwards, Col. Wellesley appointed Capt. Walker to command a select body of cav. of the Nizam's army. The Nizam's cav. were made efficient; and, during the march to Seringapatam, they displayed the utmost activity in keeping Tippoo's horse, but especially the Looties, in check. Capt. W. was always at their head, encouraging them by his example, and, by his attention to their habits and prejudices, attached them to his person.

It may not be superfluous to subjoin a few dates and details of this campaign, so far as they are connected with the services of Capt. Walker. The 4th reg. of cav. marched from Cudalore, and arrived at Arcot in the beginning of 1799: here they found most of the cav. and a considerable body of inf. assembled, under the command of Col. Wellesley. The cav. were completely mounted, and in a high state of discipline. On this occasion Capt. W. resigned the adjutantcy of the 4th, as he deemed it more honourable to act as a brevet capt. in the line, when in the field and opposed to the enemy. He had held this appointment for nine years. Col. Wellesley was ordered to move his corps near to Velore, where the army for the campaign was collected, under the Com.-in-Chief, Gen. Harris. Soon afterwards, H. M.'s 33d reg. was ordered to join the Nizam's subsidiary force, and Col. Wellesley was appointed to the command of those troops. The Nizam's army, under Meer Allum, consisted of five thousand horse, a large body of disciplined inf., and a body of regular cav., which had been instructed in the European exercise by the French partizan Perron. A train of field-pieces were attached to this force, and, to make the batt. more respectable, some British officers were appointed to them. The general charge, however, was invested in Capt., now Sir John, Malcolm, the assistant to the Resident at the court of Hyderabad; the British subsidiary force was at the same time attached to the Nizam's army.

Soon after the British army had entered the enemy's country, Gen. Floyd, at the desire of Col. Wellesley, informed Capt. Walker, that the Com.-in-Chief intended to appoint him to the command of the regular cav. with the Nizam's contingent; that he should be allowed a European and a native adjut. and a detail of men from our own cav., and that at least 1000 of Meer Allum's best horse would also be placed under his orders. It was besides intended, the Gen. observed, after the war, to raise a reg. of Native cav., which was to be paid by the Nizam, and that Capt. W. would undoubtedly retain the command of it. He was accordingly appointed to the command of the division of the allied cav., and received a handsome allowance from the Nizam, besides his captain's pay. In this conspicuous situation, opportunities continually offered, which served to distinguish an active and intelligent officer. The very day after Capt. Walker joined Col. Wellesley's army, he fell in with a large body of the enemy's horse; but they refused to wait a charge, and drew off after a few guns were fired at them. Capt. W.'s immediate duty with Col. Wellesley's line was to watch his front and flank, to protect the baggage, and to keep the cav. of the enemy at a distance. Their practice was a harassing and a daily annoyance: he had often a long and fatiguing pursuit after their partizan parties, whose object is more generally to plunder than to fight: he frequently brought in horses, and drove five times the number of the enemy before him. At the battle of Malavilly, 27th March, the cav., regular and irregular, made some fine and gallant charges, in which they cut to pieces and dispersed several corps of the enemy's infantry.

On the 6th April Capt. Walker's corps was ordered to march with

Gen. Floyd, who was detached with a large body of forces to meet the Bombay army, which was assembled on the Mysore frontiers. Sadullah Khan, one of the Nizam's best officers, and 1000 good horse, were placed under Capt. Walker's command on this occasion. The protection of the rear and flank were entrusted to his care, and a troop of Madras cav. were put under his orders, to enable him to perform more effectually this duty. Tippoo detached* Kummer-u-deen with a large force of inf. and cav., to prevent the junction of the Bombay and coast armies. On the return of these forces towards Seringapatam, Capt. Walker's post was the flank, on a line with the rear-guard. The enemy's cav. repeatedly appeared in front of the line of march, and threatened to charge; but, excepting on one occasion, when they came down on a gallop upon the rear-guard, which formed and repulsed them, they continually drew off before they reached the line. They stopped short just when they came within the reach of the British guns, at the very instant when cav. ought to advance, and exposed themselves to an useless and unnecessary danger. They continued until the troops reached Seringapatam on the 14th, this shew of charging, without the resolution of executing it, which harassed and retarded the progress of the troops. On the 15th April Gen. Floyd again marched beyond the old fort of Mysore with the cav. and Capt. Walker's party. The object was to cover the foragers of the army, and all the followers and cattle were ordered to accompany the detachment. Some supply of provisions was by this means obtained, which was of the utmost importance at the moment, and the party returned to camp in the evening, without having seen any large body of the enemy.

On the 19th April Gen. Floyd marched with the whole of the ca-

* It has been observed by an able writer, that the Sultaun's cavalry had on no occasion been so well commanded, or held themselves so effectually prepared at a moment's warning, to profit by the slightest irregularity or error, and strike a decisive blow, as throughout the whole of this march to and from Periapatam; but the only result was to compel their opponents to corresponding vigilance and care, and of course to retard their movements.

valry of the army, and a brigade of infantry, to meet the large convoys of provisions which were advancing by the Cavariporam pass, under the charge of Lieut.-Cols. Brown and Read. On this occasion Meer Allum detached all the Nizam's horse, supposed to be 5000 men, under Capt. Walker's command; his duty was to cover the flank and rear; and on the 20th these points were attacked by the enemy's horse, but the gallopers were sufficient to oblige them to draw off. The detachment were, in the same manner, attacked or threatened daily, without any thing serious following. During this service the Nizam's cavalry behaved well. Capt. W. found that temper and patience were essentially necessary in directing their operations. They might be prevailed on to do any thing, but they did not understand force or positive orders, the only infallible test which we allow of military obedience and discipline. At assembly-beating in the morning, those troops turned out with alacrity, and each division ranged round their respective chiefs, who were usually mounted on elephants. They either waited there for Capt. W.'s orders, or moved to the stations which had been previously appointed for them. Many of their chiefs were men of rank and respectability. Sadullah Khan was the superior. Some of this cavalry were remarkably well mounted; the men were good horsemen, and possessed of great personal courage, but quite unacquainted with the restraints of discipline. By treating them with mildness and attention, Capt. W. gave them confidence, and they did their duty cheerfully. They always paid due attention to his orders, and behaved to him personally with the greatest respect. In posting them to cover the flank and rear, he judiciously followed an arrangement which they observe among themselves; he very seldom separated or mixed their divisions, because, in the imperfect state of their military regulations, they conceive themselves only bound to obey their respective leaders.

The Nizam's camp was, however, at this time, in the greatest distress for grain and provisions. When the detachment came up with the supplies, to meet which it had marched, an impolitic and unjust refusal to issue rations to the Nizam's troops, excited clamours among the men, and a general disaffection. They proceeded, according to their custom when they have any grievance to redress, to place one of their chiefs, Hassain Ali Bey Khan, in dhurna; and when they found this expedient not likely to produce the result they expected, about 1000 of the men went off to their own country. The quantity of rice they required was at length supplied, and the remainder joined their standards, and returned to camp.

When the property and dominions of Tippoo fell into our possession, after our own cavalry had supplied themselves with horses, Capt. W. was directed to take charge of the remainder for his highness the Nizam. Upwards of 500 horses, and 300 mares, were delivered over, from which it was intended to mount two regiments of cavalry for the Nizam's service, but to be raised and disciplined on the same principles as our regiments. Capt. W. was, at the same time, desired to recruit for this establishment; and in a very short time collected about 300 fine young soldiers. He was ordered with this corps to Arcot, and accompanied Meer Allum, who was going that way to Madras: he had also charge of all the horses received from Tippoo's cavalry, and a brigade of gallopers. He left his corps at Arcot, and proceeded with Meer Allum to the presidency. The intention, however, of raising regs. for the service of the Nizam, was abandoned; and instead of this arrangement it was resolved, that one of our own regs. of cavalry should be added to the subsidiary force at Hyderabad. Capt. W. was soon afterwards, therefore, directed to discharge the men he had enlisted, or to enter them for the service of the Company, and to deliver over the horses and mares to one of the Nizam's officers. After the conquest of Mysore he rejoined his reg.; and on the 4th Sept. 1799 was promoted to capt. of cav. About the same period he was appointed, by the Gov.-Gen. in council, to command the escort which was to accompany Capt. Malcolm, Envoy to the court of Persia; but this appointment was vacated, in consequence of an order of the government of Madras of the 18th Sept., appointing him to be maj. of brigade, to complete the establishment of the second brigade of cavalry.

Soon after his appointment, Capt. W. proceeded to Hoolionore to join his Brig.-Col., Stevenson, and marched with him to Serah with two regs. of cavalry. Towards the end of 1799, Col. Stevenson was appointed to the command of Chittledroog, and Capt. Walker, as major of brigade, accompanied him. In the beginning of 1800 a severe intermitting fever prevailed in the garrison and country of Chittledroog. Capt. W. was seized with this fever, and being unable to shake off the disease, he came to the resolution of resigning his staff appointment. He accordingly joined the 4th reg., of which he was senior officer, and commanded it on the ensuing service. About the middle of 1800 an army was assembled at Hurryheer, under the command of Col. Wellesley, to act against Doondia Waugh*. The campaign was of the most active kind; the conduct of it displayed as much of perseverance and skill as had ever been exhibited in India. In this trying campaign, which was terminated in the death of Doondia, and the destruction of his followers, Capt. Walker had his full share of fatigue and danger. This service was remarkable for an uninterrupted succession of long and rapid marches, for the laborious duties which devolved upon the officers, and for the excessive fatigue which the troops endured.

On the 1st of July 1800 Capt. Walker was appointed subordinate agent for cavalry supplies to the 4th. reg. of cav.; but he still continued in the command of the reg. In consequence of the clashing interests and wavering politics of the Mahratta government at this period, it was found necessary to direct a large force to their frontier. Gen. Wellesley accordingly marched towards Darwar, and the 4th, commanded by Capt. W., composed part of his army. This force remained only a few weeks encamped at Hubley; and the Mahrattas

---

* This enterprising adventurer had collected a large army in the Dooaub, between the Kistna and Toombudra, where he had established himself, and placed garrisons in many of the forts: he was a bold but an unprincipled freebooter, and disguised his schemes of plunder under the specious design of driving the English out of the country, and of replacing the family of Tippoo on the throne of Mysore. By this declaration he expected to attract the officers and adherents of that family to his standard.

testifying a friendly disposition, Gen. Wellesley ordered the troops into quarters.

Almost immediately after this service, Capt. W. was employed with his reg. in the ceded districts, under Maj.-Gen. Dugald Campbell. The object of this expedition was to take possession of the districts which the Nizam had ceded to us, and in which it was necessary to establish the Company's authority by an armed force. The inhabitants of these countries are mostly of the Poligar race; they lived under their respective chiefs or leaders, and paid often but a nominal submission to the Nizam. Their revenue was consequently much in arrear; and as they possess many strong forts, they were continually able to set a weak government at defiance. The reduction of this people could only be accomplished by a series of long marches and fatiguing operations. Most of the refractory chiefs, after an ineffectual shew in some cases of resistance, submitted, and in a few instances they were punished for their temerity. Capt. W. was detached against the chiefs of Chitsill, a descendant of the ancient Rajahs of Annagoondy, and Nursum Reddy, both of whom yielded at discretion.

We find, by the government orders of Fort St. George, of Sept. 27, 1801, Capt. Walker is directed to proceed to Mangalore, for the purpose of receiving remount horses for the service of the cavalry; and he was to perform this duty without detriment to his regimental staff appointment. On the 27th March 1802, the Gov. in council at Madras appointed Capt. Walker to be general agent for cavalry supplies, and to procure, at the same time, horses for the cavalry.

On the army taking the field, in the general war against the Mahrattas, under the Com-in-Chief, Lieut.-Gen. James Stuart, Capt. W. was appointed commissary of grain and bullocks. On the 1st May 1804 he was promoted to a majority in the 8th reg. of cavalry, which he was appointed to raise. In the same year he was confirmed by government as sole agent for the purchase of horses for the cavalry, having in fact supplied the cavalry with horses since 1802, and which appointment he continued to hold until he found it necessary, for the sake of his health, to return to England towards the end of 1807. A short time before this event, and in the same year, he was promoted to the rank of lieutenant-colonel.

In mentioning the laborious and honourable offices which were successively held by Lieut.-Col. Walker, the record of the Court of Directors, which bestows a high and justly merited encomium on his integrity and talents, ought not to be omitted. In a despatch to Fort St. George they take notice of the able and satisfactory manner in which he had conducted the purchase of horses; and they remark with pleasure, as a circumstance highly creditable to Lieut.-Col. Walker, that his agency had been conducted on principles of economy and public advantage, superior to what they had before observed in that department. During the whole period that Lieut.-Col. Walker held this important appointment, the cavalry were supplied with fine horses in any number that was required, and at such reduced prices, that the government made him a present, on one occasion, of 3000 pagodas. While engaged in this important duty, Lieut.-Col. W. raised and formed the 8th reg. of cavalry. So effectually and speedily was this reg. mounted and disciplined, that, in less than a year after it had been formed, it was ordered to proceed to Bellary, and to join a force assembled there for field service. Lieut.-Col. W. marched with the reg., and put himself under the orders of Gen. Campbell; but the war at that time having blown over, the troops were sent into quarters. He from thence went to Mangalore on the duty of the agency, and returned with upwards of 1000 horses for the service. In April 1806, while he was on his route to rejoin his reg. at Bellary, the Com.-in-Chief thought his presence necessary at Grammum, which was the depot fixed for the rendezvous of the horses previous to their distribution to corps. A malignant fever raged amongst the inhabitants of this place, and committed great destruction: it seized the cavalry followers, and an alarming mortality ensued. Lieut.-Col. Walker and his family were attacked by the contagion; and although Gen. Macdowall had considerately sent a surgeon to their assistance from Seringapatam, there appeared no other way of escaping from this destructive fever than by removing to another situation. There was no time to apply to head-quarters, and Lieut.-Col. W. took the responsibility upon himself, by removing the depôt to Coondgull, about forty miles distant, on the road to Bangalore. The people soon recovered, and the Com.-in-Chief fully approved of the measure. Lieut.-Col. W.'s own illness however continued, and rendered it impossible for him to join the reg. His constitution had been much impaired by the fever contracted at Chittledroog, from which he had never entirely recovered, and this new attack, which was still more severe than the former, induced his medical attendant to recommend that he should first go to sea, and eventually to Europe. While he was proceeding to Arcot, he passed Velore a few days before the mutiny and massacre of that garrison; and he narrowly escaped the same fate, by refusing to accept the invitation of his friends to remain with them a short time. At Arcot, however, his health, in the course of a few months, had assumed a considerable degree of amendment, and he was prevailed on to give up his intention of immediately returning to Europe. His presence was thought necessary to reconcile the horse-dealers to some regulations which government was at this time desirous of introducing: difficulties were apprehended, should those men prove refractory, which might afterwards produce much inconvenience and distress to the service. Lieut.-Col. W. accordingly once more proceeded to Mangalore, settled all the existing differences, and returned with 1200 remount horses. He purchased, by commission, 1000 horses for the ensuing season, which were to be from three to eight years old, and settled their price with the dealers at the average rate of 106 star pagodas a-head. It is to be observed, that all these horses were to be transported by sea from the gulph of Kutch, or the ports of Guzerat and Scind; that many of them were drawn from Scind, Kattywar, Lahore, Cabool, and the Persian provinces adjoining. This horse-market was far beyond the political influence and controul of the British government; it depended upon a multitude of ferocious and barbarous tribes, who were led by caprice and avarice. It may readily be imagined, that it required no small share of address, intelligence, and management, to direct the co-operation of a rude and suspicious people, and to prevent them from disappointing the public service. In March 1807, Lieut.-Col. W. having finished his business at Mangalore, and dispatched the remount horses to Coondgull, proceeded to that depôt, but found himself under the necessity of signifying to the Com.-in-Chief, that he had received medical advice to go on furlough to Europe, which had now become absolutely necessary for the restoration of his health, and at the same time requested leave to visit the presidency for the settlement of his affairs. This request was complied with, and in July he arrived at Madras. In the following month, after a period of twenty-five years actual service in India, he obtained a furlough for three years; and on the 24th Oct. embarked for England.

The loss of a moderate fortune, which he had saved in the course of a long service, by the failure of a house at Madras, obliged Lieut.-Col. W., on the expiration of his furlough, to return to India. In the month of May 1811, he embarked for India, landed at Madras 10th Sep. 1811, and found himself in the 1st reg. of cav. It was his wish to have joined his reg. immediately; but it was judged expedient, by the government of the period, to remove him to the 3rd reg., at Bangalore, and very soon afterwards he was appointed to the 5th reg. of cav., which was stationed at Seroor. It was alleged that this corps required the presence of a commanding officer of judgment and experience; but the arrangement exposed Lieut.-Col. W. to a heavy expense. As some parts of the road were infested by banditti, it obliged him to proceed with his family to Bombay by sea, before he could arrive at his station. On the 23d Feb. he arrived at Bombay; from thence he proceeded to Poonah, and joined the 5th reg. at Seroor. At this station he was the second in command, but derived no emolument on that account.

Every thing at that period was quiet in India. The materials of discontent, however, were abundantly diffused, and they were ready in every direction to burst into a flame. In the beginning of the following year general symptoms of commotion began to manifest themselves, and some circumstances about this period gave the Resident at

Poonah reason to suspect the Peishwa of hostile intentions. His highness had left that capital to visit a place in the neighbourhood, on pretence of performing some religious ceremonies; and, although accompanied by one of our batts. as an honorary escort, as he had still more considerable forces of his own collected about his person, it was judged expedient to watch his motions, by the subsidiary troops stationed at Seroor. They continued marching for some time in the vicinity of that station, and at length took up a position on the banks of the Punderpore river. This happened in Feb. 1813. The troops remained in this encampment for several months; but on the approach of the monsoon they were ordered to return to their cantonments. In June, Lieut.-Col. W. arrived with his reg. at Seroor. For a short time he commanded the cantonment during the absence of Col. Montresor. In Aug. the 5th reg. was ordered to Jaulnah, and Lieut.-Col. W. consequently became attached to the Hyderabad subsidiary force. Some time in Nov. following, the whole force at that station took the field, in consequence of the general disturbed state of the country, which was infested by robbers and banditti. Travelling was rendered unsafe, and it was difficult to preserve the usual military communications. It was not before a strong remonstrance was made to the Nizam's government, and the determined appearance of using force, that these disorders were suppressed. On this arrangement, Lieut.-Col. W. and the rest of the troops returned to their cantonments. On the 4th June, a general promotion in his Majesty's army conferred on Lieut.-Col. W. the rank of colonel; and, for a short time, the command of the Hyderabad subsidiary force devolved on him.

In the course of this year the Pindarries had become very troublesome, and had committed depredations to a great extent in various directions. Some duplicity was also apprehended on the part of several of the chiefs who were in alliance with the British government, and who owed to it fidelity in return for protection. The war with Nepaul had been protracted to an unusual length, and had given rise to feelings among the native states, particularly the Mahratta governments, which it was necessary not only to watch with attention, but be prepared to check on the first decided appearance of a hostile disposition. Under these circumstances it was expedient to have our armies in the field. Towards the end of Oct. 1814, the different subsidiary forces were put in motion, and Col. Walker accompanied that of Hyderabad. They remained in this state of preparation until Sept. 1815, when the cavalry, under the command of Col. Walker, received a route for Ellichpore; but on the march he was met by a fresh and pressing order to proceed with the utmost expedition to Poonah. This sudden and unexpected destination was occasioned by the murder* of Gungathur Shastree, who had been dispatched by the Guicawar government, as its agent, to settle some pecuniary differences with the Poonah state, under the guarantee of the Company. But when Col.

---

* This assassination was contrived, and the instruments of it directed, by Trimbuckjee Danglia, the minister and favourite of the Peishwa, with the sanction and authority of the latter: it was perpetrated on the night of the 19th Sept. at Punderpore, under circumstances of the deepest perfidy and guilt. This base and atrocious deed is briefly but forcibly referred to in the proclamation of the Gov.-Gen. in India deposing the Peishwa; and Bajee Rao is expressly charged with the crime. It excited every where in India indignation and horror. It is impossible in this narrative to enter into the details of this wicked transaction; but as the prelude to it has never been fully explained to the British public, it may here be concisely mentioned, that the Peishwa being unable to corrupt the fidelity and integrity of the Shastree, resolved to effect his destruction by the hands of assassins. To succeed the better in his purpose, Bajee Rao proposed an alliance between their families, by affiancing one of his relations, the sister of his own wife, to the eldest son of the Shastree. The Shastree was distinguished by an ingenuous detestation of falsehood. The insidious caresses of the Peishwa did not for a moment deceive his acute and perspicacious understanding: from the beginning he suspected his highness of some nefarious design, and with reluctance accepted an invitation to accompany the Peishwa to Punderpore, a place of worship in the vicinity of Poonah, celebrated for its sanctity, and the whole territory of which is considered holy. On the evening of the 19th July, Trimbuckjee sent for the Shastree to meet him in the temple to perform his devotions. The Shastree twice declined the invitation, under the pretext of indisposition; but on receiving a third message, he thought it necessary to go, and proceeded with a few unarmed Brahmins, leaving, by the Peishwa's desire, his escort of English sepoys behind him. On his return from the pagoda on foot, and having hold of one of the Brahmins by the hand, he was beset by the assassins, cut down, and his body was divided in pieces by sabre wounds. This breach of faith, and violation of hospitality, called forth the indignation of every generous mind. Mr. Elphinstone, the able and distinguished Resident at Poonah, prepared with suitable dignity and spirit to resent it as an affront to his country, and as an atrocious offence committed against society. He instantly imparted to the Peishwa, that the same enquiry and investigation must take place respecting the murder of

Walker had nearly reached Poonah with his detachment, he was recalled. The same order directed him to make forced marches on Hyderabad, where symptoms of disaffection appeared, and where many of the Nizam's court and family were adverse to a connexion with the British. Some blood was shed on this occasion; but the troops on the spot were found sufficient to allay the dissensions, of which the causes, as is often the case in India, were a compound of public and private feelings. Order being restored, the forces, which this service had called out, returned to the cantonments at Jaulnah. They arrived at that station late in Oct.; but the Pindarries had now become so daring and formidable, that they had set the native governments at defiance, who were unable or unwilling, to check their depredations. It became necessary that the British government should interfere with all its power and resources, to prevent the ruin and desolation of the country. The troops had been scarcely twenty days in their cantonments at Jaulnah, when they were again obliged to take the field. An important part in these operations, most fatiguing to execute, fell to the lot of Col. Walker. He was repeatedly detached with the cavalry in pursuit of the marauders; to Basseen, or Amorawitty, to Ellichpore, and to scour the banks of the Nerbuddah. In these rapid excursions, which were frequently made in the night, and were peculiarly harassing, Col. Walker was always at the head of his troops. Although he was not successful in falling in with any of the parties of these freebooters, he kept them on the alert, and disconcerted their schemes of plunder. The superior authorities in India appre-

the Shastree, as if he had been a minister deriving his appointment directly from the British government. The Peishwa denied that he was accessory to the crime, and we were led, by motives of forbearance to an allied sovereign, to accept of a weak and mean apology. Our demands for satisfaction were limited to the apprehension of the persons of Trimbuckjee Danglia, the minister, and a few others who were publicly known to have been immediately accessory to the assassination. It was to enforce this claim, and to defeat the ultimate machinations of the miscreants at Poonah, that large bodies of forces were marched on that capital; but the Peishwa's duplicity and cowardice induced him to commit an additional act of baseness, by surrendering into the hands of the British government his servile and guilty minions. This prevented hostilities at that time.

ciated his energy, zeal, and intelligent activity*. From this period, for two years, Col. Walker may be fairly said to have been on the move and in the field. Every flying detachment that was formed, before the Nagpore force was established, and after it had rejoined Col. Doveton, was sent under Col. Walker's command. While in command of the Nagpore force, he fell in with several bodies of Pindarries, cut them up, and dispersed them. After his return to the station at Jaulnah, Col. Walker was detached with a light detachment in pursuit of Trimbuckjee Danglia, who had escaped from his confinement in the fort of Tannah, whom the Peishwa at first affected to consider as a rebel, and offered, at the requisition of the British government, two lacs of rupees for his apprehension.

This life of vigilance and constant movement continued until about the 10th of June 1816, when in consequence of a treaty of alliance with the Rajah of Berar, who accepted a subsidiary force, Col. Walker was appointed to the command of it, and directed to march a large body of troops and art. to Nagpore, the capital of that Rajah's dominions. We are now arrived at an important and interesting stage of Col. Walker's life. The command that he had attained was, at once, one of the most honourable and advantageous in India. He was to act in a country which had scarcely yet been visited by our arms or taught to confide in us by intercourse, and where the government had for the first time adopted the federative system of the Company. The situation was new and difficult; it required political as well as military talents; energy and vigilance, conciliation and address. While the peaceful and well disposed were to be gained by mildness and friendship, it was necessary, by firmness and vigour, to restrain and keep in order the turbulent and disaffected. One important duty was to check the incursions of the Pindarries, and to protect the inhabi-

* A partisan officer has always a bold and decisive part to perform; but this duty in India, besides eminent talents in the leader, requires an intimate acquaintance with the language and manners of the people: the strongest constitutions are gradually wasted by excessive fatigue in that country; by an alternate exposure to the violent heat of the day, and the cold vapours of the night.

tants from the effects of their depredations. This duty was effectually performed by Col. Walker, who compelled these marauders to flee to their retreats, and by a series of judicious movements, secured the Nagpore territories from their depredations. He was received with flattering attention at the Rajah's court, and enjoyed the confidence of the Resident.*

* The following extracts of despatches from the governments of India bear honourable testimony to the able manner in which Col. Walker conducted this service, and of the peculiar difficulties which attended it :—

The Gov.-Gen. to the Court of Directors, 12th Dec. 1816.

" The establishment of the subsidiary force in the territories of the Rajah of Nagpore has produced a most salutary effect; and its advance to the Nerbuddah, and the active pursuit by Col. Walker of a body of Pindarries, which crossed the river early in Nov., has created a degree of alarm in the minds of the Pindarry leaders, which may tend materially to restrain their excesses during the present season. Intelligence, indeed, is transmitted to us, that considerable bodies of the Pindarries have penetrated through the wide intervals between Col. Walker's posts, and have committed some devastation; but as we have not had any distinct report as to the amount or direction of these columns, we cannot judge whether they have any more distant object, or are only employed to occupy Col. Walker's attention. Col. Walker pursued the freebooters into Scindia's territory, south of the Nerbuddah, which afforded him the opportunity of compelling them to return across the river, and ultimately to break up their camp on the north bank, and retire to Satwas. The Resident had authorised Col. Walker to take this step, under a conviction that it was essential to any plan of operations for the obstruction, pursuit, or interruption of the Pindarries, and that no objection would be offered to it by Scindia or his officers.

" It is manifest that no defensive precautions can be of avail against an enemy like the Pindarries, while they occasion an annual expenditure exceeding the most extravagant calculations of the cost of a vigorous and decided system of measures, which would destroy the evil effectually. The inability of Col. Walker's force to defend the extended line of frontier committed to his charge has already been made manifest, notwithstanding the activity and exertion of that officer, and the troops under his command, by a large body of Pindarries having actually turned one of his largest detachments, so close to its position, as to have been partially engaged with the British troops, which being composed entirely of inf., was unable to offer any effectual obstruction to the rapid movements of the enemy. We have endeavoured to improve Col. Walker's means of defence, by placing at his disposal two batts. and two squadrons of cav., and we hope that with this additional force his line will be considerably more secure, though we can entertain no hopes that any system of measures founded on defensive principles will oppose an effectual barrier to the incursion of the Pindarries.

The Gov. in Council, at Bombay, to the Court of Directors, 18th Dec. 1816.

" The first advices respecting the Pindarries received from the Resident at Nagpore,

Early in 1817 the Gov.-Gen. came to the determination of furnishing the Berar subsidiary force from the Bengal army, either because Nagpore was more contiguous to the territories of that presidency, or because, to appoint the military force as well as to direct the political influence sustained by it, belonged to the supreme government. Whatever were the views of expediency for this measure, the Bengal troops relieved those of Madras at Nagpore, early in March 1817. It was near the end of April before Col. Walker himself was able to quit Nagpore, but he sent on the forces in advance, and joined them with the general staff at Amorawitty. The whole reached Ellichpore about the middle of May, and from thence joined the Hyderabad contingent. Col. Walker, after he was relieved from the command in Berar, received the most flattering testimonies* of approbation of his conduct

---

stated their number to be about 27,000, who are collected and prepared to cross the Nerbuddah; a body of about 4000 men soon afterwards crossed the river at the Buglateer-ford, but crossed it in consequence of the movements of the troops under Col. Walker, commanding the Nagpore subsidiary force. Another similar body having again crossed over at the Buglateer-ford, and it being reported that they had taken the Boorhanpoor road, Col. Walker pursued them for some time in that direction. On his return, with the hope of intercepting some of the other Pindarries, who might be expected to follow them, he succeeded in surprising and dispersing a party belonging to the first body, some of whom were killed, and a few taken prisoners. It appeared from the information they afforded, that the report of their having proceeded to Boorhanpoor was incorrect; and in consequence of Col. Walker's movement they recrossed the river, and the whole of the Pindarries assembled in that part of the north of the Nerbuddah immediately fell back."

* The following copies of letters and orders were communicated to Col. Walker, or published to the army on this occasion :—

" Sir,—On the occasion of your quitting the Rajah's territories with the principal body of the Madras troops lately serving his Highness as a subsidiary force, I perform a very pleasing duty in communicating to you the high sense which I entertain of the services and good conduct of the whole of the force under your command. Entering a foreign country in the beginning of an alliance, which rendered it of peculiar importance that the first impression on the minds of the Rajah and his subjects should be favourable, it has uniformly shewn a degree of regularity and discipline, highly creditable to the British character. The zeal and activity displayed by you in the operations on the Nerbuddah, and the meritorious exertions of the troops in that quarter, have been fully made known to the supreme government, in the reports I have from time to time forwarded of those operations. From that quarter must proceed the ultimate tribute of approbation; but, as connected with the execution of measures specially entrusted

from the Gov.-Gen., Lord Hastings, the Com.-in-Chief, the Gov. at Madras, and the Resident at Nagpore.

to my superintendance, I beg to offer you my personal thanks, and to request you will be pleased to convey them also to the officers and men of the force.

" I further beg to express my full concurrence in the approbation which you have expressed in your orders of this date (of which you have favoured me with a copy) of the zeal and ability of Lieut.-Col. Scott, and the good conduct of the troops at Nagpore; and I have no doubt that they will continue to maintain the credit of the establishment to which they belong, whilst they remain in these territories.

" In conclusion, I cannot refrain from expressing my obligations to you for the zealous and friendly co-operation which I have uniformly experienced from you in your late command. (Signed) " R. JENKINS, Resident.

" Nagpore, April 2, 1817."

To Richard Jenkins, Esq. Resident at Nagpore.

" SIR,—I am directed to acknowledge the receipt of your despatch of the 2d inst., transmitting a copy of your letter to Col. Walker of the same date.

" The sentiments expressed in that letter are fully participated in by the Gov.-Gen. in council. The judgment and activity uniformly displayed in Col. Walker's arrangements and operations in the important command which he lately held, had not failed to attract the notice of his Lordship in council; and his Lordship has derived great additional satisfaction from observing the high testimony borne by you to the discipline and good conduct of the troops, composing the force under Col. Walker's command, during the time they were stationed in the Nagpore territories. The conciliatory demeanour of Col. Walker towards the officers of the Nagpore government, and the natives in general, is also a point in that officer's conduct which his Lordship is desirous to mark with particular approbation. You are requested to make known to Colonel Walker the very favourable sense which the Gov.-Gen. in Council entertains of his merits and services.

" A copy of this letter will be transmitted to the government of Fort St. George, and to the Resident at Hyderabad.

(Signed) " J. ADAM, Act. Chief Sec. to the Government.

" Fort William, April 26, 1817."

To the Chief Secretary to Government, Fort St. George.

" SIR,—In submitting the accompanying copy of a letter from Col. Walker, late commanding the Nagpore subsidiary force, for the consideration of government, I am directed by the Com.-in-Chief to state, that his Exc. cannot refuse himself the gratification of embracing this opportunity to express his full approbation of the conduct of that part of the Madras army, under Col. Walker's command, recently employed in the Berar country.

" The conduct and exertions of Col. Walker during his command of the Nagpore

The detachment lately under the command of Col. Walker, had arrived only a few days at Ellichpore, when they were again ordered to take the field, in consequence of the defection of the Peishwa, and an open declaration of war. This event was hastened by the escape of Trimbuckjee Danglia from his confinement at Tannah; which was followed by an attack on our troops at Poonah, and a general insurrection, wherever the Peishwa's influence extended. The first direction of the Hyderabad force was a rapid movement upon Jaulnah; but when they reached the bottom of the Lucknawanay Ghaut, they received orders to proceed into Candeish, where it was supposed a large body of the insurgents were assembled. This information, however, either proved incorrect, or the enemy dispersed, and found means to conceal themselves in the fastnesses of that country. After this disappointment, Col. Walker was detached, in command of two regs. of cav., a corps of flank companies of inf., and a proportion of light art., to explore the valleys among the hill-forts of Chandore, and the whole tract of country to the westward. Notwithstanding the most diligent and persevering search, he was not able to obtain the least trace or intelligence of an enemy. The detachment halted at Wonny, or Wunn, not far from Nassuck, and about sixty miles from Surat; from hence, after remaining for some time in this position, Col. Walker marched to Jaulnah. On the 18th Aug. 1817, the 5th regiment of cav., to which he was attached, and which had served upwards of eight years in the Deccan, was ordered to return to the Carnatic; but an order from the government directed Col. W. to remain, and appointed him to the command of all the cav. with the Hyderabad force.

force, have been such as to merit every praise; and the Com.-in-Chief cannot in sufficiently adequate terms express his commendation of them. His Excellency considers it a duty incumbent upon him to recommend Colonel Walker to the favourable notice of the Right Honourable the Governor in Council.

(Signed) " J. H. S. CONWAY, Adj.-Gen. of the Army.
" *Adjutant-General's Office, Choultry Plain, May* 13, 1817."

The most formidable armies perhaps that had ever been seen in India, under an European standard, were now assembling from the three presidencies, and were gradually approaching the points from which they might most effectually co-operate, or unite, against whatever enemy might oppose the views of the British government.

The Nepaulese had submitted to the terms which we thought necessary to prescribe; and we had full leisure to collect all the resources of the empire, to maintain the peace and the security of our dominions in India. The most able and experienced officers were employed. Col. W. was placed on the staff, and attached to the third division of the army of the Deccan, which he was appointed to command during the absence of Sir John Malcolm on political affairs.

The Colonel left Jaulnah about the middle of Sept. with his staff and a reg. of cav. The division was appointed to assemble at Amorawitty, and it was expected that he should be at its head on the banks of the Nerbuddah by Oct.

After Col. Walker had received his instructions, he made every exertion to arrive at the place appointed for the rendezvous of the division. The haste with which he set out corresponded with the importance of the service, and his anxiety to answer the expectations of the Com.-in-Chief, who had confided largely in his activity and judgment. He left Jaulnah on the 14th Sept., to take the command of the third division of the army of the Deccan; but was detained on the road eight or ten days by the flooding and swelling of the rivers which lay in his route. This circumstance agitated and annoyed him exceedingly, and brought on a slight fever, which however had left him previous to the sudden and fatal stroke which deprived his family, his friends, and society, of a good man, and the Company's army of a most valuable officer. This event took place on the 12th Oct., at a village called Sirpoor, about twelve miles from Basseen: he was seized with a fit of apoplexy at eleven in the forenoon, and did not speak afterwards. He died at sunset, and his remains were interred at Basseen on the 13th, with every military honour which could be bestowed.

Col. Walker was a man of the most amiable and gentle manners of great professional ardour and talents: the loss of such an officer was not only felt by the private circle of his acquaintances, but also by the public authorities in India. It was deplored by the Com.-in-Chief, whose expressions on the occasion mark the highest admiration of Col. Walker's character and talents; and even betray a feeling of despondency, from the difficulty of making another selection so well adapted to the peculiar duties which had been assigned to him. These feelings were displayed in a letter from Sir T. Hislop to Lord Hastings, dated Camp at Nandore, 17th Oct. 1817, four days after the unfortunate event, of which the following is an extract:—

" Your Lordship will participate with me in the feelings of deep regret, as well as of a public as a private nature, which the melancholy and altogether unexpected death of Col. Walker has occasioned in my mind. By this mournful event, the public service, particularly at this moment, has sustained a loss which I acknowledge myself unequal to repair; for I know not at present of any officer, in whom an equal combination of rank, talent, experience, and local knowledge, can be found, to warrant a recommendation to be the Colonel's successor, in the important duty confided to him."

The most decisive proof of the regard and affection in which Col. Walker was held, is afforded by the determination of his brother officers of erecting a monument to his memory.

THE LATE LT.-COL. JAS. ACHILLES KIRKPATRICK.

(Madras Establishment.)

This officer was the son of Col. Kirkpatrick, formerly of the East India Company's establishment, at Fort St. George. He was born Aug.

1764; and, after receiving a liberal education, he was appointed a cadet on the Madras establishment, and proceeded, in 1779-80, to India. In 1788-9, the impaired state of his health compelled him to revisit his native country, where, however, he remained but a very short time, returning to India before the conclusion of the first war with Tippoo Sultaun; in the second campaign of which he served, with the reserve of the army, under the command of Lieut.-Col. Gowdie. Towards the end of 1793, he was appointed to the charge of the garrison of Vizianageam, which he soon relinquished, for the appointment of Persian translator to the detachment serving with his highness the Nizam. In this situation he continued till Oct. 1795, when, on the death of Lieut. William Stewart, he succeeded to the office of assistant to the Residency at Hyderabad, which was at that period filled by his brother, Maj (the late Col.) William Kirkpatrick, who being obliged, early in the year 1797, to proceed to Bombay, and subsequently to the Cape of Good Hope, for the benefit of his health, the charge of the British interests at the court of Hyderabad devolved on the subject of the present memoir.

During the period of his acting as Resident at the court of Hyderabad, Capt. Kirkpatrick had the honour, under the directions of Lord Mornington, now Marquess Wellesley, of negociating and concluding, with his highness the Nizam, the important treaty by which the alarming power and influence of France in the Deccan were completely annihilated, and that prince rendered an efficient ally of the Company, and enabled to co-operate with effect in the war soon after produced by the perfidy and restless ambition of Tippoo Sultaun.

Lord Mornington testified his approbation of this important and eminent service, by appointing Capt. K. to the vacant office of Resident at the court of the Nizam, and by conferring on him the peculiar distinction of honorary aid-de-camp to the Gov.-Gen.; and he was the first person on whom this honour was bestowed, though it was afterwards extended to others: it may be in a manner said to have been instituted to mark and dignify the merits of Capt Kirkpatrick. So high indeed was the sense which his lordship entertained of Capt. K.'s services on this occasion, that he was pleased to recommend him to his Majesty's ministers as deserving of some mark of the royal favour.

Extract of a Letter from the Gov.-Gen. to the Court of Directors, dated Nov. 21, 1798.

" *Par.* 21.—Among your servants who have been concerned in the execution of my orders, on this occasion, I have already recommended Lieut.-Gen. Harris to your favourable notice. To his name, it is my duty to add those of Capt. Kirkpatrick and of Lieut.-Col. Roberts. I found the former in the situation of Acting Resident at Hyderabad; and to his zeal, address, discretion, and firmness, I attribute the early success of the negociation entrusted to his management.

" 32.—Upon the resignation of Colonel Kirkpatrick, I took occasion to manifest my sense of Captain Kirkpatrick's merits, by appointing him Resident at the court of the Nizam."

But though the reasonableness of this recommendation was readily admitted, a compliance with it was from time to time postponed, and finally, entirely neglected. Upon the determination of the supreme government to demand adequate security against the hostile disposition and designs of Tippoo Sultaun, such were the zealous and successful exertions of Capt. Kirkpatrick to bring the Nizam's contingent into the field, that it actually reached Chittoor before General Harris was ready to proceed on his march from Velore.

Extract of a Letter from the Gov.-Gen. to the Court of Directors, dated March 20, 1799.

" 79.—The Nizam's contingent consists of 60,000 of the Hon. Company's troops, subsidized by his Highness, of about the same number of his own infantry, including a portion of M. Perron's Sepoys, now commanded by British officers, and a large body of cavalry.

" 80.—This force, under the general command of Meer Allum, formed a junction with the army on the 19th Feb.; and it is with the greatest satisfaction that I remark to your honourable Court, the beneficial effects which the Company have already derived from the recent improvements of an alliance with the court of Hyderabad. The Nizam's contingent actually arrived in the vicinity of Chittoor, in the state of preparation for the field, before Gen. Harris was ready to proceed on his march from Velore."

Ample as the political and territorial advantages were, which the Nizam derived from the partition treaty of Mysore; yet as his extravagant expectations from the spoils of Seringapatam had been necessarily disappointed, the ratification of that treaty, by the Court of Hyderabad, was not obtained without eliciting fresh proofs of the address and ability of Capt. Kirkpatrick.

In Oct. 1800, Capt. K., after a long and arduous negociation, succeeded in concluding a new treaty with the Nizam, whereby the political ties which connected the British government and the state of Hyderabad, were drawn together more closely than before; while the money subsidy hitherto paid by his highness, in defraying of the expences of the British troops employed in the defence of his country, was commuted for the territories acquired by his highness, in consequence of the wars of 1791-2, and 1799, with Tippoo Sultaun, which were now assigned in perpetual sovereignty to the Company.

The estimated revenue of these territories, according to the schedules annexed to the treaty, amounted to star pagodas 16,51,465. The sense entertained by Lord Wellesley of this officer's services on this important occasion will best appear from the following copy of a letter to Capt. Kirkpatrick, dated Nov. 10, 1800.

"SIR,—Since the commencement of my administration of the affairs of the British empire in India, frequent occasions have arisen, at the court of Hyderabad, to require the exertion of address, firmness, and perseverance on the part of the British Resident, and on the success of the negociations entrusted to his management, the most important political interests of the Company in India have essentially depended. In all these instances your general conduct has afforded me the greatest degree of satisfaction;

and I now repeat, with pleasure, the public tribute of justice which I rendered to your eminent services in accelerating the destruction of the French influence at Hyderabad, in the year 1798; and in bringing the Nizam's forces into the field with so much promptitude and alacrity during the war in Mysore, in 1799. The conclusion of the treaty of the 12th Oct. 1800 furnishes a confident expectation of the lasting security and permanent duration of the British power in the Deccan: the service which you have rendered to the Company, and to the British interests in India, by your able and assiduous exertions throughout the course of the long and intricate negociation which preceded this important measure, demands my most cordial approbation, and entitles you to the gratitude of the Company and of your country.

" I discharge a satisfactory part of my public duty in recording these sentiments on the proceedings of this government; but the peculiar merit of your services, and the great importance of the beneficial consequences which have flowed from your success, will induce me to submit to the Court of Directors my earnest recommendation, that you should be rewarded by some honourable mark of public distinction.

(Signed " WELLESLEY."

In Dec. 1800 Capt. Kirkpatrick attained the rank of maj. From this time, nothing material occurred at the court of Hyderabad, until April 1802, when Maj. K. concluded a treaty of commerce between the East India Company and his Highness the Nizam. By this treaty, the merchant acquired, for the first time, a degree of security, and the trade of the two countries a spring, that have since conduced essentially to the advantage of both. The difficulties experienced by Maj. K., in accomplishing this beneficial measure, and consequently, the merit of his success on the occasion, can only be duly appreciated by those acquainted with the extraordinary spirit, the profound ignorance of every true principle of commerce, and the obstinate prejudices which usually prevail in Asiatic, and particularly in Mahommedan, courts, on most questions of political economy.

In 1803 the British government was compelled, in defence of its own rights, and those of its allies, both of them invaded by the restless ambition of the confederated Mahratta chieftains, Dowlut Rao

Scindia, Raojie Bhosillah, and Jeswunt Rao Holkar, to appeal to arms. On this occasion, the power of the court of Hyderabad, stimulated by the unremitting exertions of the Resident, proved eminently useful, and contributed, in no small degree, to the speedy and glorious termination of the war in the Deccan. What considerably enhanced the merit of these efforts was, that they were made in the midst of difficulties, occasioned by the daily expectation of the Nizam's death, and the consequent anxiety respecting the succession to the throne. His Highness actually died on the 6th Aug., being only two days prior to the commencement of hostilities, in the attack of, and capture of, Ahmednuggur. Owing however, in a great degree, to the prudent measures adopted by Maj. Kirkpatrick, under the general direction of Lord Wellesley, Secunder Jah succeeded to the vacant musnud of his father, without the slightest opposition; and the energies of the new government were immediately directed to a vigorous co-operation with the British forces, against the common enemy.

The favourable sentiments entertained, by Lord Wellesley, of Maj. Kirkpatrick's conduct and services on this occasion, were signified to him, by direction of his lordship, in the following terms, contained in a letter, dated 30th May 1804:

" Lord Wellesley desires me to add, that as soon as the British troops are withdrawn from the field, and are returned to their usual stations, it is his intention to afford you a public testimony of his approbation of your conduct, during the late crisis of affairs, and to recommend your services to the notice of the Court of Directors, and of his Majesty's ministers. His lordship will not lose sight of your claim to some mark of distinction from his Majesty's government in England, and will not fail to urge your pretensions in the manner most likely to obtain for you those honours, to which he is of opinion you are entitled for your public services, under his lordship's administration; which he recommended strongly to government, in England, some years ago, and which, in his judgment, have been withheld from you unjustly."

The next occasion, and the last of particular importance, that exercised the vigilance and address of Maj. Kirkpatrick, presented itself in the somewhat sudden death of Azim-ul-Omrah, who fell a victim, on the 9th May 1804, to a fever of only four days duration. Numerous were the candidates, who contended for the high station of this intelligent and respectable minister; and who by various arts strenuously endeavoured to secure the succession to it. Of these candidates, some were well known to be violently disaffected to the British interest, while others were utterly disqualified, by incapacity, for the arduous trust to which they aspired. In spite, however, of the active intrigues set on foot by these different competitors, Maj. Kirkpatrick was enabled to keep the appointment of a successor to the deceased minister in suspense, until he received the sentiments and instructions of the Gov.-Gen. on the subject. The result was, that the vacant office was conferred by the Nizam, on Meer Allum, who was distinguished beyond any other for his political sagacity and experience, and reasonably believed to be a steady friend to the connexion subsisting between his master and the British government, of which he had been for more than twenty years a principal promoter and advocate; and to which, in fact, he was chiefly indebted for the rank and consideration he attained.

In Oct. 1804 Maj. Kirkpatrick was promoted to the rank of lieut.-col.; and in Sept. of the following year he proceeded to Calcutta, with the permission of the late Gov.-Gen., Lord Cornwallis, partly for the benefit of his health, which was somewhat impaired by his long residence at Hyderabad, but chiefly for the purpose of conferring with his lordship on the political affairs of that court. He reached Calcutta, under the affliction of an alarming complaint, and of which he died, on the 15th of Oct. 1805, after a short illness, in the 41st year of his age.

In private life he was eminently distinguished for all those qualities which gain esteem, and secure confidence and friendship. The high diplomatic situation in which he died, he had filled for a period of nine eventful years; and it has been shewn that, in the course of that time, he was successfully employed in some of the most important negociations which took place during the vigorous and brilliant administration of that enlightened statesman. The following, as well as those already introduced, are most honourable testimonies of the zeal and talents which Lieut.-Col. Kirkpatrick displayed in his official character:—

Extract of an Order published by the Vice-President and Dep.-Gov. of Fort William, on the occasion of the death of Lieut.-Col. Kirkpatrick.

"The Vice-President and Dep.-Gov., with sincere regret, performs the painful duty of directing the last tribute of military honours to be paid to the remains of that valuable officer, and meritorious public character, Lieut.-Col. J. A. Kirkpatrick, of the establishment of Fort St. George, late Resident at the court of the Subadar of the Deccan; in which situation he rendered the most important services to the Honourable East India Company."

Extract from a Despatch, dated Nov. 3, 1805, from Mr. Russel, Acting Resident at Hyderabad, to Sir George Barlow, Governor-General.

"The intimation of the decease of Lieut.-Col. Kirkpatrick, the late Resident at Hyderabad, was received by his highness the Subadar with expressions of the most poignant grief, and diffused a universal gloom over every individual at Durbar. The important public services, and the eminent private virtues of Lieut.-Col. Kirkpatrick, were always justly appreciated at the court of Hyderabad. He commanded the confidence and attachment of those with whom he was connected by the functions of his public office, and the love and admiration of those who participated in the happiness of his private friendship. I had long known the respectability of his public character, and long esteemed the virtues of his mind; and it was not without a bitter pang, that I directed the last tribute of respect to be paid to the memory of a man whose loss can never be sufficiently deplored."

Extract from a Despatch, dated Nov. 23, 1805, from Mr. Secretary Edmonstone to Mr. Russel, Acting Resident at Hyderabad.

"The Gov.-Gen. has received, with deep concern and regret, the intelligence of the death of Lieut.-Col. Kirkpatrick, the late Resident at the court of Hyderabad, whose eminent public services, during the long period of time that he discharged the arduous and important functions of that high station, entitled him to the distinguished approbation of the British government."

LIEUTENANT-COLONEL THOMAS STEELE.

(Madras Establishment.)

IN 1792 this officer arrived in India, and shortly afterwards was employed, as a subaltern, under Col. Maxwell, against the southern Poligars. In 1796 he was present at the capture of Ceylon. In 1798 he embarked with the force employed against Batavia and Java, and on his return was present at the storm of Seringapatam. He served also during the active campaign, under Col. Stevenson, as captain, against Doondia. In 1803, 4, and 5, he served under the Duke of Wellington in the Mahratta war. In 1814, as lieut.-col. (which rank he obtained 6th May 1813), and in command of a brigade, he served with Col. Dowse's field force; and in 1815, 16, 17, and 18, he was employed, with a similar command, to quell the disturbances in the Ganjam district, and during the invasion of that country by the Pindarries: he served also in the Goomsur hills, against the rebels of that country.

MAJ.-GEN. SIR JOHN MALCOLM, G.C.B. & K.L.S.

(Madras Establishment.)

APPOINTED a cadet on the Madras establishment in 1781; ensign, 24th Oct. 1781; lieut., 1st Nov. 1788; capt.-lieut., 29th Nov. 1797; capt., by brevet, 7th Jan. 1796; capt. regimentally, 19th Sept. 1798; maj., 27th Jan. 1802; lieut.-col., 18th Dec. 1804; col. by brevet, 4th June 1813; col. regimentally, 8th April 1818; brig.-gen.*, in May 1817; and maj.-gen., 12th Aug. 1819.

* This rank had been previously conferred on this officer in 1808 and 1809, as a temporary commission, to be held by him during his absence from the British Indian territories on his mission to Persia.

This officer arrived in India in 1783*, and in Feb. 1794 returned to England, for the recovery of his health. In 1795 he re-embarked on board the same ship with Gen. Sir Alured Clarke, who was proceeding to Madras as second in council, and Com.-in-Chief at Fort St. George, and entrusted in his way thither with the command of a secret expedition against the Cape of Good Hope. Upon the arrival of the fleet in False Bay, Gen. Clarke conferred upon Lieut. Malcolm a conditional appointment, as his aid-de-camp, and employed him in procuring 400 recruits for the Madras army from among the German troops who had been taken prisoners of war at the Cape. For these services he obtained the recorded approbation of that General, and of the Madras government, by whom he was appointed, 29th Jan. 1796, secretary to the Com.-in-Chief, and, on the 21st Jan. 1798, to succeed Major Allan as town-major of Fort St. George.

In Sept. 1798 Capt. Malcolm was appointed assistant to Capt. Kirkpatrick†, the resident at Hyderabad: in Nov. following he was called from thence, by express summons, to Calcutta, where he arrived, charged by Meer Allum with some verbal communications to the Gov.-Gen., Lord Mornington, of considerable importance. He immediately accompanied his lordship on his way from Calcutta to Madras. In Dec. he quitted the Gov.-Gen., and received instructions to proceed immediately and join the Nizam's contingent force; and in Jan. following (1799) he was invested with the chief command of the infantry of that force, and which continued to act under his direction during the campaign that terminated in the death of Tippoo Sultaun, and the surrender of his capital to the British army. The services of this officer during that campaign were various, as he was

---

* Sir John Malcolm was born in 1769, and was but thirteen years of age when sent out to India to the care of his maternal uncle, the late eminent Dr. Gilbert Pasley. Sir John is one of seventeen children, and it is a remarkable occurrence, that three brothers, Sir James, Sir Pulteney, and Sir John Malcolm, were honoured on the same occasion with the dignity of Commander of the Bath. Sir John was subsequently raised to the rank of Grand Cross of that order.

† *See* Services, p. 460.

not only political agent with the Nizam's army, and commanded all the regular troops of that prince, but was, with Sir Arthur Wellesley, Col. Close, and Maj. Agnew, one of a political commission: he had also charge of all the supplies from the Deccan. The manner in which Capt. M. fulfilled these duties is thus noticed in a letter to the Court of Directors;—

"The Com.-in-Chief reported to us, that Capt. Malcolm had, at all times during the campaign, in which he took a very conspicuous part, made the necessary arrangements for the co-operation of the contingent, in a manner which reflects the highest honour on his abilities, and which strongly marked his zeal in the public cause. The peculiar talent for conciliating the Sirdars of the allied forces, and for directing their exertions to objects of general utility, in a manner foreign to their habits of service; his ability in applying the unconnected power of resource possessed by the contingent in aid of the general supplies of the army; and the important assistance he gave with the corps of his highness the Nizam's regular infantry, under his command; are valuable points of service, entitling Capt. Malcolm to the notice of your Hon. Court.

"In consequence of the honourable testimony of the Com.-in-Chief, we conveyed to Capt. Malcolm our public thanks for the zeal, ability, and judgment, which he had shewn in the discharge of extensive duties of great political importance and delicacy."

After the fall of Seringapatam, Capt. Malcolm was appointed, jointly with Capt. (now Maj.-Gen. Sir Thomas) Munro, secretary to the commissioners, to whom was entrusted the adjustment of the affairs, and division of the territories of Mysore, and the investiture of the young Rajah with the government of that country.

Shortly after the termination of the Mysore war, and the arrangements of the conquered territory were completed, it was deemed expedient that a mission should proceed from the Supreme government of India to Baba Khan, in order to ascertain the intentions and power of that prince, and more particularly of Zemaun Shaw; and, under the apprehension that the latter was meditating the invasion of Hindostan, to engage the court of Persia to act with vigour and decision against either him or the French, should either attempt to penetrate to India through any part of the Persian territories. For this service, involving the most essential interests of the East India Company, Capt. Malcolm was selected, and ordered to quit Hyderabad, in Oct. 1799, and proceed to Bombay, there to embark for Persia, and, should the season admit of it, to touch at Muscat, in his way thither, in order to endeavour to adjust any points relating to the British interests at that place, which the Bombay government should recommend to his attention.

Capt. M. reported, on the 1st Feb. 1800, to the Gov.-Gen. his arrival at Bushire, and his having concluded an agreement with the Imaum of Muscat, which provided for the future residence there of an English gentleman in the capacity of agent of the British government; and on the 20th Feb. 1801 he transmitted to Bengal copies of two treaties which he had concluded with Persia, the one political, the other commercial. Capt. M. reached Bombay, on his return from Persia, 12th May 1801, and arrived in Calcutta in Sept. following, when he was appointed private secretary to the Gov.-Gen. The success of his mission is thus stated to the secret committee by Lord Wellesley :—

" He had succeeded," observes his lordship, " in accomplishing every object of his mission, and in establishing a connexion with the actual government of the Persian empire, which promised to the interests of the British nation in India, political and commercial advantages of the most important description." After referring to the stipulations of the treaties, his lordship adds, " Your committee will further have the satisfaction to observe, that these important advantages have been obtained without any sacrifice whatever, either of interest or of honour, on the part of the British government. The issue of Capt. Malcolm's negociations with the Imaum of Muscat, has proved highly advantageous to the interests of the British nation. The importance of cultivating a good understanding with the government of Muscat, is sufficiently obvious, and the arrangements which have taken place with that government, through the agency of Capt. Malcolm, may be expected to ensure all the benefits of which that connexion is susceptible. The intercourse which Capt. Malcolm held with the Pacha of Bagdad, appears to have produced on the mind of that prince an impression extremely favourable to the British interests, and to have laid the foundation of future essential advantages, intimately connected with the alliance so happily contracted with the court of Persia." After further adverting to the great public advantages which had resulted from Capt. M.'s mission, as well as to those which might be expected to ensue from it, his lordship observes, in conclusion, " I anxiously solicit the particular attention of the honourable committee, and the Court of Directors, to the ability, firmness, temper, and dignity, which have distinguished Capt. Malcolm's conduct throughout the whole course of the arduous and important duties committed to his charge*.

On the decease of the Persian ambassador, Hajeh Kulleel Khan, who was accidentally shot at Bombay in 1802, Maj. Malcolm was immediately dispatched to that presidency, invested with authority to conduct all affairs respecting the embassy from the King of Persia to the British government, and to make every necessary communication to the King of Persia and his minister; also, with instructions to console, and, as far as possible, compensate the family and relatives of the deceased ambassador, and to make the necessary arrangements for their return to Persia. The Bombay government were instructed upon this occasion to receive Maj. M. at Bombay, with the honours due to an envoy to any foreign state, from the supreme British authority in India. In Aug. 1802 Maj. M. quitted Bengal for Bombay, and returned in Nov., having, as is stated in a letter from Bengal to the Secret Committee, " completely succeeded in accomplishing the objects of his mission without subjecting the Hon. Company to any considerable expence, or imposing any important permanent burthen on the Hon. Company's finances." " Every measure which prudence and policy could dictate in the actual situation of affairs," the Bengal government further observe, " has been adopted under the authority vested in that officer, for the regulation of all points con-

---

* The Gov.-Gen. in advising the Court of Directors of the result of Capt. M.'s mission to Persia, in which he had been accompanied by four assistants, further stated, that his lordship's object in connecting so many assistants with the mission was not only to provide for the possible contingencies of so distant an expedition, but also with a view to the education of a suitable number of the Company's junior servants in the diplomatic line. This measure and its object were both highly approved by the Court of Directors.

nected with the Persian embassy." " The Gov.-Gen.," it is added, " is of opinion, that Maj. Malcolm has manifested a degree of judgment, ability, and zeal, in the discharge of the duties of his mission, which merits the highest approbation of this government, and the Gov.-Gen. in Council deems it to be his duty to recommend the merits and services of that able officer, on this important delicate occasion, to the distinguished notice of your Hon. Committee and the Hon. Court of Directors."

In Nov. 1802, while Maj. Malcolm was at Bombay, Gov. Duncan received a communication from the Peishwa, stating the extremity to which he was reduced by the intrigues of Jeswunt Rao Holkar, and requesting an asylum in the British territories. Before any answer was returned to this letter, it was judged proper to consult Maj. Malcolm, who, at the request of the government, communicated to them his detailed sentiments on the conduct which he judged it advisable for them to pursue on that occasion; and it appears from a letter addressed by the Bombay government to the Resident at Poonah, on the 4th Nov., conveying instructions for his guidance, " that all their proceedings on this subject had had the concurrence, and been indeed suggested in their course and purport by Maj. Malcolm." It further appears from a minute* recorded by Gov. Duncan, dated 5th Sept. 1803, that he had derived great assistance from the accidental presence and co-operation of Maj. Malcolm, in preparing instructions for the army in Guzerat.

Maj. Malcolm was nominated, in Feb. 1803, by the Gov.-Gen. to the Residency of Mysore, in the room of the late Mr. Webbe, who was transferred to Nagpore. The considerations which led to this officer's

* *Extract.*—" Under these circumstances, and the earnest wish I entertain to adopt such a line of conduct as may in general consonance to my own judgment, meet also the sentiments of the supreme government, I have availed myself of the accidental presence here of Maj. Malcolm, late private secretary to his Exc. the most noble the Gov.-Gen. (whose minute acquaintance with all the military objects at issue, joined to his accurate information of our political circumstances in Guzerat, enable him so well to afford advice on the present occasion,) to confer with him on the subject, the result of which has been our concurrence in the accompanying draft of instructions."

selection for this appointment, are thus stated in a letter from Lord Wellesley to the Madras government: " It is indispensably necessary, that the person who may be nominated to that situation should be intimately acquainted with the conditions and interests of the several states and chieftains composing the Mahratta empire, with the whole course of the late transactions in the Deccan, and with my views and sentiments with regard to the whole system of our political arrangements in that quarter of India. The complete information possessed by Maj. Malcolm in all these important points, added to the zeal, judgment, and ability, which have distinguished the conduct of that officer, in various important political stations, qualify him in a peculiar degree for the situation of Resident at Mysore." Maj. Malcolm quitted Calcutta for Fort St. George, whither it was previously the intention of the Gov.-Gen. to have proceeded in person: but his lordship observed, in the conclusion of the above quoted letter, " that his absence at such a crisis would be supplied in a considerable degree by the communication which Maj. Malcolm would be enabled to make to the Fort St. George government."

On the 1st March 1803, Maj. Malcolm received the appointment of Resident at Mysore from the Madras government, by whom it was considered unnecessary to furnish him with any specific instructions for his guidance in the immediate duties of the residency. Towards the close of the same month Lord Clive recorded a minute, in which, adverting to the extensive acquaintance of Maj. Malcolm with Lord Wellesley's sentiments, relative to the political interests of the British government in the then crisis of Mahratta affairs, he states, that he had, in compliance with his lordship's wishes, determined to employ the abilities of Maj. Malcolm on such affairs of a political nature, as the advance of the British troops into the Mahratta territory might give rise to. Maj. M. was accordingly directed to proceed to the headquarters of Lieut.-Gen. Stuart, who was recommended to repose that confidence in him " to which he was entitled by his great public services, by his distinguished zeal, and by his extensive experience."

Shortly afterwards, Maj. Malcolm joined the detachment of the army nder Maj.-Gen. Wellesley, at whose request he accompanied the force to Poonah, in order to assist the Maj.-Gen. in the adoption of measures for the conciliation of the Peishwa's southern Rajahs, Soidars, and Jageerdars, respecting whom he prepared, and in April transmitted to Lord Clive, a memorandum containing a full description of their political influence and numerical force. It is further to be observed, that the late Sir Barry Close conducted some of his personal discussions with the Mahrattas jointly, and with the assistance of Maj. Malcolm.

Maj. Malcolm was sent, in Jan. 1804, from the camp of Maj.-Gen. Wellesley on a mission to the court of Dowlut Rao Scindia, in whose camp he arrived on the 11th of that month, and with whom, on the 27th Feb. following, he concluded a treaty of defensive alliance and subsidy. Lord Wellesley, after communicating this event to the Secret Committee, adds, " I beg leave to offer my most sincere congratulations to the Hon. Committee and the Hon. Court, upon the prosperous conclusion of this important treaty, which has been established on principles highly advantageous to the British interests and honourable to the British characters."

On the 14th May, Maj. M. was compelled, by ill health, to quit Scindia's camp, but not till he had vindicated the honour of the British government upon the occasion of an insult being offered to it by Scindia's Durbar. He obtained the particular commendation of the Gov.-Gen. for the " judgment and firmness" he evinced on this occasion. Maj. M. proceeded to Mysore, whence he was called to Calcutta with all possible dispatch, on the 11th March 1805, for the reasons assigned in the following extract of a letter from the Bengal government to the Secret Committee, dated May 31, 1805:—

" The Gov.-Gen. in Council deems it proper to intimate to your Hon. Committee, in this place, that the Gov.-Gen. being desirous of receiving personally from Lieut.-Col. Malcolm, the Resident at Mysore, information on various points connected with the political interests of the British government, which that officer's employment in the field with Maj.-Gen. the Hon. Sir A. Wellesley, and subsequently at the Court of Dowlut Rao Scindia, has enabled him to acquire, had directed Lieut.-Col. M., in the month of March, to proceed to Fort William with the least practicable delay; and that, in consequence of Col. Close's detention at Nagpore, and the probability that circumstances might occur to prevent the prosecution of his journey to the camp of Dowlut Rao Scindia, the Gov.-Gen. had determined to supply the eventual defect of Col. Close's able agency at the court of Dowlut Rao Scindia, by dispatching Lieut.-Col. Malcolm to his Highness's camp. Lieut.-Col. M. arrived at the presidency of Fort William on the 15th April; and the Gov.-Gen. having judged it proper, previously to that date, to invest Col. Close with the general controul of military and political affairs in the Deccan, Lieut.-Col. M. was directed to proceed to the head-quarters of the British army, eventually to be dispatched to the Court of Dowlut Rao Scindia, for the purpose of conducting such negociations as might be prescribed directly by the orders of the Gov.-Gen., or by the instructions of his Exc. the Com.-in-Chief, under the Gov.-Gen.'s authority."

Lieut.-Col. M., shortly after his arrival at the head-quarters of the Bengal army, received instructions from Lord Lake to take charge of the office of the Gov.-Gen.'s agent, vacant by the departure of Mr. Mercer for Fort William; and from this time, June 1805, to March 1806, he continued with the Bengal army, occupied in the performance of the most active and responsible political duties, among which were the following:—The conclusion, on the 22d Nov. 1805, under the direction of Lord Lake, of a new treaty of amity and alliance with Dowlut Rao Scindia, which stipulated the cession of Gualior and Gohud to Scindia; and, by the final adjustment of boundaries, removed some doubts and misunderstandings which had arisen respecting the meaning of the former treaty. The conclusion, on the 24th Dec. following, of a treaty of peace and alliance with Jeswunt Rao Holkar; and, in Jan. 1806, of a treaty of amity with the Sikh chieftains, Rumjeet Sing and Futtch Sing, with a view to induce the Sikhs to break off their connexion with Holkar. In a letter to Lord Wellesley, upon the former of these treaties, Lord Lake observed, " Though aware how unnecessary it is to call your attention to the merits of Lieutenant-Colonel Malcolm, I feel it a justice to that officer to state the very high sense I entertain of his services on this important occasion." His lordship further observed, " To the personal influence which Lieut.-Col. M., had, during his former residence at the Court of Dowlut Rao Scindia, established over the mind of that chief and his principal officers, and to the full confidence they repose in his character, I attribute, in a very great degree, the happy commencement of the late negociation; and, from the documents I have already transmitted, you can perfectly judge how much his experience and ability have contributed to its favourable conclusion; and you will, I am sure, concur with me in thinking that this officer has, on the present occasion, greatly augmented his claims on the Hon. Company and his country, to whose favourable notice I feel confident you will derive satisfaction in recommending the distinguished services of this valuable officer." Lord Wellesley, in his reply, stated, that " He entertained a due sense of the exertions of Lieut.-Col. Malcolm in effecting the adjustment of all subjects of difference between the British government and Dowlut Rao Scindia." On the 2d treaty, that with Jeswunt Rao Holkar, Lord Lake observed, " I feel it my duty again to call your attention to the exertions of Lieut.-Col. Malcolm, by whose knowledge and abilities this treaty has been negociated under my direction, and whose many and important services will, I trust, meet that recompense to which I consider them so justly entitled."

Lord Lake, on the 29th March 1806, in a letter to the Gov.-Gen. in Council, stated, that several political discussions with Holkar, combined with the numerous unsettled points respecting the irregulars, had obliged him to detain Lieut.-Col. Malcolm at his head-quarters longer than he intended, but that he was then enabled to permit him to proceed to Fort William. In acknowledging this letter, the Bengal government observed, " We have great pleasure in expressing our high approbation of the activity, diligence, ability, and judgment, manifested by Lieut.-Col. Malcolm in the discharge of the arduous and laborious duties connected with the arrangements for the reduction of the irregular troops, and for the assignment of rewards and provisions for such individuals as had received promises or had established claims upon the government, by their conduct during the war; and we concur in opinion with your lordship, that Lieut.-Col. M. has accomplished the objects of your lordship's orders in a manner highly honourable to the reputation, and advantageous to the interests of the British government, and we consider that officer to have rendered important public services, by his indefatigable and successful exertions in the accomplishment of these important arrangements. We entirely approve of your lordship's intention of permitting Lieut.-Col. M. to return to the presidency when his services shall no longer be required by your lordship."

On his return to the presidency, Lieut.-Col. M. having addressed to the Bengal government a statement, shewing the great amount of extra expences which he had been obliged to incur during the various missions and diplomatic duties he had been called upon to perform in the preceding five years, and soliciting some remuneration, a brief review* of his services was submitted, by Sir George Barlow and

---

* " On the occasion of Lieut.-Col. Malcolm's return to the presidency, preparatory to his proceeding to resume his situation of *Resident at Mysore*, after having been an active instrument in the conclusion of peace with the Mahrattas, and in the complete settlement of affairs in Hindostan, we consider it an act of justice to that meritorious officer, to submit to the recollection of your honourable Committee the various important duties in which he has been engaged during the last five years. Since his return from his embassy to Persia in 1801, independently of private secretary to the Gov.-Gen., to which he was appointed in Sept. 1801, and which he resigned in March 1803, and of his present situation of Resident at Mysore, to which he was nominated on resigning the former office, Lieut.-Col. M. has been employed in the following extra missions: — A mission to Fort St. George, in Jan. 1802, for the purpose of explaining to the government of that presidency the sentiments of the Gov.-Gen. on a variety of important points connected with the general affairs of India at that period. A mission to Bombay, in Sept. 1802, for the purpose of consoling the relations and attendants of the late Persian ambassador, Rajee Khuleel Khan, and of making every arrangement necessary for their return to their own country, and every communication regarding the melancholy occurrence of the ambassador's death to the king of Persia and his ministers. In Feb. 1803 Lieut.-Col. M. was deputed to Fort St. George, charged with communications of the highest importance to the government of that presidency, by which he was immediately nominated Resident at Mysore, and directed to join Lieut.-Col. Stuart, who was with the army on the frontier of that province. On his arrival Lieut.-Col. M. was directed to join the Hon. Maj.-Gen. Wellesley, then on his march towards Poonah, with a considerable force under his command. Lieut.-Col. M. continued with the Hon. Maj.-Gen. Wellesley during the war,

Council, to the Secret Committee, and accompanied by a recommendation for some extra allowance, in consideration of the expences to which he had been subjected by his exertions in the public service; and in compliance with which, and a subsequent recommendation transmitted to the Court of Directors, when he came to England in 1812, they resolved to present him with the sum of 50,000 Sicca rupees, with interest from the period of his quitting India. This sum was accordingly presented to him in 1814, the grant having previously received the sanction of the general court of proprietors.

In March 1807, Lieut.-Col. M. arrived at Fort St. George, on the way to the resumption of his residency of Mysore; in the performance of the duties of which appointment he did not long continue, the political state of Europe, and the increased power and extensive projects of Buonaparte, having, towards the close of the year, furnished fresh occasion for his employment as a diplomatist. Intelligence of the French design of invading India through Persia, and that the invaders would probably be supported in it by the Turkish and Persian states, reached the Gov.-Gen., Lord Minto, late in 1807; in consequence of which, his lordship appointed Lieut.-Col. M. to be the Gov.-Gen.'s political agent, and to be vested with plenipotentiary powers in Persia, the Persian Gulph, and in Turkish Arabia. By

except about three months, during which period he was compelled to be absent by severe illness, solely occasioned by excessive fatigue, and great exposure to the climate. At the conclusion of the peace with Dowlut Rao Scindia, Lieut.-Col. M. was deputed to the court of that chieftain, in Jan. 1804, and remained in the exercise of the duties of Resident at Scindia's court till June of the same year, when he was relieved by the late Mr. Webbe. In April 1805, a few weeks after his return to Mysore, Lieut.-Col. Malcolm was called to this presidency, and on his arrival was appointed to proceed on a mission to the court of Dowlut Rao Scindia, but directed immediately to join the Right Hon. Lord Lake, and to place himself under his lordship's orders. Lieut.-Col. M. joined his lordship in the beginning of June 1805, and continued with the army during the ensuing campaign. The records of the government, and the distinguished approbation of the several authorities under whom Lieut.-Col. M. has acted, afford an honourable testimony of the value of his services, and we cannot, in justice, withhold the expression of our opinion, that the zeal and exertions of Lieut.-Col. M., in the discharge of the arduous duties of those various employments, entitle him to some public mark of the favourable consideration of the Honourable Court."

this appointment, the powers of separate political agency possessed by the Residents at Bagdad, Bussorah, and Bushire, were suspended, and Lieut.-Col. M. was authorized, at any time when he might judge it to be expedient for the benefit of the public service, to take upon himself the powers of Resident at any of those stations. He was also, in addition to his powers as political agent, furnished with credentials as envoy or ambassador to the court of Persia, and to the Pacha of Bagdad, in the event of his finding it practicable or expedient, to repair in person to either or both of those courts. In proposing this appointment, Lord Minto described Lieut.-Col. M. as an officer " in whose talents, zeal, judgment, and ability, entire confidence might be reposed," and as one, who, in his lordship's opinion, if vested with special powers, might be enabled, " by means of personal influence and address, and by negociation on the part of the British government in India, to alienate from their attachment to the interests of France those states of Persia which appeared disposed to support the designs of that nation against the British government in India."

Lieut.-Col. M., on the 17th April 1808, quitted Bombay for the Persian Gulph, and arrived at Bushire on the 10th May, from which place he transmitted to the Bengal government a paper, by them considered and represented to the Court of Directors as " a very able historical review of the late intrigues of the French in Persia, and of the military operations of Russia in the north-west frontier of that kingdom." The ascendancy which the French government had acquired in the councils of the Persian monarch having, however, rendered all attempts to procure the reception of the British mission unavailing, except through means, which Lieut.-Col. M. stated at full length in his despatches, he deemed derogatory to the British character, this officer resolved on immediately quitting Bushire, and returning to Calcutta (leaving his Sec. Capt. Pasley, to act in any emergency) for the purpose of affording the Gov.-Gen., in person, full information respecting the then existing state of affairs in Persia, and of consulting with his lordship upon the most expedient measures to be adopted in consequence thereof by the British government in India. On the

20th Aug. Lieut.-Col. M. arrived at Calcutta: his return was approved by the Bengal government, although they did not concur in the propriety of some of his anterior proceedings. The Gov.-Gen. in council, nevertheless, observed as follows:—" Notwithstanding the total failure of our views in Persia, the general tone of his (Lieut.-Col. M.'s) measures has vindicated the dignity and honour of the British government."

The Bengal government having, in Nov. 1808, determined to send an expedition to the Persian Gulph, consisting of a military force of about 2000 men, Lieut.-Col. M. was selected to conduct it, and vested with the same diplomatic powers as were conferred upon him on his former mission. In addition thereto the separate commission of Brig.-Gen., which had also been given to him on his former mission to the Persian Gulph, was ordered to be considered as being still in force, and he was invested with the command of the troops to be employed upon this occasion. When the expedition, in Feb. 1809, was on the point of sailing from Bombay, advices were received from Europe, which Lieut.-Col. M. conceived might cause an alteration in the views of the Bengal government, and he therefore resolved to delay his departure until the arrival of further instructions from that presidency. Lord Minto on the 27th Feb. transmitted to Lieut.-Col. M. the required instructions, which directed the entire abandonment of the projected expedition, to which his lordship added an expression of " his high sense of the disinterested regard for the good of the public service, evinced by Brig.-Gen. M., in resolving to suspend his departure from Bombay until apprized of the Gov.-Gen.'s sentiments regarding the expediency of prosecuting the expedition, under the altered state of circumstances which had taken place." His lordship further complimented him for " having manifested the prevalence of a solicitude for the interests of the public service, over a natural and laudable incitement to exercise the duties of a high and important station, and preferred considerations of public expediency to the allurements of a just and honourable ambition." He was then directed to proceed to his residency at Mysore, and Lord Minto in thus dispensing with his services, again declared it to be " an obligation of justice to express the acknowledgments of the Bengal government for the zeal and alacrity with which he had undertaken and discharged the arduous and responsible duties assigned to him, and the high sense entertained of his distinguished talents and abilities, and of the ardent spirit of patriotism with which he had employed them in the service of his country, and of the benefits which government had derived from his knowledge, experience, and active exertions." The Secret Committee, adverting to the circumstance of his having suspended his departure from Bombay, until the receipt of the further instructions from Bengal, declared it to be " a determination which they noticed with great satisfaction, as founded in the exercise of a sound judgment and discretion.

The state of affairs in Persia being considered by the Gov.-Gen., in Oct. 1809, to be such as again to render the presence of Brig.-Gen. Malcolm in that country expedient, provided that assurances were received of his suitable reception, he was reappointed Envoy to the Persian and Arabian courts, and early in 1810 quitted Bombay for Persia. Upon his arrival, in Feb., at Bushire, he assumed, in obedience to his instructions, the functions of Envoy Plenipotentiary on the part of the British government in India, to the court of his Persian majesty, where he met with a most gracious and distinguished reception. He remained, however, but a short time in the Persian camp, having requested leave to depart, on hearing the nomination, in Europe, of Sir Gore Ouseley, to be H. M.'s ambassador at the court of Persia. The King of Persia expressed his regret at the early departure of this officer, and instituted the Persian Order* of the Lion

---

* The Order of the Sun, which was the first of this description ever in Persia, was presented to Gen. Gerdanne, the French ambassador, and offered to Sir Harford Jones, envoy from His Britannic Majesty, who refused it because it was created for the representative of an enemy. Sir J. Malcolm, on the same offer being made, declined it on the ground that Sir Harford Jones had done so; when the King of Persia, declaring his first English friend must have a mark of his favour, instituted the Order of the Lion and Sun, which is the arms of Persia.

and Sun, to bestow it upon him; H. M. presented him with the star* of this order, ornamented with diamonds, and a sword, and also nominated him to be a Khan and Sepahdar of the empire†.

On the 6th Oct. 1810, while at Bagdad, on his return from Persia, Brig.-Gen. M. transmitted to the Bengal government his final report on the affairs of that kingdom, with an account of its geography, internal government, policy, resources, and condition, and accompanied by a map, geographical memoir, and abstracts of the merits of different officers employed under his orders. The receipt of this report was acknowledged by the Bengal government, in May 1811, in terms expressive of their highest satisfaction. In addressing the Secret Committee, they observed on " the highly meritorious qualities of temper, moderation, discretion, and ability," manifested by this officer, " under circumstances peculiarly delicate and embarrassing," and add, " while he has successfully vindicated the just pretensions of the local government of India to rank and consideration at the court of Persia, he preserved a scrupulous regard to the dignity of H. M. mission, and not only established a concert and unity of proceeding with Sir Harford Jones, but afforded to him the lights of his judgment and local knowledge, on points referred by Sir H. Jones to his consideration, in a manner highly satisfactory to that gentleman, and advantageous to the interests of the public service; and we confidentially trust that your Hon. Committee will appreciate in the same degree the merits of Brig.-Gen. M.'s conduct in this situation."

Brig.-Gen. Malcolm reached Bombay, on his return from Persia, 29th Nov. 1810, at which presidency he obtained the permission of the Bengal government to continue‡ till his embarkation from thence

---

* His acceptance of the present was sanctioned in Feb. 1813.

† For the impression made throughout Persia, and upon all ranks, by Sir J. Malcolm in his different missions to that court, see the Travels of Sir Robert Ker Porter, vol i. p. 379.

‡ The object of this officer's residence at Bombay was the compilation of an historical account of Persia, and of all the countries between the Araxes and Indus, which had been visited by him, or travelled over by the officers attached to his mission, to be pre-

for Europe, 19th Jan. 1812. His arrival in this country in July following, was accompanied by a review* of his services, and recommen-sented to His Majesty's ministers and to the Court of Directors. For this purpose, the Bengal government granted him an allowance of 2000 rupees per month for an establishment, which was afterwards approved by the Court of Directors; and the materials thus arranged were ultimately formed into a " History of Persia from the most early period," which was published by Sir John Malcolm, in England, in 2 vols. 4to., in 1815.

The following works had been previously published by this officer: 'Sketch of the Political History of India, from the introduction of Mr. Pitt's Bill, A.D. 1784, to the present date, 1811,' 1 vol. 8vo; ' Sketch of the Sikhs,' 1 vol. 8vo., 1812, (first published in the 11th vol. of the Asiatic Researches); and ' Observations on the Disturbances in the Madras Army in 1809,' in 2 parts, 8vo. He has just published Memoirs of ' Central India, including Malwa and the adjoining Provinces.'

* To the Hon. the Court of Directors, &c.

" HONOURABLE SIRS,—1st. The high estimation in which we hold the merits and services of Lieut.-Col. Malcolm coincides with the ordinary obligation of our public duty in leading us to bring under the special notice of your Hon. Court the enclosed copy of a letter addressed to us by that officer on the eve of his departure for Europe, stating his pretensions to a compensation for losses sustained by him in the execution of the various and important duties assigned to him during the last thirteen years, and the grounds on which he is led to hope that your Hon. Court may be disposed to entertain a favourable opinion of his claim to reward, for his long, laborious, and successful exertions in the service of the Hon. Company; and soliciting the support of our recommendation of these his claims and pretensions to the liberality of your Hon. Court.

" 2d. The degree in which we have deemed it within the limits of our province to afford him that solicited support, will appear from the enclosed copy of the Gov.-Gen's reply to the letter above described, and the object of this address might be perhaps essentially fulfilled by simply referring your Hon. Court to a perusal of that document, and recognizing the testimony therein afforded to the high sense which we entertain of the extent and value of his services; but we should inadequately satisfy the impulse of our sentiments by thus closing our communication on the subject now submitted to the consideration of your Hon. Court; and without exceeding the limits which we have prescribed to ourselves on this occasion, we may be permitted to manifest that degree of interest in Lieut.-Col. Malcolm's prosperity, which is naturally excited in one's mind by a recollection of his zealous, faithful, and able exertions in the ministerial duty of carrying into effect many of the most important measures and objects of the present administration, combined with a retrospect of his antecedent labours and services in situations of peculiar delicacy, difficulty, and responsibility, to which he was called by the discernment and confidence of our predecessors.

" 3d. The whole course of our reports, and the addresses of the Gov.-Gen. to the Hon. the Secret Committee of your Hon. Court, relative to the affairs of Persia, exhibit both the arduous nature of the duties in which Lieut.-Col. M. has been employed under the present

dation for a reward, contained in a letter from the Bengal government to the Court of Directors, dated 19th May 1812, which led to the grant of the 50,000 rupees mentioned in p. 479. Shortly after his arrival he received the honour of knighthood from His Majesty. He continued in this country till 1816; and during his residence the important subject of the renewal of the East India Company's charter having come under the consideration of Parliament, he was called to give evidence, in April and May 1813, before a committee of the House of Lords, and before the House of Commons, upon the various points then under discussion. The evidence which he gave on these occasions appears, by the reports of it printed by order of Parliament, to have embraced the following topics:—The religion, character, and habits of the natives of Hindostan, both within and without the Company's territories; the effects of European intercourse upon them; the possible consequences of colonization; the nature

government, and our sense of his ability and ardent zeal in the execution of them. The public advantages of Lieut.-Col. M.'s agency have also been enhanced by the extensive and valuable information relative to Persia, which his industry and talents enabled him to accumulate under all the solicitude and occupation of his diplomatic duties. Much of it has already appeared on the records of this government, and been brought under the notice of the Secret Committee and of your Hon. Court, and we are led to expect that a far greater mass of historical and political information will have resulted from the literary labours, which Lieut.-Col. M. was enabled to prosecute, by the indulgence granted to him of residing at Bombay for the express purpose of arranging the materials acquired in Persia, as reported in the Vice President in Council's address to your Hon. Court of 27th July 1811."

" 4th. The sentiments of the late Gov.-Gen. in Council, Sir G. Barlow, relative to the merits and services of Lieut.-Col. M., were submitted to the Hon. Committee in the 390th and following paragraphs of his address of 20th Aug. 1806; and the claim which, at that period of time, Lieut.-Col. M. preferred to a compensation for losses by the nature of his public employments, were then submitted to the favourable consideration of the Hon. Committee. We advert to this recommendation merely as it contains (what perhaps we are not strictly entitled to afford) an honourable testimony to the value of services, which relate to the period of former administrations, and to which Lieut.-Col. M. has specifically appealed."

" 5th. We hope we shall not presume too far, nor be thought disposed to encroach on your Hon. Court, in the gracious office of distributing favour and reward to your old and meritorious servants, if we so far yield to the impulse of our own feelings, as to submit the application of Lieut.-Col. Malcolm, transmitted with this despatch, to your favourable consideration.

(Signed) "MINTO, G. NUGENT, J. LUMSDEN, H. COLEBROOKE."

and extent of the traffic which is carried on in all parts of India, and the probable consequences of an open trade. Upon all these points Sir John stated his opinions at length, supported by a variety of facts which had come under his personal observation during his thirteen missions to the different Native states and courts of India.

The Bengal government were advised of this officer's return to India in 1816 by the following notice from the Court of Directors:—

"We have permitted brevet Col. Sir John Malcolm, K. C. B., to return with his rank upon the Fort St. George establishment. Although there can be no doubt that the high character which Sir John Malcolm has maintained through a long series of years, and particularly in the discharge of the duties of various important missions, will secure to him the favourable notice of your government; yet, in order to manifest the sense we ourselves entertain of this gentleman, we are induced to recommend him for an employment suitable to his rank and former services."

Sir John Malcolm having arrived in Bengal early in 1817, he was immediately attached, as the Gov.-Gen.'s political agent, to the force under Lieut.-Gen. Sir T. Hislop, then about to commence important operations in the Deccan. In the instructions issued to this officer on this occasion, the Bengal government observe, " It has been judged to be for the benefit of the public service, that his Exc. should have at his command the assistance of a Political Agent of character, experience, and ability, to be a channel of correspondence with the Residents at the courts of the allied Princes, and to be employed by his Exc. in the conduct of such political arrangements and negociations with the Native powers, or chiefs, with whom the course of events may bring him into communication, as he may be empowered to prosecute. The Gov.-Gen. in council, reposing entire confidence in your zeal, ability, and knowledge of our political interests generally, and in your personal acquaintance with the character, habits, and temper of the several powers and chiefs in the Deccan, is happy to avail himself of your services in this important duty." With a view to place Sir John Malcolm, in the exercise of the functions thus assigned to him, on an equal footing, in point of military rank, with the officers commanding divisions of the army under Sir T. Hislop, the Gov.-Gen. again conferred upon this officer the brevet rank of brig.-gen. Under this appointment, he was instructed by the Bengal government to procced to Madras, and place himself under the orders of Sir T. Hislop, and either to accompany him to the Deccan, or precede him, and visit the several Native courts, for the purpose of obtaining, by confidential communications with the Residents, such information as might be useful for his Exc. to possess. He was placed upon the same footing, as to allowances, &c. as the Residents at those courts: he was also to be supplied with carriages and equipments by the Madras government, and to have Maj. Agnew as an assistant.

Having equipped himself at Fort St. George, he proceeded, in the first place, to Bangalore, in order to concert arrangements for the co-operation of the troops of the Rajah of Mysore, which he found had been already accomplished by Mr. Cole, the resident. He thence proceeded to Hyderabad, to acquaint himself with the military resources of that state, and to secure the support of the Nizam's troops during the forthcoming operations. From Hyderabad he went to Poonah, to concert arrangements with the Resident connected with the approaching service; he reached Poonah on the 8th Aug., and from thence proceeded, on the Peishwa's invitation, to Mehowly, the place where his highness then resided, and with whom he had several conferences, in which Sir John fully elicited the hostile state of the Peishwa's feelings towards the British government, notwithstanding the treaty he had so lately (13th June preceding) concluded with it. Sir John Malcolm's reports of his conferences with the Peishwa were particularly pointed out to the Court of Directors, as affording the means of judging of the course of policy which was afterwards so successfully adopted towards him; and Sir John was informed by the Bengal government, that the topics of discourse chosen by him in his discussions with the Peishwa, and the tone and language in which they were urged, reflected credit on his judgment and discrimination. From Poonah he proceeded to Hyderabad, where he continued a short time, for the purpose of obtaining information regarding the resources of the country, and of making an arrangement with the local government. Having accomplished this object, he quitted Hyderabad on the 4th Sept., and proceeded to Nagpore for the same purpose.

In the war which followed the defection of the Peishwa, Sir. J. Malcolm was appointed to command the third division of the army. On the 25th Sept. Capt. Grant, under the orders of this officer, took Talym by surprise; the garrison of which place, with the exception of one individual (Wahab Khan, the adopted son of one of the principal chiefs), was disarmed, by Sir John's orders, and set at liberty. Early in Dec. he joined Sir T. Hislop at Ougein, and on the 21st of that month the battle of Mehidpoor was fought, and followed by the complete defeat and dispersion of the hostile army, under Mulhar Rao Holkar, which was pursued for eight days by the cavalry and light troops under Sir J. Malcolm. The following remarks are in the general order issued by the Com.-in-Chief upon the field of battle:— " His Exc. must here notice the undaunted gallantry with which the charge was made upon the guns, under the conduct and direction of Brig.-Gen. Sir J. Malcolm."—" The Com.-in-Chief would not feel himself justified were he to omit his warmest thanks and acknowledgments to Brig.-Gen. Sir J. Malcolm, for the important assistance he derived throughout the day from that officer's judgment, experience, and personal exertions in conducting the assault on the left of the enemy's line." Sir T. Hislop, also, in his despatch of the 23d Dec., to the Gov.-Gen., observes, " Although the conduct of every officer of the army merits the highest commendation, I gladly seize this opportunity of bringing to your lordship's notice those who were prominent from their rank and situations, and from the superior duties they had to perform. Your lordship is too well aware of the high professional character and abilities of Brig.-Gen. Sir J. Malcolm to render it necessary for me to dwell upon them; I shall therefore merely express my admiration of the style of distinguished conduct and gallantry with which the assault on the left of the enemy's position was headed by the Brig.-Gen, and my warmest thanks for the great and essential aid I have derived from his councils, as well previous to, as during the action of, the 21st inst." In the Gov.-Gen.'s letter to the Secret Committee, dated 29th Dec., his lordship observes, " When we look to the additional instance of the important victory gained by the energy of Lieut.-Gen. Sir T. Hislop, and Brig.-Gen. Sir J. Malcolm, over Holkar's army, one cannot but feel that the hand of Providence has signally chastened the profligacy of those who forced the contest upon us by the violation of the most solemn engagements. It is unnecessary for me to expatiate on the high credit due to Sir T. Hislop and Sir J. Malcolm, or on the extraordinary benefit attending the decisive correction given to an insolence of tone, which Holkar's army had carried to a daring pitch."

Lord Hastings, adverting to the same event, in his general order of 21st Feb. 1818, says, " The chivalrous intrepidity displayed by Brig.-Gen. Sir J. Malcolm in the battle of Mehidpoor, and the admirable tact manifested by him in the subsequent negociations, advanced the public interests no less than they distinguished the individual." And in a letter to the Secret Committee, dated 8th Feb., his lordship observes, " The zeal and success of Sir T. Hislop merit your complimentary attention. Sir J. Malcolm has shewn equal valour and ability, joined to indefatigable exertion, so that his behaviour deserves cordial notice." Mr. Canning, the President of the Board of Controul, after moving the thanks of Parliament to Sir T. Hislop, who commanded at this battle*, went on to say, " And also to Sir J. Mal-

* The Prince Regent also judged this to be a proper occasion for expressing his sense of the services of the Indian army, by a liberal distribution of military honours. The distinction of a Knight Commander of the Bath was conferred upon one, and the honour of being Knight Companions upon twenty-two of the Company's officers. The exclusion of Sir J. Malcolm from a participation in the highest of these distinctions, was occasioned by it not being considered consistent with military etiquette. But the Bengal government were informed, that " His Royal Highness had condescended to express his regret that the regulations of the Order precluded the advancement of Sir John Malcolm, K.C.B. to the highest rank with his then present military rank, but that it had pleased his Royal Highness to record his gracious intention to confer the dignity of a Grand Cross upon that distinguished officer, when he shall have attained the rank of Maj.-Gen." The intentions of the Prince Regent have since been fulfilled through the medium of the present Gov.-Gen., to whom the King's instructions were transmitted early in 1821, and by his lordship forwarded to Bombay, at which presidency Sir J. Malcolm was on the 6th Sept. 1821.; and upon that day he was

colm, who was second in command on that occasion, but who is second to none in valour and renown. The name of that gallant officer will be remembered in India as long as the British flag is hoisted in that country."

The Rajah of Mysore, feeling himself under obligations to Sir J. Malcolm for his attention to the Mysore troops during the whole of the Pindarry war, resolved, as an acknowledgment of that attention, and as a token of his personal regard, to present him with a sword and belt, valued at about 500 pagodas, which were taken by his highness's Silladar horse from Mulhar Rao Holkar during the action, which gift the Bengal government permitted Sir J. Malcolm to accept.

This officer, as already stated, continued in pursuit of the fugitives after the battle of Mehidpoor, having under his command the larger part of the cav. and light troops, joined by a light detachment from the Bombay army, under Col. the Hon. Lincoln Stanhope. Coming up with the retreating force, he captured the whole of the enemy's bazar, camels, 7000 bullocks, &c., and making prisoners of the men, he immediately disarmed them, and sent them about their business. Thus vigorously encountered, Holkar gave up the contest, and signed a preliminary treaty which Sir J. Malcolm had sent to him; and on the 13th Jan. 1818, Sir John negociated, under the instructions of Sir T. Hislop, upon its basis, a treaty of peace with the vanquished chief, by which the latter made very considerable cessions and remunerations to the British government, and pledged himself to a future co-operation with the British forces.

Lord Hastings immediately after employed Sir J. Malcolm in restoring and settling the distracted government and territories of

invested with the Grand Cross of the Order of the Bath, by his Exc. Sir C. Colville, the Com.-in-Chief at Bombay, acting for the Gov.-Gen. In the address from Sir Charles on this occasion, is the following paragraph.—

"In your person, Sir John, I can, without fear of the imputation of flattery, say, that in Europe, as in Asia, and in every branch of the public service, it will be freely admitted, that the distinction is most amply and in every way earned, which has been long, and will, I hope, be much longer held up, and appreciated as the proud reward alike of diplomatic and ministerial as of military merit."

Mulhar Rao, so as to render that government, in the hands of the British, an instrument for restoring the peace of India, of which it had for a series of years been one of the most active disturbers. To this charge was added the general superintendance of the distracted states of Central India. In Feb. 1818, Scindia's general, Jeswunt Rao Bhow, and a Pindarry chief, Kurreem Khan, surrendered to Sir J. Malcolm. Several other Pindarry chiefs followed the example of the latter, and were like him treated with consideration and humanity. In this month the division of the Deccan army under Sir J. Malcolm, was separated therefrom, and placed by order of the Gov.-Gen under his lordship's immediate directions, with a view to the accomplishment of some ulterior arrangements. In April the settlement of the district of Soondwarrah, and suppression of the excesses of the freebooters therein, is mentioned by Lord Hastings as having been effected by this officer in such a manner as to entitle him to his entire approbation. "The principle," his lordship observes, "upon which Sir J. Malcolm has acted, in re-establishing the legitimate authority of several of the chiefs, is calculated to exalt the reputation of the British government, and diffuse a knowledge of its principles of action, which cannot fail to be attended with the most salutary consequences." And on the 27th May, his lordship expressed his perfect approbation of the whole of this officer's proceedings with respect to the occupation of the possessions of the late Peishwa (Bajee Rao) in the Nerbuddah. But the complete suppression of that chieftain, to whose treachery was ascribed all that had given a character of importance to the war, was, in his lordship's opinion, an object at this time of great moment, as leading, in connexion with the extirpation of the Pindarries, to the entire pacification of India. To this object, therefore, the several divisions of the army in the field applied themselves; and in the pursuit of it, Sir J. Malcolm very early obtained the most accurate information respecting Bajee Rao's movements; by which means he was completely surrounded on the 30th of that month, then retaining under his command a force which did not exceed 2000 horse, 800 infantry, and 2 guns. Thus circumstanced, he resolved upon negociation, and sent two vakeels to Sir J. Malcolm, who proposed a personal conference, which was agreed to. The particulars of this conference are stated in Sir John's letter to the secretary to the Bengal government, dated June 3, 1818. Its result was, the peaceable surrender, to Sir J. Malcolm, of the fallen prince, upon an agreement that he should be allowed to reside in the British dominions, and there to enjoy a revenue of eight lacs of rupees per annum. The surrender of Bajee Rao was followed by the entire dispersion of his followers*.

By the fall of Bajee Rao the Company not only obtained a large accession of territory, but treasure to a considerable amount. It was also attended with the more important consequences of restoring complete peace to the countries of which he was sovereign, and of destroying the hopes and plans of those attached to his cause, or who still used his name as a pretext for their continued depredations. Lord Hastings indeed stated some objection to the terms, as having been granted by Sir J. Malcolm without specific authority; at the same time that his lordship expressed most decidedly a general approbation of Sir John's conduct in the war. This diversity of opinion, between the Gov.-Gen. and his political agent, gave rise to discussions that subsequently came under the consideration of the Court of Direc-

---

* In reporting this event to the Court of Directors, Lord Hastings observes, (letter 20th June 1818), " Bajee Rao having submitted and placed himself in the hands of Brig.-Gen. Sir J. Malcolm, I have the honour to congratulate you on the termination of what still bore a lingering character of war. The troops with which Bajee Rao had crossed the Tafty were completely surrounded. He found progress towards Gualior impracticable, retreat as much so, and opposition to the British force altogether hopeless; so that any terms granted to him under such circumstances were purely gratuitous, and only referable to that humanity which it was felt your Hon. Court would be desirous should be shewn to an exhausted foe. The ability with which Brig.-Gen. Sir J. Malcolm first secured the passes of the hills, and then advanced to confine Bajee Rao in front, while Brig.-Gen. Doveton closed upon him from the rear, will not fail to be applauded by your Hon. Court; nor will you less estimate the moderation with which Sir J. Malcolm held forth the assurance of liberal and decorous treatment, even to an enemy stained with profligate treachery, when that enemy could no longer make resistance. Bajee Rao is to reside as a private individual in some city within your ancient possessions, probably Benares, enjoying an allowance suited to a person of high birth, but without other pretensions."

tors, who resolved to approve the course which Sir John had adopted, considering that the circumstances in which he was placed authorised him to exercise his discretion. "This difference of opinion," it is added in the Court of Directors' letter, "does not extend to any of the military arrangements, which must be admitted to demand unqualified applause; neither is there any question respecting the zeal and public spirit, and the indefatigable and skilful exertions of Sir J. Malcolm, in the very prominent part which he took in the transaction."

The next service of this officer was the suppression of the mutiny of the Arabs in Bajee Rao's service, and in which he completely succeeded.*

* The following account of this mutiny is extracted from Lieut.-Col. Blacker's 'Memoir of the operations of the British army in India, during the Mahratta War of 1817-18, and 19.'—" All arrangements being complete, the march was commenced on the 4th June, by Beekungaum and Seeonee, towards the Raveir Ghat, on the Nerbuddah. This movement was conducted for several days by moderate stages, without any extraordinary occurrence, Bajee Rao's camp, which marched late in the day, being invariably separate from that of the British troops. Yet scarcely any diminution was made in the number of his followers, notwithstanding Sir John's occasional remonstrances on the embarrassments they were likely to produce. The Ex.-Peishwa seemed averse to any measure calculated to dispel the illusions of sovereignty, which he could yet scarcely believe to have vanished with the last treaty. The shadow still afforded a soothing deception, which required, for its banishment, some external event, independent of his unwilling mind; or perhaps he even considered this as the least painful manner of being divested of his troops, the impropriety of whose admission into Malwah he would probably confess. Experience must have shewn him that the Arabs, at all events, were a body with whom it was difficult to make a settlement, and that, in all likelihood, the intervention of Sir John's means and influence would be requisite to compromise the impending disagreement. This interference would also save him from the necessity of anticipating an active exertion, so different from the usual policy of a Mahratta government, in which, through habit, he still imagined himself to preside. These troops, amounting to about 2000 men, had been hired for Bajee Rao's service, some months previously, by Trimbuckjee; and they demanded their arrears of pay from that date; instead of which it was offered to them from the day they had joined. The comparative justice of the claim and offer, were it of importance for examination here, might not be easily determined, as it would depend on express stipulations, or on the prevailing customs in similar cases, which would generally be found in favour of the offer. But a turbulent body, like the Arabs, are not always to be satisfied by the payment of just demands, and instances are not uncommon of their rising in their exactions, in proportion to the degree of acquiescence. Matters arrived at an extremity, on the 9th of June, at

After the termination of the war, Sir John Malcolm continued in Malwah, for the purpose of making arrangements with the neighbour-

Seeonee, when the Arabs, instead of marching, clamorously surrounded Bajee Rao's tent, threatening personal injury if their demands were not satisfied on that ground, which was within ten miles of the Nerbuddah. They accompanied this violent conduct with declarations, that any movement on the part of the British troops would cause his instant destruction, and that of all the helpless people about him. The contagion of their example spreading to the Rohillahs, in a short time the whole of the infantry were in a state of mutiny. Sir J. Malcolm, though not apprehensive of the extreme crisis which was approaching, was not without the expectation of some disturbance this morning. While, therefore, he dispatched his baggage to the next ground, with the irregular horse, and part of the infantry, he retained the regular cavalry, with six companies of the battalion, and two galloper guns. In this predicament were affairs when Bajee Rao applied for assistance, at the same time that he entreated no coercive movement might take place, to bring on the fate with which he was threatened; and Sir John finding that he had not sufficient force to awe the mutineers, sent off a despatch for the troops which had marched. The day passed in messages to Sir John from Bajee Rao, declaring his apprehensions; and from Sir John to the Arabs, menacing them with extirpation if they proceeded to violence. Towards the evening, however, he had such communications with the refractory principals, who were themselves comparatively reasonable, as to enable him to send consolation to the encircled chief, whom he assured of a favourable settlement on the following morning. The Mahratta camp was established along the bank of a nullah or ravine, much divided by small water-courses, and interspersed with scattered jungle highly favourable to the efforts of irregular troops; but to the west the ground gradually rose into a commanding position. This Sir John assumed at day-break on the 10th, and was joined by the troops who had countermarched, which completed his corps to 400 regular Native cav., 700 regular Native inf., with seven guns and 600 irregular horse. These he extended in a single rank, to increase their apparent numbers, as his object was intimidation, under the apprehension of the results of mutineers' despair. This expedient was not without the desired effect, and the principal Jemidar, Syed Fyze, advanced to demand a parley, while some of his own lawless bands opened a fire, which wounded two Sepoys. The troops were under such admirable discipline, that no attempt was made to resist this aggression, though the guns were loaded and the matches lighted; but all communication was refused till this irregular firing should be discontinued; and as their chief dispatched an attendant for this purpose, he was permitted to approach. Bajee Rao had already paid the greater part of their demands; and the remaining subjects of difference consisted of trifling matters, which both parties were satisfied to refer to the arbitration of Sir John, who willingly assented to become the umpire. Syed Fyze galloped off, on this assurance, to withdraw his people from their position round Bajee Rao's tent; but these refused to be removed, till all their leaders had received a promise of security against attacks after they should relinquish the pledge they already held. As Sir John instantly gave his hand to every Jemidar, their men were drawn off without more delay; and the Mahratta chief, attended by some horse, came in front of the British line, delighted at his emancipation from such barbarous thraldom. To make the contrast of the treatment to be derived from his own troops

ing states, and of introducing and establishing the Company's authority in that province, and the other territories which had been ceded to them. With the Rajah of Dewleah and Purtaubgurh, a Rajpoot chief, and formerly a tributary of Holkar, Capt. Caulfield, under Sir John Malcolm's orders, concluded a treaty on the 5th Oct. 1818, by which the Rajah transferred to the British government his rights over Purtaubgurh, on receiving from the Company the amount of the tribute realized from that petty state. The controul over Purtaubgurh, which commands one of the principal roads from Guzerat to Malwah and Hindostan, was on that account esteemed to be a point of much interest, as well as in consideration of Purtaubgurh having been, in former times, the channel of a very considerable trade. On the 5th Dec. following, Capt. Caulfield, under the orders of this

and from the British authorities, more striking, Sir John received him with a general salute; and he acknowledged the error he had committed in neglecting previous admonition, with expressions of gratitude for the benefits recently conferred. His first mark of obedience was moving off instantly to the opposite bank of the Nerbuddah, while the British commander was engaged in granting passports to the remaining troops, and in witnessing the departure of the Arabs and Rohillas towards, what they called, their respective homes. When the mutineers began to cool, after the heated state of irritation to which they had been raised, they expressed themselves equally indebted with Bajee Rao, for the lenity and temper with which they had been treated. Nor were these sentiments entertained without sufficient grounds; for undoubtedly Sir John Malcolm had the means of annihilating a considerable portion of them, and of dispersing the remainder. But they knew well the character he bore among the natives of India, and that nothing less than the most indispensable necessity could force him into the measure of sacrificing so many lives, and among them, most probably, the numerous innocent and defenceless Natives, who, from restraint, were unable to avoid the scene of conflict. Proud and severe tribute to character! demonstrated at the hazard of life, and superior, as an evidence of individual merit, to the most gaudy trappings of victory. If there were general reasons to apprehend that the occasional practice of lenity would weaken the hand that bestows it, or render it less useful for the public service, the present instance would oppose itself to that conclusion; for the happy termination of this formidable insurrection, may be fairly referred to the influence of character and talents of a higher stamp than fall to the share of the narrow-minded Martinet. That discipline is indispensable among soldiers, cannot be questioned; but the ability sufficient to maintain, in ordinary cases, the efficacy of rules, through the previously established forms of courts martial and military punishments, sinks into nothing before that power which controuls a tumultuous multitude, or directs a military body, under circumstances which have suspended the ordinary respect for orders."

officer, concluded a treaty with the Rajah of Banswarrah, another Rajpoot chief, who thereby became a subsidiary ally of the Company. On the 11th Dec. a similar treaty was concluded, by the same officer, with the Rajah of Doongerpore, also a Rajpoot chief; and another on the following day, by Lieut. Alexander Macdonald, also acting under the orders of Sir John, with the joint Rajahs of Dewass, called the Powar chiefs of Dhar; by which the British influence was established in the territories of those chiefs.

The great object to be obtained in nearly all these settlements was the expulsion of bands of Arab and Meckerania mercenaries, who had acquired an ascendancy, which they used to the worst purposes. The Gov.-Gen., in stating to the Court of Directors, letter 31st Oct. 1818, the manner in which this object had been accomplished, after noticing the zeal and intelligence displayed by Sir John in his proceedings with respect to the states of Doongerpore and Banswarrah, adds, " the successful result must tend very much to strengthen the foundations of the future tranquillity and prosperity of that part of the country, and to secure the beneficial ascendancy of the British government." To these treaties also, as well as to the other documents, explanatory of the general arrangements which Sir John had introduced into the conquered provinces, the court are referred by the Bengal government, as containing grounds of an expectation of permanent improvement in those provinces under his administration, and as affording the means of appreciating the services of this officer, who had, among other difficulties, to encounter an insurrection raised by a pretender to the throne of the house of Holkar, but which was immediately suppressed, and tranquillity restored by the exertions of Sir John Malcolm.

The Ex-Rajah of Nagpore, who had been driven from his throne and capital, in consequence of his treachery towards the British government, continued at large, a wanderer in the neighbourhood of the strong fortress of Asseergurh, of which the Killedar, Jeswunt Rao Sar, retained possession for some time after the general pacification of Central India. Military operations against this fortress were accordingly commenced in March 1819, and on the 10th April it surrendered to the force under Brig.-Gen. Doveton, the Ex-Rajah, Appa Sahib, having previously fallen into the hands of Sir J. Malcolm, whose assistance in the reduction of the fortress was thus acknowledged by Brig.-Gen. Doveton, in the general orders issued on the occasion: " To the means placed at the Brig.-Gen.'s disposal, by the rapid advance of the division under the personal command of Brig.-Gen. Sir J. Malcolm, as well as the troops from the Nerbuddah," (&c. &c.) " are principally to be attributed the fall of so stupendous a fortress, in 11 days from the opening of the trenches." " The distinguished and well-known merits of Sir J. Malcolm, might be considered as rendering any observation on the part of the Brig.-Gen. superfluous, if not almost presumptuous, but he cannot refrain from paying the just tribute of public as well as private feeling, by expressing his warmest acknowledgments for the assistance which he has derived from his unwearied and persevering energy and activity, during the entire period of military operations."

During the remainder of Sir John's residence in Malwah, he was particularly employed in the settlement of a number of disarmed Pindarries, by the assignment to them of lands and other assistance, at a very trifling expense to government; in the amicable adjustment of the conflicting claims of Scindia and Holkar, and those of numerous other princes and chiefs; in the compilation of Notes of instruction to the several officers, civil and military, who were left by him in the province of Malwah at the time of his departure, which notes embrace a number of important points of conduct, and contain the result of his long experience among the natives of India; also in preparing a report on Malwah and the adjoining countries, which appeared to the Gov.-Gen. in council to be no less deserving of circulation* among the officers of government than Mr. Elphinstone's report on Caboul. The Bengal government, previous to this officer quitting Malwah, observed, in their letter to the Secret Committee, " that the controlling political and

* Since printed, at the expense of the Company, in a Quarto Volume of upwards of 600 pages.

military authority vested in Sir J. Malcolm, had been eminently serviceable to the public interests."

In Aug. 1821, Sir John quitted Malwah, and proceeded by way of Bombay to Calcutta, where he continued a short time, and then determined to return to England over land, for the benefit of his health. The following General Orders were issued upon this occasion.

"*Political Department, Fort William, 20th Oct.* 1821.

"Maj.-Gen. Sir J. Malcolm, having obtained the permission of government to return to Europe for the recovery of his health, His Ex. the Gov.-Gen. in council deems it due to the distinguished character and talents of that meritorious officer, on the occasion of his approaching departure from India, and consequent resignation of the high and important military and political station which he holds in Malwah, to express, in the most public manner, the sense which the government entertains of his eminent merits and services, and the regret with which it regards the necessity that now compels him to retire from the scene where his talents have been displayed with so much credit to himself, and with such signal benefit to the public interests.

"To enumerate the various occasions on which Sir J. Malcolm has been employed by successive administrations to fill the most important diplomatic situations, and for his conduct in which he has frequently received the highest approbation and applause of the government in India, and the most flattering marks of the favour and satisfaction of the authorities in England, would far exceed the limits to which this general expression of the consideration and esteem of government must necessarily be confined. Although his Exc. the Gov.-Gen. in Council refrains, therefore, from the specific mention of the many recorded services which have placed Sir J. Malcolm in the first rank of those officers of the Hon. Company's service, who have essentially contributed to the renown of the British arms and councils in India, his Lordship in council cannot omit this opportunity of declaring his unqualified approbation of the manner in which Sir J. Malcolm has discharged the arduous and important functions of his high political and military station in Malwah. By a happy combination of qualities, which could not fail to win the esteem and confidence both of his own countrymen and of the native inhabitants of all classes, by the unremitting personal exertion and devotion of his time and labour to the maintenance of the interests confided to his charge, and by an enviable talent for inspiring all who acted under his orders with his own energy and zeal, Sir J. Malcolm has been enabled, in the successful performance of the duty assigned him in Malwah, to surmount difficulties of no ordinary stamp, and to lay the foundations of repose and prosperity in that extensive province, but recently reclaimed from a state of savage anarchy, and a prey to every species of rapine and devastation. The Gov.-Gen. in Council feels assured, that the important services thus rendered to his country by Sir J. Malcolm, at the close of an active and distinguished career, will be not less gratefully acknowledged by the authorities at home, than they are cordially applauded by those under whose immediate orders they have been performed.

" By order of His Exc. the most noble the Gov.-Gen. in Council.

(Signed) " GEORGE SWINTON, Sec. to the Government."

Upon his arrival at Fort St. George, he obtained from the Gov. in Council of that Presidency permission to come to England; and upon his quitting Madras, the following general order was issued:—

" *Fort St. George, Oct.* 29, 1821.

" Maj.-Gen. Sir J. Malcolm, G. C. B. and K. L. S., having applied for permission to proceed to Europe, the Hon. the Gov. in Council has learned with deep concern that this distinguished officer is now compelled to quit India on account of the declining state of his health. The many and important services of Sir J. Malcolm in different situations, have been so often brought to the notice of the Hon. the Court of Directors by the supreme government, that no praise of this government can add to his high reputation. Although, however, it belongs to higher authority to appreciate his services in the late Mahratta war, and the settlement of central India, the Gov. in Council cannot, on this occasion, deny himself the pleasure of discharging the grateful duty of expressing, in general orders, the high sense he entertains of the Maj.-Gen.'s talents, and of his unwearied and honourable exertion of them for the benefit of his country. Among the individuals who have at different times distinguished themselves in the employment of the Hon. Company, Sir J. Malcolm will always hold a very high rank. His career has been unexampled; for no other servant of the Hon. Company has ever, during so long a period, been so constantly employed in the conduct of such various and important military and political duties. His great talents were too well known to admit of their being confined to the more limited range of service under his own presidency. The exercise of them in different situations has connected him with every presidency, and rendered him less the servant of any one of them than of the Indian Empire at large. Maj.-Gen. Sir J. Malcolm is permitted to return to Europe on sick certificate.

" By order of the Hon. the Gov. in Council.
   (Signed) " E. Wood, Chief Secretary."

Sir John arrived at Bombay early in Nov., and on the 29th of that month a splendid entertainment was given to him by the gentlemen at that presidency. He quitted it on the 2d Dec., and arrived in England on the 30th April 1822. Since his arrival, he has received a superb vase, valued at 1500*l*., as a testimony of respect from the gentlemen who acted under him in the Mahratta war of 1818 and 1819.

ADDENDA.

HONOURS CONFERRED ON OFFICERS SINCE THEIR SERVICES WERE PRINTED IN THIS WORK.

Major-General Thos. Brown, Bengal Establishment, appointed a Knight Commander of the Bath, 23d July 1823.—Services, p. 253.

Lieutenant-Colonel M. Kennedy, Bombay Establishment, appointed a Companion of the Bath, 23d July 1823.—Services, p. 300.

Major J. F. Staunton, Bombay Establishment, appointed a Companion of the Bath, 23d July 1823.—Services, p. 98.

The Editor is not aware of any other omissions in the Services published in this Volume, but should there be any, they will be introduced in an Addenda to be published with the Second Part. Communications are therefore particularly requested to be addressed to the Editor, Duke-street, Westminster.

GENERAL INDEX

TO THE

PRINCIPAL BATTLES, SIEGES, EVENTS, &c. &c., AND NAMES OF OFFICERS PARTICULARLY MENTIONED.*

ATKINSON, James, Maj., Ben. E.; Services, 194.
Aitchison, A. Lt.-Col., Bomb. E.; Services, 264.
Ashe, St. George, Maj.-Gen., Ben. E.; Services, 290.
Auburey, Maj.; 395.
Alpin, Lieut. 397.
Aid-de-Camp, Honorary, first introduced, 461.
Adjutant-General, appointment only to be held by Field Officers, 366.
Asseergurh, siege of, 167.
Anicul, reduction of in 1768, 7.
Abington, Maj 240, 409.
Arlier, action of, 1798, 7.
Assaye, battle of, 125.
Adjutant-General, the late Sir H. Cosby, the first appointed to this office in India, 10.
Agnew, Maj. 487.
Archdeacon, the late Capt. 28, 107.
Arab Mutiny in 1818, 493.
Agra, surrender of, 18th Oct. 1803, 34, 39, 40, 291.
Allygurh, capture of, 4th Sept. 1803, 59.
Argaum, battle of, 80.
Adjygurh, capture of in 1809, 406.
Adams, Maj.-Gen., 358.

Baillie, John, Lt.-Col., Ben. E.; Services, 64; 375.
Brown, J. D. Maj., M. E.; Services, 94.
Bell, Robert, Lt.-Gen., M. E.; Services, 128.
Browne, M. W., Lt.-Col., Ben E.; Services, 168.
Broughton, T. D., Lt.-Col., Ben. E.; Services, 169.
Blachford, W. H., Maj.-Gen., Bomb. E.; Services, 175.
Boyé, C., Lt.-Gen., Bomb. E.; Services, 214.
Bellasis, G. B., Lieut.-Col., Bomb. E.; Services, 233.
Baillie, John, Maj.-Gen., Bomb. E.; Services, 244.
Brown, Sir T., Maj.-Gen., K. C. B. Ben. E.; Services, 253; 308, 389, 391, 500.
Broughton, E. S., Maj.-Gen., Ben. E.; Services, 284.
Blacker, V., Lt.-Col., C. B., M. E; Services, 321; 493.
Bond, C. J, late Lt.-Col., Bomb. E.; Services, 355.
Burr, C. B., late Lt.-Col., C. B., Bomb. E; Services, 350: 97.
Bolton, late Maj., 399.
Bajee Rao, murder of Gungathur Shastree, 452. Overthrow of, 492.
Bowles, Gen. 370.
Bonjour, Maj, 5, 6, 8.
Baillie, the late Col., 5, 14, 15, (Painting of his defeat) 30; 250, 272.
Bengal Army, composition of, 132.

Brigade, Maj., highest staff situation on the coast, 1772, 9.
Brathwaite, Col., 14.
Barker, Sir Robert, late Gen., 24.
Boojee, capture of, 339.
Bangalore, siege and capture of, &c. 26, 437.
Bourguien, Gen, 59.
Bombay Army, composition of, 133.
Brass Guns with iron cylinders, description of, 60, 61, 63.
Bejighur, fall of, 58.
Blane, Lt.-Col., 89.
Bætoorah, battle of, 26th October, 1794, 117, 194, 399, 423.
Bowness, Geo, Maj.-Gen., 212.
Ball, Col., 366.
Bath, Grand Cross of the Order, extended to the Officers of the Indian Army, 384, 386.

Cosby, Sir Henry, Knt. late Lt.-Gen., M. E.; Services, 1.
Cameron, W. N., Lt.-Gen., Ben. E.; Services, 50.
Constable, Geo, Lt.-Col, Ben. E; Services, 55.
Cockerell, John, late Lt.-Col., Ben. E.; Services, 114; 26, 181, 316, 397.
Cameron, P., Maj., M. E.; Services, 206.
Cumberlege, N., Lt.-Col., Ben. E.; Services, 216.
Caldwell, Alex., Lt.-Col., Com., Ben. E.; Services, 235.
Court, M. H., Maj., M. E.; Services, 237.
Clark, T., Maj.-Gen., M. E.; Services, 250.
Chitty, E., Lt.-Col., M. E.; Services, 270.
Cleaveland, S., Maj., M. E.; Services, 274.
Cunliffe, R. H., Maj., Ben. E.; Services, 310, 397.
Close, Sir Barry, the late Gen., 212, 475.
Carpenter, W. L., Maj., Bomb. E.; Services, 424.
Cuppage, Maj.-Gen., 377.
Colebrooke, Lt.-Col., 377.
Cartwright, Maj., 396.
Culpee, capture of, 25.
Cailland, Gen., 2.
Changama, battle of, 28th Sept. 1767, 6.
Calicoil, reduction of, 1772, 10.
Canning, Right Hon. George, Speech on action of Corygaum, 97.
Chitteport, Fort, attempt to capture it in 1780, 15.
Coote, Sir Eyre, the late Gen., 39; death and character, 44, 426, 428, 432.
Campbell, Charles, Col., 3.
Champion, Col., 25.
Cutra, battle of, 25.

---

* It was found impossible to insert even a reference to names, &c. wherever they occur in this work, without increasing the Index to an inconvenient size.

Coil, defeat of the French at, 4th Sept. 1803, 59; storm of, 22d Sept. 1804, 204.
Cudalore, battle of, siege, &c. 1783, 25, 45, 87, 231, 379, 431, 432.
Collins, late Col., 64, 254.
Carnac, Col., 50.
Cornwallis, Lord, Critical Situation, 6th Feb. 1792, 28, 403.
Cadet Company, Institution of, at Barrasett, 171, 295.
Connellon, Lieut. See Corygaum.
Campbell, Dugald, Gen., 32.
Commissariat, duties of, &c. 188, 433.
Clark, Gen., 33.
Clive, Lord, 44.
Corygaum, action of, 1st Jan. 1818, 97.
Catchonra, capture of, 58.
Cummings, Sir John, 201.
Callinger, siege of in Jan. 1812, 161, 256, 311, 375, 393, 407.
Cananore, reduction of, in 1789, 351.
Cavalry Horses, Board for the Improvement in the Breed of, 366.
Cavalry Regiment, first sent to India in 1782, 426.
Carrangooly, demolition of in 1783, 428.
Cavalry Officers, Madras Establishment, 436
Commerce, Treaty of, 1802, 464.
Camac, Jacob, Col., 229.
Charter, East India Company's, Evidence before Parliament on the Renewal of it, 485.

Dick, Geo., Maj.-Gen., Ben. E.; Services, 108.
Durand, Horace, Maj., M. E.; Services, 213.
Disney, A., Col., Bomb. E.; Services, 240.
Doolan, R., Lt.-Col., Bomb. E.; Services, 277.
Donkin, Sir R., Maj.-Gen., K. C. B., 395.
Dallas, Sir Thomas, Maj.-Gen., K. C. B., 433.
Dencamicotah, reduction of, in 1768, 8.
Doudpoor, surrender of, in 1804, 36.
Dumas, Count, 46.
De Bussy, Marquess, 43, 431.
Delhi, action near, and capture of, in 1803, 59, 136, 380, 386.
Dowdeswell, Mr., 51, 205.
Doveton, Sir John, Maj.-Gen., K. C. B., 209, 454.
Doondia Waugh, actions with, &c. 211, 446.
Drury, Admiral, 183.

Eyles, J., Maj., Bomb. E.; Services, 195.
Egan, K., Lt.-Col., Bomb. E.; Services, 261.
Egypt, Expedition to, 353.
Errour, battle of, in 1767, 7.
Edmonstone, Lt.-Col., 89.
East, W., Col., C. B., 221, 360.
Elphinstone, Mr., 152, 452.

Fergusson, A., Maj.-Gen., Ben. E.; Services, 180.
Foulis, D., Lt.-Col., M. E.; Services, 222.
Farquhar, W., Lt.-Col., M. E.; Services, 267.
Fagan, C. S., Lt.-Col., Ben. E.; Services, 325.
Fagan, C. Lieut.-Col., Ben. E.; Services, 333.
Fagan, G. H. late Lt.-Col., Ben. E.; Services, 365.
Famine in the Carnatic in 1782, 427.
Floyd, Sir John, the late Gen., 259, 273, 436-7-8, 443.
Fullarton, Col., 84, 434.
Fawcett, W. D., Maj.-Gen., 326.

Frederick, Charles, late Col., 248, 279, 340.
Flint, late Col., 245.

Garner, T., Lieut.-Col., Ben. E.; Services, 193.
Gibson, T., Lieut.-Col., Bomb. E.; Services, 197.
Grant, M., Maj.-Gen., Bomb. E.; Services, 207. 287.
Gillespie, G. J., Maj., M. E.; Services, 210.
Gibbings, A., Lieut.-Col., M. E.; Services, 214.
Gall, G. H., Maj. Ben. E.; Services, 307.
Gough, Brigade-Major, 397.
Gregory, R., Maj.-Gen., C. B. 35, 52.
Gualior, capture of, 4th Feb. 1804, 36, 182, 291, 372; surprise of, 3d Aug. 1780, 50, 229, 326; ceded to Scindia in 1805, 476.
Gohud, surrender of, 1804, 36, 77, 120; ceded to Scindia in 1805, 476.
Gillespie, Sir R. R., K. C. B., late Maj.-Gen., 91, 161, 263, 309, 382, 383, 407.
Gadjnoor, battle of, 29th Dec 1791, 341.
George III., anecdote of, 113.
Goddard, the late Gen., 115, 228, 240, 247.
Gordon, the late Lieut.-Col., 58, 312.

Hussey, V. W., late Lieut.-Gen, Ben. E.; Services, 49, 127.
Hicks, John, Maj., Bomb. E.; Services, 111.
Hardwicke, T., Maj.-Gen., Ben. E.; Services, 178.
Henley, W., Maj. Ben. E.; Services. 267.
Hardyman, G., Lieut.-Gen., Ben. E.; Services, 271.
Harriot, J. S., Maj., Ben. E.: Services, 275.
Hodson, H., Maj., Ben. E.; Services, 312.
Hind, Alex., Col., Ben. E.; Services, 397.
Holmes, Sir George, late Maj.-Gen., K.C.B.; Services, 408; 289, 305, 356, 360.
Hattrass, attack and capture of, 395.
Horsford, Sir John, late Maj.-Gen., K.C.B., 395.
Hyder Ally, peace with, 1769, 7.; anecdote of, 251; character of, 408, 427, 428.
Hunter, Capt., 29.
Hughes, Admiral, 39, 282, 426.
Hobart, Lord, 57.
Hastings, Warren, 88, 114, 239.
Hartley, late Gen., 149, 176, 298, 301, 351.
Horse-dealers, 449.

Johnson, John, Lieut.-Col., C.B., Bomb. E.; Services, 220.
James, Capt., 396.
Jourdan, Major, 16.
Jones, Sir William, 64.
Jones, Lieut.; See Corygaum.
Infanticide, practice of, among the Jahrejah Rajapoots, 151, 152, 343.
Jemaulabad, capture of, 196, 336.
Jones, Sir Richard, Lieut.-Gen., 111, 357-8, 371.
Juggernauth, new road to Burdwan, 377.
Jews, favourite soldiers in the Bombay army, 134.
Jones, Sir Harford, 483.

Kennaway, Sir John, Bart., Lieut.-Col., Ben. E.; Services, 87.
Kennedy, M., Lieut.-Col., C.B. Bomb. E.; Services, 300, 500.
Kirkpatrick, J. A., late Lieut.-Col., M. E.; Services, 460, 469.
Kirkee, battle of, 97, 363.

INDEX.

Kurree, action of, 150, 288, 304, 371.
Kirkpatrick, William, the late Col., 461.

Lauriston, A., Lieut.-Col., Bomb. E.; Services, 226.
Lumsdaine, James, the late Maj., Ben. E.; Services, 421; 190.
Lally, Gen., 1, 251.
Laswarree, action of, 1st Nov. 1803, 35, 60, 136, 204, 400.
Leslie, the late Col., 114, 115.
Lake, Gen. Lord, 60, 135.
Ludlow, late Lieut.-Col., C.B., 169.
Little, late Col., 207, 226, 283, 287, 340, 410.
Lushington, J. L., Lieut.-Col., 212.

Mackay, Robt. Lieut.-Gen., M. E.,; Services, 37.
Mackenzie, Jabez., Lt.-Col., Ben. E.; Services, 77.
Monteath, A. D., Maj., M. E.; Services, 92.
Macleod, D. Lt.-Col., C.B., Ben. E.; Services, 116.
Macmorine, G., Lt.-Col., Ben. E.; Services, 141.
Mitchell, D., Maj., Bomb. E.; Services, 269.
Molesworth, A., Lt.-Col., M. E.; Services, 275.
M'Dowall, A., Lieut.-Col., C.B., M.E.; Services. 297.
Moor, Edward, Major, Bomb. E.; Services, 486; 153, 226, 279.
Marshall, Sir Dyson, Maj.-Gen., K.C.B., Ben. E.; Services, 395.
Macdonald, Sir John, Lt.-Gen., K.C.B., Ben. E.; Services, 398.
Martindell, Sir G., Maj.-Gen., K.C.B., Ben. E.; Services, 406; 308, 327, 374, 383, 391, 393.
Mounsey, G. S., Maj., Ben. F.; Services, 423.
Malcolm, Sir John, Maj.-Gen., G.C.B. & K.L.S., M. E.; Services, 468; 199, 442, 445, 459,.
Marley, B., Maj.-Gen., 382.
Madras, siege of, in 1759, 1.
Marine Sepoy corps raised in 1801, 33.
More, Major, 79th Reg., 1.
Madura, siege of, in 1764, 3.
Madras army, composition of, 133.
Munro, Sir Hector, late Gen., 14, 15, 17, 282.
Maitland, Sir Thomas, Lt.-Gen., G.C.B., 86, 434.
Macleod, Lord, 14. 20.
Muir, Col., 50.
Malet, Sir Charles, 342.
Monson, late Gen., 52, 61, 291.
Macao, expedition to, in 1808, 182.
Madras mutiny, in 1809, 81.
Monnypenny, Col., 211.
Matthews, the late Gen., 241, 278, 431.
Murray, Sir John, Lieut.-Gen. 111, 353, 356, 357.
M'Leod, Norman, Capt., 400.
Medows, the late Gen. Sir W., 403, 436.
Montana, relief of, in 1800, 411.
Malabar, acquisition of, troublesome, 411.
Moore, Sir John, late Lieut.-Gen., 420.
Madras treasury exhausted, &c. 435.
Malavilly, battle of, 27th March 1799, 442.
Mangalore, siege of, 148.
Middleton, C., Maj., 293.
Munro, Sir Thomas, Maj.-Gen, K.C.B., 470.
Morpeth, Lord, opinion on talents of officers of the Company's army, Advertisement, p. vi.
Mehidpore, battle of, 488.
Malwah, report on, 497.

Nagle, James, Lieut.-Col., M. E.; Services, 121.
Nelly, John. Lieut.-Col., Ben. E.; Services, 127.
Newall, D., Lieut.-Col., M. E.; Services, 265.
Nepaul war. 109, 380, 384, 386, 387, 452, 459.
Nagpore, action near, 16th Dec. 1817, 193.
Nair, military tribe of, 411.

O'Donnell, H. A., Lieut.-Col., C.B., Ben. E.; Services, 51.
Orr, John, Lieut.-Gen., M. E.; Services, 272.
Osborne, H. S. Lt.-Col., Bomb. E.; Services, 313.
Ochterlony, Sir D., Maj.-Gen., Bart. & G.C.B., Ben. E.; Services, 379, 193.
Ouseley, Sir Gore, 482.
Owen, Colonel, 19.
Oakley, Sir Charles, 57.
Outradroog, capture of, 319.
Onore, siege and storm of, 175.

Pearson, Jas., Lieut.-Col., Ben. E.; Services, 75.
Pennington, G., Lieut.-Col., Ben. E.; Services, 158.
Penny, G. R., Lieut.-Col., Ben. E.: Services, 192.
Pepper, H. H., Lieut.-Col., M. E.; Services, 198.
Pogson, T., Lieut.-Col., M. E.; Services, 258.
Pollock, Geo., Maj., Ben. E.; Services, 277.
Pine, G. H., Maj.-Gen., Ben. E.; Services, 280.
Price, D., Maj., Bomb. E.; Services, 282.
Prother, D., Lieut.-Col., C. B., Bomb. E.; Services, 304; 337.
Prole, Maj.-Gen., 394.
Persian Orders, 482.
Persia, mission to, and treaty with, in 1799, 471; mission to, in 1808, 480; in 1809, 481; in 1810, 483.
Popham, the late Lieut.-Gen., 170.
Partition Treaty of Mysore, 463.
Pondicherry, siege of, in 1760, 1; in 1778, 12, 47; in 1793, 440.
Picket, select corps, 24, 406.
Perambancum, or Pollelore, action of, 27th Aug. 1781, 40, 93.
Portonovo, battle of, 1st July 1781, 39.
Pearse, T. D., late Col., 40, 87, 316.
Peter Serai, reduction of, in 1808, 52.
Perron, Gen., 59, 169, 442, 462.
Pedrong, Gen., 59.
Parneiro, capture of, in 1780, 72.
Palambang, expedition to, 91.
Powell, P., Lieut.-Gen., 326, 372.
Pungalumcoorchy, storm of, 330.
Popham, Sir Home, embassy to the Arab States, 195.
Pindarry war, 1815-16, 209, 257; character of the Pindarries, 302, 452, 488.
Petrie, Col., 149, 249.
Powaghur, capture of, 355, 415.
Palicaudcherry, investment of, 433.
Plassey, victory of, 133.
Persian ambassador shot at Bombay, in 1802, 472.
Porter, Sir Robert Ker, 483.

Quarter-Master-General, appointment only to be held by field-officers, 366.

Raban, G., Lieut.-Col., C. B., Ben. E.; Services, 76.
Raban, W., Lieut.-Col., Ben. E.; Services, 90.

INDEX.

Ramsay, Sir Thomas, *Bart.*, Lieut.-Col., Ben. E.; Services, 106.
Riddell, M., Maj., M. E.; Services, 208.
Richardson, J. L., Lieut.-Col., 382.

Rajpoots, description of, 132.
Ramnadapram, reduction of, in 1792, 10.
Rajamundry, ceded to the English, 3.
Recruiting depôt, 24.
Rohillas, existence as a nation terminated, 25.
Rohilla battle, in 1774, 395, 406.
Regimental rank, 32.
Russell, George, Lieut.-Gen., 308.
Ramporah, capture of, 77.
Ryghur, siege and capture of, 11th May 1818, 305, 338.
Regulations, Bengal army, 268; Bombay army, 343.
Roberts, Geo., Lieut.-Gen., 210, 462.
Read, the late Col., 317, 444.
Regimental officer, 420.

Sentleger, Hon. A., Maj.-Gen., M. E.; Services, 78.
Symons, J. H., Maj.-Gen., M. E.; Services, 84.
Staunton, F. F., Maj., *C. B.*, Bomb. E.; Services, 95, 500.
Stewart, C., Maj., Ben. E.; Services, 200.
Shaw, T., Lieut.-Col., Ben. E; Services, 228.
Scott, J. G., Maj.-Gen., M. E.; Services, 230.
Smith, J., Lieut.-Col., Bomb. E.; Services, 286.
Stuart, C., Maj., Ben. E.; Services, 292.
Spens, A., Lieut.-Col., Bomb. E.; Services, 298.
Scott, R., Lieut.-Col., Ben. E.; Services, 315.
Sackville, Fred., Maj., Ben. E.; Services, 372.
Sandys, William, Lieut.-Col., Ben. E.; Services, 401.
Steele, Thomas, Lieut.-Col., M. E.; Services, 468.
Smith, J. N., Col., 374.
Stevenson, the late Gen., 222, 397, 439.
Semple, Capt., 414.
Smith, Joseph, late Gen., 1.
Sepoys, uniformity of dress first established, 4.
Seringapatam, battle of, 15th May 1791, 26; storm of Tippoo's entrenched camp, 6th Feb. 1792, 27, 51, 262, 273, 352, 403.
Shrapnell, Col., *C. B.*, 61.
Savendroog, fort, description of, 26.
Sibbald, Capt., 30, 181.
Serinagur, action of, 144.
Stuart, Sir Robert, late Gen., 57.
Sasnee, siege of, in 1808, 58.
Sartorius, Col., 196.
Scott, H. S., Col., *C. B.*, 193, 200, 457.
Symes, M., Lieut.-Col., 202.
Sweden, king of, anecdote, 231.

Smith, Sir Lionel, Maj.-Gen., *K. C. B.*, 360, 364.
Service, that in which energy and address are most tried, 411, 454.
Service in India, not justly estimated in England, (see advertisement, p. vii.,) 420.

Tomkyns, J., Lieut.-Col., Ben. E.; Services, 109.
Thomas, W., Lieut.-Col., Ben. E.; Services, 162.
Thompson, J., Lieut.-Col., Bomb. E.; Services, 224.
Trimbuckjee Dauglia, murder of Gungathur Shastree, 452; given up to the British, 453; escape, &c., 458.
Tanjore, siege and surrender of, in 1773, 10.
Trinomally, battle of, in 1767, 7.
Tripassoor, capture of, in July 1781, 40.
Tippoo Saib, character of, &c. &c., 409, 438, 439.
Torriano, Maj., 175.
Tellichery, siege of, 408.

Voyle, Elliot, Lieut.-Col., Ben. E.; Services, 349.
Velore, siege and capture of, 2.
Vellum, capture of, in 1771, 8.

White, Sir Henry, *K. C. B.*, late Maj.-Gen., Ben. E.; Services, 24; (see Advertisement, p. v.) 182, 291, 326, 372.
Welsh, Thomas, late Lieut.-Col., Ben. E.; Services, 71.
Webber, H., Maj.-Gen., M. E.; Services, 93.
Wood, Sir Mark, *Bart.*, Col., Ben. E.; Services, 113.
Worsley, H., Col., *C. B.*, Ben. E.; Services, 130.
Wilks, M., Col., M. E.; Services, 140.
Walker, Alex., Lieut.-Col., Bomb. E.; Services, 147; 288, 356, 371, 426.
Weguelin, T. M., Lieut.-Col., Ben. E.; Services, 180; 422.
Wood, S., Lieut.-Col., *C. B.*, Ben. E.; Services, 203.
Wilton, G., Lieut.-Col., Ben. E.; Services, 238.
Welsh, J., Lieut.-Col., M. E.; Services, 329.
Woodington, Col., 353, 414, 416.
Williams, Geo., late Maj., Bomb. E.; Services, 370.
Watson, A., Lieut.-Col., Ben. E.; Services, 387.
Walker, Patrick, late Col., M. E.; Services, 425.
Wood, S., Maj.-Gen., 382.
Ware, late Maj.-Gen., 400.
Wangenheim, Gen., 231.
Weltervreeden, action of, in 1811, 263, 309.
Wandiwash, siege of, 245; demolition of, in 1783, 428.
Wiseman, Maj., 227.

Youngoon, W., Lieut.-Col., M. E.; Services, 140.

THE END.

W. WILSON, Printer, 4, Greville-Street, Hatton-Garden, London.

www.ingramcontent.com/pod-product-compliance
Lightning Source LLC
Chambersburg PA
CBHW080417230426
43662CB00015B/2133